S0-BEB-775

HOUGHTON MIFFLIN HARCOURT

WRITE SOURCE

TEACHER'S EDITION

Grade 3

Authors

Dave Kemper, Patrick Sebranek, and Verne Meyer

Illustrator

Chris Krenzke

Education Resource Center
University of Delaware
Newark, DE 19716-2940

GREAT SOURCE®

HOUGHTON MIFFLIN HARCOURT

23414

Reviewers

Genevieve M. Bodnar
Youngstown City School District
Youngstown, Ohio

Joan Chiodo
Patricia Di Chiaro Elementary
Yonkers, New York

Kay Dooley
Naperville Community USD
Naperville, Illinois

Jean Evans
Jenks Southeast School District
Tulsa, Oklahoma

Paula Denise Findley
White Hall, Arkansas

Mary Fischer
Arlington Public Schools
Arlington, Massachusetts

Cullen Hemstreet
Jefferson Parish School District
Metairie, Louisiana

Elma G. Jones
Wallingford-Swarthmore School District
Swarthmore, Pennsylvania

Marilyn LeRud
Tucson Unified School District
Tucson, Arizona

Mary Osborne
Pinellas County School District
Largo, Florida

Amy Stenger
Millard Public Schools
Omaha, Nebraska

Pamela J. Strain
Rosemead School District
Rosemead, California

Photos: TE-8 ©Tim Pannell/Corbis; TE-10–TE-11 ©Andrzej Tokarski/Alamy; TE-12 ©Image Source/Getty Images; TE-16–TE-17 ©Big Cheese Photo LLC/Alamy.

Text: Common Core State Standards © Copyright 2010. National Governors Association Center for Best Practices and Council of Chief State School Officers. All rights reserved.

This product is not sponsored or endorsed by the Common Core State Standards Initiative of the National Governors Association Center for Best Practices and the Council of Chief State School Officers.

Copyright © 2012 by Houghton Mifflin Harcourt Publishing Company

All rights reserved. No part of this work may be reproduced or transmitted in any form or by any means, electronic or mechanical, including photocopying or recording, or by any information storage or retrieval system, without the prior written permission of the copyright owner unless such copying is expressly permitted by federal copyright law.

Permission is hereby granted to individuals using the corresponding student's textbook or kit as the major vehicle for regular classroom instruction to photocopy copying masters from this publication in classroom quantities for instructional use and not for resale. Requests for information on other matters regarding duplication of this work should be addressed to Houghton Mifflin Harcourt Publishing Company, Attn: Paralegal, 9400 South Park Center Loop, Orlando, Florida 32819.

Printed in the U.S.A.

ISBN 978-0-547-48437-2

3 4 5 6 7 8 9 10 0914 19 18 17 16 15 14 13 12

4500367122 B C D E F G

If you have received these materials as examination copies free of charge, Houghton Mifflin Harcourt Publishing Company retains title to the materials and they may not be resold. Resale of examination copies is strictly prohibited.

Possession of this publication in print format does not entitle users to convert this publication, or any portion of it, into electronic format.

In the Front Matter

Program Overview

Professional Development for Writing

THE FORMS, THE PROCESS, AND THE TRAITS

WRITING WORKSHOP AND GRAMMAR

WRITING ACROSS THE CURRICULUM, ACADEMIC VOCABULARY, AND TEST PREPARATION

DIFFERENTIATION

RESEARCH

Teacher Resources

In the Wraparound

The Writing Process

The Forms of Writing

In the Wraparound

How does *Write Source* work?

Write Source is a complete language arts curriculum focused on writing and grammar in print and digital formats.

With writing instruction at the core, grammar, usage, and mechanics are taught in an authentic writing context.

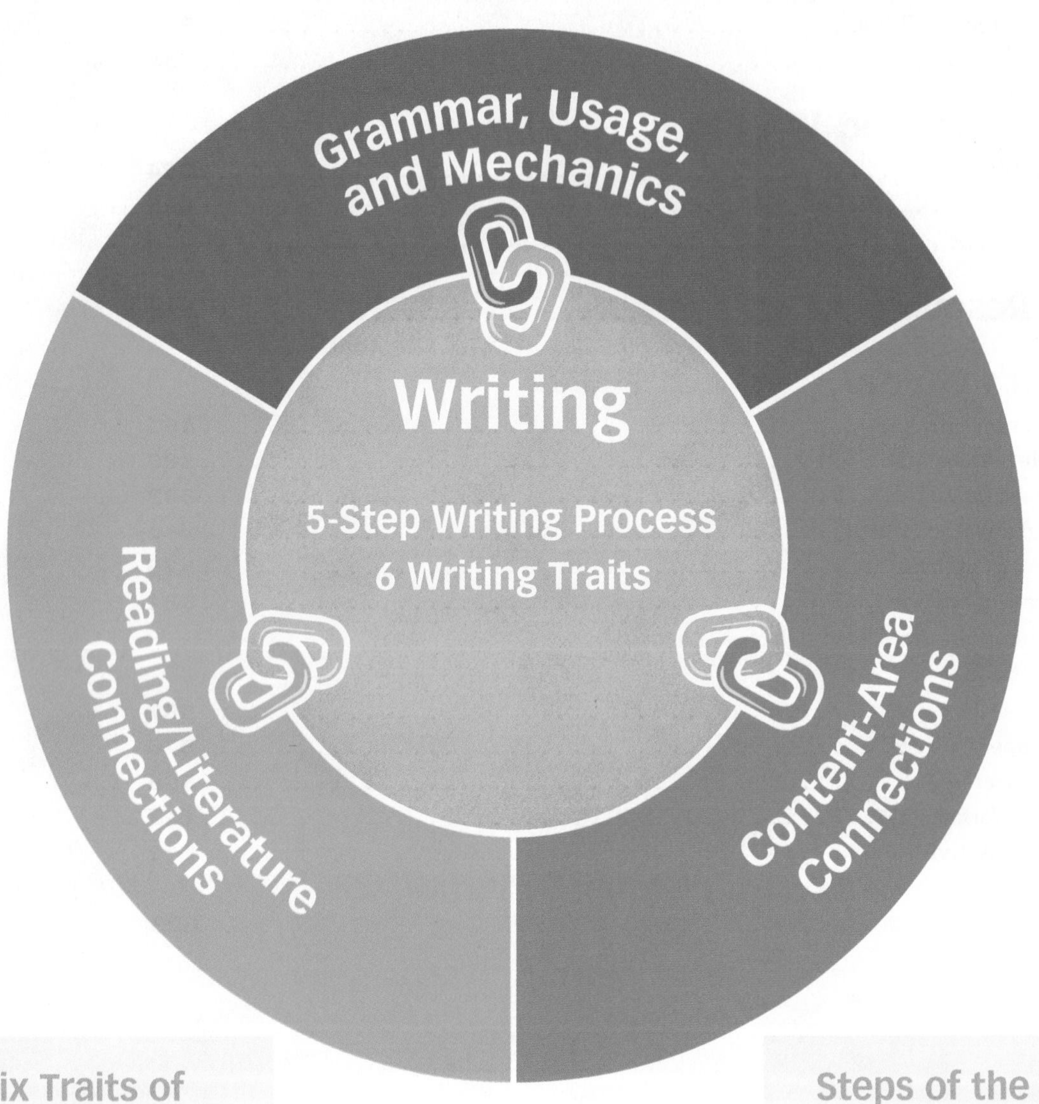

The Six Traits of Effective Writing

- Ideas
- Organization
- Voice
- Word Choice
- Sentence Fluency
- Conventions

Steps of the Writing Process

- Prewriting
- Writing
- Revising
- Editing
- Publishing

Each core forms of writing unit follows the same instructional path—a consistent writing curriculum across all grade levels.

Introduce the writing form:

- Analyze a model paragraph.
- Preview the form by responding to questions about the model and by writing a paragraph.
-  Reflect on how revising for the six traits and editing for **conventions** can improve writing.

Explore the writing form:

- Analyze a model story or essay.
-  **Read authentic real-world fiction or nonfiction** that models the writing form.
- Use the writing process to write a story or essay.
-  Use the six traits to revise and then edit the writing for **conventions**.
- Evaluate writing by first analyzing a model against a 6-point analytical, mode-specific rubric and then self-assessing.
- **Read authentic real-world fiction or nonfiction** that models the writing form.

Write in the content areas:

-  Write a piece in the same writing form **across the major content areas**—science, social studies, math, and the arts.

Write Source prepares students for success in the 21st century.

Write for assessment:

- Using the unit's writing form, write a piece for assessment.

What are the main components of *Write Source?*

The *Write Source* **Student Edition** reflects the latest research on writing instruction. The **Teacher's Edition** has all the support you need to help students become confident, proficient writers.

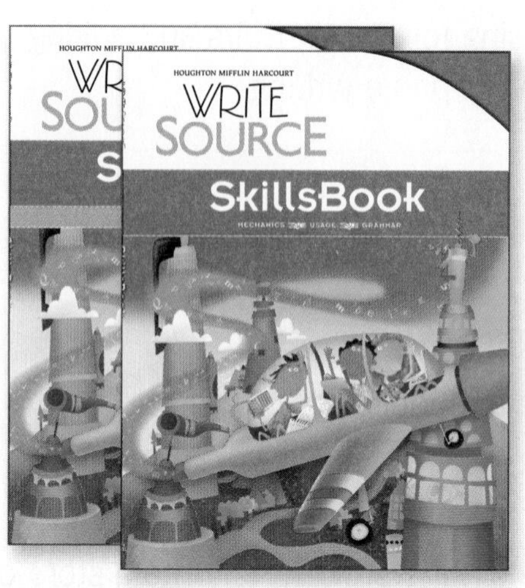

The **SkillsBook** helps students practice and improve grammar, usage, and mechanics skills.

The **Assessment** book provides a pretest, progress tests, and a post-test.

The **Daily Language Workouts** build student conventions skills through quick, daily editing and proofreading activities.

Write Source Online
www.hmheducation.com/writesource

- Discover the power of writing instruction with **Net-text**, an interactive, collaborative online worktext.
- Engage students in grammar through **GrammarSnap**, the grammar practice Web application.
- Transform writing instruction through high-functioning **Interactive Whiteboard Presentations.**
- Support instruction with a searchable **File Cabinet** teacher resource.

How does the Teacher's Edition support instruction?

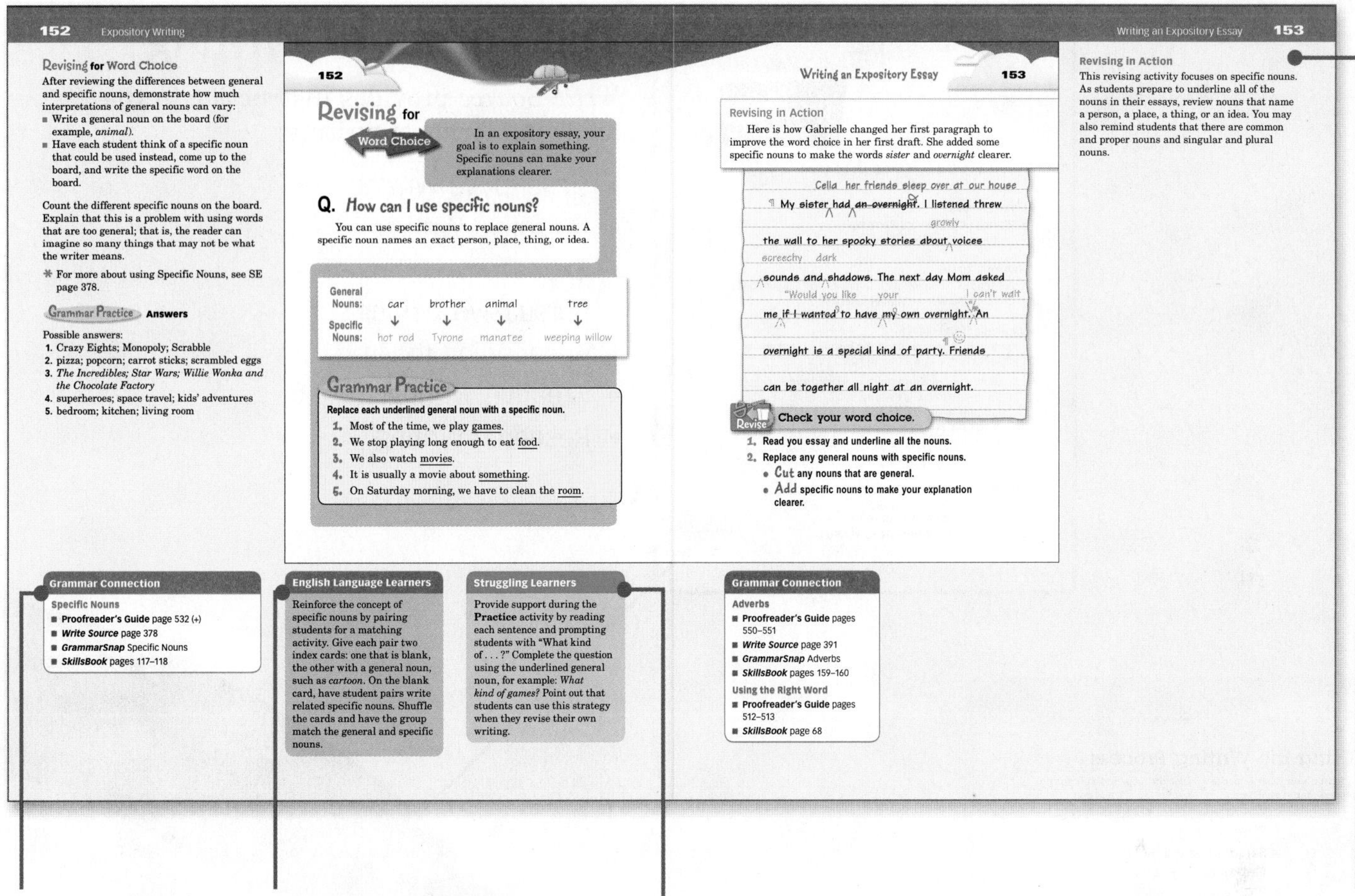

Grammar Connections support grammar, usage, and mechanics instruction.

The Teacher's Edition provides consistent support for **English language learners.**

Differentiated Instruction for struggling learners and advanced learners is provided throughout the core instructional units.

Teaching suggestions provide the support you need to implement writing instruction.

Additional Resources

- Common Core State Standard Correlation
- Yearlong Timetable
- Professional Development for Writing
- Reading–Writing Connection
- "Getting Started" Copy Masters
- Benchmark Papers
- Graphic Organizers
- Family Letters

How is *Write Source* organized?

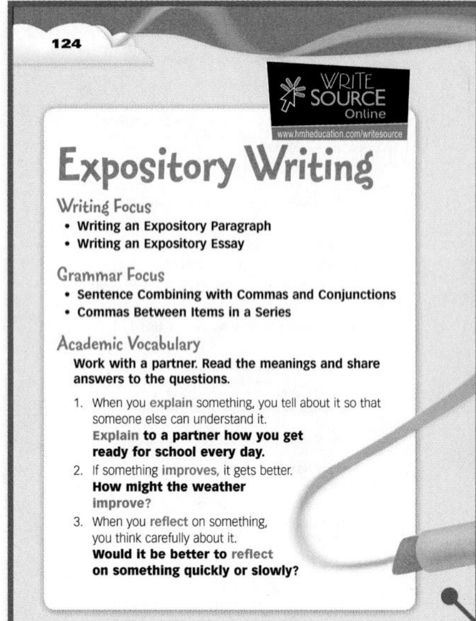

124

WRITE SOURCE Online

www.hmheducation.com/writesource

Expository Writing

Writing Focus
- Writing an Expository Paragraph
- Writing an Expository Essay

Grammar Focus
- Sentence Combining with Commas and Conjunctions
- Commas Between Items in a Series

Academic Vocabulary

Work with a partner. Read the meanings and share answers to the questions.

1. When you explain something, you tell about it so that someone else can understand it. **Explain to a partner how you get ready for school every day.**
2. If something improves, it gets better. **How might the weather improve?**
3. When you reflect on something, you think carefully about it. **Would it be better to reflect on something quickly or slowly?**

The Forms of Writing

Write Source provides instruction in the following forms of writing:

- Descriptive Writing
- Narrative Writing
- Expository Writing
- Persuasive Writing
- Responding to Literature
- Creative Writing
- Research Writing

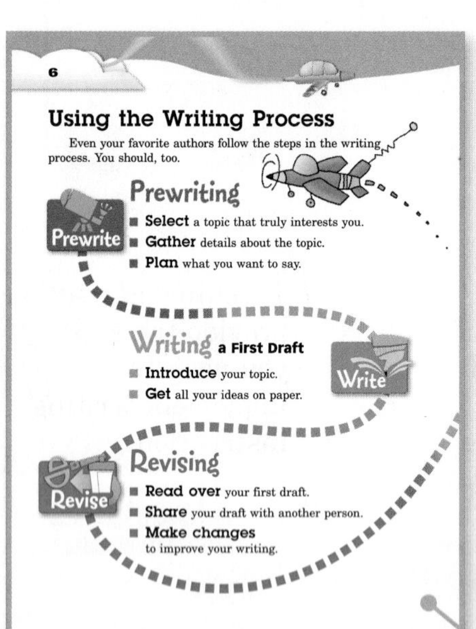

6

Using the Writing Process

Even your favorite authors follow the steps in the writing process. You should, too.

Prewriting (Prewrite)
- **Select** a topic that truly interests you.
- **Gather** details about the topic.
- **Plan** what you want to say.

Writing a First Draft (Write)
- **Introduce** your topic.
- **Get** all your ideas on paper.

Revising (Revise)
- **Read over** your first draft.
- **Share** your draft with another person.
- **Make changes** to improve your writing.

The Writing Process

This unit introduces students to the steps in the writing process and integrates instruction on the six traits of writing.

The Tools of Learning

The third section helps students improve important classroom skills: giving speeches, writing in journals and learning logs, viewing and listening skills, and taking tests.

Basic Grammar and Writing

This section covers the fundamental building blocks of writing: words, sentences, and paragraphs.

A Writer's Resource

This section is a writing guide students can refer to whenever they have questions about the development and presentation of paragraphs, reports, essays, and stories.

Proofreader's Guide

This final section addresses the conventions of standard English: punctuation, mechanics, spelling, grammar, usage, and sentences.

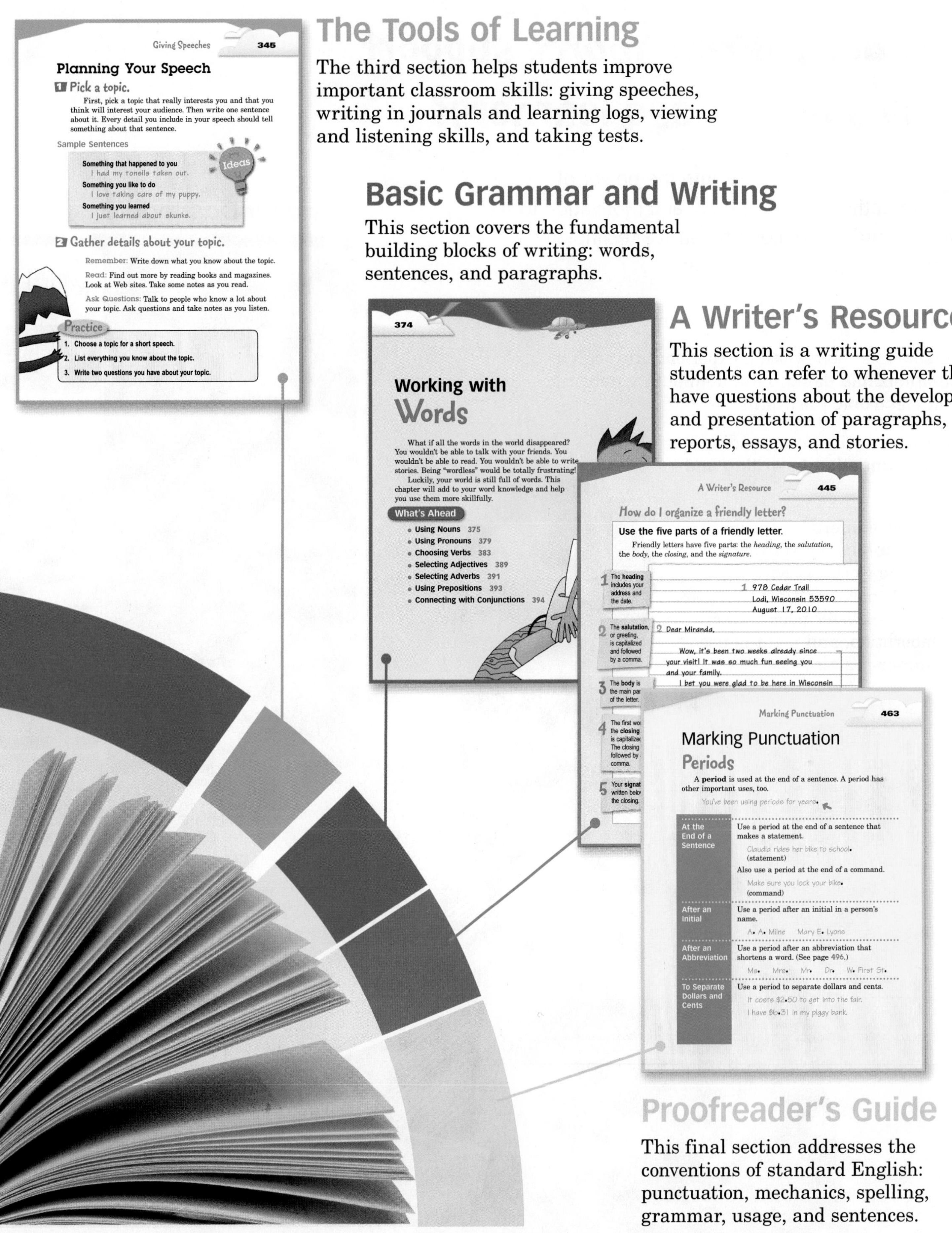

Giving Speeches 345

Planning Your Speech

1 Pick a topic.

First, pick a topic that really interests you and that you think will interest your audience. Then write one sentence about it. Every detail you include in your speech should tell something about that sentence.

Sample Sentences

Something that happened to you
I had my tonsils taken out.
Something you like to do
I love taking care of my puppy.
Something you learned
I just learned about skunks.

Ideas

2 Gather details about your topic.

Remember: Write down what you know about the topic.

Read: Find out more by reading books and magazines. Look at Web sites. Take some notes as you read.

Ask Questions: Talk to people who know a lot about your topic. Ask questions and take notes as you listen.

Practice

1. Choose a topic for a short speech.
2. List everything you know about the topic.
3. Write two questions you have about your topic.

374

Working with Words

What if all the words in the world disappeared? You wouldn't be able to talk with your friends. You wouldn't be able to read. You wouldn't be able to write stories. Being "wordless" would be totally frustrating!

Luckily, your world is still full of words. This chapter will add to your word knowledge and help you use them more skillfully.

What's Ahead

- Using Nouns 375
- Using Pronouns 379
- Choosing Verbs 383
- Selecting Adjectives 389
- Selecting Adverbs 391
- Using Prepositions 393
- Connecting with Conjunctions 394

A Writer's Resource 445

How do I organize a friendly letter?

Use the five parts of a friendly letter.

Friendly letters have five parts: the *heading*, the *salutation*, the *body*, the *closing*, and the *signature*.

1 The heading includes your address and the date.

2 The salutation, or greeting, is capitalized and followed by a comma.

3 The body is the main par of the letter.

4 The first wo the closing is capitalize The closing followed by comma.

5 Your signat written belo the closing.

1 978 Cedar Trail
Lodi, Wisconsin 53590
August 17, 2010

2 Dear Miranda,

Wow, it's been two weeks already since your visit! It was so much fun seeing you and your family.

I bet you were glad to be here in Wisconsin

Marking Punctuation 463

Marking Punctuation

Periods

A **period** is used at the end of a sentence. A period has other important uses, too.

You've been using periods for years.

At the End of a Sentence	Use a period at the end of a sentence that makes a statement. Claudia rides her bike to school. (statement) Also use a period at the end of a command. Make sure you lock your bike. (command)
After an Initial	Use a period after an initial in a person's name. A. A. Milne Mary E. Lyons
After an Abbreviation	Use a period after an abbreviation that shortens a word. (See page 496.) Ms. Mrs. Mr. Dr. W. First St.
To Separate Dollars and Cents	Use a period to separate dollars and cents. It costs $2.50 to get into the fair. I have $6.31 in my piggy bank.

How does *Write Source* support today's digital-age learners?

Write Source Online taps into the power of interactivity, collaboration, and motivation to deliver a coordinated, comprehensive technology program for writing and grammar.

With ***Write Source Online***, teachers and students:

- personalize their writing experience through a **customizable dashboard**, **community network**, and **electronic portfolios**
- easily transition from reading to build a **solid foundation in writing and grammar**
- experience **interactive guided instruction** using Net-text, an online worktext with comprehensive writing support, tools for peer-to-peer collaboration, and point-of-use grammar practice

Teacher Dashboard

Preparing students and teachers for success in the 21st century.

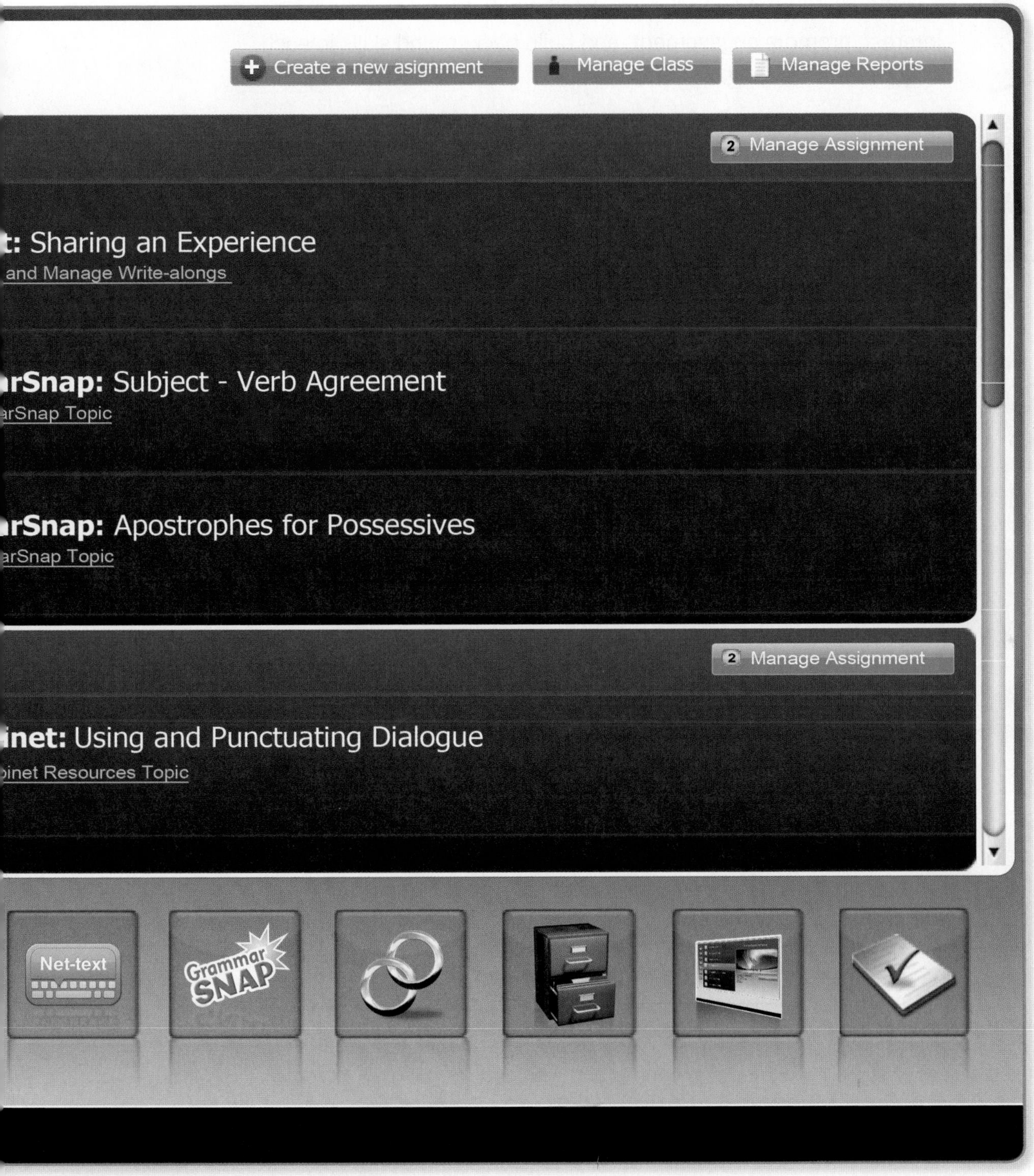

Create a new asignment
Manage Class
Manage Reports

Manage Assignment

t: Sharing an Experience
and Manage Write-alongs

rSnap: Subject - Verb Agreement
arSnap Topic

rSnap: Apostrophes for Possessives
arSnap Topic

Manage Assignment

inet: Using and Punctuating Dialogue
binet Resources Topic

Net-text
Grammar SNAP

What are the components of *Write Source Online*?

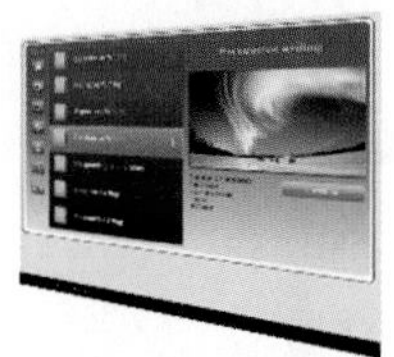

Set the stage for success with Interactive Whiteboard Lessons, high-functioning multimedia presentations that help you generate interest, promote engagement, and build background skills in each major form of writing.

Transform students into writers with Net-text, an innovative online worktext that features interactive instruction, online document creation, peer-to-peer commenting, and integrated grammar—all supported by tools that help you monitor progress and give feedback.

Engage students in grammar with GrammarSnap, a multimedia application that reinforces and extends understanding of key topics through videos, games, and quizzes that make learning about grammar fun.

Students are motivated to earn **SkillSnap points to unlock a variety of accessories** for their avatar character.

Tap into the power of publishing with the *Write Source Online* Portfolio, a customizable resource that gives students an authentic forum for sharing and reflecting on their writing.

Students and classrooms can connect in **My Network** to share and comment on each other's published portfolios.

Simplify the management of daily work with the Assignment Manager, a tool that delivers automatic student notifications about due dates and next steps while providing you with linked access to student work for commenting and grading.

Energize instruction with an innovative, integrated online writing program.

plays literature connections graphic organizers
instructional videos satire online peer reviewing
presentation creative writing
process grammar writing writing in the arts word ch
poetry descriptive writing voice mechanics collaboration
prewriting expository writing assessment
paragraph rubric publishing
stories

Write Source Online
www.hmheducation.com/writesource

traits editing
ideas writing across the curriculum interactive instrucion
essay scoring revising narrative writing essay organization
sentence fluency conventions
informative writing forms usag
benchmark papers games
writing in math persuasive writing

Additional Resources

- **Bookshelf** *Write Source* print component eBooks
- **Essay Scoring** Prompts for additional writing practice with automatic scoring and evaluation
- **File Cabinet** Thousands of printable teacher resources, such as blackline masters and additional assessments, that help you minimize planning time and differentiate instruction

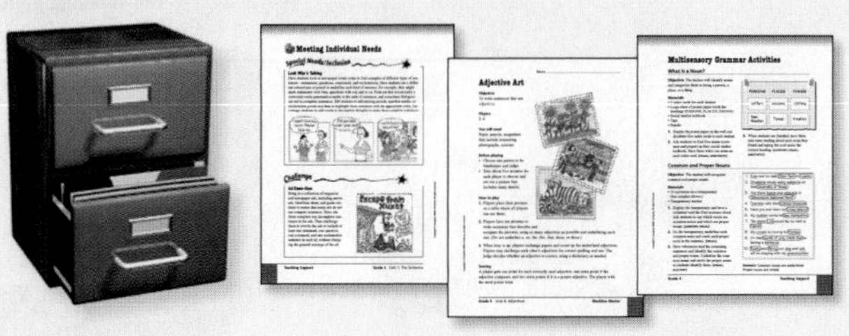

Professional Development for Writing

This section of the *Write Source* Teacher's Edition provides information to help you make the most of *Write Source* in your classroom. The program's instructional design includes comprehensive support for the topics that matter most to teachers: grammar, writing workshops, academic vocabulary, test preparation, the use of technology, and so much more. Whether you are a new teacher or a veteran, the information in the following pages will show how *Write Source* can help you meet your classroom goals.

Contents

How does *Write Source* teach the forms of writing?

Write Source provides numerous models and assignments for each major form of writing: **descriptive, narrative, expository, persuasive, response to literature, creative,** and **research**.

Writing Assignments

The core writing units provide students with comprehensive, research-based exploration of the narrative, expository, and persuasive forms of writing. Each of these units employs the following instructional sequence:

- a **start-up paragraph assignment**—complete with a writing model and step-by-step writing guidelines;
- a **multiparagraph assignment**—complete with writing models, in-depth step-by-step guidelines, and integration of traits and grammar instruction;
- an **across-the-curriculum writing assignment and a practical writing assignment**—complete with writing models and writing tips
- an **assessment writing assignment**—complete with a model response to a prompt plus writing tips.

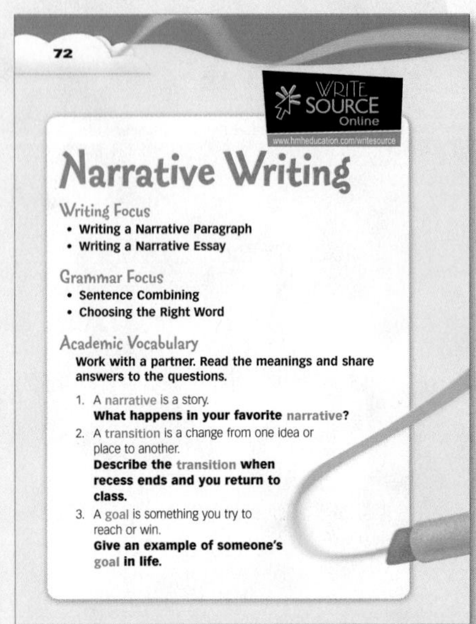

72

WRITE SOURCE Online

www.hmheducation.com/writesource

Narrative Writing

Writing Focus
- Writing a Narrative Paragraph
- Writing a Narrative Essay

Grammar Focus
- Sentence Combining
- Choosing the Right Word

Academic Vocabulary

Work with a partner. Read the meanings and share answers to the questions.

1. A narrative is a story.
   What happens in your favorite narrative?
2. A transition is a change from one idea or place to another.
   Describe the transition when recess ends and you return to class.
3. A goal is something you try to reach or win.
   Give an example of someone's goal in life.

Writing Skills and Strategies

As students develop their composition in each unit, they gain valuable experience with the following skills and strategies:

- reading and responding to texts (writing models);
- **integrating the traits of writing into the writing process;**
- using graphic organizers;
- developing beginnings, middles, and endings;
- **practicing grammar skills in context;**
- publishing (presenting) writing;
- reflecting on writing;
- **responding to an assessment prompt.**

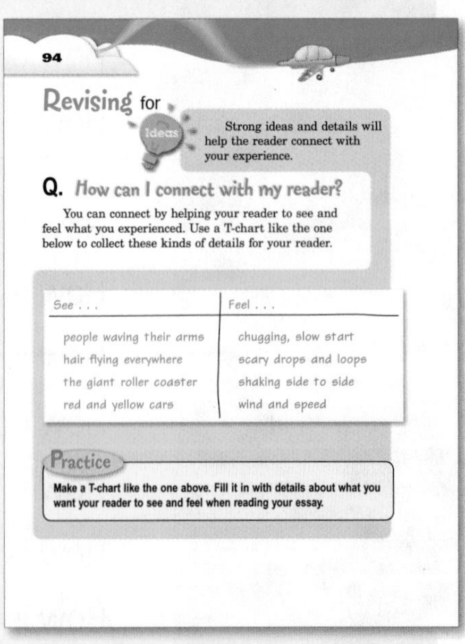

94

Revising for Ideas

Strong ideas and details will help the reader connect with your experience.

Q. How can I connect with my reader?

You can connect by helping your reader to see and feel what you experienced. Use a T-chart like the one below to collect these kinds of details for your reader.

See . . .	Feel . . .
people waving their arms	chugging, slow start
hair flying everywhere	scary drops and loops
the giant roller coaster	shaking side to side
red and yellow cars	wind and speed

Practice

Make a T-chart like the one above. Fill it in with details about what you want your reader to see and feel when reading your essay.

How does the program integrate the writing process and the six traits?

Throughout each core forms of writing unit, the six traits of effective writing are integrated into the steps of the writing process. As students develop their writing, they acquire an understanding of and appreciation for each trait of writing. In addition, a rubric, checklists, guidelines, and activities are used to ensure that each piece of writing is completely traits based.

The Process and the Traits in the Core Units

Understanding Your Goal

This page helps students understand the goal of their writing. It lists expectations for each trait as it relates to the writing form.

Revising and Editing for the Traits

When students are ready to revise and edit, they will find step-by-step traits instruction, guidelines, and strategies to help them improve their writing.

Rubrics for the Core Units

A traits-based rubric concludes each unit. This rubric ties directly to the goal chart at the beginning of the unit and the rubric strips presented on the revising and editing pages.

Special Note: For more information about the writing traits, we recommend *Creating Writers Through 6-Trait Writing Assessment and Instruction*, 4th ed., by Vicki Spandel (Addison Wesley Longman, 2005) and *Write Traits®* by Vicki Spandel and Jeff Hicks (Houghton Mifflin Harcourt, 2011).

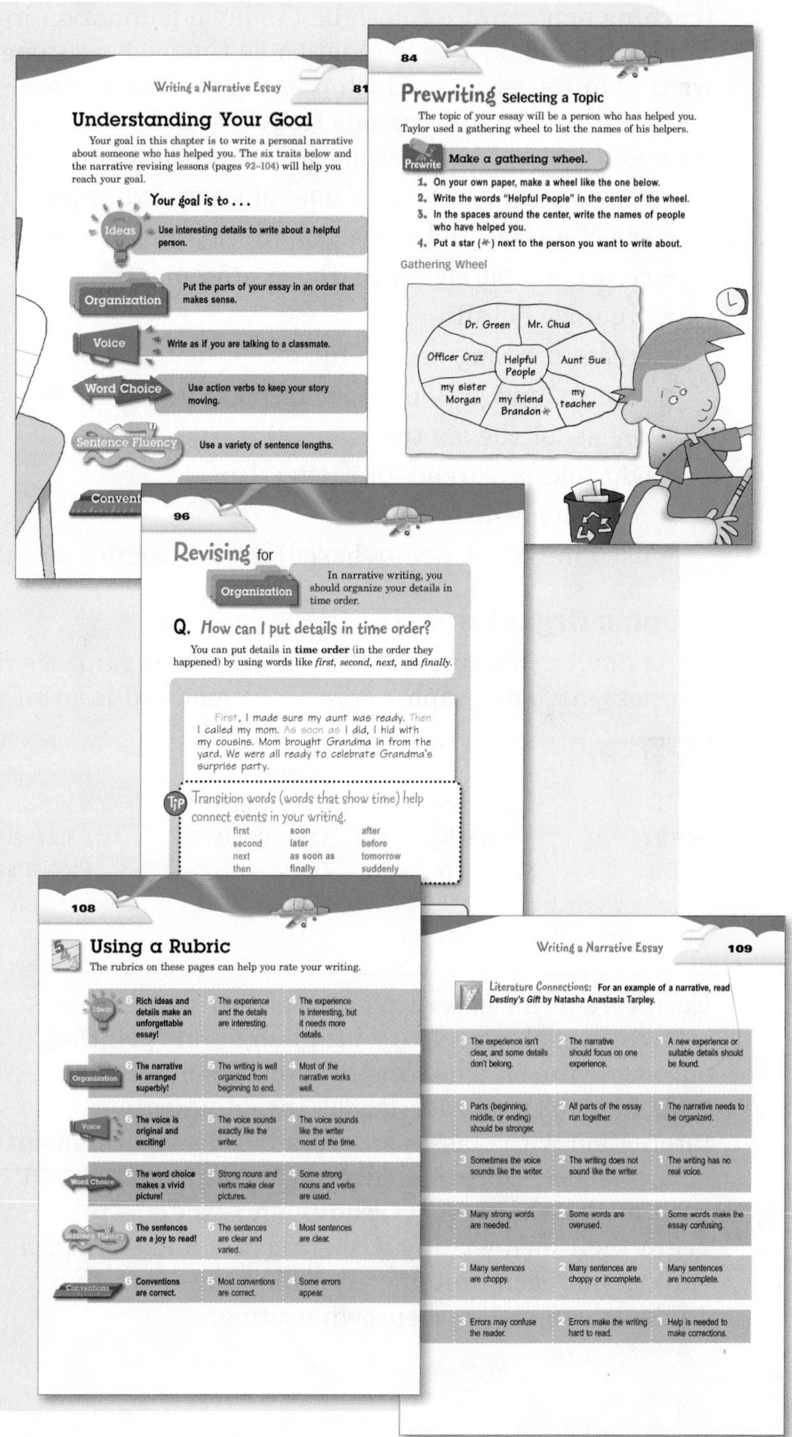

Writing a Narrative Essay 81

Understanding Your Goal

Your goal in this chapter is to write a personal narrative about someone who has helped you. The six traits below and the narrative revising lessons (pages 92–104) will help you reach your goal.

Your goal is to . . .

Ideas — Use interesting details to write about a helpful person.

Organization — Put the parts of your essay in an order that makes sense.

Voice — Write as if you are talking to a classmate.

Word Choice — Use action verbs to keep your story moving.

Sentence Fluency — Use a variety of sentence lengths.

Convent…

84

Prewriting Selecting a Topic

The topic of your essay will be a person who has helped you. Taylor used a gathering wheel to list the names of his helpers.

Prewrite — Make a gathering wheel.

1. On your own paper, make a wheel like the one below.
2. Write the words "Helpful People" in the center of the wheel.
3. In the spaces around the center, write the names of people who have helped you.
4. Put a star (*) next to the person you want to write about.

Gathering Wheel

96

Revising for Organization

In narrative writing, you should organize your details in time order.

Q. How can I put details in time order?

You can put details in **time order** (in the order they happened) by using words like *first, second, next,* and *finally.*

First, I made sure my aunt was ready. Then I called my mom. As soon as I did, I hid with my cousins. Mom brought Grandma in from the yard. We were all ready to celebrate Grandma's surprise party.

Tip: Transition words (words that show time) help connect events in your writing.

first, second, next, then, soon, later, as soon as, finally, after, before, tomorrow, suddenly

108

Using a Rubric

The rubrics on these pages can help you rate your writing.

Trait	6	5	4	3	2	1
Ideas	Rich ideas and details make an unforgettable essay!	The experience and the details are interesting.	The experience is interesting, but it needs more details.	The experience isn't clear, and some details don't belong.	The narrative should focus on one experience.	A new experience or suitable details should be found.
Organization	The narrative is arranged superbly!	The writing is well organized from beginning to end.	Most of the narrative works well.	Parts (beginning, middle, or ending) should be stronger.	All parts of the essay run together.	The narrative needs to be organized.
Voice	The voice is original and exciting!	The voice sounds exactly like the writer.	The voice sounds like the writer most of the time.	Sometimes the voice sounds like the writer.	The writing does not sound like the writer.	The writing has no real voice.
Word Choice	The word choice makes a vivid picture!	Strong nouns and verbs make clear pictures.	Some strong nouns and verbs are used.	Many strong words are needed.	Some words are overused.	Some words make the essay confusing.
Sentence Fluency	The sentences are a joy to read!	The sentences are clear and varied.	Most sentences are clear.	Many sentences are choppy.	Many sentences are choppy or incomplete.	Many sentences are incomplete.
Conventions	Conventions are correct.	Most conventions are correct.	Some errors appear.	Errors may confuse the reader.	Errors make the writing hard to read.	Help is needed to make corrections.

Writing a Narrative Essay 109

Literature Connections: For an example of a narrative, read *Destiny's Gift* by Natasha Anastasia Tarpley.

How can I implement a writing workshop?

Write Source supports a workshop approach through both print and technology resources. The program includes minilessons for instruction, high-quality models to encourage writing, support for whole-class sharing, and much more.

Integrated Minilessons

As a starting point, **Interactive Whiteboard Lessons** provide short, focused teaching opportunities designed to lay a foundation in key concepts. Students build on this foundation as they move through the core forms of writing units, where each step in the writing process presents additional opportunities for minilessons targeting individual needs. Both the print book and the **Net-text** lessons teach students to:

- preview the trait-based goal of a writing project
- select a topic and use a graphic organizer to gather details
- create a topic sentence (thesis statement)
- organize details
- create a strong beginning, a coherent middle, and an effective ending
- receive (and provide) peer responses
- revise for the six traits
- edit and proofread for conventions
- publish a finished piece
- use analytical, (traits-based) mode-specific rubrics

Mon | Tues | Wed | Thurs | Fri

Writing Minilessons
(10 minutes as needed)

Status Checks
(2 minutes)
Find out what students will work on for the day.

Individual Work
(30 minutes)
Writing, Revising, Editing, Conferencing, or Publishing

Whole-Class Sharing Session
(5 minutes)

Graphic Organizers

Write Source contains a wealth of graphic organizers that can serve as the subjects of minilessons. The graphic organizers modeled in print and technology include the following:

Pie graph	Sensory chart	Process diagram	"Why" chart	Topic list
Web	Plot chart	Venn diagram	Basics of life list	Character chart
Cluster	Storyboard	Circle graph	5 W's chart	Picture diagram
T-chart	Bar graph	Cycle diagram	Cause-effect chart	Comparison-contrast chart
Outline	KWL chart	Gathering grid	Problem-solution chart	Time line

High-Quality Models

Each core forms of writing unit begins with a high-interest model, complete with annotations pointing out key features. The **Net-text** provides additional tools for exploring each model, including online interaction with classroom peers to rate and comment on the model. Once students have read and analyzed each model, they will be ready—and excited—to begin their own writing. Other models and examples throughout each unit offer specific techniques that students can use in their own writing.

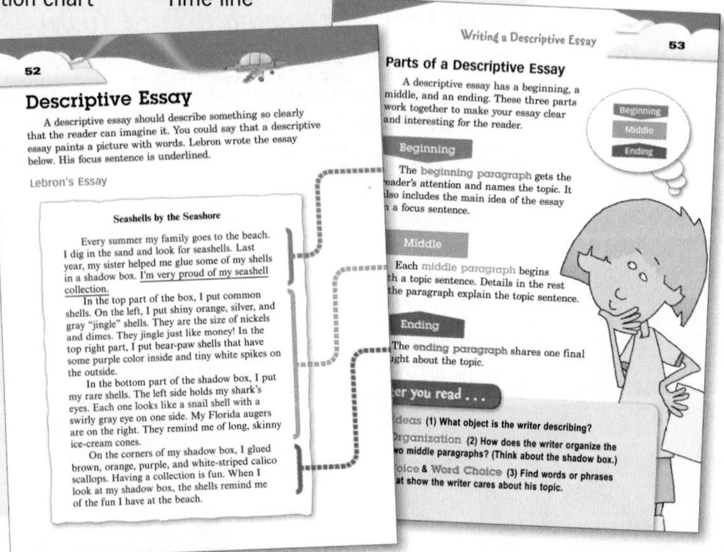

52

Descriptive Essay

A descriptive essay should describe something so clearly that the reader can imagine it. You could say that a descriptive essay paints a picture with words. Lebron wrote the essay below. His focus sentence is underlined.

Lebron's Essay

Seashells by the Seashore

Every summer my family goes to the beach. I dig in the sand and look for seashells. Last year, my sister helped me glue some of my shells in a shadow box. I'm very proud of my seashell collection.

In the top part of the box, I put common shells. On the left, I put shiny orange, silver, and gray "jingle" shells. They are the size of nickels and dimes. They jingle just like money! In the top right part, I put bear-paw shells that have some purple color inside and tiny white spikes on the outside.

In the bottom part of the shadow box, I put my rare shells. The left side holds my shark's eyes. Each one looks like a snail shell with a swirly gray eye on one side. My Florida augers are on the right. They remind me of long, skinny ice-cream cones.

On the corners of my shadow box, I glued brown, orange, purple, and white-striped calico scallops. Having a collection is fun. When I look at my shadow box, the shells remind me of the fun I have at the beach.

Writing a Descriptive Essay 53

Parts of a Descriptive Essay

A descriptive essay has a beginning, a middle, and an ending. These three parts work together to make your essay clear and interesting for the reader.

Beginning

The beginning paragraph gets the reader's attention and names the topic. It also includes the main idea of the essay in a focus sentence.

Middle

Each middle paragraph begins with a topic sentence. Details in the rest of the paragraph explain the topic sentence.

Ending

The ending paragraph shares one final thought about the topic.

After you read . . .

Ideas (1) What object is the writer describing?

Organization (2) How does the writer organize the two middle paragraphs? (Think about the shadow box.)

Voice & Word Choice (3) Find words or phrases that show the writer cares about his topic.

Individual Writing

Write Source makes it easy for writing-workshop students to work on their own. It also provides specific help whenever students have questions about their writing. Here are some of the areas that are addressed:

- catching the reader's interest
- providing background information
- developing strong paragraphs
- elaborating on ideas
- organizing ideas by time and location
- quoting
- using transitions
- drawing conclusions
- calling the reader to act

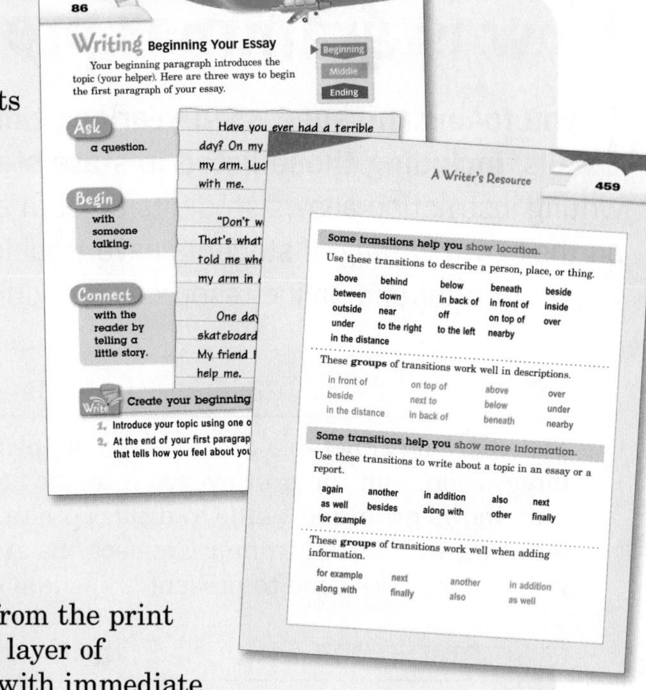
86

Writing Beginning Your Essay

Beginning
Middle
Ending

Your beginning paragraph introduces the topic (your helper). Here are three ways to begin the first paragraph of your essay.

Ask a question. — Have you ever had a terrible day? On my ... my arm. Luc... with me.

Begin with someone talking. — "Don't w... That's what... told me whe... my arm in ...

Connect with the reader by telling a little story. — One day... skateboard... My friend I... help me.

Write — Create your beginning

1. Introduce your topic using one o...
2. At the end of your first paragrap... that tells how you feel about you...

A Writer's Resource 459

Some transitions help you show location.

Use these transitions to describe a person, place, or thing.

above, behind, below, beneath, beside, between, down, in back of, in front of, inside, outside, near, off, on top of, over, under, to the right, to the left, nearby, in the distance

These groups of transitions work well in descriptions.

in front of, beside, in the distance — on top of, next to, in back of — above, below, beneath — over, under, nearby

Some transitions help you show more information.

Use these transitions to write about a topic in an essay or a report.

again, another, in addition, also, next, as well, besides, along with, other, finally, for example

These groups of transitions work well when adding information.

for example, along with — next, finally — another, also — in addition, as well

In addition to supporting these and other key concepts from the print components, the *Write Source* **Net-text** provides an extra layer of scaffolding for independent writing, including exercises with immediate feedback, at-a-click support for grammar and conventions concepts, ready access to such resources as a dictionary and thesaurus, and an application for creating and managing work online.

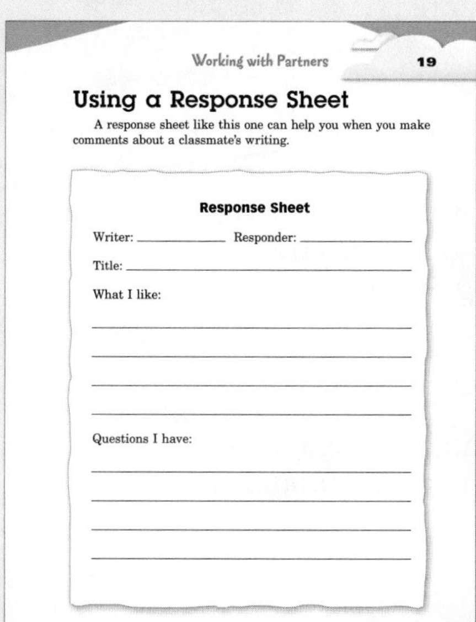
Working with Partners 19

Using a Response Sheet

A response sheet like this one can help you when you make comments about a classmate's writing.

Response Sheet

Writer: ____________ Responder: ____________

Title: ____________

What I like:

Questions I have:

Peer and Teacher Response

Write Source teaches peer responding and provides a peer response sheet. Consistent integration of the traits into the writing process allows students and teachers to speak a common language as they conduct response sessions. Traits-based checklists help pinpoint just what is working—and what could work better—in each piece of writing. The *Write Source* **Net-text** provides additional support for teacher-to-student and student-to-student response, including a commenting tool and commenting notifications.

Whole-Class Sharing

Write Source helps students prepare their work for whole-class sharing— whether in a traditional presentation or in the public section of the **Online Portfolio**. In addition, the program provides a wealth of suggestions for publishing in a variety of forms and for a variety of audiences.

How is grammar presented?

If you follow the suggested yearlong timetable, you will cover all the key grammar skills, including those listed in state standards. Grammar instruction integrated into writing instruction allows students to learn about grammar in context when they are working on their own writing. If students have trouble with a particular concept, you can refer to a wealth of print and online resources for additional support.

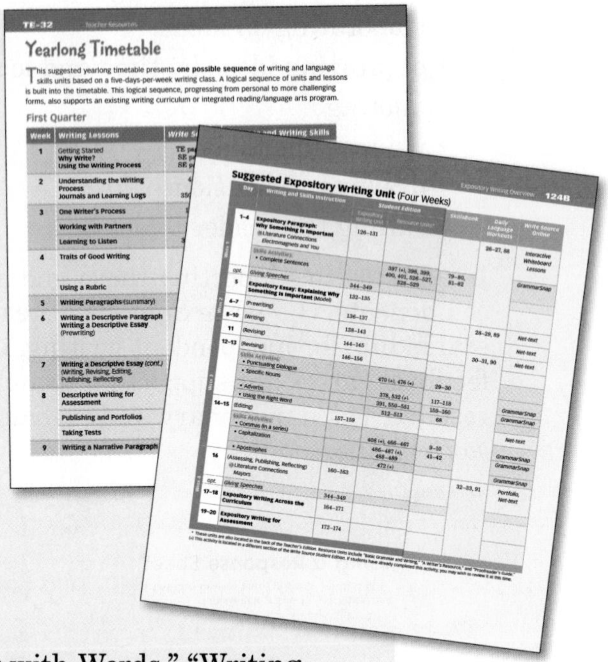

Grammar in the Teacher's Edition

The yearlong timetable provides the big picture of grammar integration, and the unit overview at the beginning of each unit shows grammar skills and concepts to teach while teaching writing. Grammar Connections at point of use help you pinpoint the time to present skills and concepts.

Grammar in the Student Edition

Forms of Writing

During the development of the main composition in each core forms of writing unit, grammar instruction is integrated into the revising and editing steps. Grammar instruction includes examples, practice, and application activities, and it links to students' writing.

Basic Grammar and Writing

For more grammar in the context of writing, refer to "Working with Words," "Writing Sentences," and "Building Paragraphs." Use these minilessons to teach specific grammar and style topics that students can apply to their writing. These pages include examples of each skill, as well as practice activities.

Proofreader's Guide

This unit serves as a complete conventions guide, providing grammar, usage, and mechanics rules, instruction, examples, and activities (including tests in standardized-test format).

Write Source Online

The *Write Source* **Net-text** offers interactive instruction and practice for the conventions topics embedded in the core writing units. **GrammarSnap** provides additional instruction, practice, and basic skills reinforcement through videos, minilessons, games, and quizzes.

Grammar in Other Program Components

The *SkillsBook* provides more than 130 grammar, usage, punctuation, mechanics, and spelling, and sentence-construction activities. The *Assessment* book contains a pretest, benchmark tests, and a post-test for basic writing and editing skills. *Daily Language Workouts* includes a year's worth of sentences (daily) and paragraphs (weekly) for editing practice.

Planning Grammar Instruction

Should I implement all of the suggested basic grammar activities?

In the course of the year, if you assigned every grammar exercise listed in the unit scope and sequence charts (located in the unit overviews of your Teacher's Edition), your students would complete **all** of the "Basic Grammar and Writing," "Proofreader's Guide," *SkillsBook*, and **GrammarSnap** activities.

Because the most effective teaching of grammar happens in context, grammar instruction appears at appropriate times during the revising and editing steps of the core writing forms units. As the teacher, you must choose the type and amount of instruction that will best meet the needs of your students.

How are all the grammar resources related?

The *SkillsBook* grammar activities parallel and expand on the rules and exercises found in the "Proofreader's Guide." In "Basic Grammar and Writing," brief exercises function well as minilessons and may be assigned on an as-needed basis. **GrammarSnap** offers additional support for key grammar topics in an engaging, interactive format.

How do I use the unit scope and sequence charts?

The sample below from the persuasive writing unit is followed by an explanation of how to read and use the charts.

Persuasive Writing Overview 176B

Suggested Persuasive Writing Unit (Four Weeks)

	Day	Writing and Skills Instruction	Student Edition: Persuasive Writing Unit	Student Edition: Resource Units*	SkillsBook	Daily Language Workouts	Write Source Online
Week 1	1–4	**Persuasive Paragraph: A Class Need** Literature Connections *The Big Cleanup*	178–183			34–35, 92	*Interactive Whiteboard Lessons*
		Skills Activities: • Using the Right Word		520–521, 522–523	72–73		
		• Spelling		502–507	63–64		
		• Fragments		403 (+), 526 (+), 528 (+)	96		*GrammarSnap*
	opt.	*Giving Speeches*	344–349				

1. The Resource Units column indicates the Student Edition pages that cover rules, examples, and exercises for corresponding skills activities.
2. The *SkillsBook, Daily Language Workouts*, and **Write Source Online** columns indicate pages and information from those particular resources.

How do I use *Daily Language Workouts*?

Daily Language Workouts is a teacher resource that provides a high-interest sentence for each day of the year and weekly paragraphs for additional editing and proofreading practice. This regular practice helps students develop the objectivity they need to effectively edit their own writing.

How is writing across the curriculum addressed?

Write Source provides a wide variety of writing-across-the-curriculum activities and assignments. It promotes *writing to show learning, writing to learn new concepts,* and *writing to reflect on learning.*

Writing to Show Learning

Writing to show learning is the most common type of writing that content-area teachers assign. The following forms of writing covered in the program are commonly used for this purpose.

- descriptive paragraph and essay
- narrative paragraph and essay
- expository paragraph and essay
- persuasive paragraph and essay
- response paragraph and book review
- response to nonfiction
- comparison of fiction and nonfiction books
- response to a poem
- summary paragraph
- research report

74

Writing a Narrative Paragraph

Donica was asked to write a few things about herself. Instead of just telling facts about herself, she wrote a narrative paragraph! In it, she told about an experience she had enjoyed.

In this unit, you will tell something about yourself in a narrative paragraph. Your paragraph will have three parts.

Paragraph Parts

1 The **topic sentence** tells the main idea of the paragraph.

2 The **body sentences** tell more about the main event or topic of your paragraph.

3 The **closing sentence** gives the reader something to think about.

126

Writing an Expository Paragraph

Elijah had a bike. It was one of the most important things in his life. How could he explain to his family and friends what makes his bike great for him? He wrote an expository paragraph.

Soon you will write your own expository paragraph. In it, you'll explain why something is important to you.

Paragraph Parts

1 The **topic sentence** tells what the paragraph explains.

2 The **body sentences** add details that help explain the topic sentence.

3 The **closing sentence** completes the explanation.

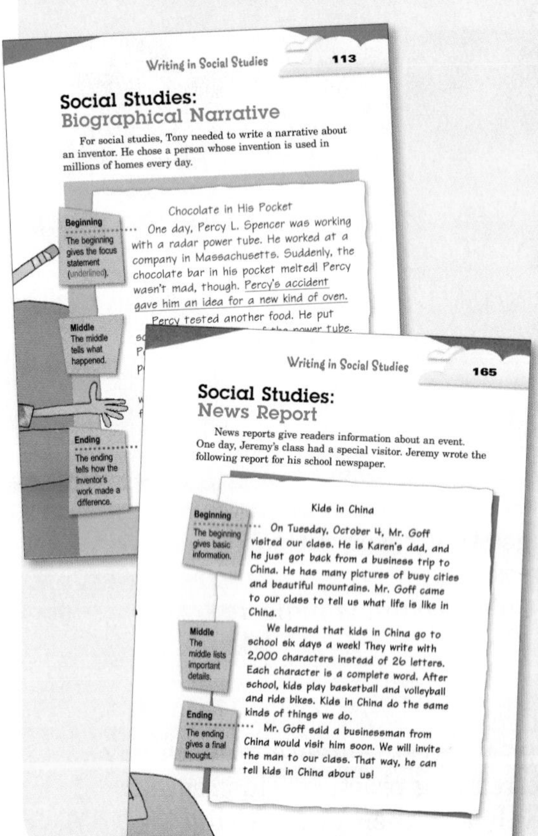

Writing in Social Studies 113

Social Studies: Biographical Narrative

For social studies, Tony needed to write a narrative about an inventor. He chose a person whose invention is used in millions of homes every day.

Beginning: The beginning gives the focus statement (underlined).

Chocolate in His Pocket

One day, Percy L. Spencer was working with a radar power tube. He worked at a company in Massachusetts. Suddenly, the chocolate bar in his pocket melted! Percy wasn't mad, though. Percy's accident gave him an idea for a new kind of oven.

Percy tested another food. He put ...

Middle: The middle tells what happened.

Ending: The ending tells how the inventor's work made a difference.

Writing in Social Studies 165

Social Studies: News Report

News reports give readers information about an event. One day, Jeremy's class had a special visitor. Jeremy wrote the following report for his school newspaper.

Beginning: The beginning gives basic information.

Kids in China

On Tuesday, October 4, Mr. Goff visited our class. He is Karen's dad, and he just got back from a business trip to China. He has many pictures of busy cities and beautiful mountains. Mr. Goff came to our class to tell us what life is like in China.

Middle: The middle lists important details.

We learned that kids in China go to school six days a week! They write with 2,000 characters instead of 26 letters. Each character is a complete word. After school, kids play basketball and volleyball and ride bikes. Kids in China do the same kinds of things we do.

Ending: The ending gives a final thought.

Mr. Goff said a businessman from China would visit him soon. We will invite the man to our class. That way, he can tell kids in China about us!

Sample Writing-Across-the-Curriculum Assignments

Narrative Writing

Social Studies: Biographical Narrative
Art: A Personal Art Story

Expository Writing

Social Studies: News Report
Music: Report

Persuasive Writing

Science: Persuasive Poster
Health: An Important Issue

How does *Write Source* teach academic vocabulary?

Write Source gives students the opportunity to learn and use academic vocabulary so essential for success in school.

Academic Vocabulary in *Write Source*

Academic vocabulary refers to the words students must know in order to understand the concepts they encounter in school. Academic vocabulary terms such as *transition, convince, compare*, and *logical* are not specific to any one subject but rather denote key ideas and skills relevant to many subject areas. In a sense, academic vocabulary is the language of school. To be successful in school, students must understand and be able to use academic vocabulary as they write about and discuss what they learn in class.

The *Write Source* Academic Vocabulary feature gives students the opportunity to learn and practice using new academic vocabulary in a collaborative activity. This feature, which appears at the beginning of each unit of the Student Edition, provides a brief explanation of each academic vocabulary word, followed by a prompt that motivates students to practice using the term.

- Academic vocabulary is taken from words appearing in the unit.
- Students work with a partner to read the explanations of the academic vocabulary.
- Each explanation is accompanied by an activity or question that prompts students to demonstrate their understanding of the word.

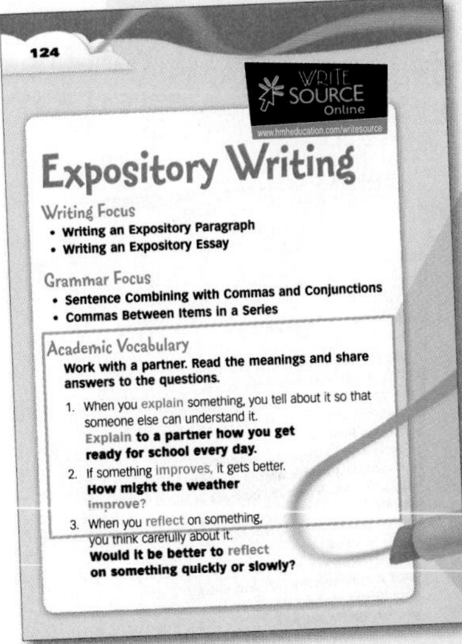
124

WRITE SOURCE Online

www.hmheducation.com/writesource

Expository Writing

Writing Focus
- Writing an Expository Paragraph
- Writing an Expository Essay

Grammar Focus
- Sentence Combining with Commas and Conjunctions
- Commas Between Items in a Series

Academic Vocabulary

Work with a partner. Read the meanings and share answers to the questions.

1. When you explain something, you tell about it so that someone else can understand it. **Explain to a partner how you get ready for school every day.**
2. If something improves, it gets better. **How might the weather improve?**
3. When you reflect on something, you think carefully about it. **Would it be better to reflect on something quickly or slowly?**

Academic Vocabulary

Work with a partner. Read the meanings and share answers to the questions.

1. When you **explain** something, you tell about it so that someone else can understand it.
   Explain to a partner how you get ready for school every day.
2. If something **improves,** it gets better.
   How might the weather improve?
3. When you **reflect** on something,

How is test preparation covered?

Each core forms of writing unit in the Student Edition prepares students for responding to testing prompts. **If students complete their work in each of the core units, they will have learned the skills necessary for success on any type of writing assessment.** Here are some of the main features in the Student Edition that address testing.

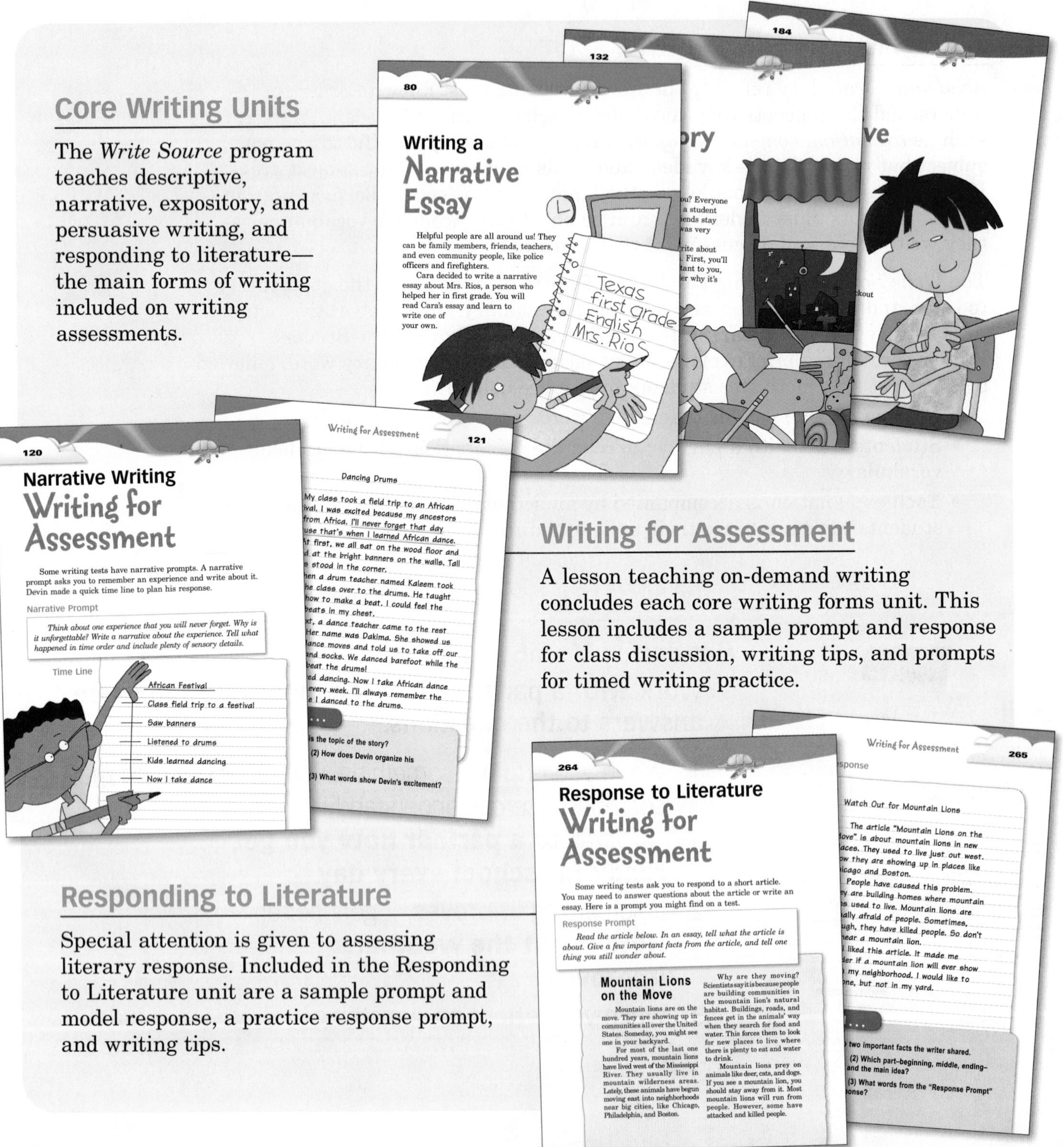

Core Writing Units

The *Write Source* program teaches descriptive, narrative, expository, and persuasive writing, and responding to literature—the main forms of writing included on writing assessments.

Writing for Assessment

A lesson teaching on-demand writing concludes each core writing forms unit. This lesson includes a sample prompt and response for class discussion, writing tips, and prompts for timed writing practice.

Responding to Literature

Special attention is given to assessing literary response. Included in the Responding to Literature unit are a sample prompt and model response, a practice response prompt, and writing tips.

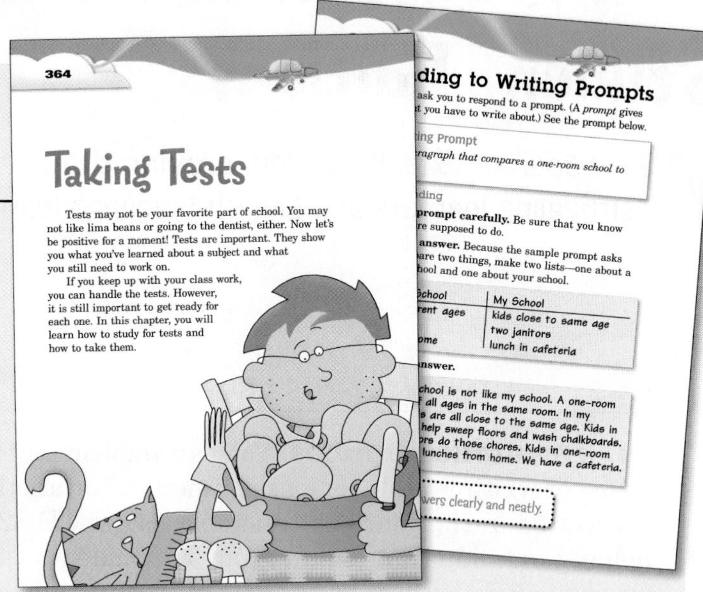

Taking Classroom Tests

The chapter on test-taking includes a section entitled "Responding to Writing Prompts" that models how to approach this type of testing.

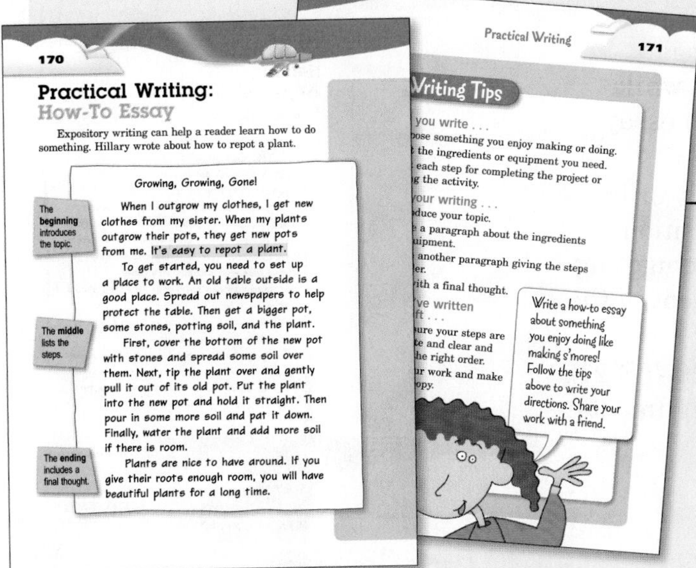

Writing Across the Curriculum

The writing-across-the-curriculum assignments at the end of the core writing units help students prepare for on-demand writing in content-based tests.

Test Prep for Grammar Skills

Tests at the end of each section in the "Proofreader's Guide" follow a standardized test format. Familiarity with this formatting will help students do their best on these important tests of writing ability.

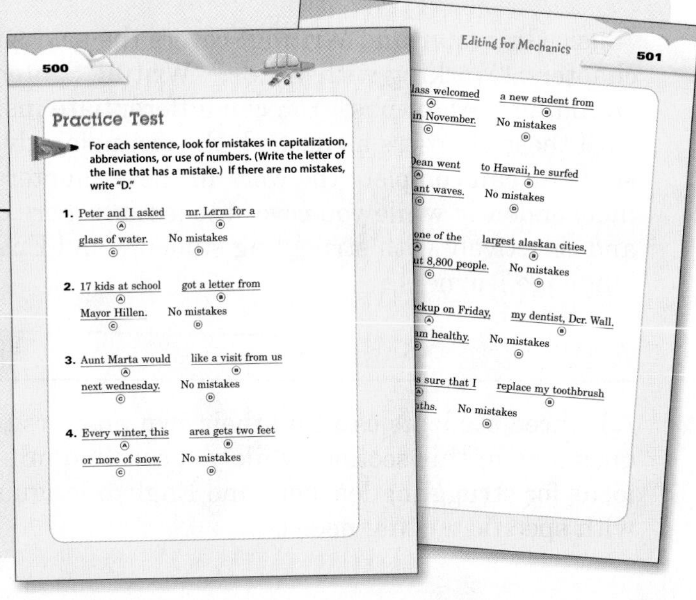

How is differentiation handled in the Student Edition?

Write Source texts, by design, **provide differentiation** in writing instruction—from struggling learners and English-language learners to advanced, independent students.

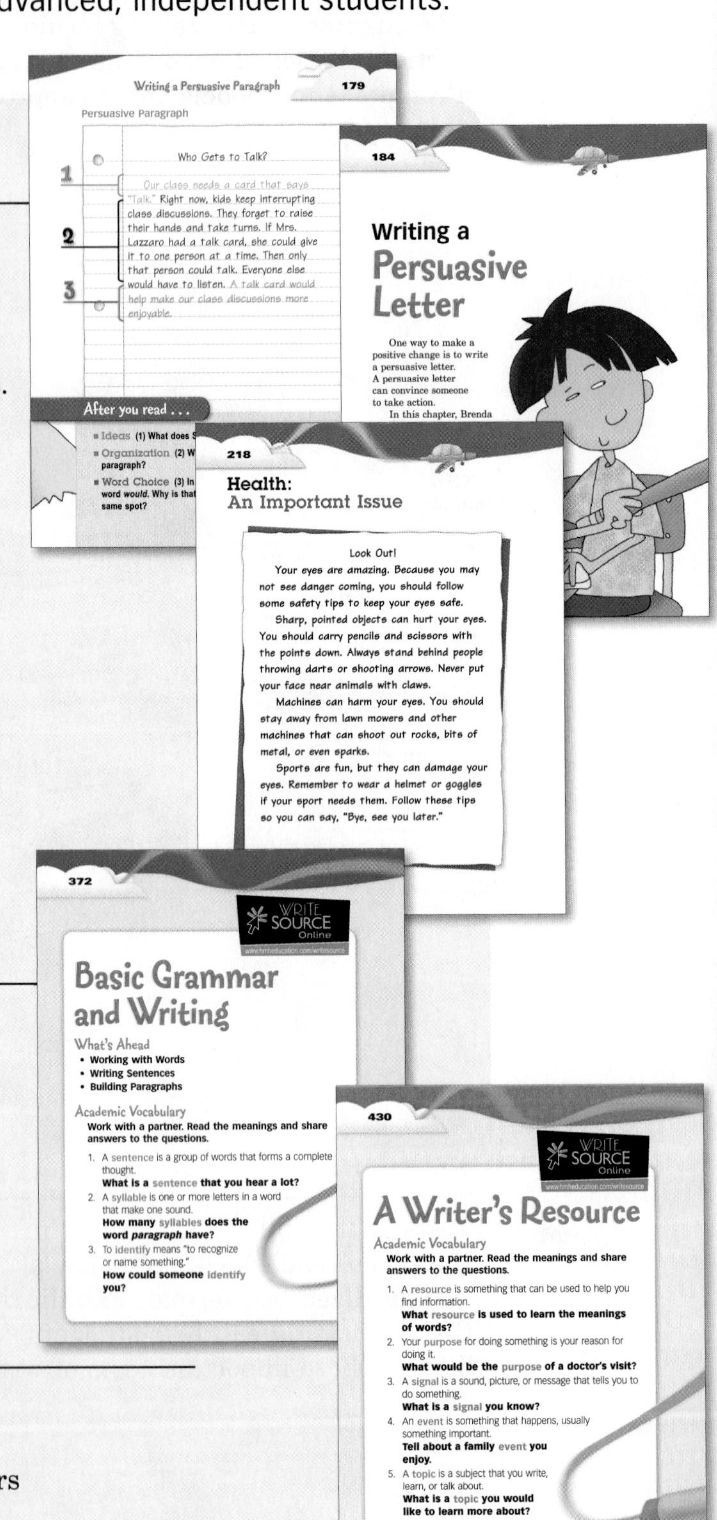

Core Forms Writing Units

Implementation Options: You can implement the forms of writing units, one assignment after another, as delineated in the yearlong timetable (pages TE-32–TE-35), helping individuals or small groups of students as needed. Or you can differentiate instruction in any number of ways. Here are three of the many possibilities:

- Have **struggling learners** focus on the single-paragraph writing assignment in each unit while other students complete the multiparagraph essay assignment.
- Have **advanced learners** work individually or in small groups on the multiparagraph composition assignment in each unit, while you guide struggling learners step by step through the development of the composition.
- Conduct a **writing workshop** (pages TE-20–TE-21), asking students to develop one or more assignments in a unit at their own pace.

Basic Grammar and Writing

"Basic Grammar and Writing" covers the basics in three chapters: "Working with Words," "Writing Sentences," and "Building Paragraphs." You can differentiate instruction with these chapters as needed. For example, advanced students can complete the work in these chapters independently while you cover the lessons more carefully and selectively with struggling students and English language learners.

A Writer's Resource

Advanced students can find their own answers to writing questions in this section, while you can find minilesson ideas for struggling learners and English language learners with specific writing needs.

How is differentiation handled in the Teacher's Edition?

The Teacher's Edition provides point-of-use differentiation for struggling learners, English language learners, and advanced learners.

Struggling Learners

The Struggling Learners notes allow you to customize lessons to meet the needs of students who may have difficulty completing the work. These notes provide alternative approaches, extra practice, or additional insights.

Struggling Learners

Provide students with extra practice using specific details to create "showing" sentences. On the board, write the following "telling" sentences:

- Dad said he enjoyed our Little League baseball game.
- We had fun at the park.

Work with students to add sensory details that turn each sentence into a "showing" sentence. Solutions might resemble the following:

- Dad said, "That was the best baseball game I've seen in a long time!"
- We played on the slide and swings all morning at the park.

Have students compare the two versions and point out specific details in the "showing" sentences.

English Language Learners

Some students may be unfamiliar with the term *scavenger hunt.* Explain that a scavenger is someone who searches for something. Tell students that a scavenger hunt is a game in which individuals or teams compete with one another to search for various items.

Demonstrate the general concept of a scavenger hunt by hiding "clues" (several symbols ¶, ✱, ☺ on sticky notes) around the room. Give students a list of the symbols and have them find the clues. They can then use the sticky notes with their own writing.

English Language Learners

The English Language Learners notes help you to guide students with limited language skills through the lessons. These notes provide extra practice, alternative approaches, connections to first languages, glossaries of new terms, demonstration ideas, and more.

Advanced Learners

The Advanced Learners notes help you enhance the lessons for students who need to be challenged. Some of the notes extend the lessons.

Advanced Learners

Students can practice toning down and building up sentences by playing the following game:

- Have students think of a topic and write one silly sentence and one boring sentence about it on two separate index cards.
- Collect all the cards and shuffle them.
- Read each card aloud to the class and have each student choose two to build up or tone down.

After students have rewritten their sentences, have them read to the class two silly and/or boring sentences with their revisions.

What research supports the *Write Source* program?

Write Source reflects the best thinking and research on writing instruction.

Applying the Process Approach to Writing

Research: The process approach, discussed by educators Donald M. Murray and Donald H. Graves, among others, breaks writing down into a series of steps—prewriting through publishing. Research has shown that students write more effectively and thoughtfully if they approach their work as a process rather than as an end product.

Graves, Donald. H. ***Writing: Teachers and Children at Work.*** Heinemann, 2003.

Murray, Donald. M.; Newkirk, Thomas; Miller, Lisa C. ***The Essential Don Murray: Lessons from America's Greatest Writing Teacher.*** Boynton/Cook Heinemann, 2009.

Write Source: All writing units and assignments are arranged according to the steps in the writing process. This arrangement helps students manage their work, especially in the case of longer essay or research report assignments.

Sequencing Assignments

Research: Writing instructor and researcher James Moffett developed a sequence of writing assignments—known as the "universe of discourse"—that has over the years served countless English/language arts classrooms. Moffett sequences the modes of writing according to their connection or immediacy to the writer. Moffett suggests that students first develop descriptive and narrative pieces because the students have an immediate, personal connection to this type of writing. Next, they should develop informational pieces that require some investigation before moving on to more challenging, reflective writing, such as persuasive essays and position papers.

Moffett, James. ***Teaching the Universe of Discourse.*** Boynton/Cook, 1987.

Related Title: Fleischer, Cathy; Andrew-Vaughn, Sarah. ***Writing Outside Your Comfort Zone: Helping Students Navigate Unfamiliar Genres.*** Heinemann, 2009.

Write Source: The writing units and assignments in the *Write Source* texts are arranged according to the "universe of discourse," starting with descriptive and narrative writing, moving on to expository writing, and so on. These assignments are designed to be used in a sequence that supports an existing writing curriculum or integrated reading/language arts program.

Implementing a Writing Workshop

Research: Countless respected writing instructors and researchers have advocated the importance of establishing a community of writers in the classroom. Teachers can establish such a community by implementing a writing workshop. In a writing workshop, students are immersed in all aspects of writing, including sharing their work with their peers.

Atwell, Nancie. ***In the Middle: New Understandings About Writing, Reading, and Learning.*** Heinemann, 1998.

Write Source: The instruction in *Write Source* is clearly presented so that most students can work independently on their writing in a workshop. In addition, the core forms of writing units contain innumerable opportunities for workshop minilessons.

Producing Writing with Detail

Research: Rebekah Caplan learned through her teaching experience that students don't automatically know how to add details to their personal, informational, and persuasive writing. She discovered with her students that adding detail to writing is a skill that must be practiced regularly. To address this problem, Caplan came up with the "show-me" sentence strategy, in which students begin with a basic idea—"My locker is messy"—and create a brief paragraph that shows rather than tells the idea.

Caplan, Rebekah. ***Writers in Training: A Guide to Developing a Composition Program.*** Dale Seymour Publications, 1984.

Related Title: Bernabi, Gretchen S.; Hover, Jayne; Candler, Cynthia. ***Crunchtime: Lessons to Help Students Blow the Roof Off Writing Tests—and Become Better Writers in the Process.*** Heinemann, 2009.

Write Source: *Daily Language Workouts* contains a series of show-me sentences that teachers can implement as a regular classroom warm-up.

Meeting Students' Diverse Needs

Research: Many students in today's classrooms struggle with writing. For struggling students, following the writing process is not enough. According to the research done by James L. Collins, struggling students need specific strategies and aids to help them become better writers. Collins found that these students benefit from skills instruction integrated into the process of writing, color coding and signposts in the presentation of instructional material, the use of graphic organizers, instructions presented in discreet chunks of copy, and so on.

Collins, James L. ***Strategies for Struggling Writers.*** Guilford Press, 1998.

Related Title: Cruz, M. Colleen; Calkins, Lucy. ***A Quick Guide to Reaching Struggling Writers, K–5.*** FirstHand/Heinemann, 2008.

Write Source: The core writing forms units contain all the key features from Collins's work. As a result, the units are well suited to struggling learners and English language learners.

Yearlong Timetable

This suggested yearlong timetable presents **one possible sequence** of writing and language skills units based on a five-days-per-week writing class. A logical sequence of units and lessons is built into the timetable. This logical sequence, progressing from personal to more challenging forms, also supports an existing writing curriculum or integrated reading/language arts program.

First Quarter

Week	Writing Lessons	*Write Source*	Grammar and Writing Skills
1	Getting Started **Why Write?** **Using the Writing Process**	TE page 76 SE page 1 SE page 3	**Skills Assessments** Pretests: Using the right word
2	**Understanding the Writing Process** **Journals and Learning Logs**	4–9 350–355	
3	**One Writer's Process**	10–15	**Skills Assessments** Pretests: Punctuation
	Working with Partners	16–19	
	Learning to Listen	362–363	
4	**Traits of Good Writing**	20–25	**Skills Assessments** Pretests: Mechanics, understanding sentences, parts of speech
	Using a Rubric	26–33	
5	**Writing Paragraphs** (summary)	416–429	Adjectives, prepositional phrases
6	**Writing a Descriptive Paragraph** **Writing a Descriptive Essay** (Prewriting)	44–49 50–55	Types of sentences, nouns, end punctuation, numbers, fragments, adjectives, prepositional phrases, specific nouns, adjectives, capitalization, apostrophes
7	**Writing a Descriptive Essay** *(cont.)* (Writing, Revising, Editing, Publishing, Reflecting)	56–66	
8	**Descriptive Writing for Assessment**	67 68–70	Capitalization (proper nouns), commas (in a series, in an appositive), using the right word
	Publishing and Portfolios	34–41	
	Taking Tests	364–371	
9	**Writing a Narrative Paragraph**	74–79	Verbs

Second Quarter

Week	Writing Lessons	*Write Source*	Grammar and Writing Skills
1	**Writing a Narrative Essay** (Prewriting, Writing)	80–91	
2	**Narrative Essay** *(cont.)* (Revising)	92–104	Punctuating dialogue, verbs, adjectives, sentence combining
	Working with Partners	16–19	
3	**Narrative Essay** *(cont.)* (Editing, Publishing, Reflecting)	105–111	End punctuation, subject-verb agreement, using the right word
	Narrative Writing for Assessment	120–122	
	Giving Speeches *(opt.)*	344–349	
4	**Writing a Response Paragraph** **Writing a Book Review for Fiction** (Prewriting, Writing)	228–233 234–241	Punctuating titles, quotations
5	**Book Review for Fiction** *(cont.)* (Revising, Editing, Publishing, Reflecting)	242–245	Sentence variety, using the right word, apostrophes
6	**Writing an Expository Paragraph** **Writing an Expository Essay** (Prewriting)	126–131 132–137	Complete sentences
7	**Expository Essay** *(cont.)*	138–143	
8	**Expository Essay** *(cont.)* (Revising)	144–156	Specific nouns, adverbs, punctuating dialogue
	Working with Partners	16–19	
9	**Expository Essay** *(cont.)* (Editing, Publishing, Reflecting)	157–163	Commas (in a series), capitalization, apostrophes
	Giving Speeches	344–349	
	Expository Writing for Assessment	172–174	

Third Quarter

Week	Writing Lessons	*Write Source*	Grammar and Writing Skills
1	**Writing a Persuasive Paragraph**	178–183	Using the right word, spelling, fragments
	Viewing and Listening Skills	356–363	
2	**Writing a Persuasive Essay (Letter)** (Prewriting)	184–189	
3	**Persuasive Letter** *(cont.)* (Writing, Revising)	190–204	Sentence combining, run-on and rambling sentences, helping verbs
	Working with Partners	16–19	
4	**Persuasive Letter** *(cont.)* (Editing, Publishing, Reflecting)	205–213	Commas (after introductory word or word groups), commas (in dates and addresses), capitalization, abbreviations, colons
	Persuasive Writing for Assessment	222–224	
	Giving Speeches *(opt.)*	344–349	
5	**Writing Across the Curriculum** (Teacher's Choice) (Biographical Narrative, Personal Art Story, News Report, Music Report, Science Poster, Important Health Issue)	112–117 164–169 214–219	
6	**Writing a Book Review for Nonfiction**	246–251	Sentence combining, plurals, fragments
	Giving Speeches	344–349	
	Response to Literature Writing for Assessment	264–266	
7	**Writing Imaginative Stories** (Prewriting, Writing)	270–276 (280, 281)	Punctuating dialogue, interjections
8	**Imaginative Stories** *(cont.)* (Revising, Editing)	277	Pronouns, using the right word
	Working with Partners	16–19	
	Creating a Play *(opt.)*	278–279	
9	**Practical Writing** (Teacher's Choice—Friendly Letter, How-To Essay, E-Mail Message)	118–119 170–171 220–221	Compound sentences, pronouns

Fourth Quarter

Week	Writing Lessons	*Write Source*	Grammar and Writing Skills
1	**Finding Information**	296–307	
2	**Writing a Summary Paragraph** (Writing, Revising, Editing)	308–311	Numbers, verb tenses, irregular verbs, capitalization
3	**Writing a Research Report** (Prewriting)	312–323	
4	**Research Report** *(cont.)* (Writing, Revising)	324–333	Sentence variety, colons, hyphens, parentheses, nouns (possessive)
	Working with Partners	16–19	
5	**Research Report** *(cont.)* (Editing, Publishing, Reflecting)	334–337	Run-on sentences, apostrophes, subject-verb agreement, spelling
	Creating a Multimedia Presentation *(opt.)*	338–341	
6	**Writing Poems: Rhyming Poem**	282–289	Adverbs, modeling sentences, parts of speech (review), spelling
7	**Poems** *(cont.)* (limerick, clerihew, 5 W's poem, alphabet poem)	290–293	Prepositions, hyphens, tenses
8	**Responding to a Poem** (Prewriting, Writing, Revising, Editing, Publishing)	258–263	Adjectives, using the right word, quotation marks
9	Freestyle Writing Project (Choice) Journal and Portfolio Review Final Reflection Essay		

Reading-Writing Connection

The literary works listed on pages TE-36–TE-43 provide high-interest **mentor texts** that you can use to inspire your students as you teach the different forms of writing. Use these texts to accentuate **writer's craft**:

- Read **strong beginnings** or **strong endings** to inspire students as they create their own beginnings and endings.
- Read paragraphs that **elaborate ideas** or demonstrate **strong organization**.
- Read from two different examples to **contrast voice** and **word choice**.
- Read from different authors to examine their **sentence fluency**.

Narrative Books for Grades 3–5

The Day Gogo Went to Vote
Eleanor Batezat Sisulu and Sharon Wilson, 1999

Roxaboxen
Alice McLerran and Barbara Cooney, 1991

Tar Beach
Faith Ringgold, 1991

My Prairie Christmas
Brett Harvey and Deborah Kogan Ray, 1993

Sofie's Role
Amy Heath and Sheila Hamanaka, 1992

Letting Swift River Go
Jane Yolen and Barbara Cooney, 1995

All the Places to Love
Patricia MacLachlan, 1994

Grandfather's Journey
Allen Say, 1994

Two Mrs. Gibsons
Toyomi Igus, 2001

My Brother Martin: A Sister Remembers Growing Up with the Rev. Dr. Martin Luther King, Jr.
Christine King Farris, 2005

Owl Moon
Jane Yolen, 1987

To Dance: A Ballerina's Graphic Novel
Siena Cherson Siegel, 2006

Childtimes: A Three-Generation Memoir
Eloise Greenfield and Lessie Jones Little, 1993

Rules
Cynthia Lord, 2006

Because of Winn-Dixie
Kate DiCamillo, 2000

Bud, Not Buddy
Christopher Paul Curtis, 1999

Through My Eyes
Ruby Bridges, 1999

A Long Way from Chicago
Richard Peck, 1998

Granny Torrelli Makes Soup
Sharon Creech, 2003

Sarah, Plain and Tall
Patricia MacLachlan, 1985

Woodsong
Gary Paulsen, 1990

Calling the Doves/El Canto De Las Palomas
Juan Felipe Herrera, 1995

Seedfolks
Paul Fleischman, 1997

Shiloh
Phyllis Reynolds Naylor, 1991

Tales of a Fourth Grade Nothing
Judy Blume, 1972

When I Was Young in the Mountains
Cynthia Rylant, 1982

Homesick: My Own Story
Jean Fritz, 1982

Under the Royal Palms: A Childhood in Cuba
Alma Flor Ada, 1998

Sing Down the Moon
Scott O'Dell, 1970

I'm in Charge of Celebrations
Byrd Baylor, 1986

Math Curse
Jon Scieszka and Lane Smith, 1995

Cyberpals According to Kaley
Dian Curtis Regan, 2006

Louis Braille: The Boy Who Invented Books for the Blind
Margaret Davidson, 1991

Marvelous Mattie: How Margaret E. Knight Became an Inventor
Emily Arnold McCully, 2006

A Weed Is a Flower: The Life of George Washington Carver
Aliki, 1998

Now & Ben: The Modern Inventions of Benjamin Franklin
Gene Barretta, 2006

Read About Walt Disney
Stephen Feinstein, 2005

Summer of Fire: Yellowstone, 1988
Patricia Lauber, 1991

Famous Trials: The Boston Massacre
Bonnie L. Lukes, 1998

The Salem Witch Trials: How History Is Invented
Lori Lee Wilson, 1997

A Multicultural Portrait of the American Revolution
Fran Zell, 1995

The Incredible Journey of Lewis and Clark
Rhoda Blumberg, 1987

Expository Books for Grades 3–5

Scientists in the Field (series)
Houghton Mifflin

Career Ideas for Kids (series)
Diane Lindsey Reeves

Team Moon: How 400,000 People Landed Apollo 11 on the Moon
Catherine Thimmesh, 2006

Kids Inventing! A Handbook for Young Inventors
Susan Casey, 2005

When Marian Sang: The True Recital of Marian Anderson
Pam Munoz Ryan, 2002

Oh, Freedom! Kids Talk About the Civil Rights Movement with the People Who Made It Happen
Casey King and Linda Barrett Osborne, 1997

The Art of Reading
Reading Is Fundamental Staff, 2005

Quest for the Tree Kangaroo: An Expedition to the Cloud Forest of New Guinea
Sy Montgomery, 2006

Barrio: José's Neighborhood
George Ancona, 2001

Pyramid
David Macaulay, 1982

Cool Stuff and How It Works
Chris Woodford, 2005

Snowflake Bentley
Jacqueline Briggs Martin, 1998

So You Want to Be President?
Judith St. George and David Small, 2000

Lights! Camera! Action!: How a Movie Is Made
Gail Gibbons, 1985

If the World Were a Village: A Book About the World's People
David J. Smith, 2002

A Drop of Water: A Book of Science and Wonder
Walter Wick, 1997

Math on Call: A Mathematics Handbook
Great Source Education Group, 2003

How to Spell Like a Champ
Barry Trinkle, Carolyn Andrews, and Paige Kimble, 2006

Cinco de Mayo: Celebrating Hispanic Pride
Carol Gnojewski, 2002

Frozen Man
David Getz and Peter McCarty, 1996

Hottest, Coldest, Highest, Deepest
Steve Jenkins, 1998

How to Dig a Hole to the Other Side of the World
Faith McNulty, 1990

How Much Is a Million?
David M. Schwartz, 1993

If Your Name Was Changed at Ellis Island
Ellen Levine, 1994

Chimpanzees I Love: Saving Their World and Ours
Jane Goodall, 2001

Fire!
Joy Masoff, 2002

What's That Bug? Everyday Insects and Their Really Cool Cousins
Nan Froman, 2001

The Kids Summer Games Book: Official Book of Games to Play
Jane Drake, Ann Love, and Heather Collins, 2002

Leonardo's Horse
Jean Fritz and Hudson Talbott, 2001

There's a Frog in My Throat!
Loreen Leedy and Pat Street, 2003

Rattlesnake Dance: True Tales, Mysteries, and Rattlesnake Ceremonies
Jennifer Dewey, 2000

It's Disgusting and We Ate It! True Food Facts from Around the World and Throughout History
James Solheim, 2001

The Real Vikings: Craftsmen, Traders, and Fearsome Raiders
Gilda Berger, 2003

Portraits of African-American Heroes
Tonya Bolden, 2005

When Bugs Were Big, Plants Were Strange, and Tetrapods Stalked the Earth
Hannah Bonner, 2004

Sea Clocks
Louise Borden, 2005

Volcanoes: Journey to the Crater's Edge
Robert Burleigh, David Giraudon, and Philippe Bourseiller, 2003

Unexplained: An Encyclopedia of Curious Phenomena, Strange Superstitions, and Ancient Mysteries
Judy Allen, 2006

Pirates & Smugglers
Moira Butterfield, 2005

How Things Work: 100 Ways Parents and Kids Can Share the Secrets of Technology
Neil Ardley, 1995

Persuasive Books for Grades 3–5

The Giant Panda: Help Save This Endangered Species!
Alison Imbriaco, 2006

Smoking
Gail B. Steward, 2002

Why Should I Turn Down the Volume?
Louise A. Spilsbury, 2003

I Can Make a Difference
Marian Wright Edelman, 2005

Get Organized Without Losing It
Janet S. Fox, 2005

Global Warming Alert!
Richard Cheel, 2007

Speak Up and Get Along!
Scott Cooper, 2005

7 Secrets of Highly Successful Kids
Peter Kuitenbrouwer, 2001

Caring Counts
Marie Bender, 2002

Make the Right Call
Drew Bledsoe, 1998

Aaron Brooks: Rise Above
Aaron Brooks with Greg Brown, 2004

Eat Your Vegetables! Drink Your Milk!
Alvin Silverstein, Virginia B. Silverstein, and Laura Silverstein Nunn, 2000

Physical Fitness
Alvin Silverstein, Virginia B. Silverstein, and Laura Silverstein Nunn, 2002

Exercise
Sharon Gordon, 2003

Vanishing from Forests and Jungles
Gail Radley, 2001

Oil Spills: Damage, Recovery, and Prevention
Laurence P. Pringle, 1992

Money: Make It • Spend It • Save It
J. E. Bogart, 2001

50 Simple Things Kids Can Do to Save the Earth
Sophie Javna, The EarthWorks Group, 1990

I Can Make My World a Better Place: A Kid's Book About Stopping Violence
Paul Kivel, 2001

Save the Rainforests
Allan Fowler, 1997

Make Someone Smile: And 40 More Ways to Be a Peaceful Person
Judy Lalli, 1996

We Can Get Along: A Child's Book of Choices
Lauren Murphy Payne, M.S.W., 1997

You Can Speak Up in Class
Sara D. Gilbert and Roy Doty, 1991

Kid's Guide to Becoming the Best You Can Be!
Jill Frankel Hauser, 2006

Something Old, Something New: Recycling (You Can Save the Planet)
Anita Ganeri, 2005

Books About Responding to Literature for Grades 3–5

How to Make a Book Report, Grades 3–6
Kathleen Null, 2004

How to Write Terrific Book Reports
Elizabeth James and Carol Barkin, 1998

Kids Review Kids' Books
Storyworks, 1999

Book Reports— I Did It on the Computer
Dr. Merle Marsh and Diane S. Kendall, 2001

Show Time!: Music, Dance, and Drama Activities for Kids
Lisa Bany-Winters, 2000

12 Fabulously Funny Fairy Tale Plays
Justin McCory Martin, 2002

Stories on Stage
Aaron Shepard, 2005

Folktales on Stage
Aaron Shepard, 2003

Readers on Stage
Aaron Shepard, 2004

Shakespeare for Kids: His Life and Times
Colleen Aagesen and Margie Blumberg, 1999

Shake-It-Up Tales!
Margaret MacDonald, 2000

Paper Cutting Stories from A to Z
Valerie Marsh, 1992

Fold-Along Stories: Quick & Easy Origami Tales for Beginners
Christine Petrell Kallevig, 2001

Frog's Riddle: And Other Draw and Tell Stories
Richard Thompson, 1990

Thirty-Three Multicultural Tales to Tell
Pleasant DeSpain, 1993

Lost!: A Story in String
Paul Fleischman, 2000

Whirlwind is a Spirit Dancing
Natalia Belting, 2006

Crafts From Your Favorite Children's Stories
Kathy Ross, 2001

Dance Me a Story: Twelve Tales from the Classic Ballets
Jane Rosenberg, 1993

Make a Book: Six Different Books to Make, Write, and Illustrate
Vivien Frank and Deborah Jaffe, 2000

Write Out of the Oven!: Letters and Recipes from Children's Authors
Josephine M. Waltz, 2005

Kids' Letters to Harry Potter: from Around the World
Bill Adler, 2002

Storybook Travels: From Eloise's New York to Harry Potter's London, Visits to 30 of the Best-Loved Landmarks in Children's Literature
Colleen Dunn Bates and Susan LaTempa, 2002

Hobbies Through Children's Books and Activities
Nancy Allen Jurenka, 2001

The Laura Ingalls Wilder Songbook: Favorite Songs from the Little House Books
Herbert Haufrecht and Eugenia Garson, 1996

Books About Creative Writing for Grades 3–5

Haiku
Patricia Donegan, 2004

Poetry Matters: Writing a Poem from the Inside Out
Ralph J. Fletcher, 2002

Once Upon a Time, Creative Writing Fun for Kids
Annie Buckley and Kathleen Coyle, 2004

Kids Write!: Fantasy & Sci Fi, Mystery, Autobiography, Adventure & More!
Rebecca Olien, 2005

Show; Don't Tell!: Secrets of Writing
Josephine Nobisso, 2004

Writing Down the Days
Lorraine M. Dahlstrom, 2000

Writing Magic: Creating Stories That Fly
Gail Carson Levine, 2006

Writing Mysteries, Movies, Monster Stories, and More
Donna Guthrie, 2001

What's Your Story?: A Young Person's Guide to Writing Fiction
Marion Dane Bauer, 1992

A Writer's Notebook: Unlocking the Writer Within You
Ralph Fletcher, 2003

Live Writing: Breathing Life into Your Words
Ralph Fletcher, 1999

A Writing Kind of Day: Poems for Young Poets
Ralph Fletcher, 2005

Rainbow Soup: Adventures in Poetry
Brian P. Cleary, 2004

Get Writing!: Write That Play
Shaun McCarthy, 2004

The Young Journalist's Book: How to Write and Produce Your Own Newspaper
Nancy Bentley, 2001

Knock at a Star: A Child's Introduction to Poetry
X. J. Kennedy and Dorothy M. Kennedy, 1999

So, You Wanna Be a Writer?: How to Write, Get Published, and Maybe Even Make It Big!
Vicki Hambleton and Cathleen Greenwood, 2001

Funny You Should Ask: How to Make Up Jokes and Riddles with Wordplay
Marvin Terban, 1992

Written by Kids:
Loving Through Heartsongs
Mattie J. T. Stepanek, 2003

Ten-Second Rainshowers: Poems by Young People
Sandford Lyne, 1996

Salting the Ocean: 100 Poems by Young Poets
Naomi Shihab Nye, 2000

The Palm of My Heart: Poetry by African American Children
Davida Adedjouma, 1998

Who Can Fix It?
Leslie Ann MacKeen, 1989

Max's Ice Age Adventure
Logan Weinman with Jeffrey Bennett, 2007

Reference Books for Grades 3–5

The American Heritage Children's Dictionary
Editors of The American Heritage Dictionaries, 2006

The American Heritage Children's Thesaurus
Paul Hellweg, 2006

The American Heritage Children's Science Dictionary
Editors of The American Heritage Dictionaries, 2003

The Encyclopedia of World Sports
John Wukovits, 2002

Art: An A-Z Guide
Shirley Greenway, 2000

Music: An A-Z Guide
Nicola Barber, 2002

Children's Atlas of the World
Malcolm Porter, 2005

Atlas of Geology and Landforms
Cally Oldershaw, 2001

The Encyclopedia of Inventions
Jessica Snyder Sachs, 2001

Libraries and Reference Materials (Straight to the Source)
John Hamilton, 2004

Native North American Voices Edition 1 (Native North American Reference Library)
Deborah Gillan Straub, 1996

African American Voices Edition 1 (African American Reference Library)
Deborah Gillan Straub, 1996

100 Inventions That Shaped World History
Bill Yenne and Morton Grosser, 1993

Children's Illustrated Encyclopedia
Dorling Kindersley Publishing, 2006

The Student Encyclopedia of the United States
Editors of Kingfisher, 2005

The World Almanac for Kids 2006
Editors of World Almanac, 2006

The Kingfisher History Encyclopedia
Editors of Kingfisher, 2004

Something About the Author Volume 180: Facts and Pictures About Authors and Illustrators of Books for Young People
Lisa Kumar, 2006

Virtual Field Trips (book series)
Gail Cooper and Garry Cooper, 2001

The Oxford Children's Book of Famous People
Oxford University Press, 1999

How to Find Almost Anything on the Internet: A Kid's Guide to Safe Searching
Ted Pedersen and Francis Moss, 2000

School Smarts Projects: Create Tons of Great Presentations, Boost Your Creativity, Improve Your Grades, and Save Time and Trouble!
Dottie Raymer and Tracy McGuinness, 2005

The Kids' Guide to Digital Photography: How to Shoot, Save, Play with & Print Your Digital Photos
Jenni Bidner, 2004

Scope and Sequence

Skills taught and/or reviewed in the *Write Source* program, grades K–8, are featured in the following scope and sequence chart.

FORMS OF WRITING	K	1	2	3	4	5	6	7	8
Narrative Writing									
sentences	■	■							
paragraph	■	■	■	■	■	■	■	■	■
narrative prompts		■	■	■	■	■	■	■	■
narrative essay			■	■	■	■	■	■	■
phase autobiography								■	■
Expository Writing									
sentences	■	■							
paragraph		■	■	■	■	■	■	■	■
expository prompts		■	■	■	■	■	■	■	■
expository essay			■	■	■	■	■	■	■
classification essay							■		■
cause-and-effect essay								■	
comparison-contrast essay								■	■
Persuasive Writing									
sentences		■							
paragraph		■	■	■	■	■	■	■	■
persuasive prompts			■	■	■	■	■	■	■
persuasive letter			■	■	■	■	■	■	■
persuasive essay				■	■	■	■	■	■
editorial								■	■
problem-solution essay								■	■
personal commentary									■
position essay									■
Response to Literature									
sentences		■							
paragraph		■	■	■	■	■	■	■	■
response prompts		■	■	■	■	■	■	■	■
book review		■	■	■	■	■	■	■	■
journal response					■	■	■	■	■
response to literature							■	■	■
letter to an author									■
theme analysis									■

Grades	K	1	2	3	4	5	6	7	8
Descriptive Writing									
sentences	■	■							
paragraph		■	■	■	■	■	■	■	■
descriptive essay			■	■	■	■	■	■	■
descriptive prompts				■	■	■			
Creative Writing									
poetry		■	■	■	■	■	■	■	■
story	■	■	■	■	■	■	■	■	■
play			■	■	■	■			
Research Writing									
research report		■	■	■	■	■	■	■	■
multimedia presentation			■	■	■	■	■	■	■
summary paragraph				■	■	■	■	■	■
Research Skills									
interview an expert		■	■	■	■	■	■	■	■
online research/using the Internet		■	■	■	■	■	■	■	■
understanding the parts of a book		■	■	■	■	■	■	■	■
using a dictionary, a thesaurus, or an encyclopedia		■	■	■	■	■	■	■	■
using diagrams, charts, graphs, and maps		■	■	■	■	■	■	■	■
using reference sources		■	■	■	■	■	■	■	■
using the library		■	■	■	■	■	■	■	■
note taking/summarizing		■	■	■	■	■	■	■	■
using a card catalog			■	■	■	■	■	■	■
using periodicals or magazines			■	■	■	■	■	■	■
using time lines			■	■	■	■	■	■	■
asking questions				■	■	■	■	■	■
bibliography (works cited)				■	■	■	■	■	■
The Tools of Learning									
improving viewing skills		■	■	■	■	■			
interviewing skills		■	■	■	■	■	■	■	
giving speeches		■	■	■	■	■	■	■	■
journal writing	■	■	■	■	■	■	■	■	■
learning logs		■	■	■	■	■	■	■	■
listening in class	■	■	■	■	■	■	■	■	■
taking classroom tests		■	■	■	■	■	■	■	■
note taking				■	■	■	■	■	■
completing writing assignments							■	■	■

THE WRITING PROCESS

Grades	K	1	2	3	4	5	6	7	8
Prewriting									
Selecting a Topic									
draw pictures		■	■						
make lists	■	■	■	■	■	■	■	■	■
sentence starters		■	■	■	■	■	■	■	■
chart			■	■	■	■	■	■	■
cluster			■	■	■	■	■	■	■
brainstorm					■	■	■	■	■
character chart					■	■		■	■
freewrite					■	■	■	■	■
Gathering Details									
drawing	■	■							
story map		■	■	■					
cluster	■	■	■	■	■	■	■	■	■
answer questions		■	■	■	■	■	■	■	■
details chart/sheet		■	■	■	■	■	■	■	■
gathering grid		■	■	■	■	■	■	■	■
list details/reasons		■	■	■	■	■	■	■	■
sensory chart	■	■	■	■	■	■	■	■	■
selecting main reasons			■	■	■	■	■	■	■
five W's			■	■	■	■	■	■	■
time line	■			■	■	■	■	■	■
table diagram					■	■	■	■	■
opinion statement							■	■	■
counter an objection								■	■
Organizing Details									
time order		■	■	■	■	■	■	■	■
Venn diagram			■	■	■	■	■	■	■
plot chart				■	■	■	■	■	■
time line				■	■	■	■	■	■
note cards				■	■	■	■	■	■
outline ideas				■	■	■	■	■	■
order of importance					■	■	■	■	■
order of location					■	■	■	■	■
Writing									
topic sentence	■	■	■	■	■	■	■	■	■
opinion statement		■	■	■	■	■	■	■	■
facts, examples	■	■	■	■	■	■	■	■	■
supporting details/reasons		■	■	■	■	■	■	■	■
interesting facts/details			■	■	■	■	■	■	■

Grades	K	1	2	3	4	5	6	7	8
make comparisons			■	■	■	■	■	■	■
dialogue			■	■	■	■	■	■	■
transitions			■	■	■	■	■	■	■
call to action			■	■	■	■	■	■	■
closing sentences			■	■	■	■	■	■	■
final comment/interesting thought			■	■	■	■	■	■	■
focus or thesis statement				■	■	■	■	■	■
action words				■	■	■	■	■	■
direct quotations				■	■	■	■	■	■
sensory details				■	■	■	■	■	■
high point of story				■	■	■	■	■	■
explain theme				■	■	■	■	■	■
reflect on a change, a feeling, an experience, a person				■	■	■	■	■	■
restate opinion/thesis					■	■	■	■	■
summarize					■	■	■	■	■
personal details						■	■	■	■
propose a solution							■	■	■
summarize a problem								■	■
share a new insight								■	■
counter an objection						■	■	■	■
emphasize a key idea								■	■
point-by-point discussion									■
Revising									
Ideas									
sensory details	■	■	■	■	■	■	■	■	■
topic sentence			■	■	■	■	■	■	■
supporting details			■	■	■	■	■	■	■
dialogue				■	■	■	■	■	■
unnecessary details				■	■	■	■	■	■
focus statement					■	■	■	■	■
Organization									
order of ideas/details	■	■	■	■	■	■	■	■	■
transition words		■	■	■	■	■	■	■	■
order of importance			■		■	■	■	■	■
overall organization			■	■	■	■	■	■	■
order of location			■	■	■	■	■	■	■
logical order			■	■	■	■	■	■	■
clear beginning			■	■	■	■	■	■	■
time order			■	■	■	■	■	■	■

Revising (Continued)

Grades	K	1	2	3	4	5	6	7	8
Voice									
natural		■	■	■	■	■	■	■	■
convincing				■	■	■	■	■	■
interested				■	■	■	■	■	■
dialogue					■	■	■	■	■
fits audience/purpose					■	■	■	■	■
formal/informal					■	■	■	■	■
knowledgeable					■	■	■	■	■
Word Choice									
sensory words/details	■	■	■	■	■	■	■	■	■
specific nouns			■	■	■	■	■	■	■
action verbs				■	■	■	■	■	■
connotation					■	■	■	■	■
modifiers					■	■	■	■	■
onomatopoeia						■	■	■	■
descriptive words						■	■	■	■
vivid verbs						■	■	■	■
connotation								■	■
Sentence Fluency									
complete sentences		■	■	■	■	■	■	■	■
variety of lengths			■	■	■	■	■	■	■
kinds of sentences			■	■	■	■	■	■	■
combining sentences				■	■	■	■	■	■
compound sentences				■	■	■	■	■	■
complex sentences					■	■	■	■	■
expanded sentences					■	■	■	■	■
variety of beginnings					■	■	■	■	■
types of sentences					■	■	■	■	■
Editing									
capitalization	■	■	■	■	■	■	■	■	■
grammar/punctuation/spelling	■	■	■	■	■	■	■	■	■
proper nouns	■		■	■	■	■	■	■	■
proper adjectives				■	■	■	■	■	■
Publishing									
publish in a variety of ways	■	■	■	■	■	■	■	■	■
review own work to monitor growth		■	■	■	■	■	■	■	■
self- and peer-assessing writing		■	■	■	■	■	■	■	■
use portfolios to save writing		■	■	■	■	■	■	■	■
use published pieces as models for writing		■	■	■	■	■	■	■	■

WRITING ACROSS THE CURRICULUM

Grades	K	1	2	3	4	5	6	7	8
Narrative Writing									
reading		■							
music		■	■						
social studies			■			■	■	■	■
practical				■			■	■	■
science				■	■		■	■	■
Expository Writing									
social studies		■		■		■	■	■	■
math		■			■	■	■	■	■
reading *		■	■	■	■	■	■	■	■
science			■		■		■	■	■
practical			■	■	■	■	■	■	■
Persuasive Writing									
health		■							
science			■	■	■	■	■	■	■
social studies			■			■	■	■	■
practical				■	■	■	■	■	■
math					■		■	■	■
Descriptive Writing									
math		■	■				■	■	■
science		■	■		■	■	■	■	■
practical			■				■	■	■
social studies					■	■	■	■	■

* The models included in the "Response to Literature" section demonstrate expository writing within the reading curriculum.

GRAMMAR

Grades	K	1	2	3	4	5	6	7	8
Understanding Sentences									
word order		■	■	■					
declarative		■	■	■	■	■	■	■	■
exclamatory		■	■	■	■	■	■	■	■
interrogative		■	■	■	■	■	■	■	■
complete sentences and fragments		■	■	■	■	■	■	■	■
simple subjects		■	■	■	■	■	■	■	■
simple predicates		■	■	■	■	■	■	■	■
correcting run-on sentences		■	■	■	■	■	■	■	■
compound			■	■	■	■	■	■	■
imperative			■	■	■	■	■	■	■
complete predicates				■	■	■	■	■	■

Understanding Sentences (Continued) — Grades	K	1	2	3	4	5	6	7	8
complete subjects				■	■	■	■	■	■
compound predicates				■	■	■	■	■	■
compound subjects				■	■	■	■	■	■
prepositional phrases				■	■	■	■	■	■
appositive phrases					■	■	■	■	■
clauses, dependent and independent					■	■	■	■	■
complex					■	■	■	■	■
modifiers					■	■	■	■	■
noun phrases					■	■	■	■	■
verb phrases					■	■	■	■	■
Using the Parts of Speech									
Nouns									
singular and plural		■	■	■	■	■	■	■	■
common/proper		■	■	■	■	■	■	■	■
possessive			■	■	■	■	■	■	■
singular/plural possessive			■	■	■	■	■	■	■
specific				■	■	■	■	■	■
abstract/concrete					■	■	■	■	■
appositives					■	■	■	■	■
collective/compound					■	■	■	■	■
object					■	■	■	■	■
predicate					■	■	■	■	■
subject					■	■	■	■	■
gender					■	■	■	■	■
Verbs									
contractions with *not*		■	■	■	■	■	■	■	■
action	■	■	■	■	■	■	■	■	■
linking		■	■	■	■	■	■	■	■
past tense		■	■	■	■	■	■	■	■
present tense		■	■	■	■	■	■	■	■
subject-verb agreement		■	■	■	■	■	■	■	■
future tense			■	■	■	■	■	■	■
helping			■	■	■	■	■	■	■
singular/plural			■	■	■	■	■	■	■
irregular				■	■	■	■	■	■
simple tense				■	■	■	■	■	■
active/passive voice					■	■	■	■	■
direct objects					■	■	■	■	■
indirect objects					■	■	■	■	■
perfect tense					■	■	■	■	■

Grades	K	1	2	3	4	5	6	7	8
transitive/intransitive					■	■	■	■	■
participles						■	■	■	■
continuous tense							■	■	■
gerunds							■	■	■
infinitives							■	■	■
Pronouns									
personal		■	■	■	■	■	■	■	■
antecedents		■	■	■	■	■	■	■	■
singular and plural		■	■	■	■	■	■	■	■
possessive		■	■	■	■	■	■	■	■
subject and object			■	■	■	■	■	■	■
demonstrative/interrogative					■	■	■	■	■
gender					■	■	■	■	■
indefinite					■	■	■	■	■
intensive and reflexive					■	■	■	■	■
relative					■	■	■	■	■
Adjectives									
adjectives	■	■	■	■	■	■	■	■	■
comparative/superlative		■	■	■	■	■	■	■	■
articles			■	■	■	■	■	■	■
compound				■	■	■	■	■	■
positive				■	■	■	■	■	■
proper				■	■	■	■	■	■
demonstrative					■	■	■	■	■
equal					■	■	■	■	■
indefinite					■	■	■	■	■
predicate					■	■	■	■	■
Interjections		■	■	■	■	■	■	■	■
Adverbs									
of manner			■	■	■	■	■	■	■
of place	■		■	■	■	■	■	■	■
of time			■	■	■	■	■	■	■
that modify verbs			■	■	■	■	■	■	■
of degree					■	■	■	■	■
that modify adjectives and adverbs					■	■	■	■	■
comparative/superlative					■	■	■	■	■
comparing with adverbs					■	■	■	■	■
irregular forms					■	■	■	■	■
positive					■	■	■	■	■

Grades	K	1	2	3	4	5	6	7	8
Conjunctions									
coordinating			■	■	■	■	■	■	■
correlative					■	■	■	■	■
subordinating					■	■	■	■	■
Prepositions									
prepositions	■		■	■	■	■	■	■	■
prepositional phrases				■	■	■	■	■	■
Mechanics									
Capitalization									
pronoun "I"		■	■	■	■	■	■	■	■
days, months, holidays		■	■	■	■	■	■	■	■
first words	■	■	■	■	■	■	■	■	■
names of people	■	■	■	■	■	■	■	■	■
proper nouns		■	■	■	■	■	■	■	■
titles used with names		■	■	■	■	■	■	■	■
titles		■	■	■	■	■	■	■	■
beginning of a quotation		■	■	■	■	■	■	■	■
geographic names			■	■	■	■	■	■	■
abbreviations			■	■	■	■	■	■	■
proper adjectives				■	■	■	■	■	■
words used as names				■	■	■	■	■	■
names of historical events					■	■	■	■	■
names of religions, nationalities					■	■	■	■	■
organizations					■	■	■	■	■
particular sections of the country					■	■	■	■	■
trade names/official names					■	■	■	■	■
letters to indicate form or direction							■	■	■
specific course names							■	■	■
Plurals									
irregular nouns		■	■	■	■	■	■	■	■
most nouns		■	■	■	■	■	■	■	■
nouns ending with *sh*, *ch*, *x*, *s*, and *z*			■	■	■	■	■	■	■
nouns ending in *y*			■	■	■	■	■	■	■
adding *'s*					■	■	■	■	■
compound nouns					■	■	■	■	■
nouns ending with *f* or *fe*					■	■	■	■	■
nouns ending with *ful*					■	■	■	■	■
nouns ending with *o*					■	■	■	■	■

Grades	K	1	2	3	4	5	6	7	8
Abbreviations									
days and months			■	■	■	■	■	■	■
state postal abbreviations				■	■	■	■	■	■
titles of people		■	■	■	■	■	■	■	■
addresses			■	■	■	■	■	■	■
acronyms				■	■	■	■	■	■
initialisms				■	■	■	■	■	■
Numbers									
numbers 1 to 9				■	■	■	■	■	■
numbers only				■	■	■	■	■	■
sentence beginnings				■	■	■	■	■	■
very large numbers				■	■	■	■	■	■
numbers in compound modifiers							■	■	■
time and money							■	■	■
Punctuation									
Periods									
after an initial/an abbreviation		■	■	■	■	■	■	■	■
at the end of a sentence	■	■	■	■	■	■	■	■	■
as a decimal point				■	■	■	■	■	■
after an indirect question							■	■	■
Question Marks									
after questions	■	■	■	■	■	■	■	■	■
after tag questions					■	■	■	■	■
to show doubt					■	■	■	■	■
Exclamation Points									
for words, phrases, and sentences	■	■	■	■	■	■	■	■	■
for interjections		■	■	■	■	■	■	■	■
Commas									
in a series		■	■	■	■	■	■	■	■
in dates		■	■	■	■	■	■	■	■
in friendly letters		■	■	■	■	■	■	■	■
after introductory words		■	■	■	■	■	■	■	■
with interjections		■	■	■	■	■	■	■	■
in a compound sentence			■	■	■	■	■	■	■
in addresses			■	■	■	■	■	■	■
to set off dialogue			■	■	■	■	■	■	■
in direct address			■	■	■	■	■	■	■
in numbers				■	■	■	■	■	■
to separate equal adjectives				■	■	■	■	■	■
to set off appositives					■	■	■	■	■

Commas (Continued)	K	1	2	3	4	5	6	7	8
to set off interrupters					■	■	■	■	■
to set off phrases					■	■	■	■	■
to set off titles of people							■	■	■
Apostrophes									
in contractions		■	■	■	■	■	■	■	■
to form plural possessive nouns			■	■	■	■	■	■	■
to form singular possessive nouns			■	■	■	■	■	■	■
to form some plurals					■	■	■	■	■
to replace omitted numbers/letters					■	■	■	■	■
with indefinite pronouns					■	■	■	■	■
to show shared possession					■	■	■	■	■
in possessives w/compound nouns							■	■	■
to express time or amount							■	■	■
Underlining and Italics									
for titles		■	■	■	■	■	■	■	■
for special words					■	■	■	■	■
for scientific and foreign words							■	■	■
Quotation Marks									
for direct quotations			■	■	■	■	■	■	■
for titles			■	■	■	■	■	■	■
for special words					■	■	■	■	■
for quotations within a quotation							■	■	■
Colons									
between hour and minutes				■	■	■	■	■	■
in business letters				■	■	■	■	■	■
to introduce a list of items				■	■	■	■	■	■
for emphasis							■	■	■
to introduce sentences							■	■	■
Hyphens									
in word division				■	■	■	■	■	■
in compound words					■	■	■	■	■
in fractions					■	■	■	■	■
to create new words					■	■	■	■	■
to join letters and words					■	■	■	■	■
to avoid confusion or awkward spelling							■	■	■
to make adjectives							■	■	■

Grades	K	1	2	3	4	5	6	7	8
Parentheses									
to add information				■	■	■	■	■	■
Dashes									
for emphasis					■	■	■	■	■
to show a sentence break					■	■	■	■	■
to show interrupted speech					■	■	■	■	■
Ellipses									
to show a pause					■	■	■	■	■
to show omitted words					■	■	■	■	■
Semicolons									
in a compound sentence					■	■	■	■	■
to separate groups (that have commas) in a series					■	■	■	■	■
with conjunctive adverbs							■	■	■
Usage									
Spelling									
high-frequency words		■	■						
consonant endings				■	■	■	■	■	■
i before *e*				■	■	■	■	■	■
silent *e*				■	■	■	■	■	■
words ending in *y*				■	■	■	■	■	■
Using the Right Word		■	■	■	■	■	■	■	■
Penmanship									
word space, letter space		■	■						
writing legibly		■	■	■	■	■	■	■	■
margins/spaces				■	■	■	■	■	■

Meeting the Common Core State Standards

The following correlation clearly shows how the *Write Source* program helps students meet grade-specific **Common Core State Standards** for English Language Arts and Literacy in History/Social Studies, Science, and Technical Subjects. The Common Core standards translate their companion **College and Career Readiness standards** into grade-appropriate expectations that students should meet by the end of the school year.

Pages referenced below appear in the Teacher's Edition as well as the Student Edition.

Writing Standards

Text Types and Purposes

College and Career Readiness Standard 1. Write arguments to support claims in an analysis of substantive topics or texts, using valid reasoning and relevant and sufficient evidence.

Grade 3 Standard 1. Write opinion pieces on topics or texts, supporting a point of view with reasons.

a. Introduce the topic or text they are writing about, state an opinion, and create an organizational structure that lists reasons.	**Student Edition pages:** 178–179, 181, 186, 190–191, 196–197, 218–219, 220–221, 223–224, 225, 234–235, 238–239, 240, 242, 252–253, 256, 258–259, 262, 424–425 **Net-text:** Persuasive Writing, Response to Literature
b. Provide reasons that support the opinion.	**Student Edition pages:** 178–179, 181, 182, 186, 190–191, 194–195, 218–219, 220, 223–224, 225, 240, 258–259, 262, 420, 424–425 **Net-text:** Persuasive Writing, Response to Literature
c. Use linking words and phrases (e.g., because, therefore, since, for example) to connect opinion and reasons.	**Student Edition pages:** 422–423, 458–459
d. Provide a concluding statement or section.	**Student Edition pages:** 178–179, 181, 186, 190–191, 218–219, 223–224, 225, 234–235, 241, 252–253, 256, 258–259, 262, 419, 425 **Net-text:** Persuasive Writing, Response to Literature

Text Types and Purposes (continued)

College and Career Readiness Standard 2. Write informative/explanatory texts to examine and convey complex ideas and information clearly and accurately through the effective selection, organization, and analysis of content.

Grade 3 Standard 2. Write informative/explanatory texts to examine a topic and convey ideas and information clearly.

a. Introduce a topic and group related information together; include illustrations when useful to aiding comprehension.	**Student Edition pages:** 44–45, 47, 52–53, 56–61, 69–71, 126–127, 129, 134–135, 138–143, 165, 167, 168–169, 170–171, 173, 175, 228–229, 231, 267, 309, 311, 313–314, 324–329, 340–341, 347, 349, 354–355, 416–417, 424–425, 460 **Net-text:** Descriptive Writing, Expository Writing, Research Writing
b. Develop the topic with facts, definitions, and details.	**Student Edition pages:** 44–45, 47, 52–53, 58–59, 69–71, 126–127, 129, 134–135, 140–141, 146–147, 165, 167, 168–169, 170–171, 173, 175, 228–229, 231, 267, 309, 311, 313–314, 326–327, 332–333, 340, 347, 349, 416–417, 420, 424–425 **Net-text:** Descriptive Writing, Expository Writing, Research Writing
c. Use linking words and phrases (e.g., also, another, and, more, but) to connect ideas within categories of information.	**Student Edition pages:** 422–423, 458–459
d. Provide a concluding statement or section.	**Student Edition pages:** 44–45, 47, 52–53, 60–61, 69–71, 126–127, 129, 134–135, 142–143, 165, 167, 168–169, 170–171, 173, 175, 228–229, 231, 267, 309, 311, 313–314, 328–329, 347, 349, 416–417, 419, 425 **Net-text:** Descriptive Writing, Expository Writing, Research Writing

Text Types and Purposes (continued)

College and Career Readiness Standard 3. Write narratives to develop real or imagined experiences or events using effective technique, well-chosen details, and well-structured event sequences.	
Grade 3 Standard 3. Write narratives to develop real or imagined experiences or events using effective technique, descriptive details, and clear event sequences.	
a. Establish a situation and introduce a narrator and/or characters; organize an event sequence that unfolds naturally.	**Student Edition pages:** 74–75, 77, 82–83, 85–89, 96–97 113, 115, 116–117, 118–119, 121–123, 272–273, 276 **Net-text:** Narrative Writing, Creative Writing
b. Use dialogue and descriptions of actions, thoughts, and feelings to develop experiences and events or show the response of characters to situations.	**Student Edition pages:** 74–75, 77, 82–83, 86–91, 113, 115, 116, 118–119, 121–123, 272–273 **Net-text:** Narrative Writing, Creative Writing
c. Use temporal words and phrases to signal event order.	**Student Edition pages:** 96–97, 422–423, 458 **Net-text:** Narrative Writing
d. Provide a sense of closure.	**Student Edition pages:** 74–75, 77, 82–83, 90–91, 113, 115, 118, 121, 123, 272–273, 425 **Net-text:** Narrative Writing, Creative Writing

Production and Distribution of Writing

College and Career Readiness Standard 4. Produce clear and coherent writing in which the development, organization, and style are appropriate to task, purpose, and audience.	
Grade 3 Standard 4. With guidance and support from adults, produce writing in which the development and organization are appropriate to task and purpose.	**Student Edition pages:** 45–47, 52–61, 69–71, 75–77, 82–91, 94–95, 96–97, 113–115, 116–117, 118–119, 121–123, 127–129, 134–143, 146–147, 148–149, 165–167, 168–169, 170–171, 173–174, 175, 179–181, 186, 188¬–191, 194–195, 196–197, 215–217, 218–219, 220–221, 223–224, 225, 229–231, 235–241, 247–250, 253–256, 259–262, 265–266, 267, 272–276, 283–288, 309–311, 313–329, 332–333, 339–341, 347, 349, 424–425 **Interactive Whiteboard Lessons:** Descriptive Writing, Narrative Writing, Expository Writing, Persuasive Writing, Response to Literature, Creative Writing, Research Writing **Net-text:** Descriptive Writing, Narrative Writing, Expository Writing, Persuasive Writing, Response to Literature, Creative Writing, Research Writing

Production and Distribution of Writing (continued)

College and Career Readiness Standard 5. Develop and strengthen writing as needed by planning, revising, editing, rewriting, or trying a new approach.	
Grade 3 Standard 5. With guidance and support from peers and adults, develop and strengthen writing as needed by planning, revising, and editing.	**Student Edition pages:** 6–7, 11–14, 17–18, 46–49, 54–65, 70–71, 76–79, 84–107, 114–115, 117, 119, 122–123, 128–131, 136–159, 166–167, 169, 171, 173–174, 175, 180–183, 188–207, 216–217, 219, 221, 224, 225, 230–233, 236–243, 248–250, 254–256, 260–262, 266, 267, 274–277, 284–289, 310–311, 316–335, 339–331, 424–425 **Interactive Whiteboard Lessons:** Descriptive Writing, Narrative Writing, Expository Writing, Persuasive Writing, Response to Literature, Creative Writing, Research Writing **Net-text:** Descriptive Writing, Narrative Writing, Expository Writing, Persuasive Writing, Response to Literature, Creative Writing, Research Writing
College and Career Readiness Standard 6. Use technology, including the Internet, to produce and publish writing and to interact and collaborate with others.	
Grade 3 Standard 6. With guidance and support from adults, use technology to produce and publish writing (using keyboarding skills) as well as to interact and collaborate with others.	**Student Edition pages:** 37, 220–221, 336, 341 **Interactive Whiteboard Lessons:** Descriptive Writing, Narrative Writing, Expository Writing, Persuasive Writing, Response to Literature, Creative Writing, Research Writing **Net-text:** Research Writing

Research to Build and Present Knowledge

College and Career Readiness Standard 7. Conduct short as well as more sustained research projects based on focused questions, demonstrating understanding of the subject under investigation.	
Grade 3 Standard 7. Conduct short research projects that build knowledge about a topic.	**Student Edition pages:** 310¬–311, 316–329, 345 **Net-text:** Research Writing
College and Career Readiness Standard 8. Gather relevant information from multiple print and digital sources, assess the credibility and accuracy of each source, and integrate the information while avoiding plagiarism.	
Grade 3 Standard 8. Recall information from experiences or gather information from print and digital sources; take brief notes on sources and sort evidence into provided categories.	**Student Edition pages:** 297¬–307, 310, 316–323, 345, 361 **Net-text:** Research Writing
College and Career Readiness Standard 9. Draw evidence from literary or informational texts to support analysis, reflection, and research.	
Standard 9. (Begins in grade 4)	

Range of Writing

College and Career Readiness Standard 10. Write routinely over extended time frames (time for research, reflection, and revision) and shorter time frames (a single sitting or a day or two) for a range of tasks, purposes, and audiences.

Grade 3 Standard 10. Write routinely over extended time frames (time for research, reflection, and revision) and shorter time frames (a single sitting or a day or two) for a range of discipline-specific tasks, purposes, and audiences.	**Student Edition pages:** 23, 41, 46–49, 54–65, 70, 76–79, 84–107, 114–115, 119, 122, 128–131, 136–159, 166–167, 171, 174, 180–183, 188–207, 216–217, 221, 224, 230–233, 236–243, 248–250, 254–256, 260–262, 266, 274–277, 278–279, 284–289, 290, 291, 292, 293, 310–311, 316–335, 339–341, 347, 351, 352, 353, 354, 358, 378, 387, 397, 400, 401, 402, 403, 406, 407, 411, 413, 424–425, 429 **Interactive Whiteboard Lessons:** Descriptive Writing, Narrative Writing, Expository Writing, Persuasive Writing, Response to Literature, Creative Writing, Research Writing **Net-text:** Descriptive Writing, Narrative Writing, Expository Writing, Persuasive Writing, Response to Literature, Creative Writing, Research Writing

Language Standards

Conventions of Standard English

College and Career Readiness Standard 1. Demonstrate command of the conventions of standard English grammar and usage when writing or speaking.

Grade 3 Standard 1. Demonstrate command of the conventions of standard English grammar and usage when writing or speaking.	
a. Explain the function of nouns, pronouns, verbs, adjectives, and adverbs in general and their functions in particular sentences.	**Student Edition pages:** 375–378, 379–382, 383–388, 389–390, 391–392, 532, 534¬, 536, 538–539, 546, 550, 558 **GrammarSnap:** Nouns, Common and Proper Nouns, Specific Nouns, Subject and Object Pronouns, Possessive Pronouns, Action Verbs, Helping Verbs, Past Tense Verbs, Compound Verbs, Adjectives, Adverbs
b. Form and use regular and irregular plural nouns.	**Student Edition pages:** 376, 492–493, 534–535 **GrammarSnap:** Nouns
c. Use abstract nouns (e.g., *childhood*).	**File Cabinet:** Understanding Abstract Nouns

Conventions of Standard English (continued)

Standard	Correlation
d. Form and use regular and irregular verbs.	**Student Edition pages:** 64, 106, 206, 334, 383–387, 542–543, 544–545 **GrammarSnap:** Action Verbs, Helping Verbs, Past Tense Verbs, Compound Verbs **Net-text:** Descriptive Writing, Narrative Writing, Persuasive Writing, Research Writing
e. Form and use the simple (e.g., *I walked; I walk; I will walk*) verb tenses.	**Student Edition pages:** 386–387, 540–541 **GrammarSnap:** Past Tense Verbs
f. Ensure subject-verb and pronoun-antecedent agreement.	**Student Edition pages:** 243, 381, 388, 406, 542–543 **GrammarSnap:** Subject-Verb Agreement **Net-text:** Response to Literature
g. Form and use comparative and superlative adjectives and adverbs, and choose between them depending on what is to be modified.	**Student Edition pages:** 390, 548–549
h. Use coordinating and subordinating conjunctions.	**Student Edition pages:** 154–155, 394–395, 410, 468–469, 554–555 **GrammarSnap:** Coordinating Conjunctions **Net-text:** Expository Writing
i. Produce simple, compound, and complex sentences.	**Student Edition pages:** 154–155, 395, 407, 410, 468–469 **GrammarSnap:** Complete Sentences, Compound Sentences **Net-text:** Expository Writing
College and Career Readiness Standard 2. Demonstrate command of the conventions of standard English capitalization, punctuation, and spelling when writing.	
Grade 3 Standard 2. Demonstrate command of the conventions of standard English capitalization, punctuation, and spelling when writing.	
a. Capitalize appropriate words in titles.	**Student Edition pages:** 334, 488 **Net-text:** Research Writing
b. Use commas in addresses.	**Student Edition pages:** 206, 468 **Net-text:** Persuasive Writing
c. Use commas and quotation marks in dialogue.	**Student Edition pages:** 106, 277, 470, 476–477 **Net-text:** Narrative Writing, Creative Writing
d. Form and use possessives.	**Student Edition pages:** 377, 380, 474–475, 534, 536 **GrammarSnap:** Apostrophes to Show Possession

Conventions of Standard English (continued)

e. Use conventional spelling for high-frequency and other studied words and for adding suffixes to base words (e.g., *sitting, smiled, cries, happiness*).	**Student Edition pages:** 454–455, 502–507
f. Use spelling patterns and generalizations (e.g., word families, position-based spellings, syllable patterns, ending rules, meaningful word parts) in writing words.	**Student Edition pages:** 502–507 **GrammarSnap:** Plurals of Words Ending in s
g. Consult reference materials, including beginning dictionaries, as needed to check and correct spellings.	**Student Edition pages:** 105, 115, 302–303, 450 **Net-text:** Narrative Writing, Research Writing

Knowledge of Language

College and Career Readiness Standard 3. Apply knowledge of language to understand how language functions in different contexts, to make effective choices for meaning or style, and to comprehend more fully when reading or listening.

Grade 3 Standard 3. Use knowledge of language and its conventions when writing, speaking, reading, or listening.

a. Choose words and phrases for effect.	**Student Edition pages:** 24, 100–101, 152–153, 200–201 **Net-text:** Narrative Writing, Expository Writing, Persuasive Writing
b. Recognize and observe differences between the conventions of spoken and written standard English.	**File Cabinet:** Informal Speech and Formal Writing

Getting-Started Activities

The *Write Source* Student Edition is full of helpful resources that students can access throughout the year while they are developing their writing skills.

Getting-started activities are provided as copy masters on TE pages 619–621. (See the answer keys on TE page 622.) These activities will

- help students discover the kinds of information available in different sections of the book,
- teach students how to access that information
- familiarize students with the layout of the book

The more familiar students are with the text, the more proficient they will be in using it as a resource.

Scavenger Hunts

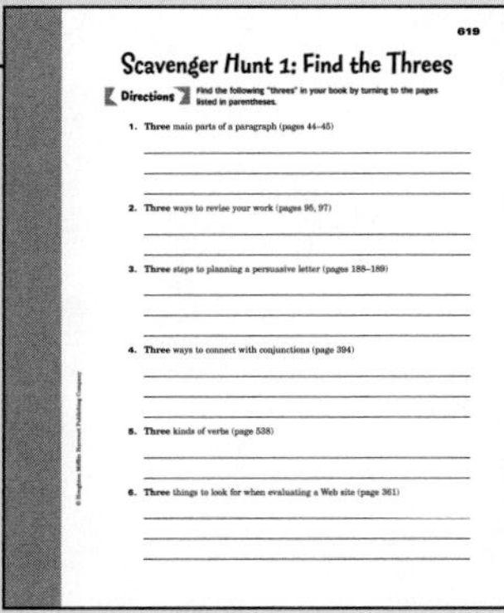

619

Scavenger Hunt 1: Find the Threes

Directions: Find the following "threes" in your book by turning to the pages listed in parentheses.

1. **Three** main parts of a paragraph (pages 44–45)
2. **Three** ways to revise your work (pages 96, 97)
3. **Three** steps to planning a persuasive letter (pages 188–189)
4. **Three** ways to connect with conjunctions (page 394)
5. **Three** kinds of verbs (page 538)
6. **Three** things to look for when evaluating a Web site (page 361)

Students enjoy using scavenger hunts to become familiar with a book. The scavenger hunts we provide can be done in small groups or as a class. They are designed for oral answers, but you may want to photocopy the pages for students to write on. You may also vary the procedure by first having students take turns finding the items and then, on the next scavenger hunt, challenging students to "race" for the answers.

After your students have completed each scavenger hunt, you can challenge them to create their own versions. For example, small groups can work together to create "Find the Fours" or "Search for Sixes" scavenger hunts and then exchange their "hunts" with other groups.

Special Challenge: Develop questions that teams of students try to answer using the book. Pattern this activity after a popular game show.

Other Activities

- **All-School Reference** Have students write down all the subject areas they study and list under each heading the parts of the *Write Source* text that might help them in that subject.
- **Pen Pal Letter** Have students imagine that they are each going to send a copy of *Write Source* to a pen pal in another state or country. Ask students to write letters telling their pen pals about the book.
- **Favorite Feature** Give your students the following assignment: Find one page, one short section, one set of guidelines, one illustration, one writing sample, or one chart you think is interesting, entertaining, stimulating, valuable, etc. Students should prepare to share their discoveries with members of their discussion group or with the entire class.
- **5 W's and H** Have students develop *Who? What? When? Where? Why?* and *How?* questions from *Write Source*—for example, *What is step one in the writing process?* Students should then exchange questions with a partner and search for answers in the textbook. Afterward, partners may discuss each other's answers. (This activity can also be used as a search contest.)

HOUGHTON MIFFLIN HARCOURT

WRITE SOURCE

Authors
Dave Kemper, Patrick Sebranek, and Verne Meyer

Illustrator
Chris Krenzke

GREAT SOURCE.
HOUGHTON MIFFLIN HARCOURT

Welcome to the Teacher's Edition!

Writing is a journey. Let the *Write Source* program be your guide.

The student edition will guide your students to many destinations. Your students will hear the voices of other writers speaking to them from the many accessible models.

The teacher's edition will guide you on this journey as well. In the following pages, you'll find not only lesson objectives and instructions, but also these special features at the points of use:

- Teaching Tips
- Grammar Connections
- Literature Connections
- Writer's Craft
- Technology Connections
- Test Prep
- Notes for English Language Learners
- Accommodations and Modifications for Struggling Learners
- Enrichments for Advanced Learners

Welcome to the journey!

Thanks to the Teachers!

This program would not have been possible without the input of many teachers and administrators from across the nation. As we developed this K–12 series, we surveyed hundreds of teaching professionals. Our grateful thanks go out to each of you. We couldn't have done it without you!

Reviewers

Genevieve M. Bodnar
Youngstown City School District
Youngstown, Ohio

Joan Chiodo
Patricia Di Chiaro Elementary
Yonkers, New York

Kay Dooley
Naperville Community USD
Naperville, Illinois

Jean Evans
Jenks Southeast School District
Tulsa, Oklahoma

Paula Denise Findley
White Hall, Arkansas

Mary Fischer
Arlington Public Schools
Arlington, Massachusetts

Cullen Hemstreet
Jefferson Parish School District
Metairie, Louisiana

Elma G. Jones
Wallingford-Swarthmore School District
Swarthmore, Pennsylvania

Marilyn LeRud
Tucson Unified School District
Tucson, Arizona

Mary Osborne
Pinellas County School District
Largo, Florida

Amy Stenger
Millard Public Schools
Omaha, Nebraska

Pamela J. Strain
Rosemead School District
Rosemead, California

Trademarks and trade names are shown in this book strictly for illustrative purposes and are the property of their respective owners. The authors' references herein should not be regarded as affecting their validity.

Copyright © 2012 by Houghton Mifflin Harcourt Publishing Company

All rights reserved. No part of this work may be reproduced or transmitted in any form or by any means, electronic or mechanical, including photocopying or recording, or by any information storage and retrieval system, without the prior written permission of the copyright owner unless such copying is expressly permitted by federal copyright law. Requests for permission to make copies of any part of the work should be addressed to Houghton Mifflin Harcourt Publishing Company, Attn: Paralegal, 9400 South Park Center Loop, Orlando, Florida 32819.

Printed in the U.S.A.

ISBN 978-0-547-48498-3

1 2 3 4 5 6 7 8 9 10 0914 19 18 17 16 15 14 13 12 11 10

4500000000 A B C D E F G

If you have received these materials as examination copies free of charge, Houghton Mifflin Harcourt Publishing Company retains title to the materials and they may not be resold. Resale of examination copies is strictly prohibited.

Possession of this publication in print format does not entitle users to convert this publication, or any portion of it, into electronic format.

Quick Guide

The *Write Source* Voice

For more than 30 years, our student books have spoken directly to students. We see ourselves as writers speaking to other writers.

As a result, the *Write Source* voice is always encouraging, like an older classmate who genuinely wants a younger one to succeed. We believe that every student can learn to write and that every writer can improve. Throughout this book, your students will hear a voice that says, "You can do it!"

In the same way, the material in the wraparound text speaks directly to you. After all, we are teachers speaking to other teachers, and so we use the same encouraging voice.

Whether you're a seasoned writing teacher or a fresh new face, we are certain that these materials in your hands can make a big difference for your students.

Understanding the Writing Process

The first section of *Write Source* provides an introduction to (or review of) the writing process.

The chapter "One Writer's Process" lets students see how another third-grade writer works through the process of prewriting, writing, revising, editing, and publishing.

Integrating the Six Traits

Write Source fully integrates the six traits of writing (plus presentation) into the writing process. Prewriting focuses on ideas and organization. Writing adds a focus on voice. Revising focuses on the first three traits and also word choice and sentence fluency. Editing zeroes in on conventions, while publishing features the trait of presentation.

contents

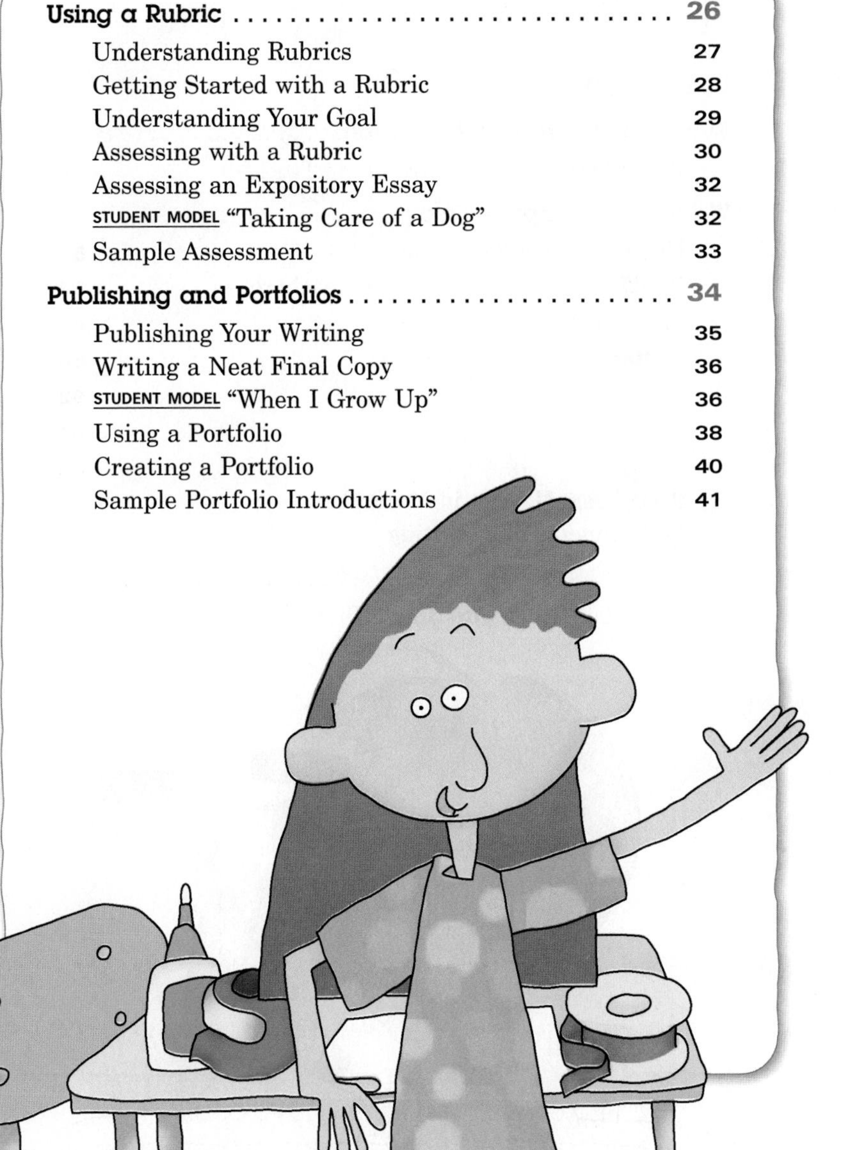

Using Rubrics Throughout the Process

The trait-based rubrics in *Write Source* are not simply for summative assessment. They help guide students throughout the process. Each core writing unit begins with goals that help students think about what they are trying to accomplish. Then, as students revise and edit, trait checklists guide their work, helping them improve their writing in ways large and small.

Peer Responding

Writing should be read and shared. Constructive feedback from a peer can supercharge student revision and editing—and *Write Source* shows your students how to give and receive constructive feedback.

Exploring Publishing Options

"Publishing and Portfolios" and the core writing units provide many options for sharing final work. Compiling a portfolio not only showcases student talent but also creates an alternative form of assessment to demonstrate progress. It's one more way that students can practice the trait of presentation!

Wraparound Feature

Teaching Tip

Boxes labeled "Teaching Tip" provide special strategies for making the lesson come alive for your students.

Creating the Forms of Writing

The writing units in *Write Source* focus on the fundamental forms of writing:

- Descriptive
- Narrative
- Expository
- Persuasive
- Responding to Literature
- Creative
- Research

Each writing assignment includes instruction, examples, and activities that lead students through the writing process. The material works well for whole-class instruction, writing workshop minilessons, and self-paced individual work.

The Forms of Writing

DESCRIPTIVE WRITING

Wraparound Features

Materials

At the beginning of each unit, consult this box to find out what materials you need to have on hand to teach the lesson.

Copy Masters

Boxes such as these tell you what classroom presentation aids exist to help you deliver the lesson.

Benchmark Papers

Check this feature to find out what benchmark papers you can use to show your students a range of performance.

Contents vii

Teaching the Core Units

The core writing units focus on the forms that are most often tested—narrative, expository, persuasive, and response to literature.

Each unit begins with an accessible model with response questions, helping students make the reading-writing connection. Afterward, concrete activities help students do the following:

- Select a topic.
- Gather details.
- Organize details.
- Create a focus statement.
- Write a strong beginning.
- Build a solid middle.
- Create an effective ending.
- Revise for ideas, organization, voice, word choice, and sentence fluency.
- Edit for conventions.
- Publish work with polished presentation.
- Assess using trait-based rubrics.

Writing Across the Curriculum

Special assignments after each of the major forms help your students write in their content areas: social studies, math, science, art, music, health, and practical writing. Whether you teach these subjects or partner with team teachers, these content-area assignments can help your students succeed throughout their day.

Wraparound Feature

Grammar Connection

Each unit overview lists possible grammar activities to cover in the unit. Grammar Connection boxes at point of use suggest the places to integrate instruction.

Differentiating Instruction

Each of the core units provides three levels of form-specific assignments:

1. **Paragraph:** Students who are struggling—or who need an introduction to the form—can create a strong paragraph in the appropriate genre.
2. **Essay:** Middle-level students can create, revise, and edit a multiparagraph essay in the form.
3. **Special Forms:** Advanced students can work on more challenging assignments that connect to science, math, social studies, or practical writing.

Also, because the *Write Source* series follows a consistent format throughout its K–12 line, students who need further differentiation can work at a grade below (or above) their classmates.

Writing Workshop

Each activity in the core writing units can function as a minilesson. You can use these minilesson activities to direct the whole class, to instruct a group of writers, or to provide scaffolding for an individual writer who gets stuck.

EXPOSITORY WRITING

Wraparound Features

English Language Learners

These boxes provide differentiation tips to help English Language Learners.

Struggling Learners

Consult this feature to adjust the lesson for those who are struggling.

Advanced Learners

These boxes feature tips for challenging students who excel.

PERSUASIVE WRITING

Reading-Writing Connections

Each unit contains numerous student models. By reading them and responding to them, students tune their minds to a given genre before beginning to write in it. The persuasive unit uses the following models:

- **Paragraph:** "Who Gets to Talk?"
- **Key Essay:** "Dear Mr. Greer"
- **Working Essay:** "Dear Mrs. Lincoln"
- **Poster:** "Come to the Science Fair"
- **Health Essay:** "Look Out!"
- **E-Mail Message:** "Library Story Hour"
- **On-Demand Essay:** "Save Our Recess"

Preparing for Assessment

Every core unit teaches students process-based strategies, which they internalize as "thinking moves" that will help them in on-demand writing situations. Each unit also ends with a sample on-demand writing prompt and response, as well as additional prompts for practice with high-stakes writing situations.

Wraparound Feature

Test Prep!
These features give suggestions for preparing your students for high- and low-stakes writing tests. Efficacy studies in numerous states have demonstrated the power of the *Write Source* series to raise students' writing scores.

Connecting to Literature

Each level of the *Write Source* series promotes age-appropriate literature. In this unit, for example, students will find responses to the following works of fiction:

- *Amber Brown Is Not a Crayon*
- *Freckle Juice*
- *Stone Fox*

This text also features nonfiction books—and a special assignment that allows students to compare a fiction and a nonfiction book about the same topic:

- *Wee and the Wright Brothers* and *To Fly, the Story of the Wright Brothers*
- *Verdi* and *Snakes*

The chapter includes a section on responding to poetry, with multiple poems to choose from:

- "The Big, Lazy Dragon"
- "Weather Forecast"
- "Bullfrog"
- "The Wolf"
- "Grandpa Frank"
- "What I Did on Saturday"

The end of the section provides a sample literature prompt and response, as well as a prompt that students can respond to.

- "Mountain Lions on the Move"
- "Still Smiling after Thousands of Years"

Wraparound Feature

Literature Connections

These features help you use age-appropriate literary works to teach students special writing techniques. You'll find interesting insights into the works and lives of favorite writers as well as fresh ways to use literature to teach writing.

Contents **xi**

CREATIVE WRITING

Tapping Creativity

The *Write Source* series promotes creativity even in academic writing assignments. However, this section allows you and your students to develop forms that are especially inventive:

- Imaginative Story
- Play
- Rhyming Poem
- Limerick
- Clerihew
- 5 W's Poem
- Alphabet Poem

Research shows a direct connection between enjoyment and learning. Think how quickly a student masters a favorite video game or learns all the words to a favorite song. By letting students write for the joy of it, you can awaken in them a lifelong love of writing.

The Craft of Writing

Art teachers teach techniques for creating perspective or formulas for the proportions of a human face. Then art students must internalize these techniques and use them to craft something new and wonderful.

Writing teachers need to do the same. Throughout the wraparound, you will find suggestions for helping students develop their writing style and voice, going beyond concrete skills to discover the art of writing.

Wraparound Feature

Writer's Craft

These features help you inspire students to write the way professional writers do. Writer's Craft notes outline techniques used by the masters as well as provide interesting anecdotes and quotations.

Training Researchers

In this Internet age, strong research skills are more important than ever. Students must be able to evaluate sources and avoid the lure of plagiarism. This section equips students to succeed using traditional and digital source materials.

The step-by-step instructions in the "Research Writing" section help students learn to do the following:

- use the library
- use the Internet
- evaluate sources
- summarize information
- cite sources (according to MLA style)
- use a gathering grid
- outline a research report

The section also helps students present their material in a traditional report form—or as a multimedia presentation!

RESEARCH WRITING

Wraparound Feature

Technology Connections

In these features, you'll see connections to *Write Source Online* www.hmheducation.com/writesource. *Write Source Online* includes *Interactive Whiteboard Lessons, Net-text, Bookshelf, GrammarSnap, Portfolio, File Cabinet,* and *Essay Scoring.*

Contents xiii

The Tools of Learning

Equipping Students to Learn

This section focuses on the so-called "soft skills" that often get neglected in the modern rush to teach academic subjects. However, the skills of speaking and listening, writing to learn, and conducting oneself in a classroom are crucial to success in all classes.

Organized topically, these chapters can be taught as minilessons when your students most need them. Here are some suggested applications:

- **Present "Giving Speeches"** after students complete a major writing assignment so that they can convert their work into speeches.
- **Teach "Writing in Journals and Learning Logs"** when students are setting up journals at the beginning of a term.
- **Work through "Viewing and Listening Skills"** when the school year begins or before showing students a documentary.
- **Use "Taking Tests"** to help students improve their test performance.

Wraparound Feature

Family Connection Letters

These boxes refer to copy masters of letters that you can send home with your students to keep their families involved in their writing progress.

Teaching Grammar and Writing

With clear rules, simple explanations, engaging examples, and fun activities, "Working with Words" provides short minilessons to help students understand and use the different parts of speech.

It's easy to integrate these minilessons into your writing program. Every writing unit includes cross-references to these pages and those in the "Proofreader's Guide." The *Write Source* series fully integrates its grammar components within its writing units. Integrated grammar instruction allows students to use the rules in context—and understand not just the "what" of grammar, but also the "why."

You can use all the grammar that is suggested—or target the grammar to your students' specific needs. The choice is yours.

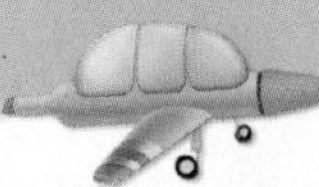

Basic Grammar and Writing

WORKING WITH WORDS

WRITING SENTENCES

Contents xv

Avoiding Errors and Creating Style

"Writing Sentences" begins on the level of correctness, ensuring that students know how to write complete, error-free sentences. The chapter then covers issues of sentence style. The chapter ends with help preparing students for a sentence-skill test—a component of many state writing tests at this grade level.

Creating Paragraphs

"Building Paragraphs" teaches students how to write topic sentences, use supporting details, and follow an organizational plan. The chapter also includes test prep for paragraph skills.

Creating Resourceful Writers

This section equips students with specific, trait-based strategies that they will use over and over during the writing process. Each new concept is introduced by a question that most third-grade writers have asked at one time or another—followed by an answer to the question and a specific strategy for implementing the answer.

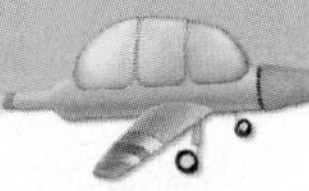

A Writer's Resource

Ideas

Organization

Voice

Contents xvii

Using Presentation

Presentation is crucial to the success of any form of writing. Each of the core units includes a page that focuses on presentation and publishing. "A Writer's Resource" also provides support for effectively presenting ideas on the page.

Perfecting Conventions

The "Proofreader's Guide" includes the rules of punctuation, mechanics, usage, sentence creation, and the parts of speech. The rules are accompanied by engaging example text and activities to test knowledge.

Also, as the "Test Prep!" box indicates, the major sections end with test-prep pages to help students study for grammar tests.

Cross-references in this TE connect to activities in the *SkillsBook* and *Write Source Online* GrammarSnap.

xviii

Proofreader's Guide

Test Prep!
The "Proofreader's Guide" includes test-prep pages to help you practice taking standardized tests on punctuation, mechanics, usage, sentences, and the parts of speech.

Wraparound Feature

Test Prep!
This feature in the wraparound points out strategies for preparing your students to succeed on writing and grammar tests.

Why Write?

When you write, you move your pencil, but you also move your mind. That's why writing helps you in so many ways.

Writing will help you . . .

- **learn more.** When you write something down in your own words, you remember it.
- **explore your mind.** Writing shows you thoughts and feelings you didn't even know you had.
- **share with others.** Letters and e-mail messages let you share your life with those you care about.
- **have fun.** In stories, poems, and plays, you can do amazing things like fly on a cloud or have a picnic on the moon.

Remember . . .

The best way to become a better writer is to write every day. Soon writing will be as natural as walking, and it will take you even farther!

Why Write?

Encourage students to talk about ways they already use writing. Focus on each of the items highlighted on the page.

- Have students ever taken notes while studying? For example, do they write out their spelling words to help memorize the words?
- Do any of them keep journals?
- Have they ever written birthday greetings, thank-you notes, or letters describing their adventures at summer camp to family members and friends?
- Have they ever written a story, poem, or play?

Point out that many everyday activities make use of writing. For example, students might write:

- a to-do list to remind themselves of everything they need to get done at busy times, or
- instructions to a neighbor about feeding a pet while the family is away for the weekend.

Advanced Learners

Have students share pieces of writing they have done. Have them identify the different purposes of their writing. For example, were they writing to explain how to do something or were they writing a funny story? As they look at each other's writing, students should see a variety of purposes.

Grammar Connection

Using the Right Word

- **Proofreader's Guide** pages 510–522 (+)
- ***SkillsBook*** page 74

The Writing Process Overview

Common Core Standards Focus

Writing 5: With guidance and support from peers and adults, develop and strengthen writing as needed by planning, revising, and editing.

Language 1: Demonstrate command of the conventions of standard English grammar and usage when writing or speaking.

Language 2: Demonstrate command of the conventions of standard English capitalization, punctuation, and spelling when writing.

Writing Process

- **Prewriting** Select a topic, gather details, and plan what to say.
- **Writing** Introduce the topic and get all ideas on paper.
- **Revising** Read over the first draft, share it with another person, and make changes to improve the writing.
- **Editing** Check spelling, capitalization, and punctuation, write a neat final copy, and check one last time for errors.
- **Publishing** Share the final copy and display it in class.

Focus on the Traits

- **Ideas** Selecting a writing topic and gathering many details about it
- **Organization** Beginning in an interesting way, and connecting the middle and ending to the beginning
- **Voice** Writing as if telling the story to a friend
- **Word Choice** Using specific words to make the meaning clear
- **Sentence Fluency** Writing different kinds of sentences that are easy to read
- **Conventions** Checking for errors in capitalization, punctuation, spelling, and grammar

Technology Connections

Write Source Online
www.hmheducation.com/writesource

- ***Net-text***
- ***Bookshelf***
- ***GrammarSnap***
- ***Portfolio***
- ***Writing Network features***
- ***File Cabinet***

Interactive Whiteboard Lessons

Suggested Writing Process Unit (Four Weeks)

	Day	Writing and Skills Instruction	Student Edition: Writing Process Unit	Student Edition: Resource Units*	SkillsBook	Daily Language Workouts	Write Source Online
Week 1	1–5	Getting-Started Activities, page TE-61 **Why Write?**	1	510–522 (+)	74	4–5, 77	
Week 2	6–10	**Understanding the Writing Process**	4–9			6–7, 78	
		Writing in Journals and Learning Logs	350–355				
Week 3	11–12	**One Writer's Process** (Prewriting, Writing)	10–12	463–482 (+)	39–40	8–9, 79	
	13–15	**One Writer's Process** (Revising, Editing, Publishing)	13–15	486–498 (+)	49–50, 59–60		
		Working with Partners	16–19				
		Learning to Listen	362–363				
Week 4	16–18	**Traits of Good Writing** (Ideas)	20–21			10–11, 80	
		(Organization, Voice)	22–23				
		(Word Choice, Sentence Fluency, Conventions)	24–25	526–528 (+)	83–84		*GrammarSnap*
	19–20	**Using a Rubric**	26–29				
		Assessing	30–33	532–554 (+)	169–170		
		Publishing and Portfolios	34–41				

* These units are also located in the back of the *Teacher's Edition*. Resource Units include "Basic Grammar and Writing," "A Writer's Resource," and "Proofreader's Guide."
(+) This activity is located in a different section of the *Write Source Student Edition.* If students have already completed this activity, you may wish to review it at this time.

Teacher's Notes for the Writing Process

This overview for the writing process includes some specific teaching suggestions for the unit.

Writing Focus

Understanding the Writing Process (pages 4–9)

Using the writing process guidelines and a steady one-step-after-another approach, children can begin to write and not be intimidated. Point out the symbols for the traits and the writing process steps that will be used throughout the book.

Traits of Good Writing (pages 20–25)

The traits of good writing are like road signs of writing. Road signs help drivers know speed limits, locate exits, and learn of road hazards. Traits of good writing help students make their writing interesting and well organized, use colorful language, and avoid errors in final copy.

Using a Rubric (pages 26–33)

If a student builds a birdhouse, measurements are important. In the same way, rubrics provide one form of measurement for writers. They can see if their paper has everything it needs or if something is missing.

Publishing and Portfolios (pages 34–41)

Most writing published by students is in the form of an assignment handed in. However, stories on a bulletin board, poems posted on a Web site, or plays acted out are other forms of publication. Publishing makes writing real, helps young writers get interested in their work, and creates a greater sense of pride and accomplishment.

Academic Vocabulary

Read aloud the academic terms, as well as the descriptions and questions. Model for students how to read one question and answer it. Have partners monitor their understanding and seek clarification of the terms by working through the meanings and questions together.

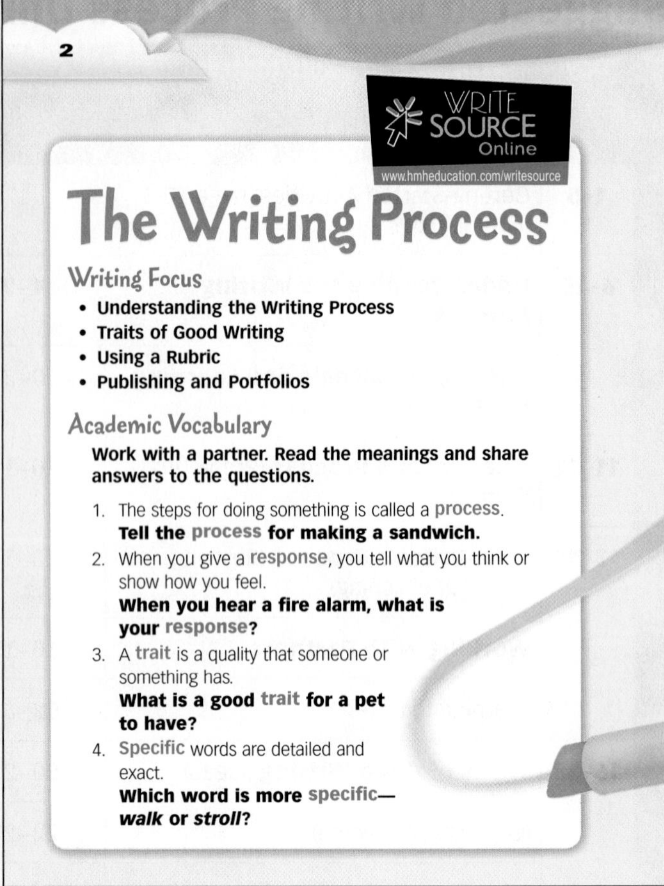
2

WRITE SOURCE Online
www.hmheducation.com/writesource

The Writing Process

Writing Focus
- Understanding the Writing Process
- Traits of Good Writing
- Using a Rubric
- Publishing and Portfolios

Academic Vocabulary

Work with a partner. Read the meanings and share answers to the questions.

1. The steps for doing something is called a process. **Tell the process for making a sandwich.**
2. When you give a response, you tell what you think or show how you feel. **When you hear a fire alarm, what is your response?**
3. A trait is a quality that someone or something has. **What is a good trait for a pet to have?**
4. Specific words are detailed and exact. **Which word is more specific—*walk* or *stroll*?**

Minilessons

"Nothing Better!" — Understanding the Writing Process

- **WRITE** a few sentences that tell how you feel about writing. You can write whatever you want to. Be honest!

Just for Fun — Working with Partners

- **PRETEND** that your teacher has asked each student in the class to write a poem about summertime.
  - **HELP** a partner decide what to write about. Also **HELP** your partner think of some good words to use in his or her poem. Then **ASK** your partner to help you—but this time pretend you are writing a funny poem about an animal.

From Top to Bottom — Traits of Good Writing

- **CHOOSE** an interesting family member or friend to describe. **ORGANIZE** your writing by describing the person's face, then work your way down. **WRITE** your description so your reader "sees" the person from head to foot.

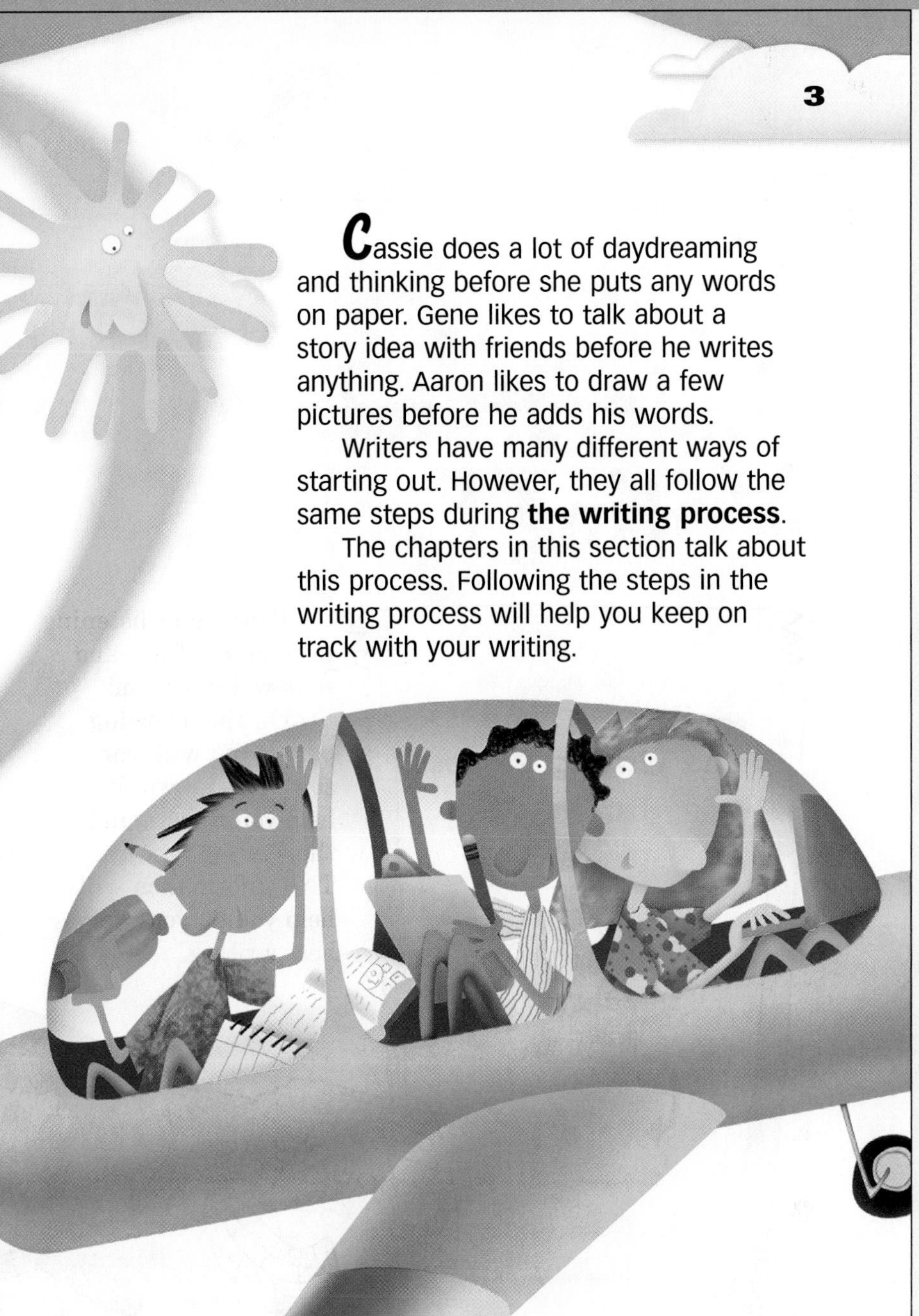

3

Cassie does a lot of daydreaming and thinking before she puts any words on paper. Gene likes to talk about a story idea with friends before he writes anything. Aaron likes to draw a few pictures before he adds his words.

Writers have many different ways of starting out. However, they all follow the same steps during **the writing process**.

The chapters in this section talk about this process. Following the steps in the writing process will help you keep on track with your writing.

Using the Writing Process

Talk about the meaning of the word *process* (a series of actions leading to a specific end or goal). Explain to students that cooks use such a process when they follow a recipe.

Explain that cooks often change ingredients to alter the taste of a dish just as writers revise their writing to change its meaning or effect. Also point out that not every writer necessarily follows the writing process in exactly the same way—just as not every cook follows the same recipe for making a salad. But good writers become familiar with all the steps and learn how to use those steps in the ways that suit them best.

Family Connection Letters

As you begin this unit, send home the Writing Process Family Connection letter, which describes what students will be learning.

- Letter in English (TE p. 601)
- Letter in Spanish (TE p. 609)

Understanding the Writing Process

Objectives

- Connect the writing process to the six traits of effective writing.
- Understand the five steps in the writing process.
- Establish good writing habits.

Discuss the different kinds of stories students enjoy, such as

- fairy tales,
- stories about historical events or characters,
- adventure tales, and
- science fiction stories.

Point out to students that their favorite authors probably follow the same process that they are about to explore in this chapter.

Literature Connections

Process: Hold up a familiar book and ask, "Does a writer just type into a computer and a book like this comes out?" The answer, of course, is no. "Most often, writers gather many ideas, write a book, and then revise it before sending it to a publisher. The publisher then has editors who help the writer edit the book and typesetters and artists to help the writer publish the book. Soon, you'll be following the same process as professional writers."

Understanding the Writing Process

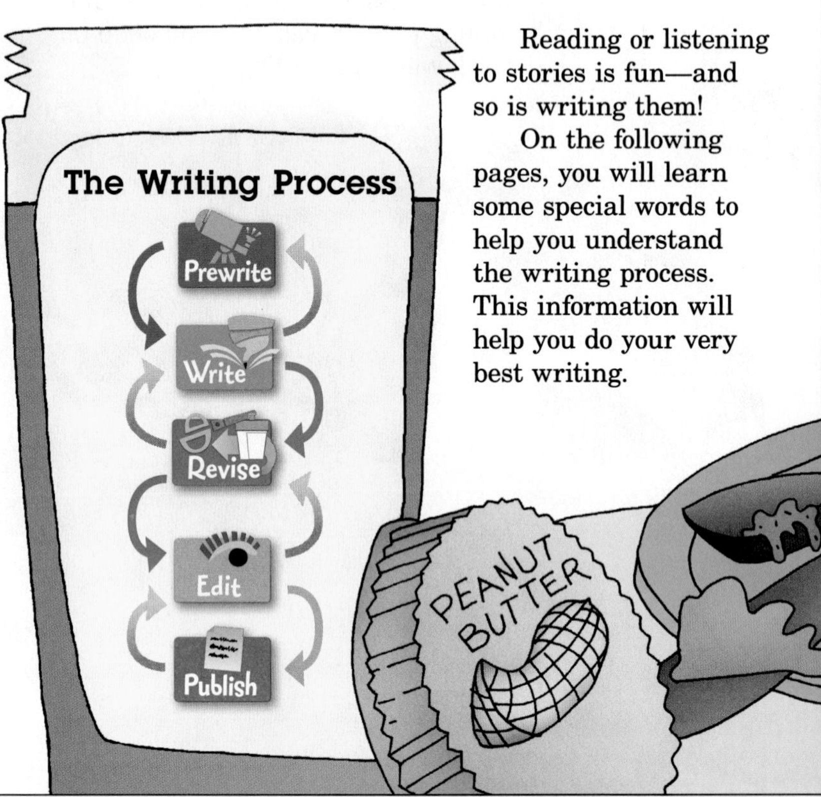

Reading or listening to stories is fun—and so is writing them!

On the following pages, you will learn some special words to help you understand the writing process. This information will help you do your very best writing.

Materials

Chart paper (TE p. 6)

Understanding the Writing Process 5

Connecting with the Traits

Do you know what can happen if you write too fast? You might leave out some important ideas or you might put ideas in the wrong order. Then again, you might use boring words. You might even forget to put periods at the end of your sentences!

When these things happen, the **writing process** gives you time to fix them. It gives you time to make each writing **trait**—and each part of your writing—the best it can be.

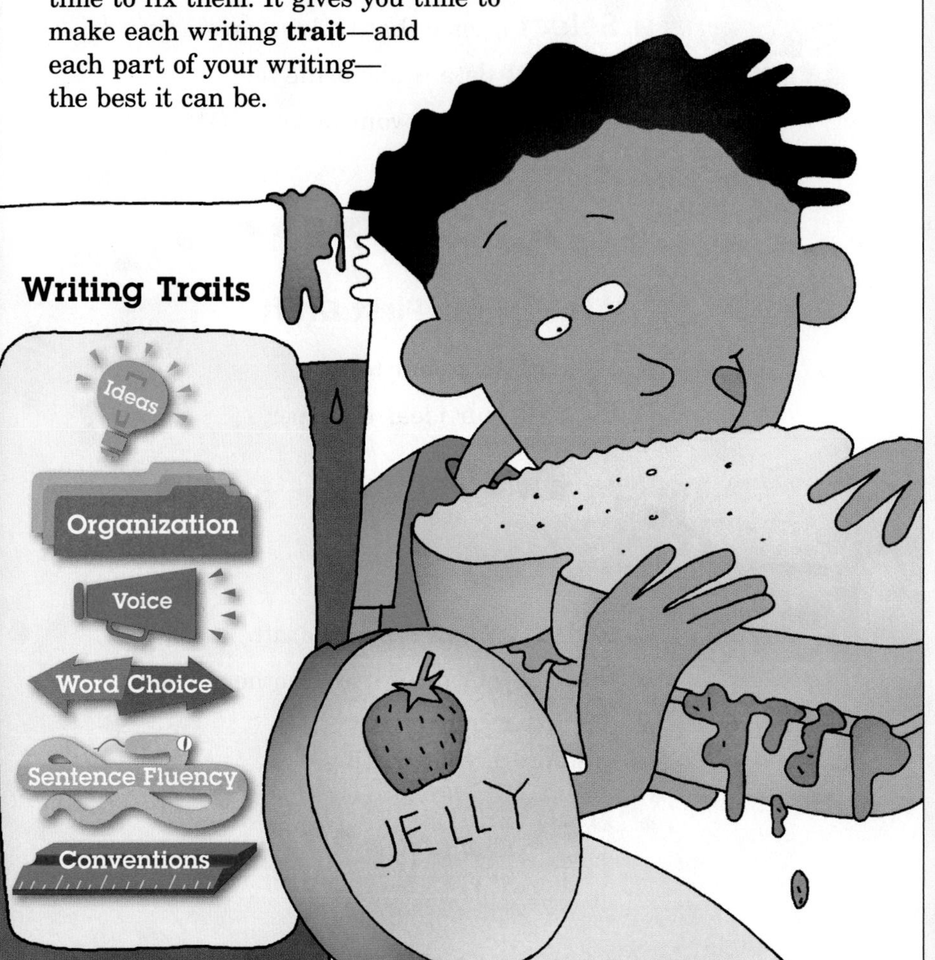

English Language Learners

Help students conceptualize the term *trait* by pointing out that people have traits, too. For example, we notice their hair and eye color and how they behave (shy, funny, or kind).

Connecting with the Traits

Tell students they'll learn more about the writing traits later (see SE page 20), but that the icons on the page tell them a little bit about each trait they'll use in the process.

- Ideas You might say getting an idea is like having a light go on in your brain. Here, the bulb symbolizes the **ideas** you might write about.
- Organization The file folder icon is a symbol for **organizing** your thoughts and ideas.
- Voice The megaphone stands for your **voice**, or the way you sound as a writer.
- Word Choice The arrows pointing different ways stand for the choices you have when **choosing words**.
- Sentence Fluency A snake gliding gracefully along symbolizes **sentence fluency**, the way sentences should glide smoothly from one to the next.
- Conventions How well you follow the capitalization, punctuation, spelling, and grammar **rules** is a kind of ruler for measuring the success of your writing.

Using the Writing Process

Assure students that even though the writing process with its five steps may seem complicated now, it will become easier and more natural after they have followed the process a few times.

Prewriting

Direct students' attention to the word *prewriting*. Remind them that the prefix *pre-* means "before." Explain that they will use this step to get ready to write.

Writing a First Draft

To help students understand that a first draft is not a final copy, talk about the word *draft*. Write the definition on the board: an early sketch, outline, or plan.

Revising

Explain that when you *revise* something, you look at it again to make good changes.

Note that an important part of this step is having another person read the draft. The new reader will have a fresh eye and may be able to spot problems or ways to improve things the writer can't see.

Using the Writing Process

Even your favorite authors follow the steps in the writing process. You should, too.

Prewriting

- **Select** a topic that truly interests you.
- **Gather** details about the topic.
- **Plan** what you want to say.

Writing a First Draft

- **Introduce** your topic.
- **Get** all your ideas on paper.

Revising

- **Read over** your first draft.
- **Share** your draft with another person.
- **Make changes** to improve your writing.

English Language Learners

Discuss ways that people think of topics before they begin to write. These may include daydreaming, doodling and drawing pictures, talking, listing ideas in a journal, or filling in a graphic organizer with words and phrases.

Ask students which prewriting activities they like to use. Assist students by using the following sentence frame:

When I'm getting ready to write I like to _______. List their responses on a "Prewriting" chart for the room.

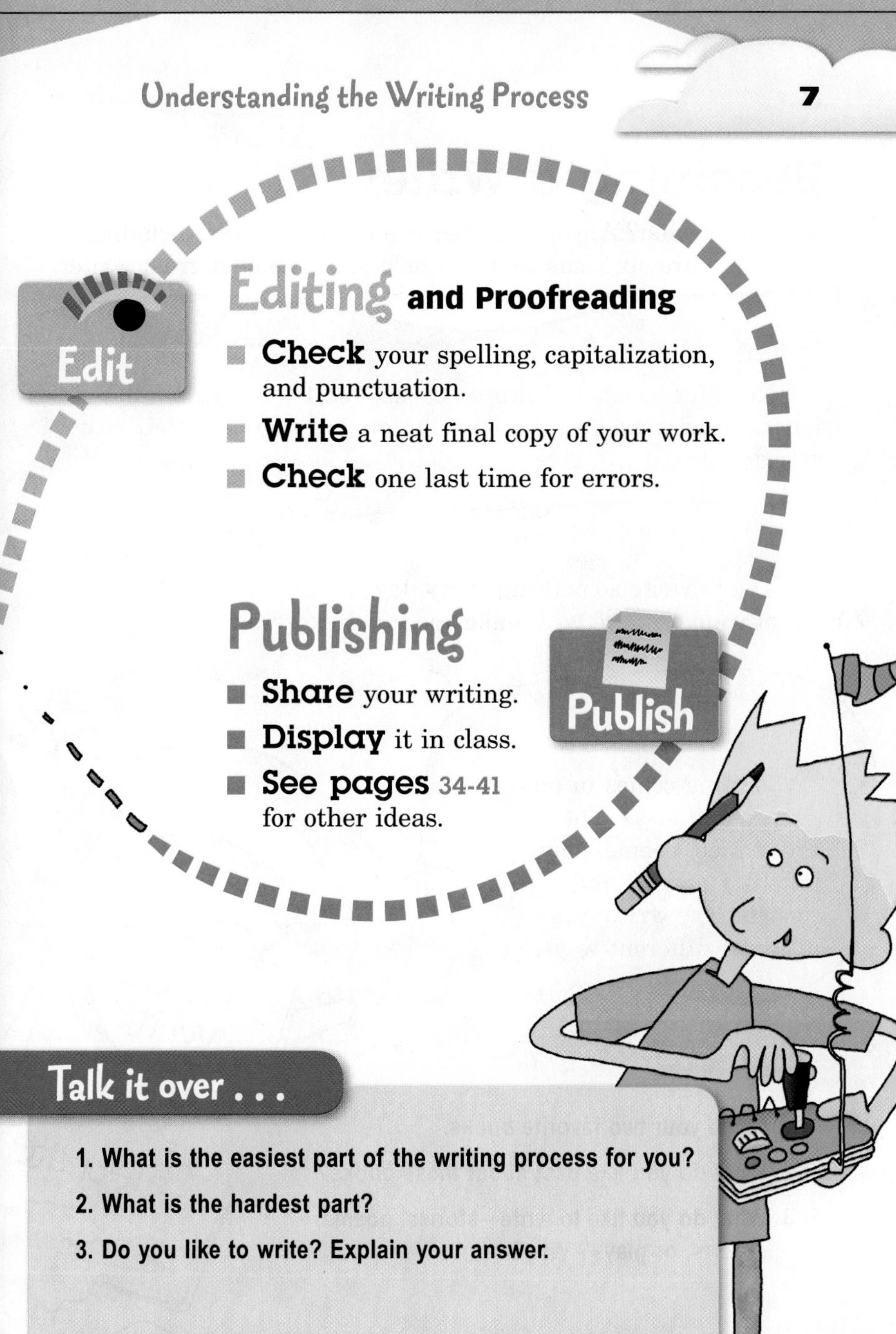

Editing and Proofreading

- **Check** your spelling, capitalization, and punctuation.
- **Write** a neat final copy of your work.
- **Check** one last time for errors.

Publishing

- **Share** your writing.
- **Display** it in class.
- **See pages** 34-41 for other ideas.

Talk it over . . .

1. What is the easiest part of the writing process for you?
2. What is the hardest part?
3. Do you like to write? Explain your answer.

Editing and Proofreading

Ask students if they've ever found a mistake in anything they've read. Point out that even professional writers and their publishers work hard to find and correct such errors.

* Direct students' attention to the Proofreader's Guide on SE pages 462–558, and suggest that they browse through it to get familiar with the information. Tell students that they can refer to the guide whenever they have a question about the rules of writing.

Publishing

Lead a discussion and brainstorm different ways writers can share their work with others. These may include the following:

- making class books
- displaying writing on bulletin boards
- submitting writing to newsletters
- performing plays
- presenting reports
- doing multimedia presentations
- creating Web sites

Advanced Learners

During the **Talk it over** activity, some students may be inclined to answer that there is no hard part of the writing process for them. Some of these students, however, may have a difficult time being patient as partners read drafts during the revising stage. Ask students questions such as:

- Why is being a good reader important?
- How can being a good listener help you?

Becoming a Writer

Discuss with students ways that they can help each other use the six ideas listed. If possible, use one or two of these ideas in the classroom:

- Post a chart with columns titled *Fat Books, Skinny Books, Picture Books,* and *Chapter Books.* Invite students to write the titles of the books they've read and enjoyed. Keep the list going all year.
- Set aside a few minutes every week for students to give a brief oral review of a book they liked.
- Invite interested students to form a writers group that could meet regularly (either during class or during free time) to share their writing with one another.
- Start a weekly or monthly class newsletter (or encourage students to create one with friends outside class) that includes examples of different kinds of writing.

Becoming a Writer

Guess what? Anyone can become a great writer, including you! Here are six ideas that can help you become a great writer.

Read a lot.

Read fat books and skinny books, short books and tall books. Reading shows you how authors put together their best stories. Also, it can give you great ideas for your own writing!

Write a lot.

Try to write something every day, even on weekends. All of your practice will make you a better writer.

Try different forms.

Writing comes in many shapes and sizes. There are stories, poems, plays, letters, journals, and reports. Try writing in all these different ways.

Talk it over . . .

1. **Name your two favorite books.**
2. **What do you like best about these books?**
3. **What do you like to write—stories, poems, reports, or plays? Why?**

Struggling Learners

Discuss how voice and word choice change depending on the audience. Give the following examples:

- An e-mail to a friend might end with *Write back soon!*
- A business letter might end with *I hope to hear from you soon.*

Write the two sentences on the board. Point out the differences in word choice and end punctuation in each sentence and discuss how they change the tone (voice) of the sentences.

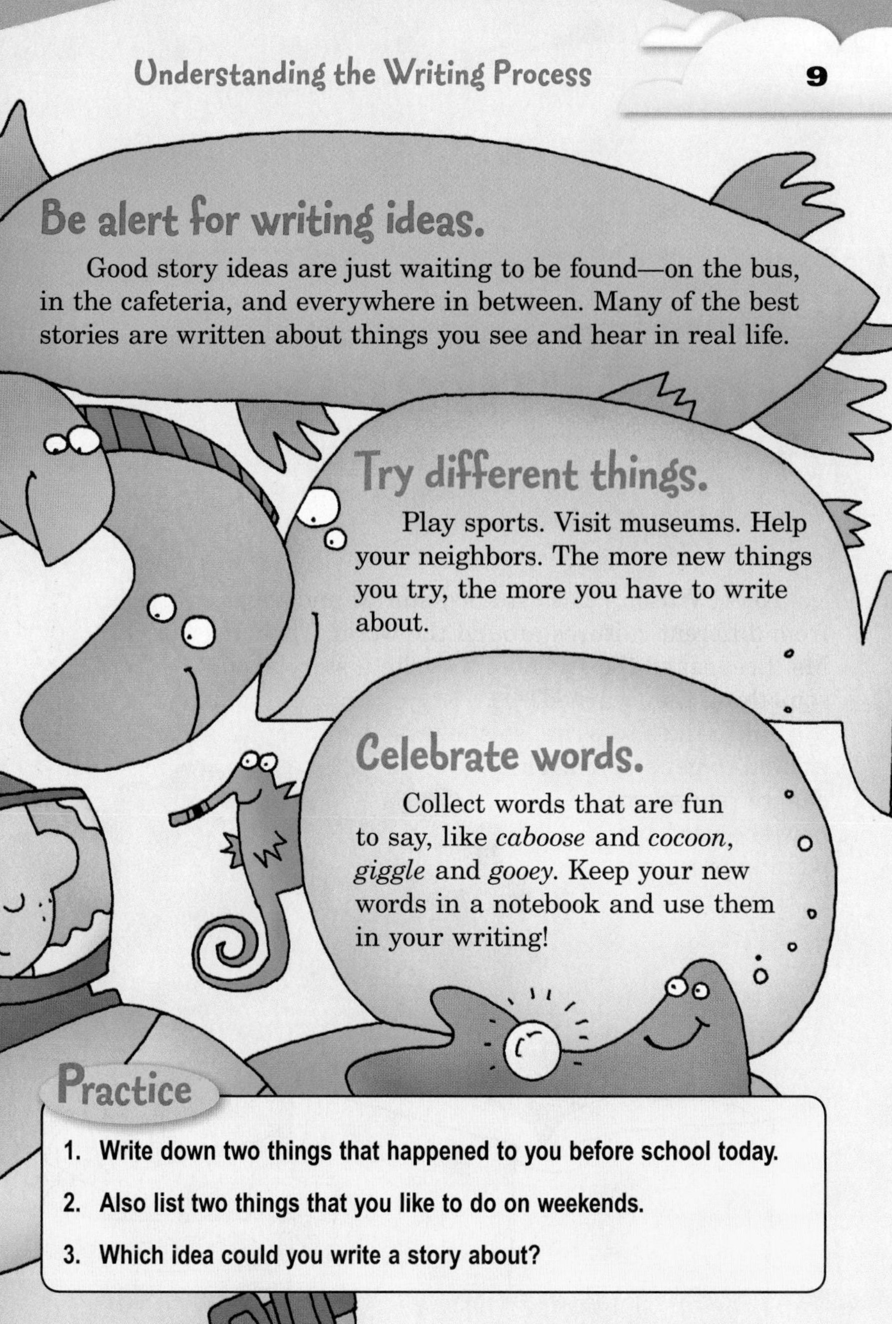

Understanding the Writing Process
9
Be alert for writing ideas.
Good story ideas are just waiting to be found—on the bus, in the cafeteria, and everywhere in between. Many of the best stories are written about things you see and hear in real life.
Try different things.
Play sports. Visit museums. Help your neighbors. The more new things you try, the more you have to write about.
Celebrate words.
Collect words that are fun to say, like *caboose* and *cocoon*, *giggle* and *gooey*. Keep your new words in a notebook and use them in your writing!
Practice
1. Write down two things that happened to you before school today.
2. Also list two things that you like to do on weekends.
3. Which idea could you write a story about?

Some students may be concerned that they won't be able to think of interesting ideas to write about. Assure them that their *Write Source* book will teach them ways to come up with ideas when they feel stuck.

✱ For more about finding story ideas, see Keep a Writer's Notebook, SE pages 432–433.

To help students add new words to their writer's vocabulary, dedicate part of a board or wall to "Word of the Day" possibilities, which include:

- Announce the word and its definition first thing in the morning. (You may want to make this an "all-school" activity.)
- Have volunteers bring in words to share with the class or make a schedule so all students will have a turn.
- Have students keep a new-word notebook and add words to the "Word of the Day" list (see SE page 449).

There are many Internet resources for finding daily words, including the Merriam-Webster site (www.m-w.com).

One Writer's Process

Objectives
- Evaluate one writer's step-by-step progress through the writing process.
- Use the 5 W's Chart for organizing details on a writing topic.

Review the stages of the writing process (prewriting, writing, revising, editing, publishing) by having students call them out. Write and leave them on the board for students to refer to.

Point out to students that the title of the section is "One Writer's Process." Direct students' attention to the word *One*. Explain to students that they are about to see how *one* writer used the writing process. Ask them to think about how they have used the writing process in the past. Remind them that the steps in the writing process are basic guidelines that they can follow in different ways.

One Writer's Process

Nikki Wilson's class studied stories and songs from different cultures around the world. Their teacher, Ms. Lee, asked the students to write a story about something they learned.

Nikki likes to write, so she was excited to get started. This chapter shows you how she used the writing process to complete her story.

Materials

Newspaper articles (TE p. 11)

Copy Masters

5 W's Chart (TE pp. 11, 12)

Prewriting Selecting a Topic

Nikki's teacher talked with the class about different topics they had studied. Afterward, Nikki decided to write about griots (GREE-ohs). Griots are special storytellers.

Gathering Details

Ms. Lee showed Nikki an interesting book about griots. Nikki read the book. When she finished, she listed the important details she had learned on a 5 W's chart.

5 W's Chart

5 W's Chart

Who?	storytellers called griots
What?	tell stories about important events
When?	a long time ago and now
Where?	in Africa
Why?	to honor people

Tip: Use a 5 W's chart the next time you have to list the important details about a writing topic.

Prewriting Selecting a Topic

Point out that Nikki's purpose was to share something she had learned. Set aside time for students to decide on a topic. Suggest some from their readings, and guide them in making their selection. Writers who are genuinely interested in their subject have more fun gathering information, and their enthusiasm shows in the writing.

Prewriting Gathering Details

Tell students that making sure a piece of writing answers the 5 W's is a technique borrowed from **newspaper writing** *(see below)*, in which it is important to give a complete account of a story.

Distribute copies of the reproducible 5 W's Chart (TE page 597) and encourage students to keep several blank charts in their notebooks so they have one ready to fill out whenever they begin a writing project.

Tell them they'll learn other ways to organize ideas in charts and lists as they go through the book.

* See SE pages 438–444 for examples of a variety of graphic organizers students can use when gathering details.

Teaching Tip: Newspaper Writing and the 5 W's

Collect short articles from the newspaper for students to read. Ask them to use the 5 W's to find information the reporter gathered.

- Divide the class into small groups, and give each group one article and a 5 W's Chart (TE page 597).
- Challenge students to read the article and fill out the chart based on the piece.
- Circulate as students work, helping as needed.
- Afterward, have groups present their findings to the class. Ask one student to read the article, and then have others read the information on the 5 W's Chart. Did the organizer help them find the information?

Grammar Connection

Marking Punctuation

- **Proofreader's Guide** pages 463–482 (+)
- ***SkillsBook*** pages 39–40

Writing Developing a First Draft

Remind students that the 5 W's are *Who? What? When? Where?* and *Why?* Distribute copies of the reproducible 5 W's Chart (TE page 597). Then read the story aloud, having students jot down any answers they hear to the 5 W's.

Talk it over . . .

Answers

Nikki used details from four of the five "W" questions about griots:

- *Who?* a griot, or special storyteller
- *What?* to remember important events
- *Where?* in Africa
- *Why?* to honor people

Writer's Craft

Voice: Use the model about storytellers to demonstrate the idea of voice. Say, "Who do you know who tells stories?" Take answers. Then say, "What kind of voice does a storyteller use?" Answers may include adjectives such as *excited* or *mysterious*. "Writers also use a storytelling voice. Readers can tell when a writer is excited. Let's read the first part of Nikki's draft and look for words that show she is excited." The word cues include *grate (great) stories, He is so good,* and *special.*

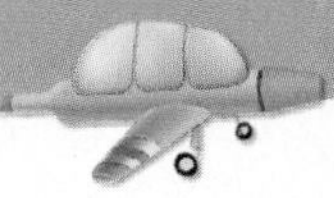

Writing Developing a First Draft

In her first draft, Nikki put all of her ideas on paper. She didn't worry about making a few mistakes. She'd fix them later.

Special Storytellers

My grandpa tells grate stories. He is so good that he could be a griot. A griot is a special storyteller in Africa.

His job was to remember important events. A griot worked for a ruler or a cheif. He also sings songs to honor people

A griot learned from his parents. They would teach him how to sing and to play musical instruments. he would also have to remember many things. When a griot got older, he helped out at festivals.

Talk it over . . .

What details does Nikki's first draft include from her 5 W's chart on page 11?

English Language Learners

During **Talk it over,** some students may have difficulty determining whom the story is about. Point out that *his* at the beginning of the second paragraph refers to the griot, not the grandpa. Explain that the story is about what a griot is.

Struggling Learners

Help students who are visual learners fill in a 5 W's Chart (TE page 597) to answer the **Talk it over** question. Point out that the title of the draft gives the reader a clue to the topic of the draft.

Advanced Learners

Have students choose a familiar story or tale and use it to fill in a copy of the 5 W's Chart (TE page 597). Tell them not to name characters when answering the *Who* question (for example, *a girl with mean stepsisters* instead of *Cinderella*). Then ask volunteers to read aloud their charts and have the group guess the title or main character of the story.

Revising Improving the Writing

Nikki read her first draft to herself. She read it to a partner, too. Then she made her story better by revising it.

Nikki added important information.

She moved an idea.

She changed an idea and started a new paragraph.

Special Storytellers

My grandpa tells grate stories. He is so good that he could be a griot. A griot (GREE-oh) is a special storyteller in Africa.

His job was to remember important events. A griot worked for a ruler or a cheif. He also sings songs to honor people

A griot learned from his parents. They would teach him how to sing and to play musical instruments. he would also have to remember many ~~things~~ stories and songs. When a griot got older, he helped out at festivals.

Talk it over . . .

1. What is one other thing that Nikki could have changed?
2. Did you wonder about any idea in Nikki's story?

English Language Learners

Point out that Nikki moved the circled sentence to the beginning of the second paragraph. Ask students why she did that. Discuss how this change will make it clear that *His* in the second sentence refers to a griot and not to Nikki's grandpa.

Revising Improving the Writing

Show students the proofreading marks on the inside back cover of the student edition. Encourage them to use the marks every time they revise their writing. Consider posting the list in your classroom for easy reference. (See the copy master on TE page 594.)

Explain each of the marks used in the revision shown on the page.

- Line 2: The *caret*, or arrowhead, pointing to the space between *griot* and *is* indicates that the pronunciation for *griot* should be inserted there.
- Lines 4 and 5: The circle drawn around this sentence reminds the writer to move the sentence to the position indicated by the arrow.
- Line 9: The line drawn through *things* means to delete that word.
- Line 9: The paragraph symbol indicates where a new paragraph begins.

Talk it over . . .

Answers will vary. Possible answers include the following.

- Add information that addresses the *when* question.
- Finish the story by referring to the grandfather again.

Editing Checking for Conventions

Suggest that when students revise and edit their writing, they use a colored pencil. Doing so will make their marks easier to see and prevent them from overlooking a correction when writing their final copy.

Encourage students to consult a dictionary when needed. Refer them to the helpful words list in their *Write Source* book (SE pages 503–507), too.

To help students avoid misspelling the same words over and over, have them highlight those words in their writing. Tell students to start a personal list of troublesome words. They should look up and spell the words correctly on the list. Then they can refer to it as they use the words in their writing.

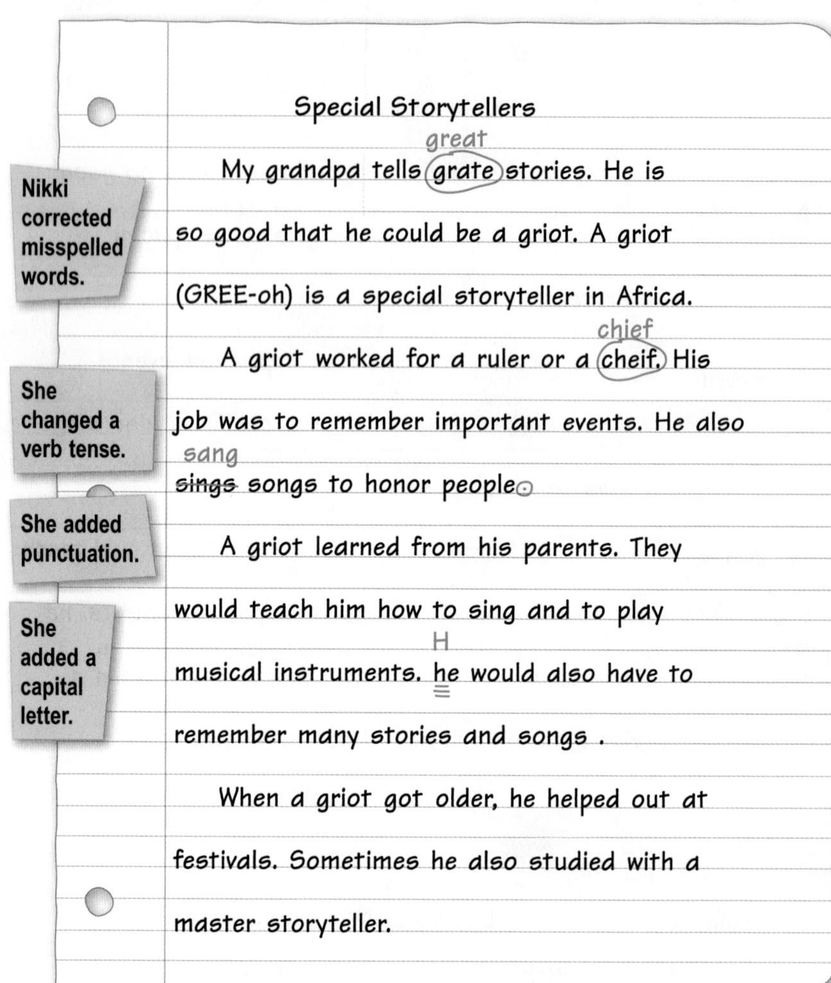
14
Edit
Editing Checking for Conventions
Next, Nikki edited her writing. She checked for mistakes in capitalization, punctuation, spelling, and grammar.
Special Storytellers
great
My grandpa tells grate stories. He is so good that he could be a griot. A griot (GREE-oh) is a special storyteller in Africa.
chief
A griot worked for a ruler or a cheif. His job was to remember important events. He also
sang
sings songs to honor people.
A griot learned from his parents. They would teach him how to sing and to play musical instruments.
H
he would also have to remember many stories and songs .
When a griot got older, he helped out at festivals. Sometimes he also studied with a master storyteller.
Nikki corrected misspelled words.
She changed a verb tense.
She added punctuation.
She added a capital letter.

Grammar Connection

Editing for Mechanics

- **Proofreader's Guide** pages 486–498 (+)
- ***SkillsBook*** pages 49–50, 59–60

English Language Learners

Point out the change in verb tense from *sings* to *sang* (an irregular verb). Explain that the past-tense form of *sings* is *sang*, not *singed*. Provide students with a list of irregular verbs (see SE page 544). Have them add new irregular verbs to their list, and use it when they write.

One Writer's Process 15

Publish Publishing Sharing Your Writing

When Nikki finished, she couldn't wait to share her final essay with her classmates . . . and her grandfather.

Special Storytellers

My grandpa tells great stories. He is so good that he could be a griot. A griot (GREE-oh) is a special storyteller in Africa.

A griot worked for a ruler or a chief. His job was to remember important events. He also sang songs to honor people.

A griot learned from his parents. They would teach him how to sing and to play musical instruments. He would also have to remember many stories and songs.

When a griot got older, he helped out at festivals. Sometimes he also studied with a master storyteller.

I'm going to tell my grandpa about griots. Then maybe I'll ask him to sing me a story.

Talk it over . . .

What do you like best about Nikki's story?

Publishing Sharing Your Writing

Tell students that the word *publishing* means "to make something *public*," that is, available to the people. Published works refer to works that are printed on paper, published on the Internet, or read aloud and performed.

Talk with the class about the ways Nikki could share her essay. She could

- mail it to her grandfather,
- read the essay to the class or at a family gathering,
- post the essay on her family's Web site, or
- print the essay in a class newsletter.

Working with Partners

Objectives

- Take the roles of the writer and the reader when working with a partner.
- Learn how to be a good listener and give helpful responses.
- Practice using a peer response sheet.

Talk with students about the experiences they have had working with partners on other kinds of projects, including those outside of school. They might bring up activities such as cooking with a sibling or parent or working with classmates on school projects.

Encourage students to think about what they learned from these experiences.

- Did the partner teach the student something about how to get the job done?
- Did working together make a challenging task easier or more enjoyable?

Working with Partners

Toshi likes writing-workshop time in her class. She gets to work on her stories and reports, and she also gets to work with her friends.

Toshi's friends help her improve her writing. Sometimes they help her think of a good writing topic. Other times they help her find ways to improve a first draft. They even help her find mistakes before she makes a final copy.

Sharing your writing will help you learn a lot about the writing process.

Materials

Index cards (TE p. 18)

Helping One Another

You can work with writing partners throughout the writing process, from prewriting to proofreading.

During Prewriting

Partners can help you . . .

- brainstorm topics to write about and
- find information about your topic.

As You Review Your First Draft

Partners can tell you . . .

- what they like and
- what parts they have questions about.

As You Revise

Partners can tell you if . . .

- the beginning gets their interest,
- the middle part sticks to the topic, and
- the ending is strong.

As You Edit and Proofread

Partners can help you . . .

- check your capitalization,
- check your punctuation, and
- check your spelling.

Talk it over . . .

1. **Has a partner ever helped you with your writing? How?**
2. **Tell your classmates about a time you worked with a partner.**

Helping One Another

Talk with students about things to consider when working with a partner. For example:

- If both partners are researching a similar topic, helping each other gather information will probably be easier.
- If your partner is a good listener, your meetings will be more productive.
- It is important to give equal time to each other's work. Partners might want to establish rules, such as agreeing to talk about one person's work for five minutes and then the other person's work for five minutes.
- Good partners prepare to meet by getting their writing done on time. It's important that partners do their part.

Writing Workshop

Partner sessions are a crucial part of any writing workshop. By having students read and respond to each other's writing, you not only help writers discover ways to improve, but you also create a writing community in the classroom.

English Language Learners

When assigning partners for the writing process, have students work with cooperative students who are proficient in English. It may be most effective if partnerships are ongoing throughout the unit, so that students feel comfortable and confident while sharing their work.

Advanced Learners

Have students write a want ad for a writing partner. Have them review the checklist on this page, and choose several items that they feel are most important. Encourage them to expand the list to include other information that might not be on the checklist.

Reviewing with Partners

Emphasize how important it is for students to respond to each other's work in a friendly, courteous way that will not hurt writers' feelings.

When You're the Writer

Remind students to read in a clear voice and not to rush. Model reading a short piece in a clear way. Remind readers that the listener is hearing the piece for the first time.

When You're the Listener

Tell students that some of the most helpful questions they can ask are those that begin with one of the 5 W words (and how), because such questions call for more than simple "yes" or "no" answers.

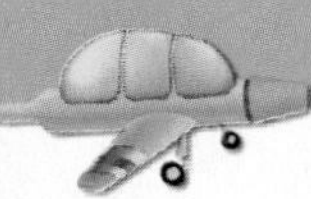

Reviewing with Partners

Use the guidelines below when you and a partner are ready to review a piece of writing.

When You're the Writer

- **Be ready to share your writing.** You can share your first draft, and you can share your changed writing.
- **Tell why you wrote this piece.** Tell just a little about it.
- **Read your writing aloud.**
- **Listen to your partner's comments.** He or she will help you improve your writing.

When You're the Listener

- **Listen carefully to the writer.**
- **Jot down a few notes to help you remember ideas.**
- **Tell the writer something you like about the writing.** "I like the way . . . "
- **Ask about things you don't understand.** "What do you mean when you say . . . ?"
- **Be positive, kind, and helpful.**

Practice

Share a first draft with a partner. Make sure to follow the guidelines listed above.

English Language Learners

Help students find the right words to provide positive feedback to their partners. Provide them with sentence frames on index cards to refer to when it is their turn to give comments. Use the following sentence frames, or create your own.

- My favorite part was ______.
- I like the way ______.
- I'd like to know more about ______.

Struggling Learners

Some students may have difficulty listening to a partner's story and jotting down notes at the same time. Remind students that the notes can be words, phrases, or pictures. Tell them they can signal their partners to pause by holding up a note card to indicate they need time to jot down notes.

Working with Partners 19

Using a Response Sheet

A response sheet like this one can help you when you make comments about a classmate's writing.

Response Sheet

Writer: __________ Responder: __________

Title: __________

What I like:

____

____

____

____

Questions I have:

____

____

____

____

English Language Learners

If students are unfamiliar with the word *response*, explain that a response is an answer or a reply. Point out that after students share their writing, they will respond, or answer, by giving feedback to their partners about the writing.

Direct students' attention to the top of the response sheet. Explain that a *responder* is the person who is the listener and that their partner's name goes after the word *writer*.

Using a Response Sheet

Emphasize the importance of responding courteously to another person's writing. Point out that there are just as many lines on the form below the *What I Like* heading as there are below the *Questions I Have* heading. Encourage students to make one positive comment for every question they ask.

Advise students to make their comments and questions specific. This will help the writers understand what is being asked and how they might approach the issue. For example, in responding to *Special Storytellers* on SE page 15, a responder might say:

- I like the way you explain what a griot does.
- I liked finding out how a person learns to be a griot.
- I'd like to find out when the griots first began telling stories.
- Is Africa the only place where griots tell stories?

Traits of Good Writing

Objectives
- Explore the six traits of effective writing.
- Apply the concepts of the traits to writing.

Explain to students that SE pages 21 through 25 cover the traits in detail and suggest ways of using them in writing.

Writer's Craft

Traits: Notice how the traits start with big ideas (topic and focus) and gradually narrow to specific conventions (every last period). When students use the writing process, they experience the traits in this order. Prewriting deals with ideas and organization. Writing focuses on these two traits and voice. Revising involves the first three traits and word choice and sentence fluency. Editing deals with conventions. By gradually adding traits all along the way, the student isn't overwhelmed at any one point.

Traits of Good Writing

To do your best writing, use the six traits listed below as a guide. You will learn all about these traits in this chapter.

Start with good ideas!

Organization — Make your writing clear and easy to follow.

Sound interested or excited about your topic.

Use specific, strong words.

Write different kinds of sentences.

Follow the rules for capitalization, punctuation, spelling, and grammar.

Materials

Drawing supplies (TE p. 20)

Tape recorder (TE p. 23)

Index cards (TE p. 23)

Four sets of index cards numbered 1–6 (TE p. 24)

Advanced Learners

To provide visual reinforcement of the traits, divide the class into six groups and assign a trait to each group. Distribute drawing supplies and have students work on their own to draw a picture that relates to their group's trait. Display the illustrations, clustered according to trait and arranged in the correct order, on a class bulletin board.

Traits of Good Writing 21

Ideas

Rachel likes collecting ideas for her stories and reports. Having plenty of information helps her to do her best writing.

First, Rachel selects a **writing topic**.

Writing topic

My cat, Henry

Next, she gathers many **details** about her topic.

Details

- weighs 16 pounds!
- has bright green eyes
- hides in many places
- loves to eat people food
- sneaks outside sometimes
- sits on my lap during meals

Practice

1. Think of a topic you would like to write about.
2. List at least five details about this topic.
3. Share your ideas with the class.

Ideas

Once students get started **looking for topics** *(see below)*, they will begin to notice interesting subjects all around them. Suggest possible sources of topics. These include the following:

- books and magazines
- movies and television
- stories told by family members or friends
- personal experiences

Also encourage students to use the questions they ask about everyday things. For example, while pouring milk on her breakfast cereal, a student might wonder, "How does milk get from the cow to the carton?"

Tell students not to worry if they can't immediately think of a topic for an assignment because their *Write Source* book contains useful suggestions for coming up with topics.

✱ Have students refer to the List of Topics on SE page 434 when they need help.

Teaching Tip: Looking for Topics

Tell students that when an idea for a topic comes to them, they should write it down as soon as possible. Have students create a special section in their notebooks for writing ideas. They could insert a divider and label it My Writing Ideas.

Organization

Work through the piece of writing with students by asking the following questions:

- What is the topic that the writer introduces in the beginning? (his Uncle Hector)
- What details does Ernesto use to tell about his topic? Which details are most interesting to you? (He and his uncle built a tree fort; Ernesto nailed some of the boards together.)
- What final thought or thoughts does Ernesto share with you about his topic? How does the ending connect to the beginning of the story? (Ernesto says again that he wants to be a carpenter when he grows up.)

Organization

Ernesto always tries to begin his stories in an interesting or exciting way. He also tries to connect the middle and ending parts to the beginning.

Beginning

The **first part** should introduce your topic in an interesting way.

Middle

The **middle part** should tell all about your topic.

Ending

The **last part** should share a final thought about the topic.

My Special Partner

Uncle Hector is a carpenter. He knows everything about building and remodeling. Some day I want to be a carpenter, too.

Last summer, my uncle and I built a tree fort in my grandma's backyard. I measured the lumber and nailed some of the boards together. It took us all day, but it sure was fun!

Uncle Hector has all kinds of power tools. I can't use any of them now. But when I grow up, my uncle says that I can be his partner. Then I can use all the tools!

Advanced Learners

Ask writing partners to rewrite the beginning of "My Special Partner" in a different way. Then have them share their rewrites in class. Have volunteers describe what they like about each beginning.

Traits of Good Writing 23

Voice

Tara likes to write about the people in her family. Her stories sound like she is telling them to a friend—that's Tara's *voice*. Writing that sounds like the writer, and no one else, has a voice.

Super Saturdays

Aunt Amita and I have great Saturdays together. We start by making blueberry pancakes. Yummy! Then we go to a store that sells used books. Amita always lets me buy two books, but I have to promise to read them.

Next, my aunt always takes me to a new place. Once she took me to a shelter for injured animals that is right in the city. I donated a dollar to help feed the animals.

At the end of our day, we always have a treat like frozen yogurt. Aunt Amita is so much fun that I never want our Saturdays to end.

Practice

Write a story about someone or something that you really like. Remember to be yourself so your reader can hear your voice.

Voice

Tell students that one of the best ways to see if their writing has *voice* is to read it aloud. As they read the words, they should sound just as if they were talking to a friend in a natural, interested voice.

After students have completed their **Practice** writing, have volunteers read their stories to the class. Ask readers if they changed any words or sentences as they read aloud. If so, ask them to write those changes into their papers.

Suggest to students that they stop from time to time when they are reading a book, and read a paragraph or two out loud to see how it sounds.

Literature Connections

Voice: Select a familiar book that has a strong storytelling voice or has dialogue that shows the voices of different characters. Read sample pieces of narration or dialogue aloud and ask students to describe the voice. Ask, "Does this person sound happy or sad? Bored or excited? Friendly or angry?" Let students suggest other adjectives to describe voice. "Your writing voice tells readers how you feel."

English Language Learners

Students may need help understanding the concept of *writing that has voice*. Before students begin the **Practice** activity, have them use a tape recorder while telling a partner about a place they like to visit. Explain that the way they used their voice as they explained their favorite place to their partner will sound the same when they write about their place.

Struggling Learners

If students need help organizing their story, provide three index cards to help them identify the beginning, middle, and ending of their story for the **Practice** activity. Have them label and number each card for each part of their story.

Word Choice

Have students explain why the first sentence does not provide enough information. What questions is the reader still asking?

- *Who* ate a big breakfast?
- *How* did the boy eat breakfast?
- *What* did the boy eat for breakfast?

Challenge students to rewrite the general sentence. For example, *Jamal's grandmother served him Texas toast with apple jelly, scrambled eggs, and a slice of melon, and he gobbled up everything!* Provide additional practice **rewriting sentences** *(see below).*

Sentence Fluency

Help students see that sentences flow more smoothly when the following strategies are used:

- There is a mix of long and short sentences—but the long ones aren't *too* long.
- The sentences don't all start the same way or repeat the same words over and over.
- Occasionally a sentence ends with an exclamation mark or a question mark for variation.

Word Choice Theo has learned an important lesson about writing: *Always use specific words.* Specific words help give the reader clear pictures and ideas.

General words (not clear)

The boy ate a big breakfast.

Specific words (clear)

Jamal gobbled up scrambled eggs and bacon.

Sentence Fluency Mori always reads over her stories before she shares them. She wants all of her sentences to be easy to read.

Smooth sentences

Max is my brother's new retriever. This crazy dog loves to chew on everything. He even chews on the remote control! Max loves to play, too. He is so big that he can knock me down.

Practice

1. Read over a story or report you have written.
2. Circle two words that could be more specific.
3. Write a specific word (or words) for each circled word.
4. Underline any sentences that are hard to read.

Teaching Tip: Rewriting Sentences

Hold a "Word Choice Olympics" to practice using stronger words.

- Choose four students to be judges, and give each a set of index cards numbered 1 to 6.
- Choose one scorekeeper.
- Choose five competitors.
- Read aloud a simple sentence you want improved—for example, *The food was good.* Give competitors time to rewrite it, using specific words.
- After each competitor reads the new sentence aloud, the judges hold up their card to score it, and the scorekeeper records the score.
- When all sentences are scored, the scorekeeper announces the winner.
- Repeat the process with five different students and a new sentence.

Grammar Connection

Understanding Sentences

- **Proofreader's Guide** pages 526–528 (+)
- ***GrammarSnap*** Complete Sentences
- ***SkillsBook*** pages 83–84

Conventions

At the end of every writing assignment, Ravi checks his writing for capital letters and for end punctuation. Then he checks his work for any spelling and grammar errors.

Conventions

Punctuation

___ 1. Did I use end punctuation after my sentences?
___ 2. Did I use commas for a series of words (red, white, and blue)?

Capitalization

___ 3. Did I start every sentence with a capital letter?
___ 4. Did I capitalize names?

Spelling

___ 5. Have I checked my spelling?

Grammar

___ 6. Did I use the right words (*one* instead of *won*)?

Conventions

Have students write out the *Conventions Checklist* in their writing folder. You may want to offer copies. (See copy masters on TE pages 561–566.) They can refer to it whenever they need to check a piece of writing.

Encourage students to use the checklist when they proofread their writing. They can ask a peer editor to use the checklist, too. Post a large version of the checklist in the room and remind students to refer to it as they proofread their work.

If students have completed the **Practice** writing from SE page 23, have them trade papers with a partner for peer editing. Ask them to use the *Conventions Checklist* to uncover any errors.

Tell students to circle the number on the checklist for any error they find more than twice. This will remind them to avoid making the same mistakes the next time they write.

English Language Learners

Using writing *conventions* means the same thing as following writing *rules*. Explain that good writers always check their writing to make sure that they have followed the rules for capitalization, punctuation, spelling, and grammar.

Use the words *conventions* and *rules* interchangeably to discuss other rules students follow, such as getting in line to leave the classroom at the end of the day or raising their hands when they want to speak. Then encourage them to name writing conventions they are familiar with, such as placing end punctuation at the end of a sentence.

Using a Rubric

Objectives
- Use the rating scale on a scoring rubric to inform writing.
- Use a scoring rubric to improve writing.

Tell students that an expository essay is writing that explains something. Refer them to the sample on SE page 32, and ask them to tell you what the essay explains (how to take care of a dog).

Tell students that a rubric can help them both when they are creating their essays and when they are evaluating a finished essay (either their own or someone else's). Ask students if a simple "I liked it" or "I didn't like it" is helpful information when someone asks them how they felt about a book. Explain that these are common responses, but that they are too general to provide any useful information. Tell students that as they judge more writing using a rubric, their responses should become more detailed and informative.

Using a Rubric

Have you ever watched figure skating in the Olympics? The judges have a list of things to look for in the skater's performance, like difficulty and variety. That's how they come up with a score for the skater.

Writing can be judged, too, with a **rubric**. A rubric is a chart of the traits of good writing. There are different rubrics for different types of writing. This chapter shows you how to use a rubric to judge an expository essay.

Learning how to use a rubric will help you write better!

Materials

Index cards (TE p. 29)

Using a Rubric 27

Understanding Rubrics

This page will tell you more about rubrics and how to use them to improve your writing.

What do the rubrics cover?

The rubrics used in this book cover the traits of writing—*ideas, organization, voice, word choice, sentence fluency,* and *conventions.*

How can I use a rubric?

During prewriting, a rubric helps you to plan your writing. During revising and editing, it can guide the changes you make. After you finish your writing, the rubric can help you judge your final copy.

How do I judge my writing with the rubric?

Each trait of your writing can be scored. A **6** is the highest score, and a **1** is the lowest score. For example, if the ideas in your essay are strong, you would get a **5** for ideas.

Should I score all of the traits in my writing?

Your teacher will tell you how many writing traits to judge. You may be told to score only one or two of the six traits.

English Language Learners

Explain what *amazing* means on the rubric strip. A paper is rated *amazing,* a score of 6, when the ideas are explained with interesting details, the parts are in the right order, the writer shows interest in the topic and uses specific words, and the sentences flow smoothly and are written correctly.

Understanding Rubrics

Point out that a rubric sums up the six traits of writing students learned about in the previous section of this unit. It describes an ideal way of addressing each trait. It also provides a point system so students can decide how close their writing is to the highest score.

Mention that different kinds of writing—narrative, expository, or persuasive—require slightly different rubrics, and refer students to the rubrics in the student edition so they can compare them.

* See SE pages 108–109, 160–161, and 208–209 for examples of rubrics for narrative, expository, and persuasive writing.

Tell students that it's a good idea to show the rubric to anyone who helps with their writing—parent, caregiver, sibling, friend. Reading the rubric will help that person understand what to look for in the student's writing.

Note: The rubrics in this book are based on a six-point scale.

Getting Started with a Rubric

After reading the pages, lead a discussion on criteria for choosing essay topics.

- Topics should be interesting to other people as well as to the writer.
- Topics need to be narrow and manageable enough to be explained in a short essay. "Sports," for example, is too general a topic for an essay. The writer should focus on a particular aspect of one sport that sets it apart from others.
- There is enough information about the topic. For example, a student should choose the topic "My Great-Great Grandfather" only if his or her family knows something about that ancestor's life.

Getting Started with a Rubric

At the beginning of each main writing unit, you will see a chart like the one on page 29. It shows you what to include in your writing. At each step in the writing process, certain traits are more important than others.

The traits of writing are very important in the writing process. For example, in prewriting, you are focusing on your ideas.

Read the entire chart before you start your writing.

Study *ideas.* This is the most important trait when you begin your writing.

Learn what you need to do. For example, when you focus on ideas, you should do two things.

- Choose an interesting topic.
- Explain it with details.

Ideas — **Choose an interesting topic and explain it with details.**

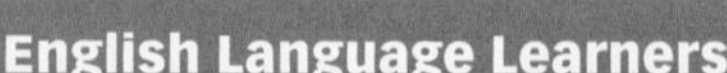

English Language Learners

Before beginning the **Ideas** activity, encourage students with limited proficiency in English to choose a topic they are very familiar with. Pair students with cooperative partners and have them take turns explaining their topic with details.

Sample Goals Page

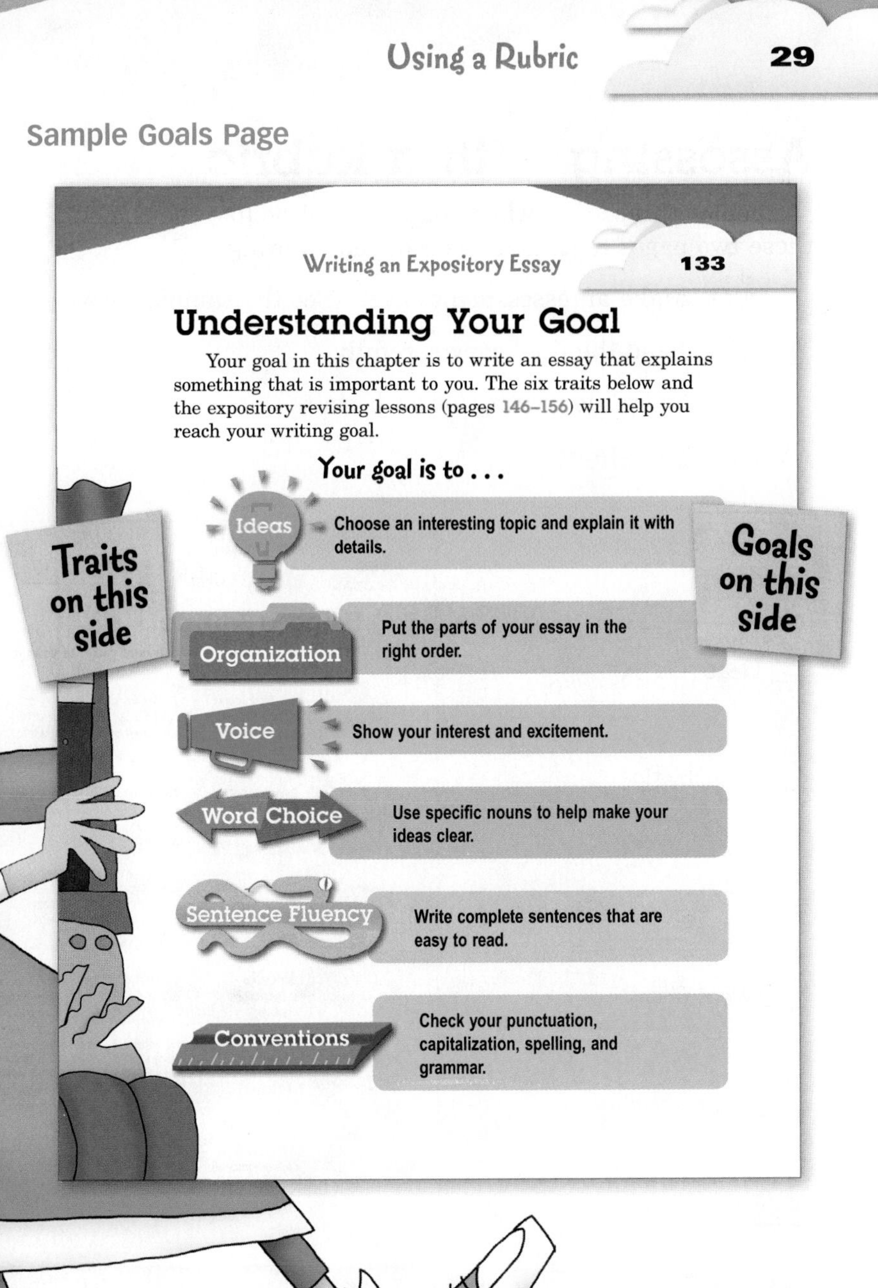

Using a Rubric
29
Writing an Expository Essay
133
Understanding Your Goal
Your goal in this chapter is to write an essay that explains something that is important to you. The six traits below and the expository revising lessons (pages 146–156) will help you reach your writing goal.
Your goal is to . . .
Traits on this side
Goals on this side
Ideas
Choose an interesting topic and explain it with details.
Organization
Put the parts of your essay in the right order.
Voice
Show your interest and excitement.
Word Choice
Use specific nouns to help make your ideas clear.
Sentence Fluency
Write complete sentences that are easy to read.
Conventions
Check your punctuation, capitalization, spelling, and grammar.

Challenge students to demonstrate their knowledge of the six traits:

- Divide the class into groups of three and give each group six index cards.
- Ask students to close their books. Read the six **traits** aloud to them, pausing after each trait so that one student in each group can write that trait on an index card.
- Read the six **goals** aloud. Hand out a set of six cards (each one with one goal on it) to each group.
- Have each group shuffle its twelve cards together. Then, have group members separate the cards, matching the traits to their corresponding goals.

Discuss with students any questions they have about the goals listed on the cards. For example, do they remember what a *noun* is (Word Choice)? Students may benefit from a **brief grammar review** *(see below).*

* Refer to Using the Parts of Speech on SE pages 532–555 for information about grammar.

Teaching Tip: Grammar Review

Review using the basic parts of speech in effective writing to provide helpful information for the students.

- noun: a person, a place, a thing, or an idea
- verb: shows action or links ideas
- adjective: describes and modifies a noun
- adverb: modifies a verb, telling how, when, or where something happened

Ask students to write smooth sentences with specific words. Encourage students to use the different parts of speech in their sentences.

Special Challenge: Have partners exchange sentences and label the parts of speech in each other's sentences.

Assessing with a Rubric

Be sure students understand the organization of the rubric. Have volunteers read across the rubric for each trait. Students should understand that a lower rating (number) means that a piece of writing needs improvement.

Encourage students to read over the rubric carefully before they write or before they evaluate a classmate's writing.

Assessing with a Rubric

Follow three steps when you use a rubric like the one on these two pages to judge a piece of your writing.

1. Make an assessment sheet. (See the sample below.)
2. Read the final copy carefully.
3. Score the writing for each trait.

Assessment Sheet

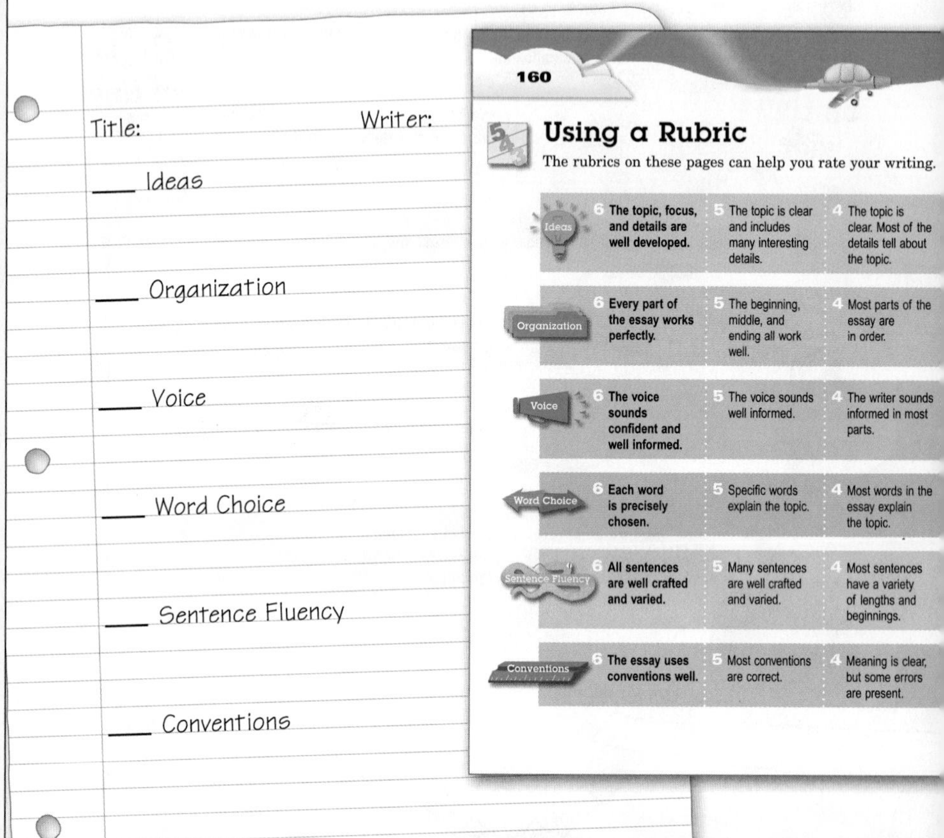

Title:
Writer:
___ Ideas
___ Organization
___ Voice
___ Word Choice
___ Sentence Fluency
___ Conventions

160

Using a Rubric

The rubrics on these pages can help you rate your writing.

Trait	6	5	4
Ideas	The topic, focus, and details are well developed.	The topic is clear and includes many interesting details.	The topic is clear. Most of the details tell about the topic.
Organization	Every part of the essay works perfectly.	The beginning, middle, and ending all work well.	Most parts of the essay are in order.
Voice	The voice sounds confident and well informed.	The voice sounds well informed.	The writer sounds informed in most parts.
Word Choice	Each word is precisely chosen.	Specific words explain the topic.	Most words in the essay explain the topic.
Sentence Fluency	All sentences are well crafted and varied.	Many sentences are well crafted and varied.	Most sentences have a variety of lengths and beginnings.
Conventions	The essay uses conventions well.	Most conventions are correct.	Meaning is clear, but some errors are present.

Struggling Learners

Students will be able to use a rubric more effectively if you have them focus on only one or two traits until they have a better grasp of scoring.

Using a Rubric 31

Each rubric helps you judge a final copy for the traits of writing. A 6 is the highest score. A 1 is the lowest score.

Writin Expository Essay 161

Literature Con ions: For an example of an expository essay, read Mayo y Shannon Knudsen.

3	2	1
The topic needs to be clearer. More details are needed.	The topic is unclear, and the details do not fit.	The topic is unclear.
Some parts of the essay could be better organized.	All parts of the essay run together.	The organization is confusing.
The writer sounds informed in some parts.	The writer sounds unsure.	The writer sounds uninterested.
The essay needs more specific words.	General or missing words make this essay confusing.	Some words are used incorrectly.
Some sentences have varied lengths and beginnings.	Many sentences are choppy or incomplete.	Many sentences are incomplete and difficult to read.
Errors may confuse the reader.	Errors make the essay hard to read.	Help is needed to make corrections.

Tell students to use a score of 5 as their standard. (A 6 is the highest score, and though many writers might score 6 for one or two traits, very few can do it for all six traits.) Suggest the following procedure for scoring:

- Read the description of a score of 5 for a trait.
- Ask yourself if the essay fits the description. If it does, write down the score of 5 for that trait.
- If the writing seems better than a 5, read about the 6 score. If the writing matches that description, give the trait a 6.
- If the writing doesn't meet the standards for a 5, read about a score of 4. Does that match? If not, keep reading the next score down until you find the right one.
- Repeat for the traits you want students to focus on first.

Grammar Connection

Parts of Speech

- **Proofreader's Guide** pages 532–554 (+)
- ***SkillsBook*** pages 169–170

Assessing an Expository Essay

Explain that when assessing an essay, it is always a good idea to read it through twice if possible—once silently and once aloud.

Tell students that both readings will help them evaluate ideas, organization, and word choice. Looking at the essay on paper is best for spotting problems with conventions. Hearing it out loud is the best way to assess voice and sentence fluency.

Have students read through the essay on their own. Then have volunteers read the essay aloud, changing readers after each paragraph.

Assessing an Expository Essay

In this essay, Kerry explains how to take care of a dog. As you read it, think about the parts that you like and the parts that you have questions about. (**You will find a few mistakes.**)

Taking Care of a Dog

At first, taking care of my dog was a lot of fun. Then I found out it was work, too. I have important jobs to do. Topper needs my help to stay healthy and safe.

Taking a dog to a veterinarien is the most important thing to do. Dogs need shots, just like people do. A veterinarien will give your dog shots and make sure that he is healthy.

Giving a dog food and water is the next most important thing to do. A dog needs the right kind of dog food. Some kinds of people food can make dogs sick. A dog also needs fresh water every day.

Exercising a dog is the last thing to remember. A dog needs a lot of exercise, so you should walk your dog and play with it. Always keep a dog on a leesh during walks. Then it won't run in front of cars and get hurt.

Dogs can cheer you up. They always seem so happy. If you take good care of your dog, you will have a friend for a long time.

English Language Learners

Use a cluster to help students to find the details in the essay. Assist students in writing words or phrases in the cluster circles.

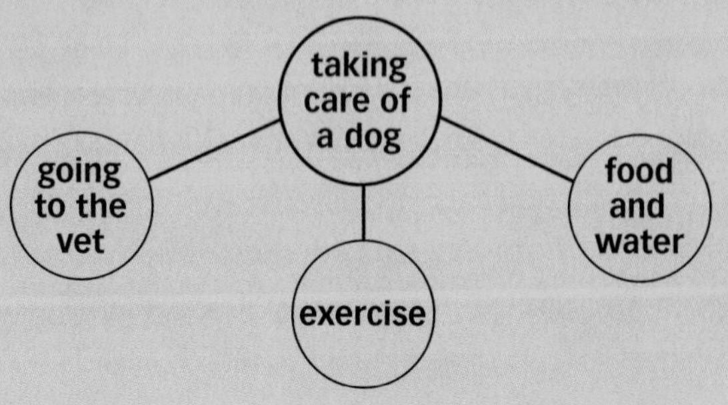

Struggling Learners

A full page of text may discourage some students. Simplify the reading process for them with a strategy they can use during reading. Have them cover the page with a large note card or half-sheet of paper to block out most of the text. They can slide the paper down one line at a time as they read to help them track print.

Using a Rubric 33

Sample Assessment

Kerry used the rubric on pages 30–31 to judge his essay. His teacher told him to score *ideas*, *organization*, and *conventions*. In addition to the numbers, Kerry wrote comments. He wrote about what he liked in his writing, as well as what he would change.

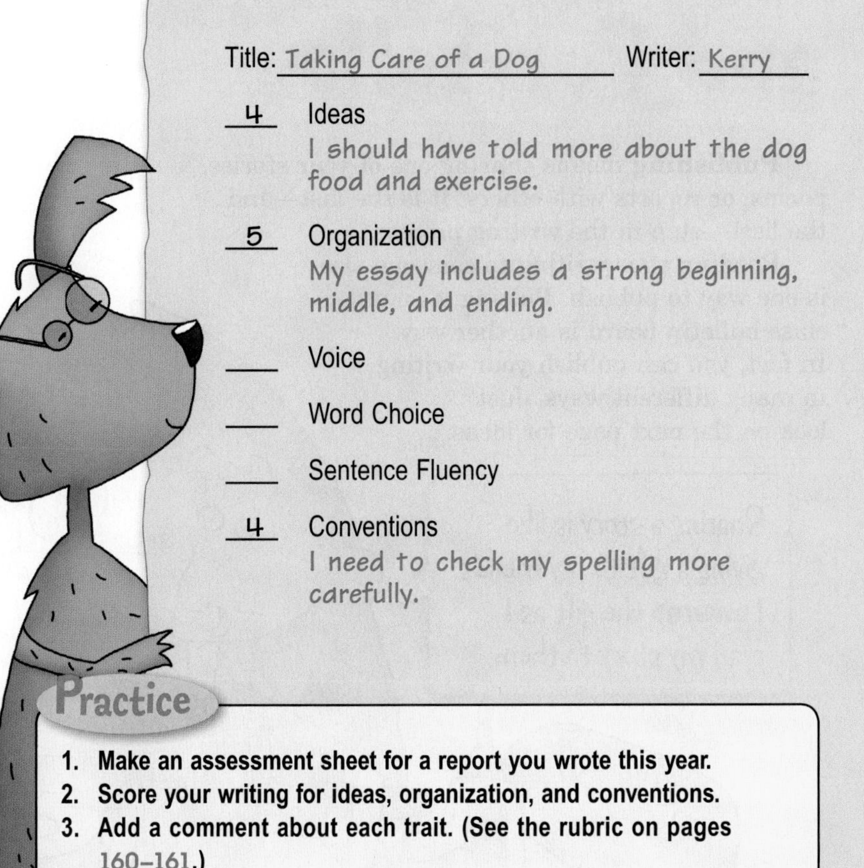

Title: *Taking Care of a Dog* Writer: *Kerry*

4 Ideas
I should have told more about the dog food and exercise.

5 Organization
My essay includes a strong beginning, middle, and ending.

___ Voice

___ Word Choice

___ Sentence Fluency

4 Conventions
I need to check my spelling more carefully.

Practice

1. **Make an assessment sheet for a report you wrote this year.**
2. **Score your writing for ideas, organization, and conventions.**
3. **Add a comment about each trait. (See the rubric on pages 160–161.)**

Sample Assessment

Discuss Kerry's self-assessment with the class. Do students agree with what he said? If not, ask them to explain why. Possible responses follow:

- **Ideas:** It might have been good to mention a specific fun thing to make the first sentence less general.
- **Organization:** The daily concerns of food, water, and exercise seem more important than taking the dog to the vet.
- **Conventions:** Ask students to identify the misspelled words that are mentioned on the assessment (*veterinarien* should be *veterinarian*, *leesh* should be *leash*).

Point out that Kerry wasn't asked to assess Voice, Word Choice, or Sentence Fluency. He did, however, address the traits in his writing. Ask students if they agree with the following evaluation of these traits:

- **Voice:** The voice sounds natural and interested.
- **Word Choice:** It might have been good to include more strong nouns. For example, Kerry could have told what kind of dog Topper is.
- **Sentence Fluency:** The sentences are easy to read and flow well from one to the next.

English Language Learners

Some students may need help assessing their own writing. Provide time to give students a personal writing conference and help them self-assess. Model the process using the Think-Aloud approach to help students understand how to use the rubric successfully.

Advanced Learners

Modify the **Practice** activity by having students score voice in a particular piece of writing. Then challenge them to rewrite a paragraph or two using a more formal or less formal voice.

Publishing and Portfolios

Objectives
- Recognize the different ways to publish writing.
- Format writing for publication.
- Choose and use one type of writing portfolio.

Talk with students about why many writers might feel that publishing is the best step in the writing process.

- Publishing is a great way to learn whether all the planning and work has paid off. If you tried to write a funny story, you'll never know if it makes people laugh if you don't share it with others.
- Getting positive feedback—listening to people laugh at your jokes or a reader tell you why she liked your story—makes you feel good.
- It's satisfying for the reader: Ask students to talk about their favorite stories. How do the stories make them feel? Has a story helped any of them face a real-life problem? Has a happy or funny story cheered them up?

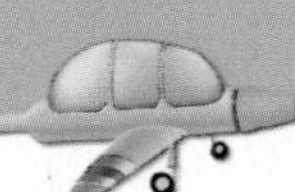

Publishing and Portfolios

Publishing means sharing one of your stories, poems, or reports with others. It is the last—and the best—step in the writing process.

Reading your writing to someone else is one way to publish. Putting it on a class bulletin board is another way. In fact, you can publish your writing in many different ways. Just look on the next page for ideas.

Sharing a story is like giving a gift to my friends. I **unwrap** the gift as I read my story to them.

Advanced Learners

Have students work in a small cooperative group to discuss the gift analogy on SE page 34. Then challenge students to develop their own analogies about writing or a particular part of the process, such as "A good story is like a fun vacation because you see things you haven't seen before."

Materials

Chart paper (TE p. 35)

Examples of different illustrated publications (TE p. 36)

Brief poem (TE p. 36)

Art supplies (TE p. 38)

Plastic sheet protectors and markers (TE p. 39)

Publishing Your Writing

Print it!
Put together a book of your stories or poems, or make a book with your classmates.

Send it!
Send a family story or a special poem to a relative who lives far away.

Submit it!
Send one of your stories or poems to the editor of a magazine. Wait to see if he or she will publish it.

Post it!
Post your writing on a class Web site.

Act it out!
Act out one of your stories or plays with the help of your classmates.

Talk it over . . .

1. **Have you ever tried one of the publishing ideas listed above? Tell the class about it.**
2. **Which new publishing idea would you like to try?**

Publishing Your Writing

Help students experience audience feedback. Ask three volunteers to share a story they've written, and have the class turn each story into a one-act play.

Divide students into groups and provide time for working on a script for the play.

After the performance, discuss students' experiences:

- Did they enjoy the process of creating and putting on a performance?
- Did writers enjoy seeing a performance of their work?
- Did the audience respond as the writers had hoped?

For students who want to submit their work, post a list of publications that welcome children's submissions. Include:

- *Crunch*, a National Center for Education Statistics e-zine (http://nces.ed.gov/nceskids/crunch)
- *New Moon* magazine, for girls (www.newmoon.org)
- *Stone Soup* magazine (www.stonesoup.com)
- *Young Writer* magazine (www.young-writer.co.uk)

English Language Learners

Some students may not be comfortable sharing their writing orally with the entire class. Provide opportunities for students to share their writing with cooperative partners. Have them review SE page 18 and talk about the "traits" of a good writing partner.

Struggling Learners

The publishing process may intimidate students who have difficulty writing. As a group, brainstorm a list of publishing ideas and jot them down on chart paper for students.

Encourage students to think of alternative forms for publishing writing, such as making picture books or putting together an anthology with classmates.

Writing a Neat Final Copy

Discuss with students the importance of making their written final copy **look as good as possible** *(see below)*. Talk about additional elements students might add to make the published paper even more interesting. These include the following:

- colored ink for the title and any subtitles (but be sure to use black or blue ink or type for the main text)
- photos or illustrations
- maps
- graphs or tables
- a decorative cover

* For more, refer to Add Graphs and Make Tables (SE pages 460–461).

Provide and examine different kinds of illustrated publications, for example, magazines, newspapers, picture books, textbooks, comic books, and history books. These examples may inspire students as they illustrate their writing.

Writing a Neat Final Copy

A neat final copy shows that you care about your writing. It also makes your writing easy to read. Follow these guidelines when you write a final copy by hand.

Handwritten Copy

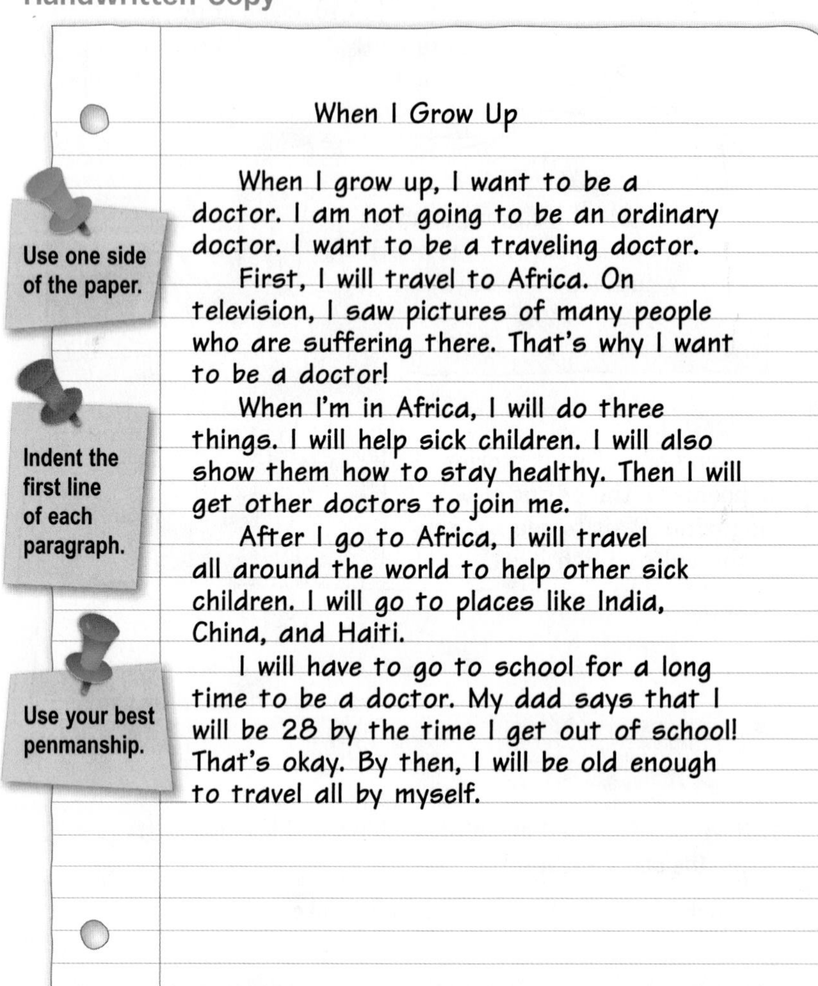

When I Grow Up
When I grow up, I want to be a doctor. I am not going to be an ordinary doctor. I want to be a traveling doctor.
First, I will travel to Africa. On television, I saw pictures of many people who are suffering there. That's why I want to be a doctor!
When I'm in Africa, I will do three things. I will help sick children. I will also show them how to stay healthy. Then I will get other doctors to join me.
After I go to Africa, I will travel all around the world to help other sick children. I will go to places like India, China, and Haiti.
I will have to go to school for a long time to be a doctor. My dad says that I will be 28 by the time I get out of school! That's okay. By then, I will be old enough to travel all by myself.
Use one side of the paper.
Indent the first line of each paragraph.
Use your best penmanship.

Teaching Tip: Look As Good As Possible

Hold a handwriting workshop to give students practice writing neatly. Review the best ways to achieve neat handwriting:

- Don't rush.
- Make sure there's plenty of elbow room on the writing surface.
- Form the letters carefully, paying special attention to such details as the loop on a lowercase *e*.
- Make sure the letters follow the lines on the paper.
- Make sure all the letters line up at the left to make a straight margin.

Write a brief poem on the chalkboard and have students copy it onto lined paper as neatly as they can. Display the poems on a bulletin board.

Advanced Learners

Some students may enjoy using a slide show or other multimedia format to compose their final copy on a computer.

For those who prefer to write their final copies by hand, encourage them to use a picture book format. Help them determine the best places to begin and end each page so that they can build the reader's interest.

Publishing and Portfolios 37

Using a Computer

Follow these guidelines when you use a computer to print out a final copy.

Computer Copy

↑ 1" ↓

Mansi Patel

When I Grow Up

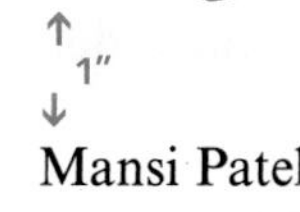

Use a font that is easy to read.

When I grow up, I want to be a doctor. I am not going to be an ordinary doctor. I want to be a traveling doctor.

First, I will travel to Africa. On television, I saw pictures of many people who are suffering there. That's why I want to be a doctor!

Try to use a list, chart, or picture.

When I'm in Africa I will do three things.

1. I will help sick children.
2. I will also show them how to stay healthy.
3. Then I will get other doctors to join me.

Indent the first line of each paragraph.

After I go to Africa, I will travel all around the world to help other sick children. I will go to places like India, China, and Haiti.

I will have to go to school for a long time to be a doctor. My dad says that I will be 28 by the time I get out of school! That's okay. By then, I will be old enough to travel all by myself.

Practice

Compare one of your final copies to the example above or the one on page 36. How are they alike? How are they different?

Using a Computer

Explain to students your requirements for using a computer for their writing. There are several important things to keep in mind:

- Save the document often. A power surge or other computer problem can cause text that took a long time to type to be lost if it hasn't been saved.
- Students should have a special folder for their work and always give documents easy-to-remember names. Finding documents on a disorganized computer can be difficult.
- Learn how to use the word-processing program. Students will need to know how to set margins and indentations for the paragraph beginnings, and how to choose a font.
- Consider learning how to touch type. It is much faster than keyboarding with one finger.

English Language Learners

Modify the **Practice** activity by asking students questions to help them compare their final copy to the one Mansi completed:

- Is your paper typed neatly?
- Did you indent the first line of each paragraph?
- Is your topic the same as Mansi's?

Point out that "yes" answers show how their papers are similar to Mansi's. "No" responses show how their papers are different from the writer's essay.

Struggling Learners

Encourage students to use a computer to write their final copy. Spelling and grammar-check features can help students catch some errors that they may have accidentally introduced into their final copy. Also, remind students to "save" their work frequently.

Using a Portfolio

Discuss with students any portfolios they have kept in the past. Students might have kept portfolios for personal writing or for tests. They also might have kept portfolios for different topics, such as science and history.

Making a Personal Portfolio

Ask students to think about what they'd like to use as a personal portfolio. Have them bring a binder, pocket folder, or box (big enough to hold sheets of regular paper) to the next class.

Have each student write his or her name and the words *Personal Portfolio* on the container.

Provide art supplies such as markers, glitter glue, sequins, ribbons, and stickers for students to use to decorate their portfolios.

Remind students that they'll be keeping three different kinds of items in their personal portfolios:

- ideas and notes for new stories
- writing in progress
- finished work with their reflections

Suggest that they keep their portfolios organized by using three folders or tabbed dividers to separate the different papers.

Using a Portfolio

Juan likes collecting pictures of horses. He keeps his pictures in a special album. Juan also collects his stories and poems. He puts them in a **portfolio**, a special place to gather your writing. When you keep a portfolio, you can look over your work and enjoy all the types of writing you have done.

Making a Personal Portfolio

A **personal portfolio** is just for you. You can use a three-ring binder, a pocket folder, a gift box, or you can make your very own portfolio. In your portfolio, you can save everything from topic ideas to finished stories. Here is one way to plan your portfolio.

Collect ideas for new stories and poems.
Store writing that you are still changing.
Save the final copies of your writing.

English Language Learners

Assist students with the selection of written pieces for their personal portfolios. Point out how their language and writing skills have improved and encourage them to reflect on which pieces they think are their best and why.

Making a Classroom Portfolio

Your teacher may ask you to make a **classroom portfolio**. There are two main types of classroom portfolios: a showcase portfolio and a growth portfolio.

Showcase Portfolio

In a **showcase portfolio**, you show your best writing. Here are some ideas for choosing your best work. Your teacher will help you decide which pieces of writing to include.

- Choose writing you really like.
- Pick a piece you worked hard on.
- Select something that shares your feelings.
- Include writing that you're proud of.

Growth Portfolio

In a **growth portfolio**, you save writing that helps you and your teacher see how you are growing as a writer. You may save something you wrote in September, in October, in November, and so on. It's amazing how your writing skills can improve by the end of the school year!

Here are some of the skills you'll want to keep track of.

- Using specific details
- Organizing your ideas
- Writing clear sentences

Practice

1. **Think of one thing you wrote from this year or last year that you would include in a showcase portfolio.**
2. **List the title of your writing and tell why you would include it.**

Making a Classroom Portfolio

Give students practical advice about assembling portfolios. For example:

- Working with a partner can be helpful when deciding which essays to put in a showcase portfolio. Read each other's work and advise each other about which pieces to choose.
- Try to include different kinds of writing in a showcase portfolio—poems, stories, and essays.
- Anything that goes into a portfolio should include the date it was written. This is especially important in a growth portfolio.

Encourage students to look back at their portfolios regularly and ask themselves how their skills are improving. Are they choosing more interesting details? Using more powerful words? Improving their spelling? Reviewing past work will reveal their progress.

English Language Learners

Some students may be unfamiliar with the word *showcase*. Explain that a showcase is a special box, case, or shelf used to show off prized possessions such as a trophy. Point out that a showcase portfolio presents the best pieces of writing, whereas a growth portfolio shows how writing has become better over a period of time.

Struggling Learners

Help students see improvement in their writing by working with them to create a growth portfolio. After you and the students have selected the pieces to include, place each one in a plastic sheet protector or tape an overhead transparency on top of it.

Then have students use markers to track skills in their writing. For example, they could circle or highlight specific details or underline clear sentences so they can easily see their progress.

Creating a Portfolio

Prepare handouts that give directions about what the portfolio must look like, what exactly should be included, and any other requirements. Go over the handouts with students immediately after distributing them and answer any questions they have.

Remind students regularly to save their prewriting notes and revisions.

Create a Writing Assignment bulletin board in the class where you can post important information about students' assignments. The bulletin board might include the following:

- a copy of the handout about what's required for a portfolio
- a sample of a finished essay that demonstrates the proper formatting
- the current assignment students are working on as well as the date it is due

Creating a Portfolio

When you put together a classroom portfolio, use these guidelines.

Follow your teacher's directions.

- Know what your portfolio should look like. You may get special instructions for making a folder.
- Know what kind of writing and how many pieces you need to include. Is any other information needed?

Be organized.

- Save all your work whenever you write.
- Sometimes you may be asked to include all of your prewriting notes and revisions for a piece of writing.

Take pride in your work.

- Finish each writing assignment on time.
- Do your best work. Keep your final copy neat and clean.

Remember: A portfolio is the story of you as a writer. Make sure that you are proud of that story.

Publishing and Portfolios 41

Sample Portfolio Introductions

Your teacher may ask you to introduce each piece of writing in your portfolio. You can say why you like the piece or where you got the idea for it. Here are some sample introductions.

Two Authors' Introductions

"I started writing *Trouble River* after our family returned from a trip west. Out there, it was easy enough to imagine pioneer days."

—Betsy Byers

"I took my dad's corny joke, and combined it with a few corny jokes of my own, and created the story, *Dog Breath: The Horrible Trouble With Hally Tosis*"

—Dav Pilkey

A Student's Introduction

My best story is "My Friend Paulo." It was fun writing about Paulo. I had so much to say about him.

—Michael

Practice

1. **Write an introduction to something you wrote earlier this year.**
2. **Tell why you like what you wrote or where you got the idea.**

Sample Portfolio Introductions

Direct students' attention to the quotation from Betsy Byers. Ask whether she is describing why she likes the piece or where she got the idea (she's describing where she got her idea—from a family trip to the West).

Suggest that students jot down a portfolio introduction for an essay or story soon after they have finished writing it while their memory of the piece is still fresh.

Point out that this introduction can be quite brief—the examples shown are only three lines long.

English Language Learners

Assist students by allowing them to complete the introduction portion of the **Practice** activity orally.

Prompt them to elaborate by asking questions, such as:

- What is this piece about?
- Why did you choose this piece?

If possible, tape-record each student's introduction so you can replay it for him or her. Students with stronger writing skills can then use the tape to write their introductions.

Descriptive Writing Overview

Common Core Standards Focus

Writing 4: With guidance and support from adults, produce writing in which the development and organization are appropriate to task and purpose.

Language 2: Demonstrate command of the conventions of standard English capitalization, punctuation, and spelling when writing.

Writing Forms

- Writing a Descriptive Paragraph
- Writing a Descriptive Essay

Focus on the Traits

- Ideas Including sensory and descriptive details
- Organization Using order of location to describe an object
- Voice Using a voice that shows excitement about the subject
- Word Choice Choosing nouns and adjectives that let the reader picture the object being described
- Sentence Fluency Writing complete sentences that flow smoothly
- Conventions Checking for errors in capitalization, punctuation, spelling, and grammar

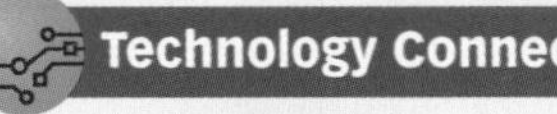

Literature Connections

- ***Spiders and Their Webs*** by Darlyne A. Murawski

Technology Connections

Write Source Online
www.hmheducation.com/writesource

- ***Net-text***
- ***Bookshelf***
- ***GrammarSnap***
- ***Portfolio***
- ***Writing Network features***
- ***File Cabinet***

Interactive Whiteboard Lessons

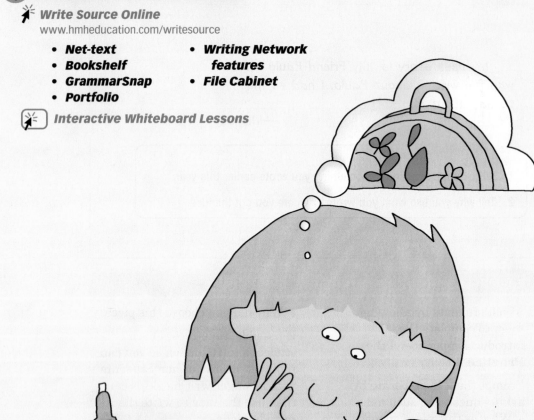

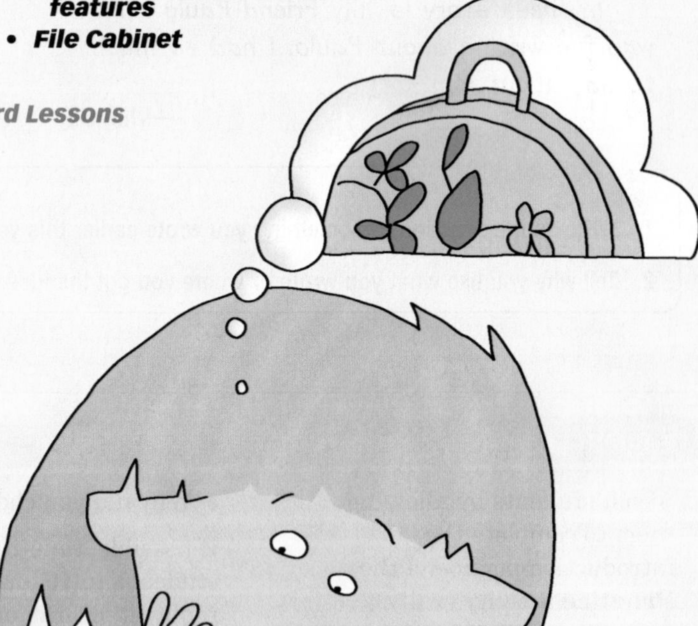

Suggested Descriptive Writing Unit (Three Weeks)

Week	Day	Writing and Skills Instruction	*Student Edition* Descriptive Writing Unit	*Student Edition* Resource Units*	*SkillsBook*	*Daily Language Workouts*	*Write Source Online*
Week 1	1–4	**Descriptive Paragraph: Something Interesting** Literature Connections *Spiders and Their Webs*	44–49			12–13, 81	*Interactive Whiteboard Lessons*
		Skills Activities: • Adjectives		389 , 546–547			*GrammarSnap*
		• Prepositional Phrases		393, 552–553	163–164		*GrammarSnap*
	5	**Descriptive Essay: Something Special** (Model)	50–53				
Week 2	6	(Prewriting)	54–55			14–15, 82	*Net-text*
	7–8	(Writing)	56–61				*Net-text*
	9–10	(Revising)	62–63				*Net-text*
		Working with Partners	16–19				
		Skills Activities: • Adjectives		389 (+), 546 (+)	151–152		*GrammarSnap*
Week 3	11–13	(Editing)	64–65			16–17, 83	*Net-text*
		Skills Activities: • Proper Nouns		375, 532–533	119–120		*GrammarSnap*
		• Capitalization (first words)		488–489	44		*GrammarSnap*
		• Apostrophes		472–473	23–24		*GrammarSnap*
		(Publishing, Reflecting)	66–67				*Portfolio, Net-text*
	14–15	**Descriptive Writing for Assessment**	68–70				

* These units are also located in the back of the *Teacher's Edition*. Resource Units include "Basic Grammar and Writing," "A Writer's Resource," and "Proofreader's Guide."
(+) This activity is located in a different section of the *Write Source Student Edition*. If students have already completed this activity, you may wish to review it at this time.

Teacher's Notes for Descriptive Writing

This overview for descriptive writing includes some specific teaching suggestions for this unit.

Writing Focus

Writing a Descriptive Paragraph (pages 44–49)

In this chapter, students will learn how they can organize sentences in a paragraph to describe something. Guidelines and a checklist are included to help students write their paragraphs about something interesting.

Writing a Descriptive Essay (pages 50–67)

A student can describe a person, a place, or an object in one paragraph. To describe someone or something in detail, a student would need to write several paragraphs, an essay. Students will follow each step of the process needed to write a descriptive essay about a special object. Drawings help students write better descriptions. Checklists as well as assessment models will help students complete their essays.

Grammar Focus

For support with this unit's grammar topics, consult the resource units (Basic Grammar and Writing, A Writer's Resource, and Proofreader's Guide).

Academic Vocabulary

Read aloud the academic terms, as well as the descriptions and questions. Model for students how to read one question and answer it. Have partners monitor their understanding and seek clarification of the terms by working through the meanings and questions together.

Minilessons

Building Blocks — Writing a Descriptive Paragraph

- **THINK** of one of your favorite toys—past or present.
  - **WRITE** a topic sentence about the toy (where you play with it, what it does, or what it looks like) without naming it. Then **WRITE** a paragraph about the toy.
  - **EXCHANGE** paragraphs with a classmate and try to guess what each other's toy is.

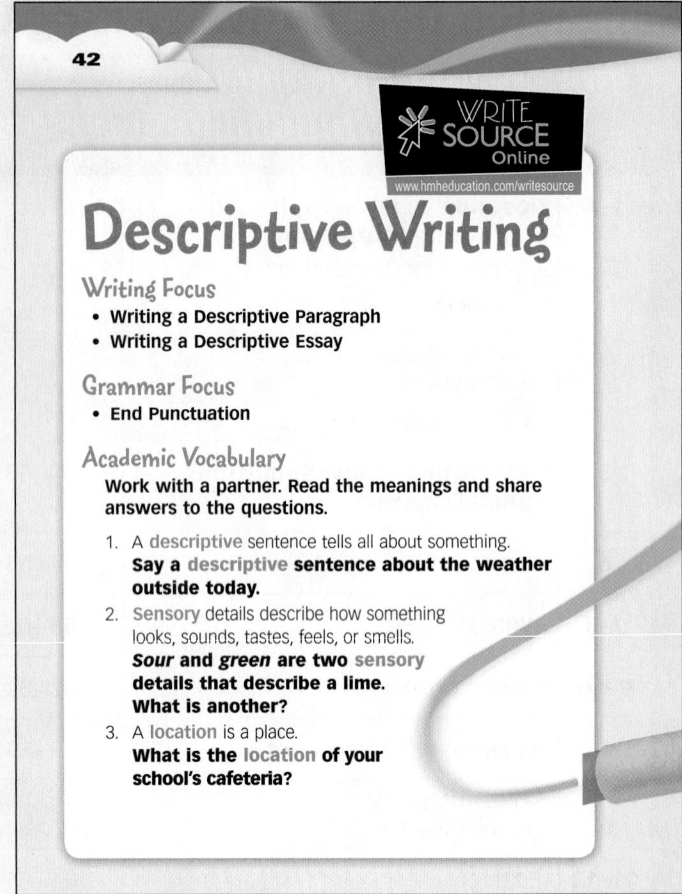

42
WRITE SOURCE Online
www.hmheducation.com/writesource
Descriptive Writing
Writing Focus
• Writing a Descriptive Paragraph
• Writing a Descriptive Essay
Grammar Focus
• End Punctuation
Academic Vocabulary
Work with a partner. Read the meanings and share answers to the questions.
1. A descriptive sentence tells all about something.
Say a descriptive sentence about the weather outside today.
2. Sensory details describe how something looks, sounds, tastes, feels, or smells.
Sour and green are two sensory details that describe a lime. What is another?
3. A location is a place.
What is the location of your school's cafeteria?

Following Orders — Building Paragraphs

- **TURN** to SE pages 422–423.
  - **CHOOSE** one of the three patterns of organizing a paragraph.
  - **WRITE** a paragraph on a topic of your choice modeled after the sample paragraphs on SE page 423. Afterward, **UNDERLINE** the order words you used.
  - **EXCHANGE** paragraphs with a partner. **TRY** to identify the pattern your partner chose.

Look and Listen — Writing a Descriptive Essay

- **THINK** about a favorite object. **WRITE** down as many details as you can about it. Now choose those details that another person needs to know to understand what your object is like. Did you include what it looks like? Did you include what sounds it might make?

Descriptive writing uses details to help the reader clearly imagine a certain person, place, thing, or idea. Sensory details help someone else *see*, *hear*, *feel*, *smell*, and *taste* what you are describing. These details also keep the reader interested in what you have to say. Whenever you write, remember to describe people, places, and things in order to make your writing clear and interesting.

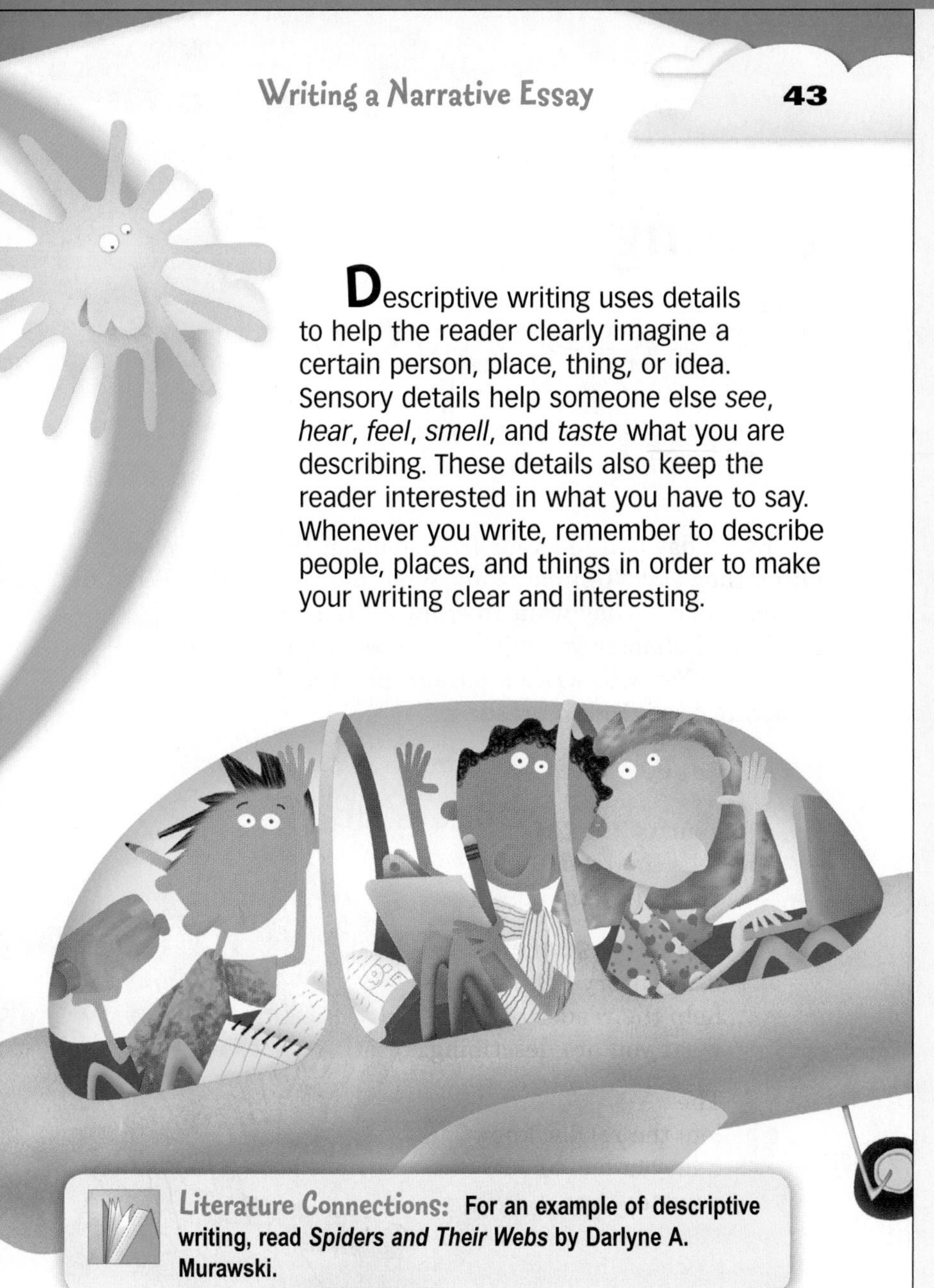

Literature Connections: For an example of descriptive writing, read ***Spiders and Their Webs*** by Darlyne A. Murawski.

Descriptive Writing

Tell students they'll find they can use what they learn in this section about descriptive writing in other kinds of writing projects, too. For example, if they're writing an expository essay about beekeeping, they can use descriptive writing to tell what a beekeeper's suit looks like and how it feels to wear it.

Write on the board the words for the five senses—*see, hear, feel, smell,* and *taste*. Tell students that using details about the senses helps to make readers feel as if they're actually experiencing what's being described.

Ask students to describe their breakfast that morning:

- How did it taste? Smell? (For example, oatmeal was sweet and milky and smelled like maple syrup.)
- How did it look or feel? (Oatmeal looked lumpy and brown and felt mushy; toast was cut into triangles and felt crisp.)
- What noises did they hear? (Perhaps a radio was playing or a pet dog was barking.)

Literature Connections

In the descriptive selection *Spiders and Their Webs,* rich details provide fascinating and specific information about various spiders and the webs they create.

Point out descriptive details that enable students to visualize the distinct spider webs. For additional models of descriptive writing, see the Reading-Writing Connections beginning on page TE-36.

Teaching Tip

As you introduce the descriptive form of writing, help students understand the specific purpose for writing—to describe. Then, discuss the concept of writing to an audience. Point out that whenever students write, they are writing for someone, themselves, teachers, friends, family members, and so on.

Family Connection Letters

As you begin this unit, send home the Descriptive Writing Family Connection letter, which describes what students will be learning.

- Letter in English (TE p. 602)
- Letter in Spanish (TE p. 610)

Writing a Descriptive Paragraph

Objectives

- Understand the content and structure of a descriptive paragraph.
- Choose an interesting topic to describe.
- Plan, write, revise, and edit a descriptive paragraph.

Remind students that a paragraph is a group of sentences about a specific topic. Longer pieces of writing, such as essays, are made up of several paragraphs.

Go over the paragraph parts again, assuring students that in this unit they will work through and thereby learn about each part.

- The topic sentence tells readers what you are going to describe and makes them want to know more.
- The body sentences contain lots of details that help readers see, hear, feel, smell, or taste what you are writing about.
- The closing sentence gives a final, interesting piece of information about the topic.

* For more about writing paragraphs, see SE pages 416–429.

Technology Connections

Use this unit's Interactive Whiteboard Lesson to introduce descriptive writing.

Interactive Whiteboard Lessons

Writing a Descriptive Paragraph

Every day you tell your friends about things you've seen. Often they say, "Tell me more. What did it look like? What did it sound like?" They want to know all the details.

In this chapter you will learn how to answer those questions. You will write a paragraph describing something you find interesting.

Paragraph Parts

1. Your **topic sentence** tells the reader what you will describe.
2. The **body sentences** use sensory details to help the reader *see* what you are describing.
3. The **closing sentence** lets the reader know how you feel about your topic.

Materials

Photo of low-rider pickup truck (TE p. 45)

Drawing supplies (TE p. 45)

Thesauruses (TE p. 45)

Tape recorder (TE p. 46)

Dictionaries (TE p. 49)

Copy Masters

Sensory Chart (TE p. 46)

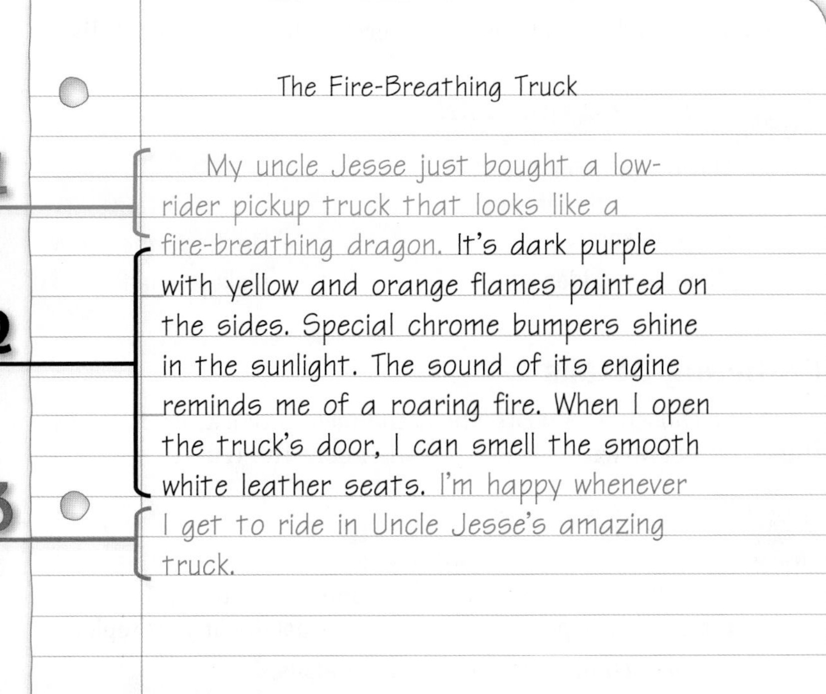

Writing a Descriptive Paragraph 45
Descriptive Paragraph
The Fire-Breathing Truck
1
My uncle Jesse just bought a low-rider pickup truck that looks like a fire-breathing dragon. It's dark purple with yellow and orange flames painted on the sides. Special chrome bumpers shine in the sunlight. The sound of its engine reminds me of a roaring fire. When I open the truck's door, I can smell the smooth white leather seats. I'm happy whenever I get to ride in Uncle Jesse's amazing truck.
2
3

After you read . . .

- **Ideas (1) Find two sensory details that help you see the truck.**
- **Organization (2) What order does the writer use to describe the truck (top to bottom, front to back, outside to inside)?**
- **Voice (3) What words in the closing sentence show how the writer feels about the truck?**

Descriptive Paragraph

Ask students if the paragraph gives them a good idea of **what the truck looks like** *(see below).*

Point out that in addition to including details about how the truck looks, the writer included other kinds of sensory details. Have students point out these details and name the senses involved.

- The engine **sounds** like a roaring fire. (hearing)
- The truck **smells** like leather inside. (smell)
- The seats **feel** smooth. (touch)

After you read . . .

Answers

Ideas 1. looks like a fire-breathing dragon, is dark purple with yellow and orange flames, chrome bumpers shine

Organization 2. order of location, from outside to inside

Voice 3. *Happy whenever I get to ride* and *amazing truck* show that the writer likes the truck.

Teaching Tip: What the Truck Looks Like

Have students draw and color the truck based on the details given in the essay. Because not all students will be familiar with low-rider pickups, begin by showing them a photo of one from the Internet or defining *low-rider* (a vehicle that has been lowered so the body is close to the ground).

- Distribute drawing supplies.
- Give students a few minutes to draw their pictures.
- Have students share their drawings with classmates to compare the details they included.

English Language Learners

For practice using synonyms, have students reread the last sentence of the essay. Ask:

- Which word describes the writer when he rides in the truck? (happy)
- What word describes Jesse's truck? (amazing)

Have students look up *happy* and *amazing* in a thesaurus and try to use the synonyms they find in the sentence.

Prewriting Finding an Idea

Write the sentence starter "I am really interested in . . . " on the board. Have volunteers complete the sentence as an example. Then have students use the sentence starter to brainstorm a few topics for their quick list.

✱ For the types of topics best suited to descriptive writing, see SE page 435.

When students have finished their list, suggest they select the topic to describe in one of these ways:

- Choose the most interesting topic to you.
- Choose the topic you have the most to say about.
- Choose the topic that lends itself to the greatest number of sensory details.

Gathering Details

Distribute copies of the reproducible Sensory Chart (TE page 596). Ask students to include details for at least four of the columns on the chart.

✱ For another example of a completed sensory chart, refer students to SE page 443, which provides more examples of sensory words.

Prewriting Finding an Idea

Ky wondered what he could describe. He made a quick list.

Make a quick list.

1. Make your quick list of interesting things you could describe.
2. Choose one idea.

Quick List

- baseball
- chess set
- Uncle Jesse's new pickup truck

Gathering Details

After choosing to write about the pickup truck, Ky filled in the chart below with sensory details about the truck.

Create a sensory chart.

1. Write the words *See*, *Hear*, *Feel*, and *Smell* across the top of your paper. List *Taste* if those details fit your topic.
2. Under each heading, list sensory details.

Sensory Chart

See	Hear	Feel	Smell
dark purple yellow and orange flames shiny bumpers	loud radio engine like a roaring fire	smooth seats hard chrome bumpers	leather seats plastic mats

English Language Learners

Some students find it easier to express ideas orally rather than in writing. Have these students use a tape recorder to dictate their quick lists, or pair them with cooperative partners who can quickly jot down their responses. Students can then play their tapes or listen to their partners read back the responses so they can jot down the list.

Writing Creating Your Paragraph

Every paragraph has three basic parts: a topic sentence, body sentences, and a closing sentence.

Topic Sentence

A good topic sentence states your topic and the main idea.

Topic **Main Idea (or Focus)**

Uncle Jesse's pickup truck looks like a dragon.

Body Sentences

The body of your paragraph includes sensory details that help the reader *see*, *hear*, *feel*, *smell*, or *taste* the topic.

Closing Sentence

The closing sentence tells how you feel about your topic.

Create your paragraph.

1. **Write a topic sentence that tells what you will describe.**
2. **Write body sentences using details from your sensory chart.**
3. **Write a closing sentence that shows your feelings about your topic.**

My Uncle Jesse's new pickup truck looks like a dragon. It's purple with yellow flames. It has shiny bumpers.

Writing Creating Your Paragraph

Suggest that students use one of the words for the five senses in their topic sentence. For example, someone writing about making angel food cake might consider the following topic sentences:

- Angel food cake *looks* like plain white cake, but it's not.
- Angel food cake *smells* heavenly when it's baking.
- Angel food cake *tastes* sweet and *feels* fluffy, like food for angels.

Encourage students to write two possible topic sentences using different sensory ideas. Then they can pick their favorite.

Tell students to refer often to their sensory charts as they write the body sentences and to check off each detail on the chart as they use it in the paragraph.

Encourage students to arrange their body sentences in the order that makes the most sense for their topic.

* For details about methods of organizing paragraphs, see SE pages 422–423.

Revising Improving Your Paragraph

Have partners take turns reading their writing. Have them discuss which revision suggestions for the page might improve the paragraph. Remind students to keep their comments friendly and specific. Then have partners switch roles and repeat the process.

Before students begin rewriting, encourage them to think about the suggestions they've received from their partner. They may not agree with everything their partner said, or they may have additional ideas for improvements.

Practice Answers

The sentence about the brother strays from the topic.

Details that could be added include:

- Replace *are great* in the first sentence with specific details, such as *have a delicious, smoky taste.*
- Give details of how cheese dogs look and smell in the second sentence, such as *plump up as they cook* and *like grilled cheese sandwiches.*

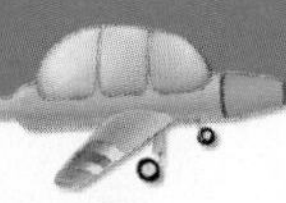

Revising Improving Your Paragraph

When you revise, you look over your paragraph and try to make it sound even better. Sometimes you may need to add more sensory details. Other times you may cut a detail that doesn't belong. After you try the minilesson below, check your own paragraph.

Check your details.

- **Read your paragraph carefully. Then try one or more of the following revising ideas:**
  - **Add at least one more sensory detail to help your reader imagine your topic even better.**
  - **Cut a detail that doesn't belong.**
  - **Move any details that seem out of place.**

Practice

Read the following paragraph. List one detail that does not belong. Then think about and write down another sensory detail you could add. Tell how it would help the reader.

Cheese dogs cooked on a campfire are great. I like the way they look and smell. When I bite into one, I can see the melted yellow cheese. My brother doesn't like them if they are burned. Roasted cheese dogs feel crunchy on the outside and creamy in the middle. I like them with lots of catsup or just plain.

English Language Learners

Students may be unfamiliar with the term *cheese dogs.* Before reading the **Practice** paragraph, explain that *dog* refers to a hot dog and that a cheese dog is a hot dog filled with cheese.

Writing a Descriptive Paragraph 49

Editing Checking for Conventions

When you edit your paragraph for conventions, you check your capital letters, punctuation, spelling, and grammar. Then you correct any errors that you find.

Conventions

Punctuation

____ **1.** Did I end each sentence with the correct punctuation?

Capitalization

____ **2.** Did I begin each sentence with a capital letter?
____ **3.** Did I use capital letters for the names of people and places?

Spelling

____ **4.** Did I check the spelling of words I'm not sure of?

Grammar

____ **5.** Did I indent the first line of my paragraph?

Grammar Practice

Tell which end punctuation each sentence needs (. period, ? question mark, ! exclamation point). Explain your answers. See pages 463–464 for help.

1. Did you ever see a kaleidoscope
2. There's one in the school library
3. Look through the kaleidoscope's eyepiece
4. Wow, I love the red, green, and blue designs

Editing Checking for Conventions

Suggest the following editing hints:

- Review the proofreading marks on the inside back cover of the student edition. (See TE page 594 for a copy master.)
- Use a colored pen or pencil so you can see your corrections.
- Read the paragraph once silently and once aloud. Some errors are easier to hear than see.
- Look up any word *(see below)* you're not sure is spelled correctly.
- Read the sentences one by one. Touch your pencil on each end punctuation mark. Be sure the next word starts with a capital letter.

* For additional information about marking punctuation, see SE pages 463–465.

Grammar Practice Answers

1. Question mark. Starting word *did* indicates a question.
2. Period: Sentence is a statement.
3. Period: Sentence is a command.
4. Exclamation point: Use of *Wow* is a clue that this is an exclamation.

Teaching Tip: Dictionary Practice

- Divide the class into teams (each with a dictionary).
- Have each team choose a name; write the names on the board.
- Call out a word for students to look up in the dictionary.
- Have students work together to find the word.
- The first group to read the correct definition aloud gets a point. Score to 10.

English Language Learners

Students whose first language is Spanish may put upside-down question marks and exclamation points at the beginning of the **Practice** sentences. For example, the phrases *How are you?* and *Hello!* are written as *¿Qué tal?* and *¡Hola!* in Spanish. Write these English and Spanish phrases on the board and point out the differences.

Grammar Connection

Adjectives

- **Proofreader's Guide** pages 546–547
- ***Write Source*** page 389
- ***GrammarSnap*** Adjectives

Prepositional Phrases

- **Proofreader's Guide** pages 552–553
- ***Write Source*** page 393
- ***GrammarSnap*** Prepositions and Prepositional Phrases
- ***SkillsBook*** pages 163–164

Writing a Descriptive Essay

Objectives

- Understand what a descriptive essay is.
- Understand the content and form of a descriptive essay.
- Plan, draft, revise, edit, and publish a descriptive essay.

A **descriptive essay** provides a detailed picture in words of a person, place, or thing.

Start students thinking about favorite things by asking them if they have ever had one of the following:

- a special toy or stuffed animal
- a book they loved to have read to them
- a favorite article of clothing

Write students' favorite objects from the past or present on the board as they speak. Encourage them to think about what the objects looked like and what experiences they had with them.

Tell students they can choose to write their essay about one of the objects on the board or about a current favorite object, as suggested on SE page 54.

Writing a Descriptive Essay

Think about something that is special to you. Do you have a great pair of shoes, a special collection, or a favorite book? It could be just about anything.

In this chapter, you will describe your special object for your classmates. Instead of just telling them about it, you will use words to help them "see" what you are describing.

Materials

Pictures (printouts from the Internet) of seashells (TE p. 52)

Drawing supplies (TE p. 55)

The picture book *Alexander and the Terrible, Horrible, No Good, Very Bad Day,* by Judith Viorst (TE p. 55)

Sticky notes (TE pp. 58, 71)

Thesauruses (TE p. 62)

Blank transparency (TE p. 65)

Index cards (TE p. 70)

Copy Masters

Editing and Proofreading Marks (TE p. 63)

Thinking About Your Writing (TE p. 67)

Writing a Descriptive Essay 51

Understanding Your Goal

Your goal in this chapter is to write a descriptive essay. The essay will describe an object that is special to you.

Your goal is to . . .

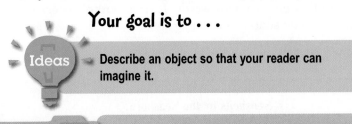

- **Ideas** — Describe an object so that your reader can imagine it.
- **Organization** — Create a strong beginning, middle, and ending.
- **Voice** — Use a voice that shows you are excited about the object.

- **Word Choice** — Choose nouns and adjectives that let the reader picture your object.
- **Sentence Fluency** — Write complete sentences that flow smoothly.
- **Conventions** — Use correct capitalization, punctuation, spelling, and grammar.

Understanding Your Goal

Point out to students that they will concentrate on different goals at different stages of the writing process.

- You try out most of your **ideas** during prewriting. You have to find an idea first to know what to write!
- You do much of the **organization** also during prewriting, when you make lists of details to mention. But you will also do some organizing during writing, when you're deciding how to approach the beginning, middle, and end.
- You develop your **voice** and make **word choices** during the writing stage, although you check these traits when you revise and edit, too.
- The best time to focus on **sentence fluency** and **conventions** is during the revising and editing stages—after you've made sure the essay includes all the necessary information.

English Language Learners

Have students who are overwhelmed by too many goals focus on Ideas and Organization. As students choose an idea (an object to describe), encourage them to choose one with which they are familiar. Point out that the more they know about the special object, the easier it will be to describe it.

Remind students that an important part of Organization is listing the details to use in the essay. Explain to students that they can refer to their list as they write the beginning, middle, and ending of their essay.

Struggling Learners

To help students use voice to show excitement, have them form small groups and assign each group a scenario, such as:

- going to a favorite movie
- greeting a favorite relative who has come for a visit

Have students role play the scenario and record words they used to convey their excitement.

Descriptive Essay

Have volunteers read the sample essay aloud, changing readers after each paragraph. Tell the class to listen carefully for descriptive details.

To help students focus on the descriptions in the essay, divide the class into small groups and give each group pictures of the types of shell mentioned—jingle shells, bear-paw shells, shark's eyes, Florida augers, and calico scallops. (Pictures are readily available on the Internet.) Make sure the pictures do not identify the shell.

Ask students to work together for a few minutes to figure out the names of the shells based on the information given in the essay. Afterward, ask if students were easily able to identify the shells. Do they think that the writer did a good job of describing them?

Descriptive Essay

A descriptive essay should describe something so clearly that the reader can imagine it. You could say that a descriptive essay paints a picture with words. Lebron wrote the essay below. His focus sentence is underlined.

Lebron's Essay

Seashells by the Seashore

Every summer my family goes to the beach. I dig in the sand and look for seashells. Last year, my sister helped me glue some of my shells in a shadow box. I'm very proud of my seashell collection.

In the top part of the box, I put common shells. On the left, I put shiny orange, silver, and gray "jingle" shells. They are the size of nickels and dimes. They jingle just like money! In the top right part, I put bear-paw shells that have some purple color inside and tiny white spikes on the outside.

In the bottom part of the shadow box, I put my rare shells. The left side holds my shark's eyes. Each one looks like a snail shell with a swirly gray eye on one side. My Florida augers are on the right. They remind me of long, skinny ice-cream cones.

On the corners of my shadow box, I glued brown, orange, purple, and white-striped calico scallops. Having a collection is fun. When I look at my shadow box, the shells remind me of the fun I have at the beach.

Teaching Tip: Using Words Correctly

Focus on compound nouns. A **compound noun** is a word made up from two or more nouns. Look at the model to find examples of compound nouns *(seashell, shadow box)*.

Focus on adjectives *(shiny, orange, long, skinny, common, tiny)* and how they add to Lebron's description. You could also have students find examples of pronouns and articles used in this model. (See SE pages 536 and 546.)

Parts of a Descriptive Essay

A descriptive essay has a beginning, a middle, and an ending. These three parts work together to make your essay clear and interesting for the reader.

Beginning

Middle

Ending

Beginning

The **beginning paragraph** gets the reader's attention and names the topic. It also includes the main idea of the essay in a focus sentence.

Middle

Each **middle paragraph** begins with a topic sentence. Details in the rest of the paragraph explain the topic sentence.

Ending

The **ending paragraph** shares one final thought about the topic.

After you read . . .

- **Ideas** **(1) What object is the writer describing?**
- **Organization** **(2) How does the writer organize the two middle paragraphs? (Think about the shadow box.)**
- **Voice & Word Choice** **(3) Find words or phrases that show the writer cares about his topic.**

English Language Learners

Allow students adequate processing time to think of a response to each **After you read** question. In addition, try not to repeat the question. Repeating the question can inhibit thinking and may frustrate students.

Parts of a Descriptive Essay

Point out that in the model on SE page 52 the focus sentence comes at the end of the opening paragraph. Note that the focus sentence may occur near the beginning of the first paragraph in an essay to tell the reader what the essay is about.

Ask students to identify the topic sentences in the middle paragraphs of the model (*In the top part . . .; In the bottom part . . .*). Note that all the sentences that follow in each middle paragraph support the topic sentence.

Have students identify the writer's final thought (the shells remind him of fun trips to the beach).

After you read . . .

Answers

Ideas 1. his shell collection

Organization 2. order of location (common shells at top, rare ones at bottom)

Voice & Word Choice 3. The use of specific names for shells shows the writer cares about the subject enough to have learned about it.

- I'm very proud of my seashell collection.
- They jingle just like money!
- Having a collection is fun.
- The shells remind me of the fun I have at the beach.

Prewriting Selecting a Topic

Model the topic-selection process by writing a list of your own favorite things on the board. Then choose one.

For the purposes of the exercise, encourage students to pick a topic that is not too complicated to draw.

Ideas List

Have a volunteer read aloud the sample focus sentence on the page. Ask students if they can think of other ways the writer could have expressed that idea. As volunteers tell classmates their suggestions, write them on the board. Alternative focus sentences might include:

- My favorite possession is my locket.
- One of the most important things I own is my locket.
- If I had to choose one thing to take with me to a deserted island, it would be my locket.

Point out to students that the topic (the locket) should be mentioned in the focus sentence, but that there are different ways of saying that it is special. Tell students they might want to think about different ways of writing their own focus sentence for their essay.

Technology Connections

Students can use the added features of the Net-text as they explore this stage of the writing process.

Write Source Online ***Net-text***

Prewriting Selecting a Topic

When you select a topic, you need to think about objects that are special to you. Amy made a list of her special objects. Then she chose the one that she wanted to write about.

List all of your ideas.

1. Write "Special Objects" on the top of a piece of paper.
2. List things that are special to you.
3. Mark (*) the one that you would like to write about.
4. Write a focus sentence that names your special object and tells how you feel about it.

Ideas List

Special Objects

skates	science kit
fuzzy sweater	stretchy bracelet
art supplies	my locket *

Focus sentence:

My locket is very special to me.

English Language Learners

Sometimes students may know what they want to say but cannot think of the particular word they want to use. Encourage them to write a similar word and draw a star next to it so they will know to come back to it later.

Struggling Learners

Students who are visual learners may find making picture diagrams helpful. If possible, make the activity more concrete by allowing students to bring their special objects to school. Encourage students to add as many details and labels to their pictures as they can generate.

Writing a Descriptive Essay 55

Gathering Details

One way to gather details about your object is to draw a picture of it and label its parts. This is called a **picture diagram**. Use words that tell about the color, shape, size, special details, and maybe even sounds of your object.

Make a picture diagram.

1. **Draw the object you want to describe.**
2. **Label your drawing with words that describe your object.**

Picture Diagram

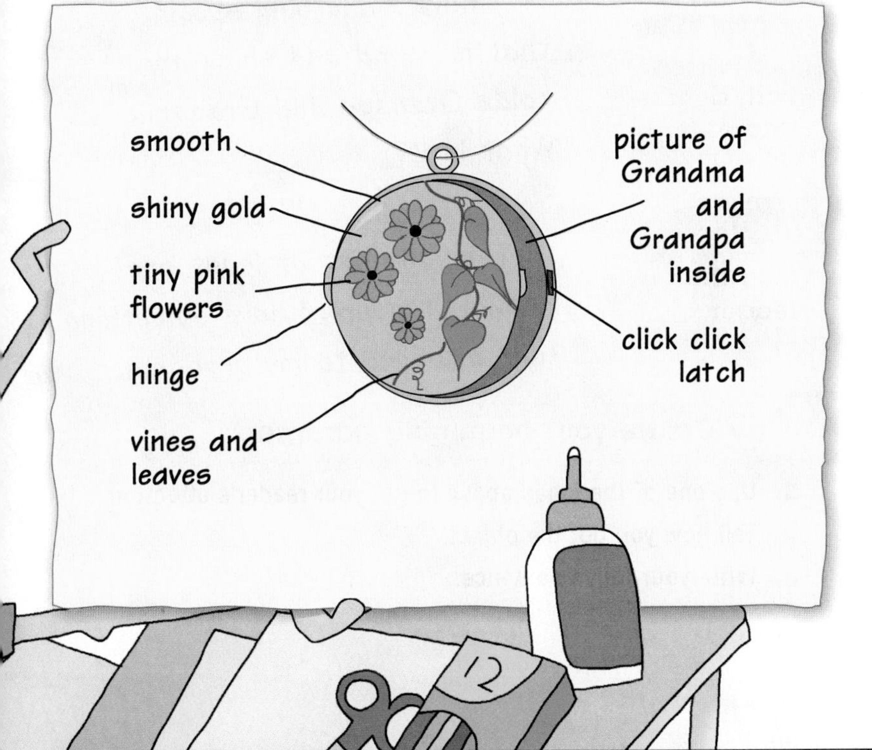

Prewriting Gathering Details

Draw a picture and label the parts. Use the diagram exercise as an opportunity to **review adjectives** *(see below)*. Ask a volunteer to tell what adjectives are (words that describe people, places, or things). Have students find the adjectives in the picture diagram on SE page 55 and tell what each describes.

- *smooth* (describes how the watch feels)
- *shiny* and *gold* (describe how the watch looks)
- *tiny* and *pink* (describe how the flowers look)

* For more information about Adjectives, see SE pages 389–390.

Distribute drawing supplies so students can color their diagrams if they choose.

Writer's Craft

Description: The goal of description is to write so clearly that readers get the same picture in their heads as the writer has. Teach this concept to students by having them sit back to back, their picture diagrams before them. One partner describes the diagram, and the other partner tries to draw it. Then the partners switch roles. See how similar the diagrams are to each other.

Teaching Tip: Review Adjectives

The familiar picture book *Alexander and the Terrible, Horrible, No Good, Very Bad Day*, by Judith Viorst, is a fun way to review word choice and provides opportunities to talk about other aspects of descriptive writing. Read the story aloud to the class.

- Pause to have students point out the adjectives used.
- Ask students to look for other ways the writer includes sensory details.
- Direct students' attention to details in the story that are reflected in the illustrations.

Writing Beginning Your Essay

After students have had the chance to create a beginning for their essays, ask them to choose partners to work with.

- Have partners tell a little about their topic and read the focus sentence.
- Have students challenge their partners to use a different attention-getting strategy to create a different opener for the topic.
- Have students read their partner's alternative focus sentence. Is it more interesting than the first one? If so, the writer should consider using it instead of the original idea.

Have students trade roles and repeat the process so that each gets an opportunity to provide an alternative focus sentence.

Technology Connections

Students can use the added features of the Net-text as they explore this stage of the writing process.

Write Source Online **Net-text**

Writing Beginning Your Essay

Beginning
Middle
Ending

The beginning paragraph in your essay should get your reader's attention. Then it should tell how you got the object. Finally, your focus sentence should tell how you feel about your object.

You could try one of the "ABC's of beginnings" shown below to get your reader's attention.

Ask a question.

Do you know what a locket is?

OR

Be creative with a riddle.

I have something special that is round and shiny and holds Grandpa and Grandma. What is it?

OR

Connect with the reader.

Everyone has at least one special treasure. I have something that belonged to my grandma.

Create your beginning paragraph.

1. Use one of the ideas above to get your reader's attention.
2. Tell how you got the object.
3. Write your focus sentence.

English Language Learners

The phrase *connect with the reader* may be confusing to some students. Explain that connecting with someone means that you try to find things both of you have in common. Point out how this is done in the example by using the words *everyone* and *I*.

Struggling Learners

Some students may get stuck before they even begin writing. To help students generate initial writing, encourage them to write a beginning that they plan to revise later. Students may even find that they want to keep a sentence or two. Point out that they can use this strategy any time they write.

Writing a Descriptive Essay 57

Amy's Beginning Paragraph

When Amy started writing her descriptive essay, she did not worry about making a few mistakes. Instead, she worked to get all of her ideas on paper.

Beginning
A question gets the reader's attention.

Details tell how the writer got this object.

The focus sentence (underlined) tells the writer's feelings.

Do you know what a locket is? Well, it's a little case that hangs on a neckless. A locket opens and has pictures inside. I have one thats been in our family for a realy long time. My grandpa gave it to my grandma before they were married. many years later, Grandma gave it to my mom, and now it's mine. My locket is very special to me.

Struggling Learners

Explain to students that Amy's paragraph begins with general information and ends with more specific information. To help visual learners see the structure of Amy's paragraph, fill in a graphic organizer similar to the following:

Amy describes a locket. It could belong to anyone.

Amy tells about a certain locket. It has been in her family for a long time.

The locket has been passed down and now belongs to Amy.

Amy's Beginning Paragraph

Ask students if they can find an important piece of extra information that Amy included in her opening paragraph, in addition to the attention-getting first sentence, the explanation of where she got the object, and the focus sentence. (She explains what a locket is.)

Point out that choosing an opening question may be especially helpful if the answer provides additional information to readers about the topic. In this case, readers who might not know what a locket is will find the essay more interesting now that they know exactly what it's about.

Ask students to think about their own essay topics.

- Do they think they might want to include a definition of their subject?
- If so, would it fit into the first paragraph?

Writing Developing the Middle

To help students practice using the different orders of location, point out an object in the classroom—for example, a poster—and have a volunteer use one of the methods given to describe it. Then have a second volunteer describe it using another method. (A poster could be described from top to bottom and left to right.)

Challenge students to think of more ways they might describe something by order of location. These include the following:

- from front to back (for example, when describing what a book looks like)
- from near to far (for a scene in a picture)
- from head to tail (for an animal)
- clockwise or counterclockwise (for details arranged in a circle)

Tell students that they may use one of these alternative methods if it suits their object. Remind them that they should choose a method that will make it easy to separate the description into two main parts, one for each middle paragraph.

* For more about order of location, see SE pages 422–423.

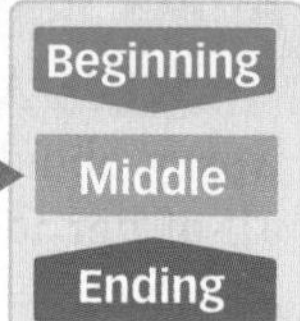

Writing Developing the Middle

Beginning
Middle
Ending

Each of your middle paragraphs should begin with a topic sentence and tell about a certain part of your topic. Use **order of location** by describing your topic in one of three ways shown below.

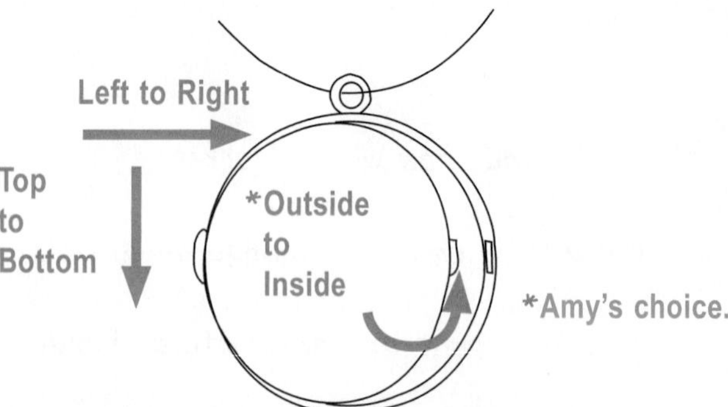

Write your middle paragraphs.

1. **Choose one way to describe your object** (left to right, top to bottom, outside to inside).
2. **Look at your picture diagram again. Now write two topic sentences that describe the main parts of your object—the left and right parts, for example.**
3. **Write two body paragraphs by adding more sentences after each topic sentence. Include details from your picture diagram to support each topic sentence.**

English Language Learners

Using their picture diagrams, have students copy the labels they wrote onto sticky notes. Have them arrange the sticky notes on a sheet of blank paper from left to right, top to bottom, back to front, and soon, until they find the best method for describing their objects.

Struggling Learners

* Some students may need to review transition words that show location. Direct students' attention to the list of transitions on SE pages 458–459. Review both pages, particularly the section about transition words that work well in description.

Writing a Descriptive Essay 59

Amy's Middle Paragraphs

In her middle paragraphs, Amy described her locket. She still didn't worry about making a few mistakes.

it to my mom, and now it's mine. My locket is very special to me.

Topic Sentence

The writer describes the outside of the locket.

Many lockets are shapped like a valentine heart, but not mine. Its shiny gold and hangs on a long chain The outside has vines and flowers carved in it. Some of the vines are smooth from mom and grandma rubbing it with there fingers. My brother wouldn't wear it for a million dollars.

Topic Sentence

Then she describes the inside of the locket.

Inside my locket, there are pictures of my grandma and grandpa when they were young. grandma was pretty. She had curly blonde hair. He had dark hair and didn't wear Glasses as he does now. Grandpa looked so different.

Amy's Middle Paragraphs

After students have read the middle paragraphs on the page, give them a few minutes to take notes about their impressions of the paragraphs. To help them organize their thoughts about what they've read, write the following questions on the board:

- What are the topic sentences?
- Does every sentence in each paragraph support the topic sentence?
- If not, which sentences don't belong?
- Do the paragraphs help you imagine what the locket looks like?
- What details are missing from the description?

Tell students that they will return to these questions when they begin working on revising their own essays (on SE page 63). Have them save their notes to refer to later.

Writing Ending Your Essay

Tell students that as they get more practice writing, they may discover that sometimes ideas for endings come to them while they're working on the earlier parts of the essay. They may even decide right at the beginning how they want the essay to end. Encourage students to jot down these possible endings in their writing journals whenever they come up. That way they won't forget a great idea.

Draw students' attention to the strategy of reminding readers about the beginning. Emphasize that if they do this, they should take care to include new information, not just repeat what was said before. Ask them to look at the sample ending shown and answer the following questions:

- How does it remind you of the beginning? (It refers to the definition of *locket*.)
- What new information is there? (The writer suggests that readers ask what's in a locket if they see one.)

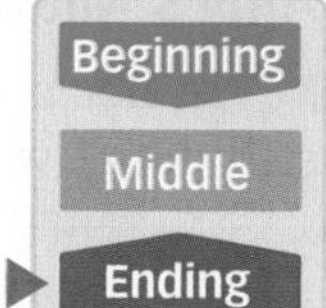

Writing Ending Your Essay

Your ending paragraph should give your reader one final thought about the topic. Here are some ways to create a strong ending.

Beginning
Middle
Ending

Remind your reader about your beginning.

Now you know what a locket is. Maybe the next time you see one, you'll ask about the pictures inside of it.

OR

Show your feelings about your topic.

I'm so glad the locket is finally mine. I always feel special when I wear it.

OR

Tie the special object to your life.

Someday, I can pass down this beautiful locket to my daughter, so she can enjoy it as much as I do.

Write **Create your ending paragraph.**

1. Try one of the ideas above to write your ending.
2. If none of these work, try your own idea.

Struggling Learners

Students may have difficulty deciding how to create a strong ending and which method to choose. Pair students and write the following sentence frames on the board:

- Now you know all about my __________. (Remind)
- I feel so ______ about my ______ because ______. (Show)
- This ______ is an important part of my life because ______. (Tie)

Have students take turns completing each sentence orally while their partners listen. After hearing the three endings, have partners tell which one they thought was the strongest.

Amy's Ending Paragraph

In Amy's first draft of her ending, she didn't worry about making a few mistakes. She just got all of her ideas on paper.

didn't wear Glasses as he does now.

Grandpa looked so different.

I open and close my locket over and over again. I like to feel it in my hand and here the click, click it makes. My mom says I shouldnt do it so much. I might ware it out. She says I should be careful with it. Someday, I can pass it down to my daughter, so she can enjoy it as much as I do

Ending
The writer connects the special object to her life.

Amy's Ending Paragraph

Focus students' attention on the sentences leading up to the final line. Point out that the writer connects the topic of her essay to her life from the very beginning of the essay, not just for the final sentence.

Point out to students that the writer continues to describe the locket in the ending paragraph. What sensory details does the writer include?

- touch (the feel of the locket in her hand)
- sound (the clicking of the latch)

Point out to students that even though the writer didn't choose the ending that shows her feelings about the locket, she still communicates her feelings and interest in her topic. Ask students to explain how she does this. Answers might include the following:

- She loves to handle the locket.
- She'd like to give it to her daughter, too.
- She says she enjoys it.

Revising Improving Your Essay

Tell students that it is always a good idea, if they have time, to set a piece of writing aside overnight—before revising it. That way, they will be fresh and problems are more likely to attract their attention than if they try to revise right after finishing the first draft.

Remind them also that it's helpful to ask a friend or family member to read the draft and comment on it. A second person's comments are a great way to learn what might be unclear in an essay.

Suggest that, if students have someone read their work, they might ask the person to answer the following specific questions:

- Can you tell what my topic is?
- Is there anything that you didn't understand? What?
- Is there anything in the essay that isn't about my topic? What?
- Are my sentences in the right order to describe the topic? If not, what seems out of place?

Technology Connections

Have students use the Writing Network features of the Net-text to comment on each other's drafts.

Write Source Online **Net-text**

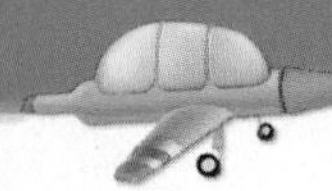

Revising Improving Your Essay

Revising is one of the most important steps in the writing process. It is your chance to make changes to your description. You can add, cut, or move details, depending on how you want to improve your essay.

Check your details.

1. **Look for places where you could add, cut, or move details.**
2. **How could you make your description even better?**

When should I add details?

You should **add** details to make your description clearer and more exciting. Use a caret ^ to show where you want to put the new detail.

When should I cut a detail?

You should **cut** any detail that does not belong in your description. Use a delete mark to show what you want to cut.

When should I move details?

You should **move** details that are out of order. Circle any idea that you want to move. Then draw an arrow → to show where you want to put it.

English Language Learners

Some students may add so many details that their essays become wordy. Often they will use synonyms to describe one thing such as *the lovely, beautiful locket.* Point out that because the words mean the same thing, only one adjective is needed in the sentence.

Advanced Learners

Encourage students to use a thesaurus to find new words for their writing as they revise their essays. For example, an *exciting* book could become a *thrilling, gripping,* or *fascinating* book. Invite students to keep a log of new words they have used in their essays and to add to their lists throughout the year.

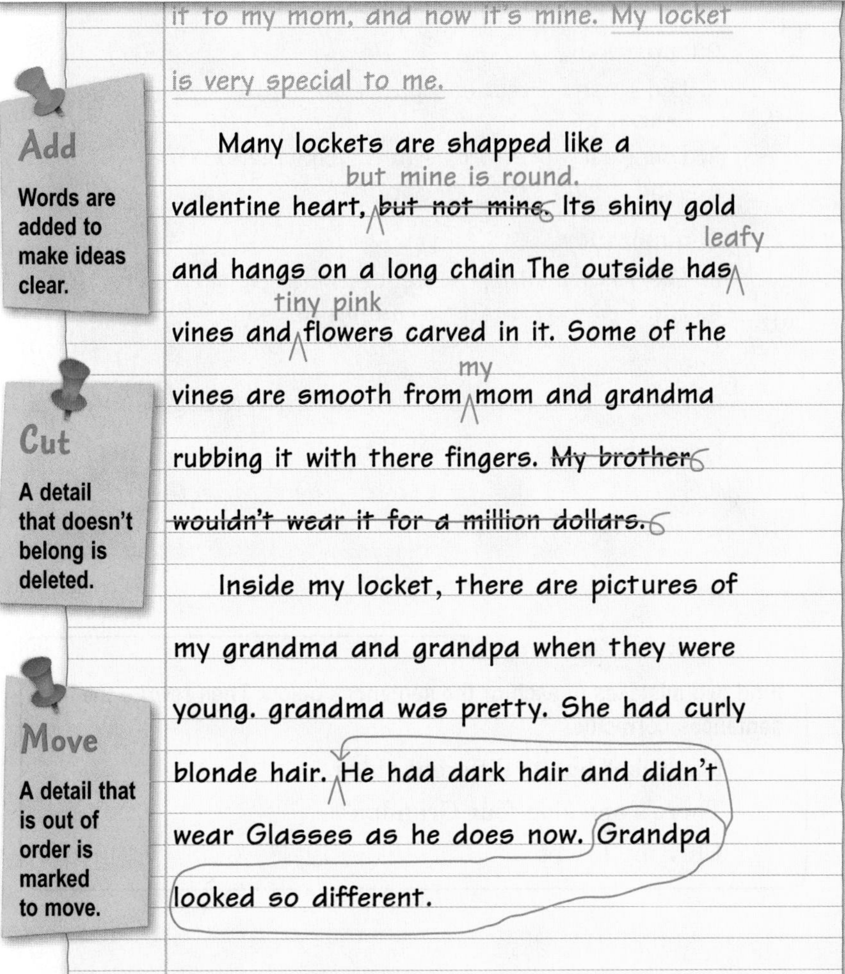

Writing a Descriptive Essay 63
Amy's Revising
Here are the changes Amy made as she revised her two middle paragraphs. She added, cut, and moved some words and sentences. By doing this, she improved her ideas and organization.
it to my mom, and now it's mine. My locket is very special to me.
Many lockets are shapped like a valentine heart, but not mine. but mine is round. Its shiny gold and hangs on a long chain The outside has leafy vines and tiny pink flowers carved in it. Some of the vines are smooth from my mom and grandma rubbing it with there fingers. My brother wouldn't wear it for a million dollars.
Inside my locket, there are pictures of my grandma and grandpa when they were young. grandma was pretty. She had curly blonde hair. He had dark hair and didn't wear Glasses as he does now. Grandpa looked so different.
Add
Words are added to make ideas clear.
Cut
A detail that doesn't belong is deleted.
Move
A detail that is out of order is marked to move.

Amy's Revising

Go through the changes marked in the sample, and ask students to explain why they were made.

- *Mine is round* was added because the writer said her locket was *not* heart-shaped but forgot to tell what shape it actually was.
- *Leafy* and *tiny pink* were added for additional sensory detail.
- *My* was added to make the language more specific.
- *My brother* . . . was cut because the sentence isn't about the topic.
- *Grandpa looked* . . . was moved because it should go before the sentence that says *why* Grandpa looks different in the locket picture.

Have students review the notes they made after working on SE page 59. Did they make note of any of the problems that were fixed in the revision? Did they find additional problems? If so, what were they?

Struggling Learners

Some students worry more about using the proper proofreading marks than about the content of their writing. Provide copies of the reproducible Editing and Proofreading Marks (TE page 594) for students to refer to as they revise.

Advanced Learners

Challenge students to consider the changes that Amy made to her middle paragraphs. Do they agree that her description is better? Have them explain why they think the changes helped or did not help. Can they think of one or two details that Amy could add to improve her description even more?

Grammar Connection

Adjectives

- **Proofreader's Guide** page 546 (+)
- ***Write Source*** page 389 (+)
- ***GrammarSnap*** Adjectives
- ***SkillsBook*** pages 151–152

Editing Checking for Conventions

Remind students that contractions are two words combined into one. The apostrophe in a contraction goes where letters were removed.

* For information about Apostrophes in Contractions, see SE pages 472–473.

For a copy master of the descriptive writing Conventions Checklist, see TE page 561.

Have students brainstorm tricky words that sound alike, such as *their, there,* and *they're.*

* See SE pages 510–525.

Ask students to share methods for remembering tricky words. For *its* or *it's,* say *it is* to see if the word can be replaced by the two words. If so, it is the contraction, and it needs an apostrophe.

Grammar Practice Answers

(Corrections are underlined.)

1. My locket has two different sides.
2. There's one side for Grandpa.
3. I love my locket.

Technology Connections

Students can use the added features of the Net-text as they explore this stage of the writing process.

Write Source Online ***Net-text***

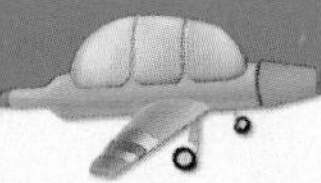

Editing Checking for Conventions

Now it's time to edit your essay. When you edit, you check your punctuation, capitalization, spelling, and grammar.

Conventions

Punctuation

___ **1.** Did I use correct end punctuation after each sentence?

___ **2.** Did I use apostrophes in my contractions (*can't, don't*)?

Capitalization

___ **3.** Did I start all my sentences with capital letters?

___ **4.** Did I capitalize all the names of people?

Spelling

___ **5.** Have I used the correct verbs (*we* ***are***, not *we* ***is***)?

Grammar

___ **6.** Have I used the right words (*there, their, they're; to, two, too*)?

Grammar Practice

Find two mistakes in each of the sentences below. Then rewrite the sentences correctly.

1. My locket has to different sides
2. There's one side four Grandpa?
3. I luv my locket

English Language Learners

Students may have difficulty checking their writing for capitalization, punctuation, spelling, and grammar mistakes. Pair students with cooperative, language-proficient partners and have them work together to review each other's work and offer suggestions.

Grammar Connection

Proper Nouns

- **Proofreader's Guide** pages 532–533
- ***Write Source*** page 375
- ***GrammarSnap*** Common and Proper Nouns
- ***SkillsBook*** pages 119–120

Capitalization

- **Proofreader's Guide** pages 488–489
- ***GrammarSnap*** Capitalization
- ***SkillsBook*** page 44

Apostrophes

- **Proofreader's Guide** pages 472–473
- ***GrammarSnap*** Contractions
- ***SkillsBook*** pages 23–24

Writing a Descriptive Essay 65

Amy's Editing

When she edited her essay, Amy carefully checked for errors.

it to my mom, and now it's mine. My locket is very special to me.

Amy corrects a spelling error.

Many lockets are shapped like a valentine heart, but mine is round. It's shiny gold and hangs on a long chain The outside has leafy vines and tiny pink flowers carved in it. Some of the vines are smooth from my mom and grandma rubbing it with there fingers.

She adds punctuation.

She corrects a wrong word.

Inside my locket, there are pictures of my grandma and grandpa when they were young. grandma was pretty. She had curly blonde hair. Grandpa looked so different. He had dark hair and didn't wear Glasses as he does now.

She fixes two capitalization errors.

Teaching Tip: Editing Corrections

To help students understand how the editing symbols are used, make an overhead transparency with a sample paragraph (written in black or blue) that has several different kinds of errors in it. Project the transparency and ask students to point out the mistakes. As they do so, demonstrate the marking of the corrections (using a green or red pen).

Point out that some editing marks are small and easy to miss when recopying a draft. Remind students that it is helpful to use a different color of pen or pencil so such corrections are more visible.

Amy's Editing

Point out to students that when Amy copied over her draft after revising, she "double-spaced" it—left every other line on the page blank—as she had done in earlier drafts. Double-spacing allows room for **editing corrections** *(see below)* and changes during revising and editing.

Have students explain why the word *grandma* starts with a lowercase *g* in lines 6 and 9 but with a capital *G* in line 10:

- In lines 6 and 9, *grandma* is a common noun; it refers to a member of the general group, grandmothers. The clue to identifying it as a common noun is the use of the possessive pronoun *my*.
- In line 10, *Grandma* is a proper noun. Grandma is the name Amy uses for her grandma. Have students share other names, such as Nana or Abuela, they may use for their grandmother. Some students may use a first name, such as Angelica. Point out that in these instances, too, the word is a proper noun and begins with a capital letter.

* More information about common and proper nouns is available on SE page 375.

Publishing Sharing Your Essay

If you plan to use the model in the book, ask students to look carefully at the sample final copy shown and to describe it. Answers should include the following:

- The title of the essay is centered on the first line of the page.
- The essay begins two lines below the title.
- The beginning of each paragraph is indented.
- The page of text ends two lines from the bottom.
- The text of any pages after the first one begins on the second line of the page.

After students have written out their final copies, display the finished essays on a class bulletin board along with the picture diagrams used to gather details. Alternatively, hold a class show-and-tell event, for which students can bring the object they wrote about for the class to see while they read their essay aloud.

Technology Connections

Remind students that they can use the Writing Network features of the Portfolio to share their work with peers.

Write Source Online ***Portfolio***

Write Source Online ***Net-text***

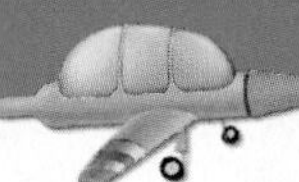

Publishing Sharing Your Essay

After you have corrected any mistakes, it is time to write a final copy of your descriptive essay.

Publish

Make a final copy.

1. **Follow your teacher's instructions, or use the model below. (For computer papers, see page 37.)**
2. **Carefully write a clean final copy and proofread it.**

Locket in My Pocket

Do you know what a locket is? Well, it's a little case that hangs on a necklace. A locket opens and has pictures inside. I have one that's been in our family for a really long time. My grandpa gave it to my grandma before they were married. Many years later, Grandma gave it to my mom, and now it's mine. My locket is very special to me.

Many lockets are shaped like a valentine heart, but mine is round. It's shiny gold and hangs on a long chain. The front has leafy vines and tiny pink flowers carved in it. Some of the vines are smooth from my mom and grandma rubbing it with their fingers.

Inside my locket, there are pictures of my grandma and grandpa when they were young. Grandma was pretty. She had curly blonde hair. Grandpa looked so different. He had dark hair and didn't wear glasses like he does now.

I open and close my locket over and over again just to feel it in my hand and hear the

...says I might
...d be careful
...pass down this
...er, so she can

Advanced Learners

Point out that Amy uses rhyme in her title. Invite students to brainstorm attention-grabbing titles for their essays, using rhyme or one of the following techniques:

- Repeat a consonant sound *(Lovely Little Locket).*
- Use the sound an object might make *(Click! Click!).*
- Use a play on words *(Lock It Up).*

Reflecting on Your Writing

Congratulations! You have finished your descriptive essay. Take a little time to think about what you have learned. Here are Amy's thoughts about her essay.

Thinking About Your Writing

Name: Amy McKekkin

Title: Locket in My Pocket

1. The best part of my essay is . . .

   telling everyone how special my locket is to me.

2. The part of my essay that still needs work is . . .

   the part where I describe the chain.

3. The main thing I learned about descriptive writing is . . .

   how to use a picture diagram. That helped me think about all of the details.

Reflecting on Your Writing

Explain to students that taking some time to think about their writing is a good way to improve their writing skills. For example, it's a good way to see if there's something they consistently have trouble with that they should focus on for the next project.

Ask students to think about the descriptive essay they wrote. Have volunteers share with the class what they liked best, what needed work, and what they learned.

Provide photocopies of the reproducible Thinking About Your Writing (TE page 593) for students to fill out. When they have finished, ask them to write the date on the assessment and to file it, along with the essay, in their portfolio.

✱ For more about portfolios, see SE pages 34–41.

Writing for Assessment

If students must take school, district, or state assessments, focus on the writing form to be tested. In addition, be sure that there are extra sharpened pencils with new erasers available and extra paper for writing planning notes on.

Explain to students that there are helpful writing tips for test-taking on SE page 70. In addition to those tips, tell students that they should also do the following:

- Decide ahead of time about how long to spend planning, writing, and revising. Watch the clock and stick to your schedule.
- Choose a simple topic—make sure you can say everything in the time given.
- Make a picture diagram if you can draw things quickly. Otherwise make a list, cluster chart, or describing wheel instead.

* For information about lists, cluster charts, and describing wheels, see SE page 436.

Descriptive Writing

Writing for Assessment

When you take a writing test, you may be given a descriptive writing prompt. It may ask you to write an essay that describes a person, a place, or a thing, using sensory details. On page 69, you can read Tola Moonbird's response to the prompt below.

Descriptive Prompt

What is your most interesting item of clothing? Write an essay in which you describe the item of clothing and how you feel when you wear it.

Sketch

Jingle Dress

Advanced Learners

Discuss the descriptive prompt on SE page 68. Point out that a good prompt is focused but not too specific. Ask students the following questions:

- What might happen if the prompt asked you to describe traditional clothing worn in a certain country? (The description would be difficult if you weren't familiar with the clothing.)
- What might happen if the prompt asked you just to write about clothing? (The description would be difficult to focus because the prompt would be too broad.)

Then challenge students to develop their own descriptive prompts.

Writing for Assessment 69

Powwow Jingle Dress

The **beginning** gives the focus sentence (underlined).

Some girls have fancy party dresses. I have a very special dress that my aunt helped me sew. It's for a festival called a powwow. My jingle dress is the best piece of clothing I have.

The **middle** gives details by order of location.

The top part of my jingle dress is called the yoke. Aunt Isa and I made it out of red satin. We sewed red and yellow ribbons in a V across the front of the yoke. Jingles hang from the ribbons. We made all the jingles by bending tin into long cones. They ring like little bells when I dance to the drums.

In the middle of my dress, I wear a wide leather belt. I sewed tiny white beads in the center. Then I used brown beads to make two running horses.

The blue skirt of my dress has ribbons and jingles. We sewed red and yellow ribbons in zigzags across the front and back. The jingles hang below the ribbons in two rows.

The **ending** tells why the object is special.

My jingle dress looks great and sounds even better! It makes me think of my tribe. I loved sewing it with my aunt, and I love wearing it when I dance at powwows!

After you read . . .

- Ideas **(1) How does the writer's dress make her feel? Why?**
- Organization **(2) How are the paragraphs organized?**
- Word Choice **(3) Find two interesting sensory words.**

Ask students to assess the essay, giving details whenever possible. Responses include the following:

- The writer did a good job explaining *yoke.*
- The writer used pronouns and adjectives to make the writing clear and easy to read.
- The writer could have told which tribe she belongs to.

After you read . . .

Answers

Ideas **1.** The dress makes her happy because she likes the way it looks and sounds, she enjoyed both making and wearing it, and it reminds her of her tribe.

Organization **2.** From top to bottom (Point out that in order to focus on the top, middle, and bottom of the dress, the writer created three middle paragraphs, one for each part.)

Word Choice **3.** Answers will vary but may include the following:

- Sight: red satin yoke, red and yellow ribbons sewed in a V or zigzags, wide leather belt, tiny white beads, running horses made of brown beads, blue skirt
- Sound: jingles that ring like little bells, drum music

Writing Tips

Students should approach writing-on-demand assignments differently from open-ended writing assignments. Such timed writing can create pressures. If, however, students know a few tips and are prepared, these pressures can be less troublesome.

Descriptive Prompt

To teach students who will take timed assessments how to approach their writing, allow them the same amount of time to write their response essay as they will be allotted on school, district, or state assessments. Break down each part of the process into clear chunks of time. For example:

- 15 minutes for note-taking and planning,
- 20 minutes for writing, and
- 10 minutes for editing and proofreading.

Start the assignment at the top of the hour or at the half-hour to make it easier for students to keep track of the time.

If your state, district, or school requires students to use and submit a graphic organizer as part of their assessment, provide a copy of one of the reproducible charts (TE pages 595–600) or refer students to SE pages 438–444.

Writing Tips

Before you write . . .

- Read the prompt carefully.
- Look for words that tell you what the prompt is asking you to do.
- Choose a topic you know well.
- Use a picture diagram to help you remember important details.

During your writing . . .

- Use key words from the prompt in your beginning paragraph.
- Be sure you write a clear beginning, middle, and ending.
- Include sensory details to describe your topic.

After you've written your first draft . . .

- Be sure your focus sentence clearly states your topic for the essay.
- Take time to correct mistakes in capitalization, punctuation, spelling, and grammar.

Descriptive Prompt

Is your favorite object a toy, a game, a picture, a football? It could be anything. Write an essay in which you describe your favorite object.

English Language Learners

Students may not understand what the prompt is asking them to do. Discuss the prompt by stressing key words that lead to their understanding such as *object, describe,* and *favorite.*

Have volunteers rephrase the prompt in their own words. Simplify the prompt by writing the following on the board: Describe your favorite object.

Advanced Learners

As a group, have students read through the writing tips and jot them down on separate index cards so they can shuffle the order. Challenge students to agree on the top five tips. Have them rank them in order from most important to least important, and have them justify their choices.

Descriptive Writing in Review

In descriptive writing, you use sensory details. Sensory details help your reader *see, feel, smell, taste,* and *hear* what you are writing about. These guidelines can help you.

Select a topic that interests you. (See page 54.)

Gather and organize sensory details about your topic. (See page 55.)

Write a focus sentence that introduces your topic. (See page 54.)

In the beginning part, introduce your topic in an interesting way. (See page 56.)

In the middle part, use sensory details to help the reader *see, hear, feel, smell,* and *taste* your topic. (See pages 55 and 58–59.)

In the ending part, share one final thought or feeling about your topic. (See pages 60–61.)

Review your essay for ideas and organization. Be sure you've included the right details. Make changes to improve your writing. (See pages 62–63.)

Check your writing for conventions and correct any errors you find. (See pages 64–65.)

Make a final copy. Proofread it again for errors. Share your final copy with classmates. (See page 66.)

Descriptive Writing in Review

Distribute sticky notes to students and have them flag SE page 71 so it will be easy to locate in their books whenever they have questions about the descriptive writing process. Encourage students to consult the page whenever they are working on a descriptive essay and need guidance. Also assure students that as they get more practice, the items on the page will become easier.

Narrative Writing Overview

Common Core Standards Focus

Writing 3: Write narratives to develop real or imagined experiences or events using effective technique, descriptive details, and clear event sequences.

Language 3a: Choose words and phrases for effect.

Writing Forms

- Writing a Narrative Paragraph
- Writing a Narrative Essay

Focus on the Traits

- Ideas Using strong ideas and details to help the reader connect with the experience described in the essay
- Organization Putting details in time order by using transition words
- Voice Creating a natural voice by writing as if telling the story to a friend
- Word Choice Choosing action verbs to make pictures for the reader to imagine
- Sentence Fluency Combining sentences to ensure a variety of sentence lengths
- Conventions Checking for errors in capitalization, punctuation, spelling, and grammar

Literature Connections

- ***Me and Uncle Romie*** by Claire Hartfield
- ***Destiny's Gift*** by Natasha Anastasia Tarpley

Technology Connections

Write Source Online
www.hmheducation.com/writesource

- ***Net-text***
- ***Bookshelf***
- ***GrammarSnap***
- ***Portfolio***
- ***Writing Network features***
- ***File Cabinet***

Interactive Whiteboard Lessons

Suggested Narrative Writing Unit (Four Weeks)

Week	Day	Writing and Skills Instruction	Student Edition: Narrative Writing Unit	Student Edition: Resource Units*	SkillsBook	Daily Language Workouts	Write Source Online
Week 1	1–4	**Narrative Paragraph: Something About Yourself** Literature Connections *Me and Uncle Romie* *Destiny's Gift*	74–79			18–19, 84	*Interactive Whiteboard Lessons*
		Skills Activities: • Verbs		383, 384, 538–539	133–134		*GrammarSnap*
		• Using the Right Word		510–511	67		
	opt.	*Giving Speeches*	344–349				
	5	**Narrative Essay: Someone Special** (Model)	80–83				
Week 2	6–7	(Prewriting)	84–85			20–21, 85	*Net-text*
	8–10	(Writing)	86–91				*Net-text*
Week 3	11	(Revising) **Working with Partners**	92–93 16–19			22–23, 86	*Net-text*
	12–13	(Revising) Organization	94–104 458–459				
		Skills Activities: • Verbs		383 (+), 538 (+)	143–144		*GrammarSnap*
		• Subject-Verb Agreement		406, 542–543	77–78, 145–146		*GrammarSnap*
		• Adjectives		389 (+), 546 (+)	154		*GrammarSnap*
		• Sentence Combining		408, 409	101–102, 103–104, 107–108		*GrammarSnap*
	14–15	(Editing) Literature Connections *Destiny's Gift*	105–107				*Net-text*
		Skills Activities: • Punctuating Dialogue		470–471, 476–477	17–18		
		• End Punctuation		397, 463–465	3–4, 7–8		*GrammarSnap*
Week 4	16	(Assessing, Publishing, Reflecting)	108–111			24–25, 87	*Portfolio, Net-text*
	opt.	*Giving Speeches*	344–349				
	17–18	**Narrative Writing Across the Curriculum**	112–119				
	19–20	**Narrative Writing for Assessment**	120–122				

* These units are also located in the back of the *Teacher's Edition*. Resource Units include "Basic Grammar and Writing," "A Writer's Resource," and "Proofreader's Guide."
(+) This activity is located in a different section of the *Write Source Student Edition*. If students have already completed this activity, you may wish to review it at this time.

Teacher's Notes for Narrative Writing

This overview for narrative writing includes some specific teaching suggestions for the unit.

Writing Focus

Writing a Narrative Paragraph (pages 74–79)

Writing personal narratives helps children establish an identity and gain self-confidence. All students have stories to tell. Have an informal sharing of "guess-what-happened" stories. To demonstrate what makes a story appealing, you may want to encourage stories about funny or unusual things that happened, and you may want to begin by sharing a story of your own.

Writing a Narrative Essay (pages 80–111)

Many experienced writers say that all writing begins with a narrative. The first stories, the most basic ones, come from an individual's own life. That is why it is so important, and so natural, to have your students write personal narratives throughout the school year. At first, your students will be most concerned with getting all their facts and details straight. Then, as they become more experienced, they will also share feelings related to their personal stories.

Grammar Focus

For support with this unit's grammar topics, consult the resource units (Basic Grammar and Writing, A Writer's Resource, and Proofreader's Guide).

Academic Vocabulary

Read aloud the academic terms, as well as the descriptions and questions. Model for students how to read one question and answer it. Have partners monitor their understanding and seek clarification of the terms by working through the meanings and questions together.

Minilessons

Great White Giant — Writing a Narrative Paragraph

- A narrative paragraph answers the question "Guess what happened?"
  - **READ** the narrative paragraph on SE page 75. Then **WRITE** two sentences that tell what happened. **SHARE** your sentences with a classmate.

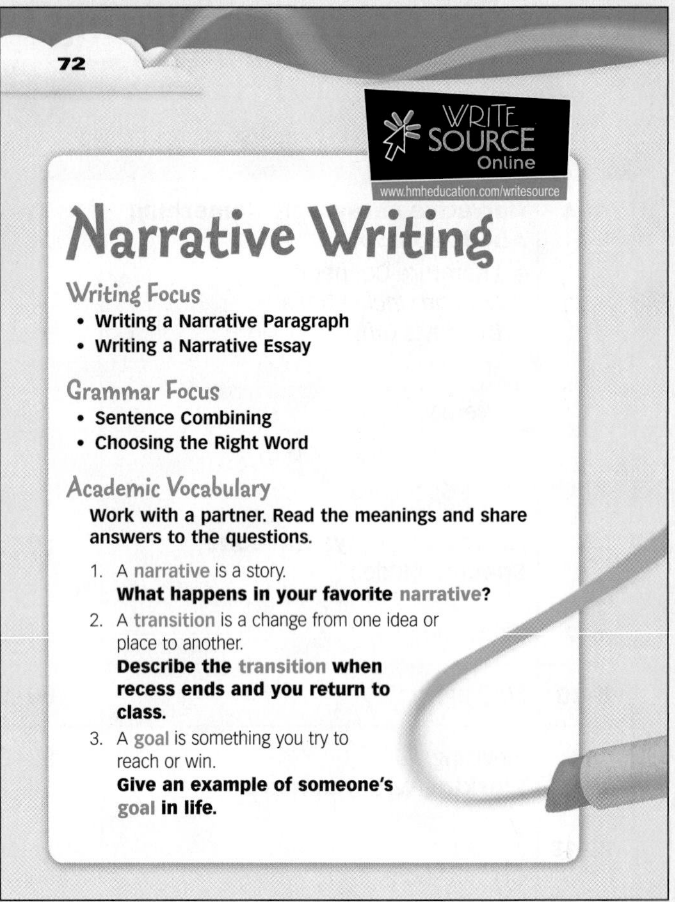

72
WRITE SOURCE Online
www.hmheducation.com/writesource
Narrative Writing
Writing Focus
• Writing a Narrative Paragraph
• Writing a Narrative Essay
Grammar Focus
• Sentence Combining
• Choosing the Right Word
Academic Vocabulary
Work with a partner. Read the meanings and share answers to the questions.
1. A narrative is a story.
What happens in your favorite narrative?
2. A transition is a change from one idea or place to another.
Describe the transition when recess ends and you return to class.
3. A goal is something you try to reach or win.
Give an example of someone's goal in life.

Happenings — Writing a Narrative Essay

- On a sheet of paper, **LIST** the following words: *happy, funny, proud, strange,* and *important.*
  - Under each word, **WRITE** one or two things that happened to you. (List happy experiences under the word "happy" and so on.) When you finish, **ASK** "Which of these happenings would my classmates be most interested in?" Then **ASK**, "Which of the interesting events do I remember the most about?" This final choice would probably make a good personal narrative.

Friendly Letters — Writing Across the Curriculum

- **WRITE** a friendly letter to someone on the staff of your school. You could write a friendly greeting to a teacher's aide, librarian, school secretary, or principal.
  - **USE** the proper form for a friendly letter on page 118 in your textbook.

"What did you do today?" Whenever you answer that question, you are creating a very short narrative. A narrative is simply a story about something that has happened.

Narratives come in all shapes and sizes. You can write a narrative in one sentence: "We went to the Milwaukee Art Museum and saw the ballerina sculptures." You can write a narrative in a paragraph, or a narrative that includes many paragraphs. This section will help you begin your adventures in narratives.

Literature Connections: For an example of a narrative, read *Me and Uncle Romie* by Claire Hartfield.

Narrative Writing

Explain to students that every time they read a story, they are reading a narrative. A **narrative** has a beginning, a middle, and an end. Tell students that sometimes the narrative writer makes up all or part of the story and that sometimes the writer tells a true story. Explain that the narratives that they will write in this unit will tell true stories about

- important events, experiences, and people in their own lives and
- important events in the life of another person.

Literature Connections

In the narrative *Me and Uncle Romie,* a boy named James shares about a summer he spent with his aunt and uncle in Harlem. After expressing initial hesitation about visiting the relatives he barely knows, James comes to enjoy the liveliness of the city and develops an appreciation for his uncle's talent as an artist.

Discuss reasons why this story is a good example of a narrative, including the fact that it is about an important experience in someone's life.

For additional models see the Reading-Writing Connections beginning on page TE-36.

Family Connection Letters

As you begin this unit, send home the Narrative Writing Family Connection letter, which describes what students will be learning.

- Letter in English (TE p. 603)
- Letter in Spanish (TE p. 611)

Teaching Tip

As you introduce the narrative form of writing, help students understand the specific purpose for writing—to tell a story. Then, discuss the concept of writing to an *audience*. Point out that whenever students write, they are writing for someone–themselves, teachers, friends, family members, and so on.

Writing a Narrative Paragraph

Objectives
- Select a personal experience to write about.
- Write a narrative paragraph.

Narrative paragraphs tell a story. They can be about a personal event or experience. They can be about another person. A narrative paragraph usually includes a topic sentence, body sentences, and a closing sentence.

* Refer to Building Paragraphs for more information. (See SE pages 416–429.)

Ask students what makes a story good enough for them to want to keep reading. List students' ideas on the board and add suggestions of your own. (Ideas may include action, excitement, colorful characters and language, suspense, humor.) Tell students to keep these ideas in mind as they read the sample writing in this unit and write their own narratives.

Explain to students that before they write their own narrative paragraphs, they will read Donica's paragraph and learn why it is a good narrative. Later, they will follow the same steps that Donica followed to write her paragraph.

Technology Connections

Use this unit's Interactive Whiteboard Lesson to introduce narrative writing.

Interactive Whiteboard Lessons

Writing a Narrative Paragraph

Donica was asked to write a few things about herself. Instead of just telling facts about herself, she wrote a narrative paragraph! In it, she told about an experience she had enjoyed.

In this unit, you will tell something about yourself in a narrative paragraph. Your paragraph will have three parts.

Paragraph Parts

1. The **topic sentence** tells the main idea of the paragraph.
2. The **body sentences** tell more about the main event or topic of your paragraph.
3. The **closing sentence** gives the reader something to think about.

Copy Masters

Time Line (TE p. 76)

Writing a Narrative Paragraph 75

Narrative Paragraph

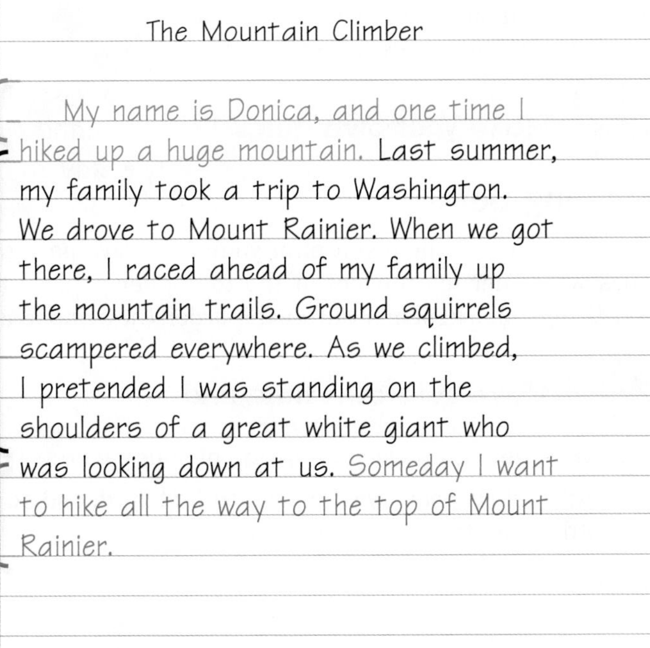

The Mountain Climber
1
My name is Donica, and one time I hiked up a huge mountain.
2
Last summer, my family took a trip to Washington. We drove to Mount Rainier. When we got there, I raced ahead of my family up the mountain trails. Ground squirrels scampered everywhere. As we climbed, I pretended I was standing on the shoulders of a great white giant who was looking down at us.
3
Someday I want to hike all the way to the top of Mount Rainier.

After you read . . .

Answer these questions about Donica's paragraph.

- **Ideas (1) What is the main idea or event of this paragraph?**
- **Organization (2) What part of the paragraph tells all about the main event?**
- **Word Choice (3) What words and phrases do you like best in the paragraph? Explain why.**

Narrative Paragraph

Review the basic parts of a paragraph by having students match each numbered section in the reading to the numbered paragraph parts on the bottom of SE page 74: topic sentence, body sentences, and closing sentence.

After you read . . .

Answers

Ideas 1. The paragraph is about Donica's hike up a huge mountain.

Organization 2. The middle, or body, sentences tell everything that Donica did and saw.

Word Choice 3. Possible answers: huge, raced, ground squirrels scampered, shoulders of a great white giant. These words help the reader picture Donica on her hike. It is like being there with her.

After students respond to the reading, discuss Donica's use of clue words to show when things happened. This will help students understand organization and prepare them for creating their time lines on SE page 76.

- Last summer
- When we got there
- As we climbed

Prewriting Finding an Idea

After students complete their quick list, tell them to **select the topic** *(see below)* they think would make the best story.

Prewriting Gathering Details

Provide photocopies of the reproducible Time Line (TE page 598) for gathering details. To ensure accurate time lines, have students first describe the event orally to a partner, using time-order transitions such as, "First, we did this. Next, we did this. Then this happened." As they list each new detail, they can jot it down on their time line.

* As students write about their event, encourage them to use transitions that show time order (SE page 458).

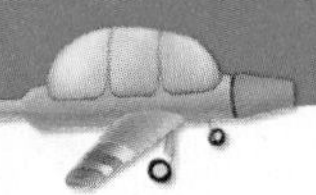

Prewriting Finding an Idea

You will be writing a paragraph about something you once did. Donica made a quick list of things she enjoyed doing.

Quick List

- *growing tomatoes*
- *Mt. Rainier trip*
- *piano recital*
- *day at water park*

Make your own quick list.

Gathering Details

A time line can help you plan your narrative paragraph. Donica wrote her main event at the top of her paper. Then she listed things she remembered in the order they happened.

Make your own time line.

1. **Write your main event at the top of your paper.**
2. **Add details about what happened first, next, and so on. Add other things you remember.**

Time Line

Hiked up a huge mountain
driving to Washington
going to Mt. Rainier
hiking up trails with family
seeing squirrels
pretending to be standing
on a giant

Teaching Tip: Selecting a Topic

Students will benefit by watching you model how to select the best topic from a list of ideas.

Write your own quick list of four events on the board. Then read aloud each idea you listed and ask these questions about it:

- Was this event really special or important to me?
- Do I remember this event well enough to describe it clearly for my readers?
- Will I be able to write at least three interesting details about the event?

If you answer "no" to any of the questions, cross out the topic. Star the topic that you know the most about and that you think will make the best story. Be sure to explain each step as you go along.

English Language Learners

Some students focus so much on getting the correct *order* of events that they forget to include *all* events. Have students generate their ideas and write them down on paper, skipping lines between ideas. Then have them cut out their ideas, order them correctly, and paste them onto another sheet of paper.

Writing a Narrative Paragraph 77

Writing Beginning Your First Draft

Each part of your narrative paragraph has a special job to do.

- Your **topic sentence** names the topic (you) and tells what event you will talk about.
- The **body sentences** tell interesting details about the event.
- Your **closing sentence** leaves your reader with a final thought about the topic.

Begin your paragraph.

1. **First write your topic sentence.**
   "My name is ___________, and I ______(event)______."
2. **Then write at least three body sentences that tell some interesting details about your event.**
3. **Write a closing sentence that leaves the reader with a final thought about the topic.**

First Draft

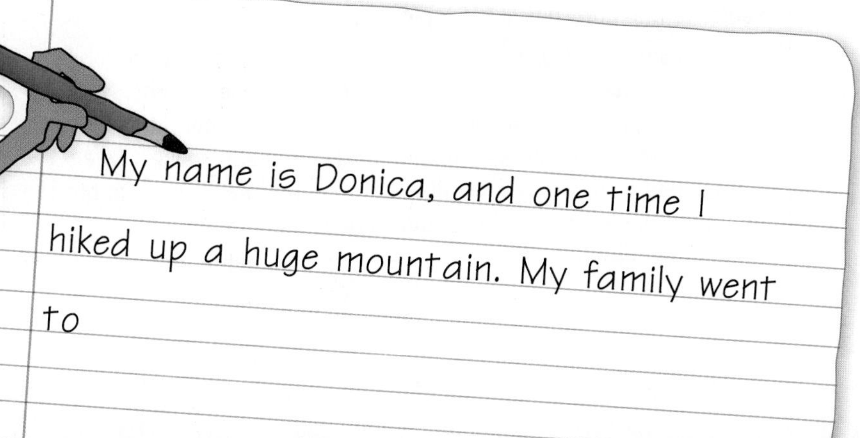

My name is Donica, and one time I
hiked up a huge mountain. My family went
to

Writing Beginning Your First Draft

Remind students to refer to the details in their time line as they write their first draft. Tell them not to worry about making their draft perfect because they will have the chance to revise and edit it later.

Instruct students working on a computer to double-space their draft and those writing by hand to write on every other line. Tell them that this will give them space to write in their changes when they revise and edit.

The sentence frame for the topic sentence will get students started, and the completed time line should ensure that students can write body sentences. Students may need, however, additional guidance with writing a solid **closing sentence** *(see below).*

Writer's Craft

Writing freely: Encourage your students to relax and write. Sometimes students get blocked because they don't know what to write about, but if students have done their prewriting, they'll have plenty of ideas. Other times, students get blocked because they want everything to be perfect from the start. Assure them that they'll be revising and editing to make everything perfect. Right now, they should just relax and write.

Teaching Tip: Closing Sentences

Most students will benefit from a refresher on how to write a good closing sentence. Use one or all of the following ideas to help them.

- Remind students that a good closing sentence makes a paragraph complete and satisfying for readers.
- Discuss different ways to write a closing sentence. See items 1 and 2 on SE page 419 for ideas that apply here.
- Create a sentence frame modeled on Donica's closing sentence on SE page 75 for students to use. (Someday, I want to _______.)
- Have students read their paragraph in a group. Group members can suggest good closing sentences for the writer to use.

Revising Improving Your Paragraph

Revising is the most difficult step in the writing process for students to apply correctly and completely. This is partly because they do not have enough experience to recognize how to make their writing better and partly because they feel pressured to complete an assignment in a set amount of time. The prewriting step should ensure that students have a workable topic with sufficient and strong details so that they can compose solid drafts. If, however, during revising, students feel that a piece of writing is not working, let them know that they can ask for additional time to start over.

Practice Answers

These two sentences don't belong:

- My uncle is a senior in high school.
- For lunch, we had sub sandwiches and shakes.

Have a volunteer reread the paragraph without the sentences that don't belong.

Revising Improving Your Paragraph

Now it's time for you to revise your paragraph. Remember that all of your body sentences should include interesting details about your topic. If they don't, you can add some now.

Revise Check your details.

Ask yourself the following questions about your paragraph.

1. **Does each body sentence include an interesting detail about my topic?**
2. **Are there any sentences that do not tell about my topic?** (If you find a sentence that doesn't fit, cross it out.)
3. **Are my sentences in the order that the event happened?** (If not, move your sentences around.)
4. **Does my paragraph have at least three body sentences?** (If it doesn't, add details in one or two new sentences.)

Practice

Read Cody's paragraph below. Write the first two words for each sentence that does not fit his topic. (There are two.)

My name is Cody, and I like race cars. Last year, my uncle took me down to the Indianapolis Speedway Hall of Fame. My uncle is a senior in high school. We walked for miles and saw more than 50 famous cars. For lunch, we had sub sandwiches and shakes. Later, we watched a movie that told all about the speedway. When I'm out of high school, I want to go to an Indianapolis 500 race.

English Language Learners

Many students with a limited English vocabulary become visual learners. Have students check for details by first reading their paragraph and highlighting or circling the details. Then have students refer to their highlighting as they follow the four **Check Your Details** steps.

Struggling Learners

Some students may have difficulty recognizing the two sentences in the **Practice** that do not fit the topic. Point out that these details are not interesting or important to Cody's story because they don't add anything about the Speedway Hall of Fame or Cody's feelings about it.

Advanced Learners

Challenge students to add vivid details to their paragraphs similar to Donica's "great white giant" comparison on SE page 75. Have them choose a place or an event and use a cluster map to fill in sensory details that describe it. Then have them use one or more details to compare the object to something similar.

Editing Checking for Conventions

When you've finished revising, you are ready to edit. Be sure you have used the right words. Words like *to, two,* and *too* are easy to confuse because they sound the same.

A computer's spell-checker won't point out a word that is spelled correctly when it is the wrong word for your sentence. It is important that you check these words yourself.

Frank has two brothers.	*Two* means the numeral "2."
I have two brothers, too.	*Too* means "also."
We all walk to the park together.	*To* means "toward."

Edit: Check your work.

1. **Did I indent the first line of the paragraph?**
2. **Did I start each sentence with a capital letter?**
3. **Did I punctuate the end of each sentence?**
4. **Have I used the right words, like *their, they're,* and *there*?** (See pages 510–522 for tips on using the right word.)

Practice

Change the incorrect word or words in each sentence below.

1. I was born right hear in California.
2. I road my bike in the holiday parade.
3. I like to swim, to.
4. At the science fare, I one a blue ribbon.
5. Every summer, I visit my grandma for a hole week.

Editing Checking for Conventions

Point out to students that a computer's spell checker cannot find mistakes in homophones—words that sound alike but are spelled differently, such as *pair, pare,* and *pear.* It also cannot find mistakes when typing errors actually create real words, such as *hem* for *her* or *form* for *from.* Have students working on a computer print out a copy of their revised draft and edit on the hard copy.

Practice Answers

1. here (not hear)
2. rode (not road)
3. too (not to)
4. fair (not fare); won (not one)
5. whole (not hole)

English Language Learners

Students may need help catching errors related to homophones because they often rely on hearing words in conversation for understanding. Have students write homophone word pairs on index cards, along with simple definitions or illustrations. They can refer to their index cards if necessary when they edit their writing.

Advanced Learners

Have students work together to develop mnemonic devices, symbols, or pictures to help writers learn the different spellings and meanings of homophones. For example, you "hear" with your "ear." Post their creations in a learning center or on a bulletin board for the class to use.

Grammar Connection

Verbs

- **Proofreader's Guide** pages 538–539
- ***Write Source*** pages 383, 384
- ***GrammarSnap*** Action Verbs
- ***SkillsBook*** pages 133–134

Using the Right Word

- **Proofreader's Guide** pages 510–511
- ***SkillsBook*** page 67

Writing a Narrative Essay

Objectives

- Choose a helpful person to write about.
- Plan, draft, revise, and edit a narrative essay telling about how the person helped the writer.

A **narrative essay** is a story that tells about a person, an event, or an experience in an interesting way. A personal narrative is a story that tells about a person, an event, or an experience in your own life. It might tell

- what you did,
- what happened to you, or
- how you felt.

Focus attention on the categories of people mentioned in the first paragraph (family members, friends, teachers, and community members). Ask students to jot down the name of at least one person from each group who helped them to do or accomplish something that really mattered to them. Provide examples from your own life to spark students' memories. Point out to students that they might want to write their essay about one of these people.

Writing a Narrative Essay

Helpful people are all around us! They can be family members, friends, teachers, and even community people, like police officers and firefighters.

Cara decided to write a narrative essay about Mrs. Rios, a person who helped her in first grade. You will read Cara's essay and learn to write one of your own.

Materials

Blank overhead transparency (TE p. 85)

Sticky notes (TE p. 93)

Copy Masters

Time Line (TE p. 84)

Response Sheet (TE p. 93)

T-Chart (TE p. 94)

Sensory Chart (TE p. 94)

Thinking About Your Writing (TE p. 111)

Writing a Narrative Essay 81

Understanding Your Goal

Your goal in this chapter is to write a personal narrative about someone who has helped you. The six traits below and the narrative revising lessons (pages 92–104) will help you reach your goal.

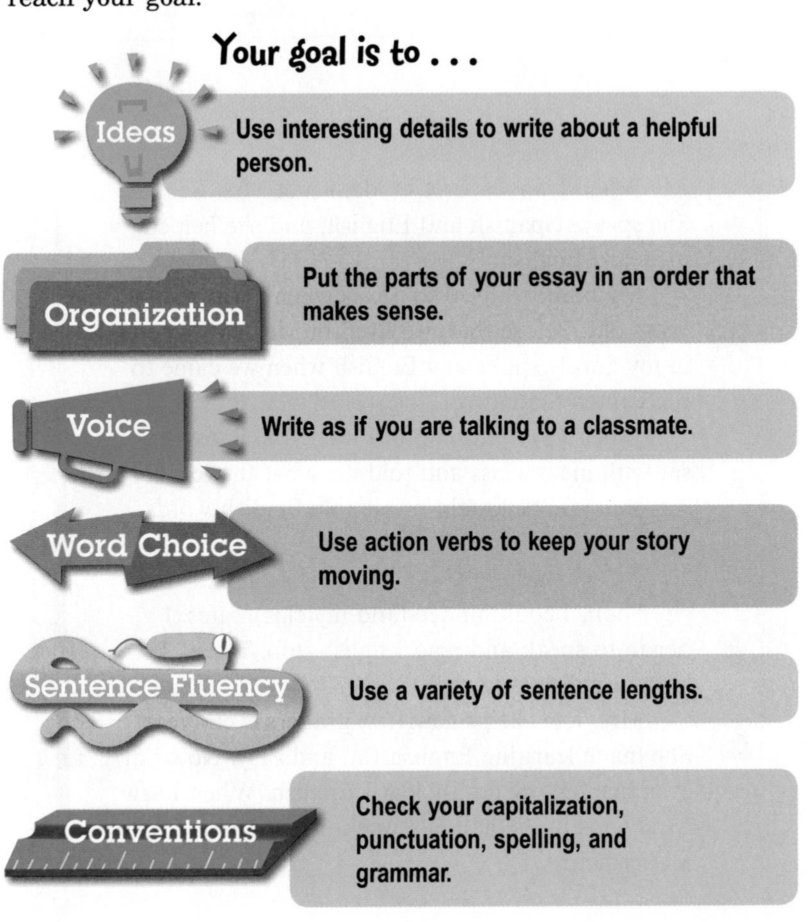

Your goal is to . . .
Ideas
Use interesting details to write about a helpful person.
Organization
Put the parts of your essay in an order that makes sense.
Voice
Write as if you are talking to a classmate.
Word Choice
Use action verbs to keep your story moving.
Sentence Fluency
Use a variety of sentence lengths.
Conventions
Check your capitalization, punctuation, spelling, and grammar.

Understanding Your Goal

Encourage students to use this page as a guide for understanding how the traits can help them write their narrative essay. Suggest that they bookmark this page so that they can flip back to it any time they need a reminder of their goals as they plan and write their essay. Reassure students that they will receive plenty of guidance throughout the writing process so that they can successfully achieve these goals.

Depending on the needs of your class, focus on one or two of the traits throughout the revising process. The revising section (SE pages 92–104) provides additional instruction and practice for each trait. The side notes and Teaching Tips throughout this section of the TE also provide suggestions to supplement the instruction and the practices.

English Language Learners

In many first languages, the manner in which a child's peers and adults are addressed is very different. A casual voice is often used with peers, while a formal voice is used when speaking to adults. Point out these differences in English and discuss which would most likely be used when talking to a classmate.

- How do you do? (formal)
- Hi! (informal)
- Who are you? (informal)
- To whom am I speaking? (formal)
- I'm sorry. (informal)
- Please accept my apology. (formal)

Narrative Essay

Work through this sample essay with the class, pointing out the elements that make it a good personal narrative essay.

Ideas

- The topic sentence names the helpful person.
- The second paragraph captures the readers' interest by telling a little story about the helpful person.

Organization

- The beginning clearly tells what the helpful person did to help the writer.
- Each middle paragraph gives details that show how the person helped and why the person is important to the writer.
- The ending shares the writer's final thoughts and feelings about the person.

Word Choice

- The writer uses specific words that suit the topic.
- The words make the helpful person seem real to the reader.

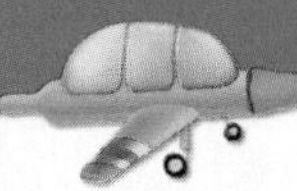

Narrative Essay

A personal narrative tells a true story about you. This narrative tells about an important helper in Cara's life.

Mrs. Rios

When I was in first grade, I met Mrs. Rios. She speaks Spanish and English, and she helped me learn English.

My family moved to Texas when I was five years old. Before that, we lived in Mexico. No one in my family spoke any English when we came to the United States.

When I started school, I met Mrs. Rios. She sat with me in class and told me what the teacher was saying. She taught me simple English words. She was always there to help me.

"You can do it, Cara," Mrs. Rios said.

Soon, I could understand my classmates. I began to speak and read English, too. Today, I know English very well.

Mrs. Rios helps new first graders every year. She made learning English fun and easy. Now I'm even helping my family learn English. When I saw Mrs. Rios in the hall last week, I thanked her for all her help.

Parts of a Personal Narrative

A narrative essay has three parts.

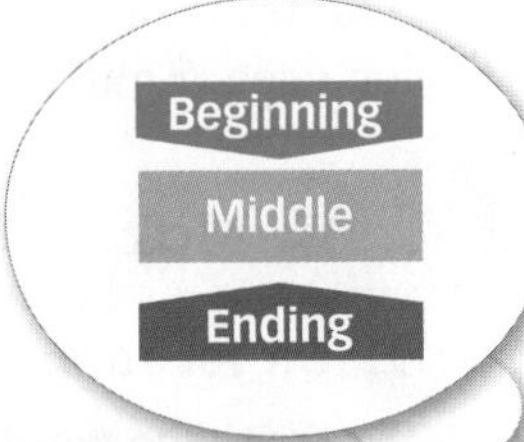

Beginning

The beginning paragraph names your topic and makes the reader want to keep reading.

Middle

The middle paragraphs tell more about the topic. They include details that make the story sound real.

Ending

The ending paragraph wraps things up. It tells how you felt and what was important to you.

After you read . . .

- Ideas (1) What is the topic (or focus) of the essay?
- Organization (2) How does Cara organize her narrative in a way that makes sense?
- Word Choice (3) What words and phrases make Mrs. Rios seem real to the reader?

Parts of a Personal Narrative

Focus on the middle paragraphs, in which the writer provides details that show why what the helpful person did was so important. Explain that if the writer doesn't include these kinds of details, then readers aren't going to care about the writer's experience or the helpful person.

- Point out the details in the first middle paragraph that explain why Cara needed to learn English.
- Point out the details in the other middle paragraphs that tell exactly how Mrs. Rios helped Cara.

After you read . . .

Answers

Ideas **1.** The topic of the essay is Mrs. Rios, who helped the writer learn English.

Organization **2.** Cara uses time order.

Word Choice **3.** Possible answers: sat with me in class, always there to help, "You can do it, Cara."

Struggling Learners

Students may need help making a story sound real. Tell them that natural-sounding dialogue is one way to bring a story to life. Point out that the dialogue in Cara's essay sounds like something a teacher would say. Have students practice writing a sentence or two of dialogue based on something a family member or friend said to them.

Prewriting Selecting a Topic

If students listed names at the beginning of this section (see TE page 80), they can write these names in their gathering wheel.

Otherwise, work with students to generate a list of categories that will help them think of helpful people. Categories may include family members, teachers and instructors, friends, neighbors, coaches, and community workers (for example, police officers, firefighters, crossing guards, doctors, and nurses).

After students have completed their gathering wheel and starred their topic, have them organize details for their narrative in a time line. Provide photocopies of the reproducible Time Line (TE page 598). Students can use the sample time line on SE page 85 as a model for writing complete but short detail sentences.

* For another example of a time line, refer students to SE page 439.

Technology Connections

Students can use the added features of the Net-text as they explore this stage of the writing process.

Write Source Online ***Net-text***

Prewriting Selecting a Topic

The topic of your essay will be a person who has helped you. Taylor used a gathering wheel to list the names of his helpers.

Make a gathering wheel.

1. **On your own paper, make a wheel like the one below.**
2. **Write the words "Helpful People" in the center of the wheel.**
3. **In the spaces around the center, write the names of people who have helped you.**
4. **Put a star (*) next to the person you want to write about.**

Gathering Wheel

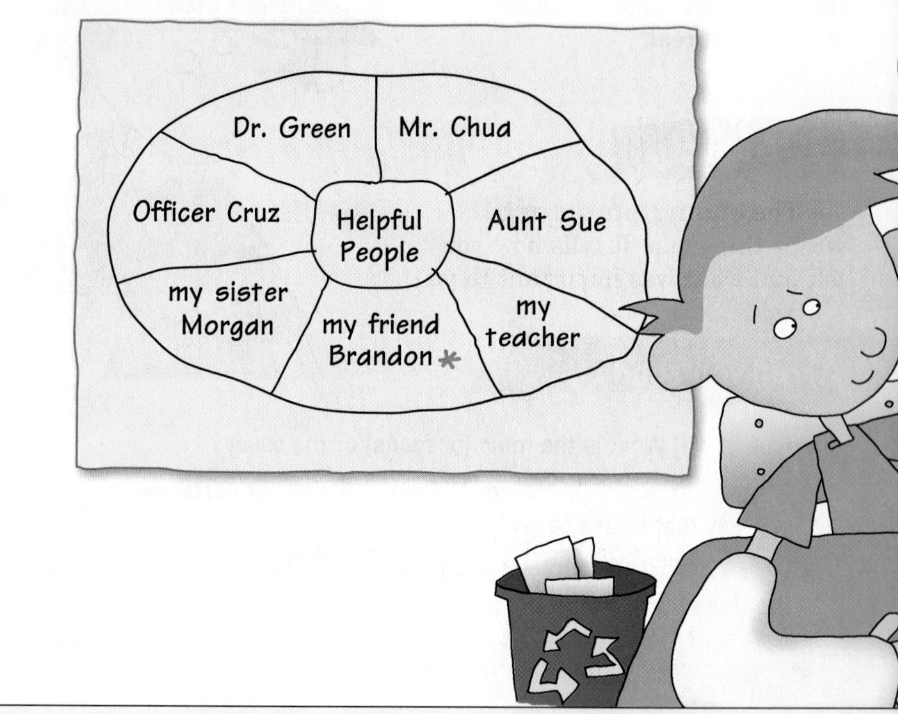

Putting Your Details in Order

Narratives are organized by time. First, one event happens, then the next event, and so on. Using a time line can help you put your events in order. You can see the time line Taylor created below.

Make a time line.

1. Draw an arrow going down the left side of your paper.
2. Next to the arrow, write a few words about the times when your helper helped you.
3. Make sure to write down the events in the right order.

Time Line

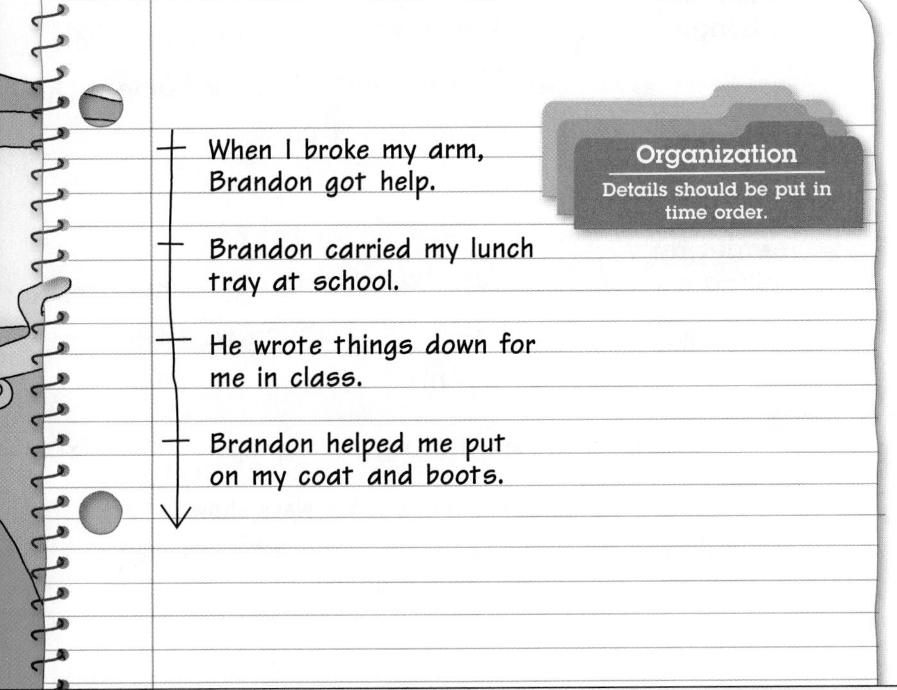

When I broke my arm, Brandon got help.
Brandon carried my lunch tray at school.
He wrote things down for me in class.
Brandon helped me put on my coat and boots.
Organization
Details should be put in time order.

English Language Learners

Because clustering may be especially helpful to students with a limited English vocabulary, be sure to provide extra practice. Create a model gathering wheel on the board or use a blank transparency on the overhead projector while students draw their own cluster on paper. For the subject, use a "helpful person" (neighbor, librarian, mail carrier, grocer, etc.) suggested by one of the students.

Putting Your Details in Order

Point out that students don't need to draw a perfect circle for their gathering wheel. Use Taylor's sample gathering wheel to show that a gathering wheel does not have to be drawn perfectly. Reinforce that the purpose of the gathering wheel is to give students a chance to list all the names that come into their minds so they might select the best topic.

Before going on to the writing step, check each time line to make sure that students have gathered enough details and arranged them in the correct time order.

Writing Beginning Your Essay

After reviewing Taylor's possible beginnings, encourage students to try all three ways—Ask, Begin, and Connect—before choosing the way to begin their essay.

Make sure students understand why a focus sentence is important (see SE page 418).

Literature Connections

Mentor texts: Model strong beginnings by reading to students from familiar books, such as *Woodsong* by Gary Paulsen or *Sing Down the Moon* by Scott O'Dell. Ask, "How did the writer get your attention at the beginning? What do you like best about this beginning? How could you begin your writing in a similar way?"

Technology Connections

Students can use the added features of the Net-text as they explore this stage of the writing process.

 *Write Source Online* ***Net-text***

Writing Beginning Your Essay

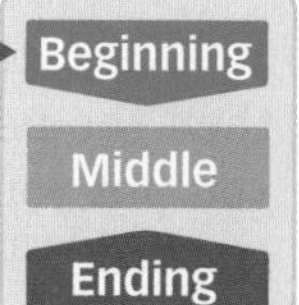

Your beginning paragraph introduces the topic (your helper). Here are three ways to begin the first paragraph of your essay.

Ask a question.

Have you ever had a terrible day? On my terrible day, I hurt my arm. Luckily, Brandon was with me.

OR

Begin with someone talking.

"Don't worry. I will help you." That's what my friend Brandon told me when I came home with my arm in a cast.

OR

Connect with the reader by telling a little story.

One day, I fell off my skateboard, and I hurt my arm. My friend Brandon was there to help me.

Create your beginning paragraph.

1. Introduce your topic using one of the ways shown above.
2. At the end of your first paragraph, write a focus sentence that tells how you feel about your helper.

Struggling Learners

Direct students' attention to the first method for beginning a paragraph, *Ask*. Point out that asking a question can be an effective way to begin a narrative because it uses the word *you*. Using *you* invites readers to connect the topic to their own experiences. If students need help with "you" questions, offer the following essay starters:

- Have you ever . . .
- Do you have . . .
- When have you . . .

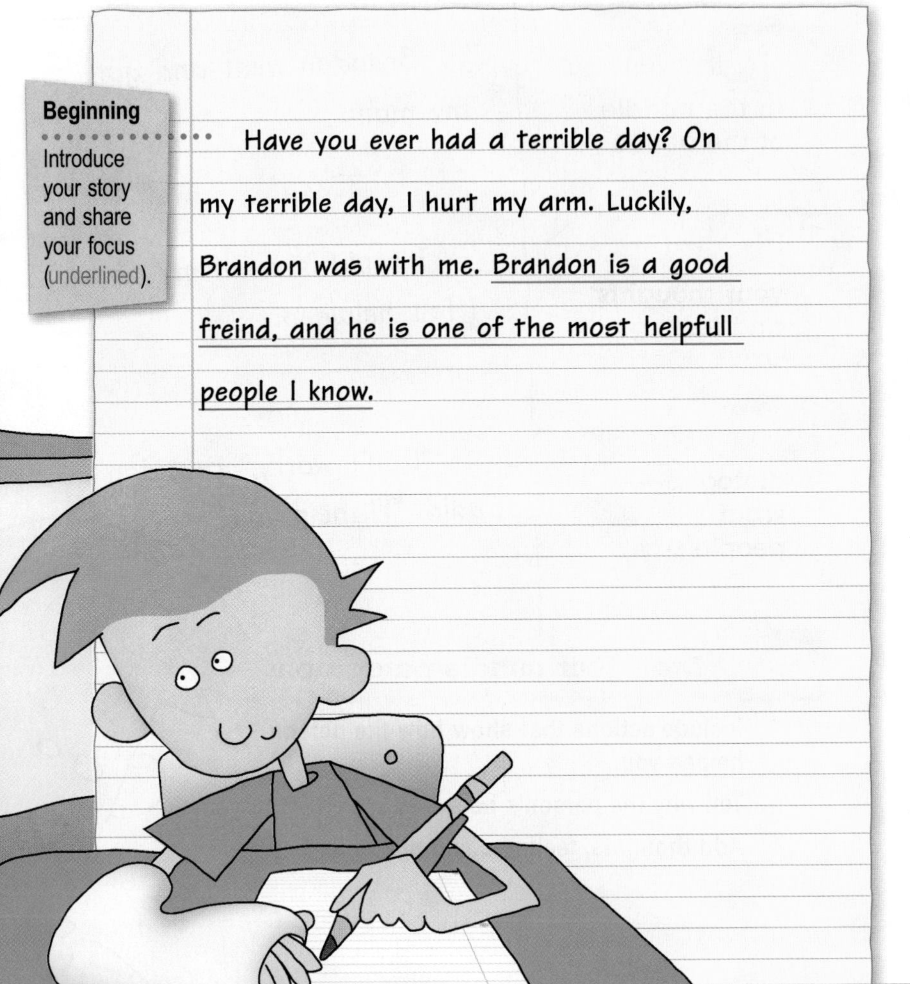

Writing a Narrative Essay 87
Taylor's Beginning Paragraph
Taylor began his narrative essay by asking a question. In his first draft, he just wanted to get his ideas down on paper. He didn't worry about errors.
Beginning
Introduce your story and share your focus (underlined).
Have you ever had a terrible day? On my terrible day, I hurt my arm. Luckily, Brandon was with me. Brandon is a good freind, and he is one of the most helpfull people I know.

Taylor's Beginning Paragraph

Point out why Taylor's beginning paragraph works well.

- It tells how Taylor feels about Brandon. (He's a good friend and one of the most helpful people he knows.)
- It reminds Taylor to include only details that show how he feels about Brandon.
- It tells readers that in the rest of the essay, Taylor is going to show why he feels this way about Brandon.

Provide strategies to help students write their focus sentence. One strategy would be to have them complete a sentence frame modeled on the sample focus sentence: _______ is a good _______, and (he or she) is one of the most helpful people I know.

Another strategy is to have them answer questions about the person.

- How do you feel about this person?
- What word best describes this person?

Students can use their answers to create their focus sentence. Suggest that students underline or highlight their focus sentence to show what is most important.

English Language Learners

Some students may be so concerned about neatness, the accuracy of word choice, or trying to remember the rules of English, that they are not able to focus on the message. Remind them that they do not need to worry about recalling every word in English in their first draft because they will have time to make changes when they revise and edit their writing.

Writing Developing the Middle

Telling students to use plenty of details can lead to essays with too many or extraneous details. Encourage students to read their middle paragraphs aloud as they draft them. This is a good way for them to find details that are unnecessary or out of order.

* For information about organizing paragraphs using time order, see SE pages 422–423.

Before asking students to draft their middle paragraphs, have them examine Taylor's middle paragraphs to see how he

- uses actions and details to show how Brandon helped,
- tells why Brandon's help was important to him, and
- adds thoughts, feelings, and **dialogue** *(see below)* to expand the ideas that he listed in his time line on SE page 85.

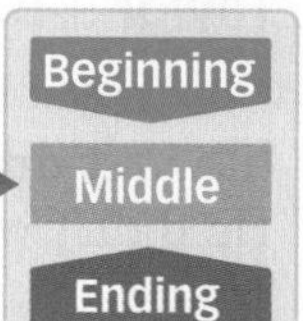

Writing Developing the Middle

Beginning
▶ Middle
Ending

In the middle part of your essay, you show how the person helped you and why that help was important. Use your *time line* from page 85 and include plenty of details.

Start in the middle of the action.

Brandon went and got my mom.

Share your thoughts and feelings.

I couldn't bend my elbow. I felt helpless.

Add dialogue—what people say.

"Don't worry," Brandon said. "I'll help you."

Draft your middle paragraphs.

1. Include actions that show how the person helped you.
2. Tell why the person's help was important to you.
3. Add thoughts, feelings, and dialogue.

Teaching Tip: Writing Dialogue

Dialogue enriches students' stories and helps create a natural narrative voice that makes the stories real and believable. Most students will benefit from a review of the conventions of writing dialogue.

Point out the quotation marks that surround Brandon's words on this page. Explain that these marks show the exact words of the person speaking.

Point out the comma before the speaker tag. Explain that the comma always goes inside the quotation marks when the name comes after the speaker's words.

* For more instruction and practice punctuating dialogue, have students turn to SE pages 476–477.

Writing a Narrative Essay 89

Taylor's Middle Paragraphs

Here are Taylor's middle paragraphs. He continues to tell what happened and adds details that show how Brandon helped him.

freind, and he is one of the the most helpfull people I know.

Middle

Use actions and details.

One Saturday, Brandon and I was skateboarding. I fell. I got hurt. Brandon went and got my mom. I came back from the hospital with a plaster cast on my write arm. that's the arm I use the most. I couldn't bend my elbow. I felt helpless.

Share thoughts and feelings.

"Don't worry about it," Brandon said. "I'll help you.

Tell what someone said (dialogue).

At school, he carried my lunch tray. We had pizza. Whenever there was something I couldn't do, Brandon was there to help me. Brandon wrote things down for me. He even helped me put on my coat and boots.

Taylor's Middle Paragraphs

Remind students that this is their story. The words, phrases, and sentences should sound natural, as if they are telling the story to a friend. This will make it real for readers. Ask students to point out words and phrases in Taylor's middle paragraphs that sound natural and real. (Possible choices include: *went and got my mom, felt helpless, Don't worry about it,* and *was there to help.*)

* For more information about writing in a narrative voice, see SE page 446.

English Language Learners

Students with limited vocabulary skills who are concerned about correct wording can try adding detail words on their time line first. Then have them use their time lines to develop their middle paragraphs. Point out that they can still make changes and corrections during the revising and editing stages.

Advanced Learners

In Taylor's paragraphs, have students replace the last sentence of the first paragraph with dialogue in order to express why Taylor feels helpless. Allow time for students to share their dialogues. Encourage them to use appropriate pitch, tone, and expression as they read aloud.

Writing Ending Your Essay

To provide an example of how ideas from earlier paragraphs can be restated, have students turn back to Taylor's beginning paragraph on SE page 87 and his middle paragraphs on SE page 89.

- Point out the use of the word *terrible* in the beginning paragraph and in the full ending paragraph on SE page 91.
- Point out the details in the middle paragraphs that express Taylor's frustration (I felt helpless . . .) and that show what Brandon did to help. Explain that the second and third sentences in the ending sum up all these ideas but in a shorter way.

After students decide on an ending and finish their first draft, have them review their time line (SE page 85) to make sure they have included all the important details they planned to include. If they have left any details out, they can circle them on their time line and, if necessary to the narrative, add them in when they revise.

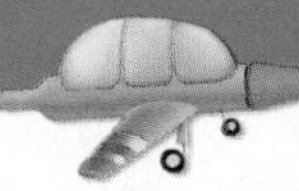

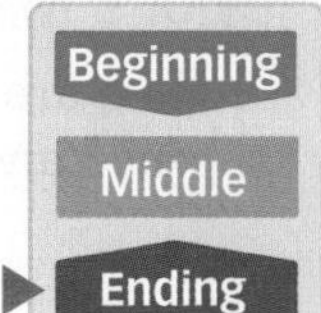

Writing Ending Your Essay

In your ending paragraph, you tell why the person's help was important to you. Here are some ideas for ending your essay.

Restate why the person's help was important.

Without Brandon's help, I don't know what I would've done.

OR

Share your feelings about the person.

I'll never forget what Brandon did for me.

OR

Talk with your reader.

Have you ever needed help? That's when you know how great it is to have a friend to help you.

Complete your ending paragraph.

1. Use one or more of the ways above to write an interesting ending.
2. Try one of your own. Use the ending you like best.

Taylor's Ending Paragraph

Here is Taylor's final paragraph. He told why the help was important and shared his feelings about Brandon.

me helped me put on my coat and boots.
Ending
The writer combines two ways of ending the essay.
The day I broke my arm was terrible, but I had a great helper. Now my arm is okay. I'll never forget what Brandon did for me.

Advanced Learners

Have students write words that describe emotions—such as *serious, funny, heartbreaking, happy,* and *nervous*—on slips of paper. Have pairs choose a slip of paper and rewrite Taylor's ending in a way that reflects the emotion they chose. Have students read their endings to the class.

Taylor's Ending Paragraph

Have students examine Taylor's ending paragraph to see how he combined restating and sharing.

Suggest students try to combine two of the three types of ending paragraphs the way Taylor did and create an alternative ending to their essay. Then they can choose the best ending for their essay.

Revising Improving Your Essay

If possible, have students set their writing aside for a day before revising so they can look at it with fresh eyes.

Before students revise, review the use of proofreading marks if necessary, as shown in the sample and on the inside back cover. (See the copy master on TE page 594.)

Begin the revision process by having students read and respond to each other's writing. For an oral review, have writers use the questions on this page to get responses from their partners. For a more in-depth response, have partners complete a response sheet like that on the facing page.

Once students have identified the strengths and weaknesses in their writing, assign them specific trait-based strategies from the revision pages that follow. Assign strategies based upon either the weaknesses discovered in the peer response or the trait(s) you are emphasizing.

Technology Connections

Have students use the Writing Network features of the Net-text to comment on each other's drafts.

Revising Improving Your Essay

When you finish your first draft, you are ready to make changes to improve your writing. Begin the revising part of the writing process by reading your narrative to yourself.

Then read your essay out loud to a partner. You may ask your partner the following questions that are based on your writing goals (see page 81).

Ideas

- Did I use interesting ideas to write about a helpful person?

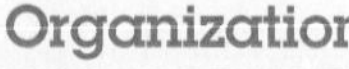

Organization

- Did I put the parts of my essay in an order that makes sense?

Voice

- Did I write as if I am talking to a classmate?

Word Choice

- Did I use action verbs to keep my story going?

Sentence Fluency

- Did I use a variety of sentence lengths?

Writing a Narrative Essay 93

Getting a Partner's Response

Here is another way a partner can help you decide how to improve your writing. This is a partner's response to Taylor's essay (pages 87–91).

Response Sheet

Writer: Taylor Responder: Antonio

Title: Skateboard Emergency 9–1–1

What I like:

I was happy Brandon went to get your mom.

That detail shows how Brandon helped you.

I liked it when Brandon said, "Don't worry."

Questions I have:

Was the cast heavy?

How did your arm feel?

Be sure to ask a classmate to read your work and fill out a response sheet.

Getting a Partner's Response

Provide photocopies of the reproducible Response Sheet (TE page 592) for students to use here. Before having students fill out the Response Sheets, discuss the sample Response Sheet.

- What I like: Point out that these comments help the writer decide what details in the essay work well.
- Questions I have: Point out that these questions help the writer think about details that he or she might want to add while revising to improve the sense and sound of the essay.

Emphasize that the comments on a Response Sheet give the writer something to think about. In the end, however, it's up to the writer to decide what revisions to make.

Divide students into pairs and have them take turns reading aloud their narratives to each other. After listening and rereading the essays, have partners fill out a Response Sheet. If necessary, review the guidelines for reviewing a piece of writing with partners (SE page 18).

English Language Learners

Schedule individual conferences for addressing response sheets. After reading through your completed Response Sheet, have students answer your questions on sticky notes. Help them locate the places in their writing where the new text belongs so they can attach their sticky notes.

Struggling Learners

Explain that feedback is most helpful when it is specific. Direct students' attention to Antonio's comments on his Response Sheet. Note that Antonio

- singles out one precise event and ties it to the focus sentence, and
- reacts to a particular line of dialogue in the story.

Revising for Ideas

Before asking students to fill in a T-chart on their own, discuss the parts of the sample T-chart, including the headings and lists of details. Point out that each detail completes the thought expressed at the top of that column.

- I want the reader to see . . . *people waving their arms.*
- I want the reader to feel . . . *the chugging, slow start.*

Draw a T-chart on the board to model how to fill out a T-chart for a personal narrative essay. Use a topic of your choice, or ask a volunteer to provide a topic. Then work together to fill in the chart with details.

Provide photocopies of the reproducible T-Chart (TE page 595) for students to fill in. As they check their essay, if they decide they need to add details to make their ideas stronger, they can choose details from their completed chart.

Revising for Ideas

Strong ideas and details will help the reader connect with your experience.

Q. How can I connect with my reader?

You can connect by helping your reader to see and feel what you experienced. Use a T-chart like the one below to collect these kinds of details for your reader.

See . . .	Feel . . .
people waving their arms	chugging, slow start
hair flying everywhere	scary drops and loops
the giant roller coaster	shaking side to side
red and yellow cars	wind and speed

Practice

Make a T-chart like the one above. Fill it in with details about what you want your reader to see and feel when reading your essay.

English Language Learners

Students may find too much information to deal with in the **Partner's Response** section on SE page 93. Individualize the task by selecting only one trait from pages 94–103 for each student to focus on during the revising process.

Further modifications can be made by doing the following:

- simplifying what each student must do
- pairing students with language-proficient partners
- focusing on only one part of the writing assignment

Advanced Learners

Extend the **Practice** activity by having students add what they want the reader to hear and smell. Distribute copies of the reproducible Sensory Chart (TE page 596) and have students write details related to each sense.

Writing a Narrative Essay 95

Revising in Action

Here are some of the changes Taylor made to improve the ideas in a middle paragraph in his first draft. He added a detail to one sentence and specific details to another sentence.

One Saturday, Brandon and I was skateboarding. I fell. I got hurt. Brandon went and got my mom. I came back from the hospital with a ^heavy plaster cast on my write arm. That's the arm I use the most. ^my arm felt hot and itchy, and I couldn't bend my elbow. I felt helpless.

Check your ideas.

1. Read your work carefully.
2. Find places to add details that connect with your reader.
   - Add details. Use a caret ∧ to show where you want to add words.
3. Remove details that don't connect with the reader.
   - Cut unnecessary details. Use a delete mark to show what you want to remove.

Revising in Action

Begin by writing the following sentence on the board or on an overhead:

One day, Brandon and I were playing.

Ask students how Taylor already used good details in his first draft.

- He named the day, Saturday.
- He told exactly what they were doing, skateboarding.

Have students look at their first drafts and identify some of their good details. Then, discuss the details that Taylor added to his first draft when he revised for ideas. Ask how these details increase the meaning of the final sentence in the paragraph.

- "Heavy" is not easy to ignore or forget. It weighs Taylor down and gets in the way.
- There is nothing Taylor can do to cool or scratch his arm under the cast.

Point out that just adding more details is never the point of revising. The point is to make the writing better. Each new idea or detail should help the reader see and feel the narrative more clearly.

Advanced Learners

Challenge students to carefully review their first drafts for ideas that may not fit in the narrative. Sometimes even a good detail does not improve the story, and it may even distract or confuse the reader.

Revising for Organization

Read the paragraph about Grandma's surprise, but leave out the transition words.

Point out that even though all the details of the story are in time order, the story sounds choppy and disconnected. Read the paragraph again with the transitions and have students listen to the difference. All the events and details are tied together for the reader.

Then read aloud the sample paragraph and have students listen carefully for words that show time order. Ask students to raise their hand every time they hear a time-order word. (See SE page 458.)

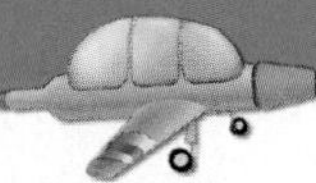

Revising for Organization

In narrative writing, you should organize your details in time order.

Q. How can I put details in time order?

You can put details in **time order** (in the order they happened) by using words like *first, second, next,* and *finally.*

First, I made sure my aunt was ready. Then I called my mom. As soon as I did, I hid with my cousins. Mom brought Grandma in from the yard. We were all ready to celebrate Grandma's surprise party.

Tip Transition words (words that show time) help connect events in your writing.

first	soon	after
second	later	before
next	as soon as	tomorrow
then	finally	suddenly

Practice

Add one more sentence to the paragraph about Grandma's surprise party. Use one of the transitions listed above.

English Language Learners

Students may have trouble conceptualizing time-order words such as *soon, later, after,* and *before.* Use a familiar picture book to ask questions about events. Turn pages back or forward to locate what happened *before* or *after* an event. Flip forward a few pages or many pages to show events that happen *soon* and *later.*

Struggling Learners

Students who experience difficulty with time-order words may benefit from a visual approach. Have them use their writing to sketch a series of events in the form of a cartoon strip or a storyboard.

Have students add time-order words, such as *soon, next, suddenly, tomorrow,* and *later* to their sketches. Have students use their sketches as visual references for correct placement of time-order words in their narratives.

Revising in Action

Here are some of the changes Taylor made to improve the organization of his first draft. He added a transition word, punctuation, and other words as needed.

One Saturday, Brandon and I was skateboarding. I fell. I got hurt. Brandon went and got my mom. When I came back from the hospital, ~~with~~ I had a heavy plaster cast on my write arm. That's the arm I use the most. my arm felt hot and itchy, and I couldn't bend my elbow. I felt helpless.

Revise Check your organization.

1. Be sure that you've used transition words to show time order and to keep your narrative moving.
   - **Add** transition words and phrases.
2. Check your essay to be sure all the events are in the order they happened.
   - **Move** any details or sentences that are not in the best order.

Revising in Action

Talk about why the word "when" is a good choice for a transition in Taylor's narrative.

- "When" reminds the reader that time has passed between getting Taylor's mom and coming home from the hospital. Lots of things happened—going to the hospital, waiting to see a doctor, seeing the doctor, and having the cast put on.
- "When" helps the reader shift from the accident to Taylor's important experience of having his arm in a cast.

Give students a chance to check their essay to make sure that all the events are in order and that they have used transition words to show the order.

To reinforce the importance of using transitions to organize and connect ideas, have volunteers read aloud paragraphs from their revised essays. Have the class listen carefully for time-order words. Afterward, have listeners suggest places where the writer might want to add a transition word.

Revising for Voice

The best way for writers to figure out how their writing will sound to readers is for them to read their writing aloud to themselves. If possible, allow students to record their writing and listen for how they can make it sound more like themselves.

Practice Answers

Answers will vary. Possible response: Pedro loved being at the Fourth of July parade. He and his dad had arrived early and were in the front of the crowd. Suddenly, Pedro saw a little girl in a red jersey and blue shorts dart into the street. She ran right in front of the team of huge horses, pulling the mayor's carriage. Pedro heard the girl's mother scream. The next thing Pedro knew, he was running into the street and shouting, "Watch out! Watch out!" Then he scooped up the frightened girl and carried her to safety. Her parents were very grateful that Pedro was there.

After completing the Practice, have students discuss how their individual voices changed the sound of the story.

Revising for

Your writer's voice is the special way you express your ideas. In narrative writing, your writer's voice should sound like you.

Q. What makes my voice sound like me?

Your writing voice sounds like you if you tell your story using your own words–the way you would tell it to a friend.

The parade was almost over. Suddenly, the girl sitting on the curb next to me darted into the street. Her big yellow balloon sailed away, and her cowboy hat flew off.

Practice

Read the following list. Then use these events to "tell the story" to a classmate. Be sure to use lots of details in your own words.

- little girl running into street
- horses coming toward them
- boy shouting and running
- boy pulling the girl to safety
- the parents thanking him

English Language Learners

Have students make up a story of their own for the **Practice** activity. Explain that the more they are familiar and comfortable with their topic, the easier it will be to tell the story.

Struggling Learners

To help students understand the use of voice in narratives, read aloud a few pages from two different books that tell similar stories. Then compare and contrast the authors' voices. The following books can be paired with their traditional fairy-tale counterparts:

- *Lon Po Po* by Ed Young (A Little Red Riding Hood story from China)
- *The Rough-Face Girl* by Rafe Martin (A Native American Cinderella tale)
- *The Stinky Cheese Man and Other Fairly Stupid Tales* by Jon Scieszka (The Gingerbread Man)

Writing a Narrative Essay 99

Revising in Action

Here are some of the changes Taylor made to improve the voice of his first draft. He added a detail that makes him sound like he's talking to a friend.

One Saturday, Brandon and I was skateboarding. I fell. I got hurt. Brandon went and got my mom. ^When^ I came back from the hospital ^I had^ ~~with~~ a ^heavy^ plaster cast on my write arm. That's the arm I use the most. ^my arm felt hot and itchy, and^ I couldn't bend my elbow. I felt ^as^ helpless ^as a baby^.

Revise: Check your writing voice.

1. Read your essay and imagine that you are telling a friend what happened.
2. Rewrite any parts of your essay that don't sound like you.
   - **Add** words to make your writing sound like you are talking to a friend.
   - **Cut** any words that sound boring or uninteresting.

Revising in Action

Explain that adding voice is something that each writer must do on his or her own. Discuss the change that Taylor made to his narrative. He made a comparison to make his feelings clear. Maybe Taylor had experience with babies (human or animal). Seeing how helpless babies can be, Taylor may have realized that's how he felt about not being able to do things for himself.

Consider asking students to work with partners. Ask them to listen for words or expressions that they use as they simply *tell* their stories to one another. Suggest that adding some of these words to their narratives might help them sound more like they are talking to a friend.

Again, remind students that adding voice is not just about adding words you would say if you were talking. Some of those words may add meaning and some may not. For example, what if Taylor had heard someone say that someone was as helpless "as a fish out of water"? Even if Taylor had been fishing and understood the saying, it doesn't fit with his narrative. A fish out of water will die. That's not the kind of helplessness that Taylor is feeling while wearing his cast.

Revising for Word Choice

Explain to students that action verbs help writers show their readers what they feel and mean, instead of just telling them. By **showing, not telling** *(see below)*, writers are able to make pictures for the reader to imagine.

Ask volunteers to describe the picture that comes into their mind for each of the three sample sentences.

As students read through their essay, tell them to

- look for places where they can use stronger action verbs,
- circle the weaker verbs with a red pencil, and
- go back and find the verbs they want to replace.

* For more about action verbs, see SE page 383.

Grammar Practice Answers

1. biked
2. raced
3. painted
4. whispered
5. galloped

Revising for Word Choice

Action verbs can help your writing come alive.

Q. How should I choose action verbs?

Choose action verbs that make pictures for the reader to imagine. An **action verb** tells what the subject is doing.

Angela tripped over the old, rotten log.

The kite dipped in the wind.

Martin slams the ball into the basket.

Grammar Practice

On your own paper, write the stronger action verb for each sentence below. The choices are shown in parentheses.

1. My dad *(went, biked)* to Mexico City.
2. Todd *(moved, raced)* toward the end zone.
3. I *(painted, made)* a picture in art class.
4. "Be quiet," Zoe *(whispered, said)*.
5. The horse *(hurried, galloped)* around the track.

Grammar Connection

Verbs

- **Proofreader's Guide** page 538 (+)
- ***Write Source*** page 383 (+)
- ***GrammarSnap*** Action Verbs
- ***SkillsBook*** pages 143–144

Subject-Verb Agreement

- **Proofreader's Guide** pages 542–543
- ***Write Source*** page 406
- ***GrammarSnap*** Subject-Verb Agreement
- ***SkillsBook*** pages 77–78, 145–146

Teaching Tip: Showing, Not Telling

"Show, don't tell" is the simple guiding principle of all good writers. It is also a refrain that students hear frequently from teachers. Use the **Practice** sentences to help students recognize the difference between a verb that tells the reader something and a specific action verb that creates a strong, vivid image in the reader's mind. Read aloud the sentences with the wrong choice and then with the correct choice. Ask students to explain in their own words the difference between the two and tell why the correct choice is better.

Revising in Action

Here are some changes Taylor made to improve the word choice in his narrative. He used better action verbs.

One Saturday, Brandon and I was skateboarding. I fell. I got hurt. Brandon ~~went~~ ran and ~~got~~ found my mom. When I came back from the hospital, I had ~~with~~ a heavy plaster cast on my write arm. That's the arm I use the most. My arm felt hot and itchy, and I couldn't bend my elbow. I felt as helpless as a baby.

Revise: Check your word choice.

1. Read your essay and underline the action verbs.
2. Be sure you have chosen action verbs that make word pictures for the reader.
   - Add better action verbs wherever you can.
   - Replace general words with specific words.

Grammar Connection

Adjectives

- **Proofreader's Guide** page 546 (+)
- ***Write Source*** page 389 (+)
- ***GrammarSnap*** Adjectives
- ***SkillsBook*** page 154

Revising in Action

The focus of this revising activity is action verbs. Remind students that word choice is not limited to verbs. Specific nouns and adjectives are also part of effective word choice.

Discuss the changes that Taylor made to his first draft for word choice. How do Taylor's new verb choices improve his narrative?

- The reader can picture "ran" more clearly than "went."
- The word "found" suggests that Brandon had to look for Taylor's mother. That adds drama to the story.

Encourage students to underline all the verbs in their essays. Point out that sometimes a simple being verb (is, are, was, were) is the best verb. It is not necessary to replace all verbs with action words. Have students try out a new word choice on a partner to see if it improves the story.

Revising for Sentence Fluency

Combining sentences is a good way to achieve sentence fluency. However, make sure students understand that it is not always a good idea to combine every short sentence with another sentence. Point out the following:

- The best writing has a variety of sentence lengths and types.
- Some ideas do not go together and should not be combined.
- Too many long sentences can be difficult to read and can confuse the reader.

* For more about combining sentences, see SE pages 408–410.

Revising for

Sometimes combining sentences can make your writing smoother.

Q. How can I combine sentences?

Here are three ways to combine short sentences into one longer sentence.

Use a series. Combine short sentences that tell different things about the same subject.

Cole is smart. Cole is funny. Cole is strong.
Cole is smart, funny, and strong.

Use compound subjects. Combine two or more subjects into the compound subject of one sentence.

My friend plays soccer. I play soccer.
My friend and I play soccer.

Use compound verbs. Combine two or more verbs into the compound verb of one sentence.

Rico wrote his essay. Rico published his essay.
Rico wrote and published his essay.

Grammar Practice

Combine these two sentences using a compound verb.

Nigel swam at the lake. He fished there, too.

Grammar Connection

Sentence Combining

- ***Write Source*** pages 408, 409
- ***GrammarSnap*** Creating a Series
- ***SkillsBook*** pages 101–102, 103–104, 107–108

English Language Learners

Some students may find it difficult to read for sentence fluency. Help them hear the differences by reading aloud the sample sentences on the page. Use a choppy, staccato rhythm for the first group of sentences in each pair. Then read the combined sentence smoothly and fluently. Ask students which sentences sound better.

Writing a Narrative Essay 103

Revising in Action

Here are some changes Taylor made to improve the flow of his writing in his first draft. He combined two short sentences by using a compound verb.

One Saturday, Brandon and I was skateboarding. I fell, ~~I~~ and got hurt. Brandon ~~went~~ ran and ~~got~~ found my mom. When I came back from the hospital ~~with~~ I had a heavy plaster cast on my write arm. That's the arm I use the most. my arm felt hot and itchy, and I couldn't bend my elbow. I felt as helpless as a baby.

Revise: Check your sentence lengths.

1. Make sure your essay has both long and short sentences.
2. If you find too many short sentences, combine some of them. Use the three suggestions on page 102.
   - Cut words, add punctuation, and add a conjunction to combine two sentences using a compound verb.

Revising in Action

Have students look at Taylor's revising change for sentence fluency. Ask them to find the other sentence in which Taylor uses a compound verb to combine ideas.

- Brandon ran and found my mom.

Ask students to find the sentence that uses a compound subject.

- One Saturday, Brandon and I was skateboarding.

Point out that Taylor also uses a compound sentence (two sentences combined using a comma and a conjunction).

- my arm felt hot and itchy, and I couldn't bend my elbow.

Have students study their own narratives or work with a partner to see if there are sentences they could combine to improve their essays. Review the suggestions and models on SE page 102.

Revising Using a Checklist

Have students check their revising for the traits of writing by using this checklist. They may work independently or with a partner.

Now, students need to make clean copies of their essays. Partners may check one another's final drafts against their first drafts that are marked with revisions. Then the writer should check his or her own letter for final editing and proofreading changes.

Revising Using a Checklist

Check your revising.

Number your paper from 1 to 9. Read each question and put a check mark after the number if the answer to a question is "yes." Otherwise, continue to work with that part of your essay.

Ideas

___ 1. Do I tell about one helpful person?
___ 2. Do I include sensory details?

Organization

___ 3. Do my beginning, middle, and ending work well?
___ 4. Are my details in time order?

Voice

___ 5. Does my voice sound like me?
___ 6. Do I use transitions to move the story along?

Word Choice

___ 7. Have I used action verbs?

Sentence Fluency

___ 8. Have I varied my sentence beginnings?
___ 9. Have I varied the lengths of my sentences?

Make a clean copy.

After revising your narrative, make a clean copy for editing.

Writing a Narrative Essay 105

Editing for Conventions

When you edit for conventions, check your spelling, capitalization, punctuation, and grammar.

Q. How can I check for the right words?

Watch for words that sound the same but have different spellings and meanings. Such words are called *homophones*.

When you use a homophone, check a dictionary to make sure you have used the right one.

are, our	rode, road
buy, by	there, their, they're
for, four	to, two, too
its, it's	you're, your

Grammar Practice

On your own paper, write the correct word or words for each sentence below. The choices are shown in parentheses.

1. We *(rode, road) (are, our)* bikes to the park.
2. *(There, They're, Their)* coming *(to, too, two)* my house later.
3. Mrs. King said *(its, it's)* fine for me to come, *(to, too, two)*.
4. *(You're, Your)* mom is looking *(for, four)* you.
5. Would you *(buy, by)* a dozen eggs and *(to, too, two)* loaves of bread?

Struggling Learners

Before completing the **Practice** activity, review homophones in which one word is a contraction such as *there, their, they're* and *your, you're.* Have students substitute the words in place of the contraction to see if the sentence makes sense such as *you are* for *you're.* For example, "Is this (your/you're) book?"

Editing for Conventions

Remind students who are working on a computer that the computer's spell checker will not find mistakes with homophones.

Students who have been working on a piece of writing for a long time often skip right over mistakes with homophones and other mistakes in spelling that the computer cannot detect, as well as errors in capitalization, punctuation, and grammar. To help students find all their mistakes suggest that they

- look for one kind of a mistake at a time;
- mark different kinds of mistakes with different colored pencils, for example, blue for homophones; and
- ask a classmate to check their writing for mistakes.

Grammar Practice Answers

1. rode, our
2. They're, to
3. it's, too
4. Your, for
5. buy, two

Technology Connections

Students can use the added features of the Net-text as they explore this stage of the writing process.

Write Source Online ***Net-text***

Editing Checking for Conventions

Students may review their narratives one last time for final editing and proofreading changes using the checklist on SE page 106.

Each paragraph in a narrative does not need a topic sentence as other essays do. A narrative essay often has dialogue, which forms a new paragraph for each change of speaker. Have students do a final review of their essays checking for paragraph indentations.

Answers

Then one day, my friend Danny . . .

106

Editing Checking for Conventions

A checklist like the one below can help you find errors in capitalization, punctuation, spelling, and grammar.

Conventions

Punctuation

____ **1.** Did I use end punctuation after all my sentences?
____ **2.** Did I put quotation marks around words people said?

Capitalization

____ **3.** Did I start all my sentences with capital letters?
____ **4.** Did I correctly capitalize proper nouns?

Spelling

____ **5.** Have I carefully checked my spelling?

Grammar

____ **6.** Did I use correct verbs *(he **plays**, not he **play**)*?
____ **7.** Did I make sure to use the right word *(to, too, two)*?

Practice

Find the place where you should indent for a new paragraph.

I told everyone that I didn't like roller coasters. They scared me. People always were screaming on the rides, and my stomach got queasy thinking about all the dips and loops and turns. Then one day, my friend Danny talked me into trying a small roller coaster with him. My stomach started doing cartwheels. I grabbed the safety bar as we chugged up the first steep climb. When we shot down the steep track, I began screaming and then laughing. I never had so much fun!

Grammar Connection

Punctuating Dialogue

- **Proofreader's Guide** pages 470–471, 476–477
- ***SkillsBook*** pages 17–18

End Punctuation

- **Proofreader's Guide** pages 463–465
- ***Write Source*** page 397
- ***GrammarSnap*** End Punctuation
- ***SkillsBook*** pages 3–4, 7–8

Struggling Learners

Many students who read their drafts too soon after writing them read right through capitalization, punctuation, and spelling errors. Have students make three separate passes through their paper. For checking capitalization, suggest that students begin with the last word of their last sentence and check each word in reverse order until they reach the beginning of their paper. This strategy focuses students on the individual words without the story meaning interfering with the editing process.

For punctuation, have students begin with the last sentence and work backward one sentence at a time.

Students can check their spelling by reading from the last word to the first word—as they did for capitalization—one word at a time.

Writing a Narrative Essay 107

Editing in Action

Here are the changes Taylor made to the first several paragraphs of his revised draft.

Have you ever had a terrible day? On my terrible day, I broke my arm. Luckily, my good friend Brandon was with me. he is one of the most helpfull people I know.

Taylor corrected a misspelled word.

One Saturday, Brandon and I was skateboarding, and I fell and got hurt Brandon ran home and found my mom. When I came back from the hospital, I had a heavy plaster cast on my write arm. That's the arm I use the most. my arm felt hot and itchy, and I couldn't bend my elbow I felt as helpless as a baby.

A verb is corrected.

He replaced a wrong word.

He added a capital letter.

"Don't worry," Brandon said. "I'll help you.

He added quotation marks.

Edit **Check for conventions in your essay.**

Editing in Action

You may want to remind students that when they revised, they made big changes—adding ideas, moving sentences, replacing and cutting words. Editing is making small changes—capitalization, punctuation, and spelling. Discuss the changes that Taylor made to his final copy. Consider putting a sentence on the board that models correct punctuation for dialogue or have students turn to SE page 476 in the proofreader's guide.

English Language Learners

Some students may be unfamiliar with the way that suffixes in Taylor's essay change the meaning of a word. Point out the words *helpful* and *helpless*. Reinforce the following meanings and provide additional examples:

- *-ful:* full of; (harmful, beautiful, wonderful, delightful)
- *-less:* without (fearless, thoughtless, careless, hopeless)

Using a Rubric

Remind students that a rubric is a chart of the traits of good writing that helps them to

- plan their writing during prewriting,
- make changes to their writing during revising (see Partner's Response, SE pages 93–104), and
- judge their final copy when they finish writing (see Writing for Assessment, SE pages 120–122).

The rubrics in this book are based on a six-point scale, in which a score of 6 indicates an amazing piece of writing and a score of 1 means the writing is incomplete.

Explain to students that they will most likely have different ratings for the traits. For example, they may give themselves a 5 for ideas but a 4 for organization.

Using a Rubric

The rubrics on these pages can help you rate your writing.

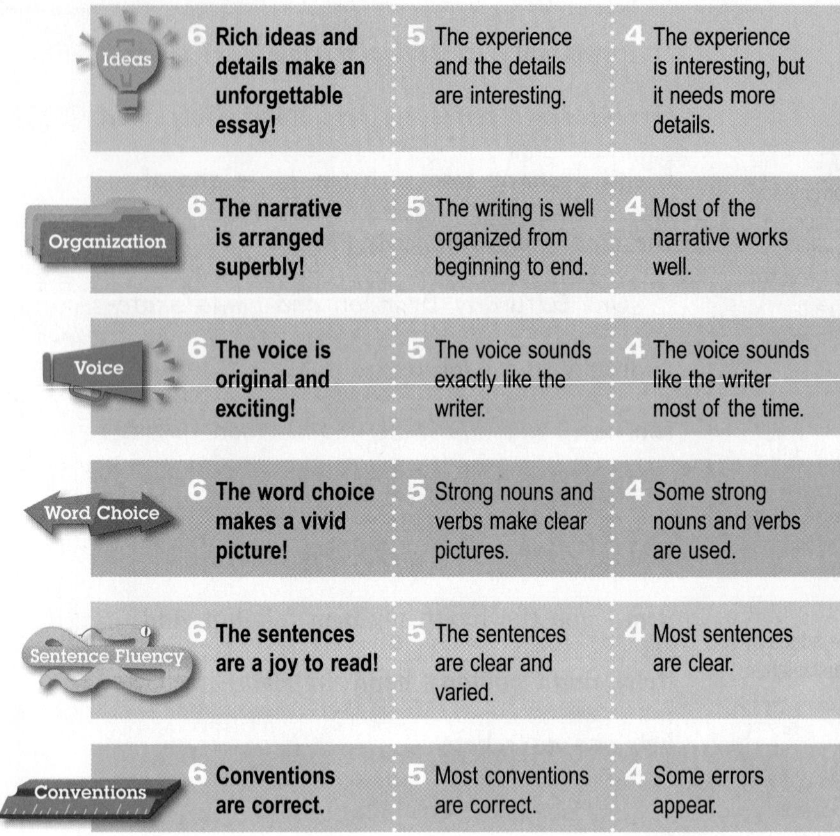

Trait	6	5	4
Ideas	**Rich ideas and details make an unforgettable essay!**	The experience and the details are interesting.	The experience is interesting, but it needs more details.
Organization	**The narrative is arranged superbly!**	The writing is well organized from beginning to end.	Most of the narrative works well.
Voice	**The voice is original and exciting!**	The voice sounds exactly like the writer.	The voice sounds like the writer most of the time.
Word Choice	**The word choice makes a vivid picture!**	Strong nouns and verbs make clear pictures.	Some strong nouns and verbs are used.
Sentence Fluency	**The sentences are a joy to read!**	The sentences are clear and varied.	Most sentences are clear.
Conventions	**Conventions are correct.**	Most conventions are correct.	Some errors appear.

Writing a Narrative Essay 109

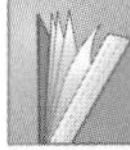

Literature Connections: For an example of a narrative, read *Destiny's Gift* by Natasha Anastasia Tarpley.

3	2	1
The experience isn't clear, and some details don't belong.	The narrative should focus on one experience.	A new experience or suitable details should be found.
Parts (beginning, middle, or ending) should be stronger.	All parts of the essay run together.	The narrative needs to be organized.
Sometimes the voice sounds like the writer.	The writing does not sound like the writer.	The writing has no real voice.
Many strong words are needed.	Some words are overused.	Some words make the essay confusing.
Many sentences are choppy.	Many sentences are choppy or incomplete.	Many sentences are incomplete.
Errors may confuse the reader.	Errors make the writing hard to read.	Help is needed to make corrections.

Writer's Craft

Rubrics: It used to be that rubrics were meant solely for those who were grading student writing, but *Write Source* rubrics are designed for students to use. Note how each of the ratings below a four indicates what the writer could do to improve the writing. By focusing on a need, the student can make specific revisions that mean real improvement.

Literature Connections

In the personal narrative *Destiny's Gift,* the narrator describes her experiences at the neighborhood bookstore and the ways in which she was supportive of the bookstore's owner.

Discuss the elements that make the story a good personal narrative, including: natural voice, focus on one event, specific details, and time order. For additional models see the Reading-Writing Connections beginning on page TE-36.

Publishing Sharing Your Essay

Review the guidelines for writing a neat final copy by hand (SE page 36), or for preparing a final copy using a computer (SE page 37).

Point out the title of Taylor's essay, "Skateboard Emergency 9–1–1." Encourage students to **add a title** *(see below)* to their essay that will grab their readers' attention.

Provide time for students to read aloud their essays to the class. Alternately, or in addition, you can have students compile their finished essays in booklet form with illustrations. Display the collected essays in the class reading center or in the school library for students to read at their leisure.

Technology Connections

Remind students that they can use the Writing Network features of the Portfolio to share their work with peers.

Write Source Online ***Portfolio***

Write Source Online ***Net-text***

Publishing Sharing Your Essay

After editing, it's time to write a neat copy of your essay to share with your classmates. If you want to, you may add an illustration.

Publish — Make a final copy.

1. **Follow your teacher's instructions, or use the model below. (For computer papers, see page 37.)**
2. **Create a clean final copy and proofread it.**

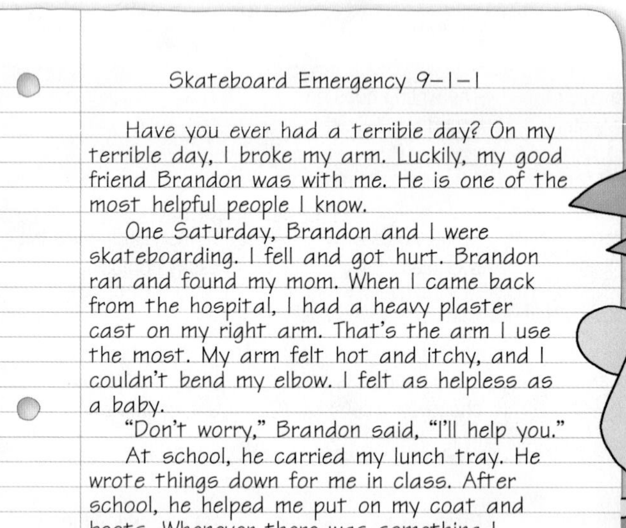

Skateboard Emergency 9–1–1

Have you ever had a terrible day? On my terrible day, I broke my arm. Luckily, my good friend Brandon was with me. He is one of the most helpful people I know.

One Saturday, Brandon and I were skateboarding. I fell and got hurt. Brandon ran and found my mom. When I came back from the hospital, I had a heavy plaster cast on my right arm. That's the arm I use the most. My arm felt hot and itchy, and I couldn't bend my elbow. I felt as helpless as a baby.

"Don't worry," Brandon said, "I'll help you."

At school, he carried my lunch tray. He wrote things down for me in class. After school, he helped me put on my coat and boots. Whenever there was something I couldn't do, Brandon was there to help me.

The day I broke my arm was terrible, but I had a great helper. Now my arm is fine. Brandon and I play ball and go skateboarding just like before. I'll never forget what Brandon did for me when I needed a helping hand.

Teaching Tip: Adding a Title

Point out to students that the title of their essay is the first thing that readers see. It should be creative and interesting, and it should make the reader want to read the essay. Suggest that students reread their essay to find key words or phrases that might work well as part of a title. Encourage students to be as creative as possible, but to keep in mind the focus of their essay.

Discuss why the sample title is a good title.

- It is creative, and it hints at what the essay is about. Most readers will know that 9–1–1 is the number that you call for help, and the essay is about a person who helps the writer.
- Young readers like to skateboard so they will want to find out about the skateboard emergency.

Writing a Narrative Essay 111

Reflecting on Your Writing

Congratulations! You have finished your narrative essay. Now it's time to think about what you have learned. Here are Taylor's thoughts about his essay.

Thinking About Your Writing

Name: Taylor Matelski

Title: Skateboard Emergency 9-1-1

1. The best part of my essay is . . .

   telling about my good friend and how he really helped me.

2. The part that still needs work is . . .

   the second paragraph. I could have used more action and dialogue.

3. The main thing I learned about narrative writing is . . .

   how to tell what happened in the right order.

Reflecting on Your Writing

If students are not keeping their writing reflections in a folder, have them start doing so now. Tell them to review their past reflections after each major writing assignment to recall what they learned before and to see how they may have applied what they learned to what they are currently writing.

Provide photocopies of the reproducible Thinking About Your Writing (TE page 593) on which students can record their reflections. To encourage students to record honest, accurate reflections, have them fill in the sheet after you have reviewed and provided written comments on their essay. If you choose to have students complete a Response Sheet (SE page 93), students can also look at those comments before filling out their reflections.

English Language Learners

Students may need help to articulate what they have learned about narrative writing and may be tempted to copy what they see on the sample reflection sheet. Help students to come up with specific and different words for their reflections by revising the statements on the sheet. For example, change #1 to: The most surprising detail in my story is. . . . Change #2 to: The sentence (or paragraph) I want to revise is . . . because. . . . Change #3 to: Writing my story helped me learn to. . . .

Advanced Learners

Challenge students to use their reflection sheets as a springboard for writing a paragraph about what they learned from revising and editing, how other students and you may have helped, and so on. Suggest that they follow the principles for creating a narrative paragraph, including adding dialogue to make the writing seem real.

Across the Curriculum

Objectives
- Apply what students have learned about narrative writing to other curriculum areas.
- Practice writing for assessment.

The lessons on the following pages provide samples of different kinds of narrative writing. The first lesson guides students through the steps of the writing process to write a biographical narrative for social studies. The second lesson provides a model and writing tips for writing a personal art story. The third lesson focuses on writing a friendly letter.

Assigning these forms of writing will depend on
- the skill level of your students,
- the subject matter they are studying in different content areas, and
- the writing goals of your school, district, or state.

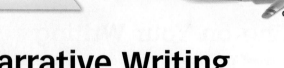

Narrative Writing Across the Curriculum

"What happened?" One way to answer that question is to write a narrative. Sometimes the narrative tells about an experience in your own life. Sometimes it tells about an experience in the life of someone else.

On the following pages, you'll learn how to write both types of narratives. You'll also learn how to respond to a narrative prompt on a writing test.

Materials

Book jackets (TE p. 113)

List of Web sites (TE p. 114)

Index cards (TE p. 114)

Age-appropriate magazines and biographies (TE p. 114)

Copy Masters

T-Chart (TE p. 114)

Five W's Chart (TE p. 114)

Sensory Chart (TE p. 119)

Time Line (TE p. 120)

Assessment Sheet (TE p. 120)

Social Studies: Biographical Narrative

For social studies, Tony needed to write a narrative about an inventor. He chose a person whose invention is used in millions of homes every day.

Beginning
The beginning gives the focus statement (underlined).

Middle
The middle tells what happened.

Ending
The ending tells how the inventor's work made a difference.

Chocolate in His Pocket

One day, Percy L. Spencer was working with a radar power tube. He worked at a company in Massachusetts. Suddenly, the chocolate bar in his pocket melted! Percy wasn't mad, though. Percy's accident gave him an idea for a new kind of oven.

Percy tested another food. He put some popcorn in front of the power tube. Pop! Pop! Pop! The kernels popped into popcorn! Microwaves had cooked it.

Percy decided to make an oven that would use microwaves. He finished his first microwave oven in 1945. It was 5 1/2 feet tall and weighed 750 pounds.

Today microwave ovens are much smaller. People still use them to pop popcorn!

Social Studies: Biographical Narrative

Analyze the sample with students to help them make the connection between the narrative paragraph and essay they wrote earlier and the biographical narrative. Use the following questions.

- How does Tony begin his narrative? (He introduces Percy L. Spencer. He connects with the reader by telling a little story about him. He ends by telling why Spencer is important.)
- How does Tony arrange the details in the middle paragraphs? (in time order)
- What story do the details in the middle paragraphs tell? (how Spencer invented the microwave oven)
- What specific words does Tony use to make Percy L. Spencer and his story sound real? (Possible choices: Percy wasn't mad, gave him an idea, Pop! Pop! Pop! 5 1/2 feet tall, 750 pounds)

Advanced Learners

Show students book reviews listed on the back covers of several books. Explain that the purpose of the reviews is to make readers want to read the book. Have pairs pretend they are reviewers assigned to write a review of "Chocolate in His Pocket." Have partners discuss the following questions:

- What is the most interesting part of this narrative?
- What fact will most people enjoy reading about?
- What words best describe this narrative in a way that people will want to read it?

Prewriting Selecting a Topic

Provide photocopies of the reproducible T-Chart (TE page 595) for students to use to create their topic chart. Provide students with a list of acceptable Web sites to search for names of inventors and inventions.

Encourage students to choose an inventor whom they will enjoy learning more about and about whom they are sure they can find enough details to tell a good story.

Prewriting Gathering Details

Suggest that students write each underlined question at the top of a new notebook page or blank index card. That way, if they want to expand their notes for each question, they will have plenty of room.

Students should organize details in time order. They can number their details, make a time line, or draw a series of pictures to show the sequence of events that tell the inventor's story.

Prewriting Selecting a Topic

Your biographical narrative will be about an inventor. Tony looked at some Web sites and some library books about inventors. He wrote down people and inventions that interested him.

Prewrite **Create a topic chart.**

1. Write "Inventors" and "Inventions" at the top of your paper.
2. Check a book or Web site and list your ideas.
3. Put a star (*) next to theinventor you choose.

Inventors	Inventions
Thomas Edison	light bulb
George Washington Carver	bleach
Percy L. Spencer*	microwave oven

Gathering Details

Questions help you gather facts. See Tony's notes below.

Prewrite **Answer these questions about your topic.**

Who is the inventor? Percy L. Spencer
What was the invention? The microwave oven
How was it invented? Chocolate in his pocket melted near a power tube.
When was it invented? 1945

Struggling Learners

Help students organize the details for their biographical narratives by reviewing the 5 W's Chart on SE page 11 (a reproducible 5 W's Chart is on TE page 597). Visual learners may prefer to use a cluster map as a way to organize their 5 W's. Point out that *How?* is a useful question to include when writing about inventors.

English Language Learners

Students may have difficulty coming up with inventors' names. Instead, have them make a list of inventions. Once they have chosen an invention to write about, have them use the library or the Internet to find out the name of the inventor.

Guide students by providing books or magazine articles that have a lot of pictures, including ones written for younger children.

Writing Creating a First Draft

Use these guidelines to write your biographical narrative.

Write your narrative.

1. Include a focus sentence in the beginning.
2. Tell the story of the inventor in the middle.
3. Share a final thought in the ending.

Revising Improving Your Writing

The following questions can help you revise your first draft.

Improve your work.

Ask yourself the following questions about your narrative.

- Did I include enough details?
- Did I put the events in the order they happened?
- Did I use a writing voice that sounds interested?

Editing Checking for Conventions

Check capitalization, punctuation, spelling, and grammar.

Check your work.

- Did I end each sentence with correct punctuation?
- Did I look up any difficult spelling words?
- Did I use the right words *(it's/its, you're/your)*?

English Language Learners

Because students think and organize ideas in their first language, have them tell the order of events aloud to a partner. Once they are orally proficient with their story, have them write down their ideas.

Advanced Learners

To extend this activity, have students develop their final thought by telling what impact their chosen inventors have made on their own lives. Point out that this is another way to connect readers with the topic.

Writing Creating a First Draft

Remind students to have their focus sentence guide their writing. If necessary, have them review the sample on SE page 113 by

- asking them to read the underlined focus sentence and
- pointing out the details in the two middle paragraphs.

Explain that by using this focus sentence as a guide, Tony knew what details to include and what details to leave out.

Revising Improving Your Writing

Have students exchange drafts with a partner. After the partner reads the narrative, the writer asks the partner the revising questions and the partner offers suggestions for improvement.

Editing Checking for Conventions

Remind students to capitalize the names of particular people and places and to check the spelling of their names.

Art:
A Personal Art Story

Writing and art both are very intimate forms of learning, involving a student's inner thoughts and perceptions of the world. A personal art story can help students explore and deepen their connection to art.

To prepare students to write such a story, read them the model on SE page 116. Then ask if any of them have had similar experiences with art. Let students tell about their experiences. Lead a discussion about how art helps students create new things and express themselves.

Writer's Craft

Art: Many writers are painters or sculptors or musicians or actors. All of these pursuits allow creativity and self-expression. It's quite likely that your students think they excel in one or more of these areas. That's because third graders are naturally creative. To help students make this connection, discuss how they might retain their creativity even when they become adults.

Art: A Personal Art Story

Texture Detectives

One day in art, Mr. Morehead had us make rubbings. We put plain paper on top of an object. Then we rubbed the side of a crayon over it. The texture of the object left a pattern on the paper.

We didn't want to stop. Mr. Morehead said, "Rub things in nature and at home. Then bring back your rubbings for a guessing game." Wow, I wanted my rubbing to be the biggest mystery.

First, I rubbed my jean jacket. That was boring. Big leaves from my backyard made awesome patterns, but looked just like leaves. My last rubbing looked like alligator skin and felt bumpy. My dad's metal watchband stumped everybody.

Writing Tips

Before you write . . .

- Think about an art experience that you could share.
- Make a time line to tell your story in the order it happened.

During your writing . . .

- Get the reader's attention in the beginning of your story.
- Then write about each part of the story in one paragraph.
- Write the way you would tell the story to a friend.

After you've written a first draft . . .

- Read your story and see if any important details are missing.
- Give your story an interesting title.
- Check capitalization, punctuation, spelling, and grammar.

Writing Tips

In addition to the writing tips on SE page 117, help students understand the importance of sensory details when writing a personal art story. Note that the model contains many sensory details: *plain paper, rubbed, texture, pattern, big leaves, awesome patterns, alligator skin, bumpy.* Details such as these help the reader see the art that students are describing.

Writing Workshop

Have students share their personal art stories with partners, who can help them decide what revisions to make and what title to add to the story. Also, make sure to leave time for whole-class sharing.

Practical Writing: Friendly Letter

Because of cell phones, instant messaging, and e-mail, children are in frequent touch with family members and friends who do not live nearby. As a result, they may not have a need or an opportunity to write friendly letters, except as part of school writing assignments. Nevertheless, writing a friendly letter, whether it is in the traditional form or as an e-mail message, is a practical and fun way for students to apply the narrative writing skills that they have learned.

Use the sample letter to review the parts of a friendly letter, including the date, salutation, body, closing, and signature. Be sure to point out that in a friendly letter, each new paragraph is indented.

Practical Writing: Friendly Letter

A narrative letter lets you share your life with people who live far away. Kerri wrote this letter to a friend who had moved to another town.

April 23, 2010

Dear Damitria,

The **beginning** tells about one event.

There was a circus at our school this week! Two real circus performers came and taught each class a circus trick. My class learned how to make balloon animals.

The **middle** shares more about a specific part of the event.

I made a funny blue poodle. The first time I tried, my balloon popped. The next time, I made the little head and legs just right. I named my poodle Tria because I miss you.

The **ending** wraps up the narrative.

On Friday, the whole school put on a circus in the gym. Mrs. Mancini played piano music. There were kids being clowns, juggling, and doing face painting. We even had popcorn. I wish you could have been here!

Your friend,

Kerri

Struggling Learners

Use the beginning, middle, and end descriptions as a basis for questioning to help students with Kerri's letter. Point out that the answer to each question should be the main idea of the paragraph, not a supporting detail.

- What one event does Kerri write about in the beginning paragraph of her letter?
- Based on the middle paragraph, what did Kerri make?
- At the end, what did Kerri say happened on Friday?

Writing Tips

Before you write . . .

- Think about a recent experience you could share.
- List things you remember seeing, hearing, smelling, tasting, and touching (sensory details).

During your writing . . .

- Introduce the topic in the body of your letter.
- Write the body of your letter in paragraphs.
- Write about events in the order they happened.
- Share your thoughts and feelings.

After you've written a first draft . . .

- Read over your letter and add missing details.
- Make sure you used the correct form for a friendly letter.
- Check capitalization, punctuation, spelling, and grammar.

Think about the experience you want to share with someone who wasn't there. Then write your friendly letter.

English Language Learners

Point out that friendly letters are written using a natural-sounding voice. As each student reads aloud his or her friendly letter, point out parts that don't sound as natural as they could, and help students reword.

Advanced Learners

Have students write their friendly letters to a parent, a grandparent, or another relative. Encourage them to end their writing by asking the reader if he or she has ever experienced a similar event. Then have students send out their letters and share the responses they receive.

Writing Tips

Explain to students that sensory details help the reader picture the experience. To emphasize this point, have students identify sensory details in the sample letter on SE page 118 and describe the pictures these details help form in their minds.

After students have chosen someone to write to and an experience to write about, suggest that they record sensory details about the experience in a sensory chart. Provide photocopies of the Sensory Chart (TE page 596) for them to use.

Writing for Assessment

If your students must take school, district, or state assessments, focus on the tested writing form.

If you have students respond to the prompt, provide photocopies of the reproducible Time Line (TE page 598) for students to use for planning their response.

Besides responding to a prompt, this lesson can also offer practice evaluating a narrative essay. Using the rubric for narrative writing (SE pages 108–109) and a copy of the Assessment Sheet (TE page 591), work with students to score the sample essay on SE page 121 (a completed assessment sheet is provided on TE page 576). Two additional essays are available in copy master form (see Benchmark Papers box below). There is an assessment sheet for each benchmark paper.

Narrative Writing
Writing for Assessment

Some writing tests have narrative prompts. A narrative prompt asks you to remember an experience and write about it. Devin made a quick time line to plan his response.

Narrative Prompt

Think about one experience that you will never forget. Why is it unforgettable? Write a narrative about the experience. Tell what happened in time order and include plenty of sensory details.

Time Line

African Festival
Class field trip to a festival
Saw banners
Listened to drums
Kids learned dancing
Now I take dance

English Language Learners

Review that the phrase *time order* in the prompt means that the events and sensory details should be written about in the order in which they happened. Discuss with students why using a time line or a sequence of events chart is more helpful than a cluster map or sensory details chart for this particular prompt.

Struggling Learners

Some students may focus so much on sensory details that they have difficulty ordering events. Direct their attention to the time line Devin made, explaining that it is easier to go back and add details after the events are clearly organized.

Benchmark Papers

The Snow Day (good)

- TE pp. 577–578

Looking for Midnight (fair)

- TE pp. 579–580

Writing for Assessment 121

Dancing Drums

The **beginning** gives the focus sentence (underlined).

My class took a field trip to an African festival. I was excited because my ancestors are from Africa. I'll never forget that day because that's when I learned African dance.

At first, we all sat on the wood floor and looked at the bright banners on the walls. Tall drums stood in the corner.

The **middle** tells about the experience.

Then a drum teacher named Kaleem took half the class over to the drums. He taught them how to make a beat. I could feel the drum beats in my chest.

Next, a dance teacher came to the rest of us. Her name was Dakima. She showed us some dance moves and told us to take off our shoes and socks. We danced barefoot while the others beat the drums!

The **ending** adds a thought about what happened.

I loved dancing. Now I take African dance lessons every week. I'll always remember the first time I danced to the drums.

After you read . . .

- **Ideas** (1) What is the topic of the story?
- **Organization** (2) How does Devin organize his experience?
- **Word Choice** (3) What words show Devin's excitement?

Discuss the narrative with students. Ask them if they think Devin has

- written a strong focus sentence,
- included enough sensory details to help them picture the experience,
- told his story in a way that is both interesting and makes sense.

Have students explain their answers, using specific examples from the narrative.

After you read . . .

Answers

Ideas 1. The topic is the day that Devin learned African dance.

Organization 2. He has used time order with transitions: At first, Then, Next, Now

Word Choice 3. Possible choices: excited, I'll never forget, I could feel the drum beats in my chest, I loved dancing, I'll always remember

Writing Tips

Point out that students must approach writing-on-demand assignments differently from open-ended writing assignments and that timed writing creates pressures for everyone.

Narrative Prompt

To teach students who must take timed assessments how to approach their writing, allow them the same amount of time to write their response essay as they will be allotted on school, district, or state assessments. Break down each part of the process into clear chunks of time. For example, you might give students

- 15 minutes for note taking and planning,
- 20 minutes for writing, and
- 10 minutes for editing and proofreading.

Tell students when time is up for each section. Start the assignment at the top of the hour or at the half-hour to make it easier for students to keep track of the time.

If your state, district, or school requires students to use and submit a graphic organizer as part of their assessment, provide a copy of one of the reproducible charts (TE pages 595–600) or refer students to SE pages 438–443.

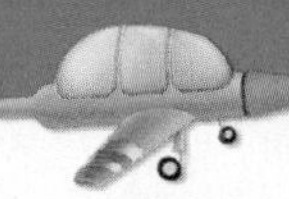

Writing Tips

Before you write . . .

- Read the prompt and underline the key words such as one *experience*, *unforgettable*, and *narrative*.
- Use a time line to list events.

During your writing . . .

- Write a focus sentence about your topic.
- Write events in time order.
- Add important details.
- Be sure to answer any question in the prompt.

After you've written your narrative . . .

- Make sure you have a clear focus and enough details.
- Check capitalization, punctuation, spelling, and grammar.

Respond to this narrative prompt. Finish your essay in the amount of time that your teacher gives you.

Narrative Prompt

Think about a time when you were surprised. How did you react? Write a narrative about the experience.

English Language Learners

Some students have trouble writing to a prompt because they fail to understand important vocabulary such as the word *react*. Provide synonyms for students and reword the question. Students are much more likely to grasp “What did you do?” instead of “How did you react?”

Narrative Writing Checklist 123

Narrative Writing in Review

In narrative writing, you tell about something that has happened in your own life or the life of another person.

Select a topic that will interest your reader. (See pages 84–85.)

Gather important details about the people and events in your narrative. Use a graphic organizer. (See pages 84–85.)

In the beginning part, give background information and introduce your topic. (See pages 86–87.)

In the middle part, tell about the events and people, using dialogue and specific details. (See pages 88–89.)

In the ending part, tell why the experience was important. (See pages 90–91.)

Review your ideas, **organization**, and **voice** first. Then review for **word choice** and **sentence fluency**. (See pages 92–104.)

Check your writing for conventions. Also have a classmate look at your writing for errors you may have missed. (See pages 105–109.)

Make a final copy and proofread it for errors before sharing it. (See page 110.)

Narrative Writing in Review

Go over the information on the page, inviting students to talk about their experiences with each step of the process.

- What was easiest or most difficult for them?
- What taught them the most?
- What did they like best?

Have students mark the page with a sticky note or paper clip, so that they can easily refer to it when they are working on a narrative assignment.

Expository Writing Overview

Common Core Standards Focus

Writing 2: Write informative/explanatory texts to examine a topic and convey ideas and information clearly.

Language 1h: Use coordinating and subordinating conjunctions.

Language 1i: Produce simple, compound, and complex sentences.

Writing Forms

- Writing an Expository Paragraph
- Writing an Expository Essay

Focus on the Traits

- Ideas Including details and dialogue that "show, don't tell"
- Organization Beginning each paragraph with a topic sentence and putting the paragraphs in the right order
- Voice Creating an excited, interested voice
- Word Choice Choosing specific nouns to make explanations clear
- Sentence Fluency Writing complete sentences and correcting run-ons
- Conventions Checking for errors in capitalization, punctuation, spelling, and grammar

Literature Connections

- ***Electromagnets and You*** by Emma Rose
- ***Mayors*** by Shannon Knudsen

Technology Connections

Write Source Online
www.hmheducation.com/writesource

- ***Net-text***
- ***Bookshelf***
- ***GrammarSnap***
- ***Portfolio***
- ***Writing Network features***
- ***File Cabinet***

Interactive Whiteboard Lessons

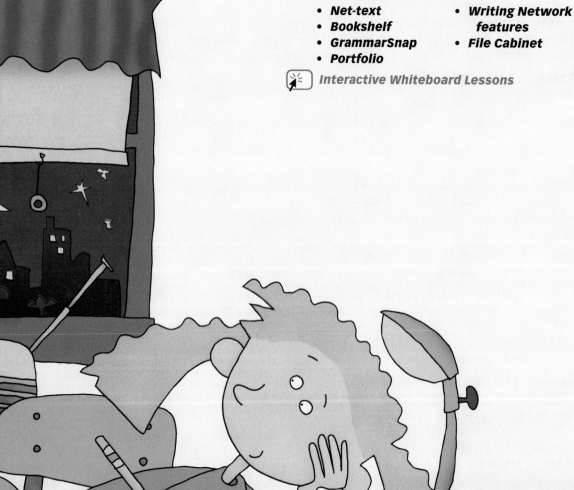

Suggested Expository Writing Unit (Four Weeks)

Week	Day	Writing and Skills Instruction	*Student Edition*: Expository Writing Unit	*Student Edition*: Resource Units*	*SkillsBook*	*Daily Language Workouts*	*Write Source Online*
Week 1	1–4	**Expository Paragraph: Why Something Is Important** Literature Connections *Electromagnets and You*	126–131			26–27, 88	*Interactive Whiteboard Lessons*
		Skills Activities: • Complete Sentences		397 (+), 398, 399, 400, 401, 526–527, 528–529	79–80, 81–82		*GrammarSnap*
	opt.	*Giving Speeches*	344–349				
	5	**Expository Essay: Explaining Why Something Is Important** (Model)	132–135				
Week 2	6–7	(Prewriting)	136–137			28–29, 89	*Net-text*
	8–10	(Writing)	138–143				*Net-text*
Week 3	11	(Revising)	144–145			30–31, 90	*Net-text*
	12–13	(Revising)	146–156				
		Skills Activities: • Punctuating Dialogue		470 (+), 476 (+)	29–30		
		• Specific Nouns		378, 532 (+)	117–118		*GrammarSnap*
		• Adverbs		391, 550–551	159–160		*GrammarSnap*
		• Using the Right Word		512–513	68		
	14–15	(Editing)	157–159				*Net-text*
		Skills Activities: • Commas (in a series)		408 (+), 466–467	9–10		*GrammarSnap*
		• Capitalization		486–487 (+), 488–489	41–42		*GrammarSnap*
		• Apostrophes		472 (+)			*GrammarSnap*
Week 4	16	(Assessing, Publishing, Reflecting) Literature Connections *Mayors*	160–163			32–33, 91	*Portfolio, Net-text*
	opt.	*Giving Speeches*	344–349				
	17–18	**Expository Writing Across the Curriculum**	164–171				
	19–20	**Expository Writing for Assessment**	172–174				

* These units are also located in the back of the *Teacher's Edition.* Resource Units include "Basic Grammar and Writing," "A Writer's Resource," and "Proofreader's Guide."
(+) This activity is located in a different section of the *Write Source Student Edition.* If students have already completed this activity, you may wish to review it at this time.

Teacher's Notes for Expository Writing

This overview for expository writing includes some specific teaching suggestions for this unit.

Writing Focus

Writing an Expository Paragraph (pages 126–131)

An expository paragraph explains something or gives information. It includes all the facts a reader needs to understand the subject. In this chapter, students will be explaining why something is important to them.

Writing an Expository Essay (pages 132–163)

An expository essay allows students to write an in-depth explanation. In this chapter, they will focus on something that is important to them.

Grammar Focus

For support with this unit's grammar topics, consult the resource units (Basic Grammar and Writing, A Writer's Resource, and Proofreader's Guide).

Academic Vocabulary

Read aloud the academic terms, as well as the descriptions and questions. Model for students how to read one question and answer it. Have partners monitor their understanding and seek clarification of the terms by working through the meanings and questions together.

Minilessons

Before First Grade — Writing an Expository Paragraph

- **NAME** a toy or an object that was important to you before you started school.
  - **LIST** at least three reasons why it was so important to you.

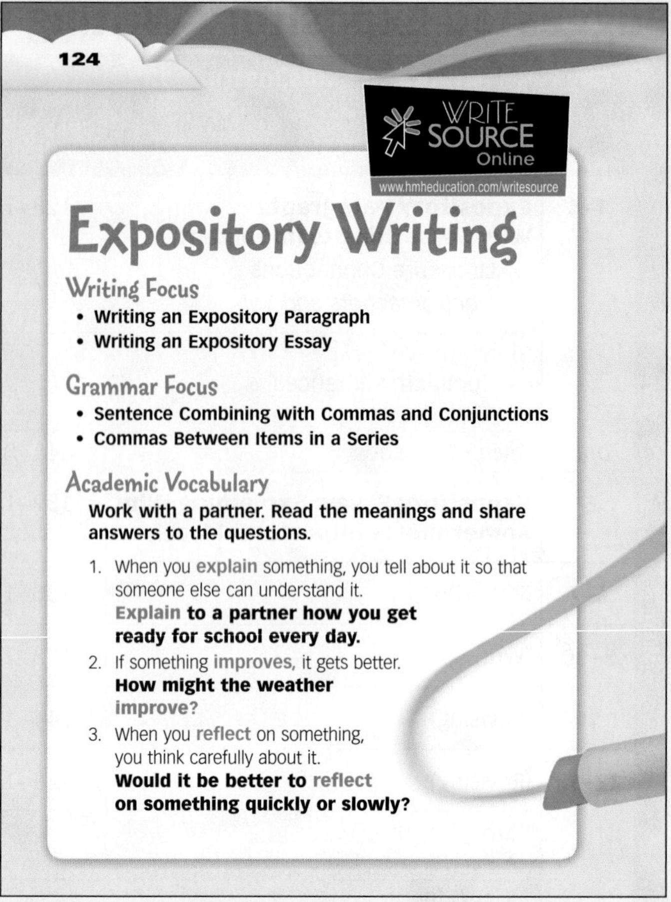

124
WRITE SOURCE Online
www.hmheducation.com/writesource
Expository Writing
Writing Focus
• Writing an Expository Paragraph
• Writing an Expository Essay
Grammar Focus
• Sentence Combining with Commas and Conjunctions
• Commas Between Items in a Series
Academic Vocabulary
Work with a partner. Read the meanings and share answers to the questions.
1. When you explain something, you tell about it so that someone else can understand it.
Explain to a partner how you get ready for school every day.
2. If something improves, it gets better.
How might the weather improve?
3. When you reflect on something, you think carefully about it.
Would it be better to reflect on something quickly or slowly?

Wish-List T-Chart — Writing an Expository Essay

- **REVIEW** the T-chart on SE page 136.
  - **MAKE** your own wish-list T-chart. **WRITE** "Foods" and "Clothing" underneath. In each group's column, **LIST** items from that group that you wish you could have. Then **CHOOSE** an item from each group that would be important to you.

Test Day — Writing for Assessment

- **IMAGINE** that you are about to take an assessment test. You will have 45 minutes to read and respond to the following prompt: What is one of the most dangerous animals?
  - **CREATE** a graphic organizer that can help you plan your essay.
  - **GATHER** details that explain why you think your chosen animal is so dangerous.

125

"What is the world's tallest mountain?"

"What is the deepest ocean?"

The world is full of questions. Writing that provides answers to these questions is called expository writing. Expository writing explains or informs.

In this section, you'll learn how to write an expository paragraph, an expository essay, and a few other forms. The world is full of questions, and here's your chance to provide some answers!

Literature Connections: For an example of an expository essay, read *Electromagnets and You* by Emma Rose.

Expository Writing

Point out that the word *expository* is based on the word *expose,* which means "to make known, or reveal." So, *expository* writing is writing that makes known, or reveals, information about a topic.

Ask students to think of where they've encountered expository writing outside school. Answers might include the following:

- newspapers and news magazines
- history books
- science and nature books
- directions for putting something together
- rules for a game

Explain that students will write many expository essays when they are in school.

Literature Connections

In the expository text *Electromagnets and You,* the author explains the use of electromagnets in commonly used machines.

Discuss how the photos in the text help the reader understand the facts and details. For additional models of expository writing, see the Reading-Writing Connections beginning on page TE-36.

Family Connection Letters

As you begin this unit, send home the Expository Writing Family Connection letter, which describes what students will be learning.

- Letter in English (TE p. 604)
- Letter in Spanish (TE p. 612)

Teaching Tip

As you introduce the expository form of writing, help students understand the specific purpose for writing—to explain. Then, discuss the concept of writing to an *audience*. Point out that whenever students write, they are writing for someone–themselves, teachers, friends, family members, and so on.

Writing an Expository Paragraph

Objectives

- Understand the content and structure of an expository paragraph.
- Choose a topic (an important object) to write about.
- Plan, draft, revise, and edit an expository paragraph.

Direct students' attention to the word *important*, and tell them they can think about this word in different ways. For example, it can refer to something that lots of people agree about (drinking water is *important,* because people can't survive without doing so). Or it can refer to something that is very personal (to someone who loves bright colors it's *important* that a new T-shirt be orange).

Remind students that a paragraph is a group of sentences about a single, specific topic.

* For more about paragraphs, see SE pages 416–429.

To get students thinking about the explanations they will find in Elijah's expository paragraph, have them brainstorm ideas about why bikes might be important to people. Write their responses on the board.

Technology Connections

Use this unit's Interactive Whiteboard Lesson to introduce expository writing.

Interactive Whiteboard Lessons

Writing an Expository Paragraph

Elijah had a bike. It was one of the most important things in his life. How could he explain to his family and friends what makes his bike great for him? He wrote an expository paragraph.

Soon you will write your own expository paragraph. In it, you'll explain why something is important to you.

Paragraph Parts

1. The **topic sentence** tells what the paragraph explains.
2. The **body sentences** add details that help explain the topic sentence.
3. The **closing sentence** completes the explanation.

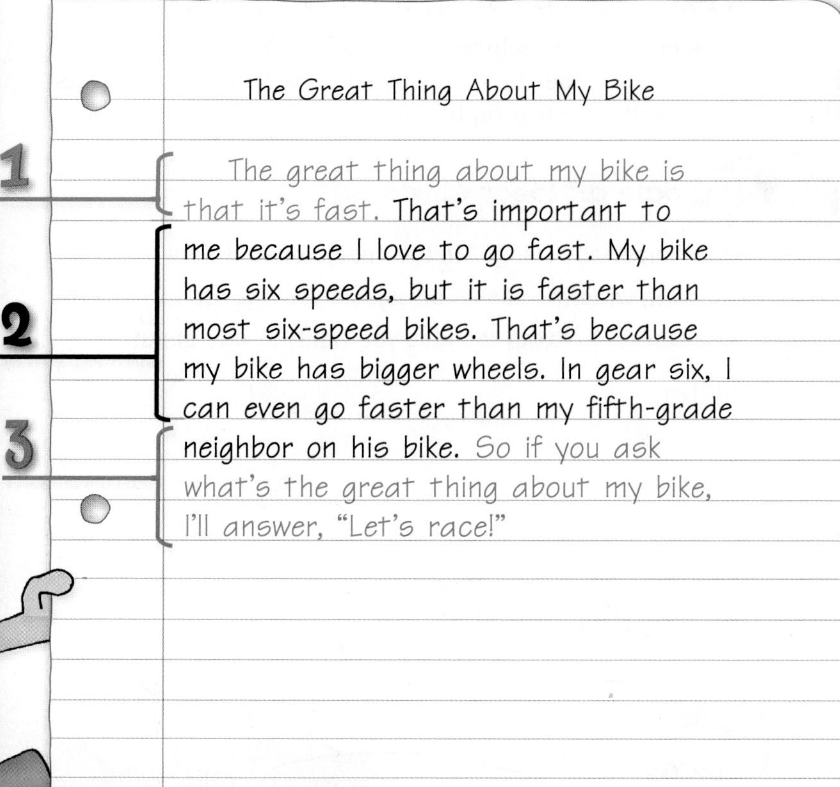

Writing an Expository Paragraph 127
Expository Paragraph
The Great Thing About My Bike
1
The great thing about my bike is that it's fast. That's important to
2
me because I love to go fast. My bike has six speeds, but it is faster than most six-speed bikes. That's because my bike has bigger wheels. In gear six, I can even go faster than my fifth-grade
3
neighbor on his bike. So if you ask what's the great thing about my bike, I'll answer, "Let's race!"

After you read . . .

- **Ideas** **(1) What details help explain the topic?**
- **Organization** **(2) What are the three parts of this paragraph?**
- **Word Choice** **(3) What three words or phrases show the writer's excitement about the topic?**

Expository Paragraph

Ask students to think about why the writer put the body sentences in this particular order. Guide them toward an understanding of the purpose of each body sentence:

- First: why a fast bike is important (Elijah loves to go fast)
- Second: one reason the bike is fast (six gears)
- Third: another reason it's fast (big wheels)
- Fourth: an example of what you can do with a fast bike (go faster than other bikes)

Point out to students that each sentence builds on the one that comes before it in a logical way that helps make the writer's explanation clear.

* For more about different ways to organize paragraphs, see SE pages 422–423.

After you read . . .

Answers

Ideas 1. writer loves to go fast; bike has six speeds; bike has big wheels

Organization 2. topic sentence, body sentences, closing sentence

Word Choice 3. Possible responses: great thing; that's important; I love to go fast; Let's race!

English Language Learners

Some students may find it difficult to tell which details explain the topic. Before students begin the **After you read** activity, write the following sentence frames on the board to help them structure their responses:

- My bike has _______.
- My bike is _______.

Using Elijah's paragraph, have students orally complete the sentence frames with details that help explain the topic such as "My bike has six speeds" or "My bike is faster than my neighbor's."

Prewriting Selecting a Topic

Suggest that students give themselves extra room for their ideas clusters by turning the sheet of paper sideways and writing the words *Important Things* in the very middle. This leaves plenty of space for the cluster.

* For more about creating a cluster, refer students to SE page 436.

If students are having difficulty filling out their clusters, ask the following questions to help them get going:

- If you were going on a long trip and could only take three things with you to help pass the time, what would they be?
- What are your favorite activities? Are there certain objects that you need for those activities?

Point out to students that they can also think about kinds of objects that are important to them in their everyday lives (for example, a diary or a favorite jacket).

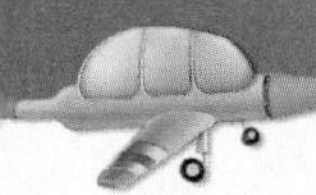

Prewriting Selecting a Topic

An ideas cluster can help you think of the important things in your life. Elijah made the cluster below. He focused on objects that he could write a paragraph about.

Create an ideas cluster.

1. Write "Important Things" in the middle of your paper.
2. Around it, write the names of objects you like. Connect them.
3. Put a star (*) next to the idea you want to write about.

Ideas Cluster

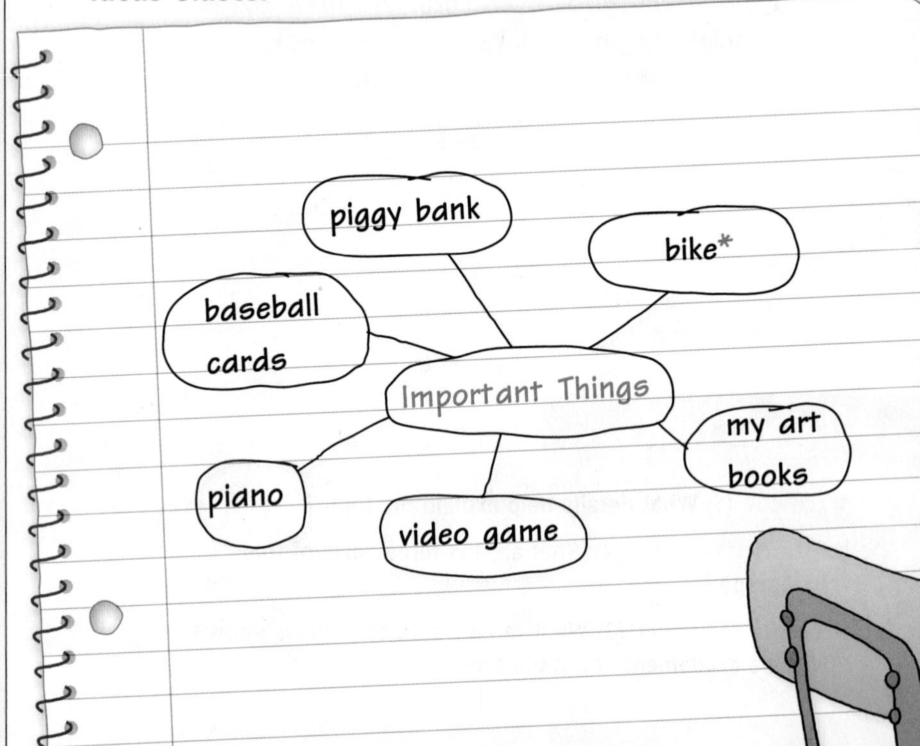

English Language Learners

Many students may benefit from oral discussions with partners because it helps them brainstorm ideas before they begin their cluster maps. To help focus the discussion on important things, have partners discuss three things they feel they cannot live without. Then have them use their ideas to create their cluster.

Advanced Learners

As a way to investigate topics, challenge students to cluster things that were important to them a year or so ago.

Writing an Expository Paragraph 129

Writing Creating Your First Draft

As you write your paragraph, remember that each part has a special job to do.

- Your **topic sentence** names the topic and tells what's great about it.
- Each **body sentence** explains your topic sentence by answering the question *why?* or *how?*
- Your **closing sentence** completes your explanation.

Write **Develop your paragraph.**

1. **Write your topic sentence using this form: "The great thing about ____________ is ____________ ."**
2. **Write sentences that answer *why?* or *how?* about the topic sentence.**
3. **Write a closing sentence that completes your explanation.**

Writing Creating Your First Draft

Help students work through the sections of their draft by **guiding them** *(see below)* during each step.

After students fill in the blanks in the suggested topic sentence (*The great thing about* ____________ *is* ____________), encourage them to express the same idea in different words.

Have students consider the following questions as they complete the body sentences:

- Why is your object or collection "great"?
- What does it do, or how do you use it?
- How do you feel when you use it or work on it?

As students complete their drafts, suggest that they

- refer to their topic sentence and add a little new information, or
- answer the question about how the object or collection of items makes them feel.

Teaching Tip: Writing Guidance

Students who need help getting started may benefit from a freewriting exercise.

- Have students take out pencil and paper.
- Instruct them to spend a few minutes writing anything they want to say about their topic, without worrying about the topic sentence or the order of details.
- Encourage students to keep writing, without pausing, for 5 to 8 minutes.

When students have finished, have them share the ideas they wrote on their topics with each other. Explain that freewriting is a good way to gather details about a topic.

Grammar Connection

Complete Sentences

- **Proofreader's Guide** pages 526–527, 528–529
- ***Write Source*** pages 397 (+), 398, 399, 400, 401
- ***GrammarSnap*** Complete Sentences
- ***SkillsBook*** pages 79–80, 81–82

Revising Improving Your Paragraph

Have students exchange papers with a partner and work together to discover things to work on when they revise their drafts.

- Have each reader answer the *how?* or *why?* question for each body sentence.
- Have each reader write one thing they learned about the topic and underline any detail that may not belong to the topic.
- Ask each writer to go over the notes made by the reader, and ask these questions: Did your reader identify the *how?* or *why?* questions you were trying to answer? Does the reader's suggestion give you an idea for how you will revise?

Let students work independently to complete their revised draft.

Practice Answers

The sentence that doesn't fit is *Some of my friends like to fish.*

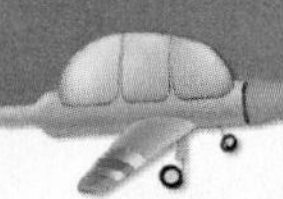

Revising Improving Your Paragraph

When you revise your paragraph, make sure your body sentences explain your topic sentence.

Check your body sentences.

1. Underline your topic sentence.
2. Check each body sentence to make sure it answers *why?* or *how?* about your topic sentence.
3. Cross out any sentence that does not explain the topic.
4. If you need to, add one or two sentences to explain your topic better.

Practice

Read the following paragraph. Which body sentence doesn't answer the question *why?* or *how?* about the topic sentence? Replace that sentence with one of your own that answers *why?* or *how?* about the topic.

I like to go to the city swimming pool on a hot day. I don't want to waste any time getting into the water. I jump into the deep end of the pool. The cool water makes me gasp. Some of my friends like to fish. I enjoy the high slide because I can make a big splash!

Struggling Learners

Some students may find it difficult to identify the body sentence that does not support the topic sentence in the **Practice**. Use the following steps to help students complete the activity:

- Have students identify the topic sentence.
- Simplify the topic sentence. For example, *I like swimming on a hot day.*
- After reading each body sentence, have students orally add *because I like swimming on a hot day.* Explain that these words answer the question *why?* For instance, *I jump into the deep end of the pool because I like swimming on a hot day.*

Help students see that *because I like swimming on a hot day* does not make sense when added to *Some of my friends like to fish.*

Writing an Expository Paragraph 131

Editing Checking for Conventions

When you edit your paragraph, make sure you have included the right punctuation after each sentence.

- Most sentences end with a period.
- Questions end with a question mark.
- Exciting sentences end with an exclamation point.

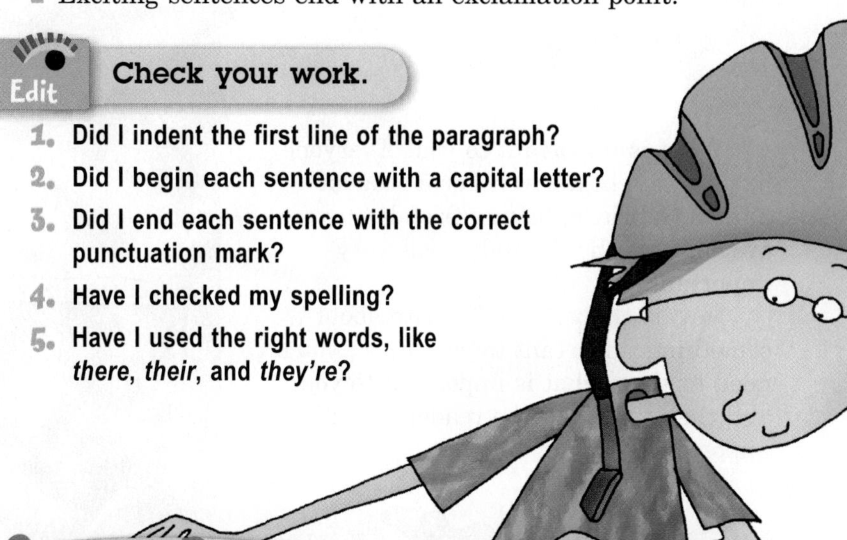

Edit Check your work.

1. **Did I indent the first line of the paragraph?**
2. **Did I begin each sentence with a capital letter?**
3. **Did I end each sentence with the correct punctuation mark?**
4. **Have I checked my spelling?**
5. **Have I used the right words, like *there*, *their*, and *they're*?**

Grammar Practice

Tell what the correct end punctuation mark would be for each sentence below.

1. How much money do you think I have in my piggy bank__
2. I wish I had a million dollars__
3. I will count my money tonight when I get home__

English Language Learners

Students may benefit from having their paragraphs read aloud by a partner, so that they can listen for places where they need to put punctuation. Have students listen for places where the voice naturally rises, usually indicating the need for a question mark, and where there is excitement, indicating an exclamation point.

Advanced Learners

After students complete the **Practice**, challenge them to write two or three sentences of their own that require commas, apostrophes, and different end punctuation. They should not include the punctuation. Then have students exchange papers with a partner and punctuate the sentences.

Editing Checking for Conventions

Focus on exclamation point use:

- Note that many sentences could end with either a period or an exclamation point, depending on what the writer wants to express.
- To demonstrate, write a short sentence on the board, such as, *Spring is the best time of year.* Have a volunteer read it as a statement and another read it with excitement as an exclamation.
- Explain that when writing expository paragraphs, it is wise not to overuse exclamation points. Remind students that the purpose of expository writing is to give information or provide answers to questions about a topic, so there shouldn't be a need for many exclamation points.

* For information about capitalization and punctuation, see SE page 402.

Grammar Practice Answers

1. question mark
2. period or exclamation point
3. period

Writing an Expository Essay

Objectives

- Understand the purpose, content, and form of an expository essay.
- Choose a topic (something important) to write about.
- Plan, draft, revise, edit, publish, and assess an expository essay.

Remind students that an essay is a piece of writing made up of several paragraphs. Explain to students that they are now going to use the information they learned about writing expository paragraphs to write an expository essay about something important to them.

Writing an Expository Essay

What is important to you? Everyone has a different answer. For a student named Gabrielle, having friends stay overnight for her birthday was very important.

In this chapter, you'll write about something important to you. First, you'll need to show what is important to you, and then you'll tell the reader why it's important.

Materials

Index cards (TE pp. 133, 140, 150, 152)

Adhesive tape (TE p. 133)

Scissors and tape (TE p. 144)

Drawing supplies (TE p. 162)

Copy Masters

T-Chart (TE p. 136)

Response Sheet (TE pp. 145, 163)

Thinking About Your Writing (TE p. 163)

Understanding Your Goal

Your goal in this chapter is to write an essay that explains something that is important to you. The six traits below and the expository revising lessons (pages 146–156) will help you reach your writing goal.

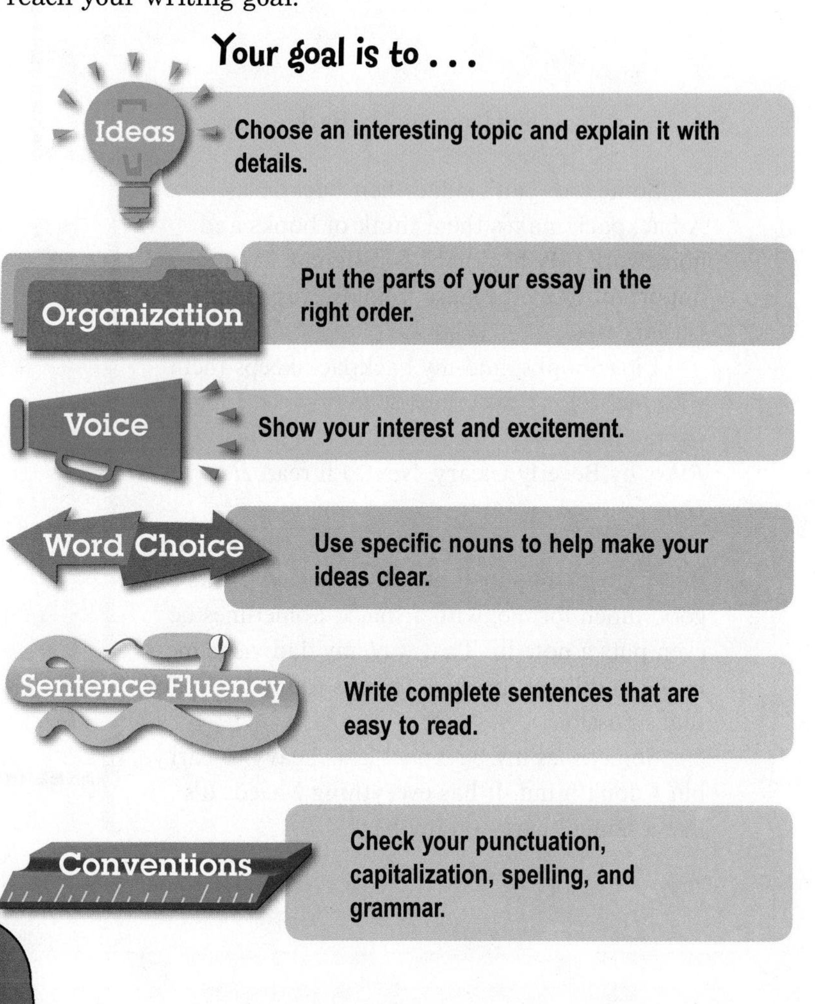

Your goal is to . . .
Ideas
Choose an interesting topic and explain it with details.
Organization
Put the parts of your essay in the right order.
Voice
Show your interest and excitement.
Word Choice
Use specific nouns to help make your ideas clear.
Sentence Fluency
Write complete sentences that are easy to read.
Conventions
Check your punctuation, capitalization, spelling, and grammar.

Understanding Your Goal

Encourage students to use this page as a guide for understanding how the traits can help them write their expository essay. Suggest that they bookmark this page so that they can flip back to it any time they need a reminder of their goals as they plan and write their essay. Reassure students that they will receive plenty of guidance throughout the writing process so that they can successfully achieve these goals.

Depending on the needs of your class, focus on one or two of the traits throughout the revising process. The revising section (SE pages 146–156) provides additional instruction and practice for each trait. The side notes and Teaching Tips throughout this section of the TE also provide suggestions to supplement the instruction and the practices.

After reviewing the goals, focus on complete sentences. A complete sentence

- contains a subject and a verb,
- expresses a complete thought,
- begins with a capital letter, and
- ends with correct end punctuation.

Struggling Learners

Give each student an index card. Then have students set a goal by choosing the trait they most need or want to work on. Have them write that goal, for example, *My goal is to improve organization in my writing.* Meet with students to discuss ways they can work to achieve their goals.

Have students tape their index cards to a prominent place such as inside their writing folders to serve as reminders and for handy reference.

Expository Essay

After students have read the model essay and reviewed the information about the beginning, middle, and ending on SE page 135, ask them to point out the

- focus sentence (It is important to me . . .),
- topic sentence for middle paragraph 1 (I love books . . .),
- topic sentence for middle paragraph 2 (Another reason . . .), and
- closing sentence (It's like a home . . .).

Have students look again at the last paragraph and discuss in their own words how they think the writer feels about his backpack.

Expository Essay

An expository essay gives information to the reader. This essay explains why Aidan's backpack is important to him.

The Home on My Back

Some kids can't stand their backpacks. A backpack makes them think of books and homework. My backpack is different. It is important to me because it holds everything I need.

I love books, and my backpack keeps them with me. I don't mean just schoolbooks. I mean my reading books, too. Right now, I'm reading *Ribsy* by Beverly Cleary. Next, I'll read *Henry Huggins*.

Another reason my backpack is important is that it holds my lunch box. Dad always packs a good lunch for me, with a snack. Sometimes he even puts a note in. That way, my dad visits me in the middle of the day! Thanks to my backpack, that's possible.

Sometimes my backpack gets heavy to carry, but I don't mind. It has everything I need. It's like a home I carry on my back.

English Language Learners

Students may need help understanding the comparison of a backpack to a home. Point out that Aidan's backpack holds the things that he needs and that are important to him. Guide students in identifying these things:

- books
- lunch
- a snack
- a note

Explain that, like a home, Aidan's backpack provides him with many things he needs and loves, and that's why it feels like a home to him.

Advanced Learners

Direct students' attention to Aidan's first sentence. Challenge students to brainstorm a list of reasons they think that some kids can't stand their backpacks. Then have students share their reasons with the class.

Parts of an Expository Essay

An expository essay has three parts.

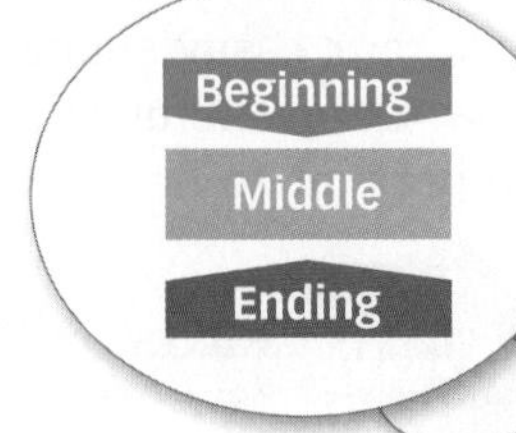

Beginning

The **beginning paragraph** names the topic and gives the focus sentence.

Middle

Each **middle paragraph** starts with a topic sentence. Details in the other sentences explain the topic sentence.

Ending

The **ending paragraph** tells how the writer feels about the topic.

After you read . . .

- **Ideas** **(1) What does the writer think is important about his backpack?**
- **Organization** **(2) How does the writer introduce his topic?**
- **Word Choice** **(3) What words or phrases help show the writer's feelings about his backpack?**

Struggling Learners

Help visual learners by making a cluster map on the board before answering the first **After you read** question. In the center circle, write *Aidan's backpack*. Have students search the paragraph for words and phrases that tell why Aidan's backpack is important to him. Cluster their responses in surrounding circles. Responses include the following:

- holds everything I need
- keeps them (books) with me
- holds my lunch box
- snack
- note

Parts of an Expository Essay

In preparation for the **After you read** exercise, discuss the way the writer introduces his topic.

- First, he draws readers in with a statement about how a lot of people feel: Some kids can't stand their backpacks.
- Then he explains why they don't like them: They don't like thinking about books and homework.
- Finally, the writer reveals how *he* feels about his backpack: He *likes* his backpack.

After you read . . .

Answers

Ideas **1.** keeps his books with him, holds his lunch box, is like a home on his back

Organization **2.** opens with an attention-getting statement (some kids can't stand their backpacks) and then says what he thinks about the topic in a focus sentence: It is important to me . . .

Word Choice **3.** It is important to me . . . , Thanks to my backpack . . . , It's like a home . . .

Prewriting Selecting a Topic

Remind students that they can choose to write about an important person, place, or activity as well as an object. Also, encourage students who still have a lot to say about the topic they chose for their paragraph (SE pages 126–131) to feel free to expand it into an essay.

Have students examine the ideas in Gabrielle's T-chart on SE page 136 and identify which ones are objects, people, places, and activities:

- Objects: pastels set
- People: family
- Places: tetherball court, bedroom
- Activities: overnights, recess, art class

Provide photocopies of the reproducible T-Chart (TE page 595). Instruct students to write *At Home* and *At School* at the top of the chart before filling it out as instructed on the page. Encourage students to consider a variety of topics—at least one of each of the types discussed above.

* Refer students who need help thinking of ideas to the topics lists on SE pages 434–435.

Technology Connections

Students can use the added features of the Net-text as they explore this stage of the writing process.

***Write Source Online* Net-text**

Prewriting Selecting a Topic

Your essay should be about something that means a lot to you. Gabrielle used a T-chart to think about things that were important to her.

Prewrite Make a T-chart.

1. Write "Important Things" at the top of your paper.
2. Write "At Home" and "At School" underneath.
3. List important things under each heading.
4. Put a star (*) next to the thing you want to write about.

T-Chart

Important Things

At Home	At School
family	the tetherball court
my bedroom	recess
overnights*	art class
my pastels set	

Advanced Learners

Have students write a focus sentence for one "At Home" and one "At School" activity on their T-charts. Then have them choose the topic they want to develop more fully. If they need help deciding, have them jot down a few details for each topic to help them choose the topic most interesting to them.

Writing an Expository Essay 137

Thinking About the Topic

(1) *What is most important about your topic?*
(2) *Why is that important?*
(3) *How is that important?*

Gabrielle answered these questions about her topic. Her first answer is her **focus sentence**. It tells *what* her essay will be about. The other two answers are the **topic sentences** for the body paragraphs. They will tell *why* and *how* about her topic.

Answer these three questions.

1. **Write "What's most important?"**
   Answer this question by writing your focus sentence.
2. **Write "Why?"**
   Answer this question by writing your first topic sentence.
3. **Write "How?"**
   Answer this question by writing your second topic sentence.

Topic Questions

1. What's most important?
   An overnight is a special kind of party.
2. Why?
   Friends can be together all night at an overnight.
3. How?
   An overnight is full of fun activities.

Teaching Tip: Extra Guidance

Circulate among students as they work. Help them to crystallize their ideas by asking questions that guide them to consider their topics in various ways:

- Can you briefly describe the object, person, or event?
- What is your favorite thing about your topic?
- Can you tell me something funny about the topic? Something sad? Serious?
- How do your friends or family feel about it?

Thinking About the Topic

Students may benefit from **extra guidance** *(see below)* in answering the three questions. If so, provide more detailed explanations such as the following to help clarify.

- Note that the answer to the first question should actually contain two pieces of information. Q: What is the topic? A: an overnight. Q: What is the main reason you chose it? A: It's a special kind of party.
- The second answer should explain why that's your main reason: because you can be with friends all night.
- The third answer should tell how your topic accomplishes what you like. Q: How is an overnight party special? A: It's full of fun activities.

Writing Beginning Your Essay

Focus on the creative strategy for beginning an essay.

- Divide the class into small storytelling groups.
- Give students a few minutes to think of a brief story about the topic they plan to write about.
- Encourage them to think of an experience they had that relates to their topic and that helps to explain why the topic is important to them.
- Suggest that students begin the story with the lead-in "Once upon a time . . . " as if it were a fairy tale.
- Have the students in each group take turns telling each other their stories.

Afterward, return to the larger group and discuss students' experiences.

- Did they enjoy telling the story? Hearing others' stories?
- Did thinking of their topic as a story give them an idea for a beginning paragraph?
- Did it give them ideas for other details to include?

Technology Connections

Students can use the added features of the Net-text as they explore this stage of the writing process.

Write Source Online ***Net-text***

Writing Beginning Your Essay

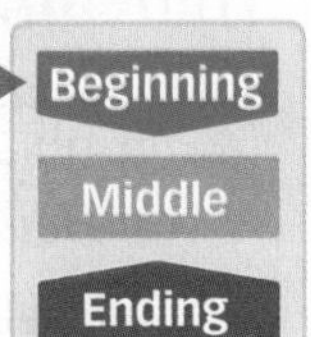

Your beginning paragraph introduces the topic. Here are three possible ways to introduce your topic.

Ask a question.

> What could be better than an overnight with friends?

OR

Be creative and tell a little story.

> At midnight, something tapped on the window, and I . . .

OR

Connect with readers.

> When my sister Celia had an overnight, I listened through the wall to the spooky stories she told.

Create your beginning paragraph.

1. Use one of the three ways above to introduce your topic.
2. Include your focus sentence. (See the bottom of page 137.)

Advanced Learners

Challenge students to write on a sheet of paper one of each type of beginning for their essay. Have students exchange their beginnings with a partner. Each reader should decide which beginning is most interesting and explain why. Students can use their partner's responses to help choose the beginning for their essay.

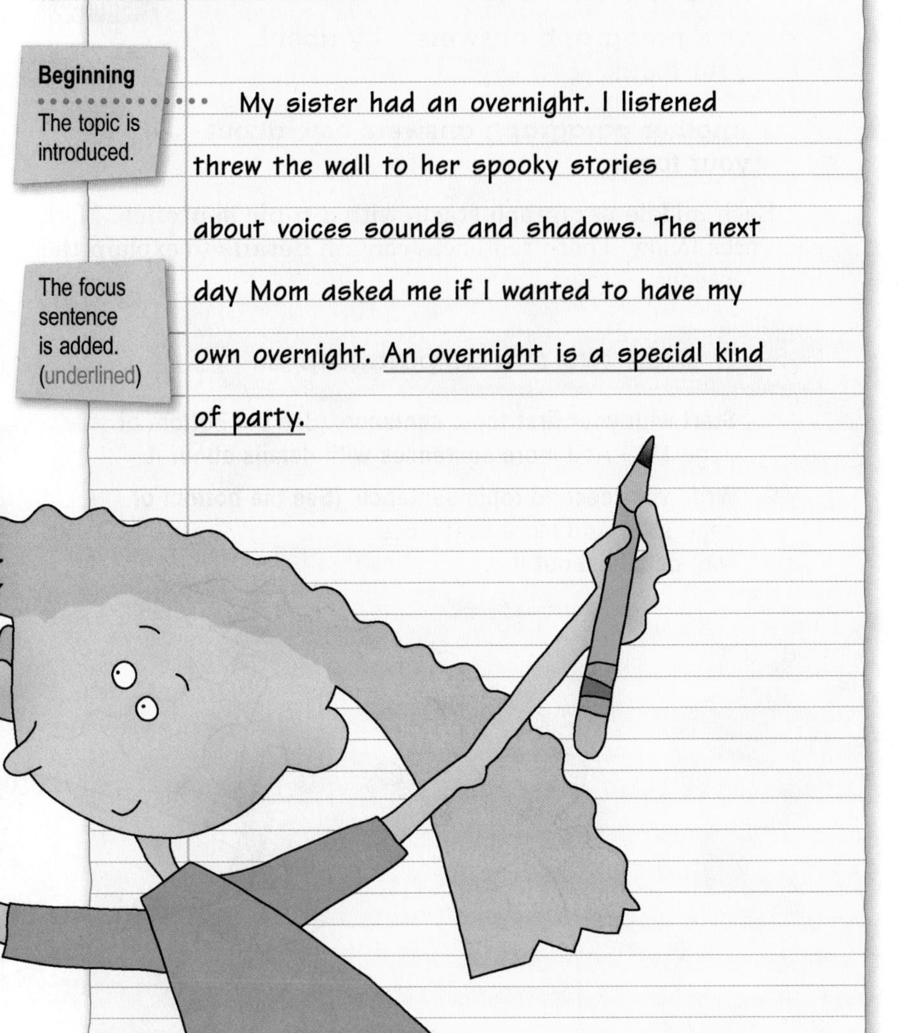

Writing an Expository Essay 139
Gabrielle's Beginning Paragraph
Gabrielle's beginning had some great ideas, and some errors. That's all right for a first draft.
Beginning
The topic is introduced.
My sister had an overnight. I listened threw the wall to her spooky stories about voices sounds and shadows. The next day Mom asked me if I wanted to have my own overnight. An overnight is a special kind of party.
The focus sentence is added. (underlined)

Gabrielle's Beginning Paragraph

Explain to students that if they think of a better idea for an opening at any stage of the writing process, they should go back and write it in.

Literature Connections

Mentor texts: Read three strong beginnings from great expository books, such as *Pyramid* by David Macaulay, *Cool Stuff and How It Works* by Chris Woodford, or *Lights! Camera! Action! How a Movie is Made* by Gail Gibbons. Then ask students to vote on which beginning is strongest. Have them tell why they voted for the beginning they chose. Ask if they could create a similar beginning for their essays.

Writing Developing the Middle

To help students with the middle paragraphs of their essays, explain that they will work with partners to "interview" each other, based on the topic sentences they've written.

Give students a few minutes to read their partner's topic sentences and think of questions. Encourage writers to take notes during the interview so they don't forget interesting details that come up.

Write sample "why" questions on the board for Gabrielle's first middle paragraph to help interviewers get going, and encourage them to ask other questions when they think of them. A student interviewing the writer of the essay about overnights might ask:

- Why do you think overnight parties are fun?
- Is it more fun than seeing friends at other times?
- What kinds of fun things do you do at overnights?

After each partner has interviewed the other, have students read through their notes and circle details they want to use in their essays.

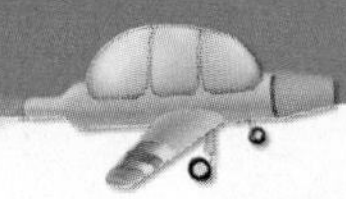

Writing Developing the Middle

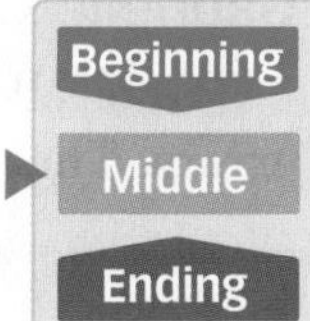

The middle part of your essay explains your focus sentence. Your middle should include two or more paragraphs.

- **One paragraph answers why about your focus.**
- **Another paragraph answers how about your focus.**

Each middle paragraph starts with a **topic sentence**. More sentences follow. Those sentences contain **details** to explain the topic sentence.

Draft two middle paragraphs.

1. **Start with your first topic sentence. (See the bottom of page 137.) Add more sentences with details about it.**
2. **Write your second topic sentence. (See the bottom of page 137.) Add more sentences with details about it.**

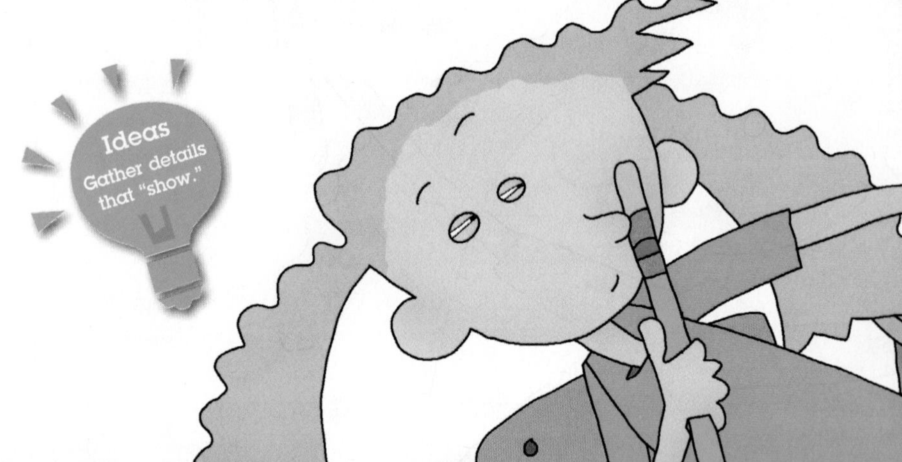

Struggling Learners

Before students draft their middle paragraphs, provide them with two index cards.

- Have them write a topic sentence on the first one and underline it.
- Then have students write details that support the topic sentence.

Have them repeat the procedure using the second index card. Tell students to refer to the details on the cards as they draft their middle paragraphs.

Writing an Expository Essay 141

Gabrielle's Middle Paragraphs

Gabrielle explained *why* and *how* about her focus sentence. Her writing has a few errors, as all first drafts do.

an overnight of my own. An overnight is a special kind of party.

Middle

A topic sentence begins the first paragraph.

Freinds can be together all night at an overnight. That's more fun than just seeing each other at school. It's great to stay up late with good freinds.

Details are added.

A topic sentence begins the second paragraph.

Another great thing about an overnight is that it is full of fun activities. Nighttime is perfect for telling spooky stories what could be better than a movie marathon, eating, board games, and sleeping on the floor in the living room.

Details are added.

Gabrielle's Middle Paragraphs

In addition to the notes students made after interviewing each other, they might also want to use the cluster chart method they learned about on SE page 128 to assemble some of the details for their paper.

Demonstrate for students how the author of the sample could have planned the second middle paragraph using a cluster. Write *Fun Things to Do at an Overnight* in the center of the board and circle it. Arrange the activities named in the paragraph around the center topic in cluster style:

- tell spooky stories
- watch a movie marathon
- play board games
- sleep on the living room floor

When students have finished writing their middle paragraphs, ask them to go back and reread their planning notes, crossing off each detail in the notes that they mentioned in the essay. Did they forget anything? Would they like to add that information to the essay?

Writing Ending Your Essay

Focus on the sample ending that Gabrielle decided to use, the one that returns to the opening idea.

Have a volunteer reread aloud the beginning paragraph on SE page 139. Ask students to think about how the ending connects to that beginning. What old information is repeated and what new information is added? Answers include the following:

- Repeated: Celia is mentioned again.
- Repeated: The writer is going to have her own overnight.
- Repeated: You tell spooky stories at an overnight.
- New: This time, Celia will be the one listening through the wall as the writer tells the stories.
- New: The overnight will happen next weekend.
- New: The writer's cousins will stay at her house instead of her aunt and uncle's house.

Remind students that the ending paragraph should always contain some new information, even if the writer chooses the strategy of returning to the beginning. This is important for holding the readers' attention all the way to the end.

Writing Ending Your Essay

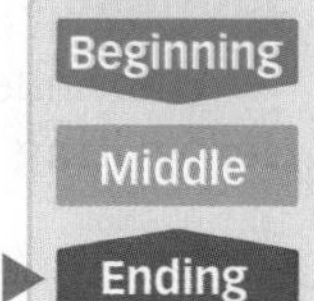

Your ending paragraph completes your explanation. Here are three possible ways to end your° essay.

Return to your beginning idea.

Now Celia will have to listen to my spooky stories because my very first overnight will be next weekend.

OR

Share something funny.

I'm so excited about my overnight, I can't sleep.

OR

Talk with your reader.

If you're like me, you've been dreaming about having an overnight.

Create your ending.

1. Use one of the three ways above to write an ending for your essay.
2. Try a second way and choose the one you like best.

English Language Learners

Choosing a method for ending a story may inhibit some students. Encourage students first to write a straightforward ending, knowing that they will change it. Then have them work with partners to adapt their ending using the method that feels most comfortable to them.

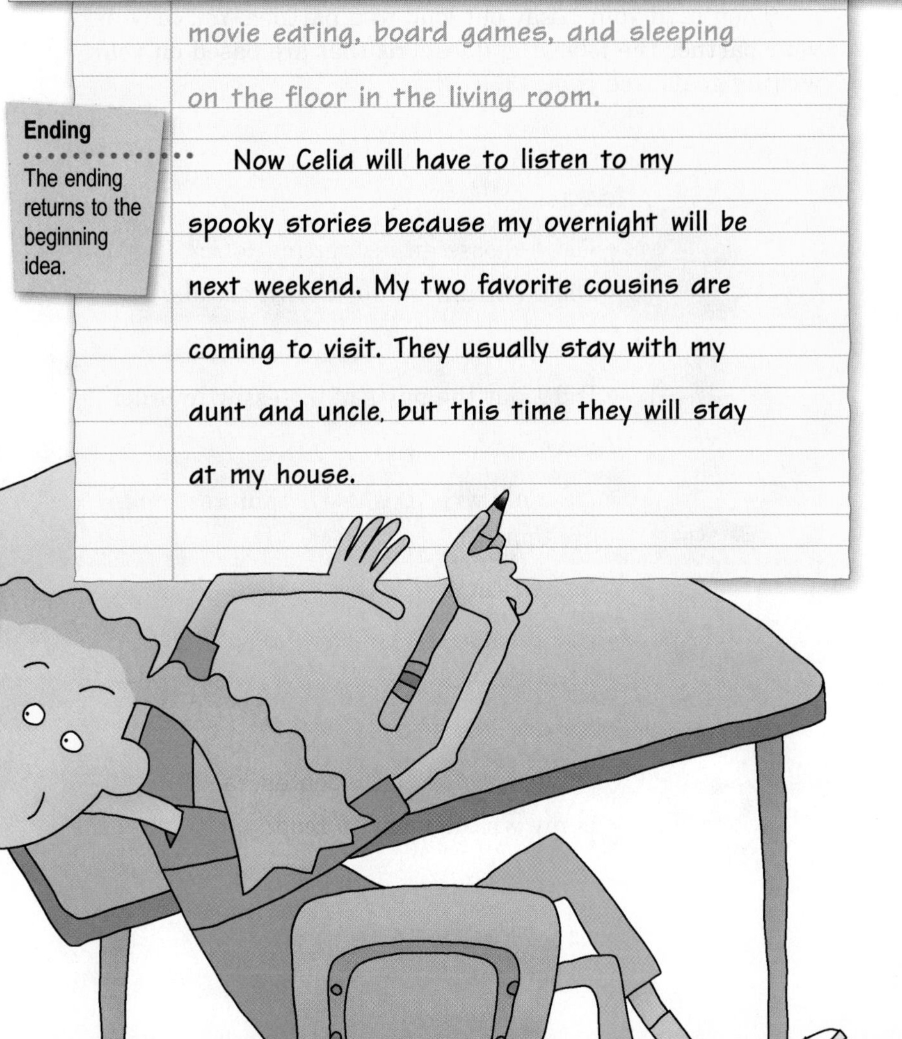

Writing an Expository Essay
143
Gabrielle's Ending Paragraph
Gabrielle created a strong ending by going back to the beginning of her essay. Her first ending contains some errors.
movie eating, board games, and sleeping on the floor in the living room.
Ending
The ending returns to the beginning idea.
Now Celia will have to listen to my spooky stories because my overnight will be next weekend. My two favorite cousins are coming to visit. They usually stay with my aunt and uncle, but this time they will stay at my house.

Struggling Learners

Help students visualize going back to the beginning idea by drawing a circle on the board.

- Read through Gabrielle's essay on SE pages 139, 141, and 143. Pause periodically and jot down details around the circle in a clockwise manner, beginning at the top.
- After you read the ending paragraph, jot down words and phrases that are also used in the beginning paragraph. Point out these similarities by focusing students' attention on the top of the circle where the essay begins and ends.

Gabrielle's Ending Paragraph

Point out to students that once they have decided on their ending idea, they have choices about how to arrange the information in the paragraph. Demonstrate how Gabrielle's closing paragraph could be changed to give the same information but in a different order. For example:

- "Next weekend, I get to have my overnight. Instead of staying with my aunt and uncle, my two favorite cousins will stay at my house. Now Celia will have to listen to my spooky stories!"

Encourage students to consider whether the information they want to include could be presented in a different order than they first planned. Sometimes it can.

Suggest that, if they decide to try alternative paragraphs, they evaluate them by reading them aloud to themselves or maybe to a friend. Does one version sound better? Is it more interesting or exciting?

Revising Improving Your Essay

In preparation for a partner revision activity, distribute scissors and have students cut their essays into four pieces with a paragraph on each piece. (If possible, photocopy the essays so students can keep the original.) After cutting the paper apart, have students trim a thin strip from each edge so it isn't possible to put the pieces back together by matching edges.

- Have partners give each other their cut-apart essays. Can they put the pieces back in the correct order?
- Ask readers to identify the topic of the essay.
- Have them circle two nouns they think should be more specific.
- Have the essays returned to their writers, who can now tape them back together and finish revising on their own.

Begin the revision process by having students read and respond to each other's writing. For an oral review, have writers use the questions on this page to get responses from their partners. For a more in-depth response, have partners complete a response sheet like that on the facing page.

Once students have identified the strengths and weaknesses in their writing, assign them specific trait-based strategies from the revision pages that follow. Assign strategies based upon either the weaknesses discovered in the peer response or the trait(s) you are emphasizing.

* For more information about specific nouns, see SE page 378.

Technology Connections

Have students use the Writing Network features of the Net-text to comment on each other's drafts.

Write Source Online ***Net-text***

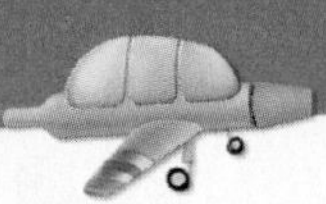

Revising Improving Your Essay

When you finish your first draft, you are ready to make changes to improve your writing. Begin the revising part of the writing process by reading your essay to yourself.

Then read your essay out loud to a partner. You may ask your partner the following questions that are based on your writing goals (see page 133).

Ideas
- Did I choose an interesting topic?
- Did I explain my topic with details?

Organization
- Did I put the parts of my essay in order?

Voice
- Does my writing show my interest and excitement?

Word Choice
- Did I use specific nouns to make my ideas clear?

Sentence Fluency
- Did I write complete sentences?
- Is my writing easy to read?

Writing an Expository Essay 145

Getting a Partner's Response

A partner can help you find ways to improve your writing. Here is a partner's response to Gabrielle's essay on pages 139–143.

Response Sheet

Writer: Gabrielle Responder: Dario

Title: All Right, an Overnight!

What I like:

Everybody likes overnights!

The part about Celia was funny.

Questions I have:

What do you eat?

Where do your cousins live?

Getting a Partner's Response

Before dividing the class into pairs, remind students that when responding to someone else's work they should always do the following:

- Keep responses friendly and polite.
- Be specific. Instead of just saying *It was good* (too general), say *It was good because . . .* and explain why.
- Ask questions that require an explanation, not just a "yes" or "no" answer.

Distribute photocopies of the reproducible Response Sheet (TE page 592), and then have students read their first drafts to each other.

Ask students to fill out the sheets, mentioning one or two things they like and one or two things they have questions about. Give partners a few minutes to review their responses together and clarify any questions.

English Language Learners

Many students speak a first language in which pronunciations of letters and combinations of letters differ from those in English.

Before having students read their work to a classmate, have them practice by reading aloud slowly and then increasing the rate to the speed of normal conversation. This strategy helps students with pronunciation and also firmly imprints vocabulary in their minds.

Advanced Learners

Challenge students to revise Gabrielle's middle paragraphs using the two questions from the Response Sheet as a basis for the revision. Post the results in the classroom for students to see that improved writing can take many different forms.

Revising for Ideas

To give students practice using detailed language, play a class game of "Show, Don't Tell":

- Give students time to think of (and write down, if they'd like) general sentences that tell rather than show.
- Have students take turns reading their "telling" sentences to the class, and have volunteers come up with detailed "showing" sentences to better express the idea.
- You might have more than one student revise each sentence. Doing so can demonstrate how the same general idea can be interpreted differently by people.
- Continue until all students have had a turn to read aloud their "telling" sentence or to come up with a "showing" one.

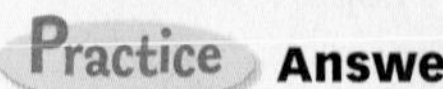

Answers

Here is one possible answer.

> Bobcat, my big brown and black tabby cat, has a purr that sounds like a little motor running. I love to listen to it at night when I am falling asleep. He curls up and keeps me company when I read books, watch TV, or play on the computer. Bobcat listens to all my stories and secrets. Whenever I see him, I just want to hug him and hold him close.

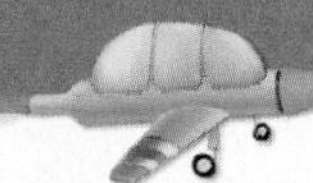

Revising for Ideas

Strong writing "shows" readers what you mean rather than just "telling" them.

Q. How can I "show" instead of "tell"?

Here are three ways you can *show* instead of *tell*.

1 Use sensory details: Include things that can be seen, heard, smelled, tasted, or touched.

Telling: Thanksgiving dinner is always good.
Showing: Thanksgiving dinner means juicy turkey, hot rolls, and steaming stuffing.

2 Use specific details: Give exact information.

Telling: I love going to baseball games.
Showing: I love sitting in the bleachers, cheering for our team, and eating hot dogs.

3 Use dialogue: Let people speak for themselves.

Telling: Mom said she was proud of me.
Showing: Mom said, "No one works harder than you do."

Practice

Rewrite the telling sentence below. Use one of the three showing strategies above.

My pet is important to me.

Struggling Learners

Provide students with extra practice using specific details to create "showing" sentences. On the board, write the following "telling" sentences:

- Dad said he enjoyed our Little League baseball game.
- We had fun at the park.

Work with students to add sensory details that turn each sentence into a "showing" sentence. Solutions might resemble the following:

- Dad said, "That was the best baseball game I've seen in a long time!"
- We played on the slide and swings all morning at the park.

Have students compare the two versions and point out specific details in the "showing" sentences.

Writing an Expository Essay 147

Revising in Action

Here are some of the changes Gabrielle made to improve the ideas in the beginning paragraph of her first draft. She changed one telling sentence and put the idea into dialogue.

My sister had an overnight. I listened threw the wall to her spooky stories about voices sounds and shadows. The next day Mom asked me, ~~if I wanted~~ "Would you like to have ~~my~~ your own overnight." An overnight is a special kind of party. Friends can be together all night at an overnight.

Check your ideas.

Find at least one place in your writing to "show" instead of "tell" using details or dialogue.

- **Add** sensory and other specific details. Use a caret ∧ to show where you want to add words or punctuation.
- **Add** dialogue if it adds information.
- **Cut** words that tell instead of show. Use a delete mark to show what you want to remove.

Revising in Action

Dialogue is a natural part of a narrative. However, there are also times when dialogue can improve an expository essay as well. Dialogue helps make details come to life. Discuss how Gabrielle's change improves her essay. Dialogue lets the reader come to her or his own conclusion. The original sentence could mean that Gabrielle's mom was upset that she had been listening to her sister's friends during their overnight. The dialogue makes it clear that is not the case.

- The dialogue shows that Gabrielle's mother thinks that she is ready for her first overnight.
- Even though Gabrielle didn't ask for an overnight, her mom knew she wanted one.

As students seek to "show" instead of "tell" as they revise their essays, consider assigning some "Show-Me" sentences from *Daily Language Workouts,* page 3.

Grammar Connection

Punctuating Dialogue

- **Proofreader's Guide** pages 470 (+), 476 (+)
- ***SkillsBook*** pages 29–30

Revising for Organization

Encourage students who like the scavenger hunt idea to come up with other things to look for and symbols they can use during revision. For example:

- Details presented in the correct order could be marked with circled numbers.
- The beginning and ending paragraphs could be marked with a circled *B* and *E*, respectively.
- Strong word choices could be noted with a check mark.
- Wording that communicates the writer's excitement could be marked with an exclamation mark.

After students brainstorm other symbols, have them create a "revision symbols key" that shows each symbol and its meaning, so they can refer to it whenever they need to revise their writing.

Revising for

Organization Your writing is well organized if it has all the parts it needs and each part is in the right place.

Q. How can I check my organization?

You can check the organization of your essay by doing the following scavenger hunt.

Organization Scavenger Hunt

1. Add a ¶ beside each paragraph indent.
2. Make a * next to your focus sentence in your beginning paragraph.
3. Put a ☺ next to the topic sentence in each middle paragraph.

Practice

Where would you place the above symbols in the passage below?

My brother and I have a tree house in a huge oak tree in the pasture. On a hot day, a breeze flows up from the valley like a cool clear stream. A tree house is a great place to play, read a book, or just be alone. Our tree house has two floors. Boards hammered into the tree make a ladder to the first floor. Then a trapdoor leads to the second level. Dad used wooden braces to make the floors and side rails strong. Our tree house even has a roof. Being up in a tree is fun. We pretend to be sailing on a ship or looking down at the world from space. We have many adventures in our tree house.

English Language Learners

Some students may be unfamiliar with the term *scavenger hunt.* Explain that a scavenger is someone who searches for something. Tell students that a scavenger hunt is a game in which individuals or teams compete with one another to search for various items.

Demonstrate the general concept of a scavenger hunt by hiding "clues" (several symbols ¶, *, ☺ on sticky notes) around the room. Give students a list of the symbols and have them find the clues. They can then use the sticky notes with their own writing.

Writing an Expository Essay 149

Revising in Action

Gabrielle checked the organization of her first draft. She marked her focus sentence and paragraph indents. She needed to create one new paragraph.

¶ My sister had an overnight. I listened threw the wall to her spooky stories about voices sounds and shadows. The next day Mom asked "Would you like me ~~if I wanted~~ to have ~~my~~ your own overnight." An ¶ overnight is a special kind of party. Friends can be together all night at an overnight.

Check your organization.

Mark your own essay for the scavenger hunt on page 148. You may need to write a focus sentence, indent a paragraph, or add a topic sentence.

Revising in Action

Review the changes that Gabrielle made to her first draft for organization based on the scavenger hunt on SE page 148. Tell students that this is a good system to remember whenever they are revising an essay for organization.

Writer's Craft

Paragraph marks: The paragraph mark might seem funny to students—a backward P with an extra leg—but the mark has a very old origin. It used to be that paper was so precious that scribes would not indent the beginnings of paragraphs, but would simply run everything together. The paragraph mark came into being as a way that scribes could indicate that a new group of ideas was beginning (much as your students are doing in this exercise). In fact, the word *paragraph* means "beside the writing" because the mark was made in the margin.

Revising for Voice

Remind students that the best way to assess voice in a piece is to read it aloud. Point out that they are much more likely to spot silly or boring sentences if they hear them spoken. Also, writing that achieves just the right interested voice is easy to read in an enthusiastic manner.

Writer's Craft

Voice: Every writer has a unique voice—a special way of expressing her- or himself. The ideas expressed, the words used, and the order of the elements all affect voice. Sometimes, when the voice is inappropriate, the idea being expressed is what needs to be toned down or built up, as in the example. Sometimes, a specific word has derailed the whole sentence, or elements need to appear in a different order. Help students discover the small changes that can make a big difference for voice.

Revising for

Voice

Your writing voice is your own special way of expressing yourself. For an expository essay, your voice should sound interested.

Q. How can I write with an interested voice?

Your voice will sound interested if your sentences aren't silly or boring. Use the ideas below to check your voice.

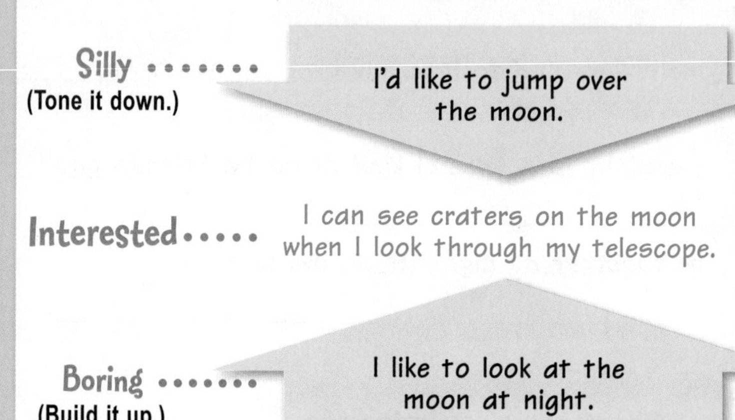
Silly
(Tone it down.)
I'd like to jump over the moon.
Interested
I can see craters on the moon when I look through my telescope.
Boring
(Build it up.)
I like to look at the moon at night.

Practice

Rewrite the boring sentence below so that you sound interested in the topic.

I have a red bicycle.

English Language Learners

Explain that to *tone down* a silly sentence means writing the sentence so that it is not silly. Also point out that a silly sentence is often an exaggerated statement such as *The only class in school should be recess.* Explain that the goal in toning down a sentence is to create an interesting sentence.

Advanced Learners

Students can practice toning down and building up sentences by playing the following game:

- Have students think of a topic and write one silly sentence and one boring sentence about it on two separate index cards.
- Collect all the cards and shuffle them.
- Read each card aloud to the class and have each student choose two to build up or tone down.

After students have rewritten their sentences, have them read to the class two silly and/or boring sentences with their revisions.

Writing an Expository Essay 151

Revising in Action

Here is how Gabrielle changed her first paragraph to improve the voice in her first draft. She added interesting words to a sentence that sounded boring. She also added a sentence to show excitement.

¶ My sister had an overnight. I listened threw
growly
the wall to her spooky stories about voices
screechy dark
sounds and shadows. The next day Mom asked
"Would you like your I can't wait
me if I wanted to have my own overnight." An
¶
overnight is a special kind of party. Friends
can be together all night at an overnight.

Revise **Check your writing voice.**

1. Read your essay and underline any sentences that sound silly or boring.
2. Rewrite underlined sentences so that you sound more interested.
   - **Cut** words or sentences that sound silly or boring.
   - **Add** words that make your writing more interesting.

Revising in Action

After students have identified the sentences that lack voice in their own essay and have rewritten them, invite volunteers to read the original versions and the revised versions aloud. (This can be done with the entire class or as a small group activity.) Have other students comment on the versions. Which do they find more interesting? Why?

Afterward, ask students what they learned from writing revisions.

- Did it help them to think of new details they might want to mention?
- Did it help them to think of new word choices?

Have students insert into their draft any new ideas they gained from revising their sentences.

Revising for Word Choice

After reviewing the differences between general and specific nouns, demonstrate how much interpretations of general nouns can vary:

- Write a general noun on the board (for example, *animal*).
- Have each student think of a specific noun that could be used instead, come up to the board, and write the specific word on the board.

Count the different specific nouns on the board. Explain that this is a problem with using words that are too general; that is, the reader can imagine so many things that may not be what the writer means.

* For more about using Specific Nouns, see SE page 378.

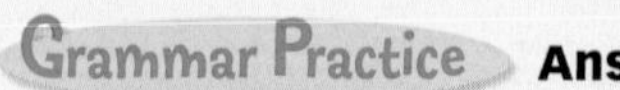

Answers

Possible answers:

1. Crazy Eights; Monopoly; Scrabble
2. pizza; popcorn; carrot sticks; scrambled eggs
3. *The Incredibles; Star Wars; Willie Wonka and the Chocolate Factory*
4. superheroes; space travel; kids' adventures
5. bedroom; kitchen; living room

152

Revising for Word Choice

In an expository essay, your goal is to explain something. Specific nouns can make your explanations clearer.

Q. How can I use specific nouns?

You can use specific nouns to replace general nouns. A specific noun names an exact person, place, thing, or idea.

General Nouns:	car	brother	animal	tree
	↓	↓	↓	↓
Specific Nouns:	hot rod	Tyrone	manatee	weeping willow

Grammar Practice

Replace each underlined general noun with a specific noun.

1. Most of the time, we play <u>games</u>.
2. We stop playing long enough to eat <u>food</u>.
3. We also watch <u>movies</u>.
4. It is usually a movie about <u>something</u>.
5. On Saturday morning, we have to clean the <u>room</u>.

Grammar Connection

Specific Nouns

- **Proofreader's Guide** page 532 (+)
- ***Write Source*** page 378
- ***GrammarSnap*** Specific Nouns
- ***SkillsBook*** pages 117–118

English Language Learners

Reinforce the concept of specific nouns by pairing students for a matching activity. Give each pair two index cards: one that is blank, the other with a general noun, such as *cartoon*. On the blank card, have student pairs write related specific nouns. Shuffle the cards and have the group match the general and specific nouns.

Struggling Learners

Provide support during the **Practice** activity by reading each sentence and prompting students with "What kind of . . . ?" Complete the question using the underlined general noun, for example: *What kind of games?* Point out that students can use this strategy when they revise their own writing.

Writing an Expository Essay 153

Revising in Action

Here is how Gabrielle changed her first paragraph to improve the word choice in her first draft. She added some specific nouns to make the words *sister* and *overnight* clearer.

Celia her friends sleep over at our house

¶ My sister had ~~an overnight~~. I listened threw

growly

the wall to her spooky stories about voices

screechy dark

sounds and shadows. The next day Mom asked

"Would you like your I can't wait

me ~~if I wanted~~ to have ~~my~~ own overnight. An

¶

overnight is a special kind of party. Friends

can be together all night at an overnight.

Check your word choice.

1. Read you essay and underline all the nouns.
2. Replace any general nouns with specific nouns.
   - **Cut** any nouns that are general.
   - **Add** specific nouns to make your explanation clearer.

Revising in Action

This revising activity focuses on specific nouns. As students prepare to underline all of the nouns in their essays, review nouns that name a person, a place, a thing, or an idea. You may also remind students that there are common and proper nouns and singular and plural nouns.

Grammar Connection

Adverbs

- **Proofreader's Guide** pages 550–551
- ***Write Source*** page 391
- ***GrammarSnap*** Adverbs
- ***SkillsBook*** pages 159–160

Using the Right Word

- **Proofreader's Guide** pages 512–513
- ***SkillsBook*** page 68

Revising for Sentence Fluency

Demonstrate on the board two other possible ways to fix run-on sentences:

- If the subject of both sentences is the same (for example, *The boy climbed the tree he untangled the kite*), consider combining them into a sentence with a compound verb. Delete the second subject and add a conjunction: *The boy climbed the tree and untangled the kite.*
- If one part of the run-on just provides description (for example, *The boy climbed the tree it was a tall magnolia tree*), you might be able to combine the two sentences into a shorter one by keeping the adjectives and deleting all other extra words. For example: *The boy climbed the tall magnolia tree.*

* For more about fixing Run-On Sentences, see SE page 404.

Revising for

Your sentences won't flow smoothly if you have too many short, choppy sentences.

Q. How can I combine sentences?

You can combine two sentences with a comma and a conjunction.

- Combine two sentences by adding a comma and one of these conjunctions: *and, but, or, for, so,* or *yet*.

Two Short Sentences
The tree changes each season. It is always beautiful.

One Compound Sentence
The tree changes each season, but it is always beautiful.

Grammar Practice

Combine the following two sentences using a comma and a conjunction.

My granola is easy to make. It doesn't even need to be cooked.

English Language Learners

Students may understand the concept of conjunctions but may have difficulty knowing which one to use. Provide meanings and examples for students to write down. Have them refer to their lists whenever they need to use a conjunction.

- **and** (together) I ate fish, **and** I ate rice.
- **yet; but** (contrast; not; unless) I'd like to come over, **but** I have homework. The horse is small, **yet** it is very strong.
- **or** (choice) Do you want ham, **or** would you like cheese?
- **so** (as a result) It rained, **so** the picnic was cancelled.

Writing an Expository Essay 155

Revising in Action

Here is how Gabrielle changed her first paragraph to improve the sentence fluency in her first draft. She combined the first two sentences.

¶ My sister had an overnight. I listened threw the wall to her spooky stories about voices sounds and shadows. The next day Mom asked me if I wanted to have my own overnight. An overnight is a special kind of party. Friends can be together all night at an overnight.

(Revisions: Celia; her friends sleep over at our house; and; growly; screechy; dark; "Would you like; your; I can't wait)

Revise **Check for smooth sentences.**

1. Read your essay and look for places that you could combine two sentences.
2. Try to create at least one compound sentence.
   - **Add** a comma and a conjunction to combine two sentences.

Revising in Action

As you discuss Gabrielle's changes to her first draft for sentence fluency, point out that sentence combining can be done with long sentences as well as with short ones.

Remind students that whenever they create a compound sentence, they must remember to use a comma and a conjunction. If they only add a conjunction, they will create a sentence error called a run-on sentence.

Consider having students work together to check one another's essays for run-on sentences.

Revising Using a Checklist

Have students check their revising for the traits of writing by using this checklist. They may work independently or with a partner.

Now, students need to make clean copies of their essays. Partners may check one another's final drafts against their first drafts that are marked with revisions. Then the writer should check his or her own essay for final editing and proofreading changes.

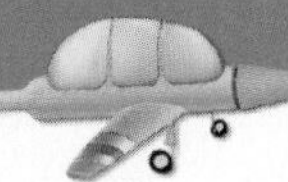

Revising Using a Checklist

Check your revising.

Number your paper from 1 to 8. If you can answer "yes" to a question, put a check mark after that number. If not, continue to work on that part of your essay.

Ideas

___ **1.** Have I used my sensory details to "show" instead of "tell"?

___ **2.** Have I used enough specific details?

Organization

___ **3.** Do I indent each new paragraph?

___ **4.** Do I have a focus sentence in my beginning paragraph?

___ **5.** Does each middle paragraph have a topic sentence?

Voice

___ **6.** Have I used an interested voice?

Word Choice

___ **7.** Have I used specific nouns that fit my topic?

Sentence Fluency

___ **8.** Have I combined some short, choppy sentences?

Make a clean copy.

After revising your essay, make a clean copy for editing.

Writing an Expository Essay 157

Editing for Conventions

When you edit for conventions, you need to be sure you have used commas in a series.

Q. How do I use commas in a series?

When you have a series (a list) of three or more things, put commas between each one. A series can have single words or groups of words.

My town has a pool, a river, and a lake.

Grammar Practice

Rewrite each sentence below. Add commas between the three or more items in a series.

1. My town is fun in spring summer winter and fall.
2. I enjoy swimming fishing and boating.
3. I also ride my bike walk my dog and play football.
4. I live with my mom a brother a sister and a hamster.
5. My family enjoys working in the garden going to the park and playing board games together.

Editing for Conventions

Challenge students to create sentences that contain different kinds of lists. For example:

- nouns (Apples, oranges, bananas, and pears are fruits.)
- adjectives (Many countries have red, white, and blue flags.)
- verbs (In a triathlon you run, bike, and swim.)

Note that *and* is the most common conjunction in lists, but *or* is used, too. *Or* implies that a choice must be made: *You may have an apple, peanuts, or juice for your snack.*

* For information about Commas Between Items in a Series, see SE pages 466–467.

Grammar Practice **Answers**

1. My town is fun in spring, summer, winter, and fall.
2. I enjoy swimming, fishing, and boating.
3. I also ride my bike, walk my dog, and play football.
4. I live with my mom, a brother, a sister, and a hamster.
5. My family enjoys working in the garden, going to the park, and playing board games together.

Technology Connections

Students can use the added features of the Net-text as they explore this stage of the writing process.

Write Source Online ***Net-text***

Struggling Learners

Visual learners may benefit from the following activity. Provide small groups with crayons and several sheets of drawing paper. Assign each group a **Practice** sentence and have them make a drawing to illustrate the different items in the series, such as *swimming, fishing,* and *boating* and label it.

Have groups take turns writing their sentences on the board, replacing each item with its corresponding picture. Have them insert commas between the pictures, making sure the last comma is inserted before the conjunction.

Grammar Connection

Commas (in a series)

- **Proofreader's Guide** pages 466–467
- ***Write Source*** page 408 (+)
- ***GrammarSnap*** Commas in a Series
- ***SkillsBook*** pages 9–10

Editing Checking for Conventions

To extend the editing checklist, use the editing page on SE page 157 in addition to this page.

After reviewing the conventions checklist, ask students to explain what a proper noun is (it names a specific person, place, or thing). Ask how readers can identify one (the first letter is capitalized). Give examples, along with brief explanations, such as:

- Elena (a person)
- Boston (a place)
- Golden Gate Bridge (a thing)

For a copy master of the expository writing Conventions Checklist, see TE page 563.

Challenge students to find proper nouns in any of the categories (person, place, thing) in their essays and read them out to classmates.

* For information about Proper Nouns, see SE page 375.

Grammar Practice Answers

(Corrections are underlined.)

1. The best thing about overnights is the fun.
2. Kids sure don't get much rest.
3. I can't wait to have my own overnight!
4. My cousins from Miami will come on Friday.
5. We laughed and played board games.

Editing Checking for Conventions

Check for capitalization, punctuation, spelling, and grammar errors in your essay.

Conventions

Punctuation

___ 1. Did I use end punctuation after all my sentences?
___ 2. Did I correctly use commas in a series?

Capitalization

___ 3. Did I start all my sentences with capital letters?
___ 4. Did I capitalize all proper names in my essay?

Spelling

___ 5. Have I carefully checked my spelling?

Grammar

___ 6. Have I used the right words *(to, two, too; there, their, they're)*?

Grammar Practice

Find two errors in each sentence. Then rewrite the sentences correctly.

1. the best thing about overnights is the fun?
2. Kids sure don't git much rest
3. I cant wait too have my own overnight!
4. my cousins from miami will come on Friday.
5. We laughed and played bored games

Grammar Connection

Capitalization

- **Proofreader's Guide** pages 486–487 (+), 488–489
- ***GrammarSnap*** Capitalization
- ***SkillsBook*** pages 41–42

Apostrophes

- **Proofreader's Guide** page 472 (+)
- ***GrammarSnap*** Contractions

English Language Learners

Many languages have structures that differ from those in English. In Spanish, for example, *mesa verde* is literally translated as *table green*. The noun precedes the adjective. In English, we would write *green table*. Pair students with cooperative, language-proficient partners who can help them find and correct such errors in their writing.

Writing an Expository Essay 159

Editing in Action

Here are some of the editing changes Gabrielle made to the first two paragraphs of her essay. She replaced a wrong word, added punctuation, and corrected misspelled words.

Gabrielle corrected a word.

She added commas in a series.

She added an apostrophe.

She changed end punctuation.

She corrected a misspelled word.

When my sister Celia had her friends sleep over at our house, and I listened threw (through) the wall to her spooky stories about growly voices, screechy sounds, and dark shadows. The next day Mom asked me, "Would you like to have your own overnight?" I can't wait! An overnight is a special kind of party.

Freinds (Friends) can be together all night at an overnight. That's more exciting than just seeing each other in school or on weekends. I love laughing and talking and staying up late with my freinds (friends).

Edit **Check for conventions in your essay.**

1. Read your own essay and look for items in a series.
2. Put commas between the items.

Editing in Action

Discuss the editing changes that Gabrielle made to her final draft. Consider having students look for one type of error at a time by using the side notes on Gabrielle's essay as a guide or by using the checklist on SE page 158.

If students need additional practice adding commas in a series, see *Daily Language Workouts* or the proofreader's guide in this book on SE pages 466–467.

Writer's Craft

Conventions: Note how the student models in this book have imperfect conventions until the very end. That's because if students focus first on improving capitalization, punctuation, spelling, and grammar, they will not think about improving ideas, organization, or voice—the traits that really make writing great. The purpose of conventions is to help the writer clearly convey an idea. Help students get the idea right before worrying about how to spell it.

Using a Rubric

Remind students that a rubric is a chart of the traits of good writing that helps you to

- plan your writing during prewriting,
- make changes to your writing during revising, and
- judge your final copy when you finish writing (see Writing for Assessment, SE pages 172–174).

The rubrics in this book are based on a six-point scale, in which a score of 6 indicates an amazing piece of writing and a score of 1 means the writing is incomplete.

Explain to students that they will most likely have different ratings for the traits. For example, they may give themselves a 5 for ideas but a 4 for organization.

Ask students to notice if there are certain traits on which they always score higher or lower. Consistently high scores show their strengths, and the lower scores will pinpoint areas to focus on for improvement.

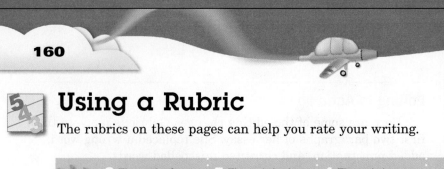

Using a Rubric

The rubrics on these pages can help you rate your writing.

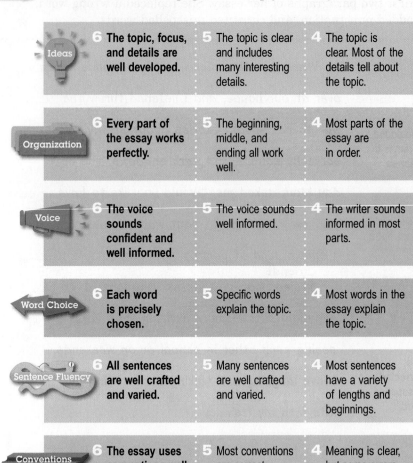

Trait	6	5	4
	**The topic, focus, and details are well developed.**	The topic is clear and includes many interesting details.	The topic is clear. Most of the details tell about the topic.
Organization	**Every part of the essay works perfectly.**	The beginning, middle, and ending all work well.	Most parts of the essay are in order.
Voice	**The voice sounds confident and well informed.**	The voice sounds well informed.	The writer sounds informed in most parts.
	**Each word is precisely chosen.**	Specific words explain the topic.	Most words in the essay explain the topic.
	**All sentences are well crafted and varied.**	Many sentences are well crafted and varied.	Most sentences have a variety of lengths and beginnings.
	**The essay uses conventions well.**	Most conventions are correct.	Meaning is clear, but some errors are present.

English Language Learners

Before reviewing the voice section of the rubric, discuss the meanings of and provide synonyms for *uninterested (bored), unsure (cautious), informed (knowledgeable),* and *confident (certain).* As you review the six levels of each trait, share examples of what each of these might sound like.

- Redwoods are big trees. (uninterested)
- I think the Mississippi River is the longest river in the country. (unsure)
- The Statue of Liberty stands near New York City. (informed)
- The awesome Rocky Mountains extend from Alaska to Mexico. (certain)

Struggling Learners

Read through the Sentence Fluency trait with students, directing their attention to number four. To help students work on sentence beginnings, have them read their essays and circle the first word of each sentence. Then have them review the circled words and replace those that are used too often.

Writing an Expository Essay 161

Literature Connections: For an example of an expository essay, read *Mayors* by Shannon Knudsen.

3	2	1
3 The topic needs to be clearer. More details are needed.	2 The topic is unclear, and the details do not fit.	1 The topic is unclear.
3 Some parts of the essay could be better organized.	2 All parts of the essay run together.	1 The organization is confusing.
3 The writer sounds informed in some parts.	2 The writer sounds unsure.	1 The writer sounds uninterested.
3 The essay needs more specific words.	2 General or missing words make this essay confusing.	1 Some words are used incorrectly.
3 Some sentences have varied lengths and beginnings.	2 Many sentences are choppy or incomplete.	1 Many sentences are incomplete and difficult to read.
3 Errors may confuse the reader.	2 Errors make the essay hard to read.	1 Help is needed to make corrections.

Test Prep!

The six traits of writing were first identified in the 1960s by Paul Diederich and a group of 50 professionals who reviewed student papers and brainstormed the qualities that made writing strong. In 1983, a group of educators in Beaverton, Oregon, replicated Diederich's work. A separate team in Missoula, Montana, simultaneously ran a study that identified the same basic group of traits. As a result, the six traits provide a universal set of criteria for strong writing.

Literature Connections

In the expository essay *Mayors,* the author explains a mayor's job responsibilities and the election process in a question-and-answer format.

Have students identify aspects of the text that make it a good example of expository writing. For example, many details show that the writer is well informed. For additional models of expository writing, see the Reading-Writing Connections beginning on page TE-36.

Publishing Sharing Your Essay

Direct students' attention to the title of the sample essay. Note that in this case, the writer decided to use a fun rhyme for her title. Suggest other strategies students can use, and challenge them to think of titles that would suit the sample essay:

- Describe the main idea—"My First Overnight"
- Repeat an important phrase from the essay—"A Special Kind of Party"
- Repeat sounds—"Oh, My Own Overnight!"

* For more on adding titles to essays, see SE page 334.

After students have chosen titles and written out their final copies (or printed them, if using a computer), distribute drawing supplies so they can illustrate their essays.

Invite volunteers to share their work with classmates by reading the essay and showing the illustration.

Technology Connections

Remind students that they can use the Writing Network features of the Portfolio to share their work with peers.

Write Source Online **Portfolio**

Write Source Online **Net-text**

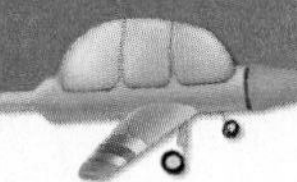

Publishing Sharing Your Essay

Finally, it's time to proofread your essay and make a neat copy to share. You can also illustrate your essay.

All Right, an Overnight!

When my sister Celia had her friends sleep over at our house, I listened through the wall to her spooky stories about growling voices, screechy sounds, and dark shadows. The next day Mom asked me, "Would you like to have your own overnight?" I can't wait! An overnight is a special kind of party.

Friends can be together all night at an overnight. That's more exciting than just seeing each other in school or on weekends. I love laughing and talking and staying up late with my friends.

An overnight also has fun activities. Nighttime is perfect for telling spooky stories. What could be better than watching movies, munching on popcorn, playing board games, and sleeping on the floor in the living room?

Now Celia will have to listen to my spooky stories because my very first overnight will be Friday night. My two favorite cousins Maria and Gina are coming to visit from Miami. They usually stay with my aunt and uncle, but this time they will stay at my house. I can't wait.

Publish **Make a final copy of your essay.**

Writing an Expository Essay 163

Reflecting on Your Writing

You're done! Take a moment to think about what you have learned. Here's what Gabrielle thought about her essay.

Thinking About Your Writing

Name: Gabrielle McGraff

Title: All Right, an Overnight!

1. The best part of my essay is . . .
   my topic. I can't wait for my first overnight!
2. The part that still needs work is . . .
   the middle. I need more details.
3. The main thing I learned about expository writing is . . .
   it's about explaining things in my own words.

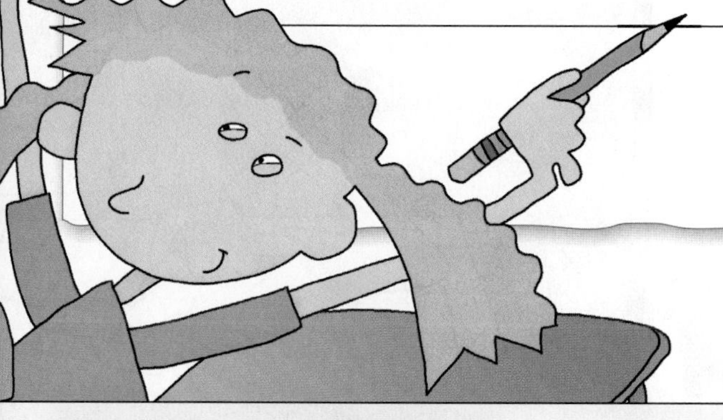

Reflecting on Your Writing

Ask students if they think the writer made a fair assessment of her essay. Have them explain their answers. Ask what they think she might mean when she says she could have used more details. Possible answers include:

- She could have said a little more about why it isn't as much fun to see friends at school.
- She could have mentioned specific friends' names.

Provide photocopies of the reproducible Thinking About Your Writing (TE page 593) so students can complete the form for their own essays.

Advanced Learners

Some students may need help identifying a part of their writing that still needs work. You may want to schedule writing response conferences with each student. Or, you may prefer that students form pairs to read each other's essays and complete a copy of the reproducible Response Sheet (TE page 592). Students can then use the Response Sheets to identify parts that need work.

Across the Curriculum

Objectives
- Apply what has been learned about expository writing to other curriculum areas.
- Practice writing for assessment.

The lessons on the following pages provide samples of different kinds of expository writing students might do. The first lesson guides students through the writing process to create a social studies news report. The second lesson provides a model and writing tips for writing a music report. The third lesson focuses on writing a how-to essay.

Ask students to talk about their experiences as *readers* of expository writing—using a recipe to cook, for example, or reading instructions to learn how to play a game. Did they have any difficulties? Have students share their experiences.

Tell students that what they learn in this unit will help them when they need to write for school. It will also help them to be better readers by giving them practice with expository text.

Expository Writing Across the Curriculum

Expository writing explains or gives information about a topic. You can find expository writing just about everywhere. A news report in a magazine, a recipe in a cookbook, the instructions for a model airplane—these are all forms of expository writing.

Expository writing also shows up in all your subjects at school. Whether you're studying science, social studies, or math, expository writing can help you explain just about anything!

Copy Masters

Five W's Chart, Time Line, Sensory Chart (TE p. 166)

Time Line (TE p. 171)

Assessment Sheet (TE p. 172)

Materials

Magazine and newspaper headlines (TE p. 165)

Drawing supplies (TE p. 171)

Social Studies: News Report

News reports give readers information about an event. One day, Jeremy's class had a special visitor. Jeremy wrote the following report for his school newspaper.

Beginning
The beginning gives basic information.

Middle
The middle lists important details.

Ending
The ending gives a final thought.

Kids in China

On Tuesday, October 4, Mr. Goff visited our class. He is Karen's dad, and he just got back from a business trip to China. He has many pictures of busy cities and beautiful mountains. Mr. Goff came to our class to tell us what life is like in China.

We learned that kids in China go to school six days a week! They write with 2,000 characters instead of 26 letters. Each character is a complete word. After school, kids play basketball and volleyball and ride bikes. Kids in China do the same kinds of things we do.

Mr. Goff said a businessman from China would visit him soon. We will invite the man to our class. That way, he can tell kids in China about us!

English Language Learners

Students may have difficulty with the word *character*, because they often think of it in the context of story characters. Explain that *character* also means a mark or a symbol used in writing. Students may need to be reminded of this as they read and discuss Jeremy's news report.

Advanced Learners

Share magazine and newspaper articles with attention-grabbing headlines. Discuss words and images that make each headline interesting. Then challenge students to rewrite the title of Jeremy's report to make it more interesting. Have students share their titles and explain how they are more effective.

Social Studies: News Report

Have students briefly review the goals for writing an expository essay on SE page 133. Then have students read the news report and ask them to discuss their impressions of the article. Does it meet the goals? Encourage students to explain their answers. Responses might include:

- Organization: Sentence 3 (*He has many pictures . . .*) does not clearly apply to the topic, kids in China.
- Organization: Paragraph 2 doesn't have a topic sentence, only sentences with details in them.
- Organization: The ending is effective because it refers to the beginning and adds that Chinese kids will hear about Jeremy's class, too.
- Word choice: The last sentence of paragraph 2 is very general. If it's just commenting on the sentence before it, it can be deleted. If it's supposed to give new information, more details should be added.
- Conventions: Two sentences end with exclamation marks. One of those could be replaced with a period.

Prewriting Selecting a Topic

If possible, give students a few days to investigate around the school as newspaper reporters to **find topic ideas** *(see below)*.

When students begin choosing a topic, have them consult the notes they took and think back to their experiences of the past few days.

Prewriting Gathering Details

Distribute photocopies of the reproducible 5 W's Chart, Time Line, and Sensory Chart (TE pages 597, 598, and 596). Ask all students to fill out the 5 W's chart and then to decide whether they need to use another chart, too.

Those who are reporting on a sequence of events may use the time line. Those describing something might use the sensory chart. Whatever their method, students should make note of *all* ideas they want to mention.

✱ For more about organizing details, see SE pages 438–444.

Prewriting Selecting a Topic

News is about "new" events. To find a topic for his school news report, Jeremy listed important events from the last week or two.

Ideas List

Events

We got a new jungle gym on the playground.

Mr. Goff visited and told us about China.*

We got a class hamster named Ziggy.

Prewrite List topic ideas.

1. **Write important events from the past week or two.**
2. **Put a star (✱) next to the event you want to write about.**

Gathering Details

Next, Jeremy used the 5 W's questions to gather details.

Prewrite Fill in the 5 W's about your event.

5 W's

Who?	What?	When?	Where?	Why?
Mr. Goff	class visitor	Tuesday, October 4	our classroom	to tell us about life in China

Teaching Tip: On the Beat to Find a Topic

Explain that a reporter calls the area he or she regularly covers a *beat* and that the students' beat is the school.

- Suggest that students carry a pencil and notepad or folded piece of paper and jot down any ideas that they have.
- Remind students that their own experiences might be newsworthy. Advise them to stay alert and take note of what they see or hear.
- Encourage them also to interview someone who might be a promising topic. Remind them to take careful notes as they listen to the answers to their questions.

Writing Creating a First Draft

It's time to write your news story! Follow the steps below.

Create your first draft.

1. In the beginning paragraph, answer the 5 W's (page 166).
2. In the middle paragraph, include other interesting details.
3. In the ending paragraph, give a final thought.

Revising Improving Your Writing

Jeremy used some questions to help him revise.

Improve your news report.

Answer the following questions as you revise your report.

1. Have I included all my information and interesting details?
2. Do I sound excited about my topic?

Editing Checking Conventions

Jeremy used these questions to check his capitalization, punctuation, spelling, and grammar.

Check your work.

1. Did I start all my sentences with capital letters?
2. Did I end all my sentences with correct punctuation?
3. Have I checked for spelling errors?

Writing Creating a First Draft

Remind students to check off each detail in their notes as they include it in their draft, so they don't forget anything.

Revising Improving Your Writing

In addition to using the revising questions on this page, refer students to the goals listed on SE page 133 for more detailed guidance.

Editing Checking Conventions

To enhance the feeling of a "class newsroom," after students use the editing checklist on this page, have them work with partner "editors" to put the finishing touches on their stories.

If time permits, encourage students to illustrate their stories. Assemble the completed articles into a class newspaper and make enough photocopies for each student to take one home.

Music: A Report

Music holds many possibilities for report writing. Musical inventions such as boomwhackers—or any other instruments from violins to harmonicas—would make good report topics. Famous musicians, whether performers or composers, could also inspire students. Types of music (from classical to jazz to hip hop) or specific songs all could produce strong reports.

Help students brainstorm ideas by asking the following questions:

- "What is your favorite song?"
- "What type of music do you like best?"
- "If you could play any instrument, which would you choose?"
- "What's the weirdest instrument?"

You could also play favorite musical selections, such as Rimsky-Korsakov's "Flight of the Bumblebee" to get students interested in specific songs or composers.

Music: A Report

Boom-Whack-a-Boom

In 1994, Craig Ramsell was cutting up a cardboard gift wrap tube. He whacked his leg with the tube and liked the sound it made. A shorter piece made a different sound. That gave him the idea for Boomwhackers.

Red, orange, yellow—each brightly colored plastic tube makes the sound of a note on the musical scale when it is whacked against a hand, a leg, or anything hard. In schools, students use sets of Boomwhackers as rhythm instruments and music makers. Color-coded song books make playing music easy.

By 2007, Whacky Music, Inc., had sold 5 million sets of tuned percussion tubes around the world. For many kids, Boomwhackers are the first instruments they learn to play!

Writing Tips

Before you write . . .

- Think of things about music that you know and care about.
- Make a cluster to gather details about your topic.

During your writing . . .

- Get the reader's attention in the beginning of your report.
- Share interesting details in the body paragraphs.
- Give readers something to think about in the ending.

After you've written a first draft . . .

- Read your report and see if any important details are missing.
- Give your report an interesting title.
- Check capitalization, punctuation, spelling, and grammar.

Writing Tips

In addition to covering the writing tips with your students, also introduce them to the idea of sound words (onomatopoeia). Sound words make the sounds that they describe. The word *whack* from the model is a sound word.

Help students think about sound words that will help their readers hear the music in their writing. For example, words like *trill* and *lilt* could describe a flute, while words like *drone* or *wail* could describe a bagpipe. Use *strum* or *pluck* for a guitar and *warble* and *swoop* for a soprano. Challenge students to incorporate sound words in their reports.

Practical Writing: How-To Essay

Ask students if any of them have ever repotted or helped to repot a plant. If they have, does the essay describe the process well? If they haven't, do they think they could do so now that they've read the essay?

Direct students' attention to the opening paragraph. What does the writer do in this paragraph? Answers include the following:

- She connects with the reader by mentioning something they have in common, outgrowing clothes.
- She compares a person outgrowing clothes to a plant outgrowing its pot.
- She ends with the focus statement: *It's easy to repot a plant.*

Note that the writer starts the first middle paragraph with a topic sentence about preparations that are needed. The second middle paragraph could use a better topic sentence. Have students make suggestions.

- Once you've got all your equipment together, repotting is simple.

Suggest that students sketch steps in this how-to essay. Is anything missing? Making sketches can help writers remember each step.

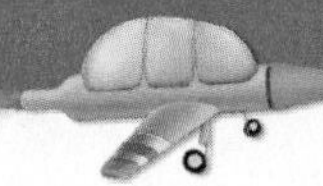

Practical Writing: How-To Essay

Expository writing can help a reader learn how to do something. Hillary wrote about how to repot a plant.

The **beginning** introduces the topic.

Growing, Growing, Gone!

When I outgrow my clothes, I get new clothes from my sister. When my plants outgrow their pots, they get new pots from me. It's easy to repot a plant.

The **middle** lists the steps.

To get started, you need to set up a place to work. An old table outside is a good place. Spread out newspapers to help protect the table. Then get a bigger pot, some stones, potting soil, and the plant.

First, cover the bottom of the new pot with stones and spread some soil over them. Next, tip the plant over and gently pull it out of its old pot. Put the plant into the new pot and hold it straight. Then pour in some more soil and pat it down. Finally, water the plant and add more soil if there is room.

The **ending** includes a final thought.

Plants are nice to have around. If you give their roots enough room, you will have beautiful plants for a long time.

Writing Tips

Before you write . . .

- Choose something you enjoy making or doing.
- List the ingredients or equipment you need.
- List each step for completing the project or doing the activity.

During your writing . . .

- Introduce your topic.
- Write a paragraph about the ingredients or equipment.
- Write another paragraph giving the steps in order.
- End with a final thought.

After you've written a first draft . . .

- Make sure your steps are complete and clear and are in the right order.
- Edit your work and make a neat copy.

Write a how-to essay about something you enjoy doing like making s'mores! Follow the tips above to write your directions. Share your work with a friend.

Struggling Learners

Help students understand why the paragraph about ingredients or equipment comes before the paragraph that gives the steps. Assign groups the following scenarios to act out

- making a sandwich
- brushing your teeth
- making a bed
- setting the table

For groups that begin their skits with the first step of the process, ask questions such as *Where did you get the bread? What else are you using?* Help students understand that first gathering necessary items makes performing a task easier.

Writing Tips

Once students have chosen their topics, do the following activity.

- Divide the class into groups of three or four.
- Ask students to take turns telling what their topic is and how you do it.
- Have group members respond by asking questions. What isn't clear? What did the teller forget to mention?

Distribute photocopies of the reproducible Time Line (TE page 598), and have students fill it out, listing steps in the correct order. Students may add sketches to their time lines to be sure they haven't forgotten a step.

✱ For more about using time lines, see SE page 85.

After students have completed their essays, distribute drawing supplies and have them illustrate their work. Display the finished papers and pictures on a class "How-To" bulletin board.

Writing for Assessment

If your students must take school, district, or state assessments this year, focus on the writing form on which they will be tested.

In addition to responding to a prompt, this lesson can also be an opportunity for students to practice evaluating an expository essay. Using the rubric for expository writing (SE pages 160–161) and a copy of the Assessment Sheet (TE page 591), work with students to score the sample essay on SE page 173 (a completed assessment sheet is provided on TE page 581 for your benefit). Two additional essays are available in copy master form (see Benchmark Papers box below). Again, a completed assessment sheet is provided for each benchmark paper.

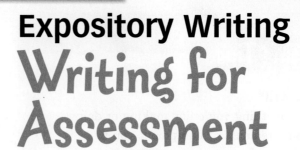

Expository Writing
Writing for Assessment

Some writing tests give you an expository topic or prompt to write about. An expository prompt asks you to explain something. Eli responded to the following prompt. He started planning his response by making a list like the one below.

Expository Prompt

> *What is your favorite school subject? Write an expository essay about your favorite subject and give details that explain why you like it.*

Ideas List

Science
- making crystals
- chicks hatching
- museum field trip
- forest field trip

Benchmark Papers

How to Bake a Cake (good)

TE pp. 582–583

A Kite (fair)

TE pp. 584–585

Learning by Doing and Going

The **beginning** gives the focus (underlined).

Some kids say their favorite school subject is recess. My favorite subject is science. I like science because the projects and field trips are exciting.

The **middle** uses details to explain the focus.

In science we do many exciting projects. One time we made crystals form in a jar by using salt in water. Another time we watched baby chicks hatch. They were slimy at first, but then the feathers dried, and we had fluffy yellow chicks.

We also take exciting field trips for science. We went to a museum and saw huge dinosaurs and tiny butterflies. On Arbor Day, we went to a forest and collected leaves. A guide told us about all kinds of trees.

The **ending** finishes the explanation.

Recess is fun, but I would rather do experiments and go on field trips. That's why science is my favorite subject.

After you read . . .

- **Ideas (1) What favorite parts of science did the writer mention in the focus sentence?**
- **Organization (2) How many paragraphs did the writer use?**
- **Word Choice (3) What words from the prompt did the writer use in the first paragraph?**

Demonstrate how Eli's planning helped him to write his response. On the board, outline the sample essay as follows, soliciting students' input as you go:

Topic: Favorite subject = Science
Focus statement: *I like science because . . .*
Topic sentence #1: *In science we do many exciting projects.*
Example #1: making crystals
Details: jar, saltwater
Example #2: hatching chicks
Details: chicks slimy then fluffy
Topic sentence #2: *We also take exciting field trips . . .*
Example #1: museum
Details: dinosaurs, butterflies
Example #2: forest
Details: leaf collecting, guide

The outline shows that the essay gives two reasons to support the focus statement, two examples for each reason, and brief details for each example. Assure students that if they use this same formula when they write in a timed setting, they will do well in writing their response.

After you read . . .

Answers

Ideas **1.** projects and field trips

Organization **2.** four

Word Choice **3.** favorite school subject, like

English Language Learners

Before reading Eli's essay, provide students with definitions of unfamiliar words, such as:

- crystals (rocks; gemstones)
- hatch (to emerge from the shell)
- slimy (slippery; greasy)
- Arbor Day (holiday to celebrate trees and plants)
- guide (leader)

Struggling Learners

Some students may be tempted to copy the first sentence of Eli's response to make sure they use words from the prompt as they write. Use the prompt on SE page 172 to craft different beginnings:

- My favorite school subject is no surprise.
- Is your favorite school subject the same as mine?
- Everyone has a favorite school subject.

Writing Tips

Point out that students must approach writing-on-demand assignments differently from open-ended writing assignments and that timed writing creates pressures for everyone.

Expository Prompt

To teach students who must take timed assessments how to approach their writing, allow them the same amount of time to write their response essay as they will be allotted on school, district, or state assessments. Break down each part of the process into clear chunks of time. For example, you might give students

- 15 minutes for note taking and planning,
- 20 minutes for writing, and
- 10 minutes for editing and proofreading.

Tell students when time is up for each section. Start the assignment at the top of the hour or at the half-hour to make it easier for students to keep track of the time.

If your state, district, or school requires students to use and submit a graphic organizer as part of their assessment, provide a copy of one of the reproducible charts (TE pages 595–600) or refer students to SE pages 438–444.

Writing Tips

Before you write . . .

- Read the prompt carefully.
- Watch for words like *define*, *explain*, and *compare*. They tell you what to do in your writing.
- Think about any questions the prompt asks.
- Use a list or graphic organizer to put your ideas in order.

During your writing . . .

- Use some main words from the prompt.
- Follow the directions. In this case, the directions said "write an essay."
- Leave time at the end to check your work.

After you've written a first draft . . .

- Check your focus sentence and details.
- Read your writing and correct any errors.

Write an expository essay in the time your teacher gives you.

Expository Prompt

Imagine that a new student has come to your class. What rules does the student need to know? Write an essay explaining the two most important class rules.

English Language Learners

During writing, some students may use words from the prompt without knowing what they mean. Have students practice reading prompts and saying them in their own words. Begin by giving students a simple prompt, such as *Explain what you like to do after school.* Have students restate the prompt using their own words: *Tell about what you like to do after school.*

Struggling Learners

Some students may struggle with the meanings of *define*, *explain*, and *compare*. Use the following examples to help students grasp the terms:

- A football is an oval-shaped ball. (define)
- A football is kicked or thrown during a game played between two teams. (explain)
- Football players can use their hands to handle the ball, but soccer players cannot. (compare)

Expository Writing Checklist 175

Expository Writing in Review

In expository writing, you share information with your reader. You may also explain how to do something. These guidelines can help.

Select an interesting topic. (See page 136.)

Gather details about your topic. Use a graphic organizer. (See page 137.)

Write a focus sentence. Name an important part of the topic. (See page 137.)

In the beginning part, introduce your topic and state your focus. (See pages 138–139.)

In the middle part, give details that explain the focus. (See pages 140–141.)

In the ending part, make a final comment. (See pages 142–143.)

Review your essay for ideas and organization. Be sure you've included the right details. Make changes to improve your writing. (See pages 144–156.)

Check your writing for conventions. Ask a classmate or parent for help. (See pages 157–161.)

Make a final copy. Proofread it for errors before sharing it. (See page 162.)

Expository Writing in Review

Use the review outline to solicit a discussion of students' experiences with the unit.

- What is the most important thing they learned?
- What did they enjoy the most?
- What is hardest for them?
- What topics are they looking forward to writing about in the future?

Encourage students to mark the page with a sticky note and to turn to it whenever they need a reminder of how the expository writing process works. Assure students that as they get more practice with the form, the steps will seem less complicated and will become easier.

Persuasive Writing Overview

Common Core Standards Focus

Writing 1: Write opinion pieces on topics or texts, supporting a point of view with reasons.

Language 3a: Choose words and phrases for effect.

Writing Forms

- Writing a Persuasive Paragraph
- Writing a Persuasive Letter

Focus on the Traits:

- **Ideas** Expressing an opinion and supporting it with strong reasons
- **Organization** Creating a beginning with a clear opinion statement, a middle that includes reasons that support it, and an ending that asks the reader to do something
- **Voice** Developing an accurate voice that convinces the reader
- **Word Choice** Using helping verbs that fit the audience
- **Sentence Fluency** Combining sentences to ensure writing that reads smoothly
- **Conventions** Checking for errors in capitalization, punctuation, spelling, and grammar

Literature Connections

- ***The Big Cleanup*** by Kate McGovern

Technology Connections

Write Source Online
www.hmheducation.com/writesource

- ***Net-text***
- ***Bookshelf***
- ***GrammarSnap***
- ***Portfolio***
- ***Writing Network features***
- ***File Cabinet***

Interactive Whiteboard Lessons

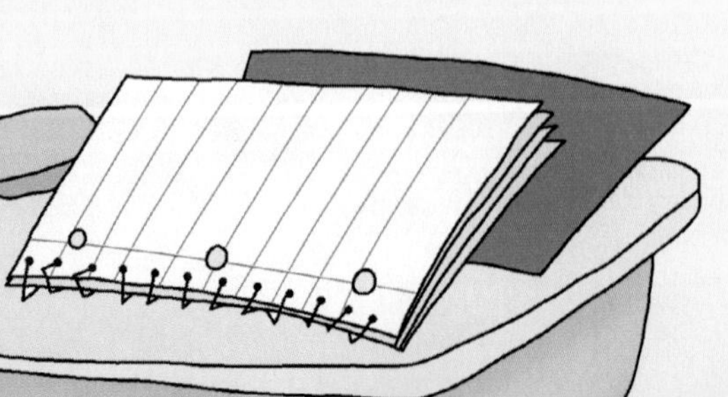

Suggested Persuasive Writing Unit (Four Weeks)

Week	Day	Writing and Skills Instruction	Student Edition: Persuasive Writing Unit	Student Edition: Resource Units*	SkillsBook	Daily Language Workouts	Write Source Online
Week 1	1–4	**Persuasive Paragraph: A Class Need** Literature Connections *The Big Cleanup*	178–183			34–35, 92	*Interactive Whiteboard Lessons*
		Skills Activities: • Using the Right Word		520–521, 522–523	72–73		
		• Spelling		502–507	63–64		
		• Fragments		403 (+), 526 (+), 528 (+)	96		*GrammarSnap*
	opt.	*Giving Speeches*	344–349				
	5	**Persuasive Essay: A Persuasive Letter** (Model)	184–187				
Week 2	6–7	(Prewriting)	188–189			36–37, 93	*Net-text*
	8–10	(Writing)	190–191				*Net-text*
Week 3	11	(Revising) **Working with Partners**	192–193 16–19			38–39, 94	*Net-text*
	12–13	(Revising)	194–204				
		Skills Activities: • Helping Verbs		385, 538 (+)	135		*GrammarSnap*
		• Sentence Combining		407	105–106		*GrammarSnap*
		• Run-On and Rambling Sentences		404, 405	97–98		*GrammarSnap*
	14–15	(Editing)	205–207				*Net-text*
		Skills Activities: • Capitalization, Abbreviations		488 (+), 496–497, 498–499	5–6, 56, 57–58		*GrammarSnap*
		• Commas (introductory word or word groups)		470 (+)	19–20, 21–22		
		• Commas (in dates and addresses)		466 (+), 468 (+)	11, 13–14		
		• Colons		480 (+)	35–36		
Week 4	16	(Assessing, Publishing, Reflecting)	208–213			40–41, 95	*Portfolio, Net-text*
	opt.	*Giving Speeches*	344–349				
	17–18	**Persuasive Writing Across the Curriculum**	214–221				
	19–20	**Persuasive Writing for Assessment**	222–224				

* These units are also located in the back of the *Teacher's Edition.* Resource Units include "Basic Grammar and Writing," "A Writer's Resource," and "Proofreader's Guide."
(+) This activity is located in a different section of the *Write Source Student Edition.* If students have already completed this activity, you may wish to review it at this time.

Teacher's Notes for Persuasive Writing

This overview for persuasive writing includes some specific suggestions for teaching this unit.

Writing Focus

Writing a Persuasive Paragraph (pages 178–183)

A student writing a persuasive paragraph states an opinion about an issue and uses facts and information to get readers to agree (and, perhaps, do something about the issue). Students will learn that persuasion calls for polite language and careful presentation of supporting facts and information.

Writing a Persuasive Letter (pages 184–213)

A business letter adds a real-life element to the classroom as students write letters to suggest solutions to a problem or ways to meet a need. Letters to company officials, government leaders, and so on produce results. Even young people can make a difference with a well-written persuasive letter. In this chapter, students will follow the necessary writing steps and proper form to write such a letter.

Grammar Focus

For support with this unit's grammar topics, consult the resource units (Basic Grammar and Writing, A Writer's Resource, and Proofreader's Guide).

Academic Vocabulary

Read aloud the academic terms, as well as the descriptions and questions. Model for students how to read one question and answer it. Have partners monitor their understanding and seek clarification of the terms by working through the meanings and questions together.

Minilessons

Not Working — Writing a Persuasive Letter

- **IMAGINE** that you have bought a 3Z Extra Cold water bottle made by the Twin Trees Corporation located at 37778 Warehouse Avenue, Waukegan, Illinois 60085. You have used the water bottle two times, and each time you used the bottle it didn't keep the water cold.
  - **WRITE** a letter to the company to request a replacement or a refund.
  - **REVIEW** the model business letter format on SE page 186 before you write your letter.

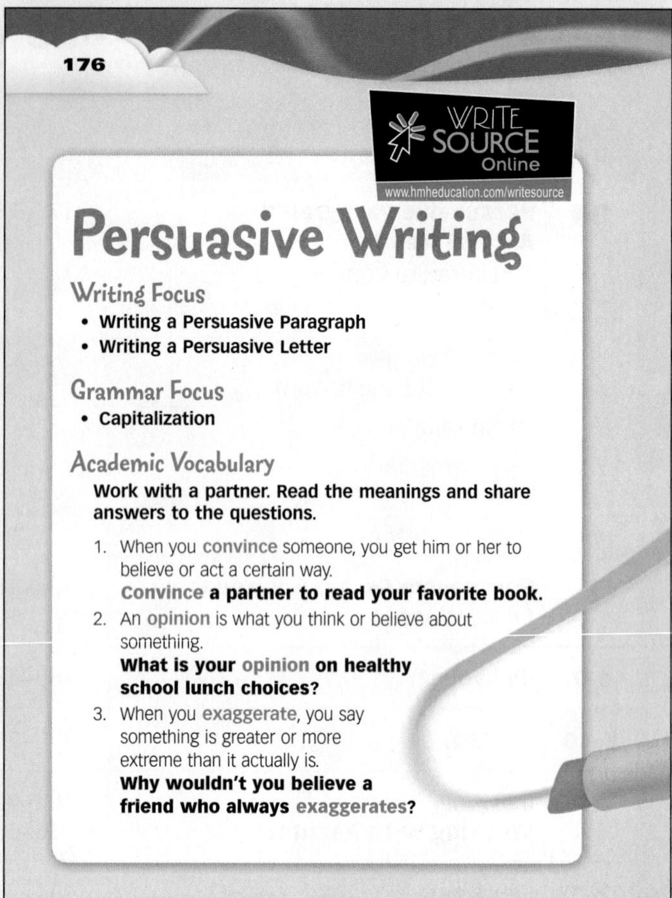

176
WRITE SOURCE Online
www.hmheducation.com/writesource
Persuasive Writing
Writing Focus
• Writing a Persuasive Paragraph
• Writing a Persuasive Letter
Grammar Focus
• Capitalization
Academic Vocabulary
Work with a partner. Read the meanings and share answers to the questions.
1. When you convince someone, you get him or her to believe or act a certain way.
Convince a partner to read your favorite book.
2. An opinion is what you think or believe about something.
What is your opinion on healthy school lunch choices?
3. When you exaggerate, you say something is greater or more extreme than it actually is.
Why wouldn't you believe a friend who always exaggerates?

Help! — Writing a Persuasive Letter

- **WRITE** a letter to the school principal recommending that five trees be planted to replace the ones destroyed by a powerful windstorm. Then **WRITE** a letter to fellow students encouraging them to give extra lunch money change to help buy the trees.
  - **EXCHANGE** your letters with a classmate.
  - **READ** the response sheet on SE page 193. On a separate sheet of paper, **MAKE UP** your own response sheet and **CHECK** each other's letters.
  - **MAKE** any recommended changes that seem to help make your letters better.

Envelope, Please . . . — Writing a Persuasive Letter

- **Address** an envelope to the president. (Put your return address on the envelope, too.)
  - **Look** at SE page 212 to make sure you do everything right. Here is the president's address: The President of the United States, The White House, 1600 Pennsylvania Avenue, Washington, DC 20500.

Announcement — Writing Across the Curriculum

- **DESIGN** a bulletin board announcement (like a poster) that tells about an upcoming event in your school. **GIVE** three reasons why students should attend.

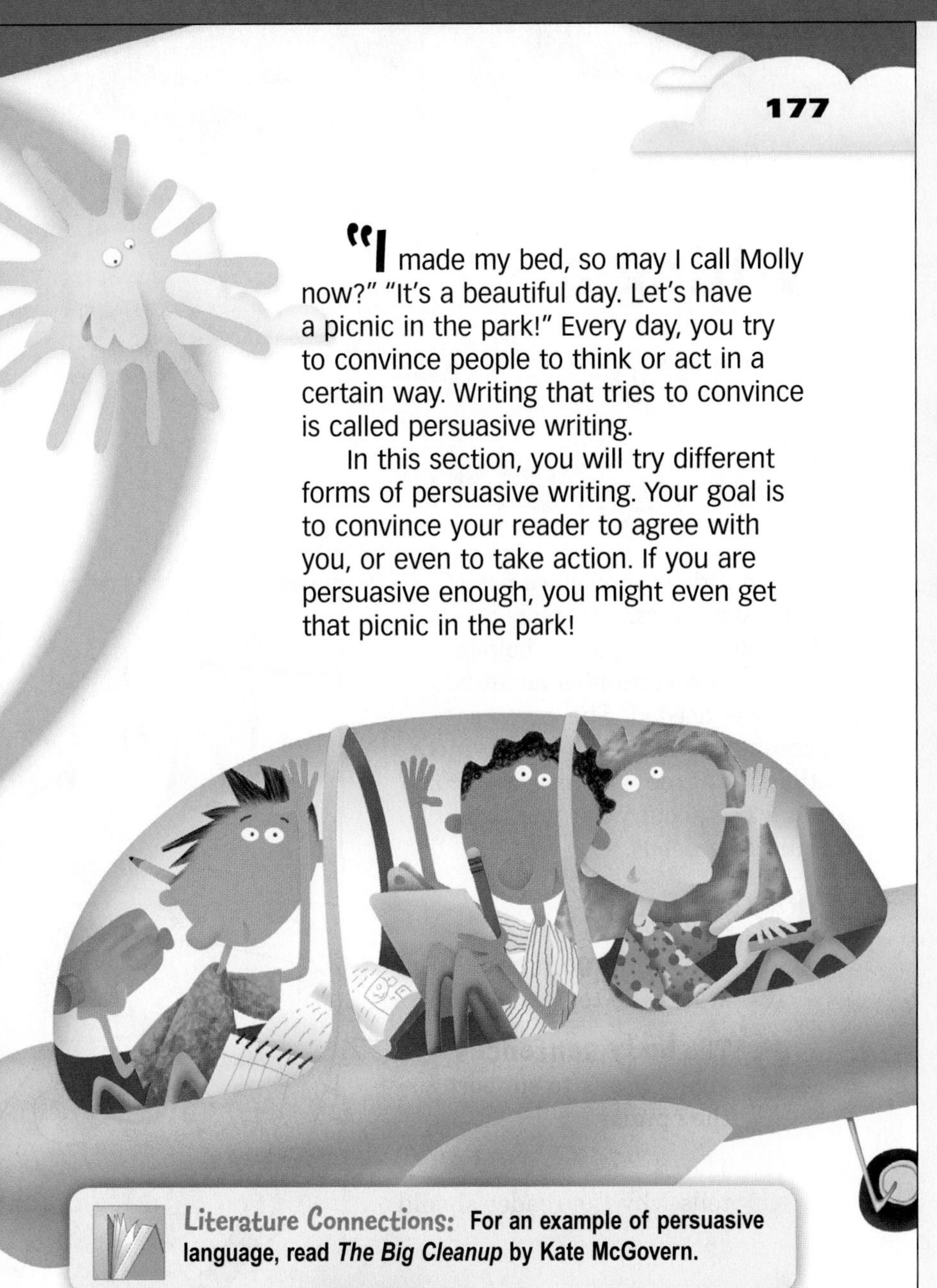

177

"I made my bed, so may I call Molly now?" "It's a beautiful day. Let's have a picnic in the park!" Every day, you try to convince people to think or act in a certain way. Writing that tries to convince is called persuasive writing.

In this section, you will try different forms of persuasive writing. Your goal is to convince your reader to agree with you, or even to take action. If you are persuasive enough, you might even get that picnic in the park!

Literature Connections: For an example of persuasive language, read *The Big Cleanup* by Kate McGovern.

Persuasive Writing

Introduce students to the concept of persuasion.

- Display print ads from magazines and newspapers aimed at a young audience. Give students time to look them over.
- Invite volunteers to describe favorite TV or Internet commercials and tell why they like them. Ask students if they think commercials are just to entertain them or if they have another purpose.
- Ask students what the print ads and commercials have in common. Help students understand that they all try to persuade or get people to do something.

Point out that the best way to persuade or convince people to do something is to give them good reasons why they should do it. To illustrate this idea, ask students to point out the reasons given by the speaker in the first paragraph on SE page 176. (I made my bed; it's a beautiful day.) Also, help students realize that the persuasive reasons they choose are dependent on their **audience** *(see below)*.

Literature Connections

In the play *The Big Cleanup,* a team of climbers clean up trash as they hike to the summit of Mount Everest. Point out persuasive language in the text. What reasons are given to convince the reader that cleaning Mount Everest is important?

This selection is from Houghton Mifflin Harcourt *Journeys*. For additional models of persuasive writing, see the Reading-Writing Connections beginning on page TE-36.

Family Connection Letters

As you begin this unit, send home the Persuasive Writing Family Connection letter, which describes what students will be learning.

- Letter in English (TE p. 605)
- Letter in Spanish (TE p. 613)

Materials

Magazine and newspaper ads (TE p. 177)

Teaching Tip: Audience

As you introduce the persuasive form of writing, help students understand the specific purpose for writing —to persuade. Then discuss the concept of writing to an *audience*. Point out that whenever students write, they are writing for someone: themselves, teachers, friends, family members, and so on.

Writing a Persuasive Paragraph

Objectives

- Understand the parts of a persuasive paragraph.
- Choose a topic (something the class needs) to write about.
- Plan, draft, revise, and edit a persuasive paragraph.

A **persuasive paragraph** tells the writer's opinion about a topic and gives good reasons that support that opinion.

* For more about writing paragraphs, see SE pages 416–429.

Ask students to recall times when they tried to persuade their parents, teachers, or friends to do something. Invite them to share the kinds of reasons they used. Make two columns on the board to list the reasons that did work and the reasons that did not work.

Explain that as they write their persuasive paragraphs, students should use only good, strong, sensible reasons to support their opinion.

Technology Connections

Use this unit's Interactive Whiteboard Lesson to introduce persuasive writing.

Interactive Whiteboard Lesson

Writing a Persuasive Paragraph

What does your class need? More computers? What about a classroom pet or parent helpers?

Sarah had an idea about what her class needed. She wrote a persuasive paragraph to convince others to agree with her. You, too, can write about what you think your class needs.

Paragraph Parts

1. The **topic sentence** states the topic (opinion).

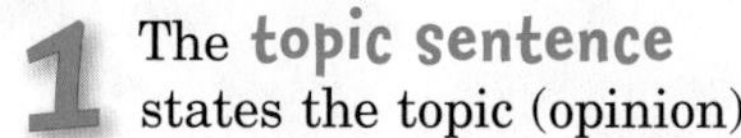

2. The **body sentences** give reasons to support the opinion.

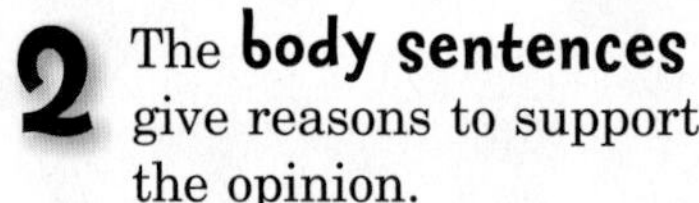

3. The **closing sentence** tells why the reader should agree.

Copy Masters

Table Diagram (TE p. 181)

Materials

Chart paper (TE p. 180)
Drawing paper (TE p. 183)

Writing a Persuasive Paragraph 179

Persuasive Paragraph

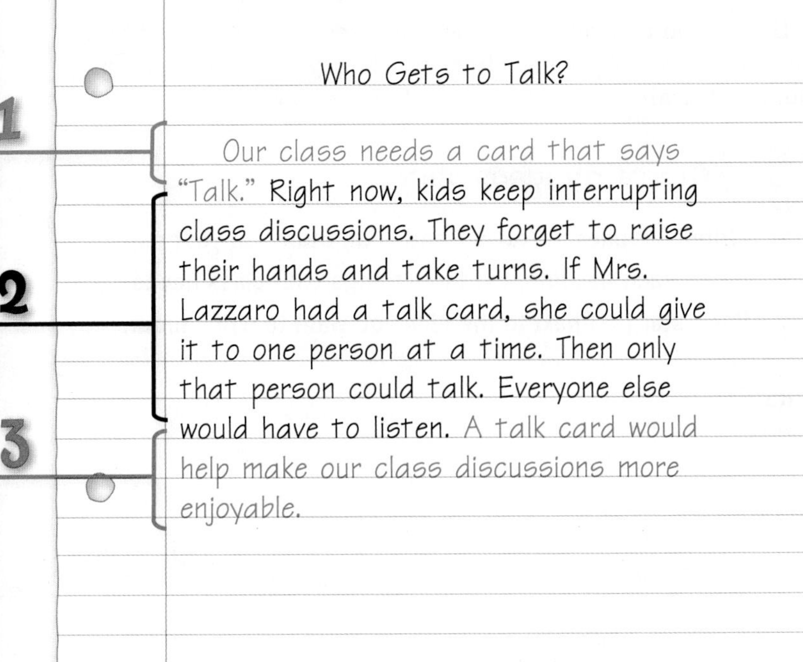

Who Gets to Talk?
1
Our class needs a card that says "Talk." Right now, kids keep interrupting class discussions. They forget to raise their hands and take turns. If Mrs. Lazzaro had a talk card, she could give it to one person at a time. Then only that person could talk. Everyone else would have to listen. A talk card would help make our class discussions more enjoyable.
2
3

After you read . . .

- **Ideas** **(1) What does Sarah think her class needs?**
- **Organization** **(2) What are the three parts of the paragraph?**
- **Word Choice** **(3) In the last sentence, Sarah uses the word *would*. Why is that a better word than *could* in the same spot?**

Persuasive Paragraph

Review the basic parts of a persuasive paragraph by having students match each numbered section in Sarah's persuasive paragraph to the numbered paragraph parts on the bottom of SE page 178: the topic sentence, the body sentences, and the closing sentence.

Point out that in "Who Gets to Talk?" the topic sentence **expresses the writer's opinion** *(see below)*. The body sentences provide the writer's reasons that support her opinion. In this paragraph, the *"If . . . then . . . "* statement provides an explanation of how the "Talk" card could be used to help solve the problem.

After you read . . .

Answers

Ideas 1. a card that says "Talk"

Organization 2. the topic sentence, which states an opinion; the body sentences, which give reasons to support the opinion; and a closing sentence, which tells why the reader should agree

Word Choice 3. The word *would* is more persuasive than *could* because it is stronger. In Sarah's opinion a talk card *will* make class discussions more enjoyable. *Could* implies that a talk card *might* make discussions more enjoyable.

Teaching Tip: Expressing an Opinion in a Topic Sentence

A good way to check whether a topic sentence states an opinion is to read it aloud with one of these phrases before it: *I believe . . . , I think . . . , or I feel . . . .* Have students add one of the phrases to the beginning of Sarah's topic sentence. Then have them read it aloud to a partner to check whether the topic sentence makes a statement of opinion. Have them use this strategy when they are writing the topic sentence for their paragraph.

Prewriting Selecting a Topic

To generate good topic ideas from which to choose, have students work as a class to create an ideas chart.

Copy the chart headings onto the board or chart paper. To stimulate ideas for the chart, use these prompts:

- Look around the classroom. Are there any supplies you wish the class had? Is there anything that needs replacing?
- Think about class and school rules. Are there any rules you think our class or school needs that we don't have now?
- What fun things do you wish you could do before school, during school, at recess, or after school?

By working together to create a class ideas chart, you can keep students on track and guide them in sharing reasonable and beneficial ideas. If you use a class ideas chart, be aware that several students will probably choose the same topic for their paragraphs.

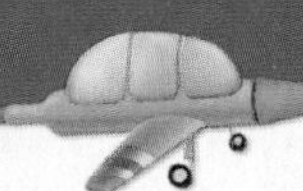

Prewriting Selecting a Topic

Before you can select a topic, you need to think about things your class needs. An ideas chart can help you organize your thoughts. Sarah created the ideas chart below.

Create an ideas chart.

1. **Write "Supplies," "Rules," and "Fun Stuff" on your paper.**
2. **Under each heading, list three things your class needs.**
3. **Put a star (*) next to the idea you want to write about.**

Ideas Chart

Supplies	Rules	Fun Stuff
good scissors	allowing gum	hat day
Bill Nye video	no line cutting	zoo trip
new reading books	a talk card*	longer recess

Writing a Persuasive Paragraph 181

Writing Creating Your First Draft

As you write your paragraph, remember that each part has a special job.

- The **topic sentence** gives your opinion about what your class needs.
- The **body sentences** give two or three reasons for your opinion.
- The **closing sentence** restates your opinion and tells why the reader should agree.

Begin your first draft.

1. Write your topic sentence: "Our class needs ____________."
2. Give two or three reasons for your opinion.
3. Write a closing sentence that restates your opinion. Use the word *would* or *should*.

Writing Creating Your First Draft

Remind students that they should not expect their first draft to be perfect. Tell them to try to get all their ideas on paper as clearly as possible but not to worry about mistakes in capitalization, punctuation, spelling, and grammar. They will have a chance to make their ideas clearer when they revise and correct mistakes when they edit.

Tell students to make sure their body sentences answer these questions:

- Why do we need this (thing or idea)?
- How can this (thing or idea) be used to solve or deal with the problem?

Suggest that students reread Sarah's persuasive paragraph on SE page 179 to see how she answered these questions in "Who Gets to Talk?"

English Language Learners

Students may find persuasive writing difficult because they cannot identify words that signal an opinion. Point out that *needs* in the topic sentence is an opinion word. Explain that some people may think an item is needed, while others do not. Provide practice by stating opinions and having students identify opinion words such as *I think, I believe, I feel, My opinion is,* and *People should.*

Struggling Learners

Visual learners may benefit from making a table diagram before starting their first drafts. Draw a table diagram on the board and model the following steps:

- Complete the "Our class needs _______" statement and write it in the tabletop.
- Have students orally provide two or three reasons for the opinion.
- Write the reasons in the legs of the main idea table.

Distribute copies of the reproducible Table Diagram (TE page 599) to students for their use.

Revising Improving Your Paragraph

Read and discuss the definitions of opinion and fact to make sure students understand the difference. Because the topics for their persuasive paragraphs are particular to their class or school, students will not be able to prove facts by checking in an encyclopedia or by asking outside experts. Instead, they will rely on their own personal observations. Explain that for this paragraph, they are the experts. Therefore, they will use facts and examples from their own experience.

Before doing the **Practice,** review ***"If . . . then . . . "* statements** *(see below)* to be sure students understand the distinction between sentences that are strictly reasons, and sentences that explain how a writer's idea can be used to solve the problem.

Practice Answers

Possible choices:

- The writer can't eat some foods because of a special diet.
- Other kids have special diets, too.

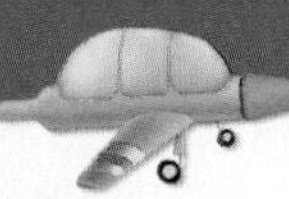

Revising Improving Your Paragraph

When you revise your paragraph, you make sure all your reasons are based on facts. A fact is different from an opinion.

An **opinion** is something you believe, think, or feel.

Our class needs a new seating order.

A **fact** is something you can prove.

Some kids talk during work time.
Other kids don't get along.
I can't see the chalkboard.

Revise Check your facts.

1. Read your paragraph.
2. Check each reason to be sure it supports your opinion. If it does not, delete the sentence.
3. Make sure your reasons are based on facts.

Practice

Read the following paragraph. List at least two reasons that support the opinion (underlined).

Our class needs a snack list. I can't eat some foods because I have a special diet. Other kids have special diets, too. We could write down what snacks we can eat. Then parents would know what to send to school for special occasions. A snack list would mean everyone could enjoy a treat.

Teaching Tip: *"If . . . then . . . "* Statements

"If . . . then . . . " statements provide students with an almost foolproof framework for presenting a solution to an issue or problem. Although the text does not tell students to present a solution, including one can make their reasons sound more convincing.

Have students reread the *"If . . . then . . . "* statement in the sample paragraph (SE page 179). The *"If . . ."* part suggests a way to use the "Talk" card. The *"then . . . "* part describes the positive results from using the "Talk" card.

Ask students to check their own paragraphs to see whether they can provide a solution in an *"If . . . then . . . "* statement. Circulate among them to offer assistance. Point out that an *"If . . . then . . . "* statement comes after the reasons in the body.

Editing Checking for Conventions

When you edit your paragraph, you need to check for proper capitalization, punctuation, and spelling.

Check your work.

1. **Did I indent the first line of my paragraph?**
2. **Did I begin each sentence with a capital letter?**
3. **Did I end each sentence with a punctuation mark?**
4. **Have I used words correctly?**
5. **Have I checked for spelling errors?**

Grammar Practice

Learn to use these sets of words correctly.

to (toward)	**there** (in that place)
two (the number 2)	**their** (belonging to them)
too (very, also)	**they're** (they are)

For each sentence below, write the correct word from those in parentheses.

1. Our class needs lockers where kids can leave *(there, their)* things.
2. Sometimes *(to, two)* backpacks get mixed up.
3. It's *(to, too)* hard for kids to find their lunches.
4. We should put lockers next *(to, two)* the door.
5. If we put them *(their, there)*, the room will be neater.

Editing Checking for Conventions

Share with students any strategies that you have for using words such as *too, to,* and *two* correctly. Give a few more examples of words that can be confused, such as *buy* and *by, dear* and *deer,* and *hour* and *our.* Then invite students to share any strategies of their own to remember other easily confused words.

* For more about Using the Right Word, see SE pages 510–525.

Grammar Practice Answers

1. their
2. two
3. too
4. to
5. there

Advanced Learners

Invite students to choose a convention from the editing checklist. Have them use it as the subject of a cartoon strip for a learning center. Explain that the cartoon strip should contain

- at least two characters,
- a process for checking writing for the convention,
- a strategy to help students, and
- an example of how the strategy is used.

Grammar Connection

Using the Right Word

- **Proofreader's Guide** pages 520–521, 522–523
- ***SkillsBook*** pages 72–73

Spelling

- **Proofreader's Guide** pages 502–507
- ***SkillsBook*** pages 63–64

Fragments

- **Proofreader's Guide** pages 526 (+), 528 (+)
- ***Write Source*** page 403 (+)
- ***GrammarSnap*** Complete Sentences
- ***SkillsBook*** page 96

Writing a Persuasive Letter

Objectives

- Understand the purpose, content, and form of a persuasive letter.
- Choose a topic (a school or community need) to write about.
- Plan, draft, revise, and edit a persuasive letter.

A **persuasive letter** is a piece of writing that

- states an opinion,
- supports the opinion with strong reasons and facts, and
- asks the reader to take action.

Point out the words *positive change* in the first paragraph. Explain that a positive change is a change that makes things better for people. Ask students to recall the positive changes they were trying to create when they wrote their persuasive paragraphs about a class need.

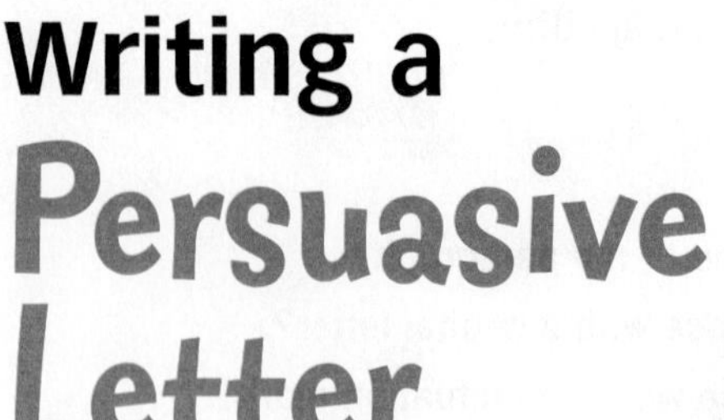

Writing a Persuasive Letter

One way to make a positive change is to write a persuasive letter. A persuasive letter can convince someone to take action.

In this chapter, Brenda writes a persuasive letter about games needed for her third-grade class. Later, Roku writes about a new library checkout rule needed at his school.

Materials

Generic business letters (TE p. 187)

Index cards, hole puncher, yarn (TE p. 196)

Tape recorder (TE p. 202)

Construction paper (TE p. 206)

Colored pencils (TE p. 207)

Chart paper (TE p. 212)

Copy Masters

T-Chart (TE pp. 188, 206)

Thinking About Your Writing (TE p. 213)

Understanding Your Goal

Your goal in this chapter is to write a persuasive letter. The letter should give your opinion about something your school or community needs. The six traits below and the persuasive revising lessons (pages 192–203) will help you reach your goal.

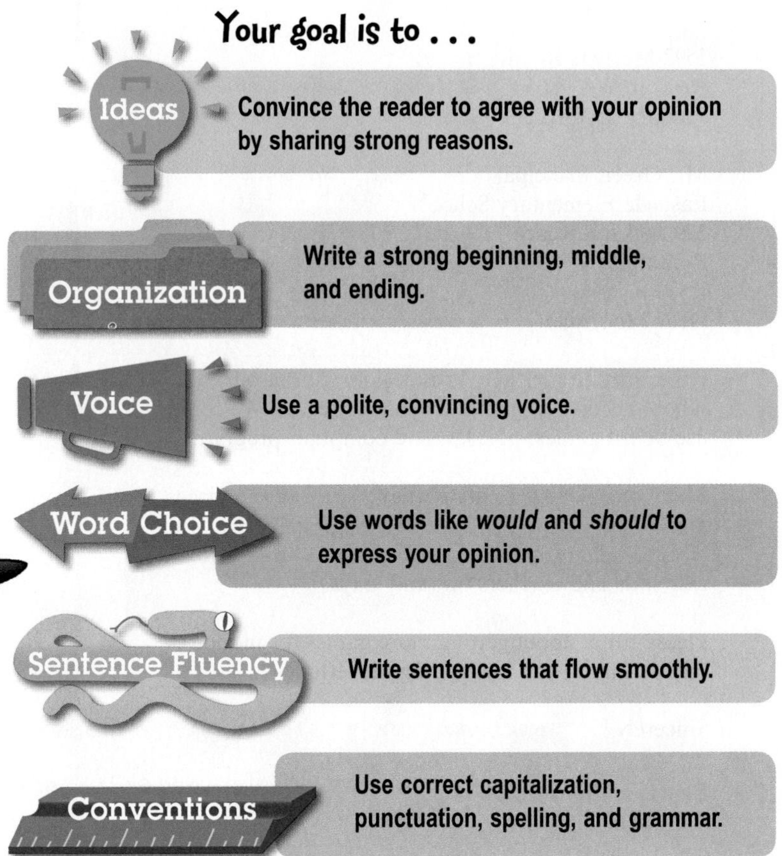

Your goal is to . . .
Ideas
Convince the reader to agree with your opinion by sharing strong reasons.
Organization
Write a strong beginning, middle, and ending.
Voice
Use a polite, convincing voice.
Word Choice
Use words like *would* and *should* to express your opinion.
Sentence Fluency
Write sentences that flow smoothly.
Conventions
Use correct capitalization, punctuation, spelling, and grammar.

Understanding Your Goal

Encourage students to use this page as a guide for understanding how the traits can help them write their persuasive letter. Suggest that they bookmark this page so that they can flip back to it any time they need a reminder of their goals as they plan and write their letter. Reassure students that they will receive plenty of guidance throughout the writing process so that they can successfully achieve these goals.

Depending on the needs of your class, focus on one or two of the traits throughout the revising process. The revising section (SE pages 194–204) provides additional instruction and practice for each trait. The side notes and Teaching Tips throughout this section of the TE also provide suggestions to supplement the instruction and the practices.

Persuasive Letter

Read this sample letter with the class, pointing out the elements that make it a good persuasive letter.

Ideas

- The topic statement clearly expresses an opinion about a need.
- The writer explains specifically what is needed.
- The writer provides strong reasons to support the opinion.
- The writer explains why the solution is a sound idea.

Organization

- The writer uses the correct form for a business letter.
- The first two body paragraphs express the opinion and provide supporting reasons that explain the opinion.
- The final paragraph asks the reader to take action.

Voice & Word Choice

- The writer uses a convincing voice.
- The writer's words are polite and fit the topic and audience.

Persuasive Letter

A persuasive letter gives your opinion and tries to convince the reader to agree with you.

1592 Mertens Road
Renton, WA 98050
January 23, 2011

Mr. Greer, Principal
Eastside Elementary School
239 Jackson Road
Renton, WA 98050

Dear Mr. Greer:

I'm a third grader here at Eastside. I think our school needs new games for indoor recess. We could use board games, puzzles, and computer programs.

Many of our puzzles are old, and some of the pieces are missing. Also, there aren't enough games, so kids have to take turns playing them. New games would help kids and teachers on rainy days.

Please think about getting more games for indoor recess. Thank you for reading my letter.

Sincerely,

Brenda Davidson
Brenda Davidson

English Language Learners

Point out examples of formal tone in Brenda's letter:

- The title *Principal* follows Mr. Greer's name.
- Brenda introduces herself in the first sentence and signs her full name.

Struggling Learners

Ask a volunteer to read the sentence in Brenda's letter that expresses her opinion *(I think our school needs new games for indoor recess).* Then ask for volunteers to read the sentences that state her reasons *(Many of our puzzles . . . are missing. Also, there aren't . . . turns playing them. New games . . . rainy days).* Also ask them which sentence introduces the writer to the reader *(I'm a third grader here . . .),* and which sentence closes the letter in a polite way *(Thank you for reading . . .).* Remind them that this is the same format they will follow to write their own persuasive letter.

Writing a Persuasive Letter 187

Parts of a Business Letter

Heading The heading includes your address and the date.

Inside Address The inside address includes the name and address of the person you are writing to.

Greeting The greeting is a polite way of saying hello. It is followed by a colon (:).

Body The body is the main part of the letter.

Closing The closing is a polite way of saying good-bye.

Signature The signature is your name at the end of the letter.

After you read . . .

- Ideas **(1) What is the writer's opinion?**
- Organization **(2) What paragraph includes the reasons that explain Brenda's opinion?**
- Word Choice **(3) What words or phrases make the letter sound polite?**

Parts of a Business Letter

Display a friendly letter and ask students to point out the differences between the parts of a friendly letter and the parts of a business letter.

* For an example of a Friendly Letter, see SE page 445.

Students should note these differences in a friendly letter.

- A friendly letter does not have an inside address.
- The greeting uses the person's first name and is followed by a comma.
- The body paragraphs are indented, and there is no extra space between them.
- The closing and signature are at the right, in line with the address and date. The writer signs only a first name.

If you have already analyzed the model as a class, focus on students' personal responses to the letter.

After you read . . .

Answers

Ideas **1.** Our school needs new games for indoor recess.

Organization **2.** second paragraph

Word Choice **3.** I think, We could use, Please, Thank you, Sincerely

English Language Learners

Some students may be unfamiliar with the word *signature*. Point out that it contains the word *sign,* as in "sign your name." Have students take turns writing their signatures on the board.

Struggling Learners

Provide several generic business letters (solicitations, advertisements, announcements, invitations, etc.), and give one to each pair of students. Have students help each other find the writer's opinion and underline several reasons. Then ask them to share their findings with the others.

Prewriting Selecting a Topic

Provide photocopies of the reproducible T-Chart (TE page 595) for students to list their topic ideas. To help students generate enough topic ideas for each heading, provide prewriting time for them to gather ideas. Suggest that they

- work with a partner to talk to other students in the school to discover school needs, and
- talk to their parents, older siblings, and teachers to identify both school and community needs.

Tell students that as they write their opinion sentence, they should have at least one specific idea in mind for how to solve the problem. They may even want to jot their idea or ideas down along with their opinion sentence.

Writer's Craft

Authentic purposes: Help students select topics that will allow them to write real letters. Inspire them with the story of Samantha Smith, a ten-year-old who wrote a letter to Soviet Premier Andropov during the height of the Cold War. He wrote back to her and invited her to the Soviet Union, making her an ambassador for peace. For the full story, go to www.samanthasmith.info.

Technology Connections

Students can use the added features of the Net-text as they explore this stage of the writing process.

Write Source Online **Net-text**

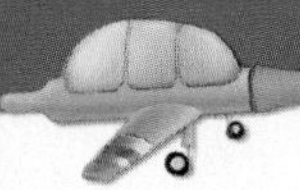

Prewriting Selecting a Topic

You can use a T-chart to help you choose your topic. (Look at Roku's T-chart below.)

List topic ideas on a T-chart.

1. Write "School Needs" and "Community Needs" on your paper.
2. List three or four ideas under each heading.
3. Put a star (✱) next to the idea you want to write about.
4. Decide who should get your letter.

T-Chart

School Needs	Community Needs
bigger lunchroom	a park to walk dogs
more jump ropes	more sidewalks
new checkout rule ✱ for the library	Ha-P Charl-E's Pizza

English Language Learners

Students may need help generating reasons to support their opinions. Have prewriting partners informally discuss their reasons with one another. If possible, have students record their conversations so they can play back their reasons. Once they have discussed their reasons, have students complete the last **Prewrite** activity.

Struggling Learners

Before writing their opinion sentence, have students write opinion statements for each of these topics:

- having a summer break from school
- living with a pet
- earning an allowance
- receiving report cards

Remind them to begin their opinion sentence with *I believe, I think,* or *I feel.*

Writing a Persuasive Letter 189

Writing an Opinion Sentence

Think about the idea you chose and your opinion about it.

Prewrite **Write your opinion sentence.**

- **Use the following form to write your opinion sentence:**
  I think our ____(place)____ needs ____(what is needed)____.

Opinion Sentence

I think our school library needs a new checkout rule.
(place) (what is needed)

Gathering Reasons

An opinion sentence should be supported by strong reasons.

Prewrite **Gather reasons for your opinion.**

- **Write at least two or three reasons that answer this question: Why is my opinion a good idea?**

Reasons List

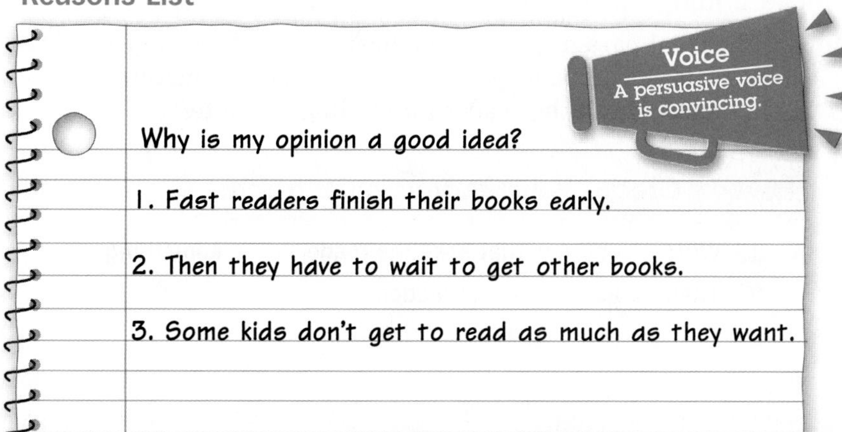

Voice
A persuasive voice is convincing.
Why is my opinion a good idea?
1. Fast readers finish their books early.
2. Then they have to wait to get other books.
3. Some kids don't get to read as much as they want.

Writing an Opinion Sentence

To help students understand the importance of how to choose a good topic, discuss how Roku may have arrived at his choice.

- Roku is probably a fast reader, so the checkout rule would affect him directly.
- The checkout rule sounds easy to change without causing other problems.
- Roku may not care that much about the other ideas, but he does care about changing the checkout rule.
- He may not know enough facts about the other issues to come up with supporting reasons.
- He may have figured out that some of the needs would be too hard or too expensive to fix.

As students gather reasons, have them keep in mind the facts that they know about the topic because they will be turning them into reasons. Hold **writing conferences** *(see below)* to provide additional guidance and to answer questions.

Teaching Tip: Writing Conferences

Brief one-on-one discussions, away from the distractions of the traditional classroom setting, can help some students focus ideas and gain confidence. If possible, meet with students in a relaxed environment to discuss their topic choice, for example, a special area in your room or their favorite spot in the school library.

To help students evaluate their topic choice, suggest that they ask themselves questions such as:

- Do I know and care about this topic?
- Is the need important to me?
- How will the change I'm suggesting affect others?
- Can I think of at least three facts about this topic that I can turn into good reasons?

Stress the importance of using strong reasons to support an opinion. Point out that whenever readers are asked to do something, they want to know the reasons for getting involved. The writer's strong, sensible reasons explain why the reader may want to help bring about the change.

Writing Starting Your First Draft

The directions for drafting a beginning paragraph ask students to tell a little more about themselves or their idea. Suggest that they

- write only one sentence about themselves, and
- make sure that their sentence is related to their idea.

Students can look at the beginning sentences of the sample draft on SE page 191 and the sample letter on SE page 186 for examples. Also have students add a sentence that further explains or makes a specific recommendation for what is needed.

Use the sample draft on SE page 191 to make sure students understand how to achieve the two purposes of the ending paragraph.

Technology Connections

Students can use the added features of the Net-text as they explore this stage of the writing process.

Write Source Online ***Net-text***

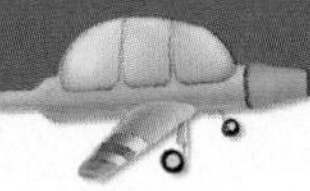

Writing Starting Your First Draft

The Beginning Paragraph

The beginning paragraph should tell the reader who you are and what your opinion is.

Draft your beginning paragraph.

1. **Remember to include your opinion sentence from page 189.**
2. **You should also write a sentence that tells a little more about you or your idea.**

The Middle Paragraph

The middle paragraph should give two or three reasons that explain your opinion.

Create your middle paragraph.

- **Include the reasons that explain your opinion. Look at the list you wrote for page 189.**

The Ending Paragraph

The final paragraph of a persuasive letter has two jobs to do: (1) It should politely ask the reader to do something. (2) It should thank the reader for reading the letter.

Create your ending paragraph.

1. **Write a sentence that asks the reader to do something.**
2. **Then politely thank the reader.**

English Language Learners

Before students draft their beginning paragraph, discuss the two beginning paragraph steps and have them look at Roku's beginning paragraph on SE page 191. Point out that Roku's first sentence tells about himself and his second sentence states his opinion. Suggest that students use Roku's paragraph as a model.

Struggling Learners

To guarantee a successful ending paragraph, suggest that students use the ending paragraph in the sample draft on SE page 186 as a model: "Please think about . . . " and "Thank you for reading my letter."

Advanced Learners

Have students write introductions that tell something unique about themselves. Have them practice modifying Roku's beginning paragraph on SE page 191. For example, "I took a break from reading an exciting book to write this important letter. I know a new library checkout rule would make many students happy."

Writing a Persuasive Letter 191

Roku's First Draft

Here is Roku's first draft, including errors. Notice how he wrote on every other line to leave room for his revisions.

Beginning
Give your opinion.

Middle
Use reasons to explain your opinion.

Ending
Use polite words such as "thank you."

Dear Mrs. Lincoln,

I'm a student who loves to read. I could eat books for breakfast, lunch, and dinner. I'm writing to you because I think our school libary needs a new checkout rule.

students must be able to check out more books. Kids can check out only a few books. That means fast readers have to wait. They have to wait forever for the next libary day. Everybody likes libary day.

Other kids like me who want to gobble up all the books they can. Think about a new checkout rule. I'm begging you. Thank you.

Sincerely,

Roku Hitsuki

English Language Learners

Some students may feel uncomfortable using the second person in their writing, as it may seem too direct or too informal. Tell them that this form of address is acceptable and even recommended when writing persuasive text in English.

Roku's First Draft

Students may notice that the draft of the persuasive letter does not use correct business-letter form. Tell students that they do not have to worry about writing the heading and inside address as they write their draft. For now, they should just concentrate on writing down all their ideas. After they revise and edit their letter, they will put it into the correct business-letter form.

Revising Improving Your Persuasive Letter

The revising process on this page focuses on the traits of ideas and organization. A Partner's Response (SE pages 193–205) extends the revising and editing processes to include all six traits of good writing. You can use the workshop section in conjunction with this page to help students revise for one or more of the six traits.

Before asking students to revise their draft, have them review and evaluate the changes that Roku made to his first draft on SE page 195.

Technology Connections

Have students use the Writing Network features of the Net-text to comment on each other's drafts.

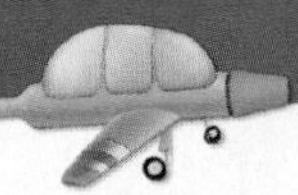

Revising Improving Your Persuasive Letter

When you finish your first draft, you are ready to make changes to improve your writing. Begin the revising part of the writing process by reading your letter to yourself.

Then read your letter out loud to a partner. You may ask your partner the following questions that are based on your writing goals (see page 185).

Ideas

- Did I convince you to agree with my opinion by sharing strong reasons?

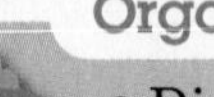

Organization

- Did I write a strong beginning, middle, and ending?

Voice

- Did I use a polite and convincing voice?

Word Choice

- Did I use the words *would* and *should* to express my opinion?

Sentence Fluency

- Do my sentences flow smoothly?

Struggling Learners

Students may think a commanding tone is necessary to be convincing. Have students look at the question "Does your voice sound convincing?" Explain that a convincing voice states reasons and facts and sounds natural. Have students explain why using command words like *you must* and *you'd better* are not necessary when they write strong reasons.

Writing a Persuasive Letter 193

Getting a Partner's Response

A partner can help you find ways to improve your writing. Here is a partner's response to Roku's letter on page 191.

Response Sheet

Writer: Roku Responder: Linda

Title: Letter to Mrs. Lincoln

What I like:

I like your idea about checking out more books.

I'm glad you are writing about kids reading more.

Questions I have:

How many books can kids check out now?

Could there be more library days?

Getting a Partner's Response

Provide photocopies of the reproducible Response Sheet (TE page 592) for students to use as they share their letter with a partner. Students can provide their partner with a copy of the letter to read, or they can read the letter aloud to their partner. Remind partners to

- provide kind and polite responses,
- comment on the writing, not the writer, and
- be specific about what they think the writer should do to improve the letter.

✱ For more information on reviewing with partners, have students turn to SE pages 17–19.

Revising for Ideas

In order for students to check that their reasons actually support their opinion statement and answer *why,* have them read aloud to a partner their opinion statement, followed by the word *because,* followed by their first reason. (They can repeat this for their second reason, and for their third reason, if they have one.) Model the process, using the examples on SE page 194.

- Our class should tour the Chicago Field Museum *because* the museum has the largest *T. rex* skeleton ever found.
- Our class should tour the Chicago Field Museum *because* the museum has other dinosaur skeletons, too.

Practice Answers

The first sentence (We are studying dinosaurs) answers *why.*

Revising for Ideas

Your writing will be convincing if your opinion is supported with good reasons.

Q. How do I know if my reasons are good?

Your reasons are good if they answer the question *why.*

Opinion: Our class should tour the Chicago Field Museum.
Why? The museum has the largest T. rex skeleton ever found.
Why? The museum has other dinosaurs, too.

Practice

Read the opinion above. Which of the following reasons answers *why* for that opinion?

1. We are studying dinosaurs.
2. The museum's founder owned a department store.
3. The Shedd Aquarium is another cool place.
4. It's fun to see what you read in books.
5. Chicago has some of the world's tallest buildings.

Writing a Persuasive Letter 195

Revising in Action

Here is how Roku improved the first draft of his letter. He added an explanation so that his reason answers the question *why*. He also cut a reason that did not support his opinion.

I love to read. I could eat books for breakfast, lunch, and dinner. I'm writing to you because I think our school libary needs a new checkout rule.

students must be able to check out more books. Kids can check out only a few books. That means fast readers ^[finish there books and] have to wait. They have to wait forever for the next libary day. ~~Everybody likes libary day.~~

Other kids like me want to gobble up all the books they can. Think about a new checkout rule ^[or more library days]. I'm begging you. Thank you.

Revise **Check your ideas.**

Read your opinion and your supporting reasons.

- **Add information so that your opinion is clear and all your reasons answer the question *why*.**
- **Cut any reasons that do not support your opinion.**

Revising in Action

This activity provides a good opportunity to stress that revising includes cutting ideas that do not fit the essay as well as adding ideas to make the writing clearer. Discuss the changes Roku made to his persuasive letter.

- He cut an idea that did not fit in his essay.
- He made one idea clearer.
- He added a totally new choice as a possible solution at the end.

Have students work with a partner to be sure their changes are making their persuasive letters better.

Revising for Organization

While the checklist is supposed to be a guide to encourage students to check their organization and help them identify weaknesses in their draft, many students will automatically check "yes" for each question and feel they are done.

To encourage students to actually look for ways to improve their draft, write the following questions on the board or on chart paper. Have students use them to revise before having them use the checklist.

- What can I add or change to make my beginning more interesting, and my opinion sentence clearer?
- On what facts did I base each reason?
- What do I ask the writer to do?
- What words and phrases make my ending sound polite?

Revising for Organization

In persuasive writing, the beginning, middle, and ending parts work together.

Q. *How can I check my organization?*

The following checklist can help you review the organization of your writing.

Organization

Beginning

___ **1.** Did I make my beginning interesting for the reader?
___ **2.** Did I write a clear opinion sentence?

Middle

___ **3.** Did I include reasons that support my opinion?

Ending

___ **4.** Did I politely ask the reader to do something?

Practice

Which ending sentences below sound polite? Write a polite final sentence for an essay in support of a fund-raiser to buy a new tree for your school grounds.

1. Please help this worthy cause.
2. I'm asking you to vote "yes."
3. Act now or you'll be sorry.

Advanced Learners

Provide students with index cards, a hole puncher, and yarn to create their own **Organization Checklist** flip charts. Challenge students to write their own beginning, middle, and ending rules for organizing persuasive writing. On each page of the chart, have them write the new rule and provide an example. Have students share their flip charts with a partner.

Writing a Persuasive Letter 197

Revising in Action

Here is how Roku improved the organization of the first draft of his letter. He moved his opinion to the end of his beginning paragraph. He added another polite word to his ending paragraph.

I love to read. I could eat books for breakfast, lunch, and dinner. I'm writing to you because I think our school libary needs a new checkout rule. students must be able to check out more books. ¶ Kids can check out only a few books. That means fast readers finish there books and have to wait. They have to wait forever for the next libary day. ~~Everybody likes libary day.~~

Other kids like me want to gobble up all the books they can. Pleese think about a new checkout rule or more library days. I'm begging you. Thank you.

Revise **Check your organization.**

Use the organization checklist on page 196 as a guide.

- **Move information as needed.**

Revising in Action

One of the big changes for revising for organization is moving words or sentences. How does the change that Roku made improve his persuasive letter?

- What Roku says about thinking the school library needs a new checkout rule sounds like an opinion statement. However, his real opinion is that students need to be able to check out more books. It's important to make a strong opinion statement in the first paragraph.
- Moving the sentence keeps the focus of the second paragraph on why the current checkout rule is a problem.

Revising for Voice

Make sure students understand that an exaggeration is a statement that stretches the truth so much that the statement is no longer true or accurate. Ask students when the use of exaggeration might be acceptable (in a tall tale, a funny story, or other kind of fiction story).

Practice Answers

Possible answers:

1. We get a snow day only if it's too dangerous for the school buses to be on the road.
2. Kids have to play outside for recess even when the weather isn't great.
3. The summer-school classrooms are really hot and stuffy.
4. This situation makes us uncomfortable.
5. When it rains, large puddles form in the playground.

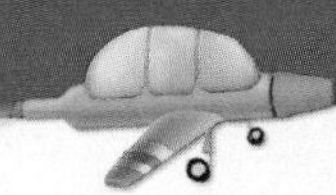

Revising for

Your writing voice is your own special way of expressing yourself. For persuasive writing, your voice should sound convincing.

Q. How can I make my voice convincing?

You can make your voice convincing by being accurate. If you exaggerate, your reader may not believe you.

Convincing: Kids have to line up outside even if it's really cold.

Exaggerating: Kids have to line up outside even if it's 50 degrees below zero!

Practice

Rewrite each exaggeration below so it sounds more convincing.

1. We get a snow day only if there's 70 feet of snow.
2. Kids have to play outside even in a hurricane.
3. The summer-school classrooms are 300 degrees.
4. This situation is hopeless.
5. When it rains, the playground turns into an ocean.

English Language Learners

Students may be unfamiliar with the word *exaggerate*. Explain that it means "to make something seem greater than it really is." Write each **Practice** sentence on the board. Model a Think-Aloud for the first sentence to identify words and phrases that show exaggeration. Then work with students to explain why each remaining sentence is an exaggeration.

Struggling Learners

Have students practice revising for a convincing voice by placing them in groups to rewrite the following exaggerations:

- Recess lasts only one second!
- My dog ate a million pounds of dog food today.
- The noise in my brother's room sounds as loud as a thousand elephants.

Writing a Persuasive Letter 199

Revising in Action

Here is how Roku improved the voice in the first draft of his letter. He added words to make his information more accurate. He also cut an exaggeration.

I love to read. I could eat books for breakfast, lunch, and dinner. I'm writing to you because I think our school libary needs a new checkout rule.

students must be able to check out more books. ¶ Kids can check out only ~~a few books.~~ as many books as the number of their grade. That means fast readers finish there books and have to wait. They have to wait ~~forever~~ for the next libary day. ~~Everybody likes libary day.~~

Other kids like me want to gobble up all the books they can. Pleese Think about a new checkout rule or more library days. I'm begging you. Thank you.

Revise **Check your voice.**

Read your letter carefully.

- **Add convincing words as needed.**
- **Cut any exaggerations.**

Revising in Action

Stress that persuasive writing calls for making a strong case for action without using words that are too strong. When someone wants to convince someone to change something, they need that person to agree with them. They do not want to make that person angry. A convincing voice uses facts to make a point.

Discuss Roku's changes to his persuasive letter. How does the information that he added help the reader understand the problem?

- A student's desire to read many books is not limited by the number of the grade he or she is in.
- One number for everyone is not going to be fair to students who want to read lots of books.
- The added information is much clearer than the phrase "a few books."

Writer's Craft

Voice: Roku's second sentence has very strong voice—"I could eat books for breakfast, lunch, and dinner." Many teachers might ask Roku to remove the sentence, but read the paragraph without it. All the personality is removed for the sake of "formal voice." By leaving in that sentence, Roku puts his unique stamp on the letter and makes it more persuasive.

Revising for Word Choice

Students may not understand exactly why *must* is not acceptable. Explain that *must* sounds like the writer is commanding the reader. The helping verbs *could* and *should* sound like the writer is suggesting an idea to the reader. Since children aren't supposed to tell grown-ups what to do, a grown-up reader is more likely to listen to an idea that is presented as a suggestion, not a command. Read aloud the samples. As you read, modulate your voice so that students can hear how each helping verb affects the sound of the sentence.

* For more about Helping Verbs, see SE page 385.

Practice Answers

Answers will vary. Possible answers:

1. Mr. Lewis, you could hire us to cut your grass.
2. Mr. Lewis, you should hire us to cut your grass.
3. Mr. Lewis, you must hire us to cut your grass.

The sentences with *could* and *should* sound polite. The sentence with *must* does not sound polite.

Revising for Word Choice

When you make a suggestion, you need to choose the best words for your audience.

Q. Which helping verbs will fit my audience?

If your audience includes people who are older than you, use the helping verbs *could* and *should*, not *must*.

Could (an acceptable choice)
Teachers could remind us to walk in the hall.

Should (an acceptable choice)
Teachers should be fair to us.

Must (**not** an acceptable choice)
Teachers must make us obey class rules.

Practice

1. **Write a polite sentence to someone older—the principal, your neighbor, or someone else. Use the word *could*.**
2. **Rewrite the sentence with the word *should*.**
3. **Rewrite the sentence again with the word *must*. How does each sentence sound?**

Grammar Connection

Helping Verbs

- **Proofreader's Guide** page 538 (+)
- ***Write Source*** page 385
- ***GrammarSnap*** Helping Verbs
- ***SkillsBook*** page 135

English Language Learners

Pair students and have them complete the **Practice** activity orally. Then have them work together to write the sentences using *could* and *should,* but not *must,* to reinforce only the acceptable choices.

Writing a Persuasive Letter 201

Revising in Action

Here is how Roku improved the word choice in the first draft of his letter. He changed a helping verb that didn't fit his audience. He rewrote his final sentence to make it more polite.

I love to read. I could eat books for breakfast, lunch, and dinner. I'm writing to you because I think our school libary needs a new checkout rule.

should
students ~~must~~ be able to check out more books. ¶ Kids can check out only ~~a few books.~~ as many books as the number of their grade.

finish there books and
That means fast readers have to wait. They have to wait ~~forever~~ for the next libary day. ~~Everybody likes libary day.~~

Other kids like me want to gobble up all the books they can. Pleese Think about a new checkout rule or more library days. ~~I'm begging you.~~ Thank you for reading my letter.

Check your word choice.

Revise

Check the words and helping verbs in your letter.

- **Add verbs that sound polite.**

Revising in Action

Discuss how Roku changed his persuasive letter to make the words more persuasive. You may want to explain the difference between the words *could* and *should*. See if students already understand the distinction between *could,* which has the sense of being able to do something or of something being possible, vs. *should,* which has a sense that one ought to do something.

Revising for Sentence Fluency

To help students identify sentences that could be combined, suggest that they look through their draft for two short sentences in a row that repeat key words. This is usually a signal that the sentences can and should be combined. Tell students to underline in red the words and phrases repeated in the two sentences. Then they can check to see if they can combine these sentences by moving to the first sentence those key words that are not repeated but that add new ideas. Students can try this using the sample sentences and Practice sentences 1, 3, and 4.

For example, in the sample sentences, they would underline the words *is crowded* in each sentence. Then they can easily see the phrase *with older kids,* which can be moved to the first sentence.

Practice Answers

1. Older kids take up many seats in back.
2. The younger kids sit together up front.
3. All the kids are cranky about the crowding.
4. Most kids would agree that they need more space.

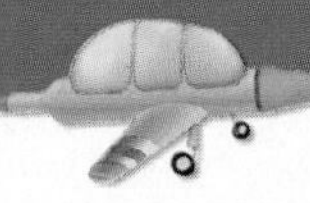

Revising for

Persuasive writing should read smoothly with no short, choppy sentences.

Q. How can I fix short, choppy sentences?

You can fix short, choppy sentences by combining them. Sometimes you can combine sentences by moving a group of words.

Two sentences:

The bus is crowded. It is crowded with older kids.

Combined sentence:

The bus is crowded with older kids.

Practice

Combine the following sentences by moving a group of words.

1. Older kids take up many seats. The seats are in back.
2. The younger kids sit together. They are up front.
3. All the kids are cranky. They are cranky about the crowding.
4. Most kids would agree. They would agree that they need more space.

Grammar Connection

Sentence Combining

- ***Write Source*** page 407
- ***GrammarSnap*** Creating a Series
- ***SkillsBook*** pages 105–106

Run-on and Rambling Sentences

- ***Write Source*** pages 404, 405
- ***GrammarSnap*** Compound Sentences
- ***SkillsBook*** pages 97–98

Struggling Learners

Students may need help evaluating the sentence fluency in their writing. Have students read what they have written into a tape recorder and then listen to the tape. Then have them play the tape again as they use their writing to follow along. Have them circle parts on their paper where they hear short, choppy sentences or repetition.

Writing a Persuasive Letter 203

Revising in Action

Here is how Roku improved the sentence fluency in the first draft of his letter. He added a conjunction and moved a group of words to combine two short sentences.

I love to read. I could eat books for breakfast, lunch, and dinner. I'm writing to you because I think our school libary needs a new checkout rule. students ~~must~~ should be able to check out more books. Kids can check out only ~~a few books.~~ as many books as the number of their grade.

That means fast readers finish there books and have to wait. ~~They have to~~ and wait ~~forever~~ for the next libary day. ~~Everybody likes libary day.~~

Other kids like me want to gobble up all the books they can. Pleese Think about a new checkout rule or more library days. ~~I'm begging you.~~ Thank you for reading my letter.

Revise **Check for smooth sentences.**

Combine short, choppy sentences by moving groups of words.

- **Move a word group to make a smoother sentence if possible.**

Revising in Action

Encourage students to look for ways to combine sentences in their persuasive letters. Review the other ways that they have learned to combine sentences in addition to using key words as shown in this activity.

- compound subjects (SE page 409)
- compound predicates (SE page 409)
- words in a series (SE page 408)
- compound sentences (SE page 410)

Revising Using a Checklist

Have students check their revising for the traits of writing by using this checklist. They may work independently or with a partner.

Now, students need to make clean copies of their essays. Partners may check one another's final drafts against their first drafts that are marked with revisions. Then the writer should check his or her own letter for final editing and proofreading changes.

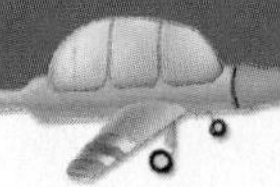

Revising Using a Checklist

Check your revising.

Number a piece of paper from 1 to 7. If you can answer "yes" to a question, put a check mark after that number. If not, continue working on that part of your essay.

Ideas

___ **1.** Do I have a clear opinion statement?
___ **2.** Do I support my opinion with good reasons that answer the question *why?*

Organization

___ **3.** Do I state my opinion in the first paragraph?
___ **4.** Does my ending ask the reader to do something?

Voice

___ **5.** Have I used a convincing voice?

Word Choice

___ **6.** Have I used polite words?

Sentence Fluency

___ **7.** Have I combined short, choppy sentences?

Make a clean copy.

After revising your essay, make a clean copy for editing.

Writing a Persuasive Letter 205

Editing for Conventions

When you edit for conventions, you check capitalization, punctuation, spelling, and grammar.

Q. How can I check my capitalization?

You can check your capitalization by following the rules listed below.

- ✔ Capitalize the **first letter of the first word** in each sentence.
- ✔ Capitalize the **first letter of the names** of people, places, streets, cities, and months.
- ✔ Capitalize **both letters of a postal state abbreviation**, such as AZ for Arizona.

Grammar Practice

Rewrite each of the following lines, using correct capitalization.

1. mr. gaul of Oil city, Pa
2. wadsworth Elementary school
3. we need a light at broad street and main street.

Check your letter for conventions.

Ask yourself the following questions about your paragraph.

1. **Add correct punctuation and capitalization.**
2. **Cut and replace any words that are the wrong word or misspelled.**

Editing for Conventions

Ask students how they would feel if they got a letter with their name spelled incorrectly. (They might feel that the writer didn't care enough about them to check the spelling.) Tell students that if they want to make a good impression on their reader, they should check the spelling and capitalization of their reader's name and address.

Students can look in a telephone book, school directory, or online directory to double-check the spelling and capitalization of their reader's name and address.

* For more about capitalization, see SE pages 486–491.

Grammar Practice Answers

1. Mr. Gaul of Oil City, PA
2. Wadsworth Elementary School
3. We need a light at Broad Street and Main Street.

Technology Connections

Students can use the added features of the Net-text as they explore this stage of the writing process.

***Write Source Online* Net-text**

English Language Learners

Students may be confused by the capitalization of common nouns that are part of proper noun phrases. Complete the **Practice** activity together on the board. Point out that words such as *city, school,* and *street* are capitalized because they are part of the name of a particular city, school, and street.

Grammar Connection

Capitalization, Abbreviations

- **Proofreader's Guide** pages 488 (+), 496–497, 498–499
- ***GrammarSnap*** Capitalization
- ***SkillsBook*** pages 5–6, 56, 57–58

Editing Checking for Conventions

To extend the editing checklist, use the editing page of the Partner's Response (SE page 205) in addition to this page.

Write the school's address and today's date on the board without proper capitalization or commas. Have students tell you what letters should be capitalized and where to add commas.

* For information about using Commas in Dates and Addresses, see SE page 468.

For a copy master of the Conventions Checklist for a persuasive letter, see TE page 564.

Practice Answers

(Corrections are underlined.)

1. There are many reasons to change the rule.
2. Kids can be responsible with more books.

Edit **Read and check your capitalization.**

Check each first word, name, and abbreviation.

Editing Checking for Conventions

When editing a letter, check for capitalization, punctuation, spelling, and grammar.

Conventions

Punctuation

___ **1.** Did I use end punctuation after all my sentences?

___ **2.** Did I use commas correctly in dates and addresses?

Capitalization

___ **3.** Did I begin all my sentences with capital letters?

___ **4.** Did I capitalize names of people, organizations, titles, streets, cities, and states?

Spelling

___ **5.** Have I carefully checked my spelling?

Grammar

___ **6.** Do I use correct forms of verbs *(go, went, gone)*?

Practice

Find two errors in each sentence below. Then rewrite the sentences correctly.

1. Their are many reasons to change the rule
2. Kids can be responsibel with more books?

English Language Learners

Pair each student with a partner proficient in English and direct partners to work together to answer the **Practice** questions at the bottom of the page. They can refer to the **Practice** section on SE page 183 to check their understanding of *their, there,* and *they're*.

Struggling Learners

Have students circle words in their writing that look wrong to them, even if they are unsure of the correct spelling. On a reproducible T-Chart (TE page 595) have them list the circled words in the first column. Have them work in pairs to find the correct spellings in the dictionary and write them in the second column.

Advanced Learners

Invite students to make up examples like those in the **Practice** activity for the class to do for additional practice. On strips of construction paper, have them write the incorrect sentences on one side and the correct versions on the other side. Laminate the strips and put them in a learning center.

Writing a Persuasive Letter 207

Editing in Action

Here are the editing changes that Roku made in his letter.

Dear Mrs. Lincoln:

I love to read. I could eat books for breakfast, lunch, and dinner! I'm writing to you because I think our school libary (library) needs a new checkout rule. students should be able to check out more books.

Kids can check out only as many books as the number of their grade Fast readers finish there (their) books and have to wait and wait for the next libary (library) day.

Other kids like me who want to gobble up all the books they can. Pleese (Please) think about a new checkout rule or more library days. Thank you for reading my letter.

Sincerely,

Roku Hitsuki

Spelling is corrected.

A capital letter is added.

A period is added.

A wrong word is replaced.

Spelling is corrected.

Editing in Action

Provide time for students to edit their drafts. Tell them to use the Conventions Checklist as a guide for finding errors in capitalization, punctuation, spelling, and grammar.

Consider having students take part in peer-editing sessions. Divide students into groups of four. Assign each student a different convention to check (capitalization, punctuation, spelling, or grammar) and give each of them a different colored pencil to mark mistakes. If possible, base your assignments on previously exhibited strengths. Tell students to pass their drafts around in round-robin fashion in the group for review. When writers get their letter back, they can easily identify the kinds of mistakes by their color.

Remind students to use the editing and proofreading marks inside the back cover of their books. (See the copy master on TE page 594.)

Grammar Connection

Commas (introductory word or word groups)

- **Proofreader's Guide** page 470 (+)
- ***SkillsBook*** pages 19–20, 21–22

Commas (in dates and addresses)

- **Proofreader's Guide** pages 466 (+), 468 (+)
- ***SkillsBook*** pages 11, 13–14

Colons

- **Proofreader's Guide** page 480 (+)
- ***SkillsBook*** pages 35–36

Using a Rubric

Remind students that a rubric is a chart of the traits of good writing that helps them

- plan their writing during prewriting,
- make changes to their writing during revising (see Partner's Response, SE pages 193–205), and
- judge their final copy when they finish writing (see Writing for Assessment, SE pages 222–223).

The rubrics in this book are based on a six-point scale, in which a score of 6 indicates an amazing piece of writing and a score of 1 means the writing is incomplete.

Explain to students that they will most likely have different ratings for different traits. For example, they may give themselves a 5 for ideas but a 4 for organization.

Using a Rubric

The rubric on these pages can help you score your writing.

Trait	6	5	4
Ideas	**The opinion and reasons are very convincing.**	The opinion is clear, and all the reasons support it.	The opinion is clear, but more reasons would be helpful.
Organization	**Every part of the writing works perfectly.**	The writing is clearly organized.	Most parts are organized and work well.
Voice	**The voice is polite and convincing.**	The voice is convincing.	The voice could be more convincing.
Word Choice	**Each word is expertly chosen.**	The words make the opinion and reasons clear.	Most words work well.
Sentence Fluency	**The sentences flow beautifully.**	The sentences read smoothly.	A few sentences sound choppy.
Conventions	**The essay uses conventions well.**	Most conventions are correct.	Some errors are present.

Writing a Persuasive Letter 209

3 The opinion needs to be clearer with more reasons.	2 The opinion is confusing and needs reasons.	1 The writer needs to state an opinion.
3 Several parts need to be organized better.	2 All parts of the essay run together.	1 The writing needs to be organized to avoid confusion.
3 The writing exaggerates or has a weak voice.	2 The voice comes and goes.	1 The writing needs voice.
3 Some words are unclear.	2 Some words make the writing confusing.	1 Help is needed to find better words.
3 Many sentences are choppy.	2 Some sentences are choppy or incomplete.	1 Many sentences are incomplete.
3 Errors may confuse the reader.	2 Errors make the writing hard to read.	1 Help is needed to make corrections.

Publishing Sending Your Letter

If possible, have students use a computer to prepare their final draft. You may want to show them how to create the heading, using your school address. Then have them print out their letter to review one final time to check that

- all the changes and corrections that they found during revising and editing have been made;
- there are no additional mistakes in capitalization, punctuation, or spelling that were created during typing; and
- the letter is in the correct business form.

Some word-processing programs have templates for creating business letters. If students feel comfortable using a template, allow them to do so. However, students still should print out their letter for one final review to make sure that the letter is complete and error free.

Technology Connections

Remind students that they can use the Writing Network features of the Portfolio to share their work with peers.

Write Source Online **Portfolio**

Write Source Online **Net-text**

Publishing Sending Your Letter

These two pages show you how to put your letter in the correct business letter form.

Heading

1. Write your street address.
2. Write your city, state, and ZIP Code.
3. Write the date. (Skip three lines.)

Inside Address

4. Write the name and title of the person you are writing to.
5. Write the school or business name.
6. Write the address: the street, city, state, and ZIP Code. (Skip a line.)

Greeting

7. Write "Dear," the person's name, and a colon. (Skip one line.)

Body

8. Don't indent paragraphs. (Skip a line between paragraphs.)

Closing

9. Write "Sincerely" or "Yours truly" and a comma. (Skip four lines.)

Signature

10. Type your name. Then sign your name above your typed name.

Writing a Persuasive Letter 211

Roku's letter

207 Broad Street
Griffith, IN 46300
February 10, 2011

Mrs. Lincoln, Librarian
Franklin Elementary School
504 Main Street
Griffith, IN 46300

[fold]

Dear Mrs. Lincoln:

I love to read. I could eat books for breakfast, lunch, and dinner! I'm writing to you because I think our school library needs a new checkout rule. Students should be able to check out more books.

Kids can check out only as many books as the number of their grade. Fast readers finish their books and have to wait and wait for the next library day.

[fold]

I know other kids like me who want to gobble up all the books they can. Please think about a new checkout rule or more library days. Thank you for reading my letter.

Sincerely,

Roku Hitsuki

Roku Hitsuki

Help students find the correct **title** *(see below)* and address for the person they are writing. If the person has a short title, the title can go on the same line as the name. If the title is long, it should probably go on its own line.

If students are handwriting their letter on unlined stationery, have them insert a lined sheet of paper under the sheet of stationery. Tell them to use the lines as a guide for preparing their letter according to the steps outlined on SE page 210. Students may have to darken the lines on the guide sheet in order to see them through the stationery.

Make sure students understand that they are not to put the fold lines or the word *fold* on their letter. They are shown here as a guide for how to fold a letter neatly to fit in an envelope.

Teaching Tip: Writing Titles Correctly

Most students will benefit from a refresher for writing titles correctly. Provide these tips.

- Titles such as *principal* or *doctor* are capitalized when they are used with names, but not capitalized when they are used alone.
- Abbreviated titles such as Dr. or Mrs. are capitalized and followed by a period.

* For more instruction and practice capitalizing and punctuating titles, see SE pages 463 and 486.

Publishing Addressing an Envelope

Tell students to copy the name and address of the person to whom they are writing from the inside address of their letter. They can, but they do not have to, include the person's title.

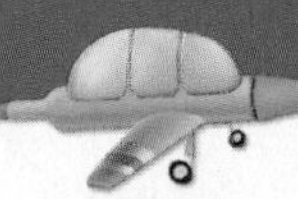

Publishing Addressing an Envelope

The United States Postal Service gives the following directions for addressing an envelope.

Address your envelope.

1. **Write your name and address in the upper left-hand corner.**
2. **Write the other person's name and address in the middle.**
3. **Place the proper postage in the upper right-hand corner.**

1 ROKU HITSUKI
207 BROAD STREET
GRIFFITH IN 46300

3 

2 MRS LINCOLN
FRANKLIN ELEMENTARY SCHOOL
504 MAIN STREET
GRIFFITH IN 46300

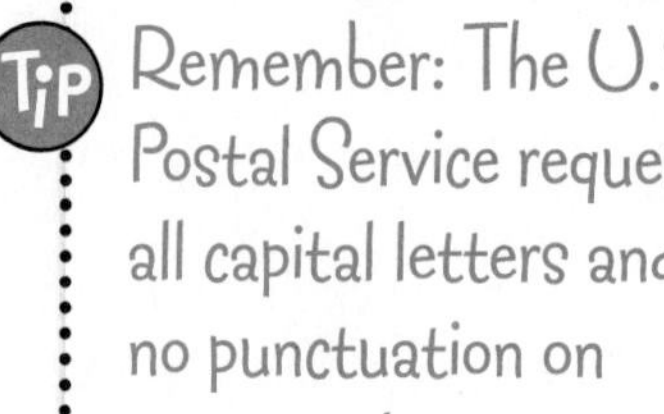

Tip: Remember: The U.S. Postal Service requests all capital letters and no punctuation on your envelope.

Struggling Learners

After students have reviewed the three elements on the envelope, draw a large rectangle on a sheet of chart paper. Draw empty blocks inside the rectangle where the address, return address, and stamp should go. Have students tell what belongs in each block. Label the parts and display the chart paper in the classroom for students to refer to.

Reflecting on Your Writing

You're done! Now it's time to think about the persuasive letter you wrote and what you learned from it. Here are Roku's thoughts about his letter.

Thinking About Your Writing

Name: Roku Hitsuki

Title: Persuasive Letter

1. The best part of my essay is . . .
   about how I could eat books for breakfast, lunch, and dinner. It gets my reader's attention for my ideas about having a new checkout rule.
2. The part that still needs work is . . .
   the last paragraph. I should have told how many books we want to check out.
3. The main thing I learned about persuasive writing is . . .
   how to use ideas and reasons to make an idea convincing.

Reflecting on Your Writing

Some students will want to adapt or copy the ideas from the sample reflection. To help them reflect on their own letter, provide time for students to actually think about their writing process before asking them to record their reflections.

Suggest that they look over their prewriting notes, their early drafts, and their final letter to recall the process they went through.

As they think about the process, tell them to ask themselves these questions.

- What part did I enjoy writing the most?
- What part was the hardest for me?
- What part do I feel most proud of?
- What part do I wish I could do over?

Provide photocopies of the reproducible Thinking About Your Writing (TE page 593) for students to record their reflections.

Struggling Learners

Students may feel overwhelmed by the parts of their letter that still need work. To make the task more manageable, have students focus on the one thing they would most like to work on and write it down on the reflection sheet.

Advanced Learners

Challenge students to write a letter to Roku from Mrs. Lincoln. Have them include the following:

- Mrs. Lincoln's checkout rule decision,
- reasons she agrees or disagrees with Roku, and
- facts that support her reasons.

Across the Curriculum

Objectives

- Apply what has been learned about persuasive writing to other curriculum areas.
- Practice persuasive writing for assessment.

The lessons on the following pages provide samples of different kinds of persuasive writing that students might do. The first lesson guides students through the steps of the writing process to create a persuasive poster for science. The second lesson provides a model and writing tips for writing about an important health issue. The third lesson focuses on writing an e-mail message.

Persuasive Writing Across the Curriculum

Scientists use their skills to create everything from space probes to submarines. Imagine a world without science! Now imagine a world without writers. There would be no books, no Web sites, and no TV shows.

In this section, you'll use your writing skills to create a poster, an e-mail message, and a response to a persuasive prompt. Thanks to students like Miko—and you—we'll never have a world without writers!

Materials

Art supplies (TE p. 215)

School calendar (TE p. 216)

Poster board (TE p. 217)

Markers (TE p. 217)

Sticky notes (TE p. 223)

Copy Masters

T-Chart (TE p. 216)

Table Diagram (TE p. 222)

Assessment Sheet (TE p. 222)

Science: Persuasive Poster

A poster gives information about an event or an idea. Miko's teacher asked students to create a poster to convince people to come to a school event. Miko made a poster for the science fair.

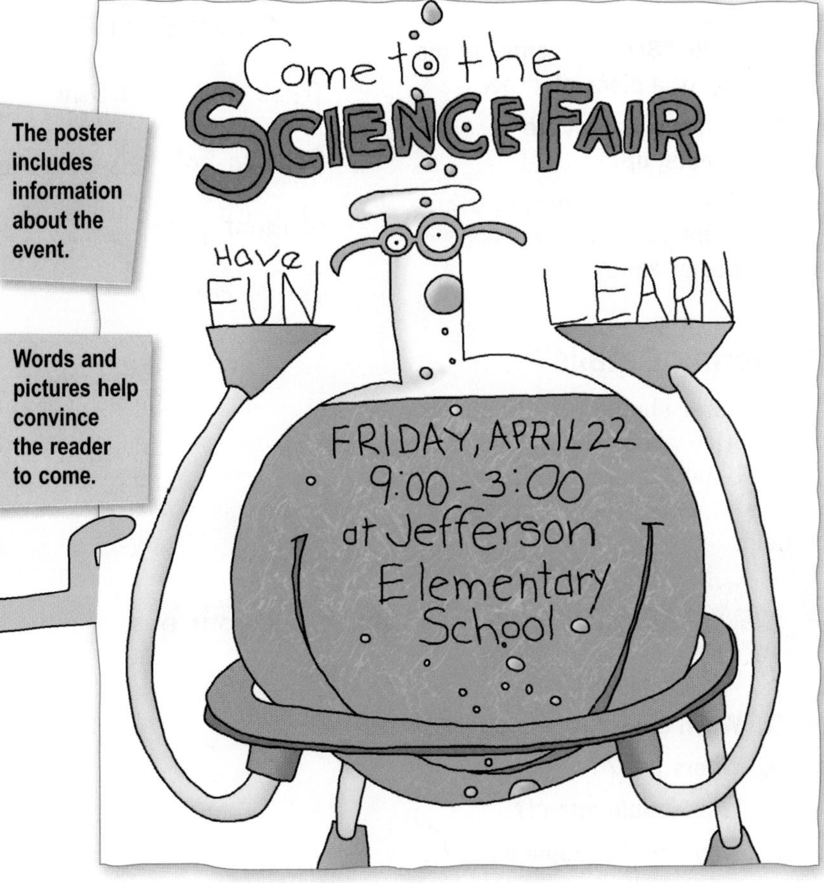

The poster includes information about the event.

Words and pictures help convince the reader to come.

Science: Persuasive Poster

Have students discuss the science poster in small groups. Share these questions with students and have them use the questions to guide their discussion.

- What do you know about the science fair from the information in the poster?
- What parts of the poster might help convince people to go to the science fair?
- What do you like most about the poster?
- How do you think Miko feels about science and the science fair?

English Language Learners

Help students identify the persuasive words Miko used in his poster by asking the following questions:

- Where does Miko think you should go? (to the science fair)
- Why should you go to the science fair? (to have fun and learn)

Point out that the remaining information on the poster is not persuasive, but it gives important facts that readers need to know, such as where and when the science fair will take place.

Advanced Learners

Challenge students to work cooperatively to develop a poster for another class or school event. Have them first discuss the words and pictures that Miko uses to help convince the reader to attend. Then have them brainstorm and create a new poster.

Prewriting Selecting a Topic

Many schools list upcoming school events on the school Web site. Most schools print school calendars to distribute to students or display a school calendar in a central location for everyone to see. Make sure students have an opportunity to look at the school calendar to get ideas for their "School Events" list. If students will be looking at the school Web site, provide the Web address, and review the rules for **Internet viewing** *(see below)*.

Prewriting Gathering Details

Have students write the answers to the questions. Then when they make their posters, they can quickly find the important information they need.

- Provide copies of the reproducible T-Chart (TE page 595).
- Tell students to copy the questions on SE page 216 in the left column, skipping space between questions.
- Have them write the answers in the right column beside the question, being careful to write the exact and correct information.

216

Prewriting Selecting a Topic

One way to think of ideas for a poster is to make a list. Miko wrote this list of upcoming school events.

Ideas List

School Events

Track and Field Day

Science Fair*

student play

spring concert

Prewrite Make a list.

1. Write "School Events" at the top of a piece of paper.
2. List events that are coming up.
3. Put a star (*) next to the event you'd like to make a poster about.

Gathering Details

A poster should give important information about the event. For example, people need to know *when* and *where* the event will be held.

Answer these questions about your event.

1. What is my event?
2. When does it happen (date and time)?
3. Where is it?
4. Who should attend?
5. Why should people come?

Teaching Tip: Internet Viewing

Most schools have established a set of rules and guidelines for Internet viewing on the school premises. If you have not yet reviewed your school's policy for Internet viewing with students, take time to do that now. If possible, distribute a printed copy of these guidelines for students to read and refer to whenever they use the Internet at school.

Parents may also have established rules for their children's use of the Internet. Be sure that you are aware of any restrictions that parents have placed on children regarding Internet viewing so that you do not inadvertently assign a task that encourages students to disregard their parents' rules.

* For more about using the Internet to find information, have students look at SE page 307.

Writing Making Your Poster

Follow these guidelines when you create your poster.

Create a first draft.

1. Sketch out your poster idea. Include the details about your event. (Refer to the bottom of page 216.)
2. Use a drawing to catch the reader's attention.

Revising Improving Your Poster

A poster must be accurate and easy to read.

Check your poster for its overall appeal.

1. Are my details correct? Do they tell what, when, where, and why?
2. Are the words large enough? Are the details spaced so the poster isn't crowded?

Editing Checking for Conventions

Before making your final poster, check your writing for errors.

Edit your poster.

1. Have I correctly capitalized any names?
2. Have I used correct punctuation in dates and addresses?
3. Have I checked my spelling?

English Language Learners

Students may need help revising their posters for persuasive details. Using a volunteer's poster, model the Think-Aloud approach using the *what, when, where,* and *why* questions. Emphasize the word *because* when you answer the *why* question. Point out that *because* signals a reason, so the answer gives the persuasive details.

Writing Making Your Poster

If you want, have students who are making a poster about the same event work together to design and create the poster. Students with strong artistic skills can concentrate on the design and drawing. Students with strong language skills can develop catchy phrases for the poster. If students do work together, monitor their work to make sure that each student has the opportunity to contribute equally to the effort.

Revising Improving Your Poster

If students copy down incorrect information during prewriting, their poster details will be incorrect. If possible, have students double-check details by looking at a school calendar or by comparing notes with a classmate who is making a poster for the same event.

Editing Checking for Conventions

Since students may make new mistakes when creating their final poster, suggest that they first write in the information for their final poster in light pencil. Then have them do one last edit for accuracy and conventions before they copy over the light pencil marks with markers or crayons.

Health: An Important Issue

Your students have heard many lectures about health, from washing hands to eating vegetables to looking both ways before crossing the street. One challenge with this assignment is to inspire students to explore health issues that are not as commonplace as these.

Ask questions to help students come up with interesting topics:

- "Have any of you gotten hurt badly? What happened? How could you make sure that doesn't happen again?"
- "Have any of you been really sick? Do you know how you got sick? How did you get better? Do you have advice to help other people not get sick or to get better?"

Try to steer the discussion to school-appropriate topics.

Health: An Important Issue

Look Out!

Your eyes are amazing. Because you may not see danger coming, you should follow some safety tips to keep your eyes safe.

Sharp, pointed objects can hurt your eyes. You should carry pencils and scissors with the points down. Always stand behind people throwing darts or shooting arrows. Never put your face near animals with claws.

Machines can harm your eyes. You should stay away from lawn mowers and other machines that can shoot out rocks, bits of metal, or even sparks.

Sports are fun, but they can damage your eyes. Remember to wear a helmet or goggles if your sport needs them. Follow these tips so you can say, "Bye, see you later."

Writing Tips

Before you write . . .

- Think about important health issues you know and care about.
- List as many supporting details for your issue as you can.

During your writing . . .

- Get the reader's attention in the beginning of your persuasive essay.
- Give your reasons in the body paragraph.
- End with a call to action that asks readers to follow your advice.

After you've written a first draft . . .

- Read your essay and see if any important details are missing.
- Give your essay an interesting title.
- Check capitalization, punctuation, spelling, and grammar.

Writing Tips

To help students decide on ways to start their essays, provide a number of strategies for strong beginnings:

- **Ask a question:** "Do you know why people go to sleep?"
- **Tell a story (anecdote):** "I sure had fun at the dunes on Sunday, but on Monday I was as red as a lobster."
- **Give a surprising fact:** "More people abuse prescription drugs than illegal drugs."
- **Use an interesting statistic:** "The human body is made up of 65 percent water."

Have students brainstorm sentences for their own essays and then decide which strategy would give them the strongest opener.

Practical Writing:
E-Mail Message

Some students may already be familiar with telephone text-messaging and online instant messaging. Both these forms of instant communication often contain a kind of shorthand that has developed among users. Discuss the importance of not using shorthand language in an e-mail that is written to an older relative, teacher, or another adult.

Tell students that they do not have to write long subject lines. They can use two or three words, similar to a title, but the subject line should contain specific information about the subject of the e-mail so that the person receiving it can tell at a glance what it is about.

220

Practical Writing:
E-Mail Message

E-mail allows you to quickly send a friendly note. Maria wrote an e-mail message to her grandpa. Remember to use a greeting and a closing just as you do in a letter.

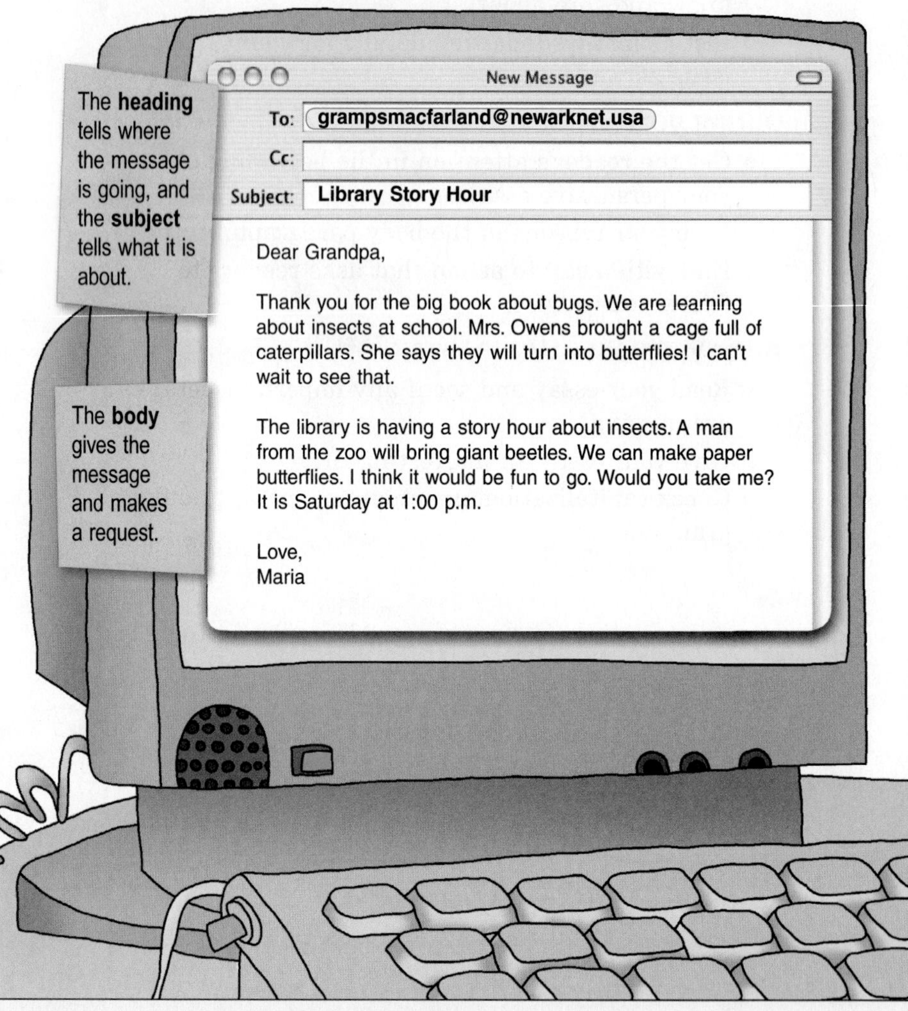

The **heading** tells where the message is going, and the **subject** tells what it is about.
New Message
To: grampsmacfarland@newarknet.usa
Cc:
Subject: Library Story Hour
Dear Grandpa,
Thank you for the big book about bugs. We are learning about insects at school. Mrs. Owens brought a cage full of caterpillars. She says they will turn into butterflies! I can't wait to see that.
The library is having a story hour about insects. A man from the zoo will bring giant beetles. We can make paper butterflies. I think it would be fun to go. Would you take me? It is Saturday at 1:00 p.m.
Love,
Maria
The **body** gives the message and makes a request.

Writing Tips

Before you write . . .

- Make sure the e-mail address is correct.
- Write a subject line about your message.

During your writing . . .

- Write *Dear*, the person's name, and a comma.
- Tell why you are writing and include all the important details.
- Write sentences that are easy to understand.
- Write a closing (a word like *Sincerely* or *Love*), a comma, and your name.

After you've written an e-mail message . . .

- Read your message carefully.
- Check capitalization, punctuation, spelling, and grammar.
- Make sure your e-mail is complete and correct before hitting "send."

Pretend a special event is coming up. Write an e-mail message to invite someone to the event. Use a computer in your school.

English Language Learners

Students may not understand the nuances of the language used in the closings of letters. Reinforce the following closings and provide examples of when to use them:

- **Sincerely; Yours truly** (a more formal way to say *from;* used when writing to an adult who you don't know personally)
- **Love** (a friendly way to end a letter; used when writing to someone you know well, such as a close friend or a family member)

Writing Tips

Have students send their e-mail invitations to each other, using the classroom e-mail address. Then it will be easy for them to check that their e-mail has been sent correctly and received. Make sure each student receives an invitation.

To extend the activity, have classmates write e-mail responses to the invitations they receive.

Writing for Assessment

If your students must take school, district, or state assessments, focus on the tested writing form.

If you have students respond to the prompt, provide photocopies of the reproducible Table Diagram (TE page 599) for students to use in planning their response.

In addition to responding to a prompt, this lesson can also be an opportunity for students to practice evaluating a persuasive essay. Using the rubric for persuasive writing (SE pages 208–209) and a copy of the Assessment Sheet (TE page 591), work with students to score the sample essay on SE page 223 (a completed assessment sheet is provided on TE page 586 for your benefit). Two additional essays are available in copy master form (see Benchmark Papers box below). Again, a completed assessment sheet is provided for each benchmark paper.

Persuasive Writing
Writing for Assessment

On some writing tests, you will need to write a response to a persuasive prompt. A persuasive prompt asks you to share an opinion about something. It also asks you to give your reasons for the opinion.

Pedro planned his response to the following prompt by making a table diagram like the one below. Then he wrote his essay.

Persuasive Prompt

Some people believe recess should be shorter. What do you think? Write a persuasive essay that tells whether you think school recesses should be shorter or should stay the same. Give reasons for your opinion.

Table Diagram

Recess should not be shorter
kids get exercise
kids learn teamwork
kids do better in reading

Advanced Learners

After students review Pedro's table diagram, challenge them to create a Table Diagram that supports the opposite view. Distribute copies of the reproducible table diagram (TE page 599). Have students work together to brainstorm reasons why a shorter recess would be beneficial. Then have them vote on the top three reasons and write them in the table diagram.

Benchmark Papers

New Sidewalks (good)

- TE pp. 587–588

A New Pool (fair)

- TE pp. 589–590

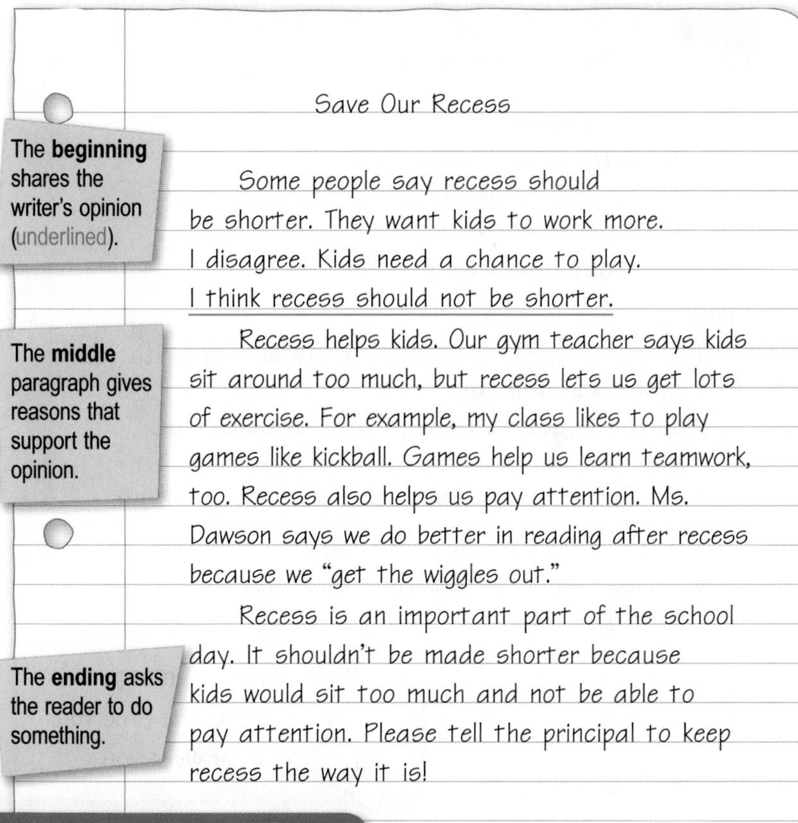

Writing for Assessment 223
Pedro's Response
Save Our Recess
The beginning shares the writer's opinion (underlined).
Some people say recess should be shorter. They want kids to work more. I disagree. Kids need a chance to play. I think recess should not be shorter.
The middle paragraph gives reasons that support the opinion.
Recess helps kids. Our gym teacher says kids sit around too much, but recess lets us get lots of exercise. For example, my class likes to play games like kickball. Games help us learn teamwork, too. Recess also helps us pay attention. Ms. Dawson says we do better in reading after recess because we "get the wiggles out."
The ending asks the reader to do something.
Recess is an important part of the school day. It shouldn't be made shorter because kids would sit too much and not be able to pay attention. Please tell the principal to keep recess the way it is!

After you read . . .

- **Ideas** **(1) What is Pedro's opinion?**
- **Organization** **(2) What sentence in the closing paragraph restates the opinion of the beginning paragraph?**
- **Word Choice** **(3) Does Pedro sound like he knows what he's talking about? Explain.**

Discuss Pedro's response. Have students explain their answers to the following questions, using details from the response.

- Has Pedro chosen a reasonable topic?
- Has he provided good, strong reasons to support his topic?
- Has he used convincing and polite language?

After you read . . .

Answers

Ideas 1. Recess should not be shorter.

Organization 2. It shouldn't be made shorter because kids would sit too much and not be able to pay attention.

Word Choice 3. Pedro does sound like he knows what he's talking about. He gives several good, strong reasons. He also includes a quotation from a teacher, which makes his ideas even more convincing.

Advanced Learners

Point out to students that Pedro uses quotations and examples from adults to make his reasons more convincing. Explain that both the gym teacher and Mr. Dawson work with students all day, so they are "experts" in student behavior. Have students discuss what kinds of experts they would quote if they wanted to support the following opinion statements:

- More city buses are needed.
- A park cleanup is necessary.
- Firefighters need to earn more money.
- Litter alongside the highway should be cleaned up.

English Language Learners

Using the table diagram on SE page 222 as a guide, have students work together to place sticky notes next to the three reasons Pedro gives in his response. As a group, review each reason and discuss the details that support it.

Writing Tips

Point out to students that they must approach writing-on-demand assignments differently from open-ended writing assignments.

Persuasive Prompt

To teach students who must take timed assessments how to approach their writing, allow them the same amount of time to write their response essay as they will be allotted on school, district, or state assessments. Break down each part of the process into clear chunks of time. For example, you might give students

- 15 minutes for note taking and planning,
- 20 minutes for writing, and
- 10 minutes for editing and proofreading.

If your state, district, or school requires students to use and submit a graphic organizer as part of their assessment, provide a copy of one of the reproducible charts (TE pages 595–600) or refer students to SE pages 438–444.

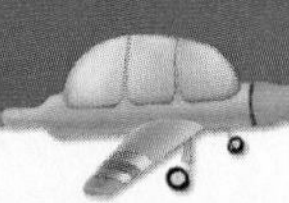

Writing Tips

Before you write . . .

- Read the prompt carefully.
- Use a graphic organizer to help you plan your answer.
- Use your time wisely.

During your writing . . .

- Use key words from the prompt as you write your opinion statement.
- In the middle paragraph, give reasons that explain your opinion.
- Restate your opinion in the closing paragraph.

After you've written a first draft . . .

- Check your capitalization, punctuation, and spelling.
- Make neat changes.

Write a persuasive essay in the time your teacher gives you.

Persuasive Prompt

Some people think students should not be allowed to have snacks at school. Do you think students should have snacks or not? Write an essay that gives your opinion and reasons.

Struggling Learners

Students may benefit from exploring their ideas orally with a partner who can help them expand their thinking before they attempt to fill in their graphic organizer and write their essay. Post different kinds of graphic organizers so students can choose the one they are most comfortable using.

English Language Learners

Read the persuasive prompt aloud to students, emphasizing the words *should have* and *not* as you read the question. Create T-chart on the board to lay out and clarify students' choices:

Should have snacks	Should not have snacks
Should have = yes I think students should have snacks.	Should not have = no I think students should not have snacks.

Persuasive Writing Checklist 225

Persuasive Writing in Review

When you write a persuasive essay, you try to convince your reader to do something or to agree with you. The guidelines below can help you do that.

Select a topic that you feel strongly about. (See page 188.)

Write an opinion statement about the topic. (See page 189.)

Gather and organize reasons to support your opinion. (See page 189.)

In the beginning part, get your reader's attention and state your opinion. (See pages 190–191.)

In the middle part, give reasons that explain your opinion. (See pages 190–191.)

In the ending part, restate your opinion and ask the reader to do something. (See pages 190–191.)

Check your **ideas, organization,** and **voice** first. Then check your **word choice** and **sentence fluency.** (See pages 192–204.)

Check your writing for conventions. Also have a classmate edit your writing. (See pages 205–209.)

Make a final copy and proofread it for errors before sharing it. (See pages 210–211.)

Persuasive Writing in Review

Encourage students to refer to these guidelines whenever they are asked to write a persuasive essay.

Continue to provide students with strong examples of persuasive writing and to offer a variety of opportunities for them to practice persuasive writing.

Remind students that the best persuasive writing includes good, strong reasons to support a topic. When they write about a topic that they know and care about, they can draw on their own knowledge and feelings to come up with good reasons. However, if they are asked to write about a topic that they do not know well, they will have to spend more time, and perhaps do some research, to come up with good reasons.

Responding to Literature Overview

Common Core Standards Focus

Writing 1: Write opinion pieces on topics or texts, supporting a point of view with reasons.

Language 2: Demonstrate command of the conventions of standard English capitalization, punctuation, and spelling when writing.

Writing Forms

- Writing a Response Paragraph
- Writing a Book Review for Fiction and Nonfiction
- Comparing a Fiction and a Nonfiction Book
- Responding to a Poem

Focus on the Traits

- Ideas Providing just enough details to capture the reader's interest
- Organization Writing about events in time order
- Voice Using a knowledgeable voice that sounds interested in the book
- Word Choice Choosing words and phrases that show that the writer likes the book
- Sentence Fluency Writing sentences that are clear and easy to understand
- Conventions Checking for errors in capitalization, punctuation, spelling, and grammar

Technology Connections

Write Source Online
www.hmheducation.com/writesource

- ***Net-text***
- ***Bookshelf***
- ***GrammarSnap***
- ***Portfolio***
- ***Writing Network features***
- ***File Cabinet***

Interactive Whiteboard Lessons

Suggested Book Review for Fiction Unit (Two Weeks)

	Day	Writing and Skills Instruction	*Student Edition*		*SkillsBook*	*Daily Language Workouts*	*Write Source Online*
			Responding to Literature Unit	Resource Units*			
Week 1	1–3	**Response Paragraph: Fiction Book**	228–233			42–43, 96	*Interactive Whiteboard Lessons*
		Skills Activities: • Punctuating Details		408 (+), 478–479	45		
		• Quotations		470 (+), 476 (+)	31–32		
	opt.	*Giving Speeches*	344–349				
	4	**Book Review for Fiction** (Model)	234–235				
	5	(Prewriting)	236–237				*Net-text*
	6–7	(Writing)	238–241			44–45, 97	*Net-text*
	8–9	(Revising)	242				*Net-text*
		Skills Activity: • Sentence Variety		411			*GrammarSnap*
	10	(Editing)	243				*Net-text*
		Skills Activities: • Verb Tenses		540–541	137–138, 139–140		*GrammarSnap*
		• Using the Right Word		514–515	69		
		• Apostrophes		377, 474–475, 534–535	25–26		*GrammarSnap*
		(Publishing, Reflecting)	244–245				*Portfolio* *Net-text*
	opt.	*Giving Speeches*	344–349				
	opt.	**Response to Literature Writing for Assessment**	264–266				

* These units are also located in the back of the *Teacher's Edition*. Resource Units include "Basic Grammar and Writing," "A Writer's Resource," and "Proofreader's Guide."
(+) This activity is located in a different section of the *Write Source Student Edition*. If students have already completed this activity, you may wish to review it at this time.

Suggested Book Review for Nonfiction Unit (One Week)

	Day	Writing and Skills Instruction	Student Edition: Responding to Literature Unit	Student Edition: Resource Units*	SkillsBook	Daily Language Workouts	Write Source Online
Week 1	1–2	**Book Review for Nonfiction** (Model)	246–247			46–47, 98	
		(Prewriting)	248–249				*Net-text*
	3	(Writing)	250				*Net-text*
	4	(Revising)	250				*Net-text*
		Skills Activity: • Sentence Combining		394, 408 (+), 409 (+), 466 (+)	111–112		*GrammarSnap*
	5	(Editing, Publishing)	250–251				*Portfolio, Net-text*
		Skills Activities: • Plurals		492–493	51–52, 53–54		*GrammarSnap*
		• Fragments		403, 526 (+), 528 (+)	95		*GrammarSnap*
	opt.	*Speeches*	344–349				
	opt.	**Response to Literature Writing for Assessment**	264–266				

* These units are also located in the back of the *Teacher's Edition.* Resource Units include "Basic Grammar and Writing," "A Writer's Resource," and "Proofreader's Guide."
(+) This activity is located in a different section of the *Write Source Student Edition.* If students have already completed this activity, you may wish to review it at this time.

Suggested Responding to a Poem Unit (One Week)

	Day	Writing and Skills Instruction	Student Edition: Responding to Literature Unit	Student Edition: Resource Units*	SkillsBook	Daily Language Workouts	Write Source Online
Week 1	1	**Poem Review** (Model)	258–259			48–49, 99	
		(Prewriting)	260–261				*Net-text*
	3	(Writing)	262				*Net-text*
	4	(Revising)	262				*Net-text*
	5	(Editing)	262				*Net-text*
		Skills Activity: • Using the Right Word		516–517	70		
		• Quotation Marks		476 (+)	33–34		
		(Publishing)	263				*Portfolio, Net-text*
	opt.	*Giving Speeches*	344–349				
	opt.	**Response to Literature Writing for Assessment**	264–266				

* These units are also located in the back of the *Teacher's Edition.* Resource Units include "Basic Grammar and Writing," "A Writer's Resource," and "Proofreader's Guide."
(+) This activity is located in a different section of the *Write Source Student Edition.* If students have already completed this activity, you may wish to review it at this time.

Suggested Book Review Comparing a Fiction and a Nonfiction Book Unit (One Week)

	Day	Writing and Skills Instruction	*Student Edition* Responding to Literature Unit	*Student Edition* Resource Units*	*SkillsBook*	*Daily Language Workouts*	*Write Source Online*
WEEK 1	1–2	**Book Review Comparing Fiction and Nonfiction** (Model)	252–253			50–51, 100	
		(Prewriting)	254–255				*Net-text*
	2	(Writing)	256				*Net-text*
	3	(Revising)	256				*Net-text*
		Skills Activity: • Compound Sentences		395, 410, 468–469, 554–555	15–16, 85–86, 165		*GrammarSnap*
	4	(Editing)	256				*Net-text*
		Skills Activities: • Pronouns		379–381, 536–537	125–126, 131–132		*GrammarSnap*
		(Publishing)	257				*Portfolio, Net-text*
	opt.	*Giving Speeches*	344–349				
	opt.	**Response to Literature Writing for Assessment**	264–266				

* These units are also located in the back of the *Teacher's Edition.* Resource Units include "Basic Grammar and Writing," "A Writer's Resource," and "Proofreader's Guide."
(+) This activity is located in a different section of the *Write Source Student Edition.* If students have already completed this activity, you may wish to review it at this time.

Teacher's Notes for Response to Literature

The overview for responding to literature includes some specific teaching suggestions for the unit.

Writing Focus

Writing a Response Paragraph (pages 228–233)

Writing a response paragraph will help students reflect upon a book of fiction they have read. The focus of this response paragraph is to draw parallels between a book's story and some event or person in the life of the reader.

Writing a Book Review for Fiction and Nonfiction (pages 234–245)

When writing a book review for fiction, a reviewer must reveal enough of the story to cause a reader to want to read the book. At the same time, the reviewer should not disclose the ending. On the other hand, a reviewer of a nonfiction book need not worry about spoiling a surprise ending. The reviewer should encourage others to read the book by pointing out some new facts the book shares on the subject. Writing book reviews brings reading and writing skills together and demonstrates comprehension.

Comparing a Fiction and a Nonfiction Book (pages 252–257)

When students write a comparison between a fiction and a nonfiction book on the same topic, they discover that both books contain facts.

Responding to a Poem (pages 258–263)

Because poetic language tends to be different from most writing, have students read simple poems at first. Once they get accustomed to responding to these poems, introduce them to more challenging poems.

Grammar Focus

For support with this unit's grammar topics, consult the resource units (Basic Grammar and Writing, A Writer's Resource, and Proofreader's Guide).

Academic Vocabulary

Read aloud the academic terms, as well as the descriptions and questions. Model for students how to read one question and answer it. Have partners monitor their understanding and seek clarification of the terms by working through the meanings and questions together.

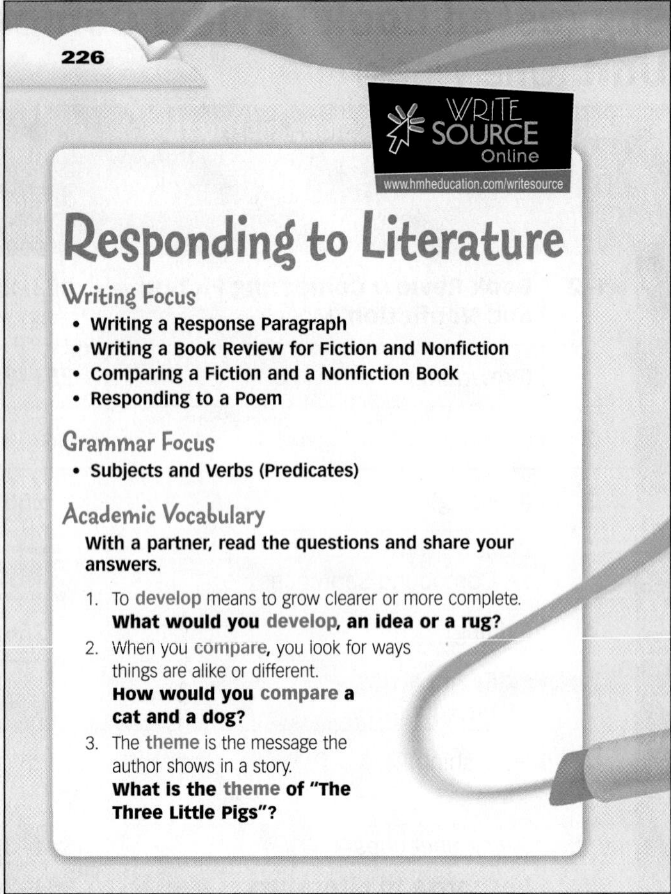
226

WRITE SOURCE Online
www.hmheducation.com/writesource

Responding to Literature

Writing Focus
- Writing a Response Paragraph
- Writing a Book Review for Fiction and Nonfiction
- Comparing a Fiction and a Nonfiction Book
- Responding to a Poem

Grammar Focus
- Subjects and Verbs (Predicates)

Academic Vocabulary

With a partner, read the questions and share your answers.

1. To **develop** means to grow clearer or more complete. **What would you develop, an idea or a rug?**
2. When you **compare**, you look for ways things are alike or different. **How would you compare a cat and a dog?**
3. The **theme** is the message the author shows in a story. **What is the theme of "The Three Little Pigs"?**

Minilessons

Book Words — Writing a Book Review for Fiction and Nonfiction

- **STUDY** the list of words on SE page 280. Then **CLOSE** your book and **EXPLAIN** each word listed below. When you finish, **OPEN** your book to check your work. (character, fiction, narrator, plot, setting)

True Story — Writing a Book Review for Fiction and Nonfiction

- **LIST** something you learned by reading nonfiction material in a book, a newspaper, a magazine, or an Internet article.
  - **WRITE** a couple sentences telling about things you learned and things that surprised you.
  - **SHARE** your discovery with a partner.

Comparing — Comparing a Fiction and a Nonfiction Book

- **CHOOSE** a topic that interests you. Then, at the library, **FIND** a nonfiction and a fiction book on that topic.
  - **READ** the books to make your comparison essay.

Poem Jumping — Responding to a Poem

- **READ** the poem on SE page 283. **LIST** the action verbs in the poem. **WRITE** down which sentence seems to be the most fun. **EXPLAIN** why.

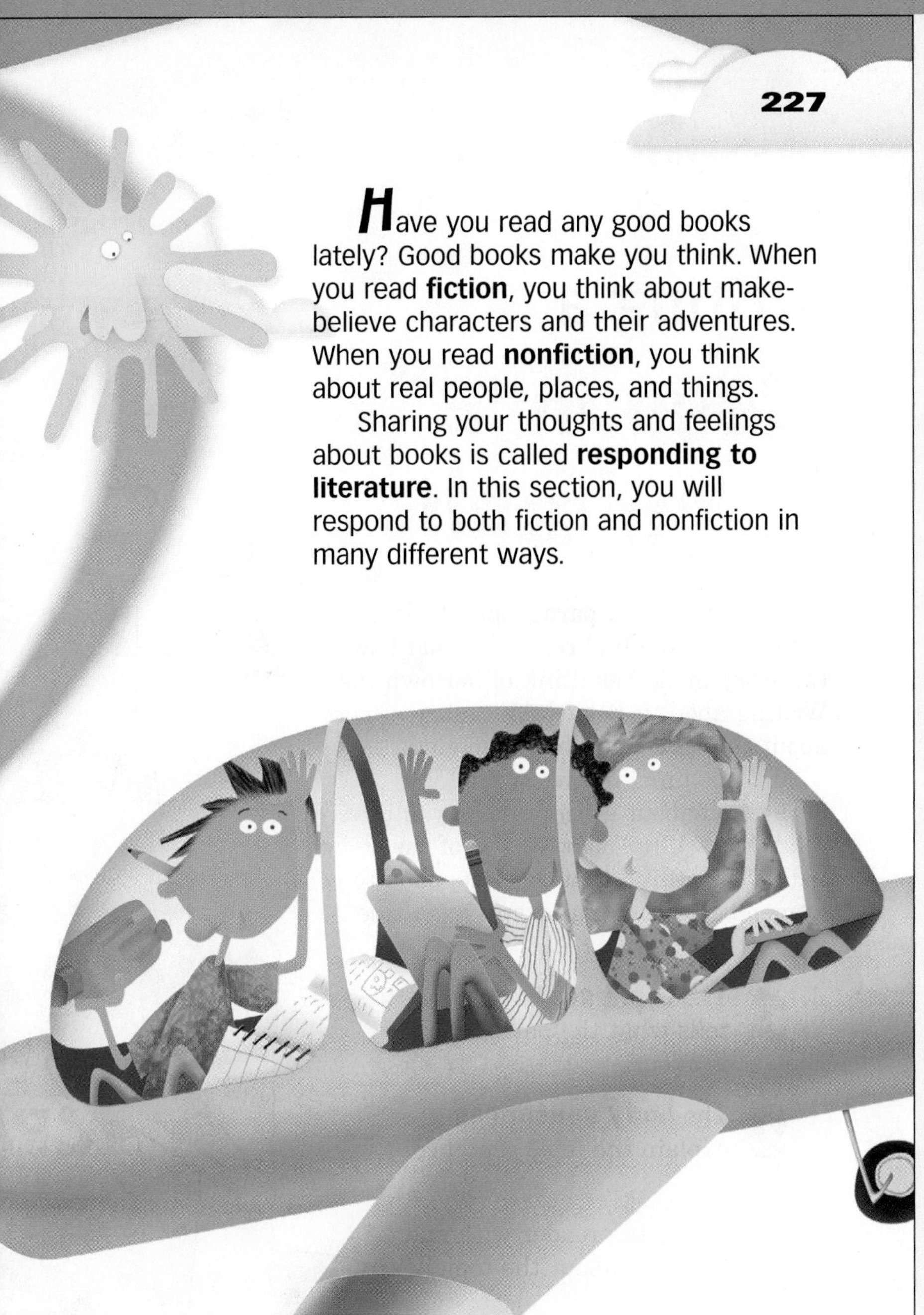

*H*ave you read any good books lately? Good books make you think. When you read **fiction**, you think about make-believe characters and their adventures. When you read **nonfiction**, you think about real people, places, and things.

Sharing your thoughts and feelings about books is called **responding to literature**. In this section, you will respond to both fiction and nonfiction in many different ways.

Responding to Literature

Ask students to name their favorite books, short stories, and poems and tell why these are favorites. Share a few of your own childhood favorites. Then ask students to share examples of literature that they didn't like and have them explain why.

The confidence to express why a person likes or dislikes a story or a poem grows as the person becomes a more confident reader. Yet, even some adults are reluctant to say that they dislike a book or a story that has received critical acclaim. To help students recognize that a response to literature is a personal and unique reaction, make sure that they are aware of the following ideas.

- Everyone's response to a piece of literature is unique because it is based on the reader's own likes, dislikes, and experiences.
- Readers do not have to like everything they read.
- While students do not have to like everything they read, they do need to be ready to explain their response.

Family Connection Letters

As you begin this unit, send home the Responding to Literature Family Connection letter, which describes what students will be learning.

- Letter in English (TE p. 606)
- Letter in Spanish (TE p. 614)

Writing a Response Paragraph

Objectives

- Understand the content and structure of a response paragraph.
- Choose a topic (main idea of a book with a real-life connection) to write about.
- Plan, draft, revise, and edit a response paragraph.

A **response paragraph** gives a summary or reaction to something the writer has read.

* For more about writing paragraphs, see SE pages 416–429.

Keep in mind that not every student will be able to connect an important event in a book to a related event in his or her own life. For example, not every reader will have a best friend who has moved away. Most of the time, however, students will be able to connect with a less important event, or perhaps, to a character's feelings about an important event. As students proceed through this section, you may need to help them identify and think about a character's response to an event, as well as about the event itself.

Technology Connections

Use this unit's Interactive Whiteboard Lesson to introduce literature response writing.

Interactive Whiteboard Lesson

Writing a Response Paragraph

Alexis wrote a paragraph about a fiction book she had read. She told how the story made her think of her own life. Writing about it helped Alexis learn more about the book and about herself.

In this unit, you will write a paragraph about a fiction book you have read. You will tell how a part of the story is like something that has happened to you. Remember that a paragraph has three main parts.

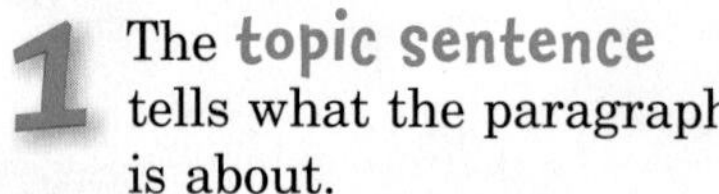

1. The **topic sentence** tells what the paragraph is about.
2. The **body sentences** explain the topic sentence.
3. The **closing sentence** leaves the reader with one last idea about the topic.

Materials

Chart paper (TE p. 230)

Index cards (TE p. 233)

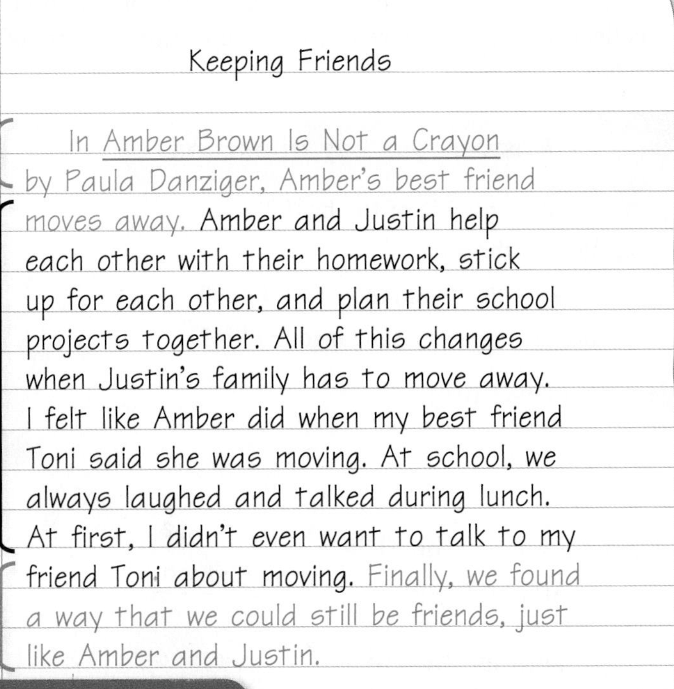

Writing a Response Paragraph
229
Alexis' Response Paragraph
Keeping Friends
1
In Amber Brown Is Not a Crayon by Paula Danziger, Amber's best friend moves away.
2
Amber and Justin help each other with their homework, stick up for each other, and plan their school projects together. All of this changes when Justin's family has to move away. I felt like Amber did when my best friend Toni said she was moving. At school, we always laughed and talked during lunch. At first, I didn't even want to talk to my friend Toni about moving.
3
Finally, we found a way that we could still be friends, just like Amber and Justin.

After you read . . .

- **Ideas** **(1) How is the writer of this paragraph like Amber, the main character in the book?**
- **Organization** **(2) What part of this paragraph gives a lot of details about the topic?**
- **Word Choice** **(3) What words or phrases do you really like? Name two or three.**

Alexis's Response Paragraph

Throughout this unit, students will be asked to write about books they have read or are reading. Many readers will not be able to recall titles, authors, or main ideas without some prompting. If students are keeping **reading journals** *(see below),* they can refer to their journal notes for this information.

Review the **After you read** questions with students to make sure they understand the parts and organization of a response paragraph.

After you read . . .

Answers

Ideas **1.** Like Amber, the writer was not happy when she learned that her best friend was moving away.

Organization **2.** the body sentences

Word Choice **3.** Possible choices: stick up for each other, laughed and talked during lunch, we found a way

Teaching Tip: Using a Reading Journal

This is an excellent opportunity for students to experience firsthand the value of keeping a reading journal. Tell students to flip through their reading journals to recall stories and books they've read that they might enjoy writing a response to.

Encourage students to review their entries carefully. Point out to students that they may be able to use details from their journal entries in their response paragraphs. If students are not yet keeping **reading journals**, take time now to initiate the practice.

* For more detailed instruction on writing in a reading journal, see SE pages 352–353.

Advanced Learners

Have students describe the kinds of details given in the body sentences. Help students see that by sharing her feelings about her best friend, Toni, Alexis connects with Amber's feelings about Justin. Ask if they understand how Amber and Alexis felt. Tell them that their response is called making a connection with the writer.

Prewriting Collecting Ideas

Explain to students that the main idea of a book is what the book is mostly about. For example, *Amber Brown Is Not a Crayon* is mostly about how Amber feels and acts after she learns that her best friend Justin and his family are moving away.

Before students can complete the **Prewrite** activity, they may need additional guidance **finding the main idea of the book** *(see below)* they have chosen.

Prewriting Collecting Ideas

Alexis decided to write about the last book she had read. To collect ideas, she answered four important questions about the book.

Prewrite **Answer four key questions.**

1. What is the title of the book?
2. Who is the author?
3. What is the main idea of the book?
4. How is the story similar to my life?

Alexis's Prewriting

1. What is the title of the book?
Amber Brown Is Not a Crayon

2. Who is the author?
Paula Danziger

3. What is the main idea of the book?
Amber's best friend moves away.

4. How is the story similar to my life?
My best friend moved away, too.

Teaching Tip: Finding the Main Idea of a Book

Help students find the main idea of the book they are writing about. Write the questions below on the board or on chart paper. Then use the sample response paragraph on SE page 229 to model how Alexis might have answered the questions to find the main idea of her book.

- Who is the main character? (Amber)
- What is the main character like at the beginning of the story? (She's happy because she and Justin are good friends. They help each other with homework; they stick up for each other; and they plan projects together.)
- What happens to change the main character? (Amber learns that Justin is moving.)

Explain that the event that causes a character to change or that creates a problem for the character usually is a clue to the main idea. Provide time for students to write answers to these questions as they relate to their book.

Writing a Response Paragraph 231

Writing Creating Your First Draft

As you write your paragraph, remember that it should include three parts: a topic sentence, the body sentences, and a closing sentence.

Write your response paragraph.

Start with a topic sentence that (1) names the title and author of your book, and (2) tells the book's main idea.

Write body sentences that tell how the story compares to something that has happened to you.

End with a closing sentence that shares a final thought about the topic.

First Draft

In Amber Brown Is Not a Crayon by Paula Danziger, Amber's best friend moves away. Amber and Justin help each other . . .

Writing Creating Your First Draft

If possible, students should have a copy of their book on hand as they write their response paragraph. Having the book on hand enables students to easily check the correct spelling of the title and author's name, as well as details to use in their body sentences.

Point out that Alexis underlined the title of the book in her first draft. Explain that underlining is the correct way to handwrite a title. Further explain to students that if they are using a computer to prepare their first draft, they should put the title in italics.

* For information about Underlining and Italics for Titles, see SE pages 478–479.

English Language Learners

Some students may have difficulty identifying how a story connects with their lives. Guide students to choose a realistic fiction book so that the characters and their adventures are more likely to mirror real life. Then work with students on a one-to-one basis, asking leading questions such as:

- Which character is most like you?
- Which event in the story reminds you of something that has happened or could happen to you?
- How did the important event change the character who is most like you?

Struggling Learners

Some students may need help beginning their response paragraphs. Review the beginning of Alexis's paragraph at the bottom of the page. Then have students use the following sentence starter to write their topic sentence: In [book title] by [author's name], [the main character] changed when [describe what happens to the main character].

Revising Improving Your Paragraph

Have students compare the three short sentences with the three body sentences in the sample response on SE page 229. Start with the sentence "I felt like Amber did when my best friend Toni said she was moving." Have students point out the details in Alexis's sentences that make them interesting to read.

Point out that the first two sentences in the middle part ("Amber and Justin . . . " and "All of this changes . . . ") help to organize the response by providing background information from the book about Amber and Justin's friendship.

Practice Answers

Have students point out the additional details in item 2 that make it more interesting and fun to read. (Possible choices: young mouse, finds a motorcycle and learns to ride, motorcycle takes Ralph on adventures, Ralph helps a boy with a fever)

Revising Improving Your Paragraph

When you revise, you make sure that the ideas in the body of your paragraph are clear. Alexis wrote five body sentences to make her idea clear. But what if she had written only three short sentences, like these?

> My best friend was moving. I was sad. It helped to talk about it.

These three short sentences would not have been very interesting or fun to read.

Revise Check your ideas.

Ask yourself the following questions. Then make changes in your paragraph.

1. **Did I explain how my life is like part of the story?**
2. **Did I write enough sentences to show how the story is like something in my life?**
3. **Did I write sentences that don't fit my topic and need to be cut?**

Practice

Which set of sentences below is clearer and more fun to read? Why?

1. Ralph is a mouse. He lives in a hotel. He finds a toy.
2. Ralph is a young mouse who lives in a hotel. One day, his life changes. He finds a motorcycle and learns to ride it. That motorcycle takes Ralph on adventures. It even lets him help a boy with a bad fever.

Grammar Connection

Punctuating Details

- **Proofreader's Guide** pages 478–479
- ***Write Source*** page 408 (+)
- ***SkillsBook*** page 45

Quotations

- **Proofreader's Guide** pages 470 (+), 476 (+)
- ***SkillsBook*** pages 31–32

English Language Learners

Some students may simply answer "yes" or "no" to the **Check Your Ideas** questions without taking time to examine their writing thoroughly. Facilitate small group discussions using modified versions of the questions to help students elaborate their answers:

- How is your life like part of the story?
- Which sentences show how the story is like your life? Could you add more sentences?
- Have you written any sentences that don't really fit with the topic? What should you do with them?

Writing a Response Paragraph 233

Editing Checking for Conventions

When you edit your paragraph, you look for errors that might confuse your reader. For example, make sure that each sentence has a subject and a verb (predicate).

Ramona Quimby writes a commercial.
(subject) (action verb)

Ramona's adventures are funny.
(subject) (linking verb)

Check your work.

1. Did I indent the first line of my paragraph?
2. Did I start each sentence with a capital letter?
3. Did I include a subject and a verb in each of my sentences?
4. Have I checked my spelling?

Grammar Practice

For each sentence below, write down the subject and the verb.

1. Aunt Dew sings a long song.
2. She is very old.
3. Michael is Aunt Dew's nephew.
4. He counts the pennies in the *Hundred Penny Box*.

Editing Checking for Conventions

Provide these reminders about sentences before asking students to do the **Practice**.

- A sentence is a group of words that expresses a complete thought.
- Every sentence has a subject and a verb, also called the predicate.
- The subject of a sentence tells who or what the sentence is about.
- The verb tells what the subject does or is.

* For information about Writing Complete Sentences, see SE pages 396–402.

Grammar Practice Answers

1. Aunt Dew, sings
2. She, is
3. Michael, is
4. He, counts

English Language Learners

Before doing the **Practice**, review **Using the Parts of Speech** (SE pages 532–558). Point out that in English the verb usually follows the subject of a sentence. Then complete the **Practice** sentences orally. For students who still have trouble identifying subjects, ask "Who?" for each sentence.

Struggling Learners

After completing the **Practice** sentences with students, provide the following hands-on activity.

Write some subjects and verbs on separate index cards, making sure to include both action verbs and linking verbs.

Form partner teams and shuffle both piles. Then have pairs take turns choosing a card, such as the noun *clown* and the linking verb *is,* from each pile. Have students use the words to create a complete sentence such as "The clown is so funny!" Have students announce their sentence aloud and ask their partner to correctly identify the subject, predicate, and the type of verb used. Invite students to add more word cards to the game.

Writing a
Book Review for Fiction

Objectives
- Understand the purpose, content, and form of a book review.
- Choose a book (fiction) to write about.
- Plan, draft, revise, and edit a book review.

A **book review for fiction** is an essay that tells what the story is about, highlights a favorite part of the story, and explains the book's main idea or theme. A book review does not usually reveal the ending of the story.

Students are more likely to enjoy writing a review if they choose a book that they enjoyed. Have students jot down a list of possible choices now. Encourage them to include books that they have read for school as well as books that they have read and enjoyed on their own. To recall titles, students can
- look in their reading and personal response journals,
- talk with friends and classmates, and
- look through their own books at home.

234

Writing a Book Review for Fiction

Writing a book review is one way to share a great book with your friends. That's what Ryan did. His book review tells what the book is about without giving away the whole story.

When you write a review, your goal is to make the book sound interesting. Your book review will have three main parts, and each part will answer a different question.

Beginning	What is the book about?
Middle	What is my favorite part?
Ending	What main idea does the author share?

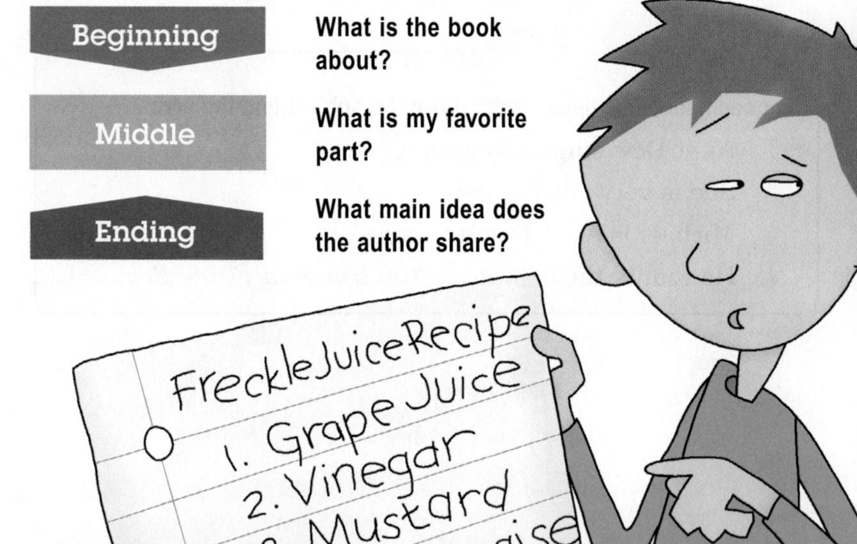

Materials

Book jackets (TE p. 235)

Drawing paper (TE p. 235)

Chart paper (TE pp. 236, 241)

Index cards (TE pp. 236, 239)

Tape recorder (TE p. 239)

Sticky notes (TE p. 242)

Orange, blue, and green crayons (TE p. 242)

Sentence strips (TE p. 242)

Copy Masters

Thinking About Your Writing (TE p. 245)

Ryan's Book Review

Freckle Juice

Beginning *Freckle Juice* by Judy Blume is a funny story about a boy named Andrew Marcus. He really wishes he could have freckles. Then a mean girl in class sells him a recipe for freckle juice.

Middle My favorite part of the story is reading about the freckle juice recipe. Freckle juice is made from grape juice, vinegar, mustard, mayonnaise, juice from one lemon, pepper, salt, ketchup, olive oil, and a speck of onion. "The faster you drink it, the faster you get freckles," the girl tells him. Then Andrew drinks it.

Ending The main idea of *Freckle Juice* is to be yourself. Andrew wants freckles because he likes how they look on a girl in his class. Does Andrew ever get his freckles? You'll have to read the book to find out!

After you read . . .

- **Ideas (1) What is *Freckle Juice* about?**
- **Organization (2) What question does the ending paragraph ask?**
- **Word Choice (3) Which sentences tell you that Ryan likes this book?**

English Language Learners

Visual learners may benefit from using a story map to answer the first **After you read** question. Use an ideas cluster to record the main characters, setting, problem, and events. Point out that the solution cannot be included at this point because a good book review does not give away the ending of the story.

Advanced Learners

Show students several books that contain book reviews on the book jacket. Point out that book jackets often contain brief reviews written by different people. Have students design book jackets for the books they are reviewing. When their book review is written, have students publish it on their book jacket. You may want to showcase these in your reading center.

Ryan's Book Review

Help students recognize how Ryan answers the three questions on SE page 234.

- Read aloud the first question (What is the book about?).
- Have students point out details in the beginning of Ryan's book review that answer the question.
- Repeat this process for the middle (What is my favorite part?) and ending (What main idea does the author share?).

After you read . . .

Answers

Ideas **1.** a boy named Andrew Marcus who wishes he could have freckles

Organization **2.** Does Andrew ever get his freckles?

Word Choice **3.** In the first sentence, Ryan says that the book "is a funny story." In the first body sentence, Ryan says, "My favorite part. . . . " Both sentences tell you that Ryan likes the book.

Prewriting Selecting a Book

If students have not yet had an opportunity to create a list of possible book titles for their review, provide time now for them to visit your class reading center or the school library to recall titles and authors of books they have read and enjoyed.

Students may want to check out a copy of the book they are reviewing so that they can refresh their memory about characters and events in the story.

Most of the books your students select will be familiar to you. If they bring you a new title, you can read a summary of the book (often available at the Web site of online bookstores) so that you can be prepared to assist students as they write.

Technology Connections

Students can use the added features of the Net-text as they explore this stage of the writing process.

Write Source Online ***Net-text***

Prewriting Selecting a Book

Kayla thought of two fiction books that she liked. Then she used sentence starters to help her decide which book to write about. Her finished sentences appear below.

Think of books to review.

1. **Write down the titles and authors of two books you have read.**
2. **Complete these two sentence starters about each book.**
   The story is about . . . I like this story because . . .
3. **Put a star (✱) next to the book you want to write about.**

Sentence Starters

Book 1: Bunnicula by James Howe
The story is about . . .
a pet bunny who is really a vampire.
I like this story because . . .
it is funny. Many of the parts made me laugh.

✱ Book 2: Stone Fox by John Reynolds Gardiner
The story is about . . .
a boy named Little Willy who enters a dogsled race.
I like this story because . . .
I like adventure stories and dogs.

English Language Learners

Use the sentence starters to model several Think-Alouds. Use a book most students know, such as one the class has read earlier in the year. Record your responses on chart paper. Then have volunteers suggest stories and complete the sentence starters as you write them. Post the chart for students to refer to as they write.

Advanced Learners

Provide students with several index cards and have them write a complete sentence starter on each card, leaving off the name of the book. Shuffle all cards, and challenge the group to guess the title of the book after the sentence starter clues are read aloud.

Gathering Important Details

Next, Kayla used a story map to gather important details about her book. She did not write about the ending because she wanted her classmates to read the book. Her story map appears below.

Make a story map.

1. Read the story map below.
2. Then fill in your own story map for the book you are writing about.

Story Map

Main Characters:
Little Willy, Searchlight, Grandpa, and Stone Fox
Setting:
Wyoming
Problem:
Willy's grandpa gets sick and may lose his farm.
He owes $500 in taxes.
Most Important Events:
- Willy helps care for Grandpa and the farm.
- Willy and his dog race against Stone Fox to try to win $500.

Teaching Tip: Book Reviews and Book Reports

Take a few minutes to compare the two forms to make sure students understand the difference between their usual content and purpose.

- Point out that both a book review and a book report tell the title of the book, the author's name, the setting, the main characters, and the problem that the main character has to solve.
- The purpose of a book report is to show that the reader has read and has understood the book. To show this, the writer tells all the important parts of the book, including its ending.
- The purpose of a book review is to make others want to read the book. To do this, the writer tells only a few important and interesting details and does not tell the ending.

Prewriting **Gathering Important Details**

To provide additional practice using story maps, complete with students a story map for a book read in class or for a familiar story that all students will know (for example, a classic fairy tale).

✱ For information about using a story map to plan a story, see SE page 440.

Be sure students understand the difference between **book reviews and book reports** *(see below)* before moving on to the next step in the writing process.

Writing Beginning Your Review

Point out to students that all the information and details for the beginning of their review can come from the story map that they created during prewriting. If students find that their story maps do not contain all the necessary information, provide time for them to go back and add more details. Some students may be reluctant to do this because it feels as if they are going backward. Returning to an earlier step in the writing process, however, should always be encouraged. In fact, students who are willing to return to an earlier step in the writing process are probably on their way to becoming better writers.

Literature Connections

Mentor texts: Bring to class well-written reviews of age-appropriate books and movies and read some of them aloud to the class. Ask students, "Which beginning is your favorite? Why? What does the writer do to catch your interest? How does the writer explain the story without giving away too much?" Challenge students to create opening paragraphs that use some of the strategies you identified.

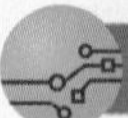

Technology Connections

Students can use the added features of the Net-text as they explore this stage of the writing process.

 ***Write Source Online* Net-text**

Writing Beginning Your Review

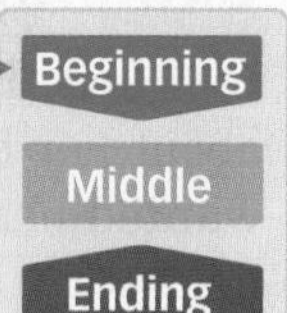

The first paragraph of your book review should name the book and its author. It should also tell what the book is about.

Create your beginning paragraph.

- Answer the following questions in your first paragraph.
  - What is the book's title, and who is the author?
  - Who are the main characters?
  - What is the book about?

Kayla's Beginning Paragraph

<u>Stone Fox</u> is a book by John Reynolds Gardiner. In the story, Little Willy's grandpa gets sick and can't pay the taxes on his farm. Willy and his dog Searchlight enter a dogsled race. The prize money would pay the taxes. They must race Stone Fox. He is a Shoshone Indian who has never lost a race.

Including Details

In a book review, you should give just enough details to make the reader want to read the whole story. Leave out unimportant details.

Don't give away the most surprising parts of the book or the ending. You don't want to spoil the story for your classmates!

Practice

Here is a different beginning paragraph for a book review of *Stone Fox*. Write down the number of each sentence that includes details that are not important.

(1) *Stone Fox* by John Reynolds Gardiner is the story of a boy named Little Willy and his grandfather. (2) Little Willy and Grandpa live on a farm in Wyoming. (3) A farm is a lot of work. (4) Grandpa is too sick to work, so he can't pay his taxes. (5) Usually Grandpa likes to play. (6) Once, he pretended to be a scarecrow. (7) Little Willy and his dog, Searchlight, enter a dogsled race to try to win the tax money. (8) They race against a Shoshone Indian named Stone Fox. (9) He wears a dark-colored headband.

Writing Including Details

Ask students how they feel when someone tells them an ending to a movie or a television program that they are in the middle of watching and enjoying. (They will probably say that it takes away some of the fun of watching.) Point out that sometimes, even when you know how a book ends, it's still fun to read. Most of the time, however, it is more enjoyable if you don't know the ending.

Point out to students that they can tell if a detail is important by asking themselves these questions.

- Does this detail make a difference to what the main character does in the story?
- Does this detail make a difference to how the story ends?

Remind students that they should include only those details that describe the story problem and tell what the main character does to try to solve the problem.

Answers

(3), (5), (6), (9)

English Language Learners

For students who have difficulty reading the book review fluently, read it aloud to them and pause after each sentence. Ask, "Does this sentence make you want to read on?" and "Does this sentence seem important to the story?" Explain that "no" answers are clues that the details are not important and should be eliminated.

Struggling Learners

Help students with the **Practice** by reading the paragraph aloud to them as they listen for unimportant details. Also have students read their own writing aloud or tape record it and listen for unnecessary details they may have written.

Advanced Learners

Ask students to write a similar paragraph with details that don't belong about short stories you have read in class. Have students print their final paragraph on a large index card with a line drawn through the unnecessary sentence(s). Post the cards in the learning center or on a bulletin board so other students can refer to them as they revise their reviews.

Writing Creating the Middle

Direct students' attention to the direct quotation in Kayla's middle paragraph. ("Morning, Mr. Stone Fox," Willy says.) Ask students to suggest why Kayla might have used this quotation. (It helps make Willy sound real. It shows that Willy wants to be friends with Stone Fox.)

Encourage students to **use direct quotations** *(see below)* from their book in their review. Explain that using direct quotations from the book can make their book review more interesting, knowledgeable, and memorable.

Writing Creating the Middle

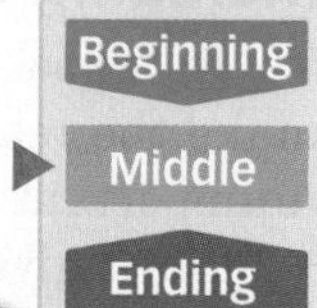

The middle paragraph should tell about your favorite part of the book.

Develop your middle paragraph.

- **Answer these questions in your middle paragraph.**
  - **What is your favorite part? Why?**
  - **What important events happen in this part?**

Kayla's Middle Paragraph

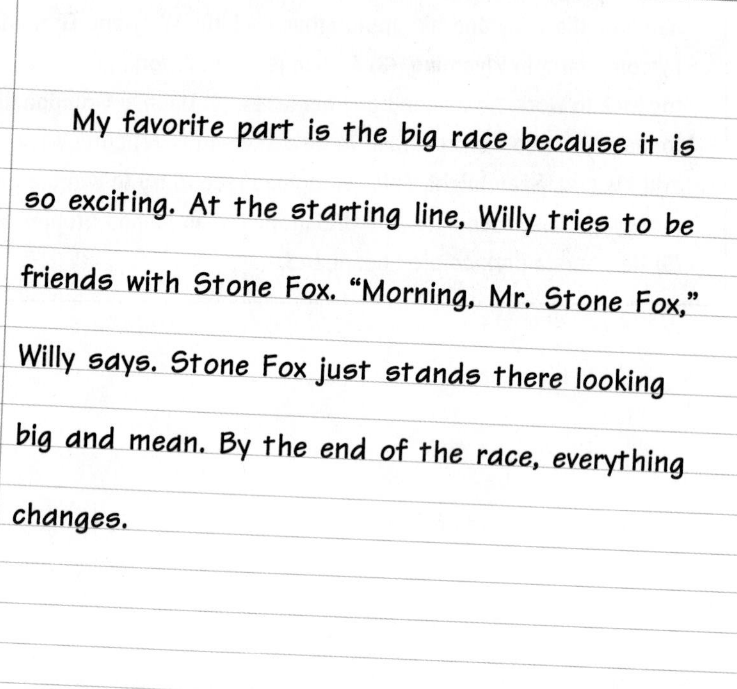

My favorite part is the big race because it is so exciting. At the starting line, Willy tries to be friends with Stone Fox. "Morning, Mr. Stone Fox," Willy says. Stone Fox just stands there looking big and mean. By the end of the race, everything changes.

Teaching Tip: Using Direct Quotations

Students may need additional guidance for selecting and writing quotations correctly in a book review. Provide these quick tips:

- Choose quotations that will help readers get a better picture of the event or character you are describing.
- Keep the quotation short. Choose a phrase or a short sentence.
- Copy the words carefully and exactly.
- Put quotation marks around the exact words that you take from the book.

* For more about using quotation marks around quoted words, see SE pages 476–477.

English Language Learners

Some students may feel uncomfortable giving opinions about their favorite part of a story. Explain that opinions are not right or wrong.

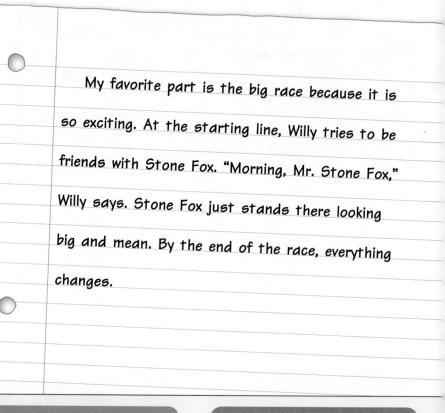

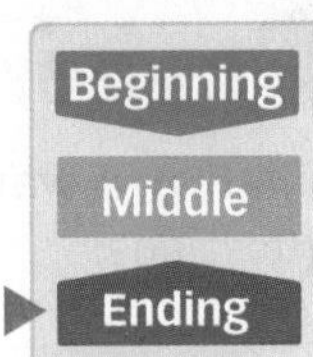

Ending Your Book Review

In the last paragraph, you tell about the main idea or theme of the story. One way to find a theme is to think about the big problem the main character faces. You can also ask yourself what the character in the story learns.

Beginning
Middle
Ending

Create your ending paragraph.

- Answer the following questions as you write the ending for your review.
  - What big problem does the main character face?
  - What does the main character learn?

Kayla's Ending Paragraph

Stone Fox shows that no one should ever give up. The race is hard for Willy and Searchlight. Still, they try to beat Stone Fox. When something terrible happens, Little Willy doesn't give up. He learns that some things are worth fighting for.

Advanced Learners

After students have completed their ending paragraphs, have them share their final paragraph in a group. Have students formulate a sentence that tells the theme, based on the character's big problem and what he or she learns. Record the title of each book and the corresponding theme sentence on chart paper. Invite students to note similarities among the themes.

Writing Ending Your Book Review

Explain to students that the theme of a book is the overall message the author wants readers to get. To provide an example, have students find the theme in the last sentence of Kayla's ending paragraph (some things are worth fighting for).

Explain that sometimes the author tells readers this message directly. Often, however, readers have to figure the message out by thinking about what the main character does and learns.

Provide additional examples of theme statements for students.

- Have them point out the theme, or message, in the ending of the sample book review on SE page 235 (to be yourself).
- Recall other stories students have read in class, and have them work together to find the theme by asking the two questions shown for the Write activity.

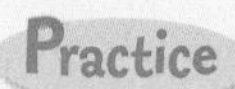

Revising Improving Your Book Review

Make revising more fun for students with this activity.

- Provide students with six sticky notes. Have them draw green dots on two notes, orange dots on two other notes, and blue dots on the last two notes.
- Tell students to put a green-dot note next to the beginning question on SE page 242, an orange-dot one next to the middle question, and a blue-dot one next to the ending question.
- Tell students to read over each part of their draft to find the sentence or sentences that answer each question and place a matching note there.

Remind students that time order is the order in which events happen. For students not familiar with "Cinderella," provide a summary of the fairy tale, or invite volunteers to summarize it.

* For information about Time Order, see SE pages 422–423.

Practice Answers

2, 3, 1, 5, 4

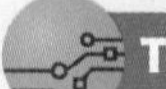

Technology Connections

Have students use the Writing Network features of the Net-text to comment on each other's drafts.

Write Source Online ***Net-text***

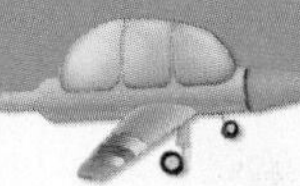

Revising Improving Your Book Review

Kayla wanted her book review to answer these three questions:

Beginning	**What is the book about?**
Middle	**Why do I like this book?**
Ending	**What is the book's main idea or theme?**

Revise Check your first draft.

- **Answer the following questions. Then make changes in your writing.**
  - **Did I answer the three questions listed above in my book review?**
  - **Did I write about events in correct time order?**

Practice

The events below are from the fairy tale "Cinderella," but they are not in the correct time order. Write the numbers of these events in the proper order.

1. Cinderella dances with the prince.
2. The prince announces a big dance.
3. Cinderella's fairy godmother gives her glass slippers.
4. The prince finds the lost glass slipper and searches for its owner.
5. The clock strikes midnight, and Cinderella runs from the dance.

Grammar Connection

Sentence Variety

- ***Write Source*** page 411
- ***GrammarSnap*** Kinds of Sentences

English Language Learners

Students unfamiliar with *Cinderella* will not be able to order the **Practice** events. Write the events on a sentence strip or piece of tag board. Then read aloud a version of *Cinderella*, pausing to let students order the events. After you finish, practice the skill by mixing up the events and having students order the sentence strips.

Editing Checking for Conventions

Next, Kayla edited her book review. She checked her writing for capitalization, punctuation, spelling, and grammar.

Conventions

Punctuation

___ **1.** Did I use end punctuation after all my sentences?
___ **2.** Did I underline the book's title?

Capitalization

___ **3.** Did I start all my sentences with capital letters?
___ **4.** Did I capitalize the names of the characters?

Spelling

___ **5.** Did I carefully check my spelling?

Grammar

___ **6.** Did I use subjects and verbs that agree *(He* **races**, not *He* **race***)*?
___ **7.** Did I use the right words *(to, two, too; there, their, they're)*?

Grammar Practice

Find two errors in each sentence and rewrite the sentences correctly.

1. Little Willy and his dog, searchlight, is brave.
2. They want to help pay the taxs for the farm
3. they know they can count on each other?

Editing Checking for Conventions

Simple mistakes in punctuation, capitalization, spelling, and grammar are often overlooked because students, like us, read what they meant to write and often miss their mistakes. Have students exchange their review with a partner who can edit it with a fresh eye for errors.

Students often make mistakes with subject-verb agreement when the subject and the verb are separated by other words and phrases. To help students catch these kinds of mistakes, suggest that they read each sentence aloud, leaving out any words that come between the subject and the verb.

* For more information about Subject-Verb Agreement, see SE pages 388 and 406.

Grammar Practice Answers

(Corrections are underlined.)

1. Little Willy and his dog, Searchlight, are brave.
2. They want to help pay the taxes for the farm.
3. They know they can count on each other.

Technology Connections

Students can use the added features of the Net-text as they explore this stage of the writing process.

Write Source Online ***Net-text***

English Language Learners

After presenting the sixth item on the checklist, for more subject-verb agreement practice, have students fill in a simple two-column chart with examples from their own writing.

Stone Fox	is
farm	is
he	can't play
They	race
He	wears

Grammar Connection

Verb Tenses

- **Proofreader's Guide** pages 540–541
- ***GrammarSnap*** Past Tense Verbs
- ***SkillsBook*** pages 137–138, 139–140

Using the Right Word

- **Proofreader's Guide** pages 514–515
- ***SkillsBook*** page 69

Apostrophes

- **Proofreader's Guide** pages 474–475, 534–535
- ***Write Source*** page 377
- ***GrammarSnap*** Apostrophes to Show Possession
- ***SkillsBook*** pages 25–26

Kayla's Final Draft

Have volunteers read aloud the beginning, middle, and ending parts of Kayla's finished book review. Then provide time for students to compare Kayla's final draft to her prewriting notes (SE pages 236–237) and first draft (SE pages 238, 240, and 241). Help them see how she used the notes from her sentence starters and story map in the review and then added details to make her ideas clearer and more interesting.

Ask students to point out details in Kayla's review that make them want to read *Stone Fox.*

Technology Connections

Remind students that they can use the Writing Network features of the Portfolio to share their work with peers.

Write Source Online **Portfolio**

Write Source Online **Net-text**

Publishing Sharing Your Book Review

Here is Kayla's finished book review.

Kayla's Final Draft

Stone Fox

Beginning

Stone Fox is a book by John Reynolds Gardiner. In the story, Little Willy's grandpa gets sick and can't pay the taxes on his farm in Wyoming. Willy decides to enter a dogsled race with his dog, Searchlight. If he wins, the prize money will pay the taxes. Stone Fox will race, too. He is a Shoshone Indian who has never lost a race.

Middle

My favorite part is the big race because it is so exciting. At the starting line, Willy tries to be friends with Stone Fox. "Morning, Mr. Stone Fox," Willy says. Stone Fox doesn't answer him. He just stands there looking big and mean. By the end of the race, everything changes.

Ending

Stone Fox shows that no one should ever give up. The race is very hard for Willy and Searchlight. Still, they try to beat Stone Fox. Even when something terrible happens, Little Willy doesn't give up. He learns that good things are worth fighting for.

Advanced Learners

Point out that the title of Kayla's final draft is the same as the book title. Challenge students to develop creative titles for their drafts. They may consider using the following:

- alliteration
- rhyme
- theme
- personal connection

Reflecting on Your Writing

Thinking about your writing can help you grow as a writer. Think about your review by completing the sentences below.

Thinking About Your Writing

Name: Kayla Martins

Title: Stone Fox

1. The best part about my book review is . . .

   the way I ended my report. I didn't give away the ending.

2. The main thing I learned about writing a book review is . . .

   that I need to choose just enough details to get my reader interested.

3. In my next book review, I would like to . . .

   write about a science-fiction book.

Reflecting on Your Writing

Provide photocopies of the reproducible Thinking About Your Writing (TE page 593), and have students record their thoughts about their review.

To create more interest in the reflecting process, offer students alternative forms of reflecting. For example, some students may enjoy recording their reflections in an audio notebook. Others may prefer to share their reflections in one-on-one discussions with you.

Always encourage students to review their previous reflections so that they can monitor for themselves their development as writers.

Struggling Learners

Tell students to reread their reviews all the way through before filling out their reflection sheets. By doing so, their writing will be fresh in their minds as they complete the sentence starters with specific details. Point out that the details will help them improve their writing.

Advanced Learners

Challenge students to elaborate their answers for the third reflection sentence by including three reasons to justify their choices. For example, "I would like to write about a science fiction book, because . . . "

- I like stories that take place in the future.
- My favorite book is the science fiction book *The Giver* by Lois Lowry.
- I like to read about things that may really happen some day.

Writing a Book Review for Nonfiction

Objectives

- Understand the purpose, content, and form of a book review.
- Choose a nonfiction book to write about.
- Plan, draft, revise, and edit a book review.

Students who do not read nonfiction books on a regular basis may not be prepared to write a nonfiction book review. To avoid this situation, provide students with a list of nonfiction books available in your school library. Choose titles based on students' interests or titles that are related to topics students are studying in social studies, science, and other curriculum areas. Then schedule a trip to the library, and have students choose a book to read and review. Make sure students are given enough time to read before they have to write.

To make it easier for students to gather details later (SE page 249), encourage them to jot down notes as they read or use sticky notes to mark important and interesting details that they may want to include in their review.

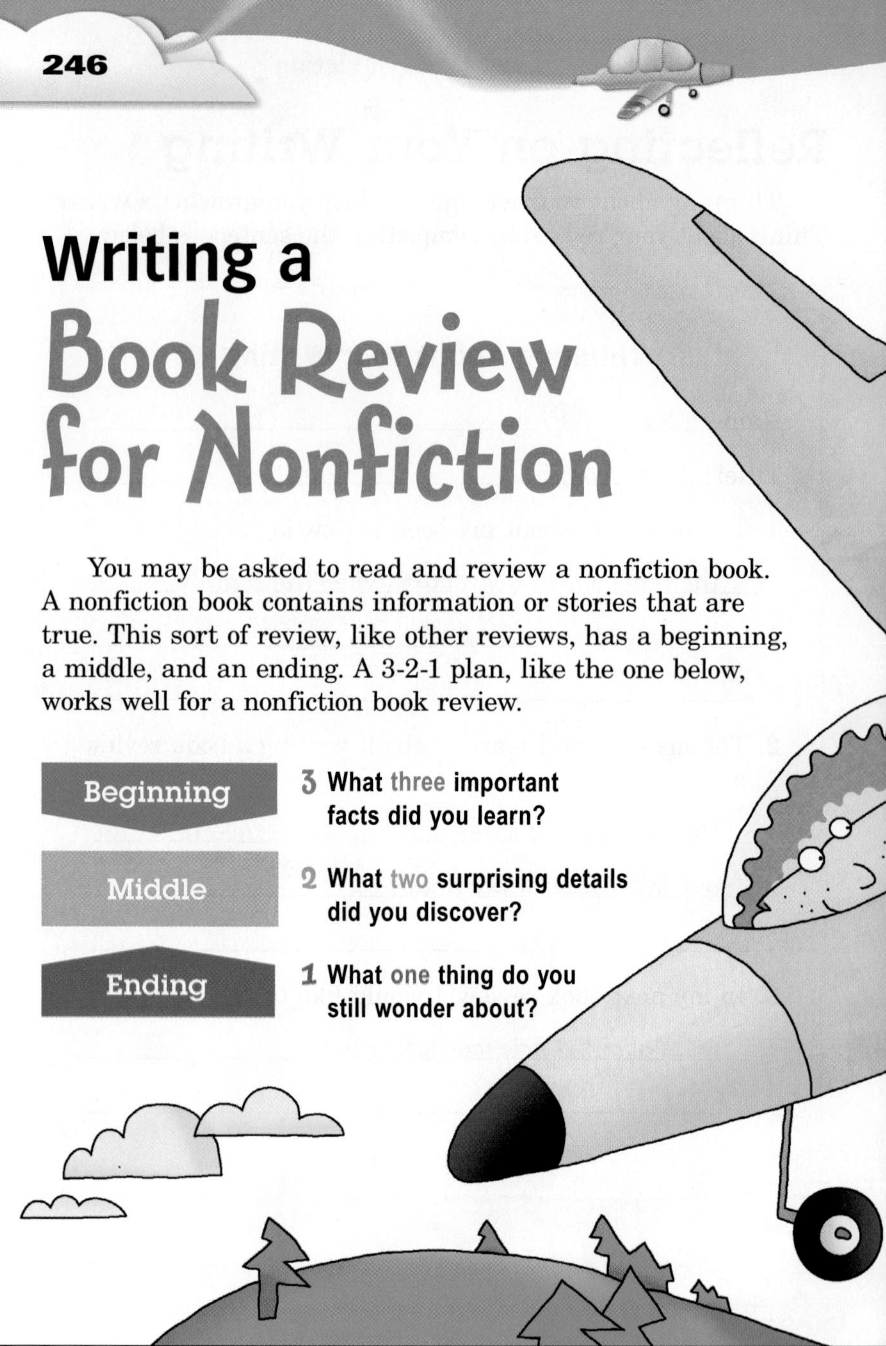

Writing a Book Review for Nonfiction

You may be asked to read and review a nonfiction book. A nonfiction book contains information or stories that are true. This sort of review, like other reviews, has a beginning, a middle, and an ending. A 3-2-1 plan, like the one below, works well for a nonfiction book review.

Beginning	3 What three important facts did you learn?
Middle	2 What two surprising details did you discover?
Ending	1 What one thing do you still wonder about?

Materials

List of available nonfiction books (TE p. 246)

Photograph of a glider (TE p. 247)

Art supplies (TE p. 247)

Nonfiction books (TE p. 248)

Drawing paper (TE p. 249)

Nonfiction Review

To Fly

Beginning

To Fly, the Story of the Wright Brothers by Wendie Old is a great book. I learned that when Orville Wright was my age, he made wonderful kites and models of flying machines. When he and his brother grew up, they built giant gliders and tried to fly in them. One day, they made an airplane that really worked.

Middle

It was so amazing when the airplane stayed in the air for 59 seconds and went 853 feet! Soon, the brothers made airplanes that could swoop, turn, and fly in a figure eight.

Ending

The Wright brothers' first airplane is in the Smithsonian Institution in Washington, D.C. I wonder if I will see it someday.

After you read . . .

- **Ideas** (1) What book is this review about? Who is the author?
- **Organization** (2) What three important facts appear in the beginning? What two surprising details appear in the middle? What one thing does the writer wonder about in the ending?
- **Word Choice** (3) What two words are most interesting to you? Why?

Nonfiction Review

Use students' responses for the **After you read** questions to discuss how the writer followed the 3-2-1 plan outlined on SE page 246 to write the sample review.

After you read . . .

Answers

Ideas 1. *To Fly, The Story of the Wright Brothers* by Wendie Old

Organization 2. **Beginning:** As a child, Orville Wright made kites and models of flying machines. He and his brother built gliders and tried to fly them. They made an airplane that worked. **Middle:** . . . *the airplane stayed in the air for 59 seconds and went 853 feet.* **Ending:** if he will see the Wright brothers' first airplane someday

Word Choice 3. Words and reasons will vary. Possible word choices:

- wonderful kites, giant gliders
- swoop, turn, figure eight
- Smithsonian Institution

English Language Learners

Students may need help to understand vocabulary in the sample nonfiction review. Explain to students that the term *flying machines* in the second sentence refers to any machine used for traveling through the air. Modern examples include jets, planes, and helicopters.

Point out that the word *glider* in the third sentence refers to a type of flying machine that does not have an engine. If possible, have a photograph of a glider to show students.

Illustrate the term *figure eight* (used in the sixth sentence) by drawing the numeral 8 on the board. You might have a volunteer show how a plane could fly in a figure eight.

Advanced Learners

Challenge students to find out more about the Wright brothers by conducting research in the library's media center or on the Internet. Invite students to share their findings by making a poster, mobile, or game.

Prewriting Choosing a Book

Remind students that the main idea of a book tells what the book is mostly about. In many nonfiction books, the main idea of the book is often introduced in the first few paragraphs or pages.

To illustrate this, read the first few paragraphs from several different nonfiction books, and ask students if they can figure out the main idea of each book. Students can find other clues to the book's main idea by looking at the cover, reading the title, and turning to the pictures and illustrations.

Students should understand, however, that in order to write the main idea for a book, they should select books they have read.

Technology Connections

Students can use the added features of the Net-text as they explore this stage of the writing process.

***Write Source Online* Net-text**

Prewriting Choosing a Book

Jared used the following steps to choose a nonfiction book to review. (See his plan below.)

1. List three nonfiction books you have read.
2. Write down the name of each author.
3. Write one sentence about the main idea of each book.
4. Put a star (*) next to the book you want to review.

Prewrite **Choose a book to review.**

1. **Read through Jared's plan below.**
2. **Then follow the steps above to make your own plan and choose a book to write about.**

Jared's Plan

Book 1: Snakes*
Author: Seymour Simon
Main Idea: Snakes are amazing animals.

Book 2: Bridges Are to Cross
Author: Philemon Sturges
Main Idea: Bridges are built in different ways.

Book 3: Lou Gehrig: The Luckiest Man
Author: David A. Adler
Main Idea: Lou Gehrig was a great baseball player and a very brave man.

Gathering Your Details

Jared gathered information for his report by making a 3-2-1 chart. He made the chart below by answering three questions.

Make a 3-2-1 chart.

- **Ask yourself the following questions about your nonfiction book.**

3-2-1 Chart

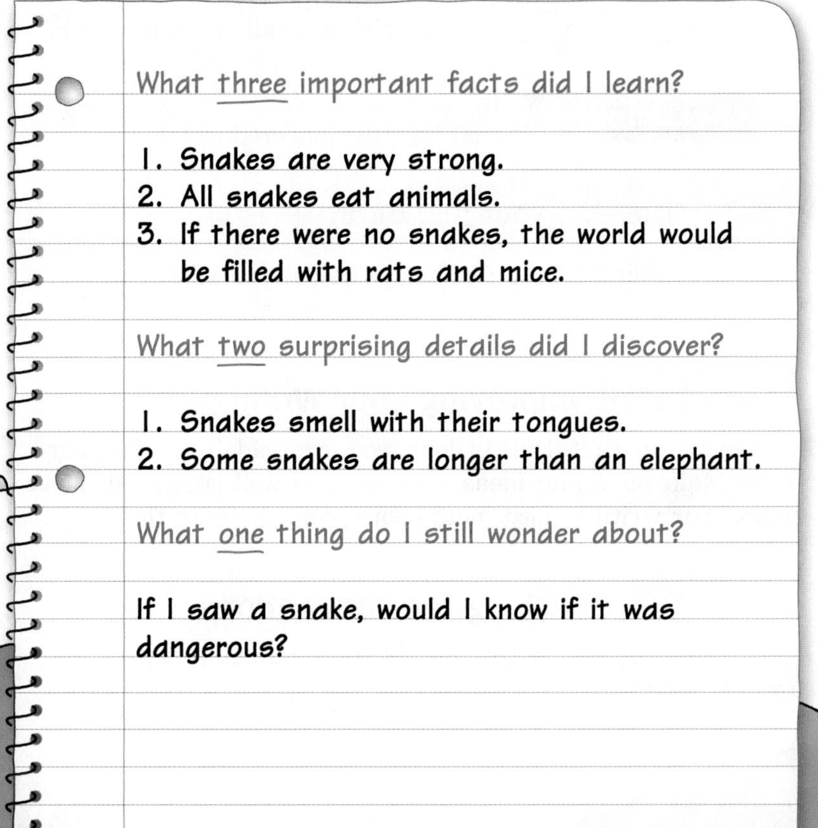

What three important facts did I learn?

1. Snakes are very strong.
2. All snakes eat animals.
3. If there were no snakes, the world would be filled with rats and mice.

What two surprising details did I discover?

1. Snakes smell with their tongues.
2. Some snakes are longer than an elephant.

What one thing do I still wonder about?

If I saw a snake, would I know if it was dangerous?

Prewriting Gathering Your Details

Students may worry about having to come up with facts and details for their review. Assure students that they do not have to remember facts and details from memory. They can look in the book for such details.

If students have taken notes or flagged important details as they read, they should be able to find details for the first two questions of their 3-2-1 chart quickly.

It may also reassure students if they understand that although the information in a nonfiction book review differs from the information in a fiction review, the purpose is the same for both: to share interesting details about a book so that others will want to read it.

English Language Learners

Many students rely heavily on picture clues as they learn English. Point out to students that they can often find important facts and surprising details in photos, illustrations, captions, subheads, and diagrams, as well as in the text.

Struggling Learners

To help visual learners organize their 3-2-1 information, have them draw an inverted pyramid on a large sheet of paper. Have students divide the pyramid into three rows of boxes and label as shown below:

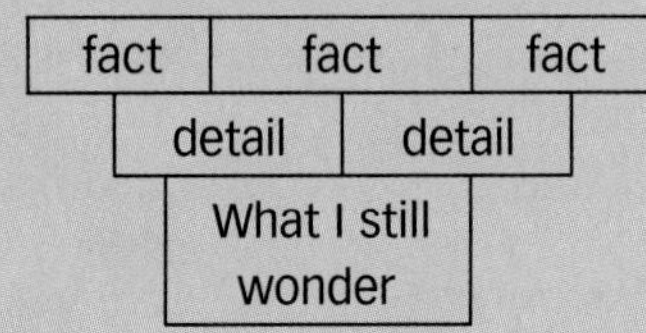

Point out that each row represents where information can be found in a particular part of the review: beginning, middle, or end.

Writing Creating Your Review

Review how to use a 3-2-1 chart to write a first draft.

- Read Jared's final draft on SE page 251.
- Then tell them to flip back to Jared's 3-2-1 chart on SE page 249. Have them read Jared's three answers for the first question.
- Next have them flip back to the sample review to find these three details in the beginning part of his review. (Repeat these steps for the middle and ending.)

Revising Improving Your Writing

Remind students that sentence variety helps their writing flow more smoothly.

* For practice combining sentences, see SE pages 408–410.

Editing Checking for Conventions

Remind students to underline or italicize the book title in their review.

Technology Connections

Students can use the added features of the Net-text as they explore this stage of the writing process.

Writing Creating Your Review

Now it is time to write your first draft. You will create a beginning, a middle, and an ending. Here is what Jared did for each part of his review.

Beginning In the **beginning**, Jared named the book and its author. He also explained *three* important facts from the book.

Middle In the **middle** part, Jared shared *two* surprising details from the book.

Ending In the **ending**, Jared told *one* thing that he still wondered about.

Develop your first draft.

- **Use your 3-2-1 chart from page 249 as you write your first draft.**

Revising Improving Your Writing

Once your first draft is done, you are ready to revise your work. Make sure your ideas are clear and well organized. Then check your writing voice, word choice, and sentence fluency.

Editing Checking for Conventions

Check your review for capitalization, punctuation, spelling, and grammar errors.

English Language Learners

Pair students with cooperative partners who are proficient in English and have good listening skills. Have students give their drafts to their partner and listen as the partner reads the draft aloud. Having the draft read aloud by another person can often help students better hear what works and what might need to be revised.

Struggling Learners

As students revise for word choice, have them circle words that they use more than two or three times in their review. Such words might include *very*, *really*, *good*, and *bad*. Encourage them to think of other more descriptive words to use in place of these words. Explain to students that they might also consider simply removing words such as *very* and *really*.

Advanced Learners

Have students work in cooperative pairs to revise their reviews. Have partners read each other's review and answer the questions of the 3-2-1 plan on SE page 246. Students should write their responses on a separate sheet of paper, which their partners can then refer to as they revise the beginning, middle, and ending of their review.

Publishing Sharing Your Book Review

Here is Jared's finished review of a nonfiction book.

Jared's Final Draft

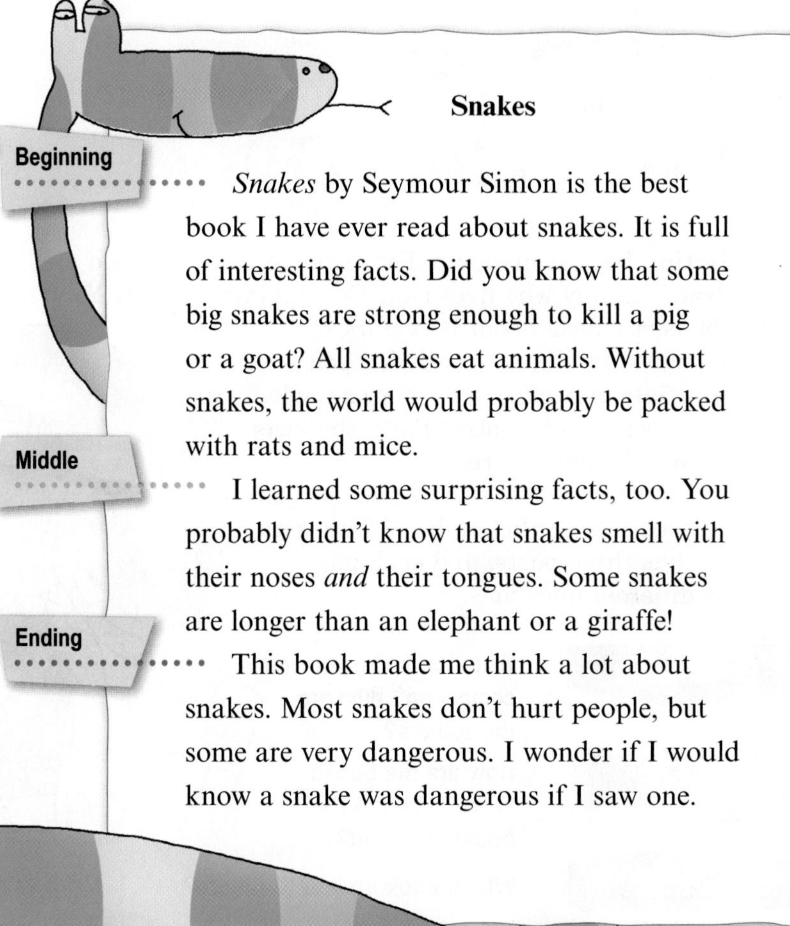

Snakes

Snakes by Seymour Simon is the best book I have ever read about snakes. It is full of interesting facts. Did you know that some big snakes are strong enough to kill a pig or a goat? All snakes eat animals. Without snakes, the world would probably be packed with rats and mice.

I learned some surprising facts, too. You probably didn't know that snakes smell with their noses *and* their tongues. Some snakes are longer than an elephant or a giraffe!

This book made me think a lot about snakes. Most snakes don't hurt people, but some are very dangerous. I wonder if I would know a snake was dangerous if I saw one.

Jared's Final Draft

Have students find an example of a statement, a question, and an exclamation in Jared's final draft. Explain to students that by using different kinds of sentences in his review, Jared makes his writing more interesting and enjoyable for his readers. Encourage students to look through their draft again to find places where they could write a different kind of sentence to improve the sound of their writing.

* For more about using Different Kinds of Sentences, see SE page 411.

Technology Connections

Remind students that they can use the Writing Network features of the Portfolio to share their work with peers.

- ***Write Source Online*** ***Portfolio***
- ***Write Source Online*** ***Net-text***

Grammar Connection

Sentence Combining

- **Proofreader's Guide** page 466 (+)
- ***Write Source*** pages 394, 408 (+), 409 (+)
- ***GrammarSnap*** Creating a Series
- ***SkillsBook*** pages 111–112

Plurals

- **Proofreader's Guide** pages 492–493
- ***GrammarSnap*** Nouns
- ***SkillsBook*** pages 51–52, 53–54

Fragments

- **Proofreader's Guide** pages 526 (+), 528 (+)
- ***Write Source*** page 403
- ***GrammarSnap*** Complete Sentences
- ***SkillsBook*** page 95

Comparing a Fiction and a Nonfiction Book

Objectives

- Understand the purpose, content, and form of a book review that compares two books.
- Choose a fiction book and a nonfiction book to compare in a book review.
- Plan, draft, revise, and edit a book review that compares a fiction and a nonfiction book.

Some students may need more time to find, read, and write about two books on the same topic. Students who are undaunted by the challenge can proceed at their own pace. Other students will need extra support and guidance throughout the writing process.

One way to help students get off to a good start is to have on hand a list of paired books on the same topic, books that will appeal to a majority of students. Your library media specialist or online resources are good sources for finding age-appropriate books on the same topic.

Comparing a Fiction and a Nonfiction Book

A **fiction** book is made-up. For example, you may read a book about a family who lives near Central Park in New York City. The book's facts about New York City may be true, but the story did not really happen.

A **nonfiction** book is true. For example, in a nonfiction book about Central Park, the facts are true and the story is real.

You can write a book review that compares a fiction book to a nonfiction book. This sort of review has three parts, and each part answers different questions.

Beginning — What two books are you comparing? Who are the authors?

Middle — How are the books alike? How are the books different?

Ending — Which book do you like more?

Materials

List of paired fiction and nonfiction books (TE pp. 252, 254)

Snakes by Seymour Simon (TE p. 254)

Verdi by Janell Cannon (TE p. 254)

Fiction and nonfiction books (TE p. 255)

Copy Masters

T-Chart (TE p. 254)

Venn Diagram (TE p. 255)

Comparing Fiction and Nonfiction 253

Fiction and Nonfiction Comparison

The Wright Brothers

Beginning

I like airplanes, so I read two books about the Wright brothers. The fiction book is *Wee and the Wright Brothers,* by Timothy R. Gaffney. The nonfiction book is *To Fly, the Story of the Wright Brothers,* by Wendie Old.

These books are alike in some ways. They happen in the same place, and both books contain many facts. For example, the famous flight took place on December 17, a freezing cold day. Orville Wright was lying on the wing of the airplane when he flew.

Middle

The biggest difference is that *Wee and the Wright Brothers* is about a made-up mouse named Wee. He is even a writer! The book says, "On a small printing press above the shop, they published the Mouse News." To get his news story, Wee hides on the airplane and goes along for the famous ride. Of course, none of this is true.

Ending

Both books had many of the same facts, but I liked *Wee and the Wright Brothers* more. The mouse character made it more fun to read. I could imagine being a mouse on the first plane flight!

After you read . . .

- **Ideas** (1) How are the ideas in the two books alike? How are they different?
- **Organization** (2) Which paragraph shows similarities? Which shows differences?
- **Word Choice** (3) What is the main character's name in the fiction book? Find words that describe him.

Struggling Learners

Have students reread the third paragraph of the review. Point out that *Wee and the Wright Brothers* is a fantasy book because the mouse acts in ways that humans act. Explain to students that they can use other types of fiction books, including realistic fiction and science fiction, when comparing nonfiction and fiction books.

Fiction-Nonfiction Comparison

Before discussing students' responses to the **After you read** questions, have students point out how the sample comparison answers the questions for the beginning, middle, and ending given on SE page 252.

After you read . . .

Answers

Ideas 1. **Alike**: Both are about the Wright brothers and contain facts about their famous first flight; the setting is the same. **Different**: *To Fly* is about the real Wright brothers and is true; *Wee and the Wright Brothers* is about a made-up mouse and is not true.

Organization 2. The second paragraph shows similarities. The third paragraph shows differences.

Word Choice 3. Wee; *made-up mouse, writer*

Prewriting Selecting a Topic

Have students work together to brainstorm topics. Have them use these questions to spark ideas.

- What topics do you usually like to read about?
- What topics are you studying in social studies or science that you would like to learn more about?
- What was the topic of the last fiction or nonfiction book that you read?

If you have a list of paired books prepared, share the list with students to see if any of these paired books will work for the topic they have chosen.

Be sure students know that they can use books that they have already read. Explain to students that they will need to have the book on hand to find details for their review.

Prewriting Gathering Details

Provide photocopies of the reproducible T-Chart (TE page 595) for students to use for listing details for their comparison. Tell students to list at least four details for each book and to look for details that will help them compare the books.

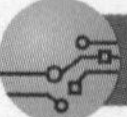

Technology Connections

Students can use the added features of the Net-text as they explore this stage of the writing process.

***Write Source Online* Net-text**

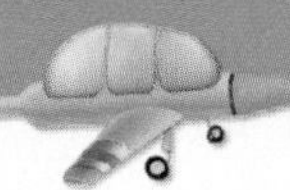

Prewriting Selecting a Topic

What topics do you love? Jared thinks snakes are amazing. He chose one fiction book and one nonfiction book about snakes.

Choose two books.

- **Find a fiction book and a nonfiction book about a topic you enjoy.**

Gathering Details

Jared gathered details about each book on a T-chart.

Create a T-chart.

1. **Read Jared's T-chart below and then make your own chart.**
2. **Write the names of your books at the top.**
3. **List interesting details from each book underneath.**

T-Chart

Verdi (fiction)	Snakes (nonfiction)
Verdi is a python.	A snake sheds its skin.
He is green.	Big snakes eat pigs and goats.
Verdi likes his color.	Snakes don't see colors well.
He sheds his skin.	The cover shows a python.
He talks and laughs.	
Umbles eats a boar.	

English Language Learners

To make SE pages 254–257 more concrete for students, set aside time to read aloud *Verdi* by Janell Cannon and *Snakes* by Seymour Simon. As you read the second book, have students point out more ways that the two stories are alike and different.

Comparing Fiction and Nonfiction 255

Organizing Your Details

Now that you've gathered your details, you need to organize them. You must decide which details are alike and which are different. A Venn diagram can help you. Jared's Venn diagram appears at the bottom of this page.

Create a Venn diagram.

1. Draw two overlapping circles.
2. Write the name of each book in the two outside circles.
3. In the center, list similarities (how they are alike).
4. On the two sides, list differences (how they are different).

Venn Diagram

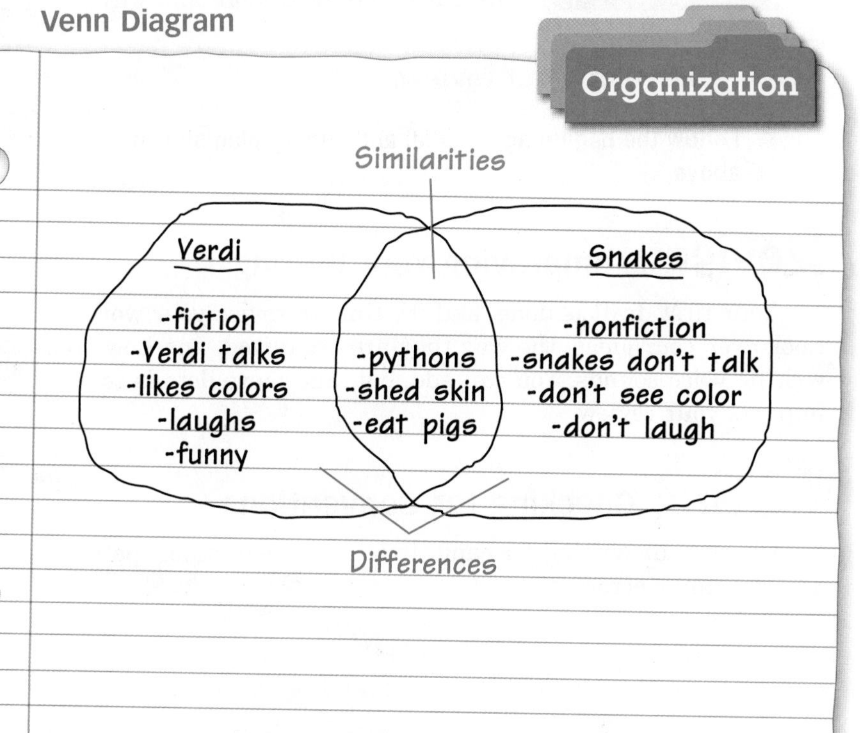

Prewriting Organizing Your Details

Provide photocopies of the reproducible Venn Diagram (TE page 600) for students to use to organize details for their comparison. Use the sample Venn diagram to show how Jared took the similarities and differences that he discovered as he created his T-chart (SE page 254) and wrote them in the Venn diagram. Point out that by using a Venn diagram, Jared could easily see how the two books were alike and different.

* For more about using a Venn Diagram, see SE page 438.

Advanced Learners

Before students create their Venn diagrams, have them work in groups to compare and contrast fiction and nonfiction elements. They can display their findings in a T-chart or Venn diagram. To help students get started, provide fiction and nonfiction books that they can examine for subheadings, chapters, bold print, diagrams, and so on.

Writing Creating Your Review

Ordinarily, students should be encouraged to be original and creative as they write, and they certainly should be allowed to be creative here. However, if students have trouble getting started, suggest that they follow the format of Jared's first paragraph (SE page 257) but replace the topic and the titles with their topic and titles. Later, if they want to go back and make their beginning more original and creative they can.

Remind students to use the details from their T-chart and Venn diagram to show how the books are alike and different.

Revising Improving Your Writing

Remind students that their writing voice is how their writing sounds to readers. The best way for them to check if their writing voice sounds natural and interested is to read their review aloud, or to have a classmate read it aloud to them.

After students have revised their review, have them put it away for a day or two before editing it for conventions.

Technology Connections

Students can use the added features of the Net-text as they explore this stage of the writing process.

Write Source Online ***Net-text***

Writing Creating Your Review

Now you are ready to write your first draft. You will create a beginning, a middle, and an ending. Here is how Jared wrote each part of his review.

Beginning In the **beginning paragraph**, Jared named the books and their authors.

Middle In the **middle paragraphs**, Jared explained how the two books were alike and different.

Ending In the **ending paragraph**, Jared told which book he liked more and why.

Develop your review.

- **Follow the beginning, middle, and ending plan shown above.**

Revising Improving Your Writing

Your first draft is done, and it's time to revise your work. Look over your ideas, the way they are organized, and how your writing voice sounds. You can add, cut, and move details to improve your review.

Editing Checking for Conventions

Check your writing for capitalization, punctuation, spelling, and grammar errors.

Grammar Connection

Compound Sentences

- **Proofreader's Guide** pages 468–469, 554–555
- ***Write Source*** pages 395, 410
- ***GrammarSnap*** Compound Sentences
- ***SkillsBook*** pages 15–16, 85–86, 165

Pronouns

- **Proofreader's Guide** pages 536–537
- ***Write Source*** pages 379–381
- ***GrammarSnap*** Pronouns, Subject and Object; Possessive Pronouns
- ***SkillsBook*** pages 125–126, 131–132

Comparing Fiction and Nonfiction 257

Publishing Sharing Your Book Review

Jared compared fiction and nonfiction books.

Jared's Final Draft

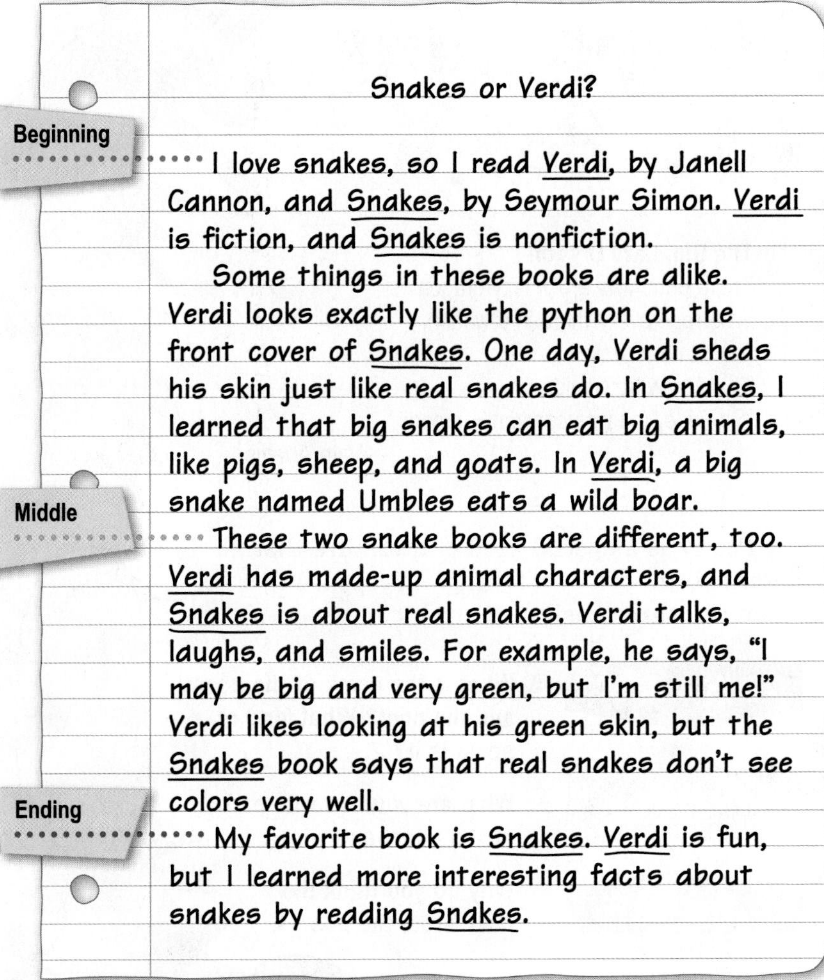

Snakes or Verdi?

Beginning

I love snakes, so I read Verdi, by Janell Cannon, and Snakes, by Seymour Simon. Verdi is fiction, and Snakes is nonfiction.

Middle

Some things in these books are alike. Verdi looks exactly like the python on the front cover of Snakes. One day, Verdi sheds his skin just like real snakes do. In Snakes, I learned that big snakes can eat big animals, like pigs, sheep, and goats. In Verdi, a big snake named Umbles eats a wild boar.

These two snake books are different, too. Verdi has made-up animal characters, and Snakes is about real snakes. Verdi talks, laughs, and smiles. For example, he says, "I may be big and very green, but I'm still me!" Verdi likes looking at his green skin, but the Snakes book says that real snakes don't see colors very well.

Ending

My favorite book is Snakes. Verdi is fun, but I learned more interesting facts about snakes by reading Snakes.

Struggling Learners

Point out that Jared's first middle paragraph discusses all the similarities between *Verdi* and *Snakes*. The second middle paragraph points out the differences between the two books. Have students refer to Jared's middle paragraphs and the way he organizes information as they revise their writing.

Jared's Final Draft

Have students identify the words in the sample review that signal to the reader that Jared is comparing the two books *(alike, like, different, but).* Invite volunteers to suggest other clue words that writers use to show how two things are alike or different. Students might suggest *both, same, similar, also, unlike.*

Have students look through their review to see if they have used clue words to make their comparisons clear for the reader.

Writer's Craft

Fiction and nonfiction: By comparing and contrasting works of fiction and nonfiction, your students will better understand each type of writing. They will see, for example, that fiction is full of imagination (snakes who admire their color) and that nonfiction is full of fact (snakes that can't see color). However, students should also note that fiction contains many actual facts (pythons can eat large animals, like boars), and nonfiction still needs to be told in an entertaining way (interesting facts about snakes). The ability to compare and contrast helps students learn more about each subject.

Technology Connections

Remind students that they can use the Writing Network features of the Portfolio to share their work with peers.

Write Source Online ***Portfolio***

Write Source Online ***Net-text***

Responding to a Poem

Objectives
- Apply what has been learned about responding to literature to the genre of poetry.
- Choose a poem to write about.
- Plan, draft, revise, and edit a response to a poem.

Writing a response to a poem will be easy for some students and difficult for others. As you progress through this section, provide extensive modeling to build their confidence.

Have several volunteers read aloud "The Big, Lazy Dragon." Then use the following questions to help students get ready to write about a poem.

- What tells you that this is a poem?
- Which lines rhyme?
- What words did the writer use to help you picture the dragon?

Assure students that they will read different kinds of poems during prewriting.

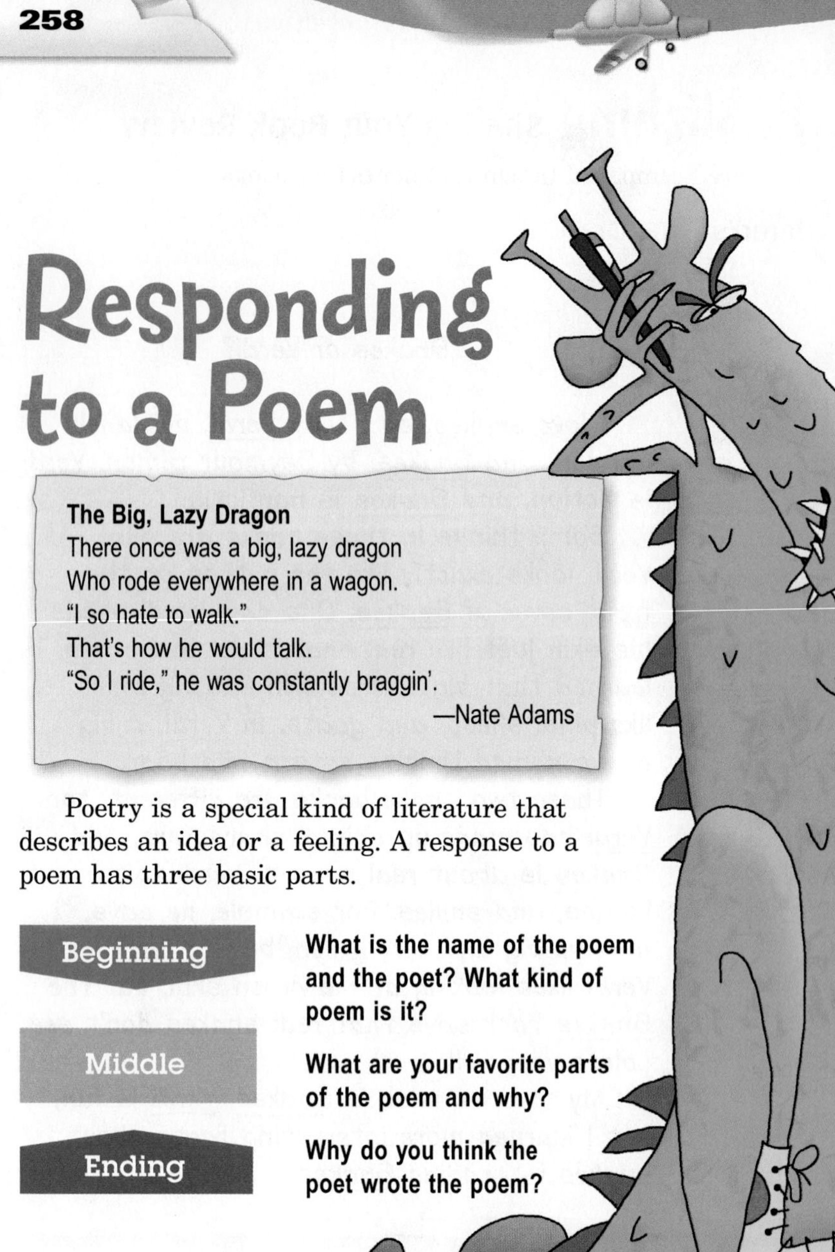

Responding to a Poem

The Big, Lazy Dragon
There once was a big, lazy dragon
Who rode everywhere in a wagon.
"I so hate to walk."
That's how he would talk.
"So I ride," he was constantly braggin'.
—Nate Adams

Poetry is a special kind of literature that describes an idea or a feeling. A response to a poem has three basic parts.

Beginning	**What is the name of the poem and the poet? What kind of poem is it?**
Middle	**What are your favorite parts of the poem and why?**
Ending	**Why do you think the poet wrote the poem?**

Materials

Poetry books (TE p. 261)

Map of the United States (TE p. 264)

Alan's Response to a Poem

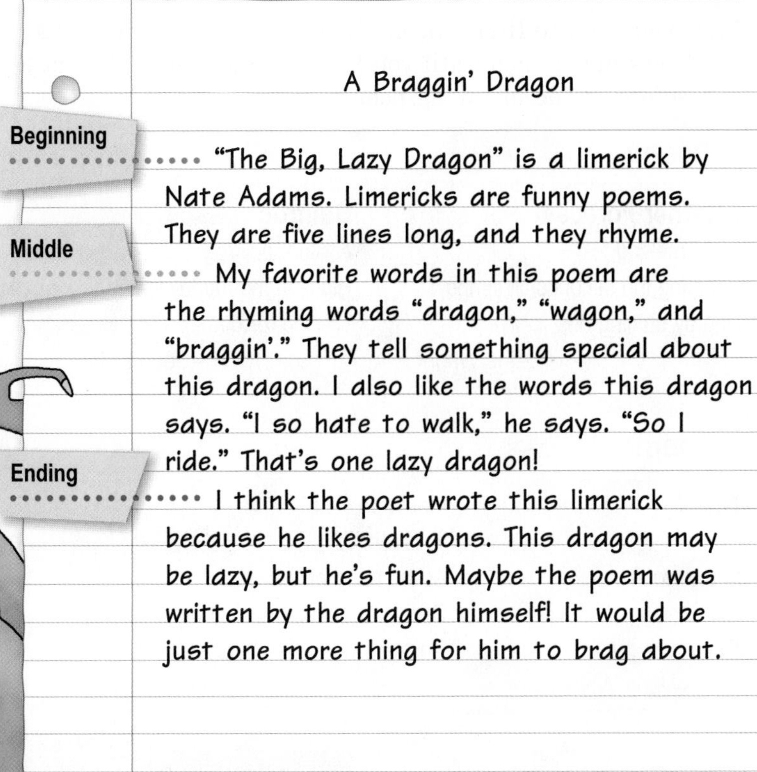

A Braggin' Dragon

Beginning — "The Big, Lazy Dragon" is a limerick by Nate Adams. Limericks are funny poems. They are five lines long, and they rhyme.

Middle — My favorite words in this poem are the rhyming words "dragon," "wagon," and "braggin'." They tell something special about this dragon. I also like the words this dragon says. "I so hate to walk," he says. "So I ride." That's one lazy dragon!

Ending — I think the poet wrote this limerick because he likes dragons. This dragon may be lazy, but he's fun. Maybe the poem was written by the dragon himself! It would be just one more thing for him to brag about.

After you read . . .

- **Ideas** (1) What is your favorite idea in this response?
- **Organization** (2) What questions does each part answer?
- **Word Choice** (3) What words from the poem appear in the response?

Alan's Response to a Poem

Call attention to the title of Alan's response ("A Braggin' Dragon"). Ask students if they think this is a good title and why. (Most students will probably like the title because it's creative, it tells the main idea of the poem, and it uses rhyming words from the poem.) Encourage students to be creative when they write their response title.

After you read . . .

Answers

Ideas 1. Possible choices:

- That's one lazy dragon!
- The dragon may have written the poem himself just to brag.

Organization 2. **Beginning:** What is the name of the poem and poet? What kind of poem is it? **Middle:** What are your favorite parts of the poem? Why are they your favorite parts? **Ending:** Why do you think the poet wrote the poem?

Word Choice 3. dragon, wagon, braggin', I so hate to walk, So I ride

Struggling Learners

Students may not be familiar with the term *limerick,* used in Alan's response. Explain that a limerick is a short, humorous poem that has five lines, a specific rhythm, and a specific rhyming pattern.

Direct students' attention to "The Big, Lazy Dragon" on SE page 258. Read it aloud, emphasizing the rhythm. Then have students identify the rhyming words in the limerick (lines 1, 2, and 5 rhyme with each other, and lines 3 and 4 have a different rhyme). Explain that most limericks have this pattern of rhyming words.

Students will have an opportunity to write their own limerick in the Creative Writing unit (SE page 290).

Prewriting Selecting a Topic

Approach this activity in different ways to make it more enjoyable for students.

- Write the poetry response as a whole-class activity.
- Have students work in small groups to write responses to the same poem. Students can share ideas and help each other develop responses. Even if the completed responses are similar, students will have had a successful experience and will be able to apply what they learn to future writing assignments.
- Encourage students to choose from one of the four poems given. Then, even if they are writing their response independently, they can discuss ideas with other classmates who have chosen the same poem, or form of poem.

For this assignment, students need only identify the **kind of poem** *(see below)* they have chosen. They don't need to explain the form.

Technology Connections

Students can use the added features of the Net-text as they explore this stage of the writing process.

Prewriting Selecting a Topic

First, you need to find a poem. Look through poetry books and children's magazines until you find one you enjoy. You may also choose one of the following poems.

Haiku Poems

Weather Forecast
Icicle melting,
Counting the seconds till spring,
Drip by shining drip.
—Lewis Wright

Bullfrog
A silent bullfrog
Hides in the muddy water
Waiting for dinner.
—Jean Netter

5 W's Poems

The Wolf
Howls
In the woods
At midnight
To call the pack.
—Jana Whiteheart

Grandpa Frank
Tells stories
At the head of the table
During Thanksgiving dinner
Because he remembers so much.
—David Moffet

Choose a poem to respond to.

- **Make sure to find out what kind of poem you have chosen. (See pages 282–293).**

Teaching Tip: Kinds of Poems

If you have time and don't think it will confuse students, explain the form of the poems mentioned in this section.

- **Haiku:** A three-line poem about something in nature. Line 1 has five syllables. Line 2 has seven syllables. Line 3 has five syllables.
- **5 W's Poem:** A poem in which each line answers a 5 W's question (who, what, where, when, why) to build a word picture.

* See SE page 290 for information about the form of a limerick, and SE page 292 for information about a 5 W's poem.

English Language Learners

Guide students in choosing poems that are fairly easy for them to interpret. Poetry filled with idioms, colloquialisms, and figurative language can hinder students' ability to write successful responses. They can be difficult to avoid, though, so be prepared to help students interpret such devices.

Responding to a Poem 261

Gathering Details

Next, you need to gather information about your poem. Answering questions can help. Here is the poem that Charise chose. Below, you can read her answers to the questions.

What I Did on Saturday

Watched cartoons. Played with spoons.
Walked the dog. Caught a frog.
Found a hole. Fought a troll.
Turned invisible. Saved our principal.
Came back home. Wrote this poem.
—Craig Eugene

Answer questions about your poem.

1. On your own paper, write the name of your poem and the poet.
2. Then write the underlined questions shown below and answer them.

Detail Questions

"What I Did on Saturday" by Craig Eugene

What kind of poem is it? It is a list poem.

What are my favorite lines or words?

"Found a hole. Fought a troll." Also, I like "Turned invisible. Saved our principal."

Why do I think the poet wrote this poem?

He likes to imagine adventures.

Prewriting Gathering Details

Point out the quotation marks around the poem's title and the words from the poem in the responses to the detail questions. Tell students to be sure to put quotation marks around the title of their poem and around any words, phrases, or sentences from the poem they use in their response.

* For information about using Quotation Marks to Punctuate Titles, see SE page 476.

If you are not writing the response as a whole-class activity, circulate among students as they gather details from their poem. Schedule a **writing conference** *(see below)* for struggling students.

Teaching Tip: Writing Conferences

Brief, one-on-one discussions can help students focus ideas and gain confidence. These students may feel more at ease sharing thoughts and feelings with you, away from their peers.

Take time to review the student's responses to the detail questions. Encourage the student to explain in his or her own words what each line says and means to him or her. Students may actually have a greater understanding of the poem than they think they do, and may just need your added assurance to see that their ideas are on track.

Struggling Learners

Students may worry about identifying different types of poems. Explain that choosing a poem they really enjoy is the most important part of writing a poetry response. For those who need more guidance, suggest they read poems by Shel Silverstein, Jack Prelutsky, Eve Merriam, Aileen Fisher, or Robert Louis Stevenson.

Writing Organizing Your Response

To be sure students follow the plan for writing a response to a poem, have them explain in their own words how they will write the beginning, middle, and ending of their response by answering the questions on SE page 258.

Revising Improving Your Writing

If students wrote responses collaboratively in small groups, read aloud each group's poem and response, and have volunteers answer the **After you read** questions on SE page 259 about each group's response.

If students wrote a response on their own, have them exchange their poem and response with a partner. The answers to the questions on SE page 259 should help them to revise their response effectively.

Editing Checking for Conventions

Tell students to make sure all their sentences begin with capital letters and end with the proper end mark.

Technology Connections

Students can use the added features of the Net-text as they explore this stage of the writing process.

Write Source Online ***Net-text***

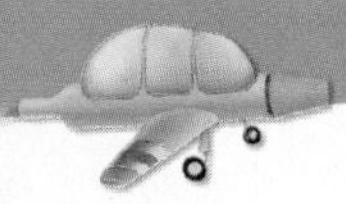

Writing Organizing Your Response

You are now ready to write a response to your poem. Here is how Charise organized her response.

Beginning	In the **beginning paragraph**, Charise named the poem and its author. She also explained what kind of poem she chose.
Middle	In the **middle paragraph**, Charise told about her favorite words or lines in the poem.
Ending	In the **ending paragraph**, Charise told why she thinks the poet wrote the poem.

Develop your response to a poem.

- **Follow the plan shown above to write your response.**

Revising Improving Your Writing

Once your first draft is done, revise your writing. Consider your ideas, the way they are organized, and how your voice sounds. Then work on your word choice and sentence fluency.

Editing Checking for Conventions

Check your response for capitalization, punctuation, spelling, and grammar errors.

Grammar Connection

Using the Right Word

- **Proofreader's Guide** pages 516–517
- ***SkillsBook*** page 70

Quotation Marks

- **Proofreader's Guide** page 476 (+)
- ***SkillsBook*** pages 33–34

English Language Learners

Some students may have difficulty explaining why they think a poet wrote a particular poem. Guide students with the following questions and remind them to support their opinions with words and lines from the poem:

- Is this poem silly, serious, happy, or sad? How do you know?
- Why might you write a poem like this?

Publishing Sharing Your Response Essay

Here is Charise's final draft of her response to a poem.

Charise's Final Draft

A Big Adventure

Beginning

"What I Did on Saturday" is a list poem by Craig Eugene. This poem rhymes, and it's funny.

Middle

My favorite part is the middle. The beginning is about usual things, like watching TV and walking a dog. Then the middle is about crazy things, like a hole and fighting a troll. This Saturday gets more and more exciting! I like the next part, too. "Turned invisible. Saved our principal." It makes me feel like I'm a character in a comic book.

Ending

I think the poet wrote this poem because sometimes he gets bored. Then he imagines wild adventures and has fun writing about them. It's like he said in the ending, "Came back home. Wrote this poem."

Charise's Final Draft

Remind students that a poem is a special type of writing that uses only a few words to tell about an idea or a feeling. Poems sometimes, though not always, have rhyming words and colorful language.

To respond to a poem, readers have to think about the special words that the poet uses to help them "see" in their mind's eye what the poet is describing. After students read Charise's final draft, have them compare their response to the poem "What I Did on Saturday" (SE page 261) to Charise's. Use questions like the following to spark ideas.

- What words from the poem helped Charise picture the poet's ideas?
- What words helped you to picture the poet's ideas?
- Why does Charise think the poet wrote the poem?
- Can you think of another explanation for why the poet wrote this poem?

Technology Connections

Remind students that they can use the Writing Network features of the Portfolio to share their work with peers.

Write Source Online ***Portfolio***

Write Source Online ***Net-text***

Writing for Assessment

If your students must take school, district, or state assessments this year, focus on the writing form on which they will be tested.

Read through the instruction and the prompt for the sample. Ask students which words and phrases in the prompt they would underline or highlight as key words to remember as they write their response (tell what the article is about, a few important facts, one thing you wonder about).

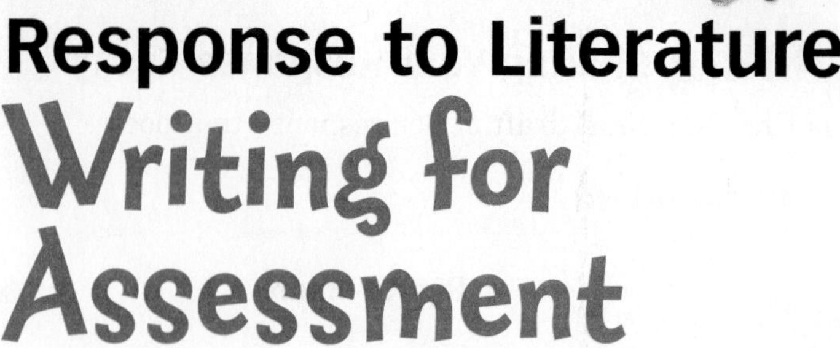

Response to Literature Writing for Assessment

Some writing tests ask you to respond to a short article. You may need to answer questions about the article or write an essay. Here is a prompt you might find on a test.

Response Prompt

Read the article below. In an essay, tell what the article is about. Give a few important facts from the article, and tell one thing you still wonder about.

Mountain Lions on the Move

Mountain lions are on the move. They are showing up in communities all over the United States. Someday, you might see one in your backyard.

For most of the last one hundred years, mountain lions have lived west of the Mississippi River. They usually live in mountain wilderness areas. Lately, these animals have begun moving east into neighborhoods near big cities, like Chicago, Philadelphia, and Boston.

Why are they moving? Scientists say it is because people are building communities in the mountain lion's natural habitat. Buildings, roads, and fences get in the animals' way when they search for food and water. This forces them to look for new places to live where there is plenty to eat and water to drink.

Mountain lions prey on animals like deer, cats, and dogs. If you see a mountain lion, you should stay away from it. Most mountain lions will run from people. However, some have attacked and killed people.

English Language Learners

Before reading the assessment article, display a map of the United States. As you read the article, pause to point out the Mississippi River and Chicago, Philadelphia, and Boston. When you read the final paragraph, explain that the homophone *prey* means "to hunt for food," as many students may be unfamiliar with the spelling and particular meaning.

Struggling Learners

Point out to students that they can adapt the 3-2-1 inverted pyramids they made before (**Struggling Learners**, TE page 249) in order to respond to "Mountain Lions on the Move." Model the process by combining the top three boxes into one box and writing the main idea in it (mountain lions are moving into neighborhoods). In the second row, write important facts (usually live in wilderness areas; now communities are in mountain lions' natural habitat; mountain lions can't find food and water). Use the bottom row for one thing you wonder about.

Writing for Assessment 265

Student Response

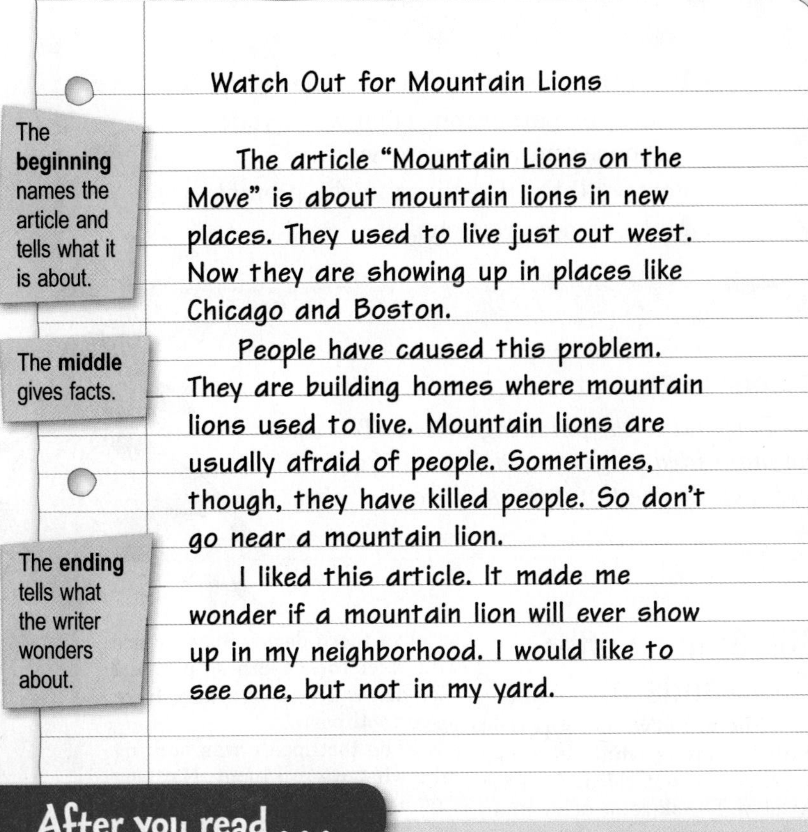

Watch Out for Mountain Lions

The article "Mountain Lions on the Move" is about mountain lions in new places. They used to live just out west. Now they are showing up in places like Chicago and Boston.

People have caused this problem. They are building homes where mountain lions used to live. Mountain lions are usually afraid of people. Sometimes, though, they have killed people. So don't go near a mountain lion.

I liked this article. It made me wonder if a mountain lion will ever show up in my neighborhood. I would like to see one, but not in my yard.

The **beginning** names the article and tells what it is about.
The **middle** gives facts.
The **ending** tells what the writer wonders about.

After you read . . .

- **Ideas** (1) Name two important facts the writer shared.
- **Organization** (2) Which part–beginning, middle, ending–named the article and the main idea?
- **Word Choice** (3) What words from the "Response Prompt" appear in this response?

Student Response

Ask students if they think the writer has written a good response. (Most students will probably say "yes" because the writer has followed all the directions in the prompt.)

Encourage students to point out other elements that make the sample a good response. (Possible choices: The writer includes only details that answer the prompt, presents ideas clearly, and uses words that go with the topic.)

Remind students that the titles of articles, poems, and shorts stories are always enclosed in quotation marks.

After you read . . .

Answers

Ideas 1. Possible choices:

- Mountain lions used to live just out west and now they are in places like Chicago and Boston.
- People built homes where mountain lions used to live.
- Mountain lions are afraid of people, but they have killed them.

Organization 2. the beginning

Word Choice 3. article is about, wonder

Writing Tips

Point out that students must approach writing-on-demand assignments differently from open-ended writing assignments and that timed writing creates pressures for everyone.

Response Prompt

To teach students who must take timed assessments how to approach their writing, allow them the same amount of time to write their response essay as they will be allotted on school, district, or state assessments. Break down each part of the process into clear chunks of time. For example, you might give students

- 15 minutes for note taking and planning,
- 20 minutes for writing, and
- 10 minutes for editing and proofreading.

Tell students when time is up for each section. Start the assignment at the top of the hour or at the half-hour to make it easier for students to keep track of the time.

If your state, district, or school requires students to use and submit a graphic organizer as part of their assessment, provide a copy of one of the reproducible charts (TE pages 595–600) or refer students to SE pages 438–444.

Writing Tips

- Read the prompt and the article carefully.
- Plan your paragraph. Then write your response and check your work.
- Follow all the directions in the prompt.
- Make neat corrections.

Response Prompt

Respond to the following article. Tell what the main idea is, give a few interesting facts, and include one thing you still wonder about.

Still Smiling after Thousands of Years

"She would've had a perfect smile." That is what scientists are saying about Europe's oldest skeleton. The skeleton of a woman is thousands of years old.

One of the most interesting things about this skeleton is her beautiful teeth. They are nearly perfect, straight, and white. In ancient times, people did not take good care of their teeth. A poor diet and poor dental care caused a lot of tooth decay. So, why are this skeleton's teeth so perfect? Scientists think she may have used toothpaste!

The toothpaste was nothing like what we use today. Not long ago, a team of scientists discovered an old Egyptian toothpaste recipe. The ingredients included rock salt, mint, and pepper. These things were pounded into a paste and then put on the teeth. Is some sort of toothpaste what gave the skeleton her beautiful smile? Nobody knows for sure.

English Language Learners

Writing to a prompt can be particularly challenging for some students. Spend as much time as possible analyzing the response prompt with students:

- Point out key words that clarify the goal of writing, such as *respond, main idea, interesting facts,* and *one thing you still wonder about.*
- Have volunteers rephrase the prompt in their own words.
- Write the rephrased prompt on the board for students to refer to when they write their responses.

Response Writing in Review

When you respond to a book, a poem, or an article, you tell what the writing is about and what it means to you.

Select a book, an article, or a poem that you enjoyed reading. (See pages 236, 248, 254, and 260.)

Gather and organize details about your reading. (See pages 237, 249, 254–255, and 261.)

In the beginning paragraph, name the title and author and give the main idea. (See pages 238, 250, 256, and 262.)

In the middle paragraph, share important details from the reading. (See pages 240, 250, 256, and 262.)

In the ending paragraph, finish with an interesting thought. (See pages 241, 250, 256, and 262.)

Look over your **ideas**, **organization**, and **voice** first. Then check your **word choice** and **sentence fluency**. (See pages 242, 250, 256, and 262.)

Check your writing for conventions. Also have a classmate edit your writing. (See pages 243, 250, 256, and 262.)

Make a final copy and proofread it for errors before sharing it.

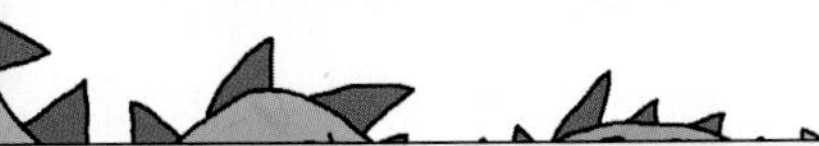

Response Writing in Review

Tell students to refer to these guidelines whenever they are asked to write a response to a book, an article, or a poem.

Continue to provide opportunities for students to read a variety of genres that include fiction, nonfiction, and poetry. Encourage students to take time to think and jot down feelings and thoughts about whatever they read. Not only is this a good way for them to practice response writing, but it is also a good way for them to grow into critical thinkers who know what they enjoy reading and why.

Creative Writing Overview

Common Core Standards Focus

Writing 3: Write narratives to develop real or imagined experiences or events using effective technique, descriptive details, and clear event sequences.

Language 2: Demonstrate command of the conventions of standard English capitalization, punctuation, and spelling when writing.

Writing Forms

- Writing Imaginative Stories
- Creating a Play
- Writing Poems

Focus on the Traits

- **Ideas** Choosing an interesting setting
- **Organization** Creating a plot about a problem and how the main character fixes it
- **Voice** Including dialogue to let characters speak for themselves
- **Word Choice** Using exciting action verbs
- **Sentence Fluency** Writing sentences that read smoothly
- **Conventions** Checking for errors in capitalization, punctuation, spelling, and grammar

Literature Connections

- **"Abuelita's Lap"** by Pat Mora

Technology Connections

Write Source Online

www.hmheducation.com/writesource

- ***Net-text***
- ***Bookshelf***
- ***GrammarSnap***
- ***Portfolio***
- ***Writing Network features***
- ***File Cabinet***

Interactive Whiteboard Lessons

Suggested Writing Stories Unit (Two Weeks)

Week	Day	Writing and Skills Instruction	*Student Edition*: Creative Writing Unit	*Student Edition*: Resource Units*	*SkillsBook*	*Daily Language Workouts*	*Write Source Online*
Week 1	1	**Writing Imaginative Stories:** (Model) Literature Connections "Abuelita's Lap"	270–273			52–53, 101	*Interactive Whiteboard Lessons*
	2–3	(Prewriting)	274–275				*Net-text*
	4–5	(Writing)	276				*Net-text*
Week 2	6–8	(Revising, Editing)	277				*Net-text*
		Skills Activity: • Punctuating Dialogue		470 (+), 476 (+)		54–55, 102	
		• Interjections		554 (+)			*GrammarSnap*
		• Pronouns		382, 536 (+)	127–128, 129–130		*GrammarSnap*
	9–10 *opt.*	*Creating a Play*	278–279				

* These units are also located in the back of the *Teacher's Edition.* Resource Units include "Basic Grammar and Writing," "A Writer's Resource," and "Proofreader's Guide."
(+) This activity is located in a different section of the *Write Source Student Edition.* If students have already completed this activity, you may wish to review it at this time.

Suggested Writing Poems Unit (Two Weeks)

Week	Day	Writing and Skills Instruction	*Student Edition*: Creative Writing Unit	*Student Edition*: Resource Units*	*SkillsBook*	*Daily Language Workouts*	*Write Source Online*
Week 1	1	**Poems: Rhyming Poem** (Model)	282–283			56–57, 103	
	2–3	(Prewriting)	284–287				*Net-text*
	4–5	(Writing)	288				*Net-text*
Week 2	6	(Revising)	289			58–59, 104	*Net-text*
		Skills Activity: • Adverbs		392, 550 (+)	161–162		*GrammarSnap*
		• Modeling Sentences		412–413			
		• Parts of Speech (review)		558 (+)	167–168		
	7–8	(Editing)	289				*Net-text*
		Skills Activity: • Spelling		503–504 (+), 506 (+)	61–62		
	9–10 *opt.*	• *Other Forms (limerick, clerihew, 5 W's, alphabet)*	290–293				

* These units are also located in the back of the *Teacher's Edition.* Resource Units include "Basic Grammar and Writing," "A Writer's Resource," and "Proofreader's Guide."
(+) This activity is located in a different section of the *Write Source Student Edition.* If students have already completed this activity, you may wish to review it at this time.

Teacher's Notes for Creative Writing

This overview for creative writing includes some specific suggestions for teaching the unit.

Writing Focus

Writing Imaginative Stories (pages 270–281)

Children love hearing stories and telling stories. Children often invent imaginative scenarios as they play. When children channel these creative energies into story writing, they can produce wonderful, finished products.

Creating a Play (pages 278–279)

Writing a play can be an inviting experience for children, especially if the play is based on a familiar fairy tale or fable. Young children often create impromptu plays in school and in their free time. Writing scripts is an outlet for students' natural speaking skills. Plays are made up of dialogue—a form of language that students know as "the way people talk." Also, writing plays, which are meant to be performed, provides students with a keen awareness of an audience for their writing. Plays, like stories, have settings, characters, and problems to be solved. Plays are stories filled with dialogue that are brought to life by actors. A way for students to understand how plays work is for them to turn the stories they have just written into plays.

Writing Poems (pages 282–293)

Like all writing, poetry depends upon the wise use of words. Young children enjoy traditional poetry with its rhyme, rhythm, and predictable structure. Students may find rhyme a challenge, but the rhyming list on SE page 287 should help them see possibilities in the words they choose. This chapter explores each step in the process, helping students to develop their poems. Students will get a chance to try several different types of poems.

Academic Vocabulary

Read aloud the academic terms, as well as the descriptions and questions. Model for students how to read one question and answer it. Have partners monitor their understanding and seek clarification of the terms by working through the meanings and questions together.

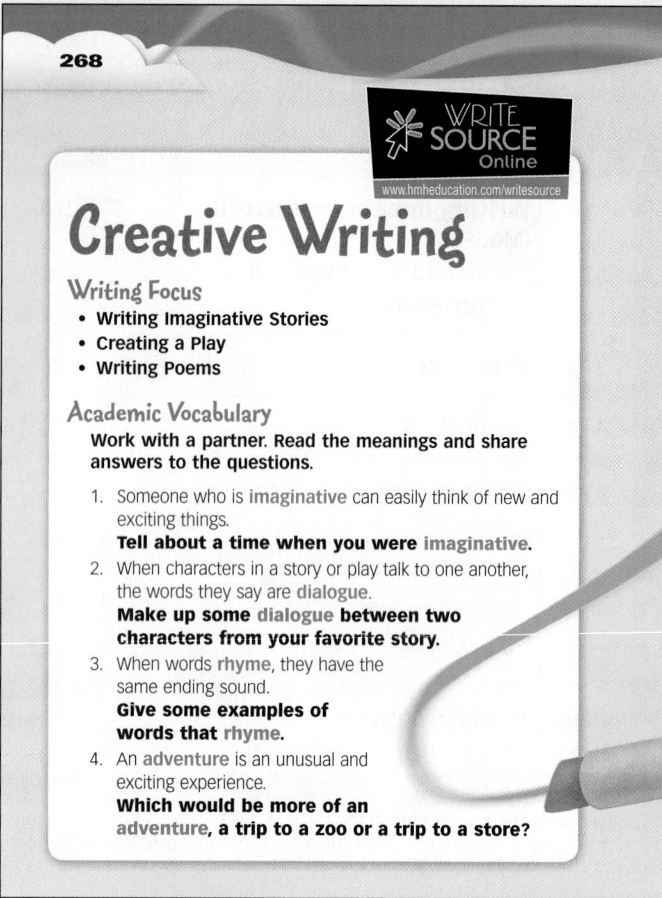

268
WRITE SOURCE Online
www.hmheducation.com/writesource
Creative Writing
Writing Focus
• Writing Imaginative Stories
• Creating a Play
• Writing Poems
Academic Vocabulary
Work with a partner. Read the meanings and share answers to the questions.
1. Someone who is imaginative can easily think of new and exciting things.
Tell about a time when you were imaginative.
2. When characters in a story or play talk to one another, the words they say are dialogue.
Make up some dialogue between two characters from your favorite story.
3. When words rhyme, they have the same ending sound.
Give some examples of words that rhyme.
4. An adventure is an unusual and exciting experience.
Which would be more of an adventure, a trip to a zoo or a trip to a store?

Minilessons

Story Talk — Writing Imaginative Stories

- **PRACTICE** writing dialogue.
  - **CHOOSE** one of the following situations to write about in a dialogue between a child and a parent or guardian.
    Planning a fun afternoon
    Doing household chores
    Having computer time
    Explaining how something got broken (or lost)

Play Along — Creating a Play

- **INVITE** your classmates to do impromptu skits.
  - **GIVE** them basic situations (at the zoo, riding a bus, planning a party, in a storm, solving a mystery) on note cards.
  - **LET** them improvise dialogue and actions.

An Ear for Words — Writing Poems

- **LOOK** at the sound words on SE page 286 and the rhyme words on SE page 287. **WRITE** as many sound words as you can think of. Then **LIST** rhyming words (don't use the ones on SE page 287).

Detective Poem — Writing Poems

- Be a detective and a poet.
  - **WRITE** a 5 W's poem.
  - **ANSWER** the five questions: Who? What? When? Where? and Why? See the poem on the top of SE page 292. Then **READ** only lines 2–5 to a partner or the class. It is a riddle. Can your listeners guess the "who" of your poem?

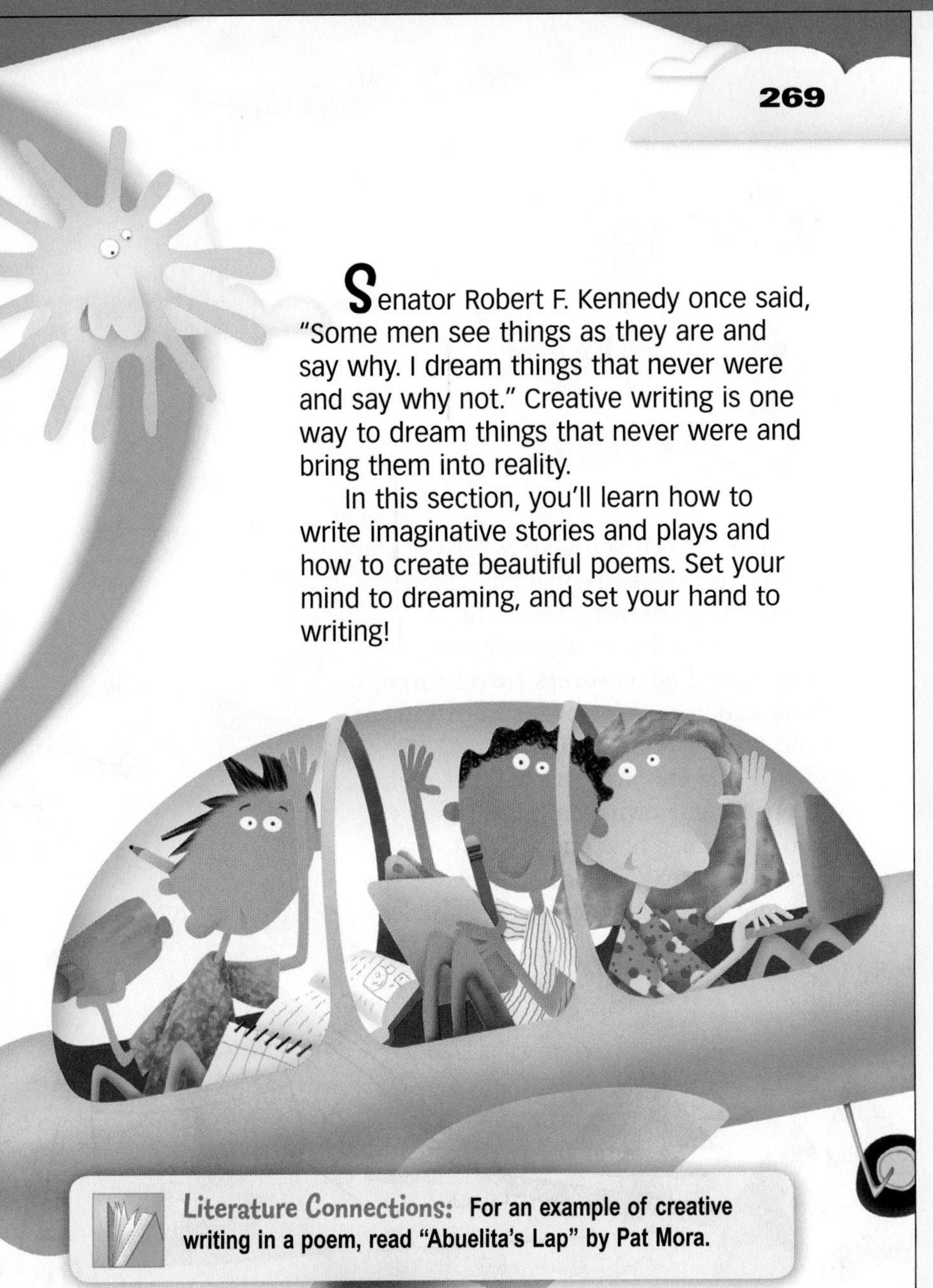

Senator Robert F. Kennedy once said, "Some men see things as they are and say why. I dream things that never were and say why not." Creative writing is one way to dream things that never were and bring them into reality.

In this section, you'll learn how to write imaginative stories and plays and how to create beautiful poems. Set your mind to dreaming, and set your hand to writing!

Literature Connections: For an example of creative writing in a poem, read "Abuelita's Lap" by Pat Mora.

Creative Writing

Tell students that the term *creative writing* usually refers to fiction (made-up stories), plays, and poems. Explain that this doesn't mean other kinds of writing aren't creative. It takes creativity to write about real people and events, too.

Ask students to think about their favorite fictional stories. Then have them name the stories and tell what they like best about

- the events: Are they action-packed, funny, sad, familiar, or strange?
- the characters: Are they brave, funny, or weird?
- the setting: Is it familiar, faraway, in the past, in the future, or entirely made up?

As students name stories, write them on the board. Have students begin making a reading list by writing down the titles of the books that appeal to them. Give them regular opportunities to respond to the books they have enjoyed reading and would recommend to classmates.

Literature Connections

In the poem "Abuelita's Lap," the author uses various poetic devices, such as rhythm and rhyme, to describe the loving relationship she has with her grandmother.

Have students identify their favorite image in the poem and share how it conveys the author's feelings. For additional models of creative writing, see the Reading-Writing Connections beginning on page TE-36.

Family Connection Letters

As you begin this unit, send home the Creative Writing Family Connection letter, which describes what students will be learning.

- Letter in English (TE p. 607)
- Letter in Spanish (TE p. 615)

Writing
Imaginative Stories

Objectives

- Understand the content and structure of short stories and plays.
- Choose a topic (an adventure with the student as the main character) to write about.
- Plan, draft, revise, and edit a short story, and then revise it as a play script.
- Become familiar with special terms related to fiction.

Play a group storytelling game.

- Begin the story with an interesting sentence. (For example: One sunny day when eight-year-old twins Samuel and Samantha were jumping on the trampoline in the backyard, they heard a strange noise.)
- Ask volunteers to add one sentence to the story.
- Ask the last few students to bring the story to an end.

Distribute drawing supplies. Have students illustrate any part of the story they wish. Display the pictures in the room.

Technology Connections

Use this unit's Interactive Whiteboard Lesson to introduce creative writing.

Interactive Whiteboard Lesson

Writing

Imaginative Stories

"Let me tell you a story!" Ever since prehistoric times, people have been telling stories. Heroes fight monsters, explorers discover new worlds, and adventurers travel through time and space. A story is born in the storyteller's imagination.

In this chapter, you will get a chance to write your own imaginative story. You'll also see how one student, Rosa, wrote her story. Before she began, she thought about how stories are made.

Materials

Drawing supplies (TE p. 270)

Copy of "Jack and the Beanstalk" (TE p. 271)

Drawing paper (TE p. 271)

Map showing Vancouver, Canada, and Puget Sound (TE p. 272)

That's Good! That's Bad! by Margery Cuyler (TE p. 273)

Drawing paper (TE p. 275)

Selection of stories (TE p. 276)

Colored pencils (TE p. 278)

Props and costumes (TE p. 279)

Copy Masters

T-Chart (TE pp. 274, 275)

Time Line (TE p. 275)

Response Sheet (TE p. 277)

Writing Stories 271

Understanding Stories

All stories have four basic ingredients:

Characters are the people or animals in the story.

Setting is the time when and the place where the story happens. The setting can change throughout the story.

Conflict is a problem or challenge the characters face.

Plot is what happens in the story. (See page 281 for more information.)

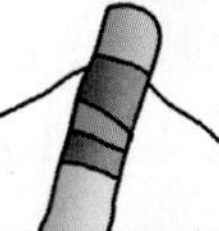

Read the beginning of "Jack and the Beanstalk." Find the characters, the setting, the conflict, and the first thing that happens in the plot.

A long time ago, in a faraway land, there lived a poor widow and her son Jack. They had nothing to live on except their cow's milk. One day, things got so hopeless that the widow sent Jack to the market to sell the cow. . . .

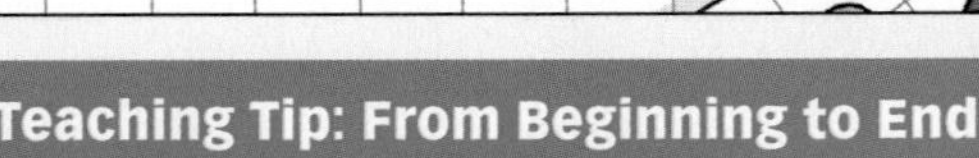

Understanding Stories

After students have read the beginning of "Jack and the Beanstalk," draw a simple story map on the board (see SE page 440) and work with students to identify the characters, setting, conflict, and first event in the plot.

- Characters: Jack and his mother (Based on this paragraph alone, the cow could be a character, but the rest of the story would show that's not the case.)
- Setting: long ago (time) and far away (place)
- Conflict: Jack and his mother are very poor and desperately need money.
- Plot: Jack goes to the market to sell the family's cow.

Emphasize that this is only the **beginning of the story** *(see below)*. Then, discuss the term *conflict*. Explain that the conflict, which the author introduces at the beginning of the story, sets the whole story in motion. Other problems and challenges will come up as the story goes on (during what's called the *rising action*).

Teaching Tip: From Beginning to End

To extend this exercise and apply the concepts to a familiar story, read students a full version of the story "Jack and the Beanstalk." Then turn to SE page 281, and read and discuss a plot line. Draw a plot line on the chalkboard, and label the various parts of the plot line as students name them. Have students identify all the parts of the plot of "Jack and the Beanstalk":

- the beginning,
- rising action (along with its complications),
- high point, and
- ending.

Struggling Learners

To review the story elements, have each student choose a familiar story—such as a folktale or fairy tale. Give each student a sheet of blank paper to be folded into four blocks. Have students label each block with one of the story elements. Then have them list or draw pictures of the characters, setting, conflict, and any event of the plot.

Imaginative Story

Have students take turns reading the paragraphs of the story aloud. Then ask them to identify the following:

- characters (Rosa, her mother, Shelly)
- settings (a rainy Saturday in Rosa's kitchen, Rosa's backyard, Puget Sound)
- conflict (Rosa misses her friend, Shelly, who has moved away.)

Talk about the other problems Rosa experiences during the story and how they are resolved:

- She meets a killer whale, but instead of harming her, it helps her.
- A seagull overturns Rosa's boat, but Shelly rescues her.

Readers may have different views of what the high point of the story is. Rosa thinks of the high point as the moment when the whale blows the boat toward Canada. Help readers see that without this action, Rosa wouldn't have been found by Shelly.

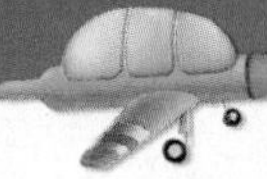

Imaginative Story

Here is the make-believe story that Rosa wrote. It tells about her adventure in a paper boat.

Beginning

The beginning tells about the characters, the setting, and the conflict or problem.

Rising Action

The rising action tells what happens in the first part of the story.

The story shares actions and speaking (dialogue).

Sailing on a Paper Dream

One rainy Saturday, I sat at the kitchen window. What a boring day! I told my mom, "I wish Shelly hadn't moved to Vancouver."

Mom said, "Maybe you can visit her, Rosa."

That gave me an idea. I drew a crayon picture of myself with a life jacket on. Then I made a paper boat and put the picture inside.

"I'm going out for a second," I told my mom. I ran out into the rain! In back of my house, there was a tiny stream of water. I put my boat in the water. It sailed away.

Then something amazing happened. The picture of me jumped on shore. The real me was in the paper boat! I floated down the stream, through a tunnel, and over a huge waterfall!

"Woo!" I shouted and held onto the side.

The boat splashed down in Puget Sound. It floated out across the water. Then the water under the boat turned hard and black. It was the back of a killer whale! "What are you doing on my back?" asked the whale.

English Language Learners

Before reading Rosa's story, help students understand one of the settings by

- pointing out Puget Sound and Vancouver, Canada, on a map and
- explaining that the multiple-meaning word *sound* means "a long inlet of the ocean."

Writing Stories 273

High Point The high point is the most exciting part.

I said, "I'm going to Vancouver."

The whale turned north and blew hard. The boat went flying through the air, halfway to Canada.

Suddenly, a seagull flew down, grabbed my boat, and dumped me out. The bird flew off, wearing my boat like a hat. I was left in the water, bobbing around in my life jacket.

Then I felt a hand on my shoulder. Someone pulled me out of the water into another paper boat.

Ending The ending tells how everything works out.

"Shelly!" I shouted when I looked up. "What are you doing here?"

My friend smiled. "I was bored, so I made a boat, and I sailed out to find you!"

Answer these questions about my story!

After you read . . .

- **Ideas** (1) What makes Rosa's story interesting?
- **Organization** (2) What problem does Rosa have, and how does she fix it?
- **Word Choice** (3) Find three strong action verbs that make Rosa's story exciting.

Focus on the surprise ending of the story: Who should Rosa meet in the middle of the sea but the very person she was going to visit! Explain that this strategy in fiction is known as a "plot twist."

To emphasize this idea to students, read them the picture book *That's Good! That's Bad!* by Margery Cuyler, which contains a funny plot twist on every other page.

After you read . . .

Answers

Ideas 1. Possible answers:

- the magical elements, such as the way Rosa gets into the boat and the talking whale
- the twist at the end—learning that Shelly did the same thing as Rosa by setting out in a paper boat to meet *her*

Organization 2. Problem: Rosa misses her friend Shelly. Solution: She decides to go visit her—in a most unusual way.

Word Choice 3. Possible choices: ran, jumped, floated, shouted, splashed, blew, went flying, was bobbing, pulled

English Language Learners

Students may have difficulty differentiating an imaginative story from a personal narrative because both can be about themselves. Remind students that the personal narratives they wrote were about real-life experiences. Point out that in a narrative, the characters speak and act as they do in real life.

Explain that in an imaginative story—which is make-believe—characters might do and say things that they could not possibly do in real life. Things can happen that do not follow the rules of nature. Have students give examples from Rosa's story.

Advanced Learners

Challenge students to think of a different event that could take place instead of Rosa's meeting the whale. Then have them tell how this would affect the rest of the story. Could the story still end the same way? If not, ask them to come up with an event that would lead the story to the same ending.

Prewriting Choosing a Setting

Before students read the page, write the sentence starter "What if I . . . ?" on the board. Explain that good ideas for stories come from different sources:

- setting
- characters
- a conflict, or problem
- even simply an image, such as seeing a boat sailing on the horizon in the rain

Have students think of two or three endings to the sentence starter, keeping themselves open to many sources of inspiration. Encourage them to let their imaginations go and to be as wild, strange, or funny as they'd like.

When students have chosen a *What if I* sentence to focus on for their story, ask them to begin thinking about the other characters involved, the setting, and the plot.

Have students read SE pages 274 and 275 and ask them to decide which page they'd like to focus on first. Some may prefer to work on plot before picking a setting.

Provide photocopies of the reproducible T-Chart (TE page 595) for students to use as their Setting List. Have students use the column headings *Places* and *Times*.

Technology Connections

Students can use the added features of the Net-text as they explore this stage of the writing process.

Write Source Online **Net-text**

Prewriting Choosing a Setting

You will be the main character in your story. First, you need to choose an interesting setting. Rosa made a list of places and times. Then she drew a line to connect a time and a place to be the setting for her story. (Remember, the setting of a story can change.)

Prewrite **Make a list of places and times.**

1. **List places in one column.**
2. **List times in another column.**
3. **Connect a place and a time with a line.**

Ideas

Setting List

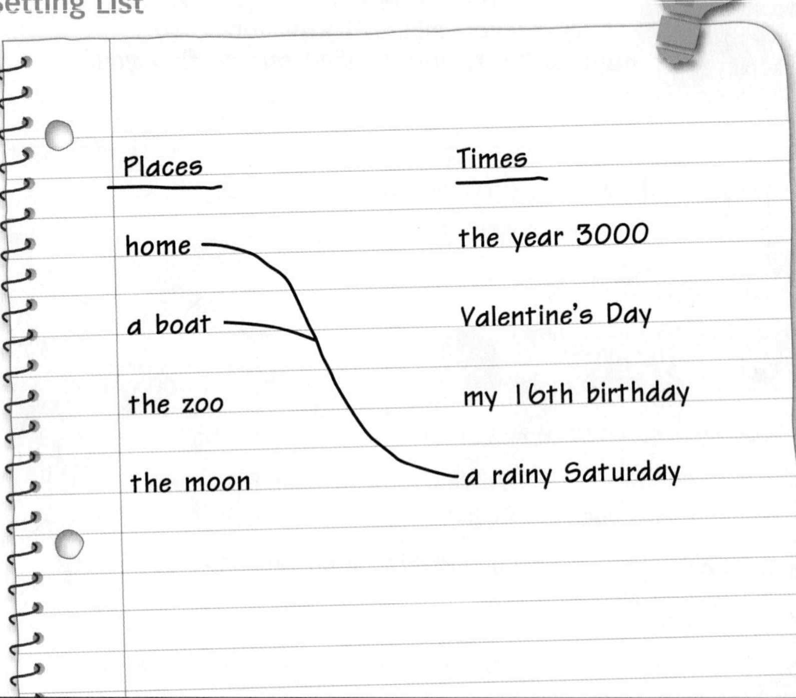

Places
Times
home
the year 3000
a boat
Valentine's Day
the zoo
my 16th birthday
the moon
a rainy Saturday

Writing Stories 275

Thinking About Your Plot

The plot is what happens in a story. Rosa imagined herself in a boat on a rainy Saturday (her setting). Then she answered the following plot questions.

Answer these plot questions.

1. What big problem do I face?
2. What amazing thing do I do?
3. What else happens?
4. What goes wrong?

Plot Questions

1. What big problem do I face?
I feel bored. I miss my friend Shelly.

2. What amazing thing do I do?
I make a paper boat and sail away to see her.

3. What else happens?
A whale blows me north!

4. What goes wrong?
A seagull takes my boat and dumps me out.

Prewriting Thinking About Your Plot

Have students plan the order of events in their stories by making storyboards of the plot:

- Give each student a large piece of drawing paper.
- Have students fold their paper in half three times, twice lengthwise and once across the width. When they unfold it, they will have eight boxes of equal size.
- Ask students to use the sections on the paper to make an eight-frame storyboard of their story.

As an alternative to making a storyboard, provide photocopies of the reproducible Time Line (TE page 598) for students to use in working out their plot. Instruct students to leave enough room between items in the time line for details they might think of later.

Remind students that since a short story is not very long, they should limit to one or two the number of characters in addition to themselves, and limit their settings and problems to two or three of each at most.

Struggling Learners

Students may be overwhelmed by the number of plot questions they must answer just to plan their stories. To simplify the task, have students use a T-Chart (TE page 595) and label the columns *Problem* and *Solution*. Have students write these questions in the appropriate column of their charts, leaving room to write the answers afterward:

- What caused the problem? (Problem column)
- Why is it a problem? (Problem column)
- How will the characters try to solve the problem? (Solution column)
- How is the problem finally solved? (Solution column)

Advanced Learners

To extend the writing activity, challenge students to think of several ways to solve the problem in their story. After they choose the solution, have them brainstorm several ways their characters can attempt to arrive at the solution. Have students include two or three of these attempts in the story before the problem is finally resolved.

Writing Putting Your Story on Paper

Suggest that students begin their stories by writing down the part of it that is clearest in their minds. Stress that this does not have to be the beginning sentence. Assure students that they can go back and fill in any missing parts of the story.

To give students different ideas of how to begin a story, read a selection of story openers to the class. Ask them if each opening sentence would make them want to read more, and why.

If the schedule permits, have students find a good opening sentence to a story they've read and share it with the class.

Point out that instead of any of the sample starting strategies shown, they might begin by setting the scene with straightforward description, as Rosa did (SE page 272): One rainy Saturday, I sat at the kitchen window.

Technology Connections

Students can use the added features of the Net-text as they explore this stage of the writing process.

Write Source Online ***Net-text***

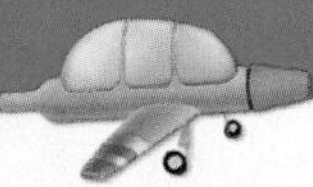

Writing Putting Your Story on Paper

Now you have a main character (you!) and a setting. You also know what happens, so you're ready to write.

Write your first draft.

1. **Follow the tips below.**
2. **When you finish, create a title for your story.**

Here are two ways to get started.

Start with action.

Lightning flashed, and rain pounded on the roof.

OR

Begin with someone talking.

"Why did Shelly have to move away?" I asked.

Here are two ways to keep going.

Introduce a new problem.

Suddenly, a seagull flew down, grabbed my boat, and . . .

OR

Add a new twist.

Someone pulled me out of the water . . .

Struggling Learners

Students may need more structure to help them begin their stories. Provide them with the following story starters and tell them they can always go back and rewrite the beginning if they find a better way.

- Once there was . . .
- One day I . . .
- A long time ago . . .

Writing Stories 277

Revising Improving Your Writing

When you revise, you make sure your story is clear and exciting, and that it reads smoothly. The questions below can help you.

Answer these questions.

1. Did I include enough interesting details?
2. Did I tell about a problem? Did I solve the problem in the end?
3. Did I use exciting action verbs?

Editing Checking for Conventions

When you edit, you make sure your writing is correct.

Check your editing.

1. Did I end my sentences with punctuation?
2. Did I begin my sentences with capital letters?
3. Have I used quotation marks for the speaking parts (dialogue)?
4. Have I checked my spelling?

Revising Improving Your Writing

Have students begin their revisions by reading their stories aloud to a partner and soliciting a **peer response** *(see below)*. Distribute copies of the reproducible Response Sheet (TE page 592) for listeners to fill out.

Editing Checking for Conventions

Focus on the conventions for writing dialogue:

- Start a new paragraph for each new speaker.
- Identify the speaker by using a "speaker tag," such as *he said* or *Mariel whispered*.
- Separate speaker tags and speech with a comma, unless an exclamation point or question mark is used:
  - He said, "That's my book."
  - "That's my book," he said.
  - "That's my book!" he yelled.
  - "Is that your book?" he asked.

* For more about using quotation marks to set off spoken words, see SE pages 476–477.

Technology Connections

Have students use the Writing Network features of the Net-text to comment on each other's drafts.

***Write Source Online* Net-text**

Teaching Tip: Peer Response

It's important for students to establish good habits in responding to other people's writing, either one-on-one or in a group. Remind them that they should always

- listen to or read the piece carefully;
- respond in a friendly, polite way;
- make their comments as specific as possible;
- ask questions that require an explanation instead of just a "yes" or "no" answer; and
- respect the ideas and feelings expressed by other group members.

Grammar Connection

Punctuating Dialogue

- **Proofreader's Guide** pages 470 (+), 476 (+)

Interjections

- **Proofreader's Guide** page 554 (+)
- ***GrammarSnap*** Kinds of Sentences

Pronouns

- **Proofreader's Guide** page 536 (+)
- ***Write Source*** page 382
- ***GrammarSnap*** Pronouns, Subject and Object
- ***SkillsBook*** pages 127–128, 129–130

Creating a Play

Have students compare Rosa's short story to the excerpt from her play and point out differences. For example, in the story, Rosa, the narrator, says, "What a boring day!" In the play, the character Rosa says, "I'm bored."

Help students start on their own scripts by:

- giving each student a photocopy of his or her finished story and two different colored pencils;
- asking students to underline all the dialogue in the story with one of the pencils;
- having them use the same pencil to underline anything they think they can turn into dialogue; and
- instructing them to switch pencils and underline everything in the story that is best presented as action.

Explain that students will have to add dialogue or action to the parts of the story that are still not underlined. Suggest that students avoid using dialogue just to "tell" what's going on, which is much less interesting than "showing."

* For more about "showing" and "telling," see SE page 146.

Creating a Play

You can turn your story into a play by acting it out. A play uses dialogue to tell the story. What the characters do is placed in parentheses. Here is the start of Rosa's play.

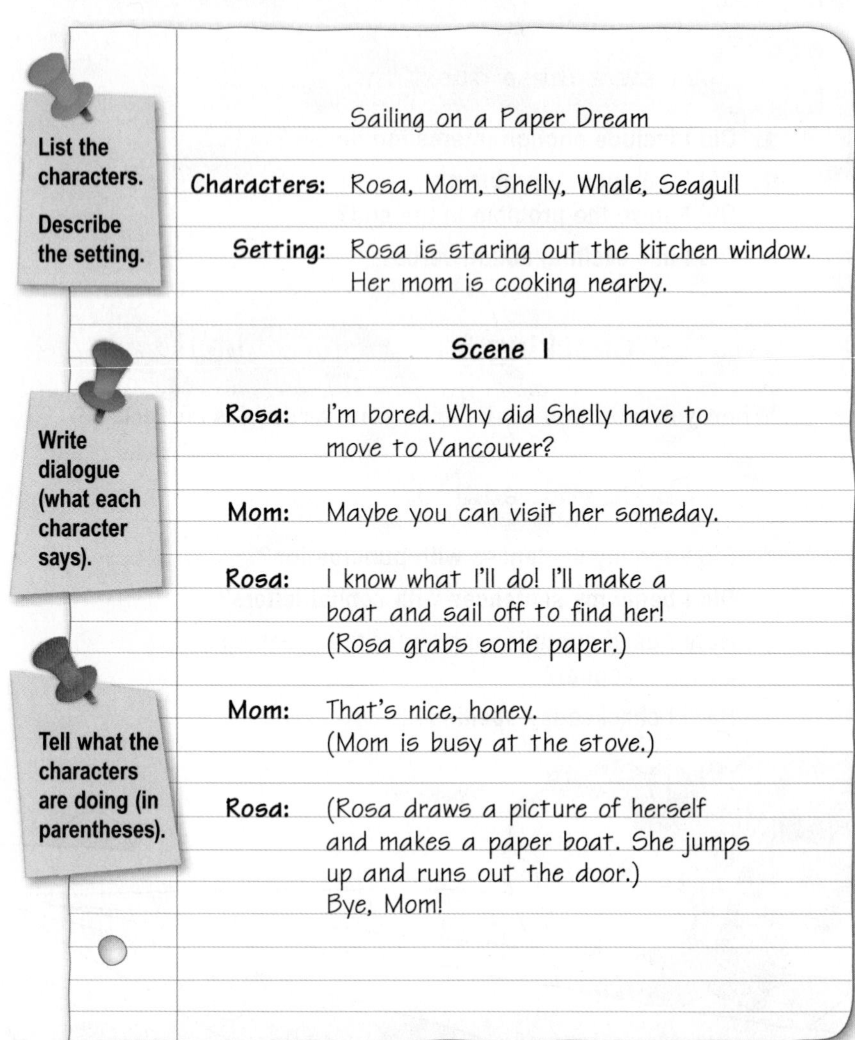

List the characters.
Describe the setting.
Write dialogue (what each character says).
Tell what the characters are doing (in parentheses).
Sailing on a Paper Dream
Characters: Rosa, Mom, Shelly, Whale, Seagull
Setting: Rosa is staring out the kitchen window. Her mom is cooking nearby.
Scene 1
Rosa: I'm bored. Why did Shelly have to move to Vancouver?
Mom: Maybe you can visit her someday.
Rosa: I know what I'll do! I'll make a boat and sail off to find her! (Rosa grabs some paper.)
Mom: That's nice, honey. (Mom is busy at the stove.)
Rosa: (Rosa draws a picture of herself and makes a paper boat. She jumps up and runs out the door.) Bye, Mom!

English Language Learners

Using the beginning of a volunteer's story, model turning it into the first scene of a play. Use the Think-Aloud process as you

- skim the story and list all the characters,
- describe the setting, and
- point out that quotation marks are not used as you write the dialogue.

Help students divide their stories into scenes by looking for places where the setting, characters, or action suddenly changes.

Advanced Learners

Have students choose a story they are all familiar with—such as a folktale or a fairy tale—to turn into a play. Divide the story into scenes, and have student pairs choose a section to turn into a script, using the process they have learned. Have students combine their scenes and act out their play for the rest of the class.

Create a new scene whenever the setting changes.

Scene 2

Setting: Rosa puts the boat in the ditch. Suddenly she is on board.

Rosa: Excellent! I'm Captain Rosa! (She floats through a tunnel.)

Oh, no! A waterfall! Woooo! (Rosa yells as the boat falls.)

That's better. Wait! This water seems hard! It's black! (The boat begins to rise on the back of a whale.)

A whale?

Whale: Who said that?

Rosa: It's me, Rosa.

Whale: What are you doing on my back?

Rosa: I'm trying to get to Vancouver.

Whale: Oh, I know where that is. Hold on! (The whale blows. Rosa and the boat fly into the air.)

Write **Turn your story into a play.**

1. **List your characters and describe the setting.**
2. **Use dialogue and lots of action to tell your story.**

Explain that each setting in a play is called a scene. When the setting—the time or location of the action—changes, the writer generally starts a new scene.

Tell students that an important part of writing stories is creating dialogue that sounds the way people really talk. Turning a story into a play focuses on the dialogue. Have the class work together in groups of three or four.

- Ask one student to read to the other group members the most interesting or exciting part of his or her story that will make up one scene of a play.
- Have students act out the scene, adding dialogue that sounds as realistic as possible.
- Tell writers to use ideas from these skits in their scripts.

Repeat the exercise until all students get a chance to be involved in the process.

Schedule readings of the finished scripts (one or two daily). If possible, create **full performances** *(see below)* of some. A script like Rosa's would make a good puppet show.

Teaching Tip: A Full Performance

Putting on a "full performance" of a play requires a large time commitment and a lot of planning, but it is a rewarding learning activity for most students. Not everyone has to perform, especially students who are self-conscious about their language skills or ability to memorize lines. Still, it is often worthwhile to encourage such students by giving them a small role, perhaps a line or two, to build self-confidence.

You could do all the planning, but it is much more fun—and educational—to have students do the work. Have them suggest costumes and props. Ask volunteers to gather or make them. They do not have to look "professional"; students enjoy seeing their work displayed. Help some students prepare written scripts, including stage directions, which you can photocopy. Show performers how to highlight their lines and cues and add stage directions as necessary.

Arrange for students to perform their play for another class or for a school assembly. Before performance day, make sure they have adequate time to practice so that they feel as comfortable as possible in front of the audience.

Learning Elements of Fiction

Tell students that the terms on this page will help them talk about their own and other writers' stories. Suggest that they refer to the page as needed. Provide longer explanations. For example:

- Not all stories have a moral. In a fable, the *moral* is written out at the end. In other stories, writers decide whether to include a moral. They usually work it into the story for readers to infer rather than state it at the end.
- A writer can have his or her own character be the story's *narrator* (as Rosa did) or have another character tell the story. Probably the most common kind of narrator, however, is an unnamed person who isn't part of the story but knows everything that happens.
- The *theme* is different from the moral, because it doesn't teach a lesson. It is the main thing the writer wants the story to communicate. The theme of Rosa's story is how strong her friendship with Shelly is.
- While some fictional stories could happen, and while some are even based on true events, the writer creates story elements, such as dialogue.

Learning Elements of Fiction

Writers use the following words and ideas when they write about stories.

The **action** is what happens in a story.

A **character** is a person or an animal in a story.

Conflict is a problem or challenge for the characters.

Dialogue is what characters say to each other.

An **event** is a specific happening.

Fiction is an imaginative or made-up story.

A **moral** is the lesson that a story (fable, tale, or myth) teaches.

The **narrator** is the person or character who is telling the story.

The **plot** is what happens, the series of events. (See the plot line on page 281.)

The **setting** is the time and place of a story.

The **theme** is the main idea or message.

Writing Stories 281

Understanding a Plot Line

Most stories follow a **plot line** that builds to the most exciting point. The plot line has four parts.

- The **beginning** introduces the characters, the setting, and the conflict.
- The **rising action** tells about problems that come up. It leads to the most exciting part of the story.
- The **high point** is the most exciting part of the story.
- The **ending** tells how things finally turn out.

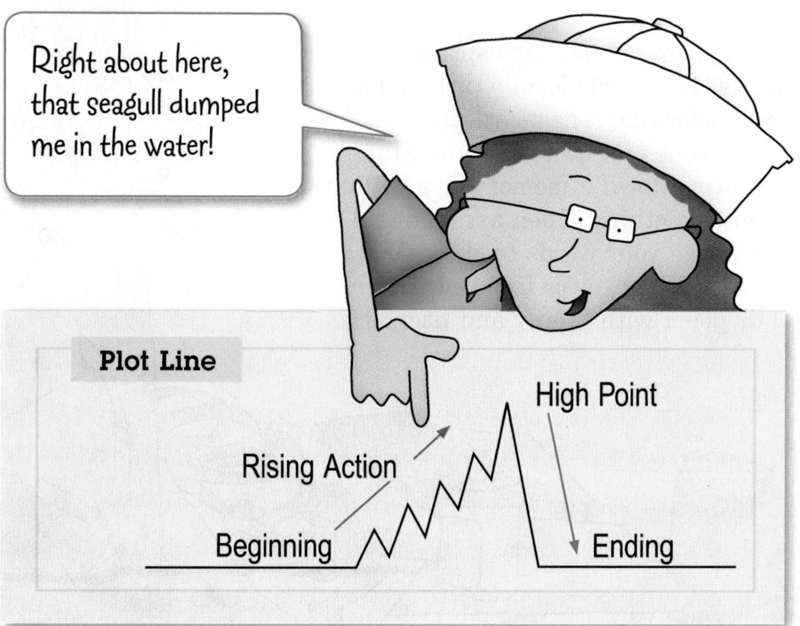

Understanding a Plot Line

On the chalkboard, draw a plot line for Rosa's story and show students how each part of the plot line applies to her story.

If the class has read and mapped out "Jack and the Beanstalk," (TE page 271), review the plot line. Then have students draw the plot line of their story, indicating what happened for each part and labeling each spike in the rising action.

Have students share their plot line with the class.

Writer's Craft

Plot Line: One way to teach the plot line is to graph a really great experience a student has had. While the student tells about the experience, note the student's level of excitement, using a graph like the following:

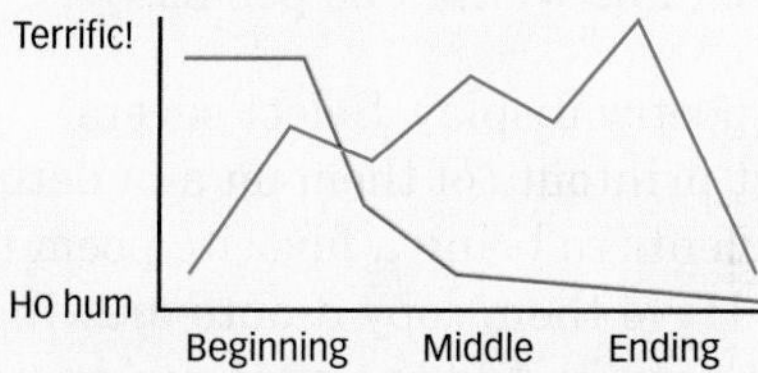

Great experiences tend to follow the plot chart. Graph a few bad experiences so that students can see the different path they take. Show students that the reason for the plot chart is that writers want readers to have a great experience as they read.

English Language Learners

Use a thermometer analogy to help students understand the plot line chart. Explain that the action rises like the column on a thermometer. The action becomes "hotter" as the events become more exciting. After the high point, problems are solved and things settle down, or cool off, like the column falling on a thermometer.

Writing Poems

Objectives

- Understand the content and form of a rhyming poem.
- Choose a topic (something happy or sad) to write about.
- Plan, draft, revise, and edit a rhyming poem.
- Practice writing poetry in different forms: limerick, clerihew, 5 W's poem, and alphabet poem.

In poetry, a writer uses words the way an artist uses paint to represent an image or idea. Ask students to name poems they know. Help them come up with ideas by mentioning that in addition to classic poetry collections such as *Mother Goose*, they probably have read picture books based on poems. Point out that the words to many songs can be written as poems.

Create a class poetry display. Select several poems and post printouts of them on a bulletin board. Ask students to bring a favorite poem to class to share. Have them copy it onto drawing paper and illustrate it. Add the students' poetry choices to the bulletin board.

Creative Writing

Writing Poems

A poem is a feeling captured in words. The words form a picture for the reader like a postcard!

Anyone can write a poem. Start by jotting down a memory or a feeling about something. Then arrange and rearrange your words to show your feeling. When you're finished, share your poem with family and friends.

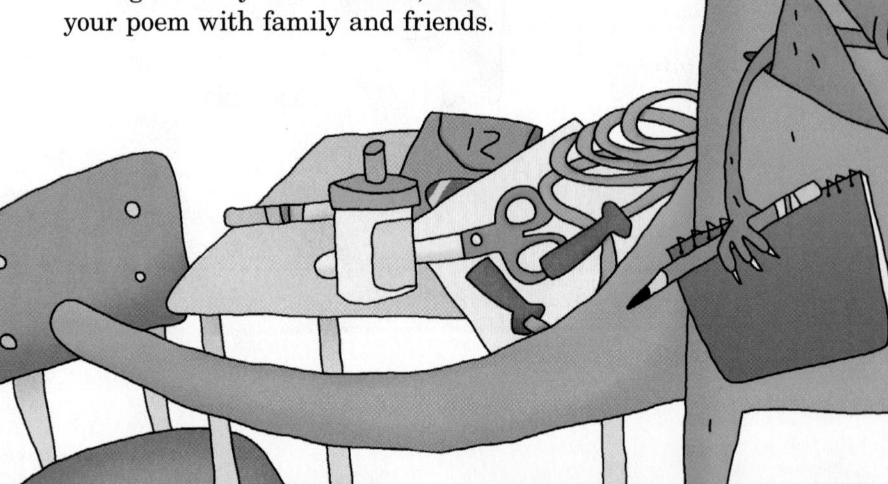

Materials

Selection of poems and drawing supplies (TE p. 282)

Selection of rhyming poems (TE p. 283)

Selection of limericks (TE p. 290)

Thesaurus (TE p. 290)

Photograph of a helicopter (TE p. 292)

Copy Masters

T-Chart and Sensory Chart (TE p. 284)

5 W's Chart (TE p. 292)

Writing Poems 283

Rhyming Poem

Some poems use pairs of rhyming words. Rhymes are fun to read and easy to remember. Marta wrote the rhyming poem below to describe how she feels about jumping rope.

Jump to It!

When a jump rope starts to spin,
I can't help but get a grin.
I like to hear a jump rope whir,
And watch it swinging in a blur.
When a jump rope slaps the street,
It gives rhythm to my feet.
I jump and jump until I pant.
Then I end my jump rope chant.

After you read . . .

- **Ideas** (1) What does the poem make you see and hear?
- **Organization** (2) What are the pairs of rhyming words in this poem?
- **Word Choice** (3) How does Marta feel about jumping rope?

English Language Learners

Help students who have trouble understanding the vocabulary in the poem by explaining the meanings of the following words and phrases:

- whir (sound of something in fast motion)
- blur (something that goes by too fast to see)
- slaps the street (hits, or smacks, the pavement)
- pant (breathe hard)
- chant (rap or song)

Rhyming Poem

Point out to students that not only do the words at the ends of the lines rhyme, but also the lines have a special rhythm. Read the poem aloud to the class, emphasizing the beats in the lines. Copy it onto the board and underline the stressed words or syllables to demonstrate:

When a <u>jump</u> rope <u>starts</u> to <u>spin</u>,
<u>I</u> can't <u>help</u> but <u>get</u> a <u>grin</u>.
<u>I</u> <u>like</u> to <u>hear</u> a <u>jump</u> rope <u>whir</u>,
<u>And</u> <u>watch</u> it <u>swinging</u> <u>in</u> a <u>blur</u>.
<u>When</u> a <u>jump</u> rope <u>slaps</u> the <u>street</u>,
<u>It</u> gives <u>rhythm</u> <u>to</u> my <u>feet</u>.
<u>I</u> <u>jump</u> and <u>jump</u> <u>until</u> I <u>pant</u>.
<u>Then</u> I <u>end</u> my <u>jump</u> rope <u>chant</u>.

Explain that students can use different rhythms for their poems. Read examples of some rhyming poems with other rhythms.

After you read . . .

Answers

Ideas **1.** Possible answers:

- jump rope spinning
- grinning girl
- jump rope slapping street
- girl jumping rope

Organization **2.** spin/grin; whir/blur; street/feet; pant/chant

Word Choice **3.** Jumping rope makes her happy.

Prewriting Selecting a Topic

Provide photocopies of the reproducible T-Chart (TE page 595) for students to fill out.

To help students think of topics, suggest occasions that might have inspired happy or sad feelings:

- a special experience or a holiday
- things they do with their best friend
- winning or losing a game with their sports team
- a time when they couldn't have what they wanted

Technology Connections

Students can use the added features of the Net-text as they explore this stage of the writing process.

 *Write Source Online* **Net-text**

Prewriting Selecting a Topic

A poem can be about anything: a pet, a friend, an adventure, a holiday, the mumps. Choose something that gives you a happy or sad feeling. To find a topic, you can list ideas on a T-chart.

Find a topic.

1. **Make a T-chart like the one below. List at least three things that make you happy and three that make you sad.**
2. **Then choose one of these happy or sad things as a topic for your poem.**

T-Chart

Organization
Happy Feelings
Sad Feelings
• a new kitten
• jumping rope
• Thanksgiving dinner
• a bubble bath
• building a dollhouse
• cold, rainy days
• when my goldfish died
• when Sandra moved away

Struggling Learners

Students may benefit from drawing a detailed picture of the topic they choose to write about. Have students label the picture with what they see, hear, and so on. Some students may want to use their pictures to draft their poems. Others may prefer to organize the information first in a sensory chart.

Gathering Details

A poem builds pictures with words that share sensory details. Once you choose your topic, you can make a sensory chart to gather details.

Gather details to create word pictures.

1. **Make a sensory chart like the one below.**
2. **In each column, list details that will help the reader see and feel your topic.**

Sensory Chart

Topic: jumping rope

See	Hear	Smell	Taste	Touch
white rope ends	whirring rope	fresh air	salty sweat on my lips	soft rope
blur	rope slapping the street			rough sidewalk
rope swingers	everybody chanting			hair in my face
line of jumpers				

Prewriting Gathering Details

Tell students to think of as many details as they can before writing their poems. However, tell them that they need not use all the details listed on their sensory chart. Do suggest, however, that students include details from two or more senses.

Have students compare Marta's sensory chart with her poem. Which details did she use?

- sight: blur
- hearing: whirring, rope slapping street, chanting

Sensory Chart

Distribute photocopies of the reproducible Sensory Chart (TE page 596) for students to use as they gather details.

Before students begin filling in the chart, have them sit quietly for a few minutes, close their eyes, and visualize the experience they're planning to write about. Have them take a moment to think about each of the five senses. What can they see, hear, smell, taste, or touch as they imagine the scene?

Literature Connections

Sensory details: To help students understand how sensory details make for a strong poem, use published poetry. See anthologies such as *Ten-Second Rainshowers: Poems by Young People* by Sandford Lyne and Virginia Halstead, and *The Palm of My Heart: Poetry by African American Children* by Davida Adedjouma, Gregory Christie, and Lucille Clifton. Read a poem aloud and have students analyze the poem by filling in a sensory details chart. Then discuss how each detail adds to the feeling of the poem.

Prewriting Using Pleasing Sounds

Tell students that their words will help their readers or listeners to visualize their images.

Encourage students to collect all kinds of words—words with interesting meanings and sounds. Suggest that they write the words and their definitions in a small notebook to keep with them.

* For information about learning new words, see SE pages 449–452.

To help students begin using onomatopoeia, challenge them to create their own sound words. Divide the class into teams. Give each team a setting to describe, for example, a busy street corner.

- Ask each team to contribute sounds they would hear.
- Have the other teams guess what setting or scenario the sounds represent.
- Write students' sound words on a class chart for them to use in poems.

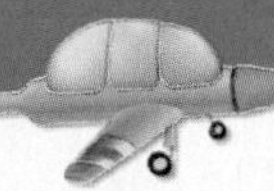

Prewriting Using Pleasing Sounds

Poets use different ways to make their writing sing!

Rhyme: Rhyme is one way to make pleasing sounds. Poets and songwriters often use rhyming words at the end of lines.

I bought my pig
A curly wig.

Summer is fun.
Give me the sun!

Sound Words: Poets use words like *buzz* and *snap* that sound like the noise they name. Using these words is called *onomatopoeia* (ŏn′ ə-măt′ ə-pē′ ə).

Buzz, buzz, hummed the bee.

Consonant Sounds: Sometimes poets use words that begin or end with the same consonant sound. This is called *alliteration* (ə-lĭt′ ə-rā′ shən).

Wind whispers through the willows.

Rhythm: Rhythm is the pattern of beats in a poem. The beat makes the lines of poetry flow from one idea to the next.

I bought my pig
A curly wig.

Summer is fun.
Give me the sun!

Prewrite Use poetry's pleasing sounds.

1. Choose some words from your sensory chart.
2. Make a list of words that rhyme with them.
3. Then use this list as you write your poem.

Advanced Learners

Discuss alliteration with students. Then have them experiment with consonant sounds by writing tongue twisters. Have students practice saying their tongue twisters quickly without making mistakes.

Writing Poems 287

Marta's Prewriting

Marta chose some words from her sensory chart. Then she listed rhyming words under each one. You can use a rhyming dictionary to help you find rhyming words.

Rhyming List

blur	chant	rope	street
fur	ant	hope	feet
purr	can't	mope	heat
sure	pant	soap	meet
whir	slant		

Sometimes poets make up rhyming words or rhyme them in funny ways. **You can't-a-rope a cantaloupe.**

Marta's Prewriting

Tell students that one good approach to use when they are having trouble coming up with rhyming words is to

- decide the sound they want to repeat,
- go through the alphabet, saying the words formed by each letter plus the sound, and then
- go back and try combinations of consonants such as *bl*, *sh*, and *tr*.

If any of the combinations that they come up with are real words (or if they make good onomatopoeia), write them down.

To get students thinking in terms of their poems, play a class rhyming game.

- Write a word in the middle of the board. Draw a circle around it (choose one that has several obvious rhymes, like the color word *blue*).
- Challenge students to name as many rhyming words as possible. Write these around the word to form a cluster of rhyming words.
- Repeat with different words for several rounds.

English Language Learners

Help students go through the alphabet to find rhyming words. Suggest that they say the words aloud and write down ones that make sense such as *blue, shoe, true,* and so on. Point out that some rhyming words are not spelled the same way such as *blur* and *whir,* but that they can correct any spelling errors while editing.

Struggling Learners

Help students generate rhyming words by listing common CVC and CVC*e* word families on the board, such as *-ate, -ike, -ip,* and *-og.*

Writing Developing Your First Draft

Suggest that students use a pencil rather than a pen when they write their drafts, so that it is easier to make changes. Have them skip lines between each line of the poem, so there is room for them to add some details without erasing.

Remind students to refer to their sensory charts as they write. Tell them that even though they've already put lots of ideas down on the charts, they're likely to think of more to include as they go along. They shouldn't hesitate to try out those new ideas.

Technology Connections

Students can use the added features of the Net-text as they explore this stage of the writing process.

***Write Source Online* Net-text**

Writing Developing Your First Draft

You've done a lot of thinking about the words you will use in your poem. Now it's time to add your feelings. Have fun writing whatever sounds and feels right! You can make changes later.

Getting Started

If you have trouble getting started, try one of these ideas.

- **Close your eyes** and picture whatever it is you are writing about. Jot down the words that come to mind.
- **Start with your favorite detail.** Then write about your second favorite, and so on.
- **Use a starter phrase,** like "When I see . . . " or "I like to . . . ," and keep going.

Write Develop the first draft of your poem.

1. **Use all your notes to write your own poem about a happy or sad time. Include the details from your sensory chart.**
2. **Stop writing when your poem sounds and feels finished to you.**

English Language Learners

Prepare students to write their first draft by having them circle the nouns on their prewriting list. Tell them to find rhyming words for these words first. Check their words and suggest where they might use them in the lines of their poem. Modify this activity for verbs and adjectives, if they have listed more of these than nouns.

Writing Poems 289

Revising Improving Your Poem

Once you finish your poem, read it aloud to see how it sounds. Next, make changes that will make your poem even better.

- **Add** new lines or details to make your ideas clearer.
- **Cut** parts that don't seem to fit with the rest of your poem.
- **Replace** words to improve your poem's rhythm and rhyme.

Make changes to your poem.

- **Add, cut, and replace words to make your poem better. Work with your poem until every word feels just right.**

Editing Fine-Tuning Your Poem

When you edit, you make your writing correct—and easier to read!

Check your poem.

- **Check your poem for punctuation, capitalization, and spelling errors. (Rhyming poems often capitalize the first word of every line.)**

Creating a Title

Every poem needs a title. Here are some ideas.

- Use the first or last line: **My Jump Rope Chant**
- Use words from the poem: **Jump Rope Whir**
- Describe the poem: **Jump Rope Song and Dance**

Revising Improving Your Poem

Encourage students to read their poems aloud as they revise so they can more easily hear the rhymes and rhythms. Suggest that each time they make a big change, they read the line aloud again so that they can hear what it sounds like.

Editing Fine-Tuning Your Poem

Before editing their own poems, have students look at the poem "Jump to It!" on SE page 283. Point out that each line begins with a capital letter. Note how commas and end punctuation marks are used.

Creating a Title

Note that the writers of sad poems will want to choose serious titles, while those who wrote happy ones might prefer more playful options. These could include using

- a familiar phrase in a new way (as in the title shown on SE page 283, "Jump to It!")
- alliteration ("Jump Rope Jingle"), or
- onomatopoeia ("Whir-slap-whir!")

When students have finished their poems, hold a class poetry festival (perhaps at snack time, so that students can enjoy refreshments as they listen).

Technology Connections

Have students use the Writing Network features of the Net-text to comment on each other's drafts.

Write Source Online* *Net-text

English Language Learners

Invite students to read their poems aloud several times so they can listen to the rhythm and rhyme. If possible, have them read their poems into a tape recorder and replay the tape so they can improve their reading. As an alternative, have a fluent partner read their poem aloud to them.

Grammar Connection

Adverbs

- **Proofreader's Guide** page 550 (+)
- ***Write Source*** page 392
- ***GrammarSnap*** Adverbs
- ***SkillsBook*** pages 161–162

Modeling Sentences

- ***Write Source*** pages 412–413

Parts of Speech (review)

- **Proofreader's Guide** page 558 (+)
- ***SkillsBook*** pages 167–168

Spelling

- **Proofreader's Guide** pages 503–504 (+), 506 (+)
- ***SkillsBook*** pages 61–62

Writing a Limerick

Bring several examples of limericks to class. Have volunteers read the rhymes aloud to classmates to give students a strong sense of the form. Emphasize how regular and strong the rhythm is by having the class chant the limerick rhythm together using the syllable *la* instead of words. Point out that the first line of a limerick always begins "There once was (were) . . . " and the second line begins with "Who . . . "

Mention that in addition to telling a silly story, a limerick has both a rhyming and a rhythm pattern that sounds humorous and that would clash with serious or sad ideas.

Writing Tips

Encourage students to treat composing a limerick as a fun word puzzle. Before they write their own limericks, have the class work together to improvise one or two, using the pattern provided.

- Read the first line, filling in the end with the syllable *la*: *There once was a la la la la.*
- Invite a volunteer to fill in the blanks.
- Repeat these two steps for each of the lines of the limerick. Then write the completed rhyme on the board.

Writing a Limerick

A limerick is a silly rhymed poem with five lines. Lines 1, 2, and 5 rhyme; and lines 3 and 4 rhyme. Limericks also have a special rhythm, as in the example below.

Pete the Fat Cat

There once was a kitten named Pete,
Who always got too much to eat.
He soon grew so fat
That he slipped and fell flat,
Too heavy to land on his feet.

Rhymning lines may not be next to each other. Notice that **eat** and **feet** are separated in this limerick.

Writing Tips

Select a topic.

- Think of something silly that an animal or a person could do.

Gather details.

- List your ideas. Then circle some funny words and find rhymes for them.

Follow the pattern.

- Write your poem using the limerick pattern.
  There once was . . .
  Who . . .
  She, He, or It . . .
  That . . .

Advanced Learners

Have students use a thesaurus to expand their vocabulary while creating their limericks. Challenge them to use as many new descriptive, colorful, or humorous words as possible. Have students share their limericks with the class.

Writing Poems 291

Writing a Clerihew

A clerihew is another funny rhymed poem. It describes a person (or a pet). A clerihew follows this pattern:

- The first line names the person.
- The second line tells a detail about the person and ends with a word that rhymes with the person's name.
- The last two lines tell more details about the person and end with rhyming words.

Ms. Doud
Our gym teacher, Ms. Doud,
must like to be loud!
It makes my hair frizzle
when she blows her whistle.

Some rhyming words match exactly, and some are near rhymes. That's okay!

My Dog Sasha
My dog Sasha
doesn't like when we wash her.
She won't stay in the tub,
but she sure likes a towel rub!

Writing Tips

Select a topic.
- Think of a pet or a person you want to write about.

Gather details.
- List details about the person (or pet).

Follow the pattern.
- Write your clerihew using the pattern above.

Writing a Clerihew

Tell students that, unlike limericks, clerihews don't have a set rhythm. Their important features are their subject—a person (or an animal) named at the end of the first line—and their rhyme scheme.

Writing Tips

Suggest that students follow this procedure for composing their clerihews:

- After deciding who the poem will be about, list all the words you can think of that rhyme with that person's name.
- Play with the name and its rhyme to create the first two lines of the poem.
- Brainstorm funny rhyming pairs of words that relate to the statement in the first half of the poem.
- Finally, play around with fitting one of those rhyming pairs into the sentence that makes up the last half of the clerihew.

Writing a 5 W's Poem

Tell students that creating a 5 W's poem is a creative way of thinking about something they are reading or writing. To help them focus and clarify their thoughts, have them

- separate out the who, what, when, where, and why of the story and
- arrange the elements into the single sentence that makes up a 5 W's poem.

Writing Tips

Provide photocopies of the reproducible 5 W's Chart (TE page 597) for students to fill out as they plan their poems. Suggest that one approach is to write their poem about a favorite book they want to recommend to their classmates.

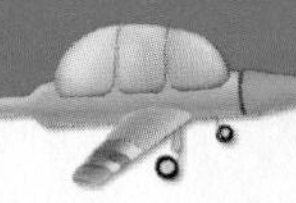

Writing a 5 W's Poem

A 5 W's poem is five lines long. Each line answers one of the 5 W's *(who? what? when? where?* and *why?)*. Usually, the lines of a 5 W's poem do not rhyme.

My Bunny Helicopter

Who? My bunny, Simon,
What? jumps and spins in midair
When? when he leaves his cage
Where? in our backyard
Why? because he is free!

Writing Tips

Select a topic.

- Make a list of silly and serious "who" ideas. Choose one as the topic for your poem.

Gather details.

- Make a 5 W's chart to list ideas for your poem.

who?	what?	when?	where?	why?

Follow the pattern.

- Write a poem that answers the 5 W's in any order, using details from your chart.
- Add, cut, and replace words until your poem feels just right.

English Language Learners

Students may find the title "My Bunny Helicopter" confusing. Show students a photograph of a helicopter and discuss how the propeller works. Then discuss how a bunny (especially a mini lop) might look as it jumps and spins in the air. Sketch a picture to help students visualize how the bunny's ears might look and draw comparisons between the bunny's ears and the helicopter's propeller.

Writing Poems 293

Writing an Alphabet Poem

An alphabet poem is a list poem in alphabetical order. It can start with any letter of the alphabet. The list of single words can be as long as you like. Alphabet poems almost never rhyme.

Parrot Music

Our
Parrot
Quotes
Rap
Songs!

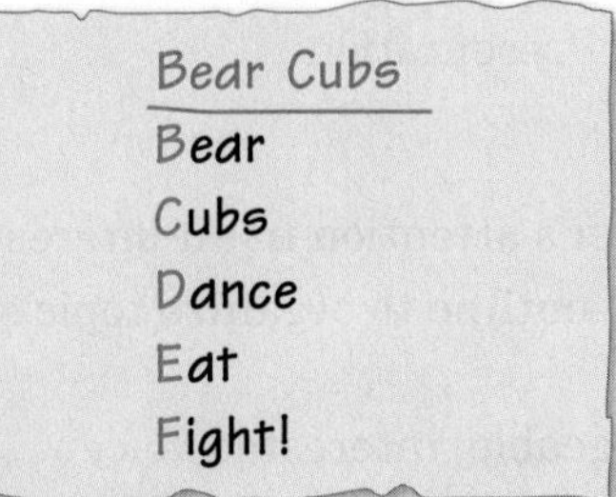

Writing Tips

Select a topic.

- Animals make great topics for alphabet poems. Think of your favorite type of animal.

Gather details.

- Freewrite about the animal you've chosen.

  I love parrots. They're really bright and colorful. They bob their heads up and down and dance from foot to foot. They squawk and talk in a funny voice.

Follow the pattern.

- Name your topic.
- Then list a group of letters from the alphabet in order.
- Be sure each word begins with the letter listed.

Writing an Alphabet Poem

Suggest that students work on this poem by listing the letters of the alphabet down the left side of a sheet of notebook paper. Once they have decided on their topic and done their freewriting, they can choose words from the freewriting that they want to use in the poem. Have them write the words next to the appropriate letters and see which sequence of letters would be best for the poem. They will probably have to fill in some missing words to make a full sentence and to use all the letters in the sequence.

English Language Learners

Formulating complete sentences can hamper some students' creativity and flow of ideas. Have them concentrate on listing words and phrases or drawing pictures to make their freewriting more productive.

Struggling Learners

Some students feel pressured and freeze up when they have to freewrite. To provide more structure, have students complete an idea cluster instead. Have them write down the name of the animal they want to write about in the center circle. Have them fill in the outer circles with words and phrases that describe the animal.

Research Writing Overview

Common Core Standards Focus

Writing 8: Recall information from experiences or gather information from print and digital sources; take brief notes on sources and sort evidence into provided categories.

Language 2: Demonstrate command of the conventions of standard English capitalization, punctuation, and spelling when writing.

Writing Forms

- Finding Information
- Writing a Summary Paragraph
- Writing a Research Report
- Creating a Multimedia Presentation

Focus on the Traits

- **Ideas** Getting the reader's attention in an interesting way
- **Organization** Using an outline to organize topic sentences and details that explain each topic sentence
- **Voice** Using a knowledgeable, interested voice
- **Word Choice** Choosing specific words to make ideas clearer
- **Sentence Fluency** Writing clear sentences that are easy to read
- **Conventions** Checking for errors in capitalization, punctuation, spelling, and grammar

Literature Connections

- ***The Power of Magnets*** by Barbara A. Donovan

Technology Connections

Write Source Online
www.hmheducation.com/writesource

- ***Net-text***
- ***Bookshelf***
- ***GrammarSnap***
- ***Portfolio***
- ***Writing Network features***
- ***File Cabinet***

Interactive Whiteboard Lessons

Suggested Research Writing Unit (One Week)

	Day	Writing and Skills Instruction	*Student Edition*: Research Writing Unit	*Student Edition*: Resource Units*	*SkillsBook*	*Daily Language Workouts*	*Write Source Online*
WEEK 1	1–2	**Finding Information** Literature Connections *The Power of Magnets*	296–307			60–61, 105	
	3	**Summary Paragraph** (Model)	308–309				*Interactive Whiteboard Lessons*
		(Prewriting)	310				
	4	(Writing, Revising)	311				
		Skills Activity: • Numbers		494 (+)	12, 55		*GrammarSnap*

* These units are also located in the back of the *Teacher's Edition.* Resource Units include "Basic Grammar and Writing," "A Writer's Resource," and "Proofreader's Guide."
(+) This activity is located in a different section of the *Write Source Student Edition.* If students have already completed this activity, you may wish to review it at this time.

	Day	Writing and Skills Instruction	Student Edition: Research Writing Unit	Student Edition: Resource Units*	SkillsBook	Daily Language Workouts	Write Source Online
Week 1	5	(Editing)	311				
		Skills Activities: • Verb Tenses		386–387, 540 (+)	141–142		GrammarSnap
		• Irregular Verbs		544–545	147–148		GrammarSnap
		• Capitalization		375 (+), 378 (+), 490–491	47–48		GrammarSnap

* These units are also located in the back of the *Teacher's Edition.* Resource Units include "Basic Grammar and Writing," "A Writer's Resource," and "Proofreader's Guide."
(+) This activity is located in a different section of the *Write Source Student Edition.* If students have already completed this activity, you may wish to review it at this time.

Suggested Research Report Unit (Four Weeks)

	Day	Writing and Skills Instruction	Student Edition: Research Writing Unit	Student Edition: Resource Units*	SkillsBook	Daily Language Workouts	Write Source Online
Week 1	1	**Research Report** (Model)	312–315			62–63, 106	
	2–5	(Prewriting)	316–323				*Net-text*
Week 2	6–10	(Writing)	324–329			64–65, 107	*Net-text*
Week 3	11-12	(Revising)	330–333			66–67, 108	*Net-text*
		Skills Activities: • Sentence Variety		401, 408–410	87–88, 109–110, 113–114		*GrammarSnap*
		• Colons, Hyphens, Parentheses		480–481, 482–483	37–38		
		• Nouns (possessive)		377 (+), 474 (+), 534 (+)	124		*GrammarSnap*
	13–14	(Editing)	334–335				*Net-text*
		Skills Activities: • Verbs (review)		383 (+), 384 (+), 385 (+), 538 (+), 542 (+)	136, 149–150		*GrammarSnap*
		• Run-On Sentences		404 (+), 526 (+), 528 (+)	99–100		*GrammarSnap*
		• Apostrophes		377 (+), 474 (+), 534 (+)	27–28		*GrammarSnap*
		• Subject-Verb Agreement		388			*GrammarSnap*
	15	(Publishing, Reflecting)	336–337				*Portfolio, Net-text*
Week 4	16–20 *opt.*	*Multimedia Presentation*	338–341			68–69, 109	
		Skills Activities: • Spelling		503–506 (+)	65–66		

* These units are also located in the back of the *Teacher's Edition.* Resource Units include "Basic Grammar and Writing," "A Writer's Resource," and "Proofreader's Guide."
(+) This activity is located in a different section of the *Write Source Student Edition.* If students have already completed this activity, you may wish to review it at this time.

Teacher's Notes for Research Writing

This overview for research writing includes some specific suggestions for teaching this unit.

Writing Focus

Finding Information (pages 296–307)

The library may seem overwhelming to some students, but once they learn basic library skills, they'll be ready to take advantage of everything that the library has to offer. Once they understand how the library works, they can become skillful researchers.

Writing a Summary Paragraph (pages 308–311)

Summary writing helps students develop competence as critical thinkers and helps them integrate important reading and writing skills. When students write summaries they are learning how to find the main ideas in reading material. Learning how to express these ideas succinctly in their own words is a valuable lifelong skill.

Writing a Research Report (pages 312–337)

Writing research reports can be a fascinating introduction to independent thinking, searching, and exploring. Students' own curiosity becomes their most valuable research tool. After finding subjects that truly interest them, young writer-researchers can follow certain steps that will lead to successful research reports. Report writing helps students understand how nonfiction material can be organized. Knowing methods for keeping track of information will always be a useful skill.

Creating a Multimedia Presentation (pages 338–341)

Although the technical side of this kind of presentation can be a challenge, children at this age are often very computer savvy. A sample media grid and a sample storyboard show how to make the presentation easier.

Academic Vocabulary

Read aloud the academic terms, as well as the descriptions and questions. Model for students how to read one question and answer it. Have partners monitor their understanding and seek clarification of the terms by working through the meanings and questions together.

Minilessons

Parts of a Book — Finding Information

- In your classroom or school library, **FIND** a reference book. Then **OPEN** your text to "Using References" on SE page 301.

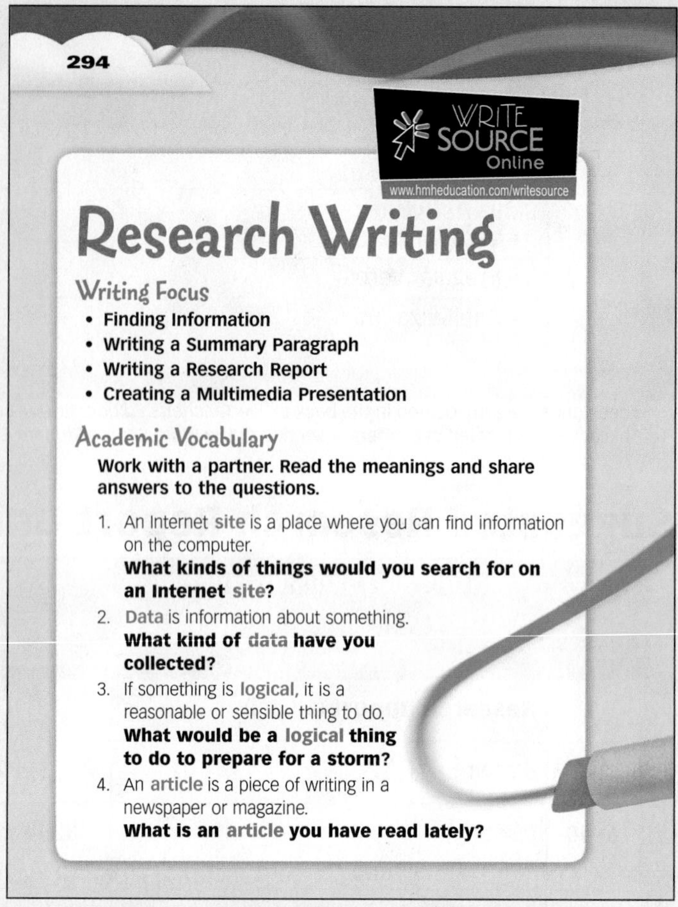

294
WRITE SOURCE Online
www.hmheducation.com/writesource
Research Writing
Writing Focus
• Finding Information
• Writing a Summary Paragraph
• Writing a Research Report
• Creating a Multimedia Presentation
Academic Vocabulary
Work with a partner. Read the meanings and share answers to the questions.
1. An Internet site is a place where you can find information on the computer.
What kinds of things would you search for on an Internet site?
2. Data is information about something.
What kind of data have you collected?
3. If something is logical, it is a reasonable or sensible thing to do.
What would be a logical thing to do to prepare for a storm?
4. An article is a piece of writing in a newspaper or magazine.
What is an article you have read lately?

  - **FIND** as many of these parts as you can in the book you selected.

Information Please — Finding Information

- **CHECK** an encyclopedia and the Internet for information about the sun.
  - **NOTICE** differences between these two sources of information. As a class, **TALK** about the advantages and disadvantages of using a reference book compared to using the Internet.

In 10 Words or Less — Writing a Summary Paragraph

- **LISTEN** to your teacher read a paragraph from a science, history, or other textbook.
  - **WRITE** a summary of the main idea in a sentence of 10 words or less.
  - **SEE** who can write the best summary topic sentence using the fewest words.

Getting Started — Writing a Research Report

- **REVIEW** SE pages 316–317. On a sheet of paper, **WRITE** at least four questions about your subject that you would like to answer. Do not write questions that can be answered with a yes or no.

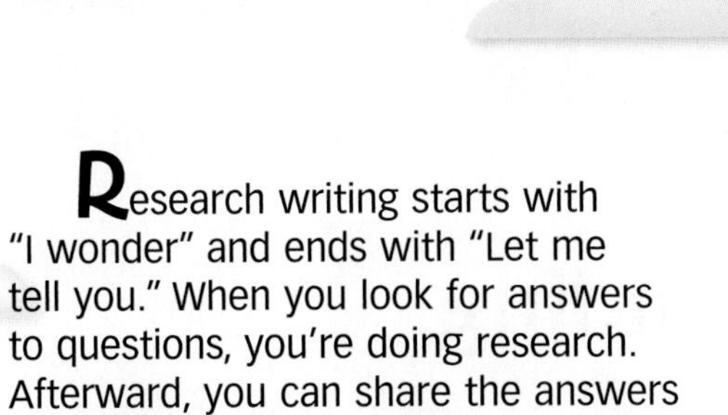

Research writing starts with "I wonder" and ends with "Let me tell you." When you look for answers to questions, you're doing research. Afterward, you can share the answers you find by writing about them.

In this section, you'll learn about doing research in the library, writing summaries, and creating a research report. When you're done, you can even make a multimedia presentation.

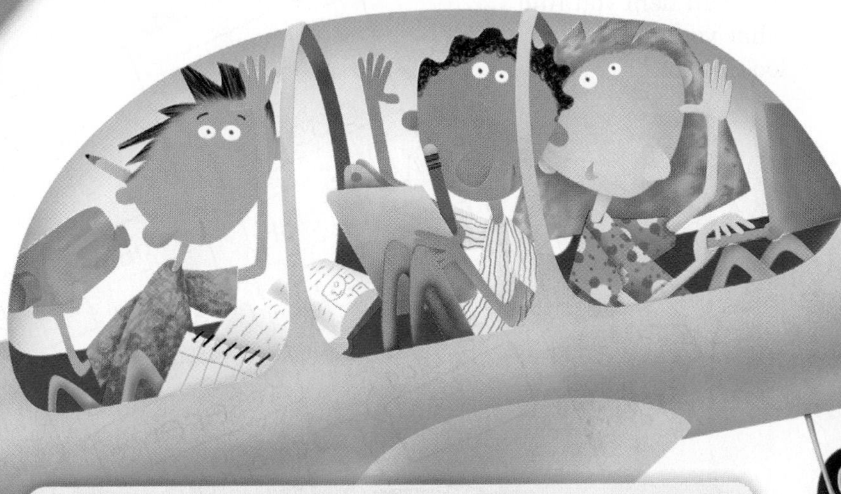

Literature Connections: For an example of report writing, read *The Power of Magnets* by Barbara A. Donovan.

Family Connection Letters

As you begin this unit, send home the Research Writing Family Connection letter, which describes what students will be learning.

- Letter in English (TE p. 608)
- Letter in Spanish (TE p. 616)

Research Writing

Research writing is based on information gathered from sources other than the writer's own imagination or everyday experience. This information might come from

- people who know a lot about the topic,
- books or other published materials about the topic, or
- experiences the writer undertakes especially to learn about the topic.

Point out to students that since research is about learning something new, it is one of the most common types of writing assignment they'll encounter in school. Note also that any time they get interested in something and decide to learn more about it, they'll be doing research.

Literature Connections

In *The Power of Magnets*, the author presents information about magnets and their various uses in a logical order and with a knowledgeable voice. This book is an example of information given like in a report.

Discuss with students possible sources the author may have used to gather information. For a list of reference books to use when writing a report, see the Reading-Writing Connections beginning on page TE-36.

Finding Information

Objectives

- Learn about the various sources of information available at a library.
- Practice using traditional references in both book and electronic form.
- Begin using the Internet for research.

Talk with students about their experiences at a public library. How often do they go there? Why do they go? Poll students to find out how many have visited a library

- for a storytelling hour,
- to check out books to read,
- to see a movie,
- to check out movies,
- to use the computers,
- to read magazines.

Tell students that the following pages will tell them about the many resources they can find at a library, some of which they might not have realized were available.

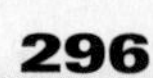

Finding Information

A library is more than just shelves of books. A library opens the door to a whole world of information. You can find books, magazines, newspapers, encyclopedias, recordings, computers, and even DVD's. Best of all, most libraries have a librarian who can help you find what you are looking for.

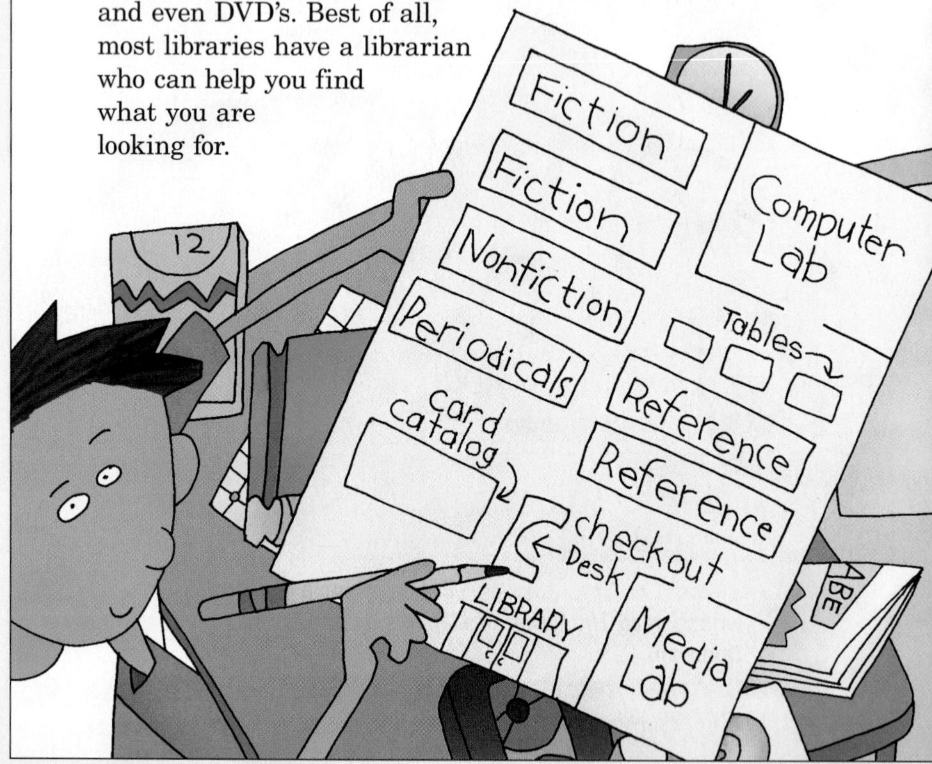

Materials

Index cards with authors' names, book titles, and subject words written on them (TE p. 298)

Index cards (TE p. 299)

Index card file boxes (TE p. 299)

Sticky notes (TE p. 301)

Nonfiction books (TE p. 301)

Dictionaries (TE p. 302)

Word list (TE p. 303)

Thesauruses (TE p. 304)

Atlas (TE p. 304)

Encyclopedias, multiple sets (TE p. 305)

Magazines (TE p. 306)

Copy Masters

Venn Diagram (TE p. 305)

Finding Information 297

Using the Library

A library is organized to help you find information. Usually, different types of books each have their own separate place.

The **books** in a library are divided into three main sections.

1. **Fiction** books include stories and novels. These books are arranged in alphabetical order by the authors' last names.
2. **Nonfiction** (factual) books are arranged on the shelves by call numbers, according to the Dewey decimal system.

> A book numbered **386** comes before a book numbered **714**. One labeled **973A** comes before one labeled **973B**. Some call numbers have decimals, like **973.19** or **973.22**. Your librarian can help you find these books.

3. **Reference** books such as encyclopedias, atlases, and dictionaries are kept in a special section of the library.

In addition to different types of books, your library may include the following:

The **periodicals** area has magazines and newspapers.

The **computer lab** has computers available to use. Some may be connected to the Internet.

The **media section** has DVD's, cassettes, CD's, and videotapes. You may also find computer software in this section.

Using the Library

To **encourage students to use the library** *(see below)*, arrange for a tour with the librarian at the school's library or a local branch of the public library. Make sure the librarian knows all the information you want students to cover. You might want to ask the librarian to

- show students the location of different kinds of materials (fiction, nonfiction, and reference books; periodicals; computers; and media);
- explain the checkout procedures for the library;
- talk briefly about the Dewey decimal system and what sorts of books they'll find organized by number;
- explain the use of the books in the reference section and the library's policy for using them; and
- explain the policy and procedures for signing up to use a computer.

Teaching Tip: Encouraging Use of the Library

Set aside time for students to check out books of their choice from the school library. Follow up with one or more of these ideas:

- **Book Chats**. On a regular basis, ask students what they're reading and invite them to talk about it.
- **Book Reviews**. Each week, have a different student write a brief review of a book he or she has completed. Post the finished reviews on a reading bulletin board.
- **Book Forums**. Acting as moderator, hold a panel discussion of a book several students have read. (Those who haven't read it will be the audience.) Try to choose a book some students liked and others didn't to create a more interesting discussion.
- **Best Sellers**. Every month, post a class "Best Sellers" list.

Using a Card Catalog

If your library maintains a print card catalog, you can use this section to familiarize your students with the basics of the Dewey decimal system. Skip to SE page 300 if your library has a computer catalog.

Card catalog users must be familiar with alphabetical order. To help them practice this,

- divide the class into groups;
- give each group a set of about ten index cards, each with an author's name, book title, or subject on it;
- remind students that author, title, and subject catalog cards are all filed together in alphabetical order according to their main word; that is, title (skipping *A, An,* or *The* at the beginning), author's last name, or subject word;
- have students shuffle their cards, and then work together to alphabetize them; and
- have groups switch card sets to check each other's work.

Using a Card Catalog

In a library full of books, how can you find the one book you need? Simple. Use the card catalog where cards are arranged in alphabetical order. Each book has one *title card* and one *author card*. It may also have a *subject card*. All of these cards tell about the book and where you can find it on the shelves.

1. **Title Card:** If you know the title of a book, look for its title card. If the title begins with *A*, *An*, or *The*, look up the next word in the title.
   - Look under PLANETS to find the book *The Planets*.
2. **Author Card:** You can also find a book by its author's last name. The last name comes first on the author card. All books by that author will be grouped together.
   - Rustad, Martha E. H.
3. **Subject Card:** If you need a book about a particular subject, look for the subject in the catalog. There you will find cards for all sorts of books about that subject.
   - Look under the subject SOLAR SYSTEM to find books about the sun and its planets.

Finding Information 299

Sample Catalog Cards

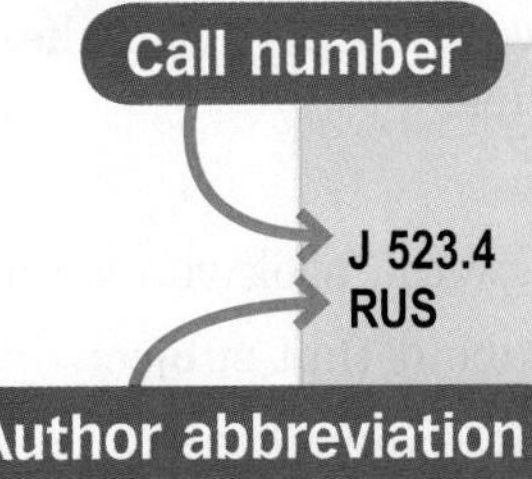

The Planets

J 523.4
RUS

Rustad, Martha E. H.
The planets/Martha Rustad.—
Mankato, Minn: Pebble Books, 2008.

Author abbreviation

Photographs and simple text introduce the planets in our solar system.

1. Solar system 2. Space 3. The Sun

Rustad, Martha E. H.

J 523.4
RUS

Rustad, Martha E. H.
The planets/Martha Rustad.—
Mankato, Minn: Pebble Books, 2008.

Description

Photographs and simple text introduce the planets in our solar system.

1. Solar system 2. Space 3. The Sun

SOLAR SYSTEM

J 523.4
RUS

Rustad, Martha E. H.
The planets/Martha Rustad.—
Mankato, Minn: Pebble Books, 2008.

Photographs and simple text introduce the planets in our solar system.

Related Topics

1. Solar system 2. Space 3. The Sun

Advanced Learners

Have students choose several nonfiction books from the library or your classroom collection and use index cards to create title, author, and subject cards for each book. Have students compile and alphabetize the cards into title, author, and subject piles.

Provide three index card boxes for students to store and maintain the card catalog. Suggest that they add cards as they encounter other nonfiction books. Invite the class to use the catalog as a quick index for finding nonfiction books.

Sample Catalog Cards

Have students look carefully at the three cards shown. Ask them to identify how they're different and how they're the same.

- They all have exactly the same information after the top line.
- The title card has the title on the top line; the author card has the author's name at the top; and the subject card has the subject at the top.

Ask students to point out the information on the cards that the student edition doesn't have labeled. (The publication information, that is, the name and location of the company that published the book, along with the year it first appeared.)

Tell students that when they use electronic catalogs at a library (a skill addressed on SE page 300), they can look up books in the same way as in the print card catalog. They will also find that the electronic catalog entries provide the same information, as well as some additional useful items.

Using a Computer Catalog

Emphasize the difference between subjects and keywords.

- Subject words are assigned by librarians based on a book's content, so a subject search will find only books about the topic.
- A keyword might be suggested in the title, summary, subject, or author's name. Choosing a good keyword helps to narrow a topic search. For example, if you were interested in learning about meteor showers on Mercury, you probably wouldn't choose *space* as a keyword because it is too broad a topic and wouldn't narrow your search sufficiently.
- Have students compare the sample computer entry to the catalog cards on the previous page. Point out a useful item found only in computer catalogs: status. This line tells whether the book is available and may also note when a checked-out book is due back. Explain that many libraries allow users to put a "hold" on a book that is checked out. That means that when the book is returned, the library will hold it so they can come borrow it.

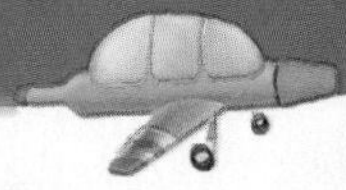

Using a Computer Catalog

Many libraries keep their catalog on computer. That makes finding a book even easier. Follow these tips.

- Always read the on-screen directions.
- Search by author or title, if you know the book you want.
- Search by subject to find all books about that subject.
- Use **keywords** in your search. For example, type in *astronomy* to find books about that subject or books with that word in the title.

Author:	Osborne, Will and Mary Pope Osborne.
Title:	*Space*
Series title:	Magic tree house research guide.
Published:	New York: Random House, 2007 137 p.: ill.
Notes:	A nonfiction companion to *Midnight on the Moon*. Jack and Annie present information about the universe, including our solar system, and briefly describe the history of space travel and of the science of astronomy.
Added entry:	Murdocca, Sal, ill.
Subjects:	Astronomy, space flight
Call number:	J 520 OSB
Status:	Checked out
Location:	Children's

English Language Learners

Some students may have difficulty generating effective keyword searches. When students need to search a computer catalog, have them use this book as a guide and pair them with students who are proficient in English.

Struggling Learners

Using SE page 300, provide students with extra practice using on-screen information:

- What is the title of this Magic Tree House research guide? (*Space*)
- When was it published? (2007)
- Where is it located in the library? (children's section)
- Which book is a companion to this research guide? (*Midnight on the Moon*)
- How many pages does this book have? (137)
- What is the call number? (J 520 OSB)
- Who is the illustrator? (Sal Murdocca)

Finding Information 301

Using References

Books are easier to use when you understand their parts.

- The **title page** lists the book's title, author, and publisher. It may also list the book's illustrator.
- The **copyright** page shows important information. It tells the year the book was published. (A new book may be more accurate than an old one.)
- The **table of contents** in the front of the book gives page numbers for chapters and sections of the book.
- Pictures in a book may have **captions** that help to explain them.
- Some books have a **glossary** near the back that defines new words.
- Many books have an **index** in the back. This alphabetical list of topics has page numbers where you can find information on each listed topic.

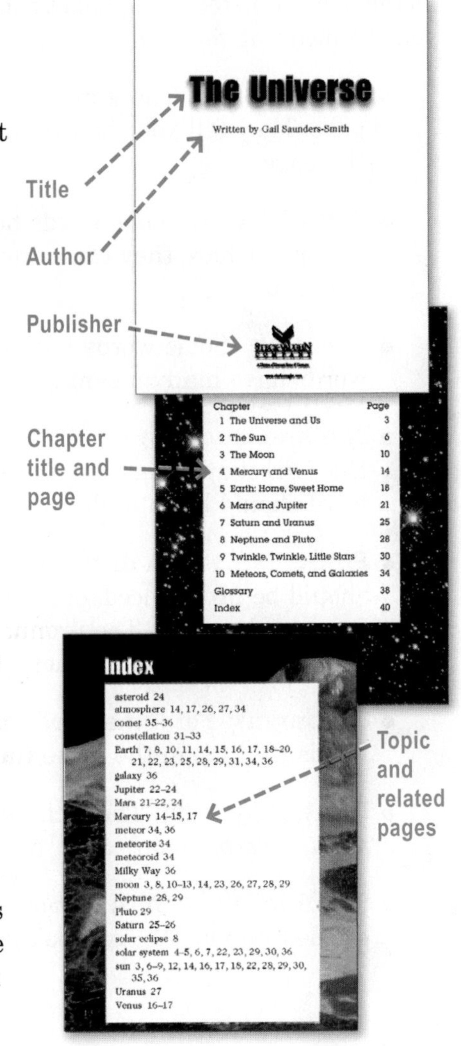

Using References

Challenge students to find examples of all the parts of a book mentioned by looking through

- their own books,
- books in the classroom, or
- school library books.

Have students bring one of these examples to share with the class. Ask students if they can make any observations based on the types of books they've read. Observations might include the following:

- Every book has a title page and a copyright page.
- Fictional works don't have indexes.

Focus on the difference between a table of contents and an index by having students compare these two features in their student editions. To demonstrate, have students find *prewriting* in the index. Note that the entry tells the pages in every chapter of the book where *prewriting* is discussed.

English Language Learners

Students with limited English vocabulary may find the names of book parts challenging. Provide support by providing students with several sticky notes so they can write the parts of a book on each note. As a group, locate the title page, copyright page, table of contents pages, and index.

Have students place each sticky note next to the corresponding book part, using the visuals on this page as a reference. Encourage students to flip to the table of contents in the front of the book when they need to refer to a particular section of the book.

Struggling Learners

For visual and kinesthetic reinforcement, have student pairs choose a nonfiction book. Then call out the parts of a book, and have partners use their nonfiction book to locate each part. Provide support as needed.

Using a Dictionary

After students have had time to read through the parts of a dictionary entry and the sample dictionary page, draw their attention to another dictionary feature: a sentence or phrase showing the word used in context. Point out where these appear on the sample page (for example, in the *danger* entry, *the danger of a cave-in* and *in danger of falling*).

Have **several dictionaries** *(see below)* on hand, and let students browse through them. Have them find differences between the dictionaries. Responses might include:

- Some dictionaries give a word history—also called an *etymology*—for every word.
- Some dictionaries show the syllable division at the beginning of the entry, instead of at the end.
- Some dictionaries don't give the plural spelling of a noun if it's formed in the usual way, by just adding *-s.* They list the plural form of a word only if it is unusual (for example *calf* and *calves*).
- Not all dictionaries include synonyms (for synonyms, see the information about thesauruses on SE page 304).

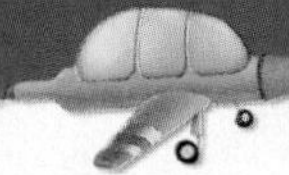

Using a Dictionary

Use a **dictionary** to look up new words. The words in a dictionary are listed in alphabetical order. The dictionary gives you the meaning for each word, plus much more.

- **Guide Words:** These are the words at the top of the page. They tell you the first and last entry words on the page.
- **Word History:** Some words have stories about their history—where they came from and what they meant long ago.
- **Meaning:** Some words have only one meaning. Other words have many meanings.
- **Spelling and Capital Letters:** The dictionary shows you the correct spelling for a word. It also shows whether a word should be capitalized.
- **Pronunciation:** A dictionary shows you how a word should be pronounced, or said. The pronunciation is given in parentheses ( ). The pronunciation key at the bottom of the dictionary page will help you, too.
- **Synonyms:** For some words, the dictionary lists other words that mean the same thing.
- **Parts of Speech:** The dictionary tells you if a word is a *noun,* a *verb,* an *adjective,* or another part of speech.
- **Syllable Division:** A dictionary shows you how a word is divided into syllables. (Look for the heavy black dots.)

Teaching Tip: Different Dictionaries—Electronic Versions

Although using book-style dictionaries is a very important skill for students to practice, many students will already be familiar with electronic dictionaries—and will prefer their use. Bookmark several of the good online dictionaries for students to use in class. These include the following:

- Merriam-Webster online dictionary (www.m-w.com),
- Web site www.onelook.com, which searches many dictionaries at once and presents all the definitions for comparison.

Finding Information 303

Dictionary Page

Guide words → **dandelion ➤ dangle**

dandelion *noun* A plant with bright yellow flowers and long notched leaves that is a common weed. Its leaves are sometimes eaten in salads.
dan·de·li·on (dăn′dl ī′ən) ◊ *noun, plural* **dandelions**

Word history →

Word History

dandelion

Dandelion comes from an old French phrase meaning "tooth of a lion." The leaves of a dandelion have jagged edges that look a little like lions' teeth.

Meaning →

dandruff *noun* Small white flakes of dead skin that are shed from the scalp.
dan·druff (dăn′drəf) ◊ *noun*

Spelling and capital letters →

Dane *noun* A person who was born in or lives in Denmark.
Dane (dān) ◊ *noun, plural* **Danes**

danger *noun* **1.** The chance of harm or destruction; peril: *the danger of a cave-in.* **2.** The condition of being exposed to harm or loss: *in danger of falling.* **3.** Something that may cause harm.
dan·ger (dān′jər) ◊ *noun, plural* **dangers**

Pronunciation →

Synonyms

Synonyms → **danger, hazard, risk**

The explorer faced many *dangers* in the jungle. ➤ People who live near active volcanoes face certain *hazards*. ➤ It is a *risk* to swim so far, but if you succeed, you will win a prize.

Part of speech →

dangerous *adjective* **1.** Full of danger; risky. **2.** Able or likely to cause harm.
dan·ger·ous (dān′jər əs) ◊ *adjective*

dangle *verb* To swing or cause to swing loosely: *A key dangled from the chain.*

Syllable division → **dan·gle** (dăng′gəl) ◊ *verb* **dangled, dangling**

Pronunciation key

ă	pat	ĭ	pit
ā	pay	ī	ride
â	care	î	fierce
ä	father	ŏ	pot
ĕ	pet	ō	go
ē	be	ô	paw, for
oi	oil	th	bath
ŏŏ	book	*th*	bathe
ōō	boot	ə	ago, item
ou	out		pencil
ŭ	cut		atom
û	fur		circus

Dictionary Page

To give students practice looking up words, play the dictionary game:

- Divide the class into teams of three or four.
- Have each team find an unfamiliar word in the dictionary from a word list you provide, jot down the word's first definition, and make up two more fun definitions.
- Have one volunteer from every team take turns reading aloud the team's word and its three possible definitions.
- Have competing teams try to pick the correct definition.
- After they announce which definition they chose, have them look up the word and read aloud its correct definition.
- Repeat until all teams have had a chance to read their word and definitions.

English Language Learners

To help students use a dictionary to check the meaning of words when they are unsure of the spelling, have them list several new words from their reading, and show them how to use guide words. This narrows their search to one or two pages.

If you have students create word cards to build their vocabulary, refer students to them whenever they write.

Teaching Tip

Review the meaning of putting words in alphabetical order. Children may locate words on the sample dictionary page by using the alphabet as a guide. Create additional practice exercises in which students arrange three or four words in alphabetical order. (Also see the spelling-word list on SE pages 503, 504, and 506.)

Struggling Learners

Help students locate words in the dictionary. First, write *carry* and *crash* on the board as guide words. Then list the following entry words: *cell, carrot, cream, cart, curb, cork.* Have students list the words in the order they would be found in the dictionary. Then ask which of the words would be found on a dictionary page with the guide words on the board (*cart, cell, cork*).

Using a Thesaurus

Display the two styles of thesaurus:

- with alphabetical entries, like a dictionary;
- with an index of keywords in the back of the book that gives numerical references to the lists of synonyms in the front.

Demonstrate the use of this second type of thesaurus for students.

Point out that students must carefully choose from among the synonyms in a thesaurus, because it is almost never a simple matter of swapping one word for another. Have students use a dictionary to look up each of the sample synonyms given for *small* to see how the meanings differ.

Using an Atlas

Demonstrate for students how to use an atlas by

- looking up a city (or geographical feature such as a mountain) in the index,
- using the map number or page number to find the general map, and then
- finding the exact location of the item by using the letter-and-number grid.

Using a Thesaurus

A thesaurus is a book that lists words and their synonyms. Synonyms are words with similar meanings. A thesaurus may also list antonyms for some words. Antonyms are words that mean the opposite. You can use a thesaurus to find just the right word and to give your writing variety. For example, the following sample thesaurus entry gives you other choices for the word *small*.

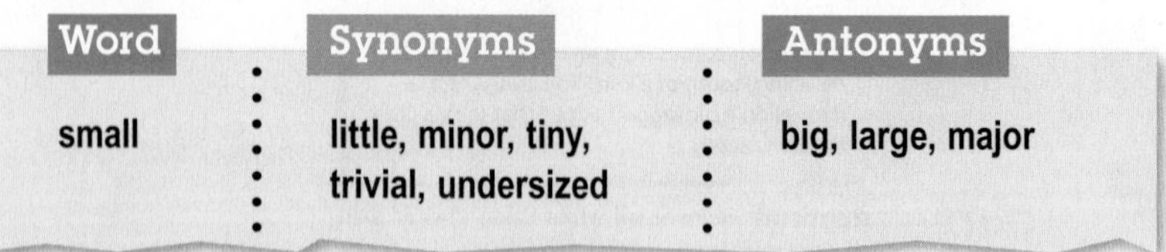

Word	Synonyms	Antonyms
small	little, minor, tiny, trivial, undersized	big, large, major

Using an Atlas

An atlas is a collection of maps. An atlas may include symbols, graphics, and tables. Always check the *key* to learn more about the map you are looking at.

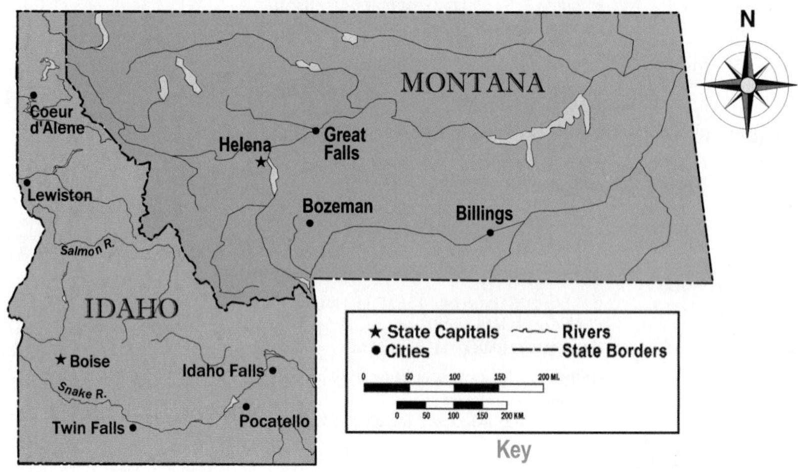

Key

English Language Learners

Provide students with a tactile-kinesthetic approach to synonyms and antonyms.

- Provide each student with a word to act out, such as *happy, little, fast,* and so on.
- Have others guess the word and provide a synonym.
- Choose another student to act out the antonym, such as *sad, big, slow,* and so on.

Struggling Learners

Reinforce atlas concepts by asking the following questions about the map of Idaho:

- Which river is closest to Twin Falls? (Snake River)
- What is the state capital of Idaho? (Boise)
- About how many miles is it from Pocatello to Idaho Falls? (about 50 miles)

Using an Encyclopedia

An encyclopedia is a set of books that contain articles on many topics. Each book is a volume labeled with letters to show what part of the alphabet it contains. Often, the last volume is an index for articles in the entire set.

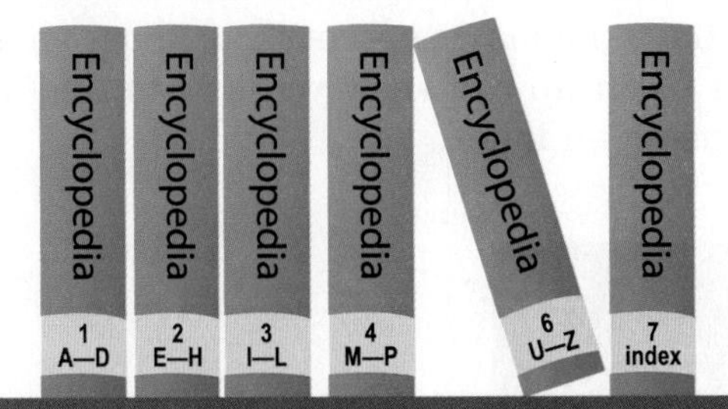

Explore Electronic Encyclopedias

Some encyclopedias are published on a CD or on the Internet. To search for your topic in an electronic encyclopedia, use keywords or words underlined in the article. (See page 300.)

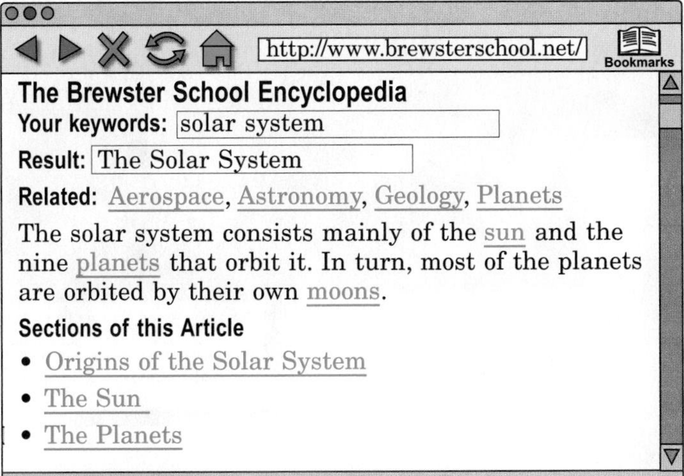

Using an Encyclopedia

During library time, assign topics and have students look up their topic in two or three of the different encyclopedias available. Have them point out ways in which the entries differ from one another. Responses should include:

- Some encyclopedias (for example, *Encyclopedia Britannica Macropedia*) have very long entries.
- Some encyclopedias have more photographs and illustrations than others.

Encourage students to begin their research with an encyclopedia geared toward grade-school students, such as *World Book*. After that, if they really want more in-depth information, they can check other encyclopedias as well.

Explore Electronic Encyclopedias

Explain that as libraries gain more access to electronic reference books, they are likely to stop buying new sets of the book versions. This means that the information may be more current in electronic encyclopedias.

English Language Learners

To give students practice using encyclopedias and at the same time reinforce their alphabetizing skills, have student pairs locate topics in encyclopedias. Using sets from the library, write the following topics on the board: *Jupiter, redwoods*, and *toads*. For each topic, have students choose the correct encyclopedia volume and work collaboratively to locate the topic. Provide assistance if needed. Have students share one thing they learned about each topic.

Advanced Learners

Have students use a copy of the reproducible Venn Diagram (TE page 600) to compare and contrast print encyclopedias and electronic encyclopedias. Suggest that they include factors such as ease of use, number of pictures, and availability.

Using Periodicals

A library that has a periodicals section usually has current newspapers and magazines on display for visitors to read. Encourage students to browse through the periodicals in their library, especially the magazines for kids. Doing so will give students an idea of the many topics covered in the periodicals. The range of titles and subjects may include the following:

- *Apple seeds* (social studies),
- *National Geographic for Kids* (nature),
- *Weekly Reader* (current events),
- *Sports Illustrated for Kids* (sports), and
- *Stone Soup* (literature).

Suggest that a great way of finding a subject to write about is to look for interesting articles in periodicals and newspapers.

Using Periodicals

Periodicals are magazines and newspapers. (*Periodic* means "occurring from time to time.") The periodicals have articles on all sorts of subjects.

Periodicals are published more often than books, so they may have more up-to-date information. Use a recent issue to be sure you have the most current facts about your topic. Your teacher or librarian can show you how to find articles in periodicals by using an index.

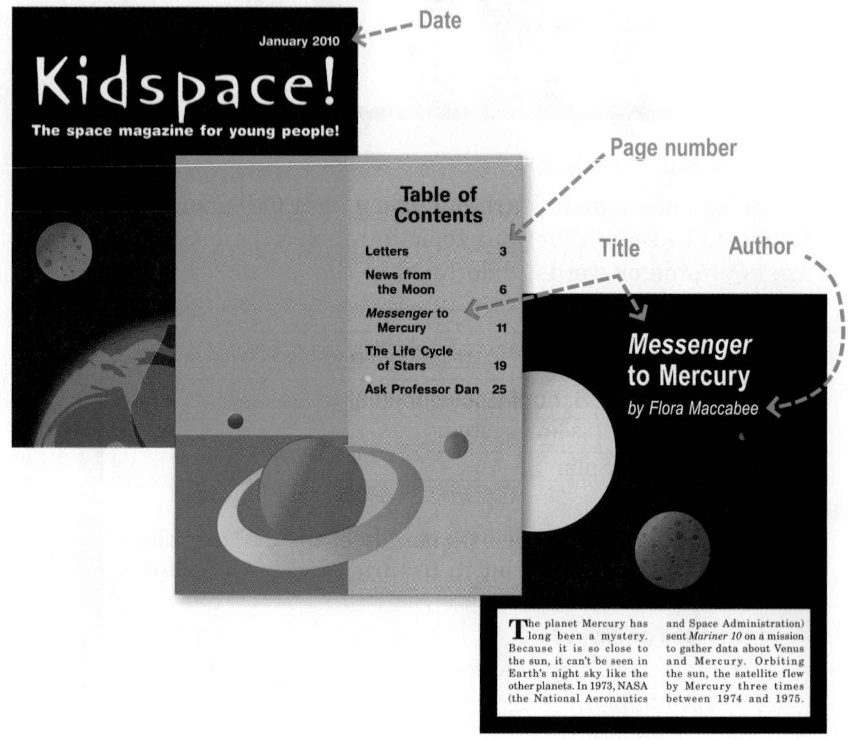

Struggling Learners

Provide extra practice using periodicals by distributing a magazine to pairs of students. Have students examine the periodical and answer the following questions:

- What is the date shown on the cover of your magazine?
- Look at the table of contents. What is the name of the second article listed?
- On which page would you find it?
- Who is the author of the article?

Using the Internet

The Internet can be a great place to find information. For example, NASA has its own Web site with lots of photos and information about space exploration. Your teacher may know of other educational sites for you to explore, as well.

Follow the Rules

Be sure to follow your school and library Internet policies. These guidelines and rules are designed to keep you safe.

Know How to Navigate

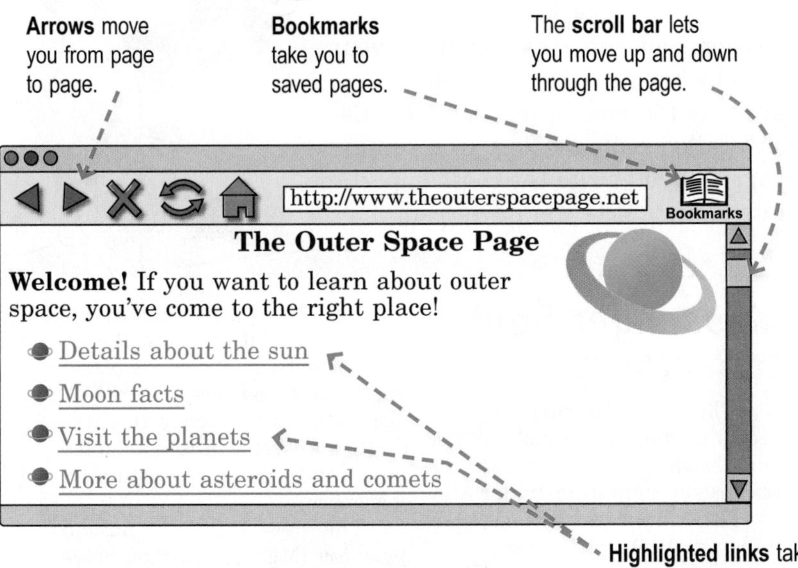

Print, Highlight, and Reword

You can print out Internet pages you find and then highlight important parts. Put information in your own words in your writing assignments.

Using the Internet

Discuss the importance of **choosing reliable sites** *(see below)* when looking for information. To get students started exploring online, list Web addresses of some useful Internet sites on the board. These could include:

- www.factmonster.com (general information and homework help for kids),
- www.howstuffworks.com (just as the title suggests),
- www.bartleby.com (many searchable reference classics), and
- www.encarta.com (free access to the concise Encarta dictionary).

Discuss plagiarism—using someone else's ideas or words without permission. Emphasize how important it is for students to rewrite all the information they get from the Internet or other sources in their own words (or to correctly attribute the sources of ideas they borrow and indicate the borrowed text with quotation marks). Point out that expressing ideas in their own words helps them to learn about the topic.

Teaching Tip: Choosing Reliable Web Sites

Explain that anyone can post a Web page about any topic, but that doesn't make the person an expert or guarantee that the information given at the Web site is correct. Suggest that students

- look at the source of information—if it comes from a university, library, government agency, or familiar reference book, then it is probably correct;
- ask a teacher, librarian, or caregiver about a site if they aren't sure about it.

Now would be a good time to remind your students of the school's policy on appropriate Internet use.

English Language Learners

Make Internet searches less overwhelming by

- providing students with a list of student-friendly sites,
- bookmarking useful sites and search engines, and
- pairing students with cooperative partners who are proficient English speakers.

Writing a Summary Paragraph

Objectives

- Understand the purpose, content, and structure of a summary paragraph.
- Choose an article to summarize.
- Plan, draft, revise, and edit a summary paragraph.

Remind students that a paragraph is a group of sentences about a specific topic.

* For more about writing paragraphs, see SE pages 416–429.

Tell students that writing summary paragraphs is a very useful skill. When researching a topic, they can summarize articles they read to help them remember important details about the article.

To reinforce the concept of summarizing, have students choose partners and tell each other what they did over the weekend. Point out to students that they probably told their partner the highlights, or important or fun things they did over the weekend. Explain that by focusing on the important details, they summarized their weekend.

Technology Connections

Use this unit's Interactive Whiteboard Lesson to introduce research writing.

Interactive Whiteboard Lesson

Writing a Summary Paragraph

When someone asks you about your day and what you did, you probably share only the most interesting details. That's called *summarizing.* In a summary paragraph, you write the most important points of an article you have read.

Messenger Sent to Mercury

The planet Mercury has long been a mystery. It is usually in the sun's bright glare, so it's hard for scientists to study it. In 1973, NASA (the **N**ational **A**eronautics and **S**pace **A**dministration) sent *Mariner 10* on a mission to gather data about Venus and Mercury. As the satellite orbited the sun, it flew past Mercury three times between 1974 and 1975. The information it sent back was based on viewing only half the planet's surface.

Now NASA has sent a new satellite to orbit Mercury. It may answer mysteries of how the planet was formed and how it can look like the moon yet have a core like Earth. It will see if there is ice in the craters at the north and south poles of Mercury.

The new satellite, named *Messenger* (**ME**rcury **S**urface, **S**pace **EN**vironment, **GE**ochemistry, and **R**anging mission), was launched on August 14, 2004. *Messenger* will begin orbiting Mercury in March of 2011. It will send back radio signals for a full year. After that it will stop working and crash into Mercury.

Materials

Photographs of Mercury and the satellite *Messenger* (TE p. 309)

Dictionary (TE p. 311)

Copy Masters

Table Diagram (TE p. 310)

Writing a Summary Paragraph 309

Summary Paragraph

After reading the "*Messenger* Sent to Mercury" article, Ugo Garrett wrote this summary paragraph.

Messenger Goes to Mercury

NASA wants to solve some of the mysteries of the planet Mercury. In 1973, NASA sent a satellite named Mariner 10 to study Mercury. In 2004, NASA sent a new satellite named Messenger to Mercury to get more information. NASA hopes Messenger will explain how the planet was formed, how it's like Earth, and if there's any ice there. Messenger will start orbiting Mercury in 2011 and send back information about the planet for a year before it crashes.

The topic sentence states the main idea.

Important details are put in the writer's own words.

A closing sentence ends the summary.

After you read . . .

- **Ideas** (1) What is the main idea of the summary?
- **Organization** (2) What does the writer do in his closing sentence?
- **Voice** (3) Did the writer use a funny or serious voice? Why?

English Language Learners

Review acronyms and vocabulary terms that may be unfamiliar to students *(NASA, Messenger, satellite, orbit, core, poles).* Build background knowledge by showing photos of Mercury and the satellite *Messenger* in books, magazines, or on Internet Web sites. Then have volunteers read the paragraphs of the report aloud.

Advanced Learners

Have students review the article "*Messenger* Sent to Mercury." Challenge them to write a different closing sentence for Ugo's summary.

Summary Paragraph

After students have had a chance to read the article and summary paragraph, ask them to look for the following:

- keywords from the article that Ugo used in his summary (for example, *mystery, the planet Mercury, Mariner 10*)
- ideas that Ugo didn't use (why Mercury is hard to study, details about the *Mariner 10* mission)
- ways Ugo presented the details in shorter form (for example, he combined the last two sentences of the article's second paragraph into one sentence with a series of three details (*NASA hopes* Messenger *will . . .*)

After you read . . .

Answers

Ideas 1. what NASA is doing to learn more about Mercury

Organization 2. refers to the beginning and adds new information by telling when NASA's plan to learn more about Mercury will take effect

Voice 3. a serious voice because it is more appropriate for nonfiction writing about factual information

Prewriting Reading an Article

Many articles geared for students are available on the Internet at news sites such as those created by

- *Time* magazine (www.timeforkids.com),
- *National Geographic* (www.nationalgeographic.com/kids/), and at
- www.kidsnewsroom.org

If students find an article on the Internet, print it out for them (if permission is given at the site) so that they can underline or highlight details. Emphasize, however, that they should read the article all the way through at least once before marking up the article. Explain that it's important to know what the whole article is about before deciding what to use in a summary.

Direct students' attention to Ugo's underlining. Point out that he forgot to underline some details in paragraph 2 that he used in his summary. Ask students to identify what those details are *(how the planet was formed; like Earth;* and *if there is ice).*

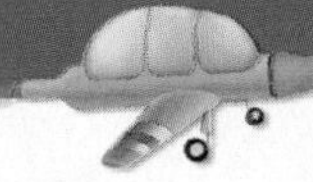

Prewriting Reading an Article

Your teacher may help you find an article to summarize. As you read, remember to look for the main idea and the most important details.

Prewrite Select and read an article.

1. **Find a short article about an interesting subject you are studying.**
2. **Read the article very carefully.**
3. **Write down the main idea and the most important details. (If you have a photocopy of the article, you may underline the details.)**

Ugo's Underlining

Messenger Sent to Mercury

The planet Mercury has long been a mystery. It is usually in the sun's bright glare, so it's hard for scientists to study it. In 1973, NASA (the **N**ational **A**eronautics and **S**pace **A**dministration) sent *Mariner 10* on a mission to gather data about Venus and Mercury. As the satellite orbited the sun, it flew past Mercury three times between 1974 and 1975. The information it sent back was based on viewing only half the planet's surface.

Now NASA has sent a new satellite to orbit Mercury. It may answer mysteries of how the planet was formed and how it can look like the moon yet have a core like Earth. It will see if there is ice in the craters at the north and south poles of Mercury.

The new satellite, named *Messenger* (**ME**rcury **S**urface, **S**pace **EN**vironment, **GE**ochemistry, and **R**anging mission), was launched on August 14, 2004. *Messenger* will begin orbiting Mercury in March of 2011. It will send back radio signals for a full year. After that it will stop working and crash into Mercury.

Struggling Learners

Explain that the topic sentence in a summary paragraph states the main idea of the article. Have students test their topic sentences.

- Read it to a partner.
- Have your partner tell the main idea in his or her own words.
- If your partner states the idea incorrectly, revise your topic sentence.

English Language Learners

Students may benefit from using a graphic organizer, such as a table diagram, for their notes. Distribute copies of the reproducible Table Diagram (TE page 599). Have students write the topic on the tabletop. Then have them write supporting details on the table legs. Other students may prefer to write their topic in the center of a cluster map and organize their details in the surrounding ovals.

Writing a Summary Paragraph 311

Writing Developing the First Draft

Use these guidelines to write your summary paragraph.

Develop your summary paragraph.

1. Tell the main idea of the article in your first sentence.
2. In your own words, give the most important details in the body of your paragraph.
3. Write the main idea in a new way in the closing sentence.

Revising Reviewing Your Writing

The following questions can help you revise your first draft.

Improve your work.

1. Did I start with a topic sentence?
2. Did I include the most important details?
3. Did I put my body sentences in a logical order?
4. Did I restate the main idea in a closing sentence?

Editing Checking for Conventions

Check capitalization, punctuation, spelling, and grammar.

Check your work.

1. Did I include accurate facts from the original article?
2. Have I checked for errors in punctuation, spelling, and grammar?

Writing Developing the First Draft

Before students write, have them work with a partner to gather their thoughts. Instruct one student to ask, "What is your article about?" and then to listen carefully and take notes as the other student explains his or her article.

After both students have described their articles, have them give each other the notes they took while listening to use as they draft.

Revising Reviewing Your Writing

Ask students to refer to their planning notes or the copy of the article with details underlined.

- Have students compare the details in their paragraph to their planning notes. Did they forget any details they wanted to mention?
- Have students compare the wording of their summaries to the original article. Are there more places where they could use their own words?

Editing Checking for Conventions

Have students double-check their spelling and practice using a dictionary by looking up at least three of the words they used.

* To work with students on Improving Spelling, see SE pages 502–509.

Advanced Learners

Provide students with the opportunity to support each other during revising by having them exchange their drafts with a partner. Have each student check his or her partner's draft using the revising questions. Then have partners discuss any questions on the checklist for which they answered "no."

Grammar Connection

Numbers

- **Proofreader's Guide** page 494 (+)
- ***GrammarSnap*** Commas in Numbers
- ***SkillsBook*** pages 12, 55

Verb Tenses

- **Proofreader's Guide** page 540 (+)
- ***Write Source*** pages 386–387
- ***GrammarSnap*** Past Tense Verbs
- ***SkillsBook*** pages 141–142

Irregular Verbs

- **Proofreader's Guide** pages 544–545
- ***GrammarSnap*** Past Tense Verbs
- ***SkillsBook*** pages 147–148

Capitalization

- **Proofreader's Guide** pages 490–491
- ***Write Source*** pages 375 (+), 378 (+)
- ***GrammarSnap*** Capitalization
- ***SkillsBook*** pages 47–48

Writing a Research Report

Objectives
- Understand the purpose, content, and form of a research report.
- Choose an interesting topic to write about.
- Plan, draft, revise, edit, and publish a research report.

If you plan to have students choose topics of their own rather than use a topic being studied in class, give students a few days to think about their topics (see TE page 316). Encourage them to

- take note of things or events that arouse their curiosity or make them wonder how or why something works;
- think of TV programs or Web sites that were interesting;
- spend time in the library looking at books, newspapers, and magazines that interest them;
- ask friends and family members if there are things they wonder about; or
- carry a little notebook with them and write down ideas as soon as they come up.

Writing a Research Report

Writing a research report can be a lot of fun. When you do research, you look for information about a topic that interests you. Then, when you write your report, you tell what you discovered! In this chapter, you will learn how to write a research report.

Materials
- Adhesive tape (TE p. 318)
- Tape recorder (TE p. 320)
- Highlighters in different colors (TE p. 322)
- Short selection from a classroom text (TE p. 323)
- Diagram of planets (TE p. 324)
- Magazine and newspaper articles (TE p. 334)
- Drawing supplies (TE p. 336)

Copy Masters
- 5 W's Chart (TE p. 320)
- Response Sheet (TE p. 330)
- Thinking About Your Writing (TE p. 337)

Writing a Research Report 313

Research Report

1

Exploring Mercury
by Ugo Garrett

If you lived on Mercury, you would celebrate your birthday every three months! That's because a year on Mercury is only about three Earth months long. Scientists have discovered amazing facts about Mercury.

Mercury is the closest planet to the sun. It is one of the inner planets of our solar system. It travels around the sun in an oval orbit. Its closest distance to the sun is 47 million miles away. Its farthest distance is 70 million miles away. The sun looks three times bigger from Mercury than it does from Earth.

Mercury can be compared to Earth. It is solid like Earth, but it is only half the size of Earth. Unlike Earth, Mercury has no moon. Also, it has no atmosphere to protect it. Meteors and comets are always crashing into

Research Report

Invite volunteers to read the essay aloud to classmates, changing readers for each paragraph. Afterward, ask students to describe what they thought of the essay. Did they think it was interesting? Why or why not?

Have students talk about the purpose of each of the five paragraphs:

- Opening paragraph mentions an amazing fact and says that scientists have discovered more such amazing facts.
- Paragraph 2 describes where Mercury is in the solar system.
- Paragraph 3 compares and contrasts Mercury with Earth.
- Paragraph 4 describes scientists' efforts to learn more about Mercury by sending probes.
- Closing paragraph mentions a mystery scientists particularly want to solve (if there's ice on Mercury) and says when they might be able to find out (2011).

Note that Ugo was able to use information from his summary paragraph (SE page 309) in his research paper. Have students identify the parts of the report that they had already learned about from reading the summary.

- In sentence 4 of the summary, Ugo mentions there are ways Mercury is *like Earth*; paragraph 3 of the essay returns to this topic.
- Paragraph 4 of the report introduces the main idea of the summary (*scientists are studying Mercury*) and gives details about the *Mariner 10* mission mentioned in the summary.
- The report's closing paragraph mentions the possibility of ice on Mercury and that *Messenger* will begin transmitting data in 2011.
- The bibliography includes the article "*Messenger* Sent to Mercury" that Ugo based his summary paragraph on.

If students choose the same topic for their report as they did for their summary paragraph, encourage them to use their summary paragraphs to add details to their report.

2

its surface. These crashes form many craters. There are no seasons on Mercury because it isn't tilted on its axis. During the day, it can be hotter than the hottest oven. At night, it can be colder than the coldest freezer. Mercury's temperature gets as high as 800 degrees Fahrenheit. At night, it can reach 300 degrees below zero!

Scientists are studying Mercury. In the 1970s, they sent a space probe called *Mariner 10* to orbit Mercury. Cameras on the probe sent back information. In 2004, another probe named *Messenger* was launched. It will send back information on a computer.

Today, scientists want to solve one of Mercury's mysteries. Old radar pictures show something shiny in the craters of the north and south poles. Scientists think the shiny part may be ice on the closest planet to the sun! After 2011, *Messenger* may send back more amazing facts about Mercury.

Writing a Research Report 315

3

Bibliography

Kipp, Steven L. *Mercury.* Bridgestone Books, Mankato, MN 2005

McIntyre, Lloyd. Interview. April 12, 2010

"Mercury (planet)." *Microsoft Encarta Online Encyclopedia 2008*

"*Messenger* Sent to Mercury." *Scholastic News,* October 4, 2004

After you read . . .

- **Ideas** **(1) How did Ugo get the reader's attention in the first paragraph?**
- **Organization** **(2) How many paragraphs are in the report?**
- **Word Choice** **(3) How can you tell that Ugo is excited about his topic?**

Explain that a bibliography is a list of the books and other sources that provide information for a report.

Ask students to identify the kinds of sources Ugo used for his paper (book, interview, encyclopedia, and news magazine).

Note that it is a good idea to use different kinds of sources, because each provides different information about a topic. For example:

- Books provide detailed information about the topic but might not have the latest information available.
- In interviews, experts can help explain confusing ideas and add a personal angle.
- Encyclopedias provide solid factual information.
- News magazines report on the most recent discoveries.

After you read . . .

Answers

Ideas 1. related an interesting fact to readers' experience

Organization 2. five

Word Choice 3. Possible answers:

- use of interesting details to create an enthusiastic voice
- use of exclamatory sentences
- the adjective *amazing*

Prewriting Choosing a Topic

If it suits your curriculum, coordinate students' research reports with a subject they are studying in class. Work with the whole group to help students choose topics:

- Write the central idea on the chalkboard.
- Ask students to brainstorm as many ideas related to it as they can.
- As they call out their ideas, create a cluster on the board.
- When the cluster is large enough, point out possible topics and have one or two students write about each of them.

If some students still have difficulty choosing among the topics, suggest that they work on their own to find something else that interests them and that fits the chosen theme.

* Refer students to SE page 436 for ways to start thinking about a topic.

Technology Connections

Students can use the added features of the Net-text as they explore this stage of the writing process.

Write Source Online **Net-text**

Prewriting Choosing a Topic

The first step in writing your report is to choose a topic. Ugo's class used a cluster to brainstorm for topic ideas about outer space. When they finished, Ugo chose Mercury as the topic for his report.

Prewrite Create your cluster.

1. **Write and circle your subject in the middle of a piece of paper.**
2. **Then write related words around the subject, as shown below.**
3. **Keep adding words until you find a topic that interests you.**

Cluster

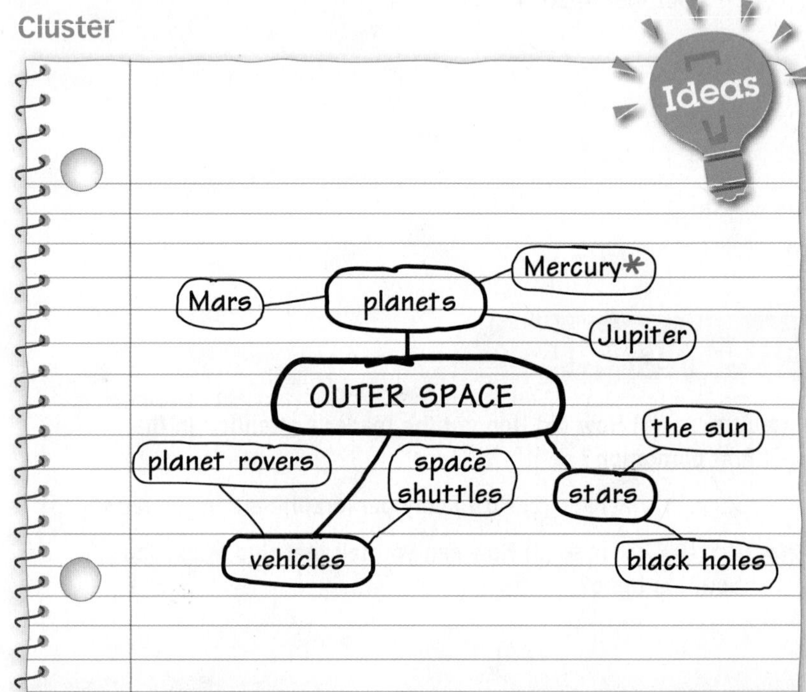

English Language Learners

If students have difficulty determining if their topics are appropriate, have them answer the following questions:

- Which one of your topics is most interesting to you?
- What do you already know about this topic?
- What would you like to learn about this topic?

Struggling Learners

Some students may find choosing a topic for their cluster difficult. Help them get started by suggesting they refer to their social studies or science textbook to find interesting topics. Point out that the topic may be something that has already been covered in class or a new topic that interests them.

Exploring Your Topic

After choosing your topic, it's time to plan your research. Ugo made the chart below. He thought about what he knew about the topic and about questions he needed to answer.

Prewrite **Plan your research.**

1. **Make a chart like Ugo's.**
2. **In the first column, write the questions you need to answer.**
3. **In the second column, write facts you already know.**
4. **In the third column, write the names of sources where you plan to look for answers.**

Questions Chart

My Questions	What I Know	Possible Sources
Where is Mercury?	Mercury is the planet closest to the sun.	our online encyclopedia
What is this planet like?	It is smaller than Earth.	book about the solar system
How did scientists learn about Mercury?		science magazine
		interview

Advanced Learners

Suggest that students choose two topics from their clusters. Have them list questions for both topics and then determine which of the two seems to have the most potential for a research report. Students should realize that the topic that generates the most questions and possible sources is probably the best choice.

Exploring Your Topic

Before having students fill out a chart as shown in the sample, ask them to change the heading of the third column to *Where could I learn about this?*

Reassure students that it's okay if they don't have a lot to put in the *What I Know* column of the chart. Explain that the point of doing research is to find out about the topic. Their main goal is to ask interesting questions and then to find the answers to them.

Mention also to students that they may think of another question or two as they learn more about the topic. Explain that they should simply add any new questions to their chart.

Prewriting Gathering Information

Encourage students not to let their gathering grid become too cramped with notes. This might make the notes difficult to read later on. If students need more space to write in, they can

- tape two pieces of paper together to make a larger grid or
- add a second page to the grid.

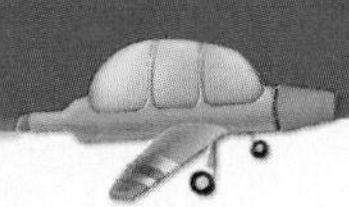

Prewriting Gathering Information

A research report usually has information from two or more sources. Ugo found information in an encyclopedia, a book, and a magazine. As he found answers to his questions, he wrote them on a gathering grid. Part of Ugo's gathering grid is shown on the next page.

Prewrite **Make a gathering grid.**

1. **Get a big piece of paper so you will have space to write your answers.**
2. **Write your research questions in the first column of your gathering grid.**
3. **Then list your sources across the top.**
4. **As you find information, fill in the spaces with answers to your questions.**

Struggling Learners

For students who need help writing research questions, suggest they use a format similar to Ugo's for their gathering grid. Such questions could include the following:

- What/who is [topic]?
- What is [topic] like?
- How do we know about [topic]?

Writing a Research Report 319

Ugo's Gathering Grid

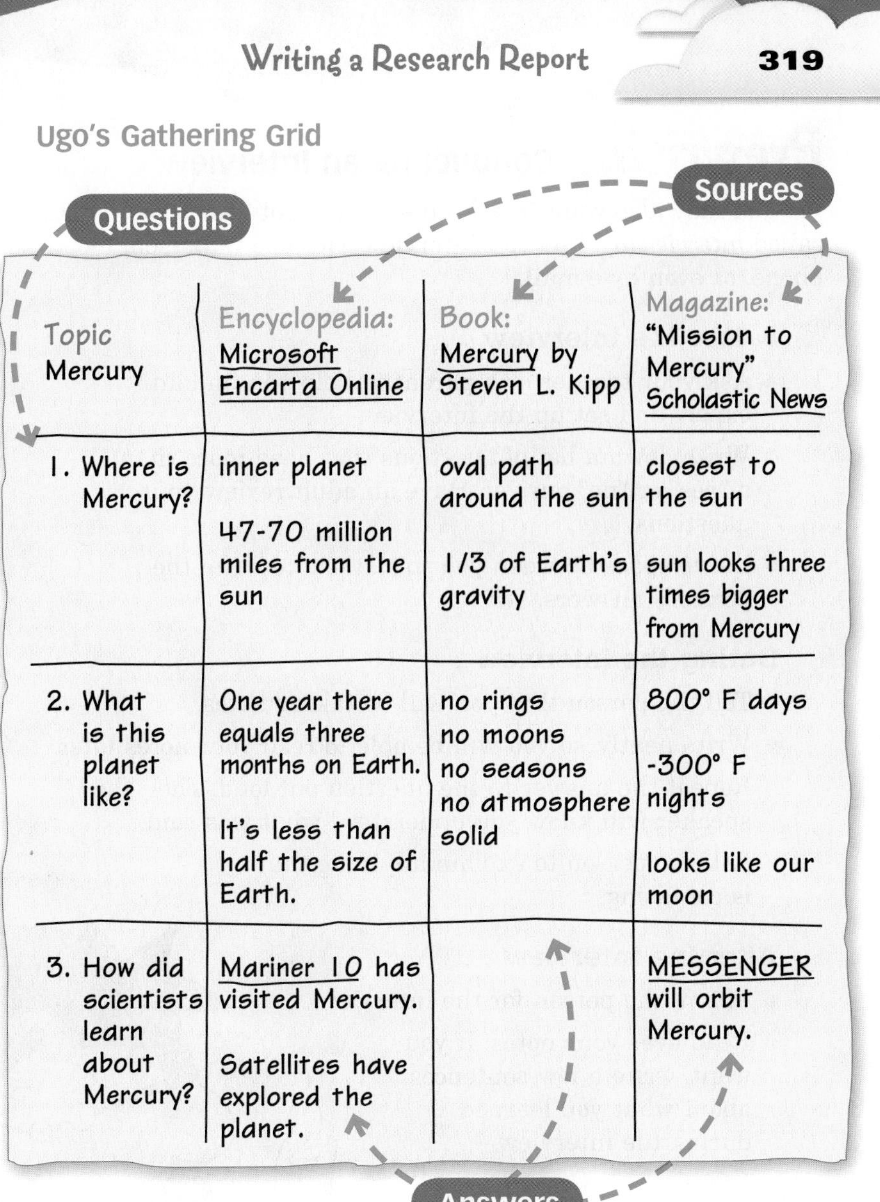

Topic Mercury	Encyclopedia: Microsoft Encarta Online	Book: Mercury by Steven L. Kipp	Magazine: "Mission to Mercury" Scholastic News
1. Where is Mercury?	inner planet 47-70 million miles from the sun	oval path around the sun 1/3 of Earth's gravity	closest to the sun sun looks three times bigger from Mercury
2. What is this planet like?	One year there equals three months on Earth. It's less than half the size of Earth.	no rings no moons no seasons no atmosphere solid	800° F days -300° F nights looks like our moon
3. How did scientists learn about Mercury?	Mariner 10 has visited Mercury. Satellites have explored the planet.		MESSENGER will orbit Mercury.

Ugo's Gathering Grid

Note that although Ugo was able to find answers to all his questions in the three sources he chose, students might find they need an additional source or two. If this happens, suggest that students

- present their question to classmates to see if anyone else has encountered details related to the question while researching their essays, and/or
- consult with a librarian for help finding a source with the answers.

Students may find that their troublesome question has an answer that is too complicated to address in their report—or that the answer isn't known yet. If so, it would probably be best to write a new question that can be answered in one of the sources they are using.

Advanced Learners

Challenge students to choose two types of sources and plan a panel discussion using the following questions as discussion prompts:

- Which type of source do you think is easier to use? Why? (Students might mention that in their source the text is easy to read, pictures and illustrations are informative and clear, and the glossary and index are easy to use.)
- Which type do you think is more reliable? Why? (Students might mention a more current copyright date, as well as up-to-date information and a familiar author.)
- Which type would you probably not use? Why? (Students might give as reasons an old copyright date, a difficult reading level, and illustrations or tables that are difficult to understand.)

Prewriting Conducting an Interview

Talk to students about the interviews they have seen or heard. These might have occurred in the following venues:

- on television or radio news shows
- in documentary films
- in school

Explain that people are interviewed for different reasons.

- Some interviewees are experts on the topic (for example, an astronaut who knows a lot about space travel).
- Others might not be experts, but they experienced what the writer is interested in (for example, a parent who saw Halley's comet the last time it passed by, in 1986).

Prewriting Conducting an Interview

You may also want to ask an expert about your topic. That's called *interviewing*. You can interview someone in person, by phone, or even by e-mail.

Before the interview . . .

- Ask your teacher or a parent to help you find an expert and set up the interview.
- Write down a list of questions that need more than a "yes" or "no" answer. Have an adult review your questions.
- Leave space between your questions to write the person's answers.

During the interview . . .

- Tell the person that you will be taking notes.
- Write neatly, so you will be able to read your notes later.
- Repeat the answer to the question out loud. Then the speaker will know you understood what was said.
- Ask the person to explain anything that is confusing.

After the interview . . .

- Thank the person for the interview.
- Read over your notes. If you want, write a few sentences about what you learned during the interview.

Teaching Tip: Questions That Encourage Talking

Distribute copies of the reproducible 5 W's Chart (TE page 597) for students to use as they develop their interview questions. Explain that questions beginning with any of the five *W* words (who, what, when, where, why)—or with the *H* word (how)—require people to explain their answer. These questions can't be answered by a simple "yes" or "no."

Encourage students to brainstorm at least one question for each row of the chart and then to choose the three questions they like best to use in their interview.

English Language Learners

Some students may want to conduct an interview but feel limited by their English skills. Suggest that students tape the interview so they can focus on speaking during the interview and listening and writing down ideas after the interview.

Writing a Research Report 321

Ugo's Interview Notes

Interviewer: Ugo Garrett Date: April 12, 2010

Expert: Lloyd McIntyre, Astronomer
Carlyle Planetarium

Question 1: What is Mercury like?

- small and rocky
- very hot
- "It's much like Earth, but smaller and closer to the sun."

Question 2: Could people live there?

- not without a special space suit
- no atmosphere
- meteors crash into it
- no air

Ugo wrote down details about the interview, his questions, notes, and one exact quotation.

Ugo's Interview Notes

- Tell students that a good way to interview people is by e-mail, because
- many experts have Web sites that provide the expert's e-mail address and encourage readers to send in questions;
- the interviewees can answer when they have time (in-person or telephone interviews must be scheduled ahead); and
- students don't have to worry whether they've written quotes correctly, because the interviewee's answers will be in the e-mail response.

No matter how they conduct the interview, emphasize that it is important to do the following:

- politely ask whether the person would be willing to answer questions,
- carefully research and plan a few important questions (not too many), and
- follow up with a note thanking the interviewee.

Set aside class time for students who interviewed someone to write thank-you notes.

Advanced Learners

Challenge students to expand on the kinds of interview questions they ask. They can do such things as the following:

- Verify facts that they can find only in one source.
- Ask questions they think of during the interview.
- Ask the expert to provide a fascinating or little known fact about the topic.

Prewriting Organizing Information

Remind students that an outline is only a sketchy version of a full draft—they aren't writing the report yet. They don't have to use the exact topic sentences they will write for their outline, or use all the details, or put them in the same order. (Of course, if they do end up following their outline, that's fine, too.)

Point out to students that because the outline is used mostly to plan the middle of the essay, Ugo hasn't put the opening and closing paragraphs on his outline.

* For more about how to Make an Outline, see SE page 444.

Prewriting Organizing Information

An outline is like a road map for writing your paper. You may not follow the map exactly, but it can guide you along the way.

1. **Give your outline a heading.**
   Ugo wrote "The Planet Mercury" as his outline heading.
2. **Write your topic sentences.**
   Each topic sentence should answer one of your research questions from your gathering grid. To write a topic sentence, just answer the question with a statement.

   Where is Mercury?
   Mercury is the closest planet to the sun.
3. **Add in your details.**
   Under each topic sentence, list details from your grid that explain the sentence or tell more about it.

Create your outline.

1. Read over Ugo's outline on the next page.
2. Then follow the directions above to write your own outline.
3. Use the information from your gathering grid on page 319.

Struggling Learners

Help students make an outline by following these steps:

- List your main points and code each one with a different color highlighter.
- Review your notes and highlight each with the color of the point it relates to.
- Use the color-coded notes as a guide for your outline.

Writing a Research Report 323

Ugo's Outline

Organization

The Planet Mercury

I. Mercury is the closest planet to the sun.

- Mercury is one of the inner planets.
- It is 47-70 million miles from the sun.
- It travels in an oval path.
- The sun looks three times bigger from Mercury.

II. Mercury can be compared to Earth.

- Mercury is solid, like Earth.
- Mercury is less than half the size of Earth.
- It has long days and short years.
- It has no moons or seasons.
- Mercury can be from 800° F to 300° F below zero.
- There is no atmosphere to protect the planet.

III. Scientists are studying Mercury.

- *Mariner 10* has explored the planet.
- *Messenger* is going to orbit the planet.

I. Where is Mercury?

II. What is this planet like?

III. How did scientists learn about Mercury?

Ugo's Outline

To help students become more familiar with the idea of outlining, work backward to create an outline based on a finished piece of writing.

- From one of your class books, choose an interesting topic that is explained in short paragraphs.
- Have a volunteer read the selection aloud.
- Point out the topic sentence for each paragraph; write these on the board, using a Roman numeral to mark each sentence and leaving plenty of room below the sentence for the details.
- Reread each paragraph separately. Ask students to identify the supporting details in each paragraph. Write these in order below the respective topic sentences, using bullet points to mark each new detail.

Stress that outlines are not used only for research reports. Encourage students to use an outline anytime they need to plan any kind of essay.

English Language Learners

Using a volunteer's gathering grid, model how to turn the words and phrases into complete sentences and write them on the outline. For extra practice, have small groups identify the subject and predicate in each of Ugo's sentences.

Struggling Learners

Help students connect the ideas on Ugo's gathering grid to the outline by comparing the two. Working in pairs, have one partner turn to the gathering grid on SE page 319 and the other turn to the outline on SE page 323. Have students first locate an idea on the gathering grid, and then find the matching sentence on the outline.

Writing Starting Your Report

Before students start their drafts, tell them that they don't necessarily have to write the opening paragraph first. Because they've been working on their outlines, they may find it easier to write the middle paragraphs first (see SE pages 326–327) and then to come back to the first paragraph.

Encourage students to begin noticing how the articles they read start out. Have them look at the article Ugo summarized (SE page 308). The opening strategy doesn't match any of the three suggested ideas—what strategy do students think is being used? (It states an interesting fact—scientists don't know much about Mercury.)

Ask students to look back at the articles they used for their summary paragraphs. Have volunteers share their article's opener with the class and describe the strategy they think the writer used. Additional opening strategies they might find include the following:

- Start with an interesting quote.
- Tell a story.
- Begin with a description of action.

Technology Connections

Students can use the added features of the Net-text as they explore this stage of the writing process.

Write Source Online ***Net-text***

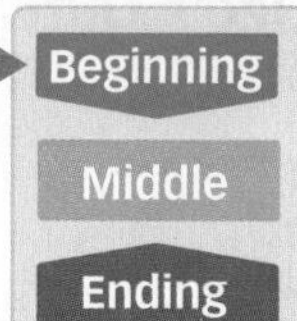

Writing Starting Your Report

Beginning
Middle
Ending

The Beginning Paragraph

The first paragraph of your report should grab the reader's attention and tell what your report is about. You can use one of the ways listed below to get started.

Ask a question.
Do you know which planet is closest to the sun?

OR

Make a clever comparison.
Being first in line isn't always best. Just ask Mercury, the planet closest to the sun!

OR

Connect with the reader.
If you lived on Mercury, you would celebrate your birthday every three months!

Write **Draft your beginning.**

1. Write a beginning paragraph that grabs your reader's attention and tells what your report is about.
2. Try one of the three ways above to get started.

English Language Learners

Some students may find the clever comparison confusing. Show students an illustration or diagram of the planets. Point out that Mercury is the closest planet to the sun, so it is the hottest planet. Explain that this is why Ugo refers to Mercury as "first in line" and that being first "isn't always fun."

Writing a Research Report 325

Ugo's Beginning Paragraph

Here is Ugo's beginning paragraph. Notice how he wrote on every other line to leave room for changes.

The Planet Mercury

If you lived on Mercury, you would celebrate your birthday every three months! That's because a year on Mercury is only about three Earth months long. This report will tell you more interesting facts about the planet Mercury. Scientists have discovered amazing facts about Mercury.

Beginning

Ugo makes a personal connection with the reader.

Ugo's Beginning Paragraph

Talk with students about Ugo's opening paragraph. Do they think it might have worked better if he had used another one of his opening ideas? If so, why? Ask students to point out anything else they might change about the opening paragraph. Answers might include the following:

- Ugo could explain a little more about what he means when he says "a year on Mercury is only about three Earth months long." (Have students look up *year* in a dictionary and note the definition that says a year is the time it takes for any planet to travel once around the sun.)
- The sentence that begins *This report will tell you . . .* isn't needed. Explain that it is always better to go ahead and present the facts rather than spend time telling readers what you're going to do.

Writing Developing Your Middle Paragraphs

To demonstrate that students don't have to follow their outline exactly, have them compare the sample middle paragraphs to the outline on SE page 323. Ask them to point out what changes Ugo made to his organization. Possible answers:

First middle paragraph:

- Changed order of details by mentioning Mercury's oval orbit before saying how far it is from the sun.

Second middle paragraph:

- Changed order of details by saying that Mercury has no atmosphere before saying it has no seasons.
- Changed information slightly. The draft says Mercury is *only* half Earth's size, but the outline says it's *less than* half the size.
- Omitted a detail that was on the outline (Mercury has short days and years).
- Added information about how the planet looks (it has holes from the meteors and comets that crash into it).
- Added explanation of why Mercury has no seasons (it isn't tilted on its axis).

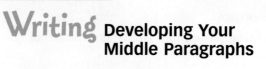

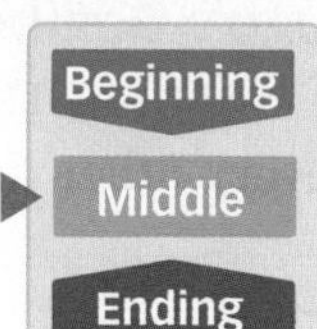

Writing Developing Your Middle Paragraphs

Beginning
Middle
Ending

The Middle Paragraphs

Each middle paragraph covers one main idea. The paragraphs begin with a topic sentence and include sentences that give supporting details.

Write Develop your middle paragraphs.

1. **Write your middle paragraphs using your outline from page 323 as a guide.**
2. **Start each paragraph with one of your topic sentences.**
3. **Then add sentences that give supporting details.**

Ugo's Middle Paragraphs

Middle Each paragraph begins with a topic sentence (underlined). Supporting details (dotted lines) are added.

Mercury is the closest planet to the sun. Mercury is one of the inner planets of our solar system. It travels around the sun in an oval orbit. Its closest distance to the sun is 47 million miles away. Its farthest distance is 70 million miles away. The sun looks three times bigger from Mercury than it does from Earth.

Writing a Research Report 327

Mercury can be compared to Earth. It is solid like Earth, but it is only half the size of Earth. Mercury has no moon. Also, it has no atmosphere too protect it. Meteors and comets are always crashing into its surface. Mercury does not have rings like Saturn. These crashes form many holes. There are no seasons on Mercury because it isn't tilted on its axis. During the day, it can be hotter than the hottest oven at night it can be colder than the coldest freezer. Mercury's tempeture gets as high as 800 degrees Fahrenheit. At night, it can reach 300 degrees below zero!

Supporting details (dotted lines) are added to each paragraph.

Supporting details are explained.

Remind students to check off each detail on their outline as they use it in the draft. Suggest to students that before beginning to write, they read over their outline as well as all the notes they took while researching. This will refresh their memories about the available information so that, if they need to, they can include a detail in their draft that isn't on the outline.

Explain that it is important that the information in their essays be correct. Tell students to be extra careful to follow their notes as they transfer the information to their drafts. Also suggest that they double-check any details they have questions about to make sure they are complete and accurate.

Writing Ending Your Report

Reassure students who are having trouble deciding how to end their report that many writers struggle over this step in the writing process. Suggest helpful ways of approaching the problem. These include the following:

- Take a break before finishing the draft. Doing so can give you a fresh outlook on your essay and sometimes help you think of a good ending.
- Write more than one ending and then choose the one you like best.
- Read the unfinished draft aloud to a parent, caretaker, or friend, and ask the person what he or she thinks should come next to bring the report to an end.

Writing Ending Your Report

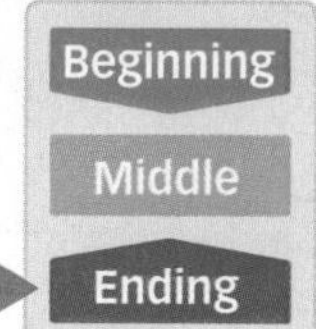

The Ending Paragraph

The ending of your report should leave the reader with something to think about.

Connect with the beginning of your report.

It would be great to have my birthday more often, but I wouldn't like Mercury's hot days and cold nights.

OR

Share a final thought.

Today, scientists want to solve one of Mercury's mysteries.

OR

Restate the main idea of the report.

There's so much to learn about Mercury. That's why scientists are sending more satellites to the planet.

Create your ending paragraph.

1. End your research paper strongly.
2. Use one of the three ideas above to leave the reader with something to think about.

English Language Learners

Have students compare the last sentence of Ugo's ending paragraph with the last sentence of his beginning paragraph on SE page 325. Have students explain how the two sentences are the same and different. Then have student pairs brainstorm different ways to end one another's papers and discuss which one they think works best.

Writing a Research Report 329

Ugo's Ending Paragraph

Here is Ugo's ending paragraph. He decided to share a final thought with the reader.

Ending
Ugo ends with an interesting detail.

Today, scientists want to solve one of Mercury's mysteries. Old radar pictures show something shiny in the craters of the north and south poles. Scientists think the shiny part may be ice on the closest planet to the sun! After 2011, Messenger may send back more amazing facts about Mercury.

Ugo's Ending Paragraph

Ask students to look at the ending strategies Ugo considered using (SE page 328). Invite a volunteer to read the ending paragraph again—substituting one of the other sentences for the one Ugo chose. Point out that the paragraph doesn't make sense anymore. The sentence he chose directly affects what comes next.

Encourage students to think of how Ugo could have ended the essay using the other sentences. Possible answers include:

- Using the Connect strategy: Move the information about temperatures on Mercury to the end. *(It would be great to have my birthday more often, but I wouldn't like Mercury's hot days and cold nights. During the day, it can be hotter than . . . At night it can reach 300 degrees below zero!)*
- Using the Restate strategy: Put the information about the latest mission at the end. *(There's so much to learn about Mercury. That's why . . . to the planet. In 2004 a probe named* Messenger *was launched. After 2011, it may send back more amazing facts about the mysterious planet.)*

Advanced Learners

Review the three ways to end a report and discuss additional ways students can think of, such as asking a thought-provoking question or offering an opinion. Then challenge students to rewrite Ugo's ending paragraph using another method. Post their endings on a bulletin board for students to review if they get stuck thinking of ways to end their papers.

Revising Using a Response Sheet

Divide the class into pairs and have students trade papers. Provide photocopies of the reproducible Response Sheet (TE page 592) for students to fill out. Refer students to the rubric for expository writing on SE pages 160–161. If necessary, review the six traits as explained on the page to help students understand what qualities to look for in the essay they read.

Have students discuss their responses to each other's reports, clearing up any questions. Then students should use their partner's responses as they revise.

Technology Connections

Have students use the Writing Network features of the Net-text to comment on each other's drafts.

Write Source Online ***Net-text***

330

Revising Using a Response Sheet

In a peer conference, you and a classmate discuss each other's reports. The ideas you share can help both you and your partner make your reports better.

Work with a partner.

1. Read your report to a partner.
2. Ask your partner to fill out a response sheet.
3. Then listen to your partner's report and fill out a response sheet about the writing.
4. Use your partner's ideas to improve your report.

Response Sheet

Response Sheet

Writer: Ugo Responder: Caitlyn

Title: "Exploring Mercury"

What I like about your writing:

I liked the part about birthdays coming every three months!

You include lots of details about Mercury. I learned a lot from your report.

You sound very interested in your subject.

Questions I have about your writing:

What is a space probe?

Why is Mercury so cold at night?

Response Sheet

Before students begin reading each other's work, have them examine the sample peer response. Do they agree with Caitlyn's assessment of Ugo's work? Have them explain their answers.

Go through each of Caitlyn's comments about what she likes. What traits do her comments address?

- The first two comments address ideas—she likes the specific detail about birthdays and, in general, she likes the number of details used.
- The third comment addresses voice. She approves of the interested voice of the report.

Point out that Caitlyn's questions start with two of the 5 W's words, *what* and *why*. Remind students that the 5 W's words are particularly good ways to begin questions, because they require responses that are explanations.

* For more about the 5 W's, see SE page 442.

Revising Improving Your Ideas

Before students begin revising, refer them to the goals for expository writing on SE page 133.

Tell students that a good way to begin the revising process is to read the report through once to themselves silently and then a second time aloud. Explain that the silent reading helps them concentrate on the traits of organization and (during the editing stage) conventions. **Hearing the words read aloud** *(see below)* can help them evaluate the voice and sentence fluency of the piece.

Revising Improving Your Ideas

Here are several ways to improve your writing. Sometimes you may need to add details to make your ideas clearer. Other times, you may need to cut or change a detail that doesn't fit.

Revise the first draft of your paper.

1. **Look for places to add ideas.**
2. **Also look for places to change or cut ideas to make your report better.**

When should I add a detail?

You should **add** a detail to make part of your paper clearer, or easier to understand. Use a ∧ (caret) to show where to put the new information.

When should I change a detail?

You should **change** a word if you think it would make an idea clearer. Cross out the word with a neat line and write the new word above it.

When should I cut a detail?

You should **cut** a detail that doesn't belong in your paper. Use a ⌒ (delete mark) to show what you are cutting.

Teaching Tip: Hearing It Aloud

To free students even more to concentrate on the sound of the words they've written, have them choose partners and each read the other's paper aloud. The student whose paper is being read should

- listen carefully,
- take notes on anything that could be changed, and
- pay attention to where the reader stumbles over the words, because this can indicate where sentences aren't as clear as they should be.

English Language Learners

Some students may have difficulty adding details. Suggest that they review the questions their partner wrote on the Response Sheet. They can use the answers to these questions as additional details. Point out that the answers will most likely belong in the same paragraph that prompted their partner's question.

Writing a Research Report 333

Revising in Action

Ugo revised his report by adding a new sentence beginning, cutting an unnecessary detail, and changing a word.

looks three times bigger from Mercury than it does from Earth.

Add

Cut

Change

Mercury can be compared to Earth. It is solid like Earth, but it is only half the size of Earth. Unlike Earth, Mercury has no moon. Also, it has no atmosphere too protect it. Meteors and comets are always crashing into its surface. ~~Mercury does not have rings like Saturn.~~ These crashes form many ~~holes~~ craters. There are no seasons on Mercury because it isn't tilted on its axis. During the day, it can be hotter than the hottest oven at night it can be colder than the coldest freezer. Mercury's tempeture gets as high as 800 degrees Fahrenheit. At night, it can reach 300 degrees below zero!

Revising in Action

Discuss why Ugo made changes. Responses include the following:

- *unlike Earth*: added as a transition
- *Mercury does not have rings like Saturn*: deleted because it doesn't apply to the topic
- *holes*: changed to the more accurate noun, *craters*

Focus students' attention on the use of *compare* in the topic sentence. Explain that, generally, *comparing* two things involves telling how they are alike. Note that Ugo's paragraph focuses on how Mercury is different from Earth, and the word for describing how things are different is *contrast*. Tell students that in later grades they will encounter a popular form of expository essay known as a comparison-contrast essay, which describes how two things are alike and how they are different.

Advanced Learners

Direct students' attention to the oven and freezer comparison that Ugo makes before discussing Mercury's temperature. This comparison to familiar objects gives readers a sense of the extreme temperatures on Mercury. Challenge students to make similar comparisons in their reports.

Grammar Connection

Sentence Variety

- **Proofreader's Guide** pages 401, 408–410
- ***GrammarSnap*** Compound Subjects, Compound Verbs
- ***SkillsBook*** pages 87–88, 109–110, 113–114

Colons, Hyphens, Parentheses

- **Proofreader's Guide** pages 480–481, 482–483
- ***SkillsBook*** pages 37–38

Nouns (possessive)

- **Proofreader's Guide** pages 474 (+), 534 (+)
- ***Write Source*** page 377 (+)
- ***GrammarSnap*** Apostrophes to Show Possession
- ***SkillsBook*** page 124

Editing Checking for Conventions

Explain that it's always a good idea to use a different colored pencil or pen for marking editing changes because some changes can be very small. For example, it would be easy to overlook an added period if the mark were made in the same color ink as the rest of the paper.

After students have checked their own papers, have them trade papers with a partner and double-check each other's work.

Creating a Title

Guide students through the process of deciding on a title by focusing briefly on each strategy:

- Creative: Bring in several newspaper and magazine articles with creative titles. Which do students like best? Why? Ask them to brainstorm a creative title or two for their papers.
- Ideas from their report: Help students skim their papers and circle two phrases that would make good titles.
- Descriptive: Note that descriptive titles are a good, solid backup. Ugo chose a descriptive title for his report.

Technology Connections

Students can use the added features of the Net-text as they explore this stage of the writing process.

Write Source Online ***Net-text***

Editing Checking for Conventions

Now that you have finished revising your report, it's time to copy it over. Check the clean copy for errors in punctuation, capitalization, spelling, and grammar.

Conventions

Punctuation

___ 1. Did I use correct end punctuation for each sentence?
___ 2. Did I use commas correctly in my sentences?

Capitalization

___ 3. Did I start all my sentences with capital letters?
___ 4. Did I capitalize all proper nouns and titles?

Spelling

___ 5. Have I spelled all my words correctly?

Grammar

___ 6. Did I use correct verbs (*it* ***flies***, not *it* ***fly***)?
___ 7. Did I use the right words *(there, their, they're; to, two, too)*?

Creating a Title

- Describe the main idea: **Exploring Mercury**
- Be creative: **Mercury, Earth's Cousin**
- Use ideas from the paper: **Mercury, a Mystery Planet**

English Language Learners

Creative titles often depend on plays on words. Such titles can cause problems for students who are not entirely familiar with word play. For example, students may not understand why Ugo wrote "Mercury, Earth's Cousin." Point out the following:

- Earth and Mercury share common characteristics, so they are related in some ways.
- Earth and Mercury are both members of the Milky Way galaxy.
- Earth and Mercury belong to the same "family" of planets.

Writing a Research Report 335

Editing in Action

Ugo found some mistakes in his revised report.

looks three times bigger from Mercury than it does from Earth.

Mercury can be compared to Earth. It is solid like Earth, but it is only half the size of Earth. Unlike Earth, Mercury has no moon. Also, it has no atmosphere ~~too~~ to protect it. Meteors and comets are always crashing into its surface. These crashes form many craters. There are no seasons on Mercury because it isn't tilted on its axis. During the day, it can be hotter than the hottest oven. at night, it can be colder than the coldest freezer. Mercury's ~~tempeture~~ temperature gets as high as 800 degrees Fahrenheit. At night, it can reach 300 degrees below zero!

An incorrect word is replaced.

A run-on sentence is corrected with a period and a capital letter.

A spelling error is corrected.

Editing in Action

After reviewing the editing changes Ugo made, focus on the nouns *Mercury* and *Earth* in the paragraph. Why do students think these nouns are capitalized? (They are proper nouns that name specific planets.)

Note that students may often see the word *earth* without a capital letter. The form without a capital letter occurs when *earth* is used as a synonym for *ground* or *soil*.

* For more information about Proper Nouns, see SE page 375.

Note another example of specialized use that appears in Ugo's paper: underlining—or italicizing when writing on a computer—the names of space probes (see SE page 314). Explain that the names of sailing ships and aircraft are always treated this way.

* For more about underlining and italics, see SE page 478.

Grammar Connection

Verbs (review)

- **Proofreader's Guide** pages 538 (+), 542 (+)
- ***Write Source*** pages 383 (+), 384 (+), 385 (+)
- ***GrammarSnap*** Action Verbs, Helping Verbs
- ***SkillsBook*** pages 136, 149–150

Run-On Sentences

- **Proofreader's Guide** pages 526 (+), 528 (+)
- ***GrammarSnap*** Compound Sentences
- ***Write Source*** page 404 (+)
- ***SkillsBook*** pages 99–100

Apostrophes

- **Proofreader's Guide** pages 474 (+), 534 (+)
- ***Write Source*** page 377 (+)
- ***GrammarSnap*** Apostrophes to Show Possession
- ***SkillsBook*** pages 27–28

Subject-Verb Agreement

- ***Write Source*** page 388
- ***GrammarSnap*** Subject-Verb Agreement

Publishing Sharing Your Report

Note that the final version of Ugo's report was printed out on a computer. If students will be writing their final copy by hand, refer them to SE page 36 for the format.

Distribute drawing supplies and invite students to create one or two illustrations to accompany their report.

When students have finished their report, set aside time for them to share their work with the class. Have students read their report aloud and show the illustrations. Then invite the listeners to ask questions, and have the presenter respond.

Technology Connections

Remind students that they can use the Writing Network features of the Portfolio to share their work with peers.

- *Write Source Online* **Portfolio**
- *Write Source Online* **Net-text**

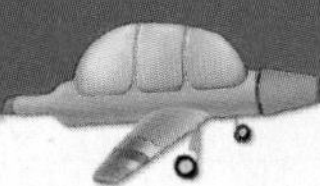

Publishing Sharing Your Report

Good job! You have worked hard on your report. Now it's time to make a neat final copy and share it.

Make a final copy.

Use the following guidelines to prepare your report.

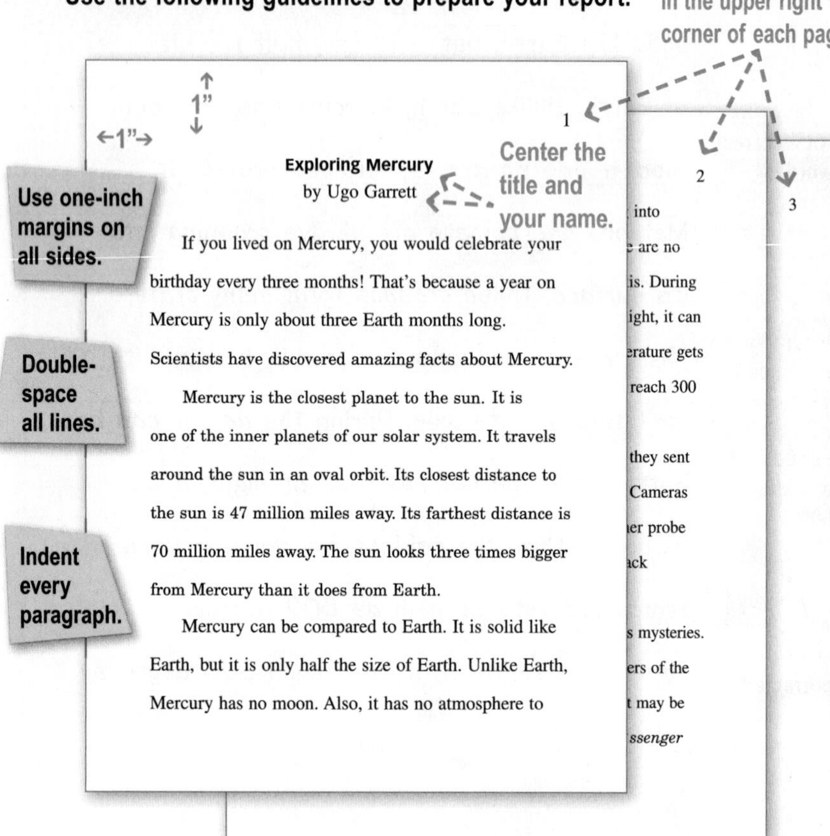

Put the page number in the upper right corner of each page.
1"
←1"→
1
2
3
Exploring Mercury
by Ugo Garrett
Center the title and your name.
Use one-inch margins on all sides.
Double-space all lines.
Indent every paragraph.
If you lived on Mercury, you would celebrate your birthday every three months! That's because a year on Mercury is only about three Earth months long. Scientists have discovered amazing facts about Mercury.
Mercury is the closest planet to the sun. It is one of the inner planets of our solar system. It travels around the sun in an oval orbit. Its closest distance to the sun is 47 million miles away. Its farthest distance is 70 million miles away. The sun looks three times bigger from Mercury than it does from Earth.
Mercury can be compared to Earth. It is solid like Earth, but it is only half the size of Earth. Unlike Earth, Mercury has no moon. Also, it has no atmosphere to

Reflecting on Your Writing

After you finish your report, complete each sentence below. Thinking about your work will help you grow as a writer.

Thinking About Your Writing

Name: Ugo Garrett

Title: Exploring Mercury

1. The best part of my essay is . . .

   the last paragraph. I still wonder if there's ice on Mercury.

2. The main thing I learned about writing a report is . . .

   that I have to carefully gather details and then I have to organize them before I start writing.

3. In my next report, I would like to research . . .

   sea turtles.

Reflecting on Your Writing

Provide photocopies of the reproducible Thinking About Your Writing (TE page 593) for students to fill out.

When students have finished writing their reflections, ask them to write the date at the top of the paper and keep the reflection, along with all their planning notes and the final essay.

Encourage students to read their past reflections regularly. This will help them to get an idea of the following:

- how they are improving as a writer
- skills they could work on
- possible interesting topics for future essays

Creating a Multimedia Presentation

Objectives

- Plan, draft, revise, and edit a multimedia presentation.
- Create a storyboard.

Talk about the word *multimedia*. Ask students to think of other words that begin with *multi-* and tell what they mean. Examples might include the following:

- multicolored (many colored)
- multimillionaire (someone with millions of dollars)

Explain that *media* is the plural form of *medium,* which means "a way of communicating" (writing, pictures, speech, music).

Have students combine the two ideas—*multi* and *media*—so they understand that *multimedia* means "many forms of communication."

Note that the section will help them create a report using a speech and a slide show, but there are other forms of multimedia presentation, too. A documentary, for example, combines talking, pictures, and, often, music.

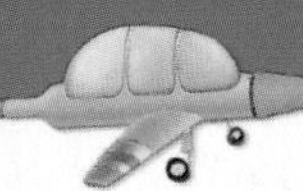

Creating a Multimedia Presentation

People can read a written report and listen to a speech. But they can do both with a multimedia presentation. A multimedia presentation is a report or speech that has been turned into a computer slide show. As you read your report aloud, the slide show illustrates each main idea.

Copy Masters

T-Chart (TE p. 340)

Creating a Multimedia Presentation 339

Prewriting Selecting a Topic and Details

You can turn almost any report or speech into a multimedia presentation.

Choose a topic and gather details.

1. Choose a report (or speech) that you would like to share with other people.
2. Next, make a list of the main ideas in your report. Each idea will be shown on one slide in your multimedia presentation.
3. Choose pictures, sounds, and animations to go with the words in your report. Make a media grid.

Media Grid

Words from your report	Pictures or videos	Animations	Music or sounds
1. Exploring Mercury	NASA photo of Mercury		exciting music
2. On Mercury, your birthday would happen every three months.		balloons circling the planet	

Prewriting Selecting a Topic and Details

If students will be preparing a presentation using an essay other than the research report they wrote for the previous section, evaluate the essay first to ensure that it's suitable. It is best for the purposes of the exercise if

- the essay is a research report,
- it is between three and five paragraphs long, and
- the student still has the planning notes used for the report.

As students begin preparing their media grid, remind them that the references they listed in their planning notes may lead them to pictures for the report.

They may also find it helpful to consult the outline they used, because all the important points in the report will be listed there.

English Language Learners

Decide ahead of time whether students will work together to create a presentation using a short article they have read and enjoyed. Create a short presentation to model your expectations. Ask students what they liked about it. Have them jot down the ideas they could incorporate into their own multimedia presentation. Provide suggestions and materials as they begin work.

Writing Making a Storyboard

Have students compare Ugo's storyboard to the sample research report shown on SE pages 313–315. How did he organize the information on his storyboard panels?

- Panel 1 shows the title and author.
- Panel 2 covers the main idea of the essay's introductory paragraph.
- Panel 3 uses the topic sentence from paragraph 2.
- Panels 4–6 cover the information in paragraph 3, but in a different order.
- Panel 7 covers the information in paragraph 4.
- Panel 8 involves the audience by asking them a question.

Tell students that they can shift information around a little, as Ugo did. Suggest that a different strategy might have been to follow the original paper more closely by making one panel for each paragraph of the essay, plus a title panel for the beginning.

Note that Ugo plans to have a sound effect and a picture for each panel. Tell students that having only sound or only a picture for some of their panels is fine.

Writing Making a Storyboard

Use your media grid to create a storyboard like the one below.

Create a storyboard.

1. **In each box, write the words that will appear on the screen.**
2. **In other colors, make notes about pictures and sounds.**

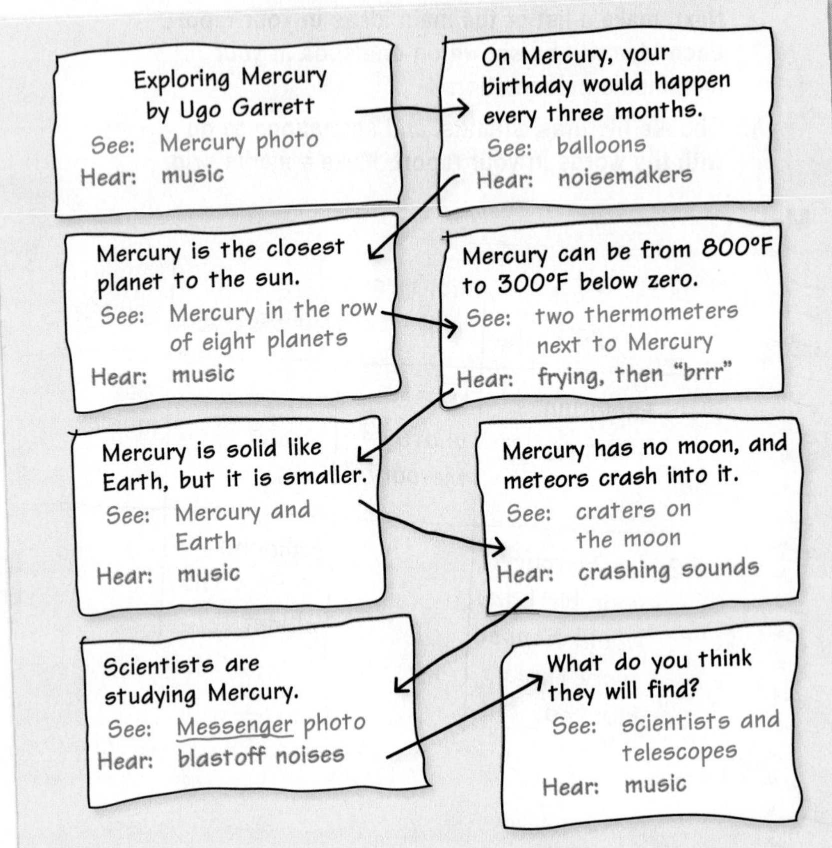

English Language Learners

To simplify the task, distribute a copy of the reproducible T-Chart (TE page 595). In the left column, have students write the words that will appear on the screen. In the right column, they can draw pictures, make speech bubbles, or jot words and phrases to help them think about the pictures and sounds.

Creating the Slides

Use a computer program to create your slides. You can find pictures and sounds in your software program, on the Internet, or on special CD's.

Create your slides.

1. **Find pictures and sounds for each slide.**
2. **Design your slides so they are easy to read.**

Revising Improving Your Presentation

Practice changing the slides as you speak. You may need to add, cut, or change slides to make your presentation clearer.

Make changes in your presentation.

1. **Practice giving your presentation to family and friends.**
2. **Listen to their suggestions for making it better.**

Editing Checking for Conventions

In a multimedia presentation, even little mistakes on the screen will distract your listeners from your message. So be sure to make everything just right.

Check your presentation for conventions.

1. **Check the text on each slide for errors in punctuation, capitalization, spelling, and grammar.**
2. **Ask someone else to check your report, too.**

Hold a class workshop to teach students how to use the presentation-making software on the computer. Provide additional guidance as students work on their presentations. Designate students who have more experience using computers as helpers, and encourage those with less computer experience to go to those students for help.

Revising Improving Your Presentation

Students may not have access to computers at home. Help them print out the pages of their presentations so they can practice for family and friends.

Editing Checking for Conventions

If possible, print out the pages of the presentation for students to read when looking for editing errors. It is generally easier to spot errors on a printed page than on a screen.

When students have finished their slides, host a class "conference day" so students can give their presentations in front of an audience. You may wish to design this as an event to which parents are invited.

English Language Learners

Before creating a slide presentation, have students review their storyboard draft to make sure they have the details in the correct order. They can cut apart their slides to make changes in the order of the presentation based on the flow of information. Point out that using too many visuals or adding too many sounds can be confusing and distracting to the audience.

Advanced Learners

As students create their slide presentations, invite them to jot down procedures they follow to make sure that things are working smoothly. After they have finished, have them use their notes to create a troubleshooting guide for other students who may be less comfortable with multimedia presentations.

Grammar Connection

Spelling

- **Proofreader's Guide** pages 503–506 (+)
- ***SkillsBook*** pages 65–66

The Tools of Learning

Common Core Standards Focus

Writing 10: Write routinely over extended time frames (time for research, reflection, and revision) and shorter time frames (a single sitting or a day or two) for a range of discipline-specific tasks, purposes, and audiences.

Skills

- Giving Speeches
- Writing in Journals and Learning Logs
- Viewing and Listening Skills
- Taking Tests

Tools and Techniques

- journals
- learning logs
- using the 5 W's to view media

Test-Taking

- test preparation
- four basic types of objective tests (true/false, matching, multiple choice, and fill-in-the-blank)
- writing prompts
- remembering for tests

Unit Pacing

Giving Speeches: 1.5–2 hours

In this section, students are shown how to prepare and present a speech about a topic of interest. Following are some of the topics that are covered:

- Learning more about the topic
- Deciding what to say
- Using note cards
- Practicing delivery
- Presenting the speech

Writing in Journals and Learning Logs: 1.5 hours

This section offers tips on keeping journals and learning logs. Following are some of the topics that are covered:

- Keeping personal and reading journals
- Writing, drawing, and asking questions in learning logs

Viewing and Listening Skills: 1–2 hours

This section explores ways to become a better television and Web site viewer. Following are some of the topics that are covered:

- Watching and evaluating the news
- Viewing and responding to television specials
- Understanding selling methods in commercials
- Evaluating Web sites
- Improving listening skills

Taking Tests: 45–90 minutes

This section helps students understand the test-taking process. The following are some of the topics that are covered:

- Developing good study habits
- Taking objective tests (true/false, matching, multiple choice, fill-in-the-blanks)
- Responding to writing prompts
- Using an idea map, flash cards, and a memory trick to remember for tests

Teacher's Notes for The Tools of Learning

This overview for the tools of learning includes some specific suggestions for teaching this unit.

Giving Speeches (pages 344–349)

Learning to give speeches will help young students become more comfortable with public speaking.

Writing in Journals and Learning Logs (pages 350–355)

A journal can be a notebook with blank or lined pages. It can also be a stack of paper stapled together. Journals can hold students' observations, ideas about favorite topics and hobbies, and notes that can be used in future writing tasks. Journal writing helps students discover their writing voices.

Share some of your own journal-writing experiences. Then share sections from a published journal, such as *Amelia's Notebook* by Marissa Moss. Allow class time for personal journaling on a regular basis, although not necessarily daily.

Whenever your class has a celebration, field trip, special guest, and so on, have each student write a journal entry about it. Then collect the pages and add photos or illustrations to create a special set of memoirs for your class library.

Viewing and Listening Skills (pages 356–363)

Television and the Internet shape what children know and believe about their world. Therefore children need to become educated viewers of both media.

Students spend more time listening than they do speaking, reading, and writing combined. With that much "practice," you might expect students to develop good listening skills automatically. But, of course, they don't. Students become good listeners by working at it.

Taking Tests (pages 364–371)

Tests are an inescapable part of school, and, for some, not always a pleasant part. Yet tests are an important way for both teachers and students to assess how they are doing. Understanding how to prepare for and take various kinds of tests can empower students.

Academic Vocabulary

Read aloud the academic terms, as well as the descriptions and questions. Model for students how to read one question and answer it. Have partners monitor their understanding and seek clarification of the terms by working through the meanings and questions together.

Minilessons

Talking Points
Giving Speeches

- On a sheet of paper, **MAKE** a series of columns with one word at the top of each column such as *animals, people, places, games,* and *holidays.* Under each heading, write as many examples as you can. For example, under *animals* you might write *dog, cat, elephant,* and so on.
  - **GO** through each list and **CHECK** the ones that interest you.
  - **DO** brief (30–60 second) impromptu speeches that focus on one special memory, experience, idea, or fact about the topic.

My Life!
Writing in Journals and Learning Logs

- **WRITE** an entry in your personal journal.
  - **WRITE** about something you saw, did, or heard about.
  - **GET** your ideas down on paper.

Whales, Hurricanes, or Rivers
Writing in Journals and Learning Logs

- **READ** an article in an encyclopedia about whales, hurricanes, or rivers.
  - **WRITE** a few sentences telling what you learned about the topic you chose. This could be the beginning of your own reading journal.

Storytelling
Viewing and Listening Skills

- **READ** the listening tips on SE page 363. Then **LISTEN** carefully while a classmate tells you a personal story.
  - **RETELL** the story in as much detail as you can.
  - **ASK** your partner how well you did. When you finish, **SWITCH** roles.

Seeing the World
Viewing and Listening Skills

- **REVIEW** SE page 358. In the first paragraph, **LOOK** over the list of things you can see on television.
  - **THINK** of one person, place, or thing you saw on television that you have never seen in person.
  - **WRITE** a few sentences about it. *What do you remember most? What did you learn? What did you like or not like about the program?*

Lunchtime
Taking Tests

- **COMPARE** a hot lunch from the school cafeteria to a cold lunch brought to school by a student.
  - **REVIEW** the tips for responding to a writing prompt on SE page 370 before you begin.

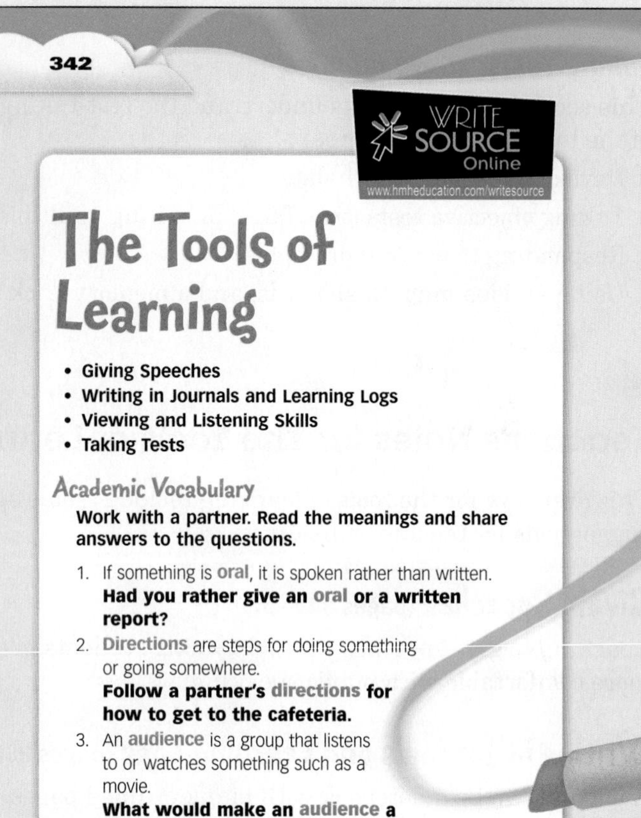
342

The Tools of Learning

- Giving Speeches
- Writing in Journals and Learning Logs
- Viewing and Listening Skills
- Taking Tests

Academic Vocabulary

Work with a partner. Read the meanings and share answers to the questions.

1. If something is **oral**, it is spoken rather than written.
   Had you rather give an oral or a written report?
2. **Directions** are steps for doing something or going somewhere.
   Follow a partner's directions for how to get to the cafeteria.
3. An **audience** is a group that listens to or watches something such as a movie.
   What would make an audience a good audience?

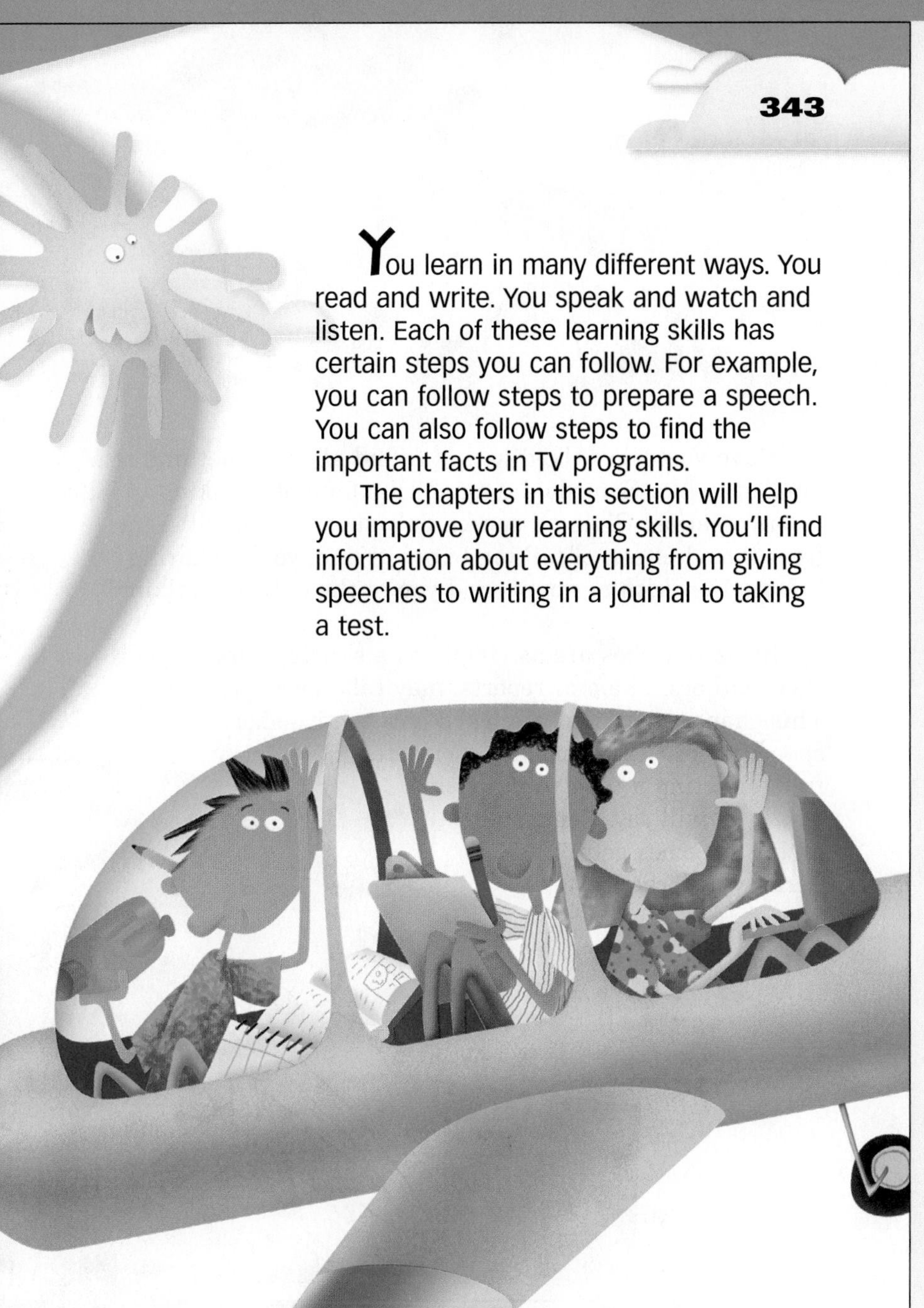

343
You learn in many different ways. You read and write. You speak and watch and listen. Each of these learning skills has certain steps you can follow. For example, you can follow steps to prepare a speech. You can also follow steps to find the important facts in TV programs.
The chapters in this section will help you improve your learning skills. You'll find information about everything from giving speeches to writing in a journal to taking a test.

Speaking and Listening Skills

Ask students to think about the questions listed below before they rate each question using this scale:

- one star for "never,"
- two stars for "sometimes,"
- three stars for "always" or "most of the time."

Point out that their rating for each question may be different. Assure them that they will improve as they learn how to become better speakers and listeners. You may want to use the questions again after completing this unit, or later on in the year.

Speaking skills questions:

- When you are assigned time to speak in class, do you prepare and practice what you're going to say before you speak?
- When you talk or read in class, do you speak loudly and clearly enough for everyone to hear?

Listening skills questions:

- When you listen to a teacher give directions, are you able to repeat them?
- When you listen to others give a talk in class, do you take notes on their main ideas?

Giving Speeches

Objectives

- Select an interesting topic for a short speech.
- Prepare and organize a short speech.
- Practice and present a short speech using notes and visual aids.

For some students, giving a speech may be more of a frightening experience than a positive learning experience. Assure students that almost everyone can feel nervous about speaking in front of an audience. If you would like to, share your early speaking experiences.

Describe one of the first times you had to speak in front of a classroom. Explain how you prepared and what you felt before and after that experience.

Write the words *Planning* and *Practice* on the board or on chart paper. Tell students that these two words are the key to feeling relaxed and confident about giving a good speech. Keep the words on display in the classroom as a reminder for students as they prepare to give their speech.

Giving Speeches

Have you ever talked with a friend about something really amazing—like Komodo dragons? This kind of speaking is called a conversation. Giving a speech or a short talk is different from that. Instead of talking to one friend, you're sharing information with a group—and you're the only one talking!

Some speeches are as simple as a sharing time in your class. Others, like oral reports, may take more planning. This chapter will help you learn how to give short speeches. You'll find tips for every step, from selecting a topic to practicing what you will say. Remember, giving speeches gets easier with practice.

Materials

Index cards (TE p. 347)

Giving Speeches 345

Planning Your Speech

1 Pick a topic.

First, pick a topic that really interests you and that you think will interest your audience. Then write one sentence about it. Every detail you include in your speech should tell something about that sentence.

Sample Sentences

Something that happened to you
I had my tonsils taken out.

Something you like to do
I love taking care of my puppy.

Something you learned
I just learned about skunks.

2 Gather details about your topic.

Remember: Write down what you know about the topic.

Read: Find out more by reading books and magazines. Look at Web sites. Take some notes as you read.

Ask Questions: Talk to people who know a lot about your topic. Ask questions and take notes as you listen.

Practice

1. Choose a topic for a short speech.
2. List everything you know about the topic.
3. Write two questions you have about your topic.

Planning Your Speech

If students need help coming up with an interesting topic for a speech, suggest that they look through their journals or writing portfolios. They may discover that a topic they wrote about earlier would make a good topic for a speech. The advantage of choosing a topic they have already explored for their speech is that they will already know about the topic and may also be able to use their prewriting notes when gathering details for their speeches.

Make sure students understand that if they do decide to choose a topic from a previous writing assignment, they are only to use their writing as a starting point for their speech. They are not simply to copy and deliver as a speech what they wrote.

English Language Learners

Students may find picking a topic overwhelming. To provide support, structure a group brainstorming session in which you list ideas students generate about the following categories:

- Something funny that happened to me
- An exciting event in my life
- An interesting problem I solved

Struggling Learners

Help students do the **Practice** by using a three-column KWL chart. Have students choose a topic. Ask them to list what they already know about the topic under the column heading *Know*. Then have them think about what they would like to know and list at least two questions under the *Want to Know* column. If students have trouble thinking of questions, have them discuss their topic with a partner.

Ask students to recall speeches that they have heard at school. These may include speeches by other students, teachers, coaches, and visiting speakers. Use the following questions to discuss these speeches and to help students recognize what makes a speech enjoyable.

- How did the speaker get your attention and make you want to keep listening?
- What kinds of details did the speaker use to help you understand the topic?
- What kinds of visual aids (for example, pictures, posters, charts, and maps) did the speaker use to make ideas clearer and more interesting?
- Could you hear everything the speaker said?
- Did you ask questions after the speech?
- What part of the speech did you like the best and why?

3 Know your purpose.

Decide why you want to tell people about your topic. Your reason for telling them is called your **purpose**. Your purpose can be to . . .

- **tell a good story,**
- **share interesting information, or**
- **convince people to do something.**

4 Decide what you will say.

Next you must decide which ideas to include in your speech. Here are some tips.

To begin your speech . . .

- **say something interesting or surprising to get your listeners' attention, and**
- **name your topic.**

In the middle of your speech . . .

- **give important details or facts about the topic, and**
- **tell how you feel about it.**

To end your speech . . .

- **remind listeners what your topic is, and**
- **repeat an important idea about it.**

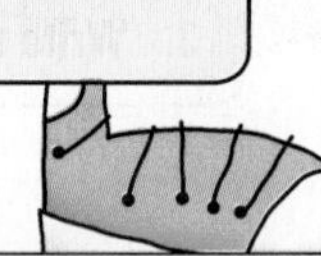

Practice

Decide what you will say in each part of your speech. Use the information above as a guide.

English Language Learners

Have students work with partners or in small groups to share the details they would like to include in the middle of their speeches. Suggest that they ask one another questions about the topic to generate more discussion. Point out that they can write a better beginning and ending once they decide which details they will include.

Writing Your Speech

5 Put it all together.

To prepare for your speech, write down what you want to say on paper. There are two ways to do this. You can write the main ideas on note cards, or you can write your whole speech on a sheet of paper. (See page 349.)

Note Cards

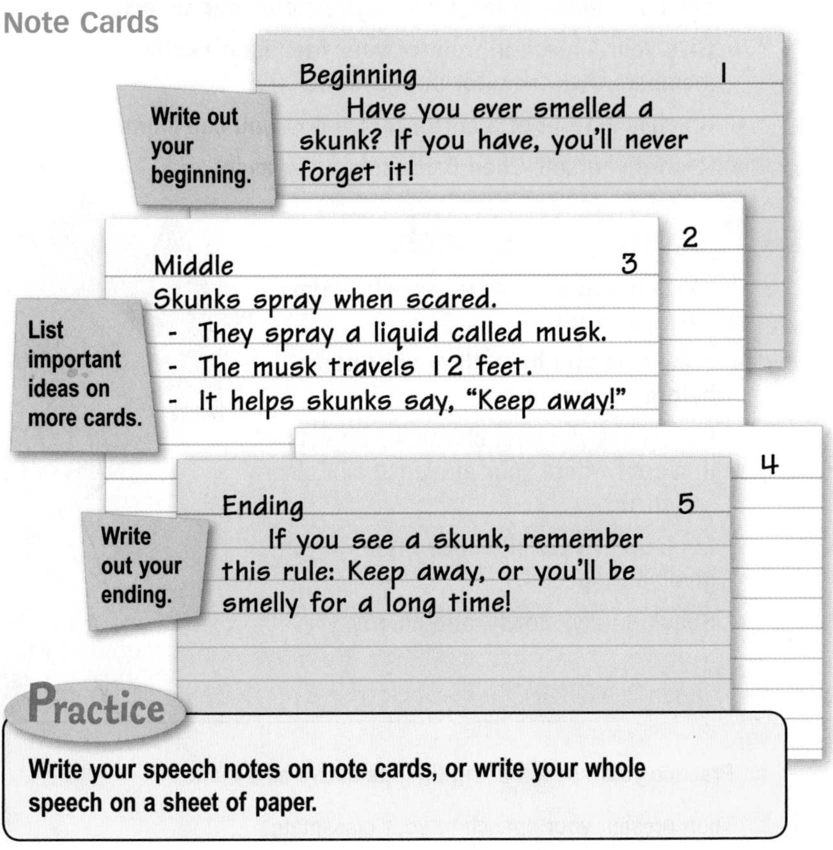

Beginning 1
Have you ever smelled a skunk? If you have, you'll never forget it!
Write out your beginning.
2
Middle 3
Skunks spray when scared.
- They spray a liquid called musk.
- The musk travels 12 feet.
- It helps skunks say, "Keep away!"
List important ideas on more cards.
4
Ending 5
If you see a skunk, remember this rule: Keep away, or you'll be smelly for a long time!
Write out your ending.

Practice

Write your speech notes on note cards, or write your whole speech on a sheet of paper.

Writing Your Speech

Provide the following additional tips if you have students make note cards to prepare their speech:

- Use large note cards for your speech. Each card should feature an important detail or new paragraph in the speech.
- Double-check your note cards to make sure they are in the correct order before assigning each card its number.
- Write the word *Beginning* at the top of note card 1 and write out the beginning.
- For the middle section label the cards *Middle* and list short sentences or phrases.
- Write the word *Ending* on the last note card and write out the ending.
- If you plan to **use a visual aid** *(see below)*, make a note at the place in your speech where you will use the visual aid.

Teaching Tip: Using Visual Aids

Students can make their speech more interesting and entertaining with diagrams, tables, graphs, and other visual aids.

Make sure students understand that visual aids are used to make ideas in a speech clearer. Students should also keep in mind that they are going to be speaking at the same time they are trying to handle their visual aids. Because of this, students should not use too many visual aids or visual aids that are too large or awkward to handle during the speech.

Encourage students to practice their speech, using their visual aids to make sure that they can handle them and that their audience will be able to see the visual aids.

* For examples of graphic organizers that can be used as visual aids, have students turn to SE pages 438–439.

Teaching Tip: Note Cards

If students prepare note cards for a speech, remind them that they should write their words as neatly as possible. Also stress that proper spacing between words makes the note cards easier to read as they give their presentations.

Giving Your Speech

Even with practice and encouragement, some students will be anxious about giving a speech.

To ease their anxiety, you might consider having some students present their speech to a small group instead of to the whole class. A smaller audience can sometimes reduce anxiety.

You might also consider having students prerecord their speech. After the audience has heard the prerecorded speech, speakers could answer questions or respond to comments from the audience. This would give them some experience responding to a live audience.

Remind students of the words *Planning* and *Practice* (see TE page 344). Point out that a good way to prepare is to practice giving their speech in front of their friends or family members before presenting it to the class.

Giving Your Speech

6 Practice many times.

If you're using note cards, practice saying the ideas listed on each card. Do this over and over until you can repeat all of the ideas easily. If you have written out your speech word for word, practice reading it. Here are some more tips.

- **Start practicing at least two days before your speech.**
- **Give your speech in front of your friends or family members. Ask them for suggestions.**
- **Practice in front of a mirror to see how you can improve.**
- **Record yourself. Then listen to your speech.**

7 Present your speech.

When you give your speech, keep these tips in mind.

- **Make sure you have all of your notes before you begin.**
- **Put up any posters, charts, or objects in a spot where your audience can clearly see them.**
- **Look up at your audience often as you give your speech.**
- **Speak loudly, slowly, and clearly.**

Practice

1. **Practice your speech using the tips above as a guide.**
2. **Then present your speech to your classmates.**

English Language Learners

For students who still feel uncomfortable speaking in front of their peers, consider scheduling one-on-one conferences in which you listen to students present their speeches and then offer one positive comment and one way they could improve.

Giving Speeches 349

Sample Speech

Here's a speech that shares facts about skunks.

Name the subject in an interesting way.

Share specific facts.

Repeat the most important idea.

Skunks

Have you ever smelled a skunk? If you have, you'll never forget it!

If you've seen a skunk, it was probably a striped one. They are black with white stripes on their backs, and they're about the same size as a cat. But there are also spotted skunks. They are very small. They weigh only about one pound. When spotted skunks spray, they stand up on their front paws—like doing a handstand!

Skunks spray only when they're scared. They spray a liquid called musk. Musk smells awful and can travel about 12 feet. It's the skunk's way of saying, "Keep away!" It works, too!

When you get sprayed by a skunk, you smell really bad. And it's hard to get the smell off. Our dog scared a skunk in our yard. My mom poured tomato juice all over the dog. For some reason, tomato juice helps get rid of the skunk smell.

If you see a skunk, remember this rule: Keep away, or you'll be smelly for a long time!

Sample Speech

Model giving a speech of your own, or present the one about skunks. Model excellent presentation skills:

- stand up straight
- speak clearly and project well
- gesture when appropriate
- speak in your natural voice or at a normal rate
- be enthusiastic about your topic
- look at your audience

Ask students to point out positive things about your presentation.

After students present their speech, have them look back at the star rating they gave themselves as speakers at the beginning of the unit (TE page 343). Suggest that they revise their rating and add comments based on what they have learned about giving speeches.

Writing in Journals and Learning Logs

Objectives

- Understand the purpose of keeping personal and reading journals.
- Understand the purpose of keeping learning logs in different curriculum areas.
- Learn strategies for writing in journals and learning logs.

Share the kinds of events and ideas that people typically include in a personal journal, for example,

- descriptions of places and interesting people,
- feelings and reflections on special events and moments,
- everyday thoughts on life, and
- new discoveries and insights.

Explain to students that beyond keeping a journal to practice their writing skills, their journal can become a record of growth as a writer and a resource of writing ideas they will use (or turn to) again and again.

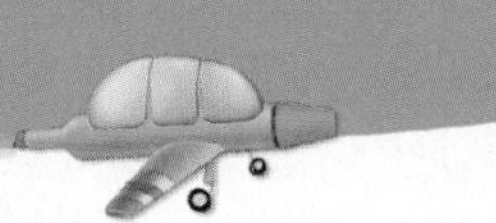

Writing in Journals and Learning Logs

Can you imagine a gymnast who doesn't practice? She would have a hard time doing flips, cartwheels, or spins. A writer won't do very well without practice, either. In fact, to become a good writer, you should try to write something every day!

Writing in a **personal journal** is the best way to practice. All you need is a notebook and a pencil. You can write about anything and everything. The choice is yours. Just make sure to write something every day.

Keeping a Personal Journal

A **personal journal** is your own special place to write. You can . . .

- write about whatever you see and hear around you,
- jot down things you wonder about,
- record what has happened in your life, and
- collect ideas for future writings (stories, poems, plays).

Practice

Start a personal journal notebook. Write your first entry about something you saw, heard, or did today. Be sure to date every entry you write. (See the sample below.)

Sample Journal Entry

Tim's great-grandmother told him about going to school in England. He wrote about what he learned from her in his journal.

March 10, 2010

In Great-Grandma's school, everyone had to learn to swim. They even had to pass a swimming test, and it was hard. She said that because England is an island, the teachers wanted everyone to know how to swim. I was surprised when she told me that the girls and boys had to play on different playgrounds! She had only one dress for school!

Keeping a Personal Journal

If you plan to make journal writing a class requirement, set aside a specific time each day for students to write in their journal for at least five or ten minutes. First thing in the morning, when students are anticipating the day ahead, or at the end of the day, when students enjoy reflecting on the day that has just passed, are probably the best times.

Make sure students know ahead of time whether or not you will be reviewing their journal writing. Keep in mind that students are likely to be more relaxed about writing and will write freely if they are not required to share every entry. If you want to check that they are writing on a regular basis and still maintain their privacy, tell students that you will flip through their journals without reading the entries.

Advise students that they should not write things in their journal that they would not want anyone else to read. Journals can be misplaced or lost. Also students should not write things that would hurt others.

Sample Journal Entry

As students read the sample entry, have them notice that Tim jumps from one idea to another as people often do when they are talking to good friends. Tell students to try to think of writing in a personal journal as talking to a friend with whom they want to share their thoughts and feelings.

English Language Learners

Students may find the freewriting process intimidating because of a limited English vocabulary. Point out that they are the audience for their personal journal notebooks, so they can write any words or phrases to express their ideas. For students who need more structure, provide a topic or sentence starter as a springboard to writing.

Writing in a Reading Journal

Point out that keeping a reading journal is another opportunity for students to relax and write about things that interest them. If students are required to keep a reading log, encourage them to apply the ideas here to their log entries.

Fiction Books

Provide these additional ideas for writing about fiction books:

- Did you like the ending? Why or why not? If not, how would you change it?
- Who else do you think would enjoy reading the book? Why?

Students can write an entry for a book they are currently reading so they don't have trouble recalling their feelings and thoughts about characters and events.

Sample Journal Entry for Fiction

Point out that Kim underlined the book title in the sample entry. Remind students that this is the correct way to write a book title when they are writing by hand. Point out that if they were keeping a reading journal on a computer, they would use italics for a book's title.

* For information about Underlining and Italics for Titles, see SE pages 478–479.

Writing in a Reading Journal

A **reading journal** is a place to write about the books and stories you read. Writing about books helps you think about them and enjoy them a second time.

Fiction Books

For a fiction book or story, you can write about . . .

- an exciting or scary part,
- something funny or sad that happens,
- your feelings about one of the characters,
- how your life is like the story, or
- a question that you have.

Practice

Write a reading journal entry for a fiction book or story that you have just read. To get started, use one of the ideas listed above.

Sample Journal Entry for Fiction

Kim read a historical fiction book, and she really liked the main character, Sarah. Kim shares her feelings in her journal.

> February 25, 2010
> The Courage of Sarah Noble by Alice Dalgliesh is about being brave. Sarah's mother said, "Keep up your courage." That was before Sarah and her dad went into the wilderness to make a new home for their family. This book made me feel brave. I learned about courage from Sarah.

Struggling Learners

To provide extra support when assigning reading journals, gather students into a group and have them all read and respond to the same book. Then hold a group discussion in which students work together to answer questions and record responses in a group reading journal.

Advanced Learners

To extend the **Practice** activity, have students use their reading journals to write a conversation between a favorite character and themselves. Suggest that the conversations focus on one or more of the following ideas:

- ways in which your lives are similar
- what it might be like to switch places for a day
- how you both feel about a certain event or character in the story

Suggest that students pair up and use their entries to create dramatic presentations.

Writing in Journals and Learning Logs 353

Nonfiction Books

For nonfiction books, you can write about . . .

- a main idea in the book,
- some surprising or unusual details, or
- your personal thoughts or questions about the topic.

Practice

Write a journal entry for a nonfiction book or article that you have just read. To get started, use one of the ideas above.

Sample Journal Entries for Nonfiction

James read a biography about a famous runner. James' journal entry shows his personal thoughts about this runner.

February 6, 2010
I read about Jesse Owens for Black History Month. Jesse was a track star. He said, "In America, anybody can become somebody." He won four gold medals in the 1936 Olympics. He was named the World's Fastest Human. Jesse is my hero. I want to be somebody, too!

Eva read a magazine article about volcanoes. Her journal entry tells about some surprising details that she learned.

May 5, 2010
Yesterday, I read an article about volcanoes. I learned that Earth has about 1,500 volcanoes and that Mount St. Helens might erupt again. Many people are watching Mount St. Helens to see what will happen.

Nonfiction Books

To ensure that everyone has a book to write about, help students recall a nonfiction book or article that you read together in class. Give students the option of writing about this book or article.

Sample Journal Entries for Nonfiction

After students read the first sample journal entry, call their attention to the direct quotation in the entry ("In America, anybody can become somebody"). Ask students why they think James chose this quotation (it was meaningful to him). Point out that James refers to the quotation in his last sentence.

Encourage students to **use direct quotations** *(see below)* from the books they have read that have special meaning for them. Tell them to be sure that they explain why the quotation is important to them.

Most students won't be able to provide a direct quotation or recall specific facts and details unless they have the book or article they are writing about on hand.

Teaching Tip: Using Direct Quotations

Explain to students that using direct quotations from a book can help them recall how they felt about characters and ideas in the book when they go back and reread their journal entries. Remind students to follow the conventions for writing direct quotations. Provide these quick tips:

- Choose a short, meaningful quotation for your journal entry.
- Refer to the original source and copy the words carefully and exactly.
- Put quotation marks around the exact words that you copy from the book or article.

* For more about using quotation marks around quoted words, see SE pages 476–477.

Writing in a Learning Log

You can have students keep a response journal with a special focus, or have them keep a learning log in a class where new information is challenging. Establish how students should **organize their response journals and learning logs** *(see below)*.

Sample Math Entry

Ask students how they can tell that David understands how to make change (he's able to explain the method in his own words). Clarifying concepts is one major benefit of writing in learning logs.

Sample Social Studies Entry

Ask students how writing questions about what they don't understand can help them become better students. (The questions usually point out what you need to study further or what you might want to learn more about.)

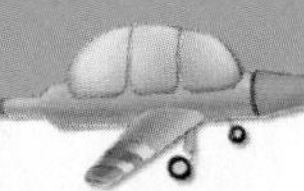

Writing in a Learning Log

A **learning log** is a place to write about the subjects you are studying. Here are some tips to help you get started.

- **Divide** your log into separate parts for each subject.
- **Write** and draw about what you have learned.
- **List** questions that you have about the subject.

Practice

Write about something you have learned in math, social studies, or science. If possible, include a drawing that will help you remember.

Sample Math Entry

In math class, David is learning how to make change. His learning-log entry explains what he knows so far.

May 18, 2010

Today in math we talked about money and how to make change. One way to make change is to do a subtraction problem to see how much change to give back. If I can make change, I can help my aunt at her garage sale.

Sample Social Studies Entry

Rosie's class visited a Native American burial ground. In her learning log, she tells what she learned and asks a question.

September 20, 2010

Our class visited a Native American burial ground. These burial grounds were used hundreds of years ago, right in our city. What was it like to live then?

Teaching Tip: Organizing Journals and Learning Logs

Some students may find that one notebook can work as both a personal journal and a learning log. Suggest that they divide the notebook into two sections, using the front for a personal journal and the back for learning log entries. They can make each section identifiable by inserting different color dividers or by using different color sticky tabs.

Some students may find it easier to use separate notebooks for a journal and a learning log.

Encourage students to write organized and complete notes in their learning logs by asking them to star the most important ideas. If you ask them questions in a learning log entry, they should highlight or circle the question, and be sure to find the answer. Then, if students want to use their learning log as a study aid to prepare for a test or a quiz, they can find important ideas quickly by looking for the stars and the questions they have answered.

Sample Science Entry

In science, Theo's class conducted an experiment. They made a balloon rocket. In Theo's learning log, he tells about the experiment and draws a picture.

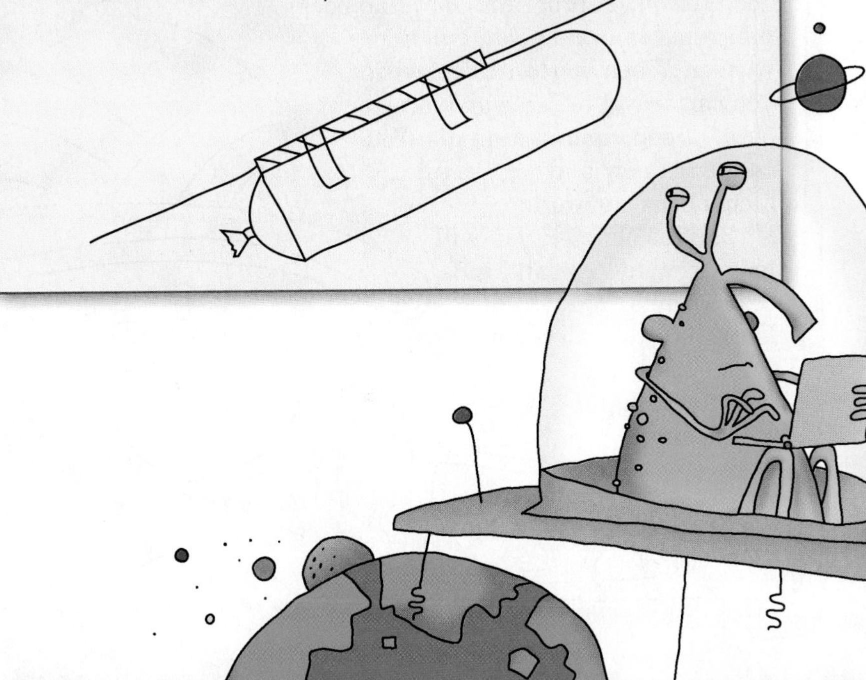

November 8, 2010
Today we studied force and motion. We made a balloon rocket with a balloon, a straw, and some string. We predicted how it would work. We also timed how fast it moved up the string. I want to try this experiment at home because it was fun. Here is a picture of our balloon rocket.

Sample Science Entry

If you plan to assess students' learning logs, separate students into groups. Assign each group a different weekday or date for submitting learning logs and receiving feedback.

If students are required to complete standardized lab reports for science experiments, compare the more detailed step-by-step scientific approach of writing a lab report to the less detailed, more personal tone of the sample science entry.

This is a good opportunity to guide students in keeping detailed, organized learning logs so that when it is time to study for a test, they can easily review important facts and details.

As an added incentive to keep up-to-date and detailed learning logs, allow students to use their learning logs during some tests and quizzes.

English Language Learners

Students may be unfamiliar with the word *log* as used to mean "diary." Explain that a log is a book in which people keep track of events or information so they can refer back to it later on. Explain to students that, in the same way, they can use a learning log to record what they have learned and then refer back to it to refresh their memory about a topic.

Struggling Learners

Invite students to share any learning log activities they have developed on their own that have consistently worked for them (for example, creating visual icons to highlight key ideas or using memory tricks to make it easier to recall factual information).

Viewing and Listening Skills

Objectives

- Learn how to assess information when watching the news, television specials, and commercials.
- Learn how to evaluate Web sites for reliability.

It's possible that some students are not allowed to watch television at home, or are allowed to watch only certain kinds of programs. Also, there may be some families who do not have a television in the home. Keep this in mind as you introduce the material in this section and make assignments.

Take a short poll of the different kinds of television programs students watch. Explain that in this section they are going to learn about some different kinds of programs they may or may not have seen.

Viewing and Listening Skills

Reading a good book is fun, and so is watching a good television program. Just like books, TV programs can make you laugh, cry, or wonder. When you watch television, you can travel to faraway places or observe endangered animals. You can learn new and wonderful facts about our world.

In this chapter, you will learn how to view all kinds of programs. You will also learn how to understand commercials and how to evaluate a Web site.

Materials

DVD recording of children's news program (TE p. 357)

DVD recording of TV commercials (TE p. 360)

Magazine and newspaper ads (TE p. 360)

Chart paper (TE p. 362)

Copy Masters

5 W's Chart (TE p. 357)

Viewing and Listening Skills 357

Viewing News Programs

Some news programs cover news from your area. Other programs cover news from across the country and around the world. Remember these three things when you watch the news.

1. **News programs show only some of what happens each day.** Program directors decide which events to cover.
2. **News programs share some of the details from each news story.** Reporters don't have time to give all the details.
3. **News reporters don't always know all of the facts.** They can only give the ones they have.

Covering the Basic Facts

A good news story will give you the basic facts. It should answer the 5 W's.

Who? zookeepers
Where? in cold northern states
What? have problems with elephants
When? during winter months
Why? There is not enough room inside to exercise the elephants.
Solution? Maybe elephants should live in warmer southern zoos.

Practice

1. **Watch a news report with an adult.**
2. **Write down the 5 W's for one of the news stories.**
3. **Did the report answer all of the questions?**

Viewing News Programs

Students probably do not watch television news on a regular basis, if at all. Many parents may feel that the news is too violently graphic or that it introduces topics that are not suitable for their children. Make sure that you are aware of family policies when you discuss specific news topics with students and when you have students watch a news program.

Some children's networks have news telecasts written, produced, and performed by children. If possible, record a segment from one of these news programs. Show the segment in class and have students apply the **Practice** activity to one of the stories from this program.

Provide photocopies of the reproducible 5 W's Chart (TE page 597) and have students use it to take notes for the **Practice** activity.

Advanced Learners

Extend the **Practice** activity by challenging students to write their own news story. Suggest that they write about a recent event that has happened at school or in their neighborhood or community. Point out that they should answer the 5 W's. Have students read their news stories aloud to the class.

Viewing TV Programs

Use the following questions to explore students' prior knowledge about TV programs.

- What was the last TV program you watched? Why did you like or not like it?
- What is something you learned from watching a TV program?
- What is something you would like to learn more about because of a TV program you watched?

If possible, check television listings for an upcoming program on a topic students are studying in social studies or science. Send a note home that advises parents of the date and time, or have students write their own, so students may watch it with their family.

Have students set up a KWL chart to use before, during, and after viewing. Then they can refer to their completed chart to write their journal response. Be sure students have read the sample journal response on SE page 359 before they write their own response.

Viewing TV Programs

TV programs and educational videos give us information about interesting subjects. These programs can be about animals, people, places, or events. There are even programs about strange creatures like Big Foot. Here are some tips that will help you watch TV programs.

Before Viewing

- Think about what you already know about the subject.
- If your teacher gives you questions to answer, make sure you understand them.

During Viewing

- Listen for new and interesting information.
- Write down key words to help you remember important ideas.
- List any questions you have about the program.

After Viewing

- Talk about the program with someone else who has watched it.
- Answer your teacher's questions.
- Write about the program in your journal.

Practice

1. **Watch a TV program and use the viewing guidelines above.**
2. **Then write about the program in your journal.**

Struggling Learners

Have students work in pairs, and help students prepare for and view the TV special by providing them with the following tips:

- **Before Viewing:** Jot down two or three things you already know about the topic of the TV special.
- **During Viewing:** Write down one question you have about the topic or about the TV special.
- **After Viewing:** Ask your partner what he or she thought about the TV special.

Have students write their own response to the special in their personal journal or learning log.

Viewing and Listening Skills 359

Responding to a TV Program

Ellie watched a nature program about zebras. She wrote about the program in her journal.

Ellie's Journal Response

October 17

"Zebras on the Open Plains"

I didn't know that the stripes on zebras protect them. The stripes help zebras hide from their enemies, especially lions. I always thought that zebras looked kind of cuddly, but they are really strong fighters. The program showed two zebra stallions fighting.

Some people in South Africa tame zebras for work. I wish they would just leave them alone. Zebras used to be all over Africa. Now many of them have been killed for food and their hides.

Zebras are part of the horse family. The colts are so cute with their long legs. The narrator of the program said that the young colts sometimes stay together in kindergartens when the mother is away. A male zebra watches the kindergartners. It sounds funny to call a zebra a kindergartner.

Responding to a TV Program

Have students identify the following details in Ellie's Journal Response:

- What Ellie thought about zebras before watching the program
- Facts Ellie learned about zebras while watching the program
- Ellie's personal feelings and reactions to what she saw and learned

Encourage students to include similar kinds of details in their journal response.

English Language Learners

To alleviate anxiety about how to organize a response, suggest that students organize their journal response the way Ellie organized hers:

- Paragraph 1: Mention and correct any misconceptions held about the topic.
- Paragraph 2: Offer an opinion about the topic.
- Paragraph 3: Provide additional facts about the topic.

Understanding Commercials

Discuss each selling method and ask students to recall a commercial that they have seen or heard about that uses this method. If possible, provide examples of current commercials on the networks to illustrate each method.

Ask them which commercials they especially like, and why.

To extend the ideas on this page, divide students into pairs or small groups and have them look through magazines and newspapers to find print ads that use the selling methods described here.

Understanding Commercials

Television stations show many commercials! They use different selling methods to make the products seem great. Knowing these methods can make you a smart viewer.

Selling Method	Commercial	Purpose
Bandwagon	Everybody enjoys a certain snack. You should, too!	The ad wants you to feel left out if you don't have the snack.
Famous Faces	A famous runner is shown drinking Superade.	The ad wants you to drink Superade because a famous person drinks it.
Survey Results	Someone may say, "Nine out of ten kids use Stay White Toothpaste."	The ad wants you to feel that you should use the product, too.
Name-Calling	A commercial might say that Healthbars have more protein than Supersnacks.	The ad wants you to believe one product is better than another one.

Practice

1. **Watch two commercials.**
2. **Can you tell which selling method is used in each one?**

English Language Learners

The term *bandwagon* may confuse students. Explain that the expression *jumping on the bandwagon* means "to do something because everyone else is doing it." Point out that advertisers use this method to suggest that if everyone is buying a certain product, the product must be good.

Advanced Learners

Have students work together in small groups to invent a product that could be used in school (for example, a self-cleaning chalkboard) and create a commercial for it, using one of the four selling methods. As an option, have students choose an existing product and create two different commercials for it. Then have them decide which is most effective and justify their reasons.

Viewing and Listening Skills 361

Evaluating Web Sites

Like television, Web sites can present great information. Many sites include facts that can be checked. Other sites only share people's opinions. How can you be sure the information you find is true? Ask an adult to help you find the best Web site for the information that you need. Then follow the tips below.

Who publishes the Web site?

Find sites that end in .org, .gov, or .edu. These sites are published by organizations, government offices, and educational groups such as schools or universities. These sites usually list true information.

Is the Web site up-to-date?

Information on the Internet is constantly changing. So look at the date of each site. Be sure the information you find is the latest about your topic.

Do all the facts agree?

Search for information on more than one site. Then compare the facts given on each site. If the facts aren't the same, you may need to check more sites.

Practice

As a class, look up a topic on a few Web sites.

- **Who publishes each site?**
- **Is each site up-to-date?**
- **Are the facts the same on all the sites?**

Advanced Learners

Challenge small groups to evaluate the Web sites they have visited by creating their own rating scales. Suggest that they consider the following:

- Is the information easy to read and understand?
- Are the graphics helpful?
- Does the Web site provide helpful links?

Students could then use the rating scale to evaluate some Web sites that you have directed them to (for example, National Geographic and the Smithsonian Institute). They could also create a bulletin board display of their evaluations for class reference.

Evaluating Web Sites

Remind students about the school's procedures and policies related to using the Internet. Also remind them of the following:

- Students should always follow their parents' rules for using the Internet, whether at home, at the library, or at school.
- They should never provide personal information (name, age, address, or telephone number) to anyone on the Internet.
- They should tell an adult immediately if anyone on the Internet asks them for personal information.

Learning to Listen

To make sure students understand the difference between hearing and listening, analyze the examples in the chart. Then create a similar chart on the board or on chart paper, and have volunteers give more examples of hearing versus listening (a sports broadcast/ knowing the score of the game).

Ask students to recall the last time they had to listen to someone. It might have been a parent giving instructions, a classmate's speech, or a public address announcement at school. Ask the following questions:

- Do you remember what the person was talking about?
- Did you talk while the other person was speaking?
- Did you have trouble paying attention to what was being said?

Explain to students that they are going to learn some strategies that will help them become better listeners.

Learning to Listen

You've learned how to be a smart viewer. Now you'll learn how to become a better listener. You already practice listening every day when you listen to your friends and your teacher.

Remember that you *hear* with your ears, but it takes both your ears and your brain to *listen*. The examples below compare hearing and listening.

Hearing	Listening
A friend's voice	**A classmate asking a question**
A teacher's voice	**A teacher giving directions**
Music playing	**Paying attention to the words in a song**

Are you listening?

Listening is one important way to learn things. The better you listen, the more you'll learn. It isn't easy, though. You have to make sure you don't daydream. You must "stay tuned" to what a speaker is saying.

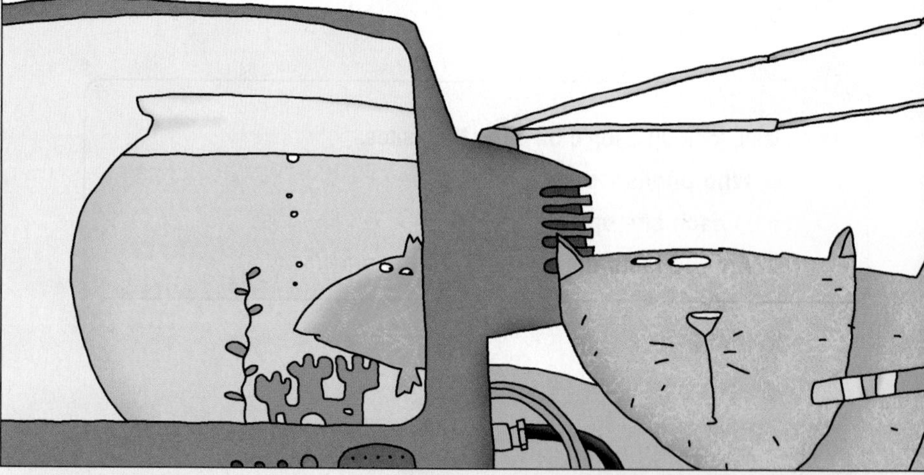

English Language Learners

Sharpen students' listening skills with the following auditory activity:

- Make an oral statement of fact, offer an opinion, or provide a simple direction.
- Have students take turns repeating the information back to you in their own words.
- Have the other students listen to determine if the student has accurately repeated what you said.

Have volunteers repeat the process to reinforce speaking, listening, and comprehension skills.

Viewing and Listening Skills 363

Good-Listener Checklist

✔ Look at the speaker.
- Don't look around.
- Keep your mind and your eyes on the speaker.
- Do not talk while the speaker is talking.

✔ Listen with your eyes as well as your ears.
- Watch the speaker's expressions.
- Decide how the speaker feels about the subject.

✔ Listen for key words.
- The *biggest* planet is Jupiter.
- The planet *closest* to the sun is Mercury.

✔ Think about what is being said.
- Do you understand what the speaker is saying?
- What do the speaker's ideas mean to you?

✔ Take notes.
- List only the most important words and ideas.
- Write down questions you may want to ask.

✔ Ask questions.
- When the speaker is through, ask the questions you wrote down.

Good-Listener Checklist

Give students a few moments to look over the Good-Listener Checklist and to think about how they listen. Have students identify the things on the checklist that they do and those things that they do not do.

Then have students refer to the star rating they gave themselves as listeners at the start of this unit (TE page 343). Based on the checklist here, they may wish to change their original rating and add comments now.

Struggling Learners

Review SE page 346 with students. Point out that the beginning of a speech names the topic, the middle gives facts and details, and the end repeats an important idea about the topic. Have students make a listening chart by folding a sheet of paper in thirds, creating three boxes, one for each part of a speech (beginning, middle, end). Have students then jot down phrases as tips to help them remember what they will hear in each part of a speech. The next time students listen to a speech in class, have them use their listening charts as they take notes for each part.

Taking Tests

Objectives

- Understand how to study for tests.
- Learn about the different types of tests.
- Learn how to read and respond to writing prompts.
- Learn methods for recalling information for a test.

Keep in mind that some students, no matter how well they understand the material and no matter how much they study, will perform poorly on tests as a result of anxiety specifically related to taking tests. These students may generally pay attention in class, participate in class discussions, complete all their homework assignments, and give correct oral responses. Whenever possible, provide alternate testing methods for these students, at least until they are able, with guidance or on their own, to overcome the anxiety associated with taking tests.

Taking Tests

Tests may not be your favorite part of school. You may not like lima beans or going to the dentist, either. Now let's be positive for a moment! Tests are important. They show you what you've learned about a subject and what you still need to work on.

If you keep up with your class work, you can handle the tests. However, it is still important to get ready for each one. In this chapter, you will learn how to study for tests and how to take them.

Materials

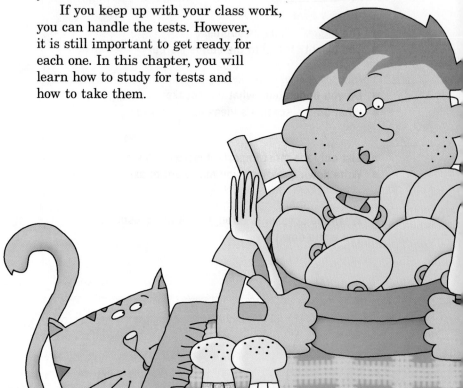

Sample tests (TE p. 366)

Stiff paper for making bookmarks (TE p. 367)

Sample writing prompts (TE p. 370)

Chart paper (TE p. 371)

Index cards (TE p. 371)

Studying for a Test

Here are four smart things you can do to get ready for a classroom test. As you develop these good study habits, you will be ready for every test!

1 Listen well.

When your teacher starts talking about your next test, listen carefully to everything he or she says. Write down when the test will be given and what will be on it.

2 Gather all of your materials.

Collect everything you need to study. Find your study guide, your review notes or cards, and your textbook.

3 Plan study time with a partner.

If your test is a week away, ask a friend or an adult to study with you. Do this for a little while each day before the test. Don't wait until the night before the test to start studying.

4 Look over everything.

Start with your textbook. Look over the chapter page by page. Pay special attention to the headings, diagrams, and words in bold print. Answer the review questions at the end of the chapter. Then look over your study guide and review notes or cards.

Studying for a Test

In addition to the four ideas listed here, you may want to post these suggestions for smart things to do to get ready for a test.

- Find a quiet place to study.
- Turn off the TV, CD player, or radio.
- Use your notes and textbook to make up some sample test questions. Ask a partner to do the same. Then exchange questions to see how well you can answer them.
- Get a good night's sleep the night before the test. Eat a good breakfast the morning of the test.

English Language Learners

Suggest that students discuss test material orally with their study partners or in a group. Students can readily cement meaning by talking with others about the content, because they rely on their own words instead of repeating word-for-word sentences from the text.

If students have difficulty discussing a certain part of a text, suggest that they review the material until they can explain it in their own words.

Advanced Learners

Have students create their own cartoons to illustrate one of the four tips on the page, or invite them to think of their own tip. Have students write a sentence or two summarizing their cartoon. Set aside time for them to present their cartoons to the class and share their tips. Post their final cartoons as reminders for classmates.

Understanding Types of Tests

If possible, display a sample of each of the five types of test listed here from tests students have taken. Ask students which kind of test they like the most and which they like the least. Then discuss why they prefer one kind of test to another.

Remind students that any type of test is easier if they have been listening in class, have taken good notes, have kept their learning logs up-to-date, have reviewed their notes, and have studied for the test.

True/False Test

Read the test-taking tip at the bottom of the page. Then review the sample True/False test. Discuss why item 2 is false. Have volunteers suggest ways to change item 2 to make it a true statement. (Some people vote to elect local and state officials.)

Understanding Types of Tests

There are different types of tests. The five most common types are **true/false, matching, multiple-choice, fill-in-the-blank,** and **responding to a writing prompt**. You can learn more about these tests on the next five pages.

True/False Test

A **true/false test** is a list of sentences. After reading each sentence, you decide if it is *true* or *false*. Here are some tips.

- If any part of the sentence is false, the answer is false.
- If the whole sentence is true, the answer is true.

Read each sentence below carefully. Then put a "T" before each true statement and an "F" before each false statement.

___ 1. Citizens pay taxes for goods and services.

___ 2. Everyone votes to elect local and state officials.

___ 3. Local government provides fire and police protection.

Answers: 1. T 2. F – "Everyone" is the key word that makes this statement false. 3. T

Words like *always, never, every, all,* or *none* make true/false sentences tricky. Read them carefully.

Advanced Learners

Have volunteers make up one true statement and two false ones about a topic the class is studying. Tell them to use the tip at the bottom of the page to help them create the false statements. Have volunteers read aloud their statements. Then have the class identify the true and false statements and discuss ways to make the false statements true.

Taking Tests 367

Matching Test

A **matching test** is two lists of words or phrases. You need to find the words from each list that match, or go together. Here are some tips.

- Before making any matches, read through both lists.
- Put a mark next to each answer you use. Then it will be easier for you to see which answers you have left.

Match the words in the first column with the correct definition in the second column. Write the letter of the definition on the line.

___ 1. taxes	**a.** a group of people who work with the mayor to run the city government
___ 2. immigrant	**b.** money paid for community services
___ 3. city council	**c.** someone who comes to live in a country in which he or she was not born

Answers: 1. b, 2. c, 3. a

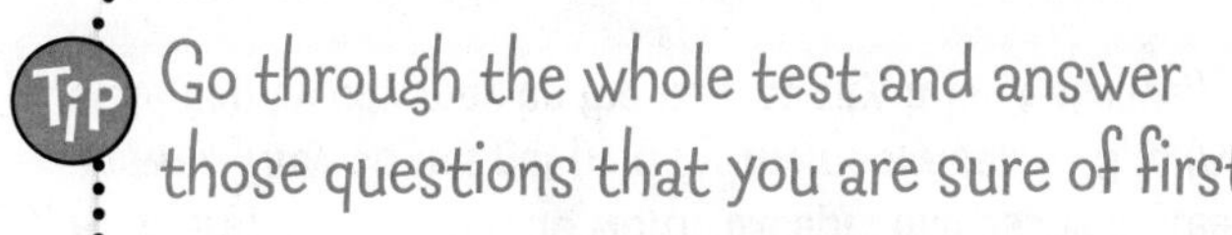

TIP
Go through the whole test and answer those questions that you are sure of first.

Matching Test

If students have covered the concepts presented in this matching test, they may enjoy trying to complete the test without looking at the answers.

The test-taking tips that appear at the bottom of these pages are part of successful test-taking strategies that good students use to take tests. The more times that students are reminded of these tips, the more likely they are to apply them when they take a test. Provide students with stiff paper cut into a large bookmark shape. Give students time to copy down each of the tips on SE pages 366–370 onto the bookmark. Students can then refer to the tips easily and frequently. If possible, laminate the bookmarks for students.

Multiple-Choice Test

Discuss each item in the sample test, having volunteers explain why each correct answer is correct, if possible without looking at the explanations that follow the questions.

Point out to students that test writers put in wrong answers that students who haven't read the question carefully may think are correct. For example, some students might choose (b) Washington, D.C., as the right answer to item 3 in the sample test because they skipped over the word *state* in the question. Remind students always to read each word of a question carefully.

Multiple-Choice Test

A **multiple-choice test** is a list of statements or questions with several answer choices. Pick the best choice to complete the statement or answer the question. Here are some tips.

- Read each statement or question very carefully.
- Look for words like *not*, *never*, or *except*. They can change the meaning of a statement.
- Study all of the choices. Then pick the best one.

Read each statement below carefully. Then write the letter that best completes each sentence.

___ **1. Many city governments are led by a**
(a) mayor (c) president
(b) police officer

___ **2. Most community workers earn pay for their services except**
(a) police officers (c) teachers
(b) volunteers

___ **3. The state government is always located in**
(a) the largest city (c) the state capital city
(b) Washington, D.C.

Answers: 1. a 2. b (The word "except" makes "volunteers" the right answer. They do not get paid for their services.) 3. c (Although the state capital city may be the largest city, it isn't always.)

If you have time, go back to any questions you may have skipped and work on them.

Struggling Learners

Many students find it helpful to eliminate wrong answer choices when taking a multiple-choice test.

In most cases, they can eliminate wrong answers if they read each question carefully and ask themselves: "Is there an answer choice that uses the word *not, never*, *none*, *except, all,* or *always*?" Have them scratch through the eliminated choices so that choosing the correct answer becomes more manageable.

Taking Tests 369

Fill-in-the-Blank Test

A **fill-in-the-blank test** is a list of sentences with blanks you must fill in. The test may also have a list of possible answers. You select the correct word and write it in the blank. Before you write, however, reread the sentence to check your choice. Here are some tips.

- Be sure you have studied your vocabulary words.
- Ask yourself what kind of information fits in the blank. Does the sentence need a word that answers *who? what? when?* or *where?*

Carefully read each sentence. Choose a word from the list that would make sense and complete the sentence. Write the word on the line.

communities rural urban

1. **Places where people live, work, and play are called ______________.**
2. **A city with many neighborhoods is called an ______________ area.**

Answers: 1. communities 2. urban

Make sure that you have answered every question. If you have time, read over the whole test to be sure your answers sound right.

Fill-in-the-Blank Test

Remind students that each blank in a fill-in-the-blank test usually stands for one missing word. Also point out that word clues in the question can help them figure out the correct answer as well as which answer choices would *not* be correct. Point out the following word clues in the sample test:

- In item 1, the word *places* is a plural noun. That tells them that the correct response will also be a plural noun. *(communities)*
- In item 2, the word *an* comes before the blank. That tells them that the correct word to complete the sentence begins with a vowel and not a consonant. *(urban)* On the other hand, if the word *a* had come before the blank, then they would have known to look for a word that begins with a consonant.

English Language Learners

Students with limited English skills can benefit from answering items in which the blank falls at the end of the sentence. Questions structured in this way enable students to use the sentence to build context.

Responding to Writing Prompts

Assure students that any writing-prompt tests you give will be based on material they have learned and discussed in class. If they have listened in class and have studied their notes, they can apply the writing skills they've learned to write a good response.

Tell students that they are ready to respond to a writing prompt when they can state what the prompt is asking them to do. Underlining or highlighting key words in the prompt can help them understand what it is asking.

Have students identify the words they would underline in the sample prompt *(paragraph, compares, one-room school, your school)*.

Read additional writing prompts to students. Have students identify the key words in each prompt and then explain in their own words what they need to do to respond to the prompt. Use former writing prompts or the following:

- In a paragraph, explain the steps you follow in a grocery store to buy a gallon of milk.
- Describe two different kinds of public transportation which you have seen or used.

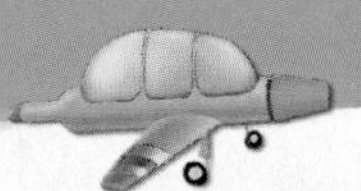

Responding to Writing Prompts

Some tests ask you to respond to a prompt. (A *prompt* gives you an idea that you have to write about.) See the prompt below.

Sample Writing Prompt

Write a paragraph that compares a one-room school to your school.

Tips for Responding

- **Read the prompt carefully.** Be sure that you know what you are supposed to do.
- **Plan your answer.** Because the sample prompt asks you to compare two things, make two lists—one about a one-room school and one about your school.

One-Room School	My School
kids of different ages	kids close to same age
no janitor	two janitors
lunch from home	lunch in cafeteria

- **Write your answer.**

A one-room school is not like my school. A one-room school has kids of all ages in the same room. In my classroom, the kids are all close to the same age. Kids in one-room schools help sweep floors and wash chalkboards. In my school, janitors do those chores. Kids in one-room schools bring their lunches from home. We have a cafeteria.

Write your answers clearly and neatly.

English Language Learners

To give students more practice understanding writing prompts, focus on the concept of reading a prompt and then repeating it in one's own words. Begin by giving a series of simple prompts and having students identify key words and explain how the prompts differ:

- Describe your favorite kind of pet.
- Compare two kinds of pets.
- Choose a type of pet and tell why you think it would make the best pet.
- Explain what you would do if you found a lost pet.

Remembering for Tests

Idea Maps

An idea map will help you put information in order. It can help you picture and remember what you need to know for a test.

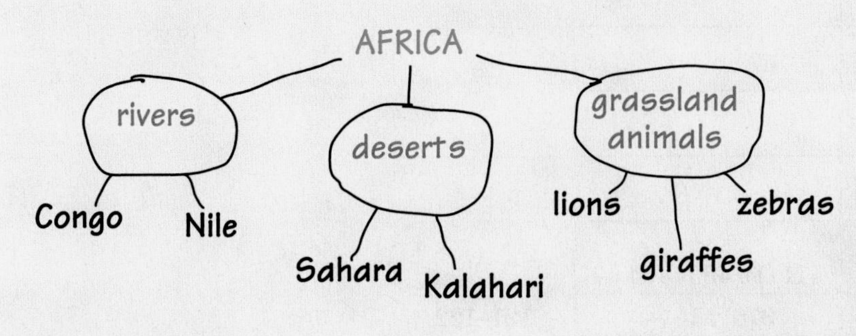

Flash Cards

Write one fact on each card. Carry the cards with you and read one whenever you have a chance. Ask family members or friends to "test" you with the cards.

Memory Tricks

A memory trick can help you remember lists of important names or information. Suppose you want to remember the names of the five Great Lakes.

You could put the names in a special order in which the first letters spell a word. For example, the word HOMES is spelled with the first letters in the names of the lakes: Huron, Ontario, Michigan, Erie, and Superior.

Remembering for Tests

Idea Maps

After reviewing the idea map shown here, have students work together to create an idea map on chart paper for a topic they are studying in social studies or science.

Flash Cards

Students are more likely to use flash cards if they make them in class. Have a batch of empty index cards on hand. Then, schedule enough time after discussing a topic or new concept for students to create their own set of flash cards, using the facts they learned during the discussion. You may want to create a class set so that students can match their set to the "official" set.

Memory Tricks

Share with students other memory tricks you have used to remember facts. For example, some people use the name Roy G. Biv to recall the seven colors of the rainbow. Perhaps you have a memory trick for remembering the name and order of the planets or how to spell a particular word. Have students share memory tricks of their own.

Struggling Learners

Have student pairs use their flash cards to play the following game:

- One student flashes a card with a fact to his or her partner.
- The partner responds with a question that would be answered by the fact. For example, the first student flashes this fact: *The three forms of matter are solids, liquids, and gases.* The partner would respond: *What are the three forms of matter?*
- Have students take turns flashing cards and forming questions.

Suggest to students that the next time they make a set of flash cards, they write the question for each fact on the back of the card. They can then use the cards to help them study for tests on their own.

Advanced Learners

Have students make a collection of memory tricks. They could ask older siblings, parents, or guardians for memory tricks they use. They could gather the memory tricks in a booklet for the class or create a bulletin board display.

Writing Paragraphs (One Week)

	Day	Writing and Skills Instruction	*Student Edition*		*SkillsBook*
			Basic Grammar and Writing Unit	Resource Units*	
WEEK 1	1	**Building Paragraphs** (Model)	416–417		
		(Topic and Closing Sentences)	418–419		
	2	(Details)	420–421		
		(Order)	422–423		
	3–4	(Guidelines)	424–425		
		Skills Activities: • Types of Sentences		411 (+), 463–464 (+)	
		• Nouns		376, 534 (+)	121–122
		Skills Activities: • End Punctuation		402, 411 (+), 463–464 (+)	
		• Numbers		494–495	
		• Fragments		403 (+), 526 (+), 528 (+)	93–94
		(Marking Paragraphs)	426–427		
	5	(Test Prep)	428–429		

* These units are also located in the back of the *Teacher's Edition.* Resource Units include "Basic Grammar and Writing," "A Writer's Resource," and "Proofreader's Guide."

(+) This activity is located in a different section of the *Write Source Student Edition.* If students have already completed this activity, you may wish to review it at this time.

Academic Vocabulary

Read aloud the academic terms, as well as the descriptions and questions. Model for students how to read one question and answer it. Have partners monitor their understanding and seek clarification of the terms by working through the meanings and questions together.

Basic Grammar and Writing

What's Ahead

- Working with Words
- Writing Sentences
- Building Paragraphs

Academic Vocabulary

Work with a partner. Read the meanings and share answers to the questions.

1. A **sentence** is a group of words that forms a complete thought.
   What is a sentence that you hear a lot?
2. A **syllable** is one or more letters in a word that make one sound.
   How many syllables does the word *paragraph* have?
3. To **identify** means "to recognize or name something."
   How could someone identify you?

Carpenters work with wood, cooks with food, tailors with fabric . . . and what do writers work with? Words. As a writer, you arrange words into sentences, and sentences into paragraphs, and paragraphs into stories or essays.

The chapters in this section cover the two most basic parts of writing—**words** and **sentences**. As you learn more about these parts, you will begin to build stronger stories, essays, and reports.

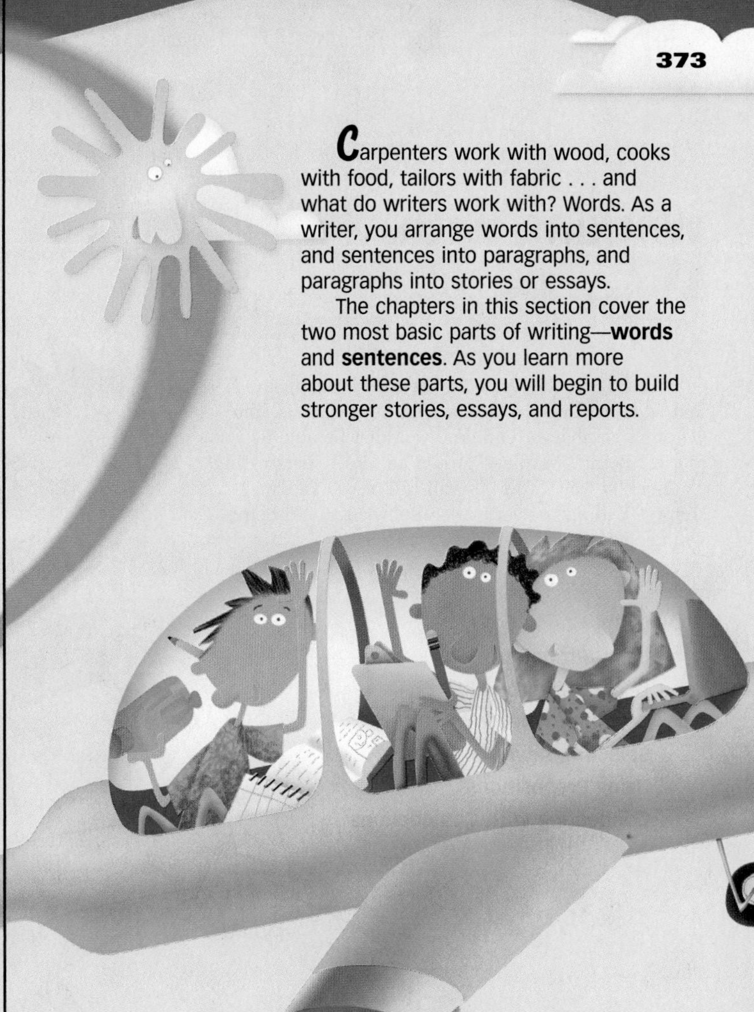

Working with Words

What if all the words in the world disappeared? You wouldn't be able to talk with your friends. You wouldn't be able to read. You wouldn't be able to write stories. Being "wordless" would be totally frustrating!

Luckily, your world is still full of words. This chapter will add to your word knowledge and help you use them more skillfully.

What's Ahead

Using Nouns

A **noun** names a person, a place, a thing, or an idea. **Common nouns** name a general person, place, thing, or idea. They are not capitalized. **Proper nouns** name a specific person, place, thing, or idea. They are capitalized.

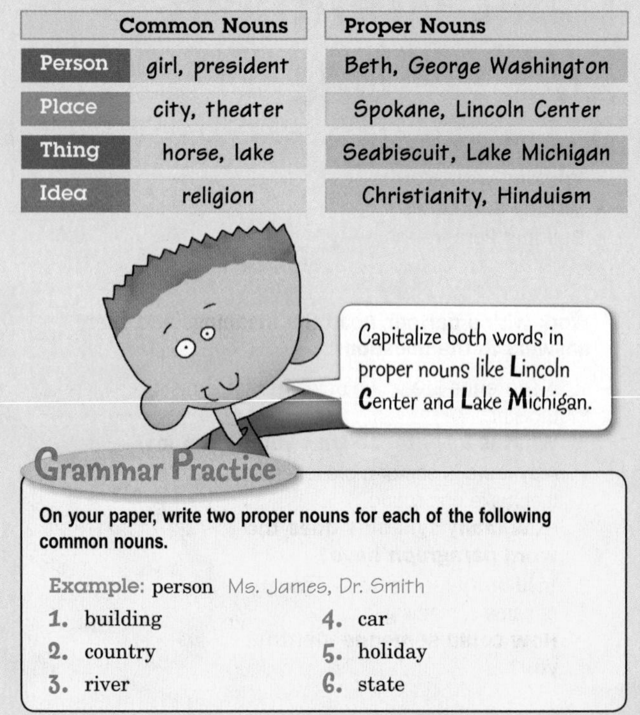

	Common Nouns	Proper Nouns
Person	girl, president	Beth, George Washington
Place	city, theater	Spokane, Lincoln Center
Thing	horse, lake	Seabiscuit, Lake Michigan
Idea	religion	Christianity, Hinduism

Capitalize both words in proper nouns like Lincoln Center and Lake Michigan.

Grammar Practice

On your paper, write two proper nouns for each of the following common nouns.

Example: person Ms. James, Dr. Smith

1. building
2. country
3. river
4. car
5. holiday
6. state

Grammar Practice Possible Answers

1. Bradley Center, Willis Tower
2. Canada, France
3. Missouri River, Hoback River
4. Lumina, Sebring
5. Thanksgiving, Labor Day
6. California, Maine

Singular and Plural Nouns

A **singular noun** names one person, place, thing, or idea. A **plural noun** names more than one person, place, thing, or idea.

To form the plural of most nouns, add an *-s* to a singular noun. For nouns that end in *s, sh, ch,* or *x,* add an *-es* to make the plural form. For nouns that end in *y* (with a consonant just before the *y*), change the *y* to *i* and add *-es* to form the plural.

Singular Nouns	Plural Nouns
train, cup, star	trains, cups, stars
bus, wish, box	buses, wishes, boxes
sky, puppy	skies, puppies

Some nouns are irregular, which means they change their spelling when they become plural. For example, **child** becomes **children**.

Grammar Practice

Write the plural form for each of the following singular nouns. Use each plural noun in a sentence.

Example: beach
beaches The beaches were crowded.

1. cow
2. fox
3. body
4. guess
5. pencil
6. lunch
7. uncle
8. library

Possessive Nouns

A **possessive noun** shows ownership. Singular nouns are usually made possessive by adding an apostrophe and *-s.* In most cases, a plural noun that ends in *s* just needs an apostrophe to make it possessive.

Singular Noun	Singular Possessive	Plural Noun	Plural Possessive
cup	cup's handle	cups	cups' handles
lion	lion's mane	lions	lions' manes

If the plural noun does not end in **s**, make it possessive by adding an apostrophe and an **-s—children's**.

Grammar Practice

Rewrite each sentence below. In your new sentence, turn the underlined noun into a possessive noun.

Example: The books belonging to the girls are here.
The girls' books are here.

1. The fur on Henry is shiny.
2. The erasers on the pencils are worn down.
3. The information in that book is helpful.
4. The screen on the computer needs cleaning.
5. The petals on the flowers are very soft.

Grammar Practice Answers

1. cows
2. foxes
3. bodies
4. guesses
5. pencils
6. lunches
7. uncles
8. libraries

Grammar Practice Answers

1. Henry's fur is shiny.
2. The pencils' erasers are worn down.
3. That book's information is helpful.
4. The computer's screen needs cleaning.
5. The flowers' petals are very soft.

Q. *How can I improve my writing with nouns?*

A. You can improve your writing by using specific nouns. A **specific noun** names a particular person, place, thing, or idea. Using specific nouns will make your writing more interesting than using general nouns will.

	General Nouns	Specific Nouns
Person	performer	juggler, Selena
Place	park	ball park, Wrigley Field
Thing	apple	crab apple, Macintosh
Idea	celebration	birthday, Lincoln's birthday

Grammar Practice

Number your paper from 1 to 10. For each of the following general nouns, write a specific noun.

Example: car convertible

1. book
2. bread
3. mountain
4. city
5. athlete
6. song
7. street
8. holiday
9. car
10. country

On your own paper, write some sentences about your favorite meal. Use at least four specific nouns in your writing, and underline them.

Using Pronouns

A **pronoun** is a word that takes the place of a noun. **Personal pronouns** are the most common type of pronoun. Some personal pronouns are used as subjects: *I, you, he, she, it, we, they.* Some are used as objects: *me, you, him, her, it, us, them.*

- A **subject pronoun** is used as the subject of a sentence.

  She wrapped a ribbon around the big tree.
  They called a reporter.

- An **object pronoun** is used after an action verb or in a prepositional phrase.

  Suki threw me the ball. (after an action verb)
  My grandma plays with us. (in a prepositional phrase)

Remember that **I** is a subject pronoun and is always capitalized, while **me** is an object pronoun and is not capitalized.

Grammar Practice

Number your paper from 1 to 5. For each of the following sentences, write the pronoun and tell whether it is a subject pronoun (SP) or an object pronoun (OP).

Example: I love apples. I, SP

1. We pick apples during the fall.
2. Many people eat them for snacks.
3. Dad takes an apple to work with him.
4. Mom makes us apple pie.
5. She uses Cortland apples.

Grammar Practice Possible Answers

1. encyclopedia
2. whole wheat bread
3. Mt. Everest
4. New York
5. Lance Armstrong
6. "America the Beautiful"
7. Maple Lane
8. Halloween
9. Prius
10. Ireland

Grammar Practice Answers

1. We, SP
2. them, OP
3. him, OP
4. us, OP
5. She, SP

Possessive Pronouns

Possessive pronouns show ownership. They can be either singular or plural. (Possessive pronouns act as adjectives when they come before a noun.)

Billy found my red hat.
The red hat is mine.

Yes, that's our art project.
That art project is ours.

Singular Possessive Pronouns	Plural Possessive Pronouns
my, mine, his, her, hers, its, your, yours	our, ours, your, yours, their, theirs

Always check to make sure you use the correct singular or plural possessive pronoun.

Grammar Practice

Number your paper from 1 to 10. Skip one or two lines between each number. Then write a sentence for each possessive pronoun listed below.

Example: their
The Smiths keep their car clean.

1. my
2. her
3. your
4. mine
5. his
6. yours
7. ours
8. theirs
9. our
10. its

Q. How can I use pronouns correctly?

A. You can check for pronoun-antecedent agreement. The **antecedent** of a pronoun is the noun that it refers to. If the antecedent is singular, the pronoun must be singular. If the antecedent is plural, the pronoun must be plural.

antecedent pronoun
The big dog broke its leash.
(The pronoun *its* and the antecedent *dog* are both singular.)

antecedent pronoun
The students walked to their classrooms.
(The pronoun *their* and the antecedent *students* are both plural.)

Grammar Practice

For each of the following sentences, write the correct pronoun from the two in parentheses. Also name the noun it refers to (the antecedent).

Example:
Maria and *(her, their)* friends wanted to go waterskiing.
her, Maria

1. Before Maria left, *(she, they)* finished her chores.
2. Maria's older brother said *(he, they)* would take Maria.
3. When Maria and her brother got into the car, *(she, they)* talked about waterskiing.
4. Maria's brother and *(his, their)* best friend ski often.
5. The father of one of Maria's friends has *(his, their)* own boat.

Grammar Practice Possible Answers

1. My lunch tastes good.
2. Her voice is pretty.
3. Eat your vegetables.
4. That book is mine.
5. Look at his artwork.
6. Is this coat yours?
7. This game is ours.
8. That house is theirs.
9. Our school is huge.
10. The dog wagged its tail.

Grammar Practice Answers

1. she, Maria
2. he, brother
3. they, Maria and brother
4. his, brother
5. his, father

Plural Pronouns

Plural pronouns refer to more than one person or thing. Some plural pronouns are used as subject pronouns. Other plural pronouns are used as object pronouns. It is important to know when to use each type of pronoun.

Plural Subject Pronouns	Plural Object Pronouns
we, you, they	us, you, them

- When you use the pronouns *we* and *us*, you are including yourself.
- When you use the pronoun *you*, you are writing about an audience.
- When you use the pronouns *they* and *them*, you are writing about others.

Grammar Practice

Rewrite the sentences below. Replace the underlined words with the correct plural pronoun *(we, they, us, them)*.

Example: Grandma took Andy and me to the circus.
Grandma took us to the circus.

1. Andy and I shared a box of popcorn.
2. The boys sat in the front row.
3. A clown threw confetti at Trent and Jake.
4. Grandma, Andy, and I laughed at the clowns.
5. The clown with big shoes shot water at Andy and me from a flower in his hat.

Choosing Verbs

A **verb** is a word that usually tells what is happening. It is the main word in the predicate. There are three types of verbs: **action verbs**, **helping verbs**, and **linking verbs**.

Action Verbs

An **action verb** tells what the subject is doing. If you use specific action verbs, your sentences are more fun to read.

General Action Verbs	Specific Action Verbs
walked	skipped, strolled, pranced
talks	tattles, chatters, whispers
fell	tripped, stumbled, crashed
laugh	chuckle, giggle, hoot

Grammar Practice

Rewrite each of the sentences below. Replace the underlined general verb with a more specific one from the list of "Specific Action Verbs" above.

Example: The poodle walked around the show ring.
The poodle pranced around the show ring.

1. The happy child walked down the sidewalk.
2. My parrot talks all the time!
3. Dad fell over the roller skate.
4. Little kids laugh a lot.

Grammar Practice Answers

1. We shared a box of popcorn.
2. They sat in the front row.
3. The clown threw confetti at them.
4. We laughed at the clowns.
5. The clown with the big shoes shot water at us from a flower in his hat.

Grammar Practice Possible Answers

1. The happy child skipped down the sidewalk.
2. My parrot chatters all the time!
3. Dad tripped over the roller skate.
4. Little kids giggle a lot.

Linking Verbs

A **linking verb** links, or connects, a subject to a noun or to an adjective in the predicate.

She is the best math student. (The linking verb *is* links the subject *she* to the noun *student.*)

Linking Verbs
am, is, are, was, were, being, been, appear, become, feel, grow, look, remain, seem, smell, sound, taste

To tell if a word is used as a linking verb or an action verb, change the verb to *is, am,* or *are*. If the sentence still makes sense, the verb is a linking verb.

That soup tastes sour. (*That soup is sour* still makes sense, so *tastes* is a linking verb in this sentence.)

He tastes the soup. (*He is the soup* does not make sense, so *tastes* is an action verb in this sentence.)

Grammar Practice

Number your paper from 1 to 4. Then write down the verb from each sentence and write "A" for action verb or "L" for linking verb.

Example: Pablo seemed very excited.
seemed, L

1. Lightning struck the big tree in our yard.
2. He was happy about the gift.
3. Boats sailed across the quiet lake.
4. Their school was really big.

Helping Verbs

A **helping verb** comes before a main verb. This extra verb helps *to show time* or *to state an action.* Some sentences can have more than one helping verb.

Common Helping Verbs					
has	will	do	may	am	was
have	could	did	can	is	were
had	should	does		are	been
	would				

Ms. Daniels has organized a kickball tournament.
(*Has* is the helping verb, and *organized* is the main verb.)

Our team should have won the tournament.
(*Should* and *have* are helping verbs, and *won* is the main verb.)

Grammar Practice

Copy the following sentences on your own paper. Then circle the helping verbs and underline the main verbs twice. (One of the sentences has more than one helping verb.)

Example: Each class could enter one or two teams.
Each class could enter one or two teams.

1. Our team did win our first two games.
2. We had scored seven runs in the second inning.
3. My friend's team should have won their game, too.
4. Pat's team could beat every other team.
5. We will win the next tournament.

Grammar Practice Answers

1. struck, A
2. was, L
3. sailed, A
4. was, L

Grammar Practice Answers

1. Our team did win our first two games.
2. We had scored seven runs in the second inning.
3. My friend's team should have won their game, too.
4. Pat's team could beat every other team.
5. We will win the next tournament.

Q. *How can I show time in my writing?*

A. You can show time by using the proper verb tense. The **tense** of a verb tells when the action takes place. The tense of a verb may be either **present**, **past**, or **future**.

- **Present tense verbs** state an action that is happening now or continues happening.

  My bicycle squeaks.

  I swim in the lake every day.

- **Past tense verbs** state an action that happened in the past and is over.

  My bicycle squeaked yesterday.

  Last week, I swam in the pool.

Verbs like *squeak* form the past tense by adding *-ed*. They are called **regular verbs**. Other verbs, like *swim*, change their spelling to form the past tense. These types of verbs are called **irregular verbs**. (See page 542.)

Grammar Practice

Number your paper from 1 to 4. For each sentence below, write the verb. Then write "PR" for present tense or "Past" for past tense.

Example: My Aunt Alicia tells me stories about my family.
tells, PR

1. My mother and my aunt played softball.
2. They traveled to many tournaments.
3. My grandmother still keeps the trophies.
4. Now I know something about my mother's life.

- **Future tense verbs** state an action that will take place at a later time, or in the future.

  My bicycle will squeak until I get it fixed.

  I will swim in the lake next year.

If the present tense verb is singular and ends in **s**, the **s** is dropped from the main verb in the future tense. He **talks**. He **will talk**.

Grammar Practice

Number your paper from 1 to 5. Rewrite the following sentences, changing the underlined present tense verbs to future tense. Underline the new verb.

Example: We travel on the train.
We will travel on the train.

1. It zooms through the city.
2. I watch the buildings change.
3. The scenery changes to rolling hills.
4. Juni rides with me.
5. We have a lot of fun on the train.

Write Now **Write three sentences about riding a bicycle.**

1. **Write one sentence using a present tense verb.**
2. **Write one sentence using a past tense verb.**
3. **Write a third sentence using a future tense verb.**

Grammar Practice Answers

1. played, Past
2. traveled, Past
3. keeps, PR
4. know, PR

Grammar Practice Answers

1. It will zoom through the city.
2. I will watch the buildings change.
3. The scenery will change to rolling hills.
4. Juni will ride with me.
5. We will have a lot of fun on the train.

Q. How can I use verbs correctly?

A. You can check carefully for subject-verb agreement. All verbs must agree in number with their subjects. If the subject in a sentence is singular, the verb must be singular. If the subject is plural, the verb must be plural.

Freddi hikes with the outdoor club.
(The subject *Freddi* and the verb *hikes* are both singular.)

Many students hike with the outdoor club.
(The subject *students* and the verb *hike* are both plural.)

Freddi and Jeff love hiking. (The compound subject *Freddi* and *Jeff* and the verb *love* are both plural.)

Tip Singular verbs often end in **s**. Plural verbs usually do not end in **s**.

Grammar Practice

Number your paper from 1 to 5. For each sentence below, write the verb in parentheses that agrees with the subject. Then write "S" if the subject and verb are singular and "P" if they are plural.

Example: Good shoes *(makes, make)* hiking much easier.
make, P

1. Our first hike *(is, are)* planned for Saturday.
2. We *(needs, need)* our parents' permission to go.
3. The bus *(leaves, leave)* at 8:00 a.m.
4. The handout *(says, say)* that we can wear shorts.
5. Parents and teachers *(has, have)* snacks for us.

Selecting Adjectives

An **adjective** is a word that describes a noun. Adjectives answer four questions about nouns: *what kind? how much? how many?* and *which one?*

What kind?	large **dog**, American **flag**, yellow **birds**
How much?	some **salt**, more **water**, less **snow**
How many?	three **steps**, fewer **questions**, one **basket**
Which one?	that **book**, this **music**, those **geese**

Tip The words **a, an,** and **the** are special adjectives called articles.

Grammar Practice

On your own paper, write the adjectives in each sentence below, but do not list the articles *a, an,* or *the.* (The number in parentheses tells you how many adjectives you should find.)

Example: A desert is a hot, empty region. *(2)*
hot empty

1. Deserts have a wide variety of prickly plants. *(2)*
2. Most deserts are in warm climates. *(2)*
3. African deserts are home to many herders who wear long robes. *(3)*
4. Sand dunes take many shapes and are formed by high winds. *(3)*
5. The Bedouin people live in desert tribes. *(2)*

Grammar Practice Answers

1. is, S
2. need, P
3. leaves, S
4. says, S
5. have, P

Grammar Practice Answers

1. wide, prickly
2. most, warm
3. African, many, long
4. sand, many, high
5. Bedouin, desert

Q. How can I use adjectives correctly?

A. You can check the form of each adjective you use. Adjectives have three forms: *positive* (used to describe one thing), *comparative* (used to compare two things), and *superlative* (used to compare three or more things).

Single-Syllable Adjectives

When the adjective is just one syllable, add *-er* to make the comparative form. Add *-est* to make the superlative form.

Positive: Our dog is small.
Comparative: Our dog is smaller than your dog is.
Superlative: Our dog is the smallest one in the neighborhood.

Multi-Syllable Adjectives

When the adjective is two or more syllables, you usually use the word *more (*or *less)* to make the comparative form. Use *most (*or *least)* to make the superlative form.

Positive: Tonight's sunset is beautiful.
Comparative: Tonight's sunset is more beautiful than yesterday's sunset was.
Superlative: That is the most beautiful sunset ever.

Grammar Practice

Write the comparative and superlative forms for each adjective below. (Remember to count the syllables in each word first.)

Example: green
greener, greenest

1. clean 2. enjoyable 3. dull 4. old 5. afraid

Selecting Adverbs

A word that describes a verb is an **adverb**.

Lori sang softly during the concert.
(The adverb *softly* describes how Lori *sang.)*

Marcus loudly bangs his drums.
(The adverb *loudly* describes how Marcus *bangs* his drums.)

Kinds of Adverbs

- **Adverbs of time** tell *when* or *how often*.

  The kite club met yesterday.
  (The adverb *yesterday* tells *when* the club met.)

  Mr. Lee always arrives on time.
  (The adverb *always* tells *how often* he arrives on time.)

- **Adverbs of place** tell *where* something happens.

  We held our meeting outside.
  (The adverb *outside* tells *where* the meeting was held.)

- **Adverbs of manner** tell *how* something is done.

  Andy worked carefully on his kite.
  (The adverb *carefully* tells *how* Andy worked.)

Grammar Practice

1. **Write two sentences using adverbs that tell when or how often an action is done.**
2. **Write two sentences using adverbs that tell where an action is done.**
3. **Write two sentences using adverbs that tell how an action is done.**

Grammar Practice Answers

1. cleaner, cleanest
2. more enjoyable, most enjoyable
3. duller, dullest
4. older, oldest
5. more afraid, most afraid

Grammar Practice Possible Answers

1. Scruffy never barks at strangers.
   She barked at Billy today.
2. We stayed inside to read.
   The dog wanted to go outside.
3. Scruffy barked loudly.
   She ran quickly to the door.

Q. How can I improve my writing with adverbs?

A. You can use adverbs to make your writing more specific. Adverbs will make your sentences clearer and more interesting to read. In the following example, notice how specific adverbs make the sentence clearer and more interesting.

Maggie trapped the frog under the pail.
Maggie calmly trapped the frog under the pail.
Maggie carefully trapped the frog under the pail.

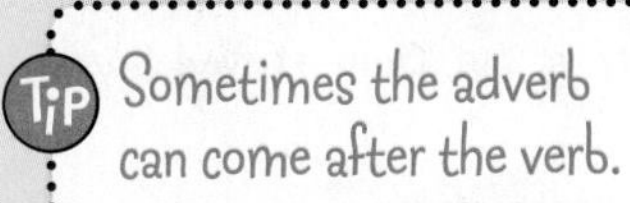

TIP Sometimes the adverb can come after the verb.

She spoke softly to her little prince.

Grammar Practice

Rewrite each sentence below, adding one of the following adverbs:

slowly easily politely poorly calmly quickly

Example:
Meg walked up the driveway, bouncing a ball.
Meg walked slowly up the driveway, bouncing a ball.

1. She had played yesterday.
2. Up ahead, her brother stood with his arms crossed.
3. He asked her to play one-on-one.
4. He scored two points.
5. Meg made the next three baskets.

Using Prepositions

A **preposition** is a word that often shows direction or position. It introduces a **prepositional phrase**, which begins with a preposition and ends with the nearest noun or pronoun.

Common Prepositions							
in	at	to	for	with	over	after	before
on	by	up	of	near	from	about	through

The bike in the yard needs a new tire.
(The preposition *in* introduces the prepositional phrase *in the yard.*)

We hid behind the garage.
(The preposition *behind* introduces the prepositional phrase *behind the garage.*)

Grammar Practice

On your own paper, identify the prepositional phrase in each of the following sentences. (One sentence has two of them.)

Example:
Mr. Cosford has a huge train set in his basement.
in his basement

1. He always works on the train set.
2. One part of the set includes a little town.
3. Another part includes a big bridge over a river.
4. He is now making a tunnel through a mountain.
5. Mr. Cosford worked for a railroad company, so he knows a lot about trains.

Grammar Practice Possible Answers

1. She had played poorly yesterday.
2. Up ahead, her brother calmly stood with his arms crossed.
3. He politely asked her to play one-on-one.
4. He scored two points quickly.
5. Meg easily made the next three baskets.

Grammar Practice Answers

1. on the train set
2. of the set
3. over a river
4. through a mountain
5. for a railroad company, about trains

Connecting with Conjunctions

A **conjunction** connects words or groups of words. Coordinating conjunctions like *and, but, so,* and *or* are used to connect words, phrases, and simple sentences.

Coordinating Conjunctions
and but or so yet

Connecting a Series of Words

At the zoo, we saw elephants, seals, and tigers.

Connecting Two Phrases

The lions eat in the morning or at night.

Connecting Two Simple Sentences

Sally was stung by a bee, but she didn't make a big fuss.

Grammar Practice

On your own paper, write each of the following sentences. First, circle the conjunction in each sentence. Then underline the words, phrases, or simple sentences that the conjunction connects.

Example:
Are grizzly bears or black bears found in our state?
Are grizzly bears (or) black bears found in our state?

1. Seals and otters are fun to watch.
2. A buffalo has a huge head, but the rest of its body seems small.
3. The hippos rest in the river or on the grassy bank.
4. Hyenas look very odd, and they do not really laugh.

Q. How can I use conjunctions in my writing?

A. You can use conjunctions to combine your ideas. For example, you can use conjunctions like *and, but,* and *or* to combine two simple sentences into a compound sentence. A **compound sentence** is two simple sentences joined by a comma and a conjunction.

Two Simple Sentences

Jack went to the store. Sam stayed home.

One Compound Sentence

Jack went to the store, but Sam stayed home.

Grammar Practice

On your own paper, combine each set of short sentences into a compound sentence. (Use the conjunction in parentheses.)

Example:
Mr. Snyder blew his whistle. He started practice. *(and)*
Mr. Snyder blew his whistle, and he started practice.

1. Most of us took batting practice. Two players practiced pitching. *(but)*
2. Next, the infielders caught ground balls. The outfielders caught fly balls. *(and)*
3. Then Mr. Snyder blew his whistle again. We had to line up for base running. *(and)*
4. At the end of practice, we could play a game. We could have a hitting contest. *(or)*

Grammar Practice Answers

1. Seals (and) otters are fun to watch.
2. A buffalo has a huge head, (but) the rest of its body seems small.
3. The hippos rest in the river (or) on the grassy bank.
4. Hyenas look very odd, (and) they do not really laugh.

Grammar Practice Answers

1. Most of us took batting practice, but two players practiced pitching.
2. Next, the infielders caught ground balls, and the outfielders caught fly balls.
3. Then Mr. Snyder blew his whistle again, and we had to line up for base running.
4. At the end of practice, we could play a game, or we could have a hitting contest.

Writing Sentences

Does "I spinach" make sense? No, something is missing. Does "I like spinach" sound better? It should (even if you don't like spinach). The second example states a complete thought.

A group of words that states a complete thought is called a **sentence**. You use sentences when you talk to other people. You also use them in your writing and read them in your favorite stories and books. In other words, you use sentences all the time.

This section will show you what you need to know about sentences.

What's Ahead

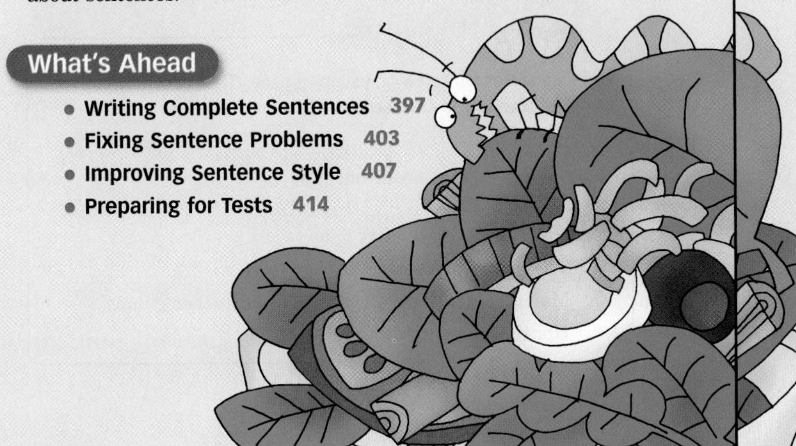

Writing Complete Sentences

Q. How can I write clear sentences?

A. You can write clear sentences by making sure each sentence expresses a complete thought. A sentence begins with a capital letter and ends with a period, a question mark, or an exclamation point.

travel trucks the on freeway

The group of words above does not make sense. But these same words can be arranged into a sentence that does express a complete thought.

Trucks travel on the freeway.

Grammar Practice

On your own paper, rearrange each group of words below so that it is a clear sentence. Remember to capitalize and punctuate your sentences.

Example: food our from places many comes
Our food comes from many places.

1. Florida our from come oranges
2. potatoes come some Idaho from
3. lakes and oceans fish caught are in
4. are many farms on raised vegetables huge
5. countries sugar and tea other produce

Write NOW **Write at least five sentences about your favorite meal. Remember: A sentence starts with a capital letter and ends with a period, a question mark, or an exclamation point.**

Grammar Practice Answers

1. Our oranges come from Florida.
2. Some potatoes come from Idaho.
3. Fish are caught in lakes and oceans.
4. Many vegetables are raised on huge farms.
5. Other countries produce sugar and tea.

Complete Subjects

All sentences have a subject and a predicate (verb). The **subject** tells who or what the sentence is about. The **complete subject** may be just one word or more than one word.

Ronnie **scored a touchdown.**
(*Ronnie* is the complete subject.)
Many fans **cheered loudly.**
(*Many fans* is the complete subject.)
The team's new kicker **made the extra point.**
(*The team's new kicker* is the complete subject.)

The subject usually comes at the beginning of a sentence.

Grammar Practice

Write the sentences below on your own paper. Then underline the complete subject in each one.

Example:
The crowd watched the football game in the rain.
The crowd watched the football game in the rain.

1. A marching band performed at halftime.
2. Our team's uniforms are red and white.
3. My favorite player is the quarterback.
4. The linemen block for the quarterback.
5. Long passes are fun to watch.

Complete Predicates

The **predicate** includes the verb and tells something about the subject or what it does. The predicate can also tell what is being done to the subject. The **complete predicate** may be just one word, or it may be several words.

Maria celebrated.
(*Celebrated* is the verb and the complete predicate.)
We ate cold slices of watermelon.
(*Ate cold slices of watermelon* is the complete predicate.)
Her party was so much fun.
(*Was so much fun* is the complete predicate.)

The complete predicate contains the verb and all the words that describe it or complete it.

Grammar Practice

Write the sentences below on your own paper. Then underline the complete predicate in each sentence.

Example:
Maria was excited about her party.
Maria was excited about her party.

1. Her friends arrived at noon.
2. They played shadow tag.
3. Maria's older sister organized many other games.
4. Her dad made hamburgers.

Grammar Practice Answers

1. A marching band performed at halftime.
2. Our team's uniforms are red and white.
3. My favorite player is the quarterback.
4. The linemen block for the quarterback.
5. Long passes are fun to watch.

Grammar Practice Answers

1. Her friends arrived at noon.
2. They played shadow tag.
3. Maria's older sister organized many other games.
4. Her dad made hamburgers.

Simple Subjects and Predicates

The **simple subject** is the subject without the words that describe it. The **simple predicate** is the verb without the words that modify it.

Our art teacher **draws funny cartoons.**
(*Our art teacher* is the complete subject, and *teacher* is the simple subject.)

Our chorus teacher sings very well.
(*Sings very well* is the complete predicate, and *sings* is the simple predicate, or verb.)

Grammar Practice

Copy sentences 1 to 5 on your own paper. Then underline the simple subjects with one line and the simple predicates with two lines.

Example:
Our teacher announced the date of our art show.
Our teacher announced the date of our art show.

1. The parents received invitations.
2. My mom marked the date on the calendar.
3. We painted pictures for weeks.
4. Every student was ready on the big day.
5. My best friend wished me good luck.

Write three sentences about a special program at your school. Then underline the simple subjects with one line and the simple predicates with two lines.

Compound Subjects and Predicates

A **compound subject** has two or more simple subjects. A **compound predicate** has two or more simple verbs.

Lions **and** tigers **do not look alike.**
(*Lions* and *tigers* make up the compound subject.)

Tigers move **with speed and** attack **with power.**
(*Move* and *attack* make up the compound predicate.)

Compound subjects and predicates are usually joined by **and, but,** or **or.**

Grammar Practice

Copy sentences 1 to 5 on your own paper. Then underline the simple subjects with one line and the simple predicates with two lines. (Watch for compound subjects and compound predicates.)

Example:
Lions and tigers are huge.
Lions and tigers are huge.

1. Some tigers grow 10 feet long and weigh 500 pounds.
2. Tigers eat deer, wild boars, and even cattle.
3. Tigers hunt alone at night.
4. Lions and tigers in the wild live about 15 years.
5. Wild lions live only in Africa and India.

Write three sentences about an animal you find interesting. Try to use a compound subject or a compound predicate in at least one of your sentences.

Grammar Practice Answers

1. The parents received invitations.
2. My mom marked the date on the calendar.
3. We painted pictures for weeks.
4. Every student was ready on the big day.
5. My best friend wished me good luck.

Grammar Practice Answers

1. Some tigers grow 10 feet long and weigh 500 pounds.
2. Tigers eat deer, wild boars, and even cattle.
3. Tigers hunt alone at night.
4. Lions and tigers in the wild live about 15 years.
5. Wild lions live only in Africa and India.

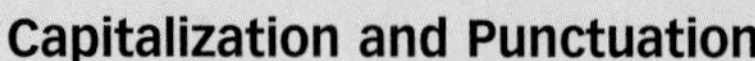

Capitalization and Punctuation

Every sentence should begin with a capital letter. A sentence that tells something is called a **statement**. It should end with a period. A sentence that asks something is called a **question**. It should end with a question mark.

Statements

Popcorn is a popular snack.

It has an interesting history.

Questions

Do you like popcorn?

How do you make it?

Grammar Practice

Write sentences 1 to 5 on your own paper. Begin each sentence with a capital letter and end it with a period or a question mark.

Example:
native americans made popcorn a long time ago
Native Americans made popcorn a long time ago.

1. they ate popcorn and used it for necklaces
2. where is popcorn grown
3. popcorn is grown in many Midwestern states
4. why does popcorn pop
5. heat causes the kernels to pop

Write three sentences about your favorite snack. At least one of your sentences should ask a question. Remember to use correct capitalization and punctuation.

Fixing Sentence Problems

Q. How can I write correct sentences?

A. You can learn to avoid fragments and other sentence errors. A **sentence fragment** is a group of words that looks like a sentence but isn't. It is missing a subject, a verb, or both.

Fragment	Sentence
My yo-yo smoothly. (The verb is missing.)	My yo-yo spins smoothly. (A verb is added.)
Were first made in China. (The subject is missing.)	Yo-yos were first made in China. (A subject is added.)
From the Philippines. (The subject and the verb are missing.)	Modern yo-yos come from the Philippines. (A subject and a verb are added.)

Grammar Practice

Number your paper from 1 to 4. Write "S" for each complete sentence and "F" for each fragment below. Rewrite each fragment to make it a complete sentence.

Example:
One of the oldest toys.
F, The yo-yo is one of the oldest toys.

1. Dolls are as old as yo-yos.
2. Made of clay.
3. Yo-yos in India looked like little boxes.
4. Went only up and down.

Write five sentences about your favorite toy. Make sure that each sentence has a subject and a predicate.

Grammar Practice Answers

1. They ate popcorn and used it for necklaces.
2. Where is popcorn grown?
3. Popcorn is grown in many Midwestern states.
4. Why does popcorn pop?
5. Heat causes the kernels to pop.

Grammar Practice Answers

Corrected fragments will vary.

1. S
2. F, The first dolls were made of clay.
3. S
4. F, Those yo-yos went only up and down.

Run-On Sentences

A **run-on sentence** is two sentences that run together. To correct this problem, add end punctuation and a capital letter between the two sentences.

Run-On Sentence

Sarah and I rode our bikes to school we left my house at 7:30. (Two sentences run together.)

Corrected

Sarah and I rode our bikes to school. We left my house at 7:30. (A period ends the first sentence. The capital **W** begins the second sentence.)

Grammar Practice

On your own paper, rewrite the following run-on sentences. Add end punctuation and a capital letter between the two sentences.

Example:
Most of our trip was easy we had only one big hill to go over.
Most of our trip was easy. We had only one big hill to go over.

1. Sarah's bike is red my bike is yellow.
2. We took a shortcut through the park I liked going that way.
3. Sarah always rides her bike to school I was doing it for the first time.
4. We talked all along the way the trip went really fast.
5. We parked our bikes in the bike rack I made sure to use my lock.

Rambling Sentences

A **rambling sentence** is one that goes on and on. A writer may use the word *and* too many times in a rambling sentence. To correct this problem, the writer can drop the *and* whenever possible. Then add capital letters, commas (if needed), and end punctuation to make new sentences.

Rambling Sentence

Josie and I went to our Girl Scout meeting and we learned about making bead necklaces and each of us made one and we also planned our summer camping trip. (The word *and* is used too often.)

Corrected

Josie and I went to our Girl Scout meeting. We learned about making bead necklaces, and each of us made one. We also planned our summer camping trip. (The word *and* is dropped in two places. Then capital letters, periods, and a comma are added to make three sentences.)

Grammar Practice

On your own paper, turn the rambling sentence below into shorter sentences. (You will need to drop the word "and" two or three times. Also, use capital letters, periods, and commas correctly.)

On rainy days, we don't have outside recess and everyone has to do things in the room and we play board games and we also build things with construction sets.

Grammar Practice Answers

1. Sarah's bike is red. My bike is yellow.
2. We took a shortcut through the park. I liked going that way.
3. Sarah always rides her bike to school. I was doing it for the first time.
4. We talked all along the way. The trip went really fast.
5. We parked our bikes in the bike rack. I made sure to use my lock.

Grammar Practice Possible Answers

On rainy days, we don't have outside recess. Everyone has to do things in the room. We play board games, and we also build things with construction sets.

Subject-Verb Agreement

The subject and the verb must agree in a sentence. If the subject is singular, the verb must be singular, too. If the subject is plural, the verb must be plural, too.

Sentences with Singular Subjects and Verbs

Ms. Peterson writes funny stories.

She reads them to us.

Sentences with Plural Subjects and Verbs

My older sisters write a lot of notes.

They talk on the phone, too.

Remember that singular means **one**, and plural means **more than one.**

Grammar Practice

Number your paper from 1 to 5. For each sentence below, select the verb in parentheses that agrees with the subject. Write that verb on your paper.

Example: Mr. Hayes *(play, plays)* softball with us.
plays

1. Mr. Hayes *(pitch, pitches)* to us.
2. Travis usually *(hit, hits)* the ball on the ground.
3. Sam and Mike *(hit, hits)* long fly balls.
4. My best friends *(like, likes)* running the bases.
5. Our games *(is, are)* four innings long.

Write three sentences about one of your favorite games. Be sure that the subject and the verb agree in each of your sentences.

Improving Sentence Style

Q. How can I write better sentences?

A. There are four ways to improve the sentences that you use in your paragraphs, essays, and stories.

1. **Combine short sentences.**
2. **Use compound sentences.**
3. **Use different kinds of sentences.**
4. **Model sentences written by other writers.**

Basic Sentences

My friends and I went bowling. We went on Saturday. I was throwing gutter balls. In the first five frames my score was 26. I got better. I had only one more gutter ball. I got one spare. My score was 70.

Improved Sentences

On Saturday morning, my friends and I went bowling. In the first five frames, I threw some gutter balls. My score was only 26. Then I started to do better. I had only one more gutter ball, and I even got one spare. One of my friends asked me, "How did you do that?" By the end of the game, my score was 70!

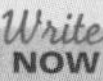
Write four or five sentences about something that you really like to do. Be sure that your sentences are fun to read.

Grammar Practice Answers

1. pitches
2. hits
3. hit
4. like
5. are

Combine Sentences with Key Words or Words in a Series

You can combine short sentences using a **key word** or a **series of words**.

Short Sentences

The butterfly landed on me. It was a monarch butterfly.

Combined with a Key Word

The monarch butterfly landed on me.

Short Sentences

Monarchs have beautiful black wings. They also have white and orange on their wings.

Combined with Words in a Series

Monarchs have beautiful black, white, and orange wings.

Grammar Practice

On your own paper, combine each set of short sentences below. Use the examples above as a guide.

Example:
Butterfly wings have scales. The scales are powdery.
Butterfly wings have powdery scales.

1. Butterflies live in rain forests. They also live in woodlands and fields.
2. Most butterflies have thin bodies. The bodies are hairless.
3. A butterfly's body has a head. It also has a thorax and an abdomen.
4. Butterflies have two antennae. The antennae are slender.

Combine Sentences with Compound Subjects and Predicates

You can combine two sentences by making a **compound subject** or a **compound predicate**.

Short Sentences

Stuart speaks Spanish. Olivia speaks Spanish.

Combined with a Compound Subject

Stuart and Olivia speak Spanish.

Tip: You may need to change a singular verb to a plural verb for a compound subject.

Short Sentences

Anna plays the clarinet. She sings in the chorus.

Combined with a Compound Predicate

Anna plays the clarinet and sings in the chorus.

Grammar Practice

Combine each of the sentence pairs below. Use a compound subject or a compound predicate to make your new sentence.

Example:
Julia is in gymnastics. Missy is in gymnastics, too.
Julia and Missy are in gymnastics.

1. Kyle swims on Mondays. He plays soccer on Tuesdays.
2. Ruby loves to read. Sheri also loves to read.
3. Luke reads comic books. He draws superheroes.
4. Erin joined the computer club. Her brother also joined.

Grammar Practice Answers

1. Butterflies live in rain forests, woodlands, and fields.
2. Most butterflies have thin, hairless bodies.
3. A butterfly's body has a head, a thorax, and an abdomen.
4. Butterflies have two slender antennae.

Grammar Practice Answers

1. Kyle swims on Mondays and plays soccer on Tuesdays.
2. Ruby and Sheri love to read.
3. Luke reads comic books and draws superheroes.
4. Erin and her brother joined the computer club.

Use Compound Sentences

A **compound sentence** is two or more simple sentences joined by a comma and a conjunction *(and, but, or)*. When you revise your writing, use simple and compound sentences correctly by making sure your subjects and verbs agree in number.

Two Sentences

Most spiders spin webs. They use their webs to catch food.

One Compound Sentence

Most spiders spin webs, and they use their webs to catch food.

Grammar Practice

Combine each of the sentence pairs below by making a compound sentence. (Use the conjunction in parentheses.) Then talk with a partner about an insect. Use compound sentences. Make sure your subjects and verbs agree.

Example:

Some spiders live in buildings. Many other spiders live outside. *(but)*

Some spiders live in buildings, but many other spiders live outside.

1. Many people call spiders insects. Scientists call them arachnids. *(but)*
2. Spiders cannot chew food. They eat only liquids. *(and)*
3. A spider can drop from its web. It can hang from a dragline in the air. *(or)*
4. Jumping spiders have short legs. They can jump very far. *(but)*

Use Different Kinds of Sentences

You can add variety to your writing by using different **kinds of sentences**.

- **Declarative** sentences make a statement.

  Mercury is the closest planet to the sun.
- **Interrogative** sentences ask a direct question.

  What other planets can you name?
- **Imperative** sentences give a command.

  Name the largest planet.
- **Exclamatory** sentences show strong emotion or surprise.

  Jupiter has more than 60 moons!

Practice

On your paper, label each sentence as "D" for declarative, "Int" for interrogative, "Imp" for imperative, or "Ex" for exclamatory. Add the correct end punctuation mark for each sentence.

Example:

Did you know that Venus is the planet closest to Earth

Int, ?

1. The solar system is amazing
2. Scientists are still studying the planets
3. Will they find new information
4. People use telescopes to view the planets
5. Please name the planets

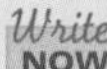

Write NOW **Write at least five sentences about the solar system. Include the four kinds of sentences.**

Grammar Practice Answers

1. Many people call spiders insects, but scientists call them arachnids.
2. Spiders cannot chew food, and they eat only liquids.
3. A spider can drop from its web, or it can hang from a dragline in the air.
4. Jumping spiders have short legs, but they can jump far.

Practice Answers

1. Ex, ! (or D, .)
2. D, .
3. Int, ?
4. D, .
5. Imp, .

Try Sentence Modeling

You can improve your writing by following the patterns of sentences written by professional authors. This type of practice is called **sentence modeling**.

Guidelines for Modeling

1. Find a sentence that you really like.
2. Decide what you will write about in your own sentence.
3. Following the author's pattern, build your sentence one part at a time.

One Student's Modeling

Anthony decided to model two of the author's sentences from his favorite book.

See how the book's sentences line up with Anthony's sentences.

1. Remy just stands <u>at the door</u> <u>on the train</u>, calling <u>to Sue</u>.

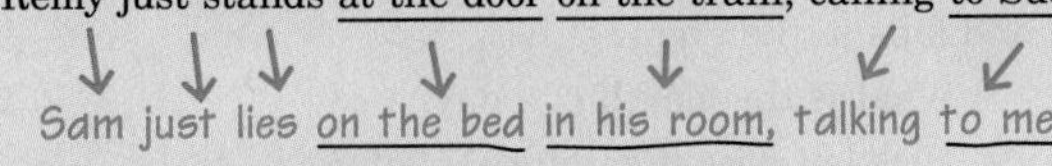

Sam just lies <u>on the bed</u> <u>in his room,</u> talking <u>to me.</u>

2. The train rolls along the tracks, and Remy reads and enjoys the ride.

The milk spills on the floor, and Jenna cries and runs outside.

Grammar Practice

Write your own sentence modeled after one of the sentences above.

Study Model Sentences

Here are some sentences that you can use as models.

- "It was Sunday, and I was riding my bike back from Robbie's."
  —from *The Journal of Ben Uchida* by Barry Denenberg
- "She looks at me closely, and I see a change in her face."
  —from *Train to Somewhere* by Eve Bunting
- "My grandmother is lining up the rolled and folded tamales ready for cooking."
  —from *Family Pictures* by Carmen Lomas Garza
- "Down the well she went, step over step."
  —from *Addie Across the Prairie* by Laurie Lawlor

Grammar Practice

Choose three of the sentences above to model. Write your own sentences, using the "Guidelines for Modeling" on page 412 to help you.

Save a spot in your notebook to list special sentences from books that you really like. Use these sentences as models to write your own sentences.

Preparing for Tests

Check Sentence Sense

1 **Choose the group of words that is a complete sentence.**
- Ⓐ Last time others in the sun.
- Ⓑ Warm weather near the favorite.
- Ⓒ Rain helps the crops grow.
- Ⓓ Thunder and lightning in the sky.

2 **Choose the group of words that is not a complete sentence.**
- Ⓐ Two teams with their coaches.
- Ⓑ Our team played hard during the whole game.
- Ⓒ The home team scored the first points.
- Ⓓ Fans shouted and cheered for the players.

3 **Find the sentence that is not correct.**
- Ⓐ The girls play outside all day.
- Ⓑ They build a snow fort.
- Ⓒ The sun were shining all afternoon.
- Ⓓ Slowly the fort melted away.

4 **Which sentence best combines the following short sentences?**
I like pizza. I like pizza with pepperoni. I like mushrooms on pizza, too.
- Ⓐ Mushrooms on pepperoni pizza taste great.
- Ⓑ I like pizza with pepperoni and mushrooms.
- Ⓒ The best pizza for me has pepperoni.

Answer Questions with Sentences

1 **Which sentence answers the following question?**
Question: What is the largest planet in our solar system?
- Ⓐ Earth and Venus are close to the same size.
- Ⓑ The largest planet in our solar system is Jupiter.
- Ⓒ Mercury is the smallest planet in the solar system.

2 **Which question would have this answer?**
Answer: The best speller wins a trophy.
- Ⓐ Who will be the best speller in our class?
- Ⓑ Will Jen or Aaron win the spelling trophy?
- Ⓒ What will the best speller in the spelldown win?
- Ⓓ Who will give the winner a trophy?

3 **Which question would be best for this answer?**
Answer: The temperature usually rises during the day and falls in the evening.
- Ⓐ What is the length of a day?
- Ⓑ How hot does it get during July?
- Ⓒ How does the temperature change from day to night?

4 **Which sentence answers the following question?**
Question: What book would you use to find the meaning of a word?
- Ⓐ You would use the dictionary to find word meanings.
- Ⓑ The encyclopedia would help you find information.
- Ⓒ You would use the thesaurus to find different words.

Answers

1. c. Rain helps the crops grow.
2. a. Two teams with their coaches.
3. c. The sun were shining all afternoon.
4. b. I like pizza with pepperoni and mushrooms.

Answers

1. b. The largest planet in our solar system is Jupiter.
2. c. What will the best speller in the spelldown win?
3. c. How does the temperature change from day to night?
4. a. You would use the dictionary to find word meanings.

Building Paragraphs

You could tell someone why living with your little brother is hard. You could also write a paragraph about it. A **paragraph** is made up of several sentences, all about the same subject.

A paragraph has three main parts. The first part is the **topic sentence**. The second part includes the **body sentences,** or middle, of the paragraph. The last part is the **closing sentence**.

Paragraph Parts

1. The **topic sentence** tells what the paragraph is about.
2. The **body sentences** support the topic.
3. The **closing sentence** wraps up the paragraph.

Parts of a Paragraph

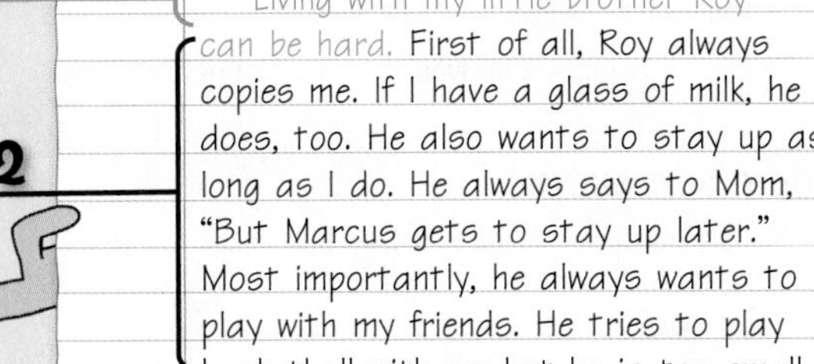

My Little Brother Roy

1 Living with my little brother Roy can be hard.

2 First of all, Roy always copies me. If I have a glass of milk, he does, too. He also wants to stay up as long as I do. He always says to Mom, "But Marcus gets to stay up later." Most importantly, he always wants to play with my friends. He tries to play basketball with us, but he is too small.

3 I keep trying to understand Roy, but it is not always easy.

After you read . . .

- **Ideas** (1) What is the topic of this paragraph? What three reasons does Marcus give to explain the topic?
- **Organization** (2) What words are used to put the reasons in order?
- **Voice** (3) How does Marcus show he's interested in the topic?

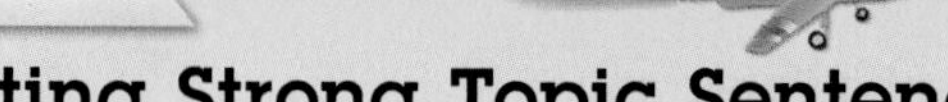

Writing Strong Topic Sentences

A strong topic sentence does two things: (1) It names the topic, and (2) it states the main idea (or focus) of the topic.

Topic	Main Idea (or Focus)
Living with my little brother Roy	can be hard.
Our neighborhood	needs better sidewalks.
My baseball team	won the championship game.

Special Topic Sentences

Numbers ■ A topic sentence can use a number to tell what the paragraph will be about.

Topic	Main Idea (or Focus)
My cat Henry	hides in three different places.

Lists ■ A topic sentence can list the things that the paragraph will cover.

Topic	Main Idea (or Focus)
The fitness test	includes running, jumping, and throwing.

Practice

Choose the best main idea (or focus) for the topic below.

Topic	Main Idea (or Focus)
Our school	1. has hundreds of students.
	2. is brick.
	3. needs new playground equipment.

Writing Closing Sentences

The closing sentence in a paragraph should be just like a special treat—something the reader will like and remember. Here are three ways to write closing sentences.

1. **Remind the reader of your main idea.**

   Topic sentence:
   Living with my little brother Roy can be hard.

   Closing sentence:
   I'm trying to understand Roy, but it is not always easy.

2. **Give a final thought about the topic.**

   Topic sentence:
   The fitness test includes running, jumping, and throwing.

   Closing sentence:
   The fitness test is fun, and I don't even have to study for it.

3. **Convince the reader of your opinion.**

   Topic sentence:
   Our neighborhood needs new sidewalks.

   Closing sentence:
   Better sidewalks will make our neighborhood safer for everyone.

A good closing sentence wraps up the paragraph.

Using Details

The sentences in the **body**, or middle part, of a paragraph include details. **Details** are the specific words and ideas that tell about the topic. Details can include reasons and facts.

Reason: A reason *answers the question* why?

Topic sentence: Living with my little brother Roy can be hard. First of all, Roy

Reason: always copies me.

Fact: A fact *adds information.*

Topic sentence: Last summer, my baseball team won the championship game.

Fact: We beat the Cardinals 2 to 1.

Practice

Choose two facts that tell more about the topic sentence below.

Topic sentence: My cat Henry hides in different places.

Facts: Henry has black fur and long whiskers.
His main hiding place is under my bed.
Cats are nosy animals.
Henry also curls up in my sister's closet.

Other Details

Most paragraphs also include examples and explanations. They give the reader even more information about the topic.

Example: An example *shows something.*

Topic sentence: Living with my little brother Roy can be hard. First of all,

Reason: Roy always copies me. If I have

Example: a glass of milk, he does, too.

Explanation: An explanation *makes an idea clearer.*

Topic sentence: Last summer, my baseball team won the championship game.

Fact: We beat the Cardinals 2 to 1.

Explanation: We scored both of our runs in the last inning.

Organizing Paragraphs

The sentences in a paragraph must be organized so the reader can follow your ideas. Here are three ways to organize your paragraphs.

Time Order . . .

When you use time order, you give the details in the order in which they happened. You can use words like *first, next,* and *then* to help organize your ideas.

My grandpa takes very good care of his garden. First, he walks up and down the rows pulling weeds. Next, he gathers any vegetables that are ready to eat. He always seems to find something that needs to be picked. Then, he plants new seeds in the open spaces. Finally, he waters everything.

Order of Location . . .

With order of location, you describe a topic from one point to another, like top to bottom. Use words and phrases like *on top, down the sides,* and *at the bottom* to help you organize your ideas in this way.

McKinley Hill towers over our neighborhood. There are oak trees on top of the hill. My friends and I sometimes climb the trees. Steep paths run down the sides of the hill. We ride down these paths on old pieces of cardboard. At the bottom of the hill, we have a homemade baseball diamond where we play baseball all summer.

Order of Importance . . .

With order of importance, you give the most important detail first or last. You can use words or phrases like *first of all, also,* and *most importantly* to help you organize your ideas in this way.

Living with my little brother Roy can be hard. First of all, Roy always copies me. If I have a glass of milk, he does, too. He also wants to stay up as long as I do. He always says to Mom, "But Marcus gets to stay up later." Most importantly, he always wants to play with my friends. He tries to play basketball with us, but he is too small. I keep trying to understand Roy, but it is not always easy.

Practice

Which type of organization would you use to write about each of these topics? (There may be more than one answer.)

- describing a pet
- baking cookies
- making a snowman
- telling why recess should be longer

Writing Guidelines

The guidelines on these two pages will help you write strong paragraphs.

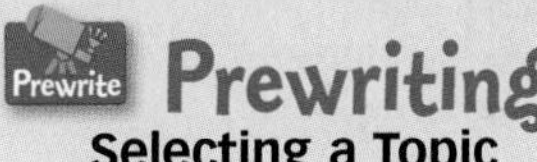

Prewriting

Selecting a Topic

- **Choose a topic that interests you.**
- **Make sure that the topic is the right size.**
  Too big: *Our team's whole baseball season*
  Too little: *One time at bat*
  Just right: *Our championship game*

Collecting Details

- **Gather plenty of details.**
  For **narrative** or story paragraphs, answer the questions *who? what? where?* and *when?*

  For **descriptive** paragraphs, collect *sights, sounds, smells,* and *tastes.*

  For **expository** (factual) paragraphs, gather important *facts* and *examples.*

  For **persuasive** paragraphs, list *reasons* that explain your opinion.
- **Use graphic organizers.**
  Choose a cluster, time line, sensory chart, 5 W's chart, or story map to help you organize your details. (See pages 438–444 for sample organizers.)

Writing

Creating Your First Draft

- Write a topic sentence that tells the main idea (or focus) of your paragraph.
- Explain the topic in the body or middle sentences.
- End with a sentence that wraps up the paragraph.

Revising

Improving Your Paragraph

- Have I included a topic sentence, the body, and a closing sentence in my paragraph?
- Did I include enough details about my topic?
- Did I put my sentences in the best order?
- Have I used the best words to explain my topic?

Editing

Checking for Conventions

- Did I start each sentence with a capital letter?
- Did I end each sentence with a punctuation mark?
- Did I indent the first line of my paragraph?
- Did I spell words correctly?

Practice

1. Write a paragraph about your favorite hobby.
2. Include two reasons that explain why this is your hobby.

Marking Paragraphs

If you're really excited about a story idea, you may keep writing and writing to get all your thoughts on paper. In the end, you may have a long piece of writing that must be divided into paragraphs. If that happens, try the following idea.

Mark-Ask-Read-Find

You can find the paragraphs in your stories and essays by following these steps.

1. **Mark the first sentence with a paragraph sign.** ¶
2. **Ask yourself what the main idea of the writing is.**
3. **Read until you find a new main idea.**

1. **Mark that sentence with a paragraph sign.** ¶
2. **Ask yourself what the main idea of this part is.**
3. **Read until you find another new main idea.**

Response to a Book (No Paragraphs)

Grow It Again

Grow It Again by Elizabeth Macleod tells how to grow plants from fruits and vegetables. This book tells how to grow plants from beans, potatoes, and peanuts. I guess I never thought about all the plants that produce the foods I eat. I didn't know potatoes and peanuts grow underground. This book also tells how fruits and vegetables are good for you, and beautiful, too. There are lots of food surprises in Grow It Again.

Following the Steps

Notice how the model book response can be divided into paragraphs using the **Mark-Ask-Read-Find** steps.

1. **Mark the first sentence with a paragraph sign.**
   ¶ Grow It Again by Elizabeth Macleod tells how to grow plants from fruits and vegetables.
2. **Ask yourself what the main idea of the writing is.**
   The main idea is what the book is about.
3. **Read until you find a new idea.**

1. **Mark that sentence with a paragraph sign.**
   ¶ I guess I never thought about all the plants that produce the foods I eat. I didn't know potatoes and peanuts grow underground.
2. **Ask yourself what the main idea of this part is.**
   The main idea is what the writer thinks.
3. **Read until you find a new idea.**

1. **Mark with a paragraph sign.**
   ¶ This book also tells how fruits and vegetables are good for you, and beautiful, too. There are lots of food surprises in Grow It Again.
2. **Ask what the main idea is.**
   It tells what else the book is about.

Grow It Again

Grow It Again by Elizabeth Macleod tells how to grow plants from fruits and vegetables. This book tells how to grow plants from beans, potatoes, and peanuts.

I guess I never thought about all the plants that produce the foods I eat. I didn't know potatoes and peanuts grow underground.

This book also tells how fruits and vegetables are good for you, and beautiful, too. There are lots of food surprises in Grow It Again.

Preparing for Tests

On a test, you may be asked to write a paragraph that summarizes a reading selection. A **summary** includes only the most important ideas found in the reading.

Writing Tips

Before you write . . .

- Read the selection at least twice.
- Use a graphic organizer to plan your paragraph and make notes.

During your writing . . .

- Start with a topic sentence that names the main idea of the reading.
- Write about the information in your own words.

After you've written . . .

- Make sure that your ideas are clear.

Reading Selection

Little Horses Take the Lead

Miniature horses make fine guide animals for the blind. They are the size of large guide dogs. These horses are usually only 20 to 34 inches at the tallest part of their back.

Miniature horses can be trained to stay calm. They are hard workers that are not bothered by noises.

Horses have their eyes on the sides of their heads. This allows them to see in almost all directions. Horses can also see very well at night.

Horses are good guides because they seem to know when danger is near. They naturally look for a safe way to get somewhere else.

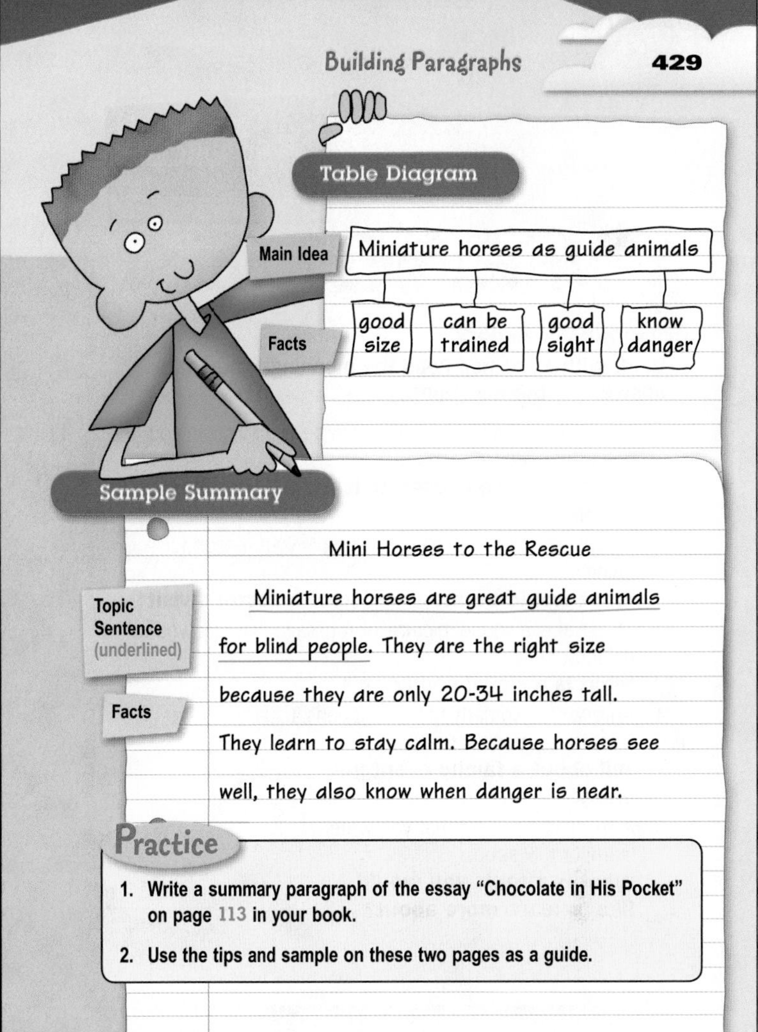

Table Diagram

Sample Summary

Mini Horses to the Rescue

Topic Sentence (underlined)

Miniature horses are great guide animals for blind people. They are the right size because they are only 20-34 inches tall. They learn to stay calm. Because horses see well, they also know when danger is near.

Facts

Practice

1. Write a summary paragraph of the essay "Chocolate in His Pocket" on page 113 in your book.
2. Use the tips and sample on these two pages as a guide.

A Writer's Resource

Academic Vocabulary

Work with a partner. Read the meanings and share answers to the questions.

1. A **resource** is something that can be used to help you find information.
   What resource is used to learn the meanings of words?
2. Your **purpose** for doing something is your reason for doing it.
   What would be the purpose of a doctor's visit?
3. A **signal** is a sound, picture, or message that tells you to do something.
   What is a signal you know?
4. An **event** is something that happens, usually something important.
   Tell about a family event you enjoy.
5. A **topic** is a subject that you write, learn, or talk about.
   What is a topic you would like to learn more about?

Writing is fun, but sometimes it's hard to get started. Finding a topic to write about is the first step. The best topics are often things that you already know about.

This chapter will help you get started. You will also find ways to put your ideas in order and get them on paper. Remember that good writing is like walking—you take one step at a time.

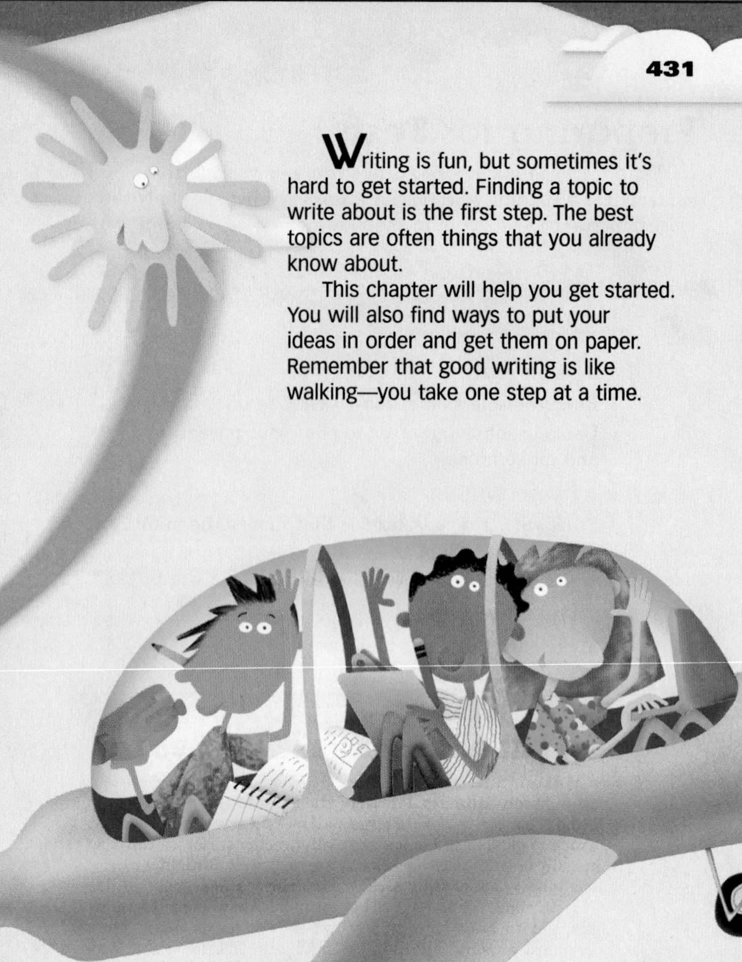

How can I find a good topic to write about?

Keep a writer's notebook.

Keep a list of writing ideas in a notebook. Then use them for your writing assignments. Here are some ways to collect ideas.

Tip: When you see or hear a good idea for a topic, write it down!

1 Keep your eyes open.

Sometimes a topic will find you! You might see a cat sitting on a fence. What is it looking for? Does it belong to someone? What is its name? Write ideas in your notebook about things that you see.

2 Make a list of your bests, worsts, and favorites.

Here are a few ideas to get you started. Look over your list when you need a writing idea.

Bests	Worsts	Favorites
My best day	My worst subject	My favorite book
My best subject	My dumbest moment	My favorite animal
What I'm best at	My worst accident	My favorite place
My best sport	My worst mistake	My favorite person
My best friend	My least favorite chore	My favorite food
		My favorite music

3 Read a lot.

Read books and magazines. Read about things you've never read about before—space travel, raising rabbits, the Civil War. Write ideas in your notebook as you read.

4 Try different things.

Try new games. Join new clubs. Help people in your neighborhood. The more you do, the more you'll have to write about.

5 Write often.

In a journal, or in your writer's notebook, write about things you see, hear, and do.

6 Finish sentence starters.

Finish some of these sentence starters in as many ways as you can.

I wonder how . . .
I just learned . . .
Everyone should . . .
Here's how to . . .
I'm afraid of . . .
I hope our school . . .
One place I like . . .
I remember . . .
When I grow up . . .
I wish I . . .

Where can I find more writing ideas?

Look at a list of topics.

You can look at a basics-of-life list to think about topic ideas.

animals	art	books	community
environment	exercise	family	food
friends	health	hobbies	jobs
music	school	sports	weather

Here's how to use the "Basics-of-Life" list:

1. Choose one of the topics.
2. Connect it to your writing assignment.
3. Make a list of possible subjects.

My topic is hobbies.

My assignment:
Write an expository essay explaining one of your hobbies.

I could write about . . .
- collecting old postcards.
- making my poetry notebook.
- learning how to ride a unicycle.

Consider topics for each form of writing.

Descriptive Writing

People: someone in your family, a friend, your bus driver, your family doctor/veterinarian, a teacher, a babysitter, a coach

Places: the dentist's office, a campground, a noisy place, a forest, a neighborhood store, your classroom

Things: a leaf falling from a tree, rain on the roof, a very old object, a special gift

Narrative Writing

Tell about . . . your first ride on a roller coaster, being surprised, learning to do something, playing with a friend, helping someone

Expository Writing

Explain how to . . . care for a pet, make a snow fort, pitch a tent, play a favorite board game, make pancakes

Explain different kinds of . . . trucks, horses, airplanes, rocks, storms, dances, skateboards, trees

Explain the meaning of . . . family, teamwork, bravery, love, fear, friendship

Explain why . . . you like or don't like where you live, you like a certain school subject, you need to be organized

Persuasive Writing

Convince your reader about the importance of . . . getting enough sleep, playing an instrument, having recess, having a classroom pet, having quiet times

How can I start learning about a topic?

Start thinking.

To begin with, you should start thinking about your topic. Here are ways to do this.

Listing Write your topic on the top of a piece of paper. Then start listing ideas about it.

The Big Blizzard
-two feet of snow
-howling wind
-huge drifts
-buried cars
-closed roads

Cluster (Web) Write your topic in the middle of a piece of paper and circle it. Then write related ideas around it. Write as many ideas as you can!

Describing Wheel Write your topic in the middle. Write words that describe the topic on the wheel's spokes.

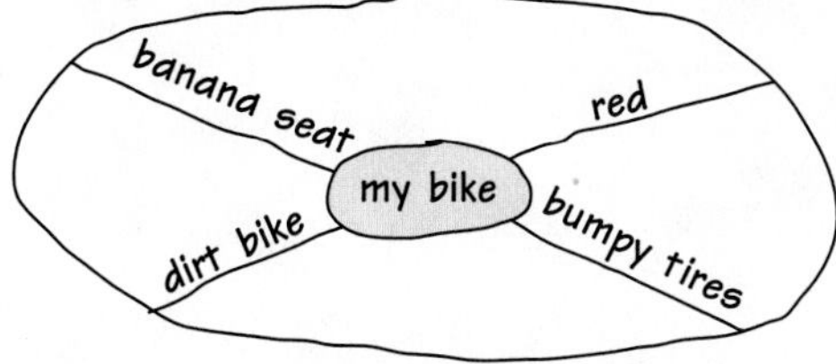

How can I write good topic sentences?

Check your purpose first.

Your topic sentence should fit the purpose of the paragraph: *to share a story, to describe, to explain,* or *to persuade.*

Remember: A topic sentence does two things: (1) it names the topic and (2) it tells what you plan to say about the topic (the *focus*).

To Describe

Descriptive paragraphs describe a topic. Here is a topic sentence for a descriptive paragraph.

Our dog **(topic)** looks like an old dust mop **(focus)**.

To Share a Story

Narrative paragraphs share a story. Here is a topic sentence for a narrative paragraph.

I swam in deep water **(topic)**
for the first time **(focus)**!

To Explain

Expository paragraphs explain or tell about a topic. Here is a topic sentence for an expository paragraph.

You can make a snowman **(topic)** in four steps **(focus)**.

To Persuade

Persuasive paragraphs give an opinion. Here is a topic sentence for a persuasive paragraph.

Afternoon recess **(topic)** should be longer **(focus)**.

Which graphic organizers should I use?

Try a Venn diagram to compare subjects.

Use a **Venn diagram** to show how two subjects are alike and how they are different. Begin by drawing two interlocking circles like the example below.

In area 1, list details about one of your subjects.

In area 2, list details about the other subject.

In area 3, list details that are true for both subjects.

Sample Venn Diagram

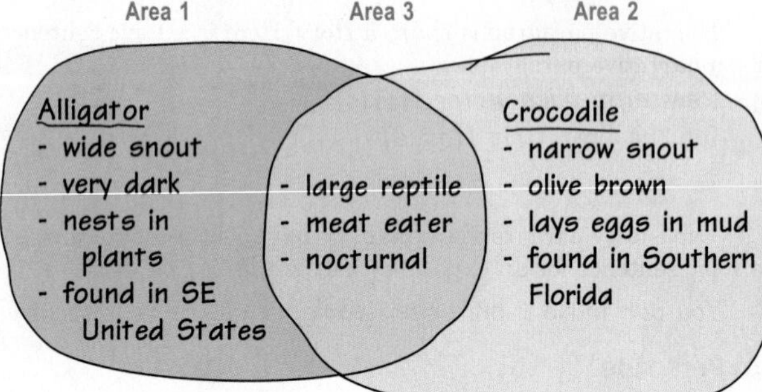

Make a time line to put events in order.

Use a **time line** to put events or actions in the order they happen in a story. You can also use a time line to list the steps in a process.

Sample Time Line

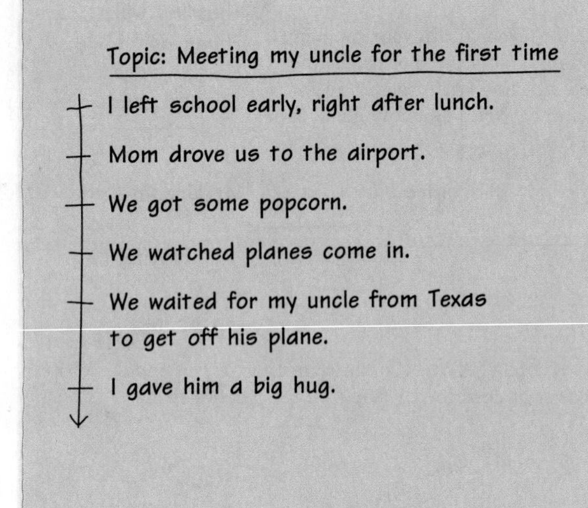

Topic: Meeting my uncle for the first time
I left school early, right after lunch.
Mom drove us to the airport.
We got some popcorn.
We watched planes come in.
We waited for my uncle from Texas to get off his plane.
I gave him a big hug.

Use a story map to make a plan.

Use a **story map** to plan your next story. Just fill in the main ideas and events. (You do not have to tell everything.)

Sample Story Map

Title:	A Very Far Hit
Main character:	Billie, a baseball player
Other characters:	Billie's coach his grandmother
Setting:	A baseball diamond
Conflict (Problem):	Billie was afraid he would strike out.
Plot (What happens?):	1. His team comes up to bat, and Billie is getting nervous.
	2. He remembers his coach's advice.
	3. Billie smashes a hit.
Ending:	Billie tells his grandmother about his hit.

Draw a life map to remember events.

You can use a **life map** to help you remember and choose an experience you want to write about. Start with the day you were born and map out events up to the present time.

Sample Life Map

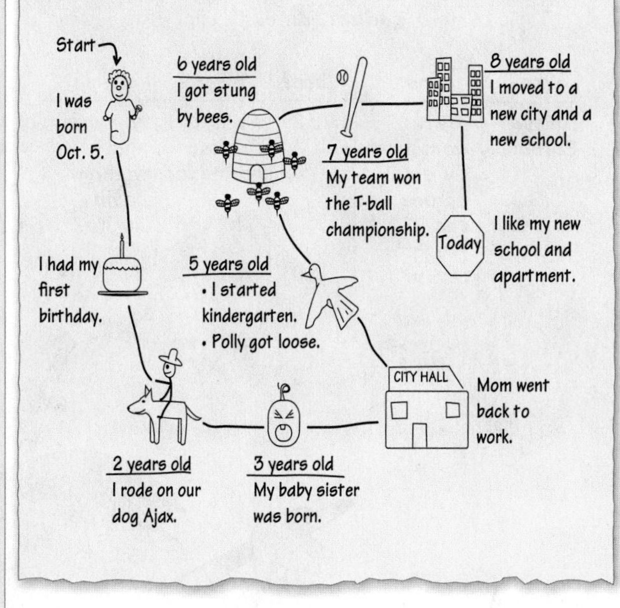

Make a 5 W's chart to list ideas.

Use a **5 W's chart** to list the important information that you need for an essay or a report. Try to answer each of the 5 W's.

Sample 5 W's Chart

Topic: Amelia Earhart, an early pilot

Who?	What?	When?	Where?	Why?
Amelia Earhart	first woman to fly solo across the Atlantic Ocean	1932	from Canada to Ireland	to prove that a woman could do it

Make a sensory chart to find details.

Use a **sensory chart** to organize details for a description. List details for each of the five senses.

Sample Sensory Chart

Topic: My picnic party

Sight	Sound	Smell	Taste	Touch
big slices of water-melon	people talking	popcorn	salty peanuts	new soft shirt
picnic tables piled with food	party noisemakers	hot dogs	crunchy pretzels	sticky table-tops
red and yellow balloons	kids laughing and shouting	smoke from the grill	sour pickles	warm hot-dog buns

Make an outline to organize details.

One way to organize the information for a report or a short talk is to make a topic outline.

Sample Topic Outline

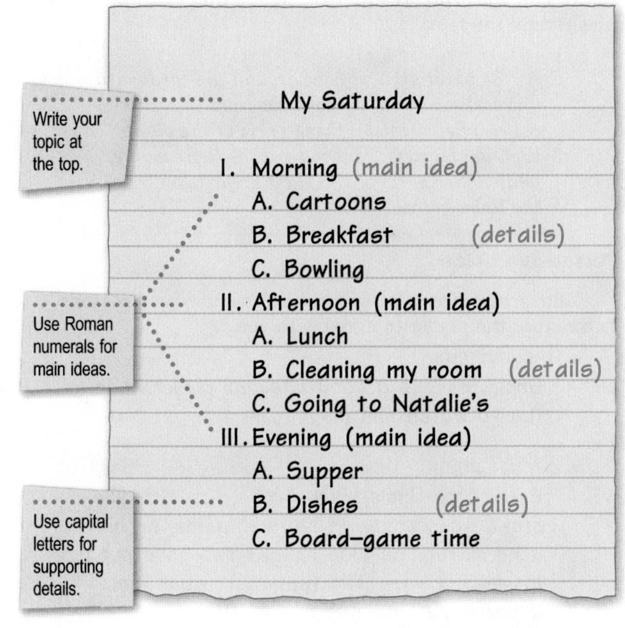

Write your topic at the top.
Use Roman numerals for main ideas.

My Saturday
I. Morning (main idea)

B. Breakfast (details)
C. Bowling
II. Afternoon (main idea)

B. Cleaning my room (details)
C. Going to Natalie's
III. Evening (main idea)

B. Dishes (details)
C. Board-game time

How do I organize a friendly letter?

Use the five parts of a friendly letter.

Friendly letters have five parts: the *heading*, the *salutation*, the *body*, the *closing*, and the *signature*.

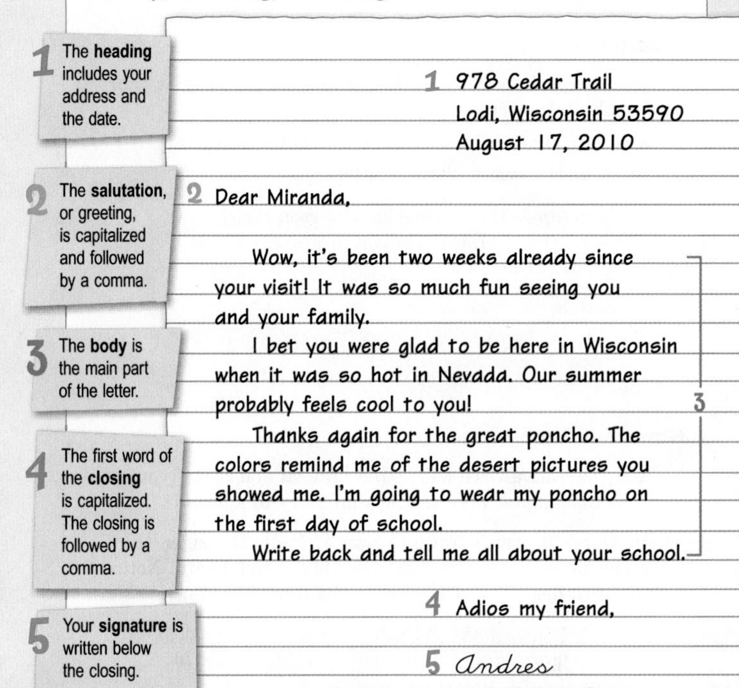

1 The **heading** includes your address and the date.
2 The **salutation**, or greeting, is capitalized and followed by a comma.
3 The **body** is the main part of the letter.
4 The first word of the **closing** is capitalized. The closing is followed by a comma.
5 Your **signature** is written below the closing.
1 978 Cedar Trail
Lodi, Wisconsin 53590
August 17, 2010
2 Dear Miranda,
Wow, it's been two weeks already since your visit! It was so much fun seeing you and your family.
I bet you were glad to be here in Wisconsin when it was so hot in Nevada. Our summer probably feels cool to you!
Thanks again for the great poncho. The colors remind me of the desert pictures you showed me. I'm going to wear my poncho on the first day of school.
Write back and tell me all about your school.
3
4 Adios my friend,
5 Andres

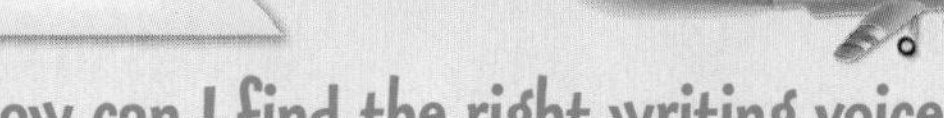

How can I find the right writing voice?

Make your voice fit your purpose.

Your writing voice will be right if you think about why you are writing and who will be reading it.

Descriptive Voice

One way to improve your descriptive voice is to show your reader what's happening.

- Telling: The writer simply tells about a character.

  Muriel always chewed gum.

- Showing: Author Katherine Paterson clearly describes a character's action in *The Great Gilly Hopkins.*

  Galadriel Hopkins shifted her bubble gum to the front of her mouth and began to blow gently.

Narrative Voice

Your narrative voice will sound natural and real if you write as though you were telling your story to a friend.

In *Amber Brown Is Not a Crayon* by Paula Danziger, the main character, Amber, thinks about her friend Justin. Notice how natural her words sound when she describes him.

> *Who else is going to make faces when some goofy grown-up says, "So your name is Justin, like in the song 'Justin-Time' "?*

Expository Voice

Your expository voice will work well when you use specific details to explain the topic, as in the following example. Notice how the sentences provide details that help the reader understand the topic.

> *As the plant grew, it bent around the cardboard maze like a snake to reach the light in a process called phototropism. Some parts of the plant, such as the stem, bent toward the light source, while other parts of the plant grew away from the light source.*

Persuasive Voice

Your persuasive voice will work if you use good reasons to convince the reader to agree with you.

- Unconvincing:

  Uncle Mark is a good baseball player. It is fun to watch him play.

- Convincing:

  Every time Uncle Mark gets up to bat, the crowd goes crazy. In his last game, he hit a home run. He also tagged two guys out at second base. His teammates call him a power player.

What forms of writing can I try?

Try these forms of writing.

You can learn a lot by writing in different forms. Here are some that you should try.

Personal Journal A personal journal is your own special place to write about anything and everything.

Lists Making lists can help you remember things, think in different ways, or just have fun. For example, you could make a list of winter words.

Family Stories These stories show how families can be brave, funny, or kind.

Alphabet Books An alphabet book puts funny or interesting information in alphabetical order.

Newspaper Stories A news story reports on an important event.

Photo Essays A photo essay tells a story using words and photographs.

Tall Tale A tall tale is a funny story about a character who can do impossible things.

Time-Travel Fantasy In this type of story, you write about any time and place that interests you.

Free-Verse Poems A free-verse poem can be short or long. It can rhyme, but it doesn't have to. You can choose!

How can I learn new words?

Keep a new-word notebook.

Make a special notebook for new words. Write the meaning and a sentence for each new word.

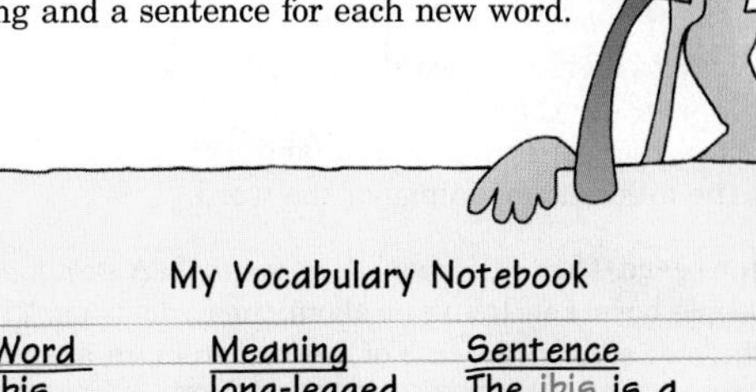

My Vocabulary Notebook

Word	Meaning	Sentence
ibis	long-legged wading bird	The ibis is a wading bird with a long, curved bill.
microscope	an instrument used to see very small objects	Carla's mom uses a microscope to study water pollution.

Tip **Read, read, read!**
The best way to learn new words is to read a lot.

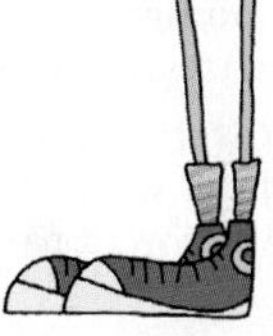

What other ways can I learn new words?

Use the dictionary.

The dictionary can teach you many facts about words. (See pages 302–303.) Each entry shows . . .

- how to divide the word into syllables,
- how to say the word,
- how the word can be used, and
- the different meanings of the word.

> **gen•e•ra•tion** *(jen´ə ra´ shən) noun* **1.** A group of people born and living at about the same time. **2.** A stage or step in the line of descent from an ancestor.

Use the context of a word.

When you are reading and you come to an unfamiliar word, look at the context (the words around it) to help you figure out what the word means. (See the next page for more ways to use context.)

Use a thesaurus.

A thesaurus can help you find just the right words to use in your writing. You can learn synonyms for the word you are trying to replace. (See page 452 for more.)

Think about word parts.

You can figure out the meanings of new words by learning about prefixes, suffixes, and roots. (See pages 453–457.)

Root words: The main part of the word, or base word
Prefix: A word part that comes before the root word
Suffix: A word part that comes after the root or base word

Use the context of a word.

"Context" means the words around a word. Looking at the context can help you figure out its meaning. Try the hints below to help you. The key words and phrases are underlined.

- Read the sentence that includes the word. Also read the sentence before and after it for clues to its meaning.

> From the edge of the <u>prairie</u>, we watched the **kestrel** <u>dive from the air into the grass and swoop up with a mouse</u>.

(A *kestrel* is a small falcon or hawk.)

- Search for synonyms (words with the same meaning).

> The **aroma** of the odd-looking plant reminded me of the unmistakable <u>scent</u> of a skunk.

(*Aroma* means the same thing as *scent*.)

- Search for antonyms (words with the opposite meaning).

> The weatherman said the sky would be **overcast**, <u>but it was completely clear</u>.

(*Overcast* means "cloudy." The word *but* is a clue that "clear" means the opposite of *overcast*.)

- Look for a definition of the word.

> I dug through the pile of rocks looking for a **geode**, <u>a rock with crystals in its center</u>.

(A *geode* is a hollow rock that has crystals inside.)

Use a thesaurus.

Use a **thesaurus** to find the right word for your sentence. A thesaurus is a book of synonyms, or words that mean almost the same thing. For example, if you look up *walk* in a thesaurus, you may find *stroll, hike,* and *step.*

Look for the Right Word

Let's say you use a thesaurus to find just the right word for *hop* in the following sentence.

Cassie and her friends ________ over the pile of snow.

Look up the word *hop* in the thesaurus.

Entry word → **hop** *verb* **bounce, bound, jump, leap, skip, spring** The boys *hop* over the sleeping dog.

Part of speech: *verb*
Synonyms: **bounce, bound, jump, leap, skip, spring**
Example sentence: The boys *hop* over the sleeping dog.

Choose the Right Word

Review the list of synonyms. Choose the word that works best for your sentence. In the example, the best word seems to be *leap.*

Cassie and her friends <u>leap</u> over the pile of snow.

How can I figure out what a new word means?

Divide the word into parts.

You can figure out the meaning of new words by learning about the three basic word parts: prefixes, roots, and suffixes.

unicyclist
1. Prefix: **uni** means *one*
2. Root: **cycl** means *wheel*
3. Suffix: **ist** means *someone who does something*

A *unicyclist* is someone who rides a one-wheeled cycle.

Learn prefixes.

Prefixes are word parts that come at the beginning of a word, *before* the root. They often change the meaning of the root. Here are some common prefixes.

anti- *[against]*
antibody (part of the blood that works against germs)

bi- *[two]*
bicycle (two-wheeled cycle)

dis- *[apart]*
disagree (apart from agreeing)

ex- *[out]*
external (outside)

mis- *[wrong]*
misbehave (behave wrongly)

non- *[no, not]*

nonfiction (not fiction; factual)

pre- *[before]*

preview (view before)

re- *[again]*

retry (try again)

sub- *[under]*

submarine (underwater ship)

un- *[not]*

unhealthy (not healthy)

Study suffixes.

Suffixes are word parts that come at the end of a word, *after* the root. They often change the meaning of the root. Here are some common suffixes.

-able *[can do]*

changeable (can change)

-ed *[past tense]*

learned (to learn something in the past)

-er, -or *[a person who]*

baker (a person who bakes)

-est *[most]*

funniest (most funny)

-ful *[full]*

helpful (full of help)

-ing *[doing something]*

talking (doing what it is to talk)

-ist *[a person who]*

pianist (a person who plays the piano)

-less *[without]*

careless (without care)

-ly *[in some manner]*

completely (in a complete manner)

-logy *[study of]*

biology (study of living things)

-ment *[act of]*

movement (the act of moving)

-ness *[state of]*

carelessness (state of being careless)

-s, -es *[plural, more than one]*

trees (more than one tree)

-sion, -tion *[state of]*

expansion (state of expanding)
addition (state of adding)

-y *[having]*

rosy (having a rose color)

Remember root words.

The **root** is the main part of a word. It helps you understand the word's meaning. Here are some common roots.

aud *[hear]*

auditorium (a place to hear something)

bio *[life]*

biography (writing about a person's life)

chron *[time]*

chronological (the time order in which things happened)

cycl, cyclo *[wheel, circular]*

bicycle (a vehicle with two wheels)
cyclone (a circular wind)

dent, dont *[tooth]*

dentist (a person who treats teeth)
orthodontist (a person who straightens teeth)

derm *[skin]*

dermatology (the study of skin)

flex *[bend]*

flexible (able to bend)

geo *[earth]*

geology (the science that describes the earth)

hab, habit *[live]*

inhabit (to live in)

meter *[measure]*

thermometer (an instrument that measures heat)

phon *[sound]*

telephone (far sound)

photo *[light]*

photograph (a picture formed by light)

port *[carry]*

portable (able to be carried)

scope *[see]*

otoscope (an instrument used for seeing inside the ear)

tele *[far]*

telescope (an instrument for seeing things that are far away)

vid, vis *[see]*

video (part of an electronic program that can be seen)
supervise (to oversee or look over)

How can I make my sentences easy to follow?

Use transitions.

Transitions are words that help the reader to follow your ideas. Each transition is a signal that a new, important idea is coming. In the following paragraph, four transitions are used.

A butterfly leads an incredible life. ***First,*** it starts out as an egg. The eggs are very tiny and round. ***Second,*** a larva hatches from the egg. Butterfly larvae are usually called caterpillars. ***Third,*** when a caterpillar finishes growing, it becomes a pupa. The pupa often forms inside a cocoon. ***Finally,*** when the pupa finishes changing, an adult butterfly comes out.

Some transitions help you show time.

Use these transitions to explain the steps in a process. (See the paragraph above.)

first	**second**	**third**	**next**	**last**
then	**now**	**soon**	**later**	**finally**
today	**yesterday**	**tomorrow**	**before**	**after**

These **groups** of transitions work well when showing time.

first	yesterday	now	before	first
second	today	soon	during	next
third	tomorrow	later	after	finally

Some transitions help you show location.

Use these transitions to describe a person, place, or thing.

above	**behind**	**below**	**beneath**	**beside**
between	**down**	**in back of**	**in front of**	**inside**
outside	**near**	**off**	**on top of**	**over**
under	**to the right**	**to the left**	**nearby**	
in the distance				

These **groups** of transitions work well in descriptions.

in front of	on top of	above	over
beside	next to	below	under
in the distance	in back of	beneath	nearby

Some transitions help you show more information.

Use these transitions to write about a topic in an essay or a report.

again	**another**	**in addition**	**also**	**next**
as well	**besides**	**along with**	**other**	**finally**
for example				

These **groups** of transitions work well when adding information.

for example	next	another	in addition
along with	finally	also	as well

How can I make my writing look better?

Add graphs to your writing.

Are you ever confused when you read about numbers? Graphs can show how numbers are related to each other. Put graphs in your writing to help your reader understand the information. A sample bar graph is shown below.

Bar Graph

A **bar graph** uses bars to compare two or more things. The bar graph below compares the number of different-colored jackets in one classroom.

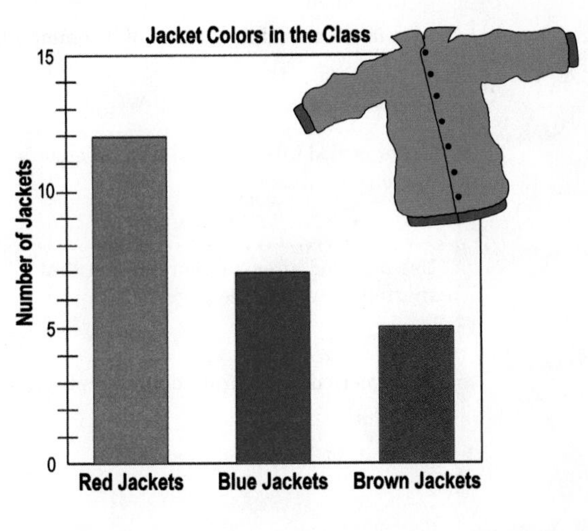

Editing and Proofreading Marks

You can use the marks below to show where and how your writing needs to be changed. Your teachers may also use these marks to point out errors in your writing.

Mark	Meaning	Example	Corrected Example
≡	Capitalize a letter.	Sable is a book by Karen hesse.	*Sable* is a book by Karen Hesse.
/	Make a capital letter lowercase.	Tate Marshall loves Dogs.	Tate Marshall loves dogs.
⊙	Add a period.	Mam doesn't want to keep Sable⊙	Mam doesn't want to keep Sable.
⌒	Take something out.	Doc Winston he will take Sable.	Doc Winston will take Sable.
∧	Insert a word or letter.	Tate was ∧very sad.	Tate was very sad.
∨ ∨ ∨	Insert an apostrophe or a quotation mark.	Sables stealing caused trouble.	Sable's stealing caused trouble.
? ! ∧ ∧ ∧	Insert punctuation.	Tate built a good∧ strong fence.	Tate built a good, strong fence.
⬭ sp.	Correct the spelling error.	Pap was (prowd) sp. of Tate.	Pap was proud of Tate.
¶	Start a new paragraph.	Tate liked to help Pap. ¶One summer day, Tate had a surprise . . .	Tate liked to help Pap. One summer day, Tate had a surprise . . .

Proofreader's Guide

What's Ahead

Academic Vocabulary

Work with a partner. Read the meanings and share answers to the questions.

1. When you **express** an idea or feeling, you show what you think or feel.
   How would you express happiness? Surprise?
2. **Language** is the way that people communicate, or talk, with each other.
   What are some languages that you know?
3. A **proofreader** is a person who edits writing for mechanics, spelling, and grammar.
   When have you been a proofreader?
4. A **guide** gives information.
   How might a guide to your town be helpful?

Marking Punctuation

Periods

A **period** is used at the end of a sentence. A period has other important uses, too.

You've been using periods for years. 

At the End of a Sentence	Use a period at the end of a sentence that makes a statement. *Claudia rides her bike to school.* (statement) Also use a period at the end of a command. *Make sure you lock your bike.* (command)
After an Initial	Use a period after an initial in a person's name. *A. A. Milne Mary E. Lyons*
After an Abbreviation	Use a period after an abbreviation that shortens a word. (See page 496.) *Ms. Mrs. Mr. Dr. W. First St.*
To Separate Dollars and Cents	Use a period to separate dollars and cents. *It costs $2.50 to get into the fair.* *I have $6.31 in my piggy bank.*

Related Skills Activities

- **Basic Grammar and Writing**
  Writing Complete Sentences, p. 397
  Capitalization and Punctuation, p. 402
  Using Different Kinds of Sentences, p. 411
- ***GrammarSnap***
  End Punctuation
  Kinds of Sentences
- ***SkillsBook***
  Periods 1 and 2, pp. 3–6
  End Punctuation, pp. 7–8
  Using Abbreviations, p. 56
- ***Daily Language Workouts***
  Period After an Initial and After an Abbreviation, pp. 6–7
  Good Books, p. 78

Question Marks

A **question mark** is used at the end of a direct question.

At the End of a Question

Who put the hot sauce on my taco?
Will I ever be able to taste again?
Where's the mild sauce?

Exclamation Points

An **exclamation point** is used to express strong feeling. It may be placed after a word, a phrase, or a sentence.

To Express Strong Feeling

Awesome!
(word)

Happy birthday!
(phrase)

There's an alligator!
(sentence)

Don't use too many exclamation points in your writing. They lose their value when they are used again and again.

End Punctuation

Write a period, a question mark, or an exclamation point to end each sentence.

Example: Do you like fruit ?

1. Fruit is a healthful food choice
2. Strawberries contain vitamin C
3. Do nectarines or peaches have a fuzzy skin
4. Brazil grows the most oranges in the world
5. Over 200 different kinds of raspberries are grown
6. Wow, settlers once used watermelons as canteens
7. Most cranberries are eaten during the Thanksgiving and Christmas holidays
8. Did you know there were so many interesting facts about fruit

Next Step: Write a question about a fruit. Then answer the question.

Related Skills Activities

- **Basic Grammar and Writing**
  Capitalization and Punctuation, p. 402
  Using Different Kinds of Sentences, p. 411
- ***GrammarSnap***
  End Punctuation
  Kinds of Sentences
- ***SkillsBook***
  End Punctuation, pp. 7–8
- ***Daily Language Workouts***
  End Punctuation, pp. 4–5
  Underground Steam Engine, p. 77

Answers

1. .
2. .
3. ?
4. .
5. .
6. !
7. .
8. ?

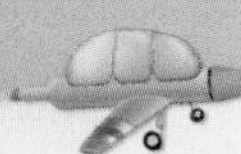

Commas

Commas tell a reader where to rest, or pause, in a sentence. They make your writing easier to read.

Reed likes to read books, and his dog Chase likes to chase squirrels.

Between Items in a Series

Use a comma between words or phrases in a series. (A series is a list of three or more things.)

I like pizza, pickles, and pretzels. (words)

Shawn drinks orange juice every morning, milk after school, and water with dinner. (phrases)

In Letter Writing

Use a comma after the greeting in a friendly letter.

Dear Auntie Liz, (greeting)

Use a comma after the closing in all letters.

Yours truly, (closing)
Sally

To Keep Numbers Clear

Use a comma in numbers of four or more digits.

Our school collected 22,000 soda cans!
My brother's used car cost $1,500.

Commas 1

Commas in a Series

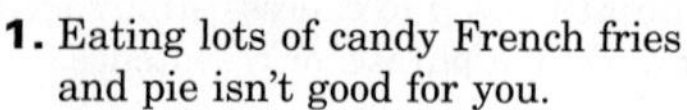

Rewrite each sentence below, placing commas where they belong.

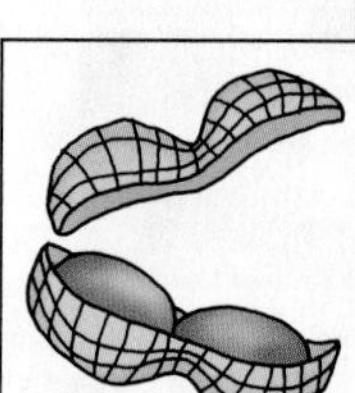

Example: I learn about food health and fitness at school.
I learn about food, health, and fitness at school.

1. Eating lots of candy French fries and pie isn't good for you.
2. Avoid eating too many sweets fats and oils.
3. At least three servings of low-fat milk yogurt and cheese should be eaten each day.
4. Meat eggs and nuts contain iron and many other nutrients.
5. Eat lots of vegetables and fruits (such as grapes apples and bananas).
6. About half of the bread cereal and pasta you eat should be made with whole grains.

Next Step: Write a sentence that lists a series of vegetables.

Related Skills Activities

- **Basic Grammar and Writing**
  Combine Sentences with Key Words or Words in a Series, p. 408
- ***GrammarSnap***
  Commas in a Series
  Commas in Numbers
  Creating a Series
- ***SkillsBook***
  Commas Between Items in a Series, pp. 9–10
  Commas in Letter Writing, p. 11
  Commas to Keep Numbers Clear, p. 12
- ***Daily Language Workouts***
  Comma Between Items in a Series, pp. 8–9
  Comma to Keep Numbers Clear, pp. 10–11
  The Great Outdoors, p. 79
  Thousands of Seats, p. 80

Answers

1. Eating lots of candy, French fries, and pie isn't good for you.
2. Avoid eating too many sweets, fats, and oils.
3. At least three servings of low-fat milk, yogurt, and cheese should be eaten each day.
4. Meat, eggs, and nuts contain iron and many other nutrients.
5. Eat lots of vegetables and fruits (such as grapes, apples, and bananas).
6. About half of the bread, cereal, and pasta you eat should be made with whole grains.

Commas . . .

Between a City and a State

Use a comma between a city and a state in a sentence or in an address at the top of a letter.

He moved to Sleepy Hollow**,** New York. (sentence)

In Addresses

110 Hill Street

Hannibal**,** MO 63401

(address)

Do not use a comma between a state and a ZIP code.

In Dates

Use a comma between the day and the year in a sentence or in the heading of a letter.

I saw Uncle Sam on July 4**,** 2010. (sentence)

July 4**,** 2010 (heading of a letter)

Do not use a comma between a month and a year.

July 2010

In Compound Sentences

Use a comma before the connecting word in a compound sentence. A compound sentence is made up of two simple sentences that are connected by *or, and, but, so, yet,* and *for*.

I usually feed Linus**,** but I don't clean his litter box!

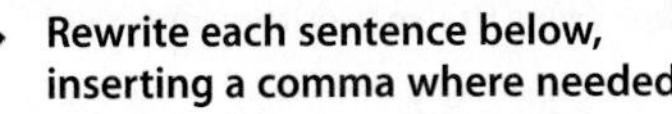

Commas 2

■ In Compound Sentences

Rewrite each sentence below, inserting a comma where needed.

Example: I had seen the car before but I had to look again.
I had seen the car before, but I had to look again.

1. Its headlights looked like eyes and the grille looked like a mouth.
2. This car was laughing at me or maybe it was just smiling.
3. I couldn't believe my eyes so I rubbed them to make sure they were okay.
4. I looked at the car again and it still had that goofy grin!
5. I must have been dreaming that day for I never saw the car "smiling" after that.

Next Step: Write a compound sentence about a time your eyes played tricks on you. Don't forget the comma!

Related Skills Activities

- **Basic Grammar and Writing**
  Use Compound Sentences, p. 410
- ***GrammarSnap***
  Compound Sentences
- ***SkillsBook***
  Commas in Dates and Addresses, pp. 13–14
  Commas in Compound Sentences, pp. 15–16
- ***Daily Language Workouts***
  Comma in Dates and Between a City and a State, pp. 12–13
  Comma in Compound Sentences, pp. 14–15
  Wish You Were Here, p. 81
  Hide-and-Seek Beans, p. 82

Answers

1. Its headlights looked like eyes, and the grille looked like a mouth.
2. This car was laughing at me, or maybe it was just smiling.
3. I couldn't believe my eyes, so I rubbed them to make sure they were okay.
4. I looked at the car again, and it still had that goofy grin!
5. I must have been dreaming that day, for I never saw the car "smiling" after that.

Commas . . .

To Set Off a Speaker's Words

Use a comma to set off the exact words of a speaker from the rest of the sentence.

Maddie said, "If I have four eggs and you have six eggs, what do we get when we put them together?"

"We get scrambled eggs," said her mother.

After an Introductory Word or Group of Words

A Word That Shows Surprise
Use a comma to set off an interjection. An interjection is a word that shows surprise.

Wow, you hit that ball a mile!

The Name of a Person Spoken To
Use a comma to set off the name of someone you are speaking to.

Mom, why didn't you come to the game?

A Group of Words
Use a comma to set off a group of words that comes before the main part of a sentence.

Because she had to work late, Mom missed the game.

Between Describing Words

Use a comma between two words that describe the same noun.

His pet is a hairy, black spider!

Commas 3

■ After Introductory Words

For each sentence below, write the word or group of words that should be followed by a comma. Also write the comma.

Example: Gee that frog looks big!
Gee,

1. Jamal did you see it?
2. Before we let it go let's weigh it.
3. Cristi see if you can grab it.
4. If I stand over here the frog can't escape.
5. Uh-oh it's getting away!
6. Hopping into the pond the frog made a big splash.
7. Aw maybe we will catch it another time.

Next Step: Write a sentence about an experience with a wild animal. Include an introductory group of words and use commas correctly.

Related Skills Activities

- ***SkillsBook***
  Commas to Set Off a Speaker's Words, pp. 17–18
  Commas After an Introductory Word, pp. 19–20
  Commas After a Group of Words, pp. 21–22
- ***Daily Language Workouts***
  Comma to Set Off A Speaker's Words, pp. 16–17
  Comma After an Introductory Word, pp. 18–19
  Comma Between Describing Words, pp. 20–21
  All Alike, p. 83
  Good Books, Good Friends, p. 84
  A Big, Beautiful Garden, 85

Answers

1. Jamal,
2. Before we let it go,
3. Cristi,
4. If I stand over here,
5. Uh-oh,
6. Hopping into the pond,
7. Aw,

Apostrophes

An **apostrophe** is used to make contractions or to show ownership. An apostrophe looks like a comma, but it is placed between letters like this:

It's lunchtime!

In Contractions

Use an apostrophe to form a contraction. The apostrophe takes the place of one or more letters.

"Not" Contractions

aren't (are not)	hasn't (has not)
can't (can not)	haven't (have not)
couldn't (could not)	isn't (is not)
didn't (did not)	wasn't (was not)
doesn't (does not)	weren't (were not)
don't (do not)	won't (will not)
hadn't (had not)	wouldn't (would not)

Other Common Contractions

I'm (I am)	I'll (I will)
you're (you are)	you'll (you will)
they're (they are)	I've (I have)
we're (we are)	they've (they have)
should've (should have)	I'd (I would)
it's (it is **or** it has)	you'd (you would)
that's (that is)	she's (she is)

Apostrophes 1

■ In Contractions

For each sentence below, write the contraction for the underlined words.

Example: I was not able to go to school yesterday.
wasn't

1. I had a fever, so my mom would not let me go.
2. I am feeling better today.
3. Some other kids also were not in school.
4. The teacher did not assign homework yesterday.
5. We will not have to do makeup work.
6. All the kids say they are happy about that.
7. It is hard to do lots of homework at once.
8. Sometimes I can not do it by myself.
9. Luckily, I have always gotten help from Dad.

Next Step: Write two sentences about homework. Use a contraction in each sentence.

Related Skills Activities

- ***GrammarSnap***
  Contractions
- ***SkillsBook***
  Apostrophes 1, pp. 23–24
- ***Daily Language Workouts***
  Apostrophe in Contractions, pp. 24–25
  Recess!, p. 87

Answers

1. wouldn't
2. I'm
3. weren't
4. didn't
5. won't
6. they're
7. It's
8. can't
9. I've

Apostrophes . . .

To Show Possession (Ownership)

Singular Possessive

An apostrophe plus an *s* is added to a singular noun to show ownership. (Singular means "one.")

We took my friend's dog for a walk.
(The friend owns the dog.)

The dog's fur is fluffy and white.

The dog wanted to chase the neighbor's cat.

Plural Possessive

An apostrophe is usually added after the *s* in a plural noun to show ownership. (Plural means "more than one.")

The students' paintings are posted on the bulletin board. (More than one student owns the artwork.)

Ms. Worth went to the teachers' workroom.
(More than one teacher uses the workroom.)

Some plurals, such as "children" or "men," do not end in *s*. For these plurals, an apostrophe plus an *s* must be added.

We looked at the women's quilts on display.
(The word for more than one woman is *women*. The women own the quilts.)

Apostrophes 2

■ Possessives

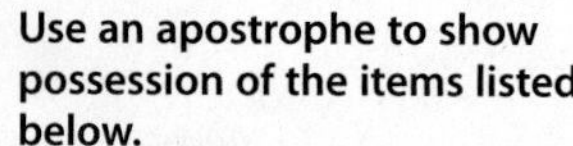

Use an apostrophe to show possession of the items listed below.

Example: soup that Aunt Ida makes
Aunt Ida's soup

1. a pencil that belongs to Mark
2. the funny ears on those dogs
3. the flowers that Ms. Gardner grows
4. the fruit salad that our neighbors brought
5. the ringtone on my phone
6. the glasses that Dr. Wiler wears
7. the new movie that Hilary Duff is in
8. homework that Tracy dropped
9. the color of the sky

Next Step: Write a sentence about something that belongs to a friend. Use an apostrophe to show ownership.

Related Skills Activities

- ***GrammarSnap***
  Apostrophes to Show Possession
- ***SkillsBook***
  Apostrophes 2 and 3, pp. 25–28
- ***Daily Language Workouts***
  Apostrophe to Form Possessives, pp. 26–29
  Nicole's Borrowing Day, p. 88
  Girls' Dress-Up Day, p. 89

Answers

1. Mark's pencil
2. those dogs' funny ears
3. Ms. Gardner's flowers
4. our neighbors' fruit salad
5. my phone's ringtone
6. Dr. Wiler's glasses
7. Hilary Duff's new movie
8. Tracy's homework
9. the sky's color

Quotation Marks

Quotation marks are used to punctuate titles and to set off a speaker's exact words. Remember that quotation marks always come in pairs. One set comes before the quoted words, and one set comes after them, like this:

Porky Pig says, "That's all, folks!"

To Set Off Spoken Words

Use quotation marks before and after the exact words of the speaker in a sentence.

"What's that?" I asked.

Dad said, "It's just a pile of rags."

"Dad," I asked, "do rags have a pink nose?"

Dad looked carefully into the chicken coop. "It's a possum!" he said, surprised.

In almost all cases, punctuation (periods, commas, question marks) is placed inside quotation marks.

To Punctuate Titles

Use quotation marks to punctuate titles of songs, poems, and short stories.

"This Land Is Your Land" is a great song.

Ms. Barr read a poem called "Whispers."

Lu read a story called "Swamp Monster."

Use underlining or italics for titles of books, magazines, and movies. (See page 478.)

Quotation Marks

■ In Dialogue

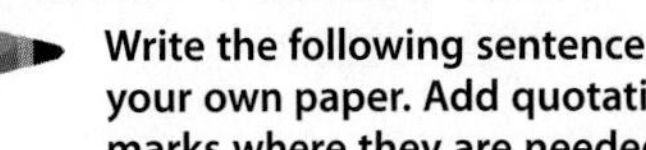

Write the following sentences on your own paper. Add quotation marks where they are needed.

Example: Mom said, Here's a surprise.
Mom said, "Here's a surprise."

1. What is it? I asked.
2. She said, We are going to get a dog!
3. Wow! I exclaimed.
4. Mom explained, We will choose a dog from the animal shelter.
5. You will need to help take care of it, she added.
6. I said, I'm so glad we are getting a dog. I will be happy to take care of it.
7. Great! Let's go, Mom said.

Next Step: Write a few lines of dialogue without quotation marks (like those above). Then exchange papers with a classmate and add quotation marks to each other's sentences.

Related Skills Activities

- ***SkillsBook***
  Quotation Marks 1 and 2, pp. 29–32
  Quotation Marks, Underlining, and Italics to Punctuate Titles, pp. 33–34
- ***Daily Language Workouts***
  Quotation Marks to Set Off Spoken Words, pp. 30–31
  Quotation Marks to Punctuate Titles, pp. 32–33
  What About Rocky?, p. 90

Answers

1. "What is it?" I asked.
2. She said, "We are going to get a dog!"
3. "Wow!" I exclaimed.
4. Mom explained, "We will choose a dog from the animal shelter."
5. "You will need to help take care of it," she added.
6. I said, "I'm so glad we are getting a dog. I will be happy to take care of it."
7. "Great! Let's go," Mom said.

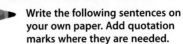

Underlining and Italics

Underlining is used to mark titles of books, plays, movies, television programs, and magazines. If you use a computer, you can put titles in *italics* instead of underlining them.

For Titles

Underlining: The Ghostmobile
or
Italics: ***The Ghostmobile*** (a book)

Fantasia or ***Fantasia*** (a movie)

Nature or ***Nature*** (a television program)

Cricket or ***Cricket*** (a magazine)

Tip: Use quotation marks (" ") for titles of poems, songs, and short stories. (See page 476.)

For Names of Aircraft and Ships

Use underlining (or italics) to mark the names of aircraft and ships.

Pinta, Santa Maria, Niña or ***Pinta, Santa Maria, Niña*** (Columbus' ships)

Discovery or ***Discovery*** (spacecraft)

Underlining and Italics

In Titles

For each sentence below, write the word or words that should be in italics. Underline them.

Example: In the movie Babe, all the animals could talk.
Babe

1. Grandma gave me The Boxcar Children, a book about orphans.
2. I get the magazine Highlights once a month.
3. Tay saw a TV show he liked called Reading Rainbow.
4. Tiff is reading the book Henry Huggins.
5. My dad likes to watch Nova, a TV science show.
6. The Iron Giant is a cartoon movie about a robot.
7. I like to read the jokes in old Reader's Digest magazines.

Next Step: Write a sentence about a book you have read recently. Underline its title.

Related Skills Activities

- ***SkillsBook***
  Quotation Marks, Underlining, and Italics to Punctuate Titles, pp. 33–34
- ***Daily Language Workouts***
  Ramona and Ralph, p. 91

Answers

1. The Boxcar Children
2. Highlights
3. Reading Rainbow
4. Henry Huggins
5. Nova
6. The Iron Giant
7. Reader's Digest

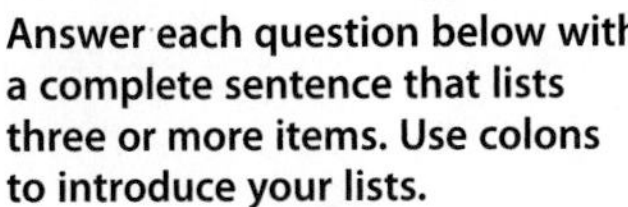

Colons

A **colon** is used in three special cases: to show time, to introduce a list, and after the greeting in a business letter. To make a colon, put one dot on top of another one (:).

Between Numbers in Time

Use a colon between the parts of a number showing time.

My school starts at 7:45 a.m.

I'll meet you on the playground at 3:30.

To Introduce a List

Use a colon to introduce a list.

I don't like to do these things: go shopping, do chores, or go to bed early.

Here are my favorite foods: pizza, spaghetti, and pancakes.

When introducing a list, the colon is used after words like *the following* or *these things*. Do not use a colon after a verb or preposition.

In a Business Letter

Use a colon after the greeting in a business letter.

Dear Ms. Yolen: Dear Editor:

Dear Mr. Wilson: Dear Office Manager:

Colons

To Introduce a List

Answer each question below with a complete sentence that lists three or more items. Use colons to introduce your lists.

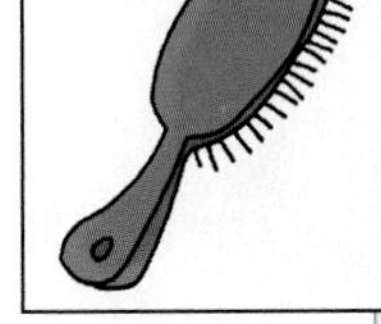

Example: What things do you use every morning?
I use these things every morning: a hairbrush, a toothbrush, and lip balm.

1. What are some funny names for dogs?
2. What three things do you like about yourself?
3. How do you spend your free time?
4. Which colors might you see in a rainbow?
5. Which chores might you be asked to do?
6. Which three foods do you like best?
7. What are the names of some of your friends?

Next Step: Write a question that could be answered with a list. Exchange papers with a classmate. Then answer each other's question in a complete sentence with a colon.

Related Skills Activities

- ***SkillsBook***
  Colons, pp. 35–36
- ***Daily Language Workouts***
  Colon, pp. 22–23
  Call It a Day, p. 86

Possible Answers

1. Here are some funny names for dogs: Skipper, Clyde, and Howler.
2. I like these three things about myself: my hair, my teeth, and my eyes.
3. Some ways I spend my free time include the following: reading, writing, and watching movies.
4. I might see these colors in a rainbow: red, yellow, and blue.
5. Mom listed the following chores for me: take out the garbage, feed the dog, and vacuum the rug.
6. These are three of the best foods in the world: spaghetti, pudding, and pizza.
7. Here are the names of some of my friends: Carla, Miguel, Tina, and Maria.

Hyphens

A **hyphen** is used to divide words. Hyphens can come in handy when you run out of room at the end of a line.

To Divide a Word

Hawks really like to eat mice, grass-
hoppers, and even snakes. A hawk can
see a mouse from a mile in the sky.

Divide words only between syllables. (The word *grass-hop-per* can be divided in two places.) If you are not sure where the word gets divided, check your dictionary.

Parentheses

Parentheses are used to add information. Parentheses always come in pairs.

To Add Information

The map (see figure 2) will help you understand the trail.

When you find important information, write down only the main ideas. (This is called note taking.)

Hyphens

Divide each of the following words into syllables using hyphens. (Check a dictionary if you're not sure how.)

Example: swimming
swim-ming

1. almost
2. question
3. something
4. people
5. before
6. pencil
7. circus
8. happen
9. subtract
10. prepare
11. breakfast
12. winter
13. insect
14. monster

Next Step: Write two sentences about the last time you went swimming. Use a hyphen to divide a word at the end of the line if you need to.

Related Skills Activities

- ***SkillsBook***
  Hyphens, p. 37
  Parentheses, p. 38

Answers

1. al-most
2. ques-tion
3. some-thing
4. peo-ple
5. be-fore
6. pen-cil
7. cir-cus
8. hap-pen
9. sub-tract
10. pre-pare
11. break-fast
12. win-ter
13. in-sect
14. mon-ster

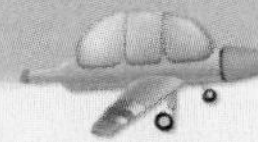

Practice Test

Which punctuation mark should replace the blank in each sentence? Write the letter of the correct answer.

1. Maggie, Darren__ and I love to read.
   - Ⓐ question mark (?)
   - Ⓑ comma (,)
   - Ⓒ apostrophe (')
   - Ⓓ period (.)

2. Do you have a library card__
   - Ⓐ period (.)
   - Ⓑ comma (,)
   - Ⓒ apostrophe (')
   - Ⓓ question mark (?)

3. Robert__s mom works in the school library.
   - Ⓐ apostrophe (')
   - Ⓑ comma (,)
   - Ⓒ period (.)
   - Ⓓ question mark (?)

4. I couldn__t find the book I wanted.
   - Ⓐ period (.)
   - Ⓑ comma (,)
   - Ⓒ apostrophe (')
   - Ⓓ question mark (?)

5. Mrs. Ramer helped me find it__
   - Ⓐ period (.)
   - Ⓑ question mark (?)
   - Ⓒ apostrophe (')
   - Ⓓ comma (,)

6. I read a whole chapter last night__ and I can read some more today.
   - Ⓐ period (.)
   - Ⓑ comma (,)
   - Ⓒ apostrophe (')
   - Ⓓ question mark (?)

7. Wow, you read fast__
   - Ⓐ period (.)
   - Ⓑ exclamation point (!)
   - Ⓒ question mark (?)
   - Ⓓ apostrophe (')

8. When I am done with the book__ I will return it to the library.
   - Ⓐ period (.)
   - Ⓑ apostrophe (')
   - Ⓒ question mark (?)
   - Ⓓ comma (,)

9. Then I__ll get a new book!
   - Ⓐ period (.)
   - Ⓑ apostrophe (')
   - Ⓒ question mark (?)
   - Ⓓ comma (,)

10. How many books can I check out__
    - Ⓐ period (.)
    - Ⓑ apostrophe (')
    - Ⓒ question mark (?)
    - Ⓓ comma (,)

11. We are allowed to get six books at a time__
    - Ⓐ period (.)
    - Ⓑ apostrophe (')
    - Ⓒ question mark (?)
    - Ⓓ comma (,)

12. Once I had to put two of my books in Anna__s backpack.
    - Ⓐ period (.)
    - Ⓑ apostrophe (')
    - Ⓒ question mark (?)
    - Ⓓ comma (,)

Answers

1. B
2. D
3. A
4. C
5. A
6. B

Answers

7. B
8. D
9. B
10. C
11. A
12. B

Related Skills Activities

- ***SkillsBook***
  Punctuation Review, pp. 39–40
- ***Daily Language Workouts***
  Mixed-Review Sentences, pp. 34–43

Editing for Mechanics

Capitalization

Proper Nouns and Proper Adjectives

Capitalize all proper nouns and proper adjectives. A proper noun names a specific person, place, or thing. Proper adjectives are formed from proper nouns.

Do you know who Rosa Parks is?
She worked for civil rights in Alabama.
(proper nouns)

Where's my Spanish book?
You left it on the Great Lakes ferry.
(proper adjectives)

Words Used as Names

Capitalize words such as *mother, father, mom, dad, aunt,* and *uncle* when these words are used as names.

If Dad goes, Uncle Terry will go, too.

No capital letter is needed if you use *our* mother, *my* dad, and so on.
My dad asked me to set the table.

Titles Used with Names

Capitalize official titles used with names.

President Abraham Lincoln

Mayor Barbara Long

Do not capitalize titles when they are used alone: the president, a mayor.

Capitalization 1

■ Proper Nouns and Adjectives

For each sentence, write the word or words that should be capitalized.

Example: A russian speed skater won the gold medal.
Russian

1. The first Olympic Games were held in athens, greece.
2. Devon understands the french language.
3. He has been to paris.
4. Rodrigo will live in kansas with aunt tanya this summer.
5. The author of the Sherlock Holmes stories is sir Arthur Conan Doyle.
6. A black iron fence surrounds the white house in Washington, D.C.
7. I like learning about president Thomas Jefferson.

Next Step: Write a sentence about a famous person. Remember to capitalize correctly.

Related Skills Activities

- **Basic Grammar and Writing**
  Using Nouns, p. 375
- ***GrammarSnap***
  Capitalization
- ***SkillsBook***
  Capitalizing Proper Nouns, pp. 41–42
  Capitalizing Official Titles, p. 43
- ***Daily Language Workouts***
  Planets, pp. 34–35
  U.S. History 1, pp. 40–41
  Science and Inventions 1, 2, and 3, pp. 64–69
  All About Ben, p. 107

Answers

1. Athens, Greece
2. French
3. Paris
4. Kansas, Aunt Tanya
5. Sir
6. White House
7. President

Capitalization . . .

Abbreviations	Capitalize abbreviations of titles and organizations. Mr. (Mister) Dr. (Doctor) NFL (National Football League)
Titles	Capitalize the first word of a title, the last word, and every important word in between. "There's a Hole in the Bucket" (song) ***Beauty and the Beast*** (movie)
First Words	Capitalize the first word of every sentence. The first day at school is exciting. Capitalize the first word of a direct quotation. Mr. Hon said, "Welcome to my class."
Days, Months, and Holidays	Capitalize the names of days of the week, months of the year, and special holidays. Friday April Memorial Day Thanksgiving Arbor Day
Official Titles	Capitalize the official title of a person when it is used before the name. Mayor Barton Mrs. Denny President Obama Doctor Pham

Capitalization 2

- First Words
- Days, Months, and Holidays

Number your paper from 1 to 10 (for each line in the following paragraph). Write the word or words from each line that should be capitalized. There are 12 mistakes in all.

Our
1 our family's birthdays are
2 at different times of the year. my
3 sister Margy's birthday was last tuesday, october
4 12. I have to wait until november 26, the day after
5 thanksgiving this year, for my birthday. Dad's
6 birthday, june 5, was on a saturday this year. he
7 liked that! Mom's day was february 16, which
8 was presidents' day. Margy gave her a quarter
9 with Washington's picture. a penny with Lincoln's
10 picture was my gift!

Next Step: Write a sentence that tells the day and date of your birthday this year.

Related Skills Activities

- **Basic Grammar and Writing**
  Capitalization and Punctuation, p. 402
- ***GrammarSnap***
  Capitalization
- ***SkillsBook***
  Capitalizing First Words, p. 44
  Capitalizing Official Titles, p. 43
  Capitalizing Titles, p. 45
- ***Daily Language Workouts***
  Using Reference Materials 2, pp. 46–47

Answers

1. Our
2. My
3. Tuesday, October
4. November
5. Thanksgiving
6. June, Saturday, He
7. February
8. Presidents' Day
9. A

Capitalize geographic names and places in your writing. Geographic names are the names of natural features, such as mountains or rivers. Geographic places, such as cities or countries, are man-made. Also, capitalize historical periods in your writing, such as the *Middle Ages* and *World War I.*

Capitalize Names of Places

Planets and heavenly bodies	Earth, Mars, Milky Way
Continents	Europe, Asia, Africa, North America, South America, Australia, Antarctica
Countries	Canada, Mexico, United States of America
States	Utah, Ohio, Washington, Maine, Indiana
Provinces	Nova Scotia, Quebec, Newfoundland
Cities and counties	Buffalo, New York City, Travis County
Bodies of water	Red Sea, Lake Michigan, Mississippi River, Atlantic Ocean
Landforms	Rocky Mountains, Mount Everest, Hawaiian Islands
Public areas	Liberty Island, Yellowstone National Park
Streets, roads, and highways	Main Street, Skyline Drive, Park Avenue, Interstate 95
Buildings	Willis Tower, Petronas Towers

Capitalize	Do Not Capitalize
January, October	spring, summer, winter, fall
Mother (as a name)	my **mother** (describing her)
President Washington	our first **president**
Mayor Hefty	Ms. Hefty, our **mayor**
Lake Erie	the **lake** area
the **South** (section of the country)	**south** (a direction)
planet **Earth**	the **earth** under our feet

Capitalization 3

- Geographic Names and Places
- Historical Periods

For each sentence, write the word or words that should be capitalized.

Example: Some people in parts of asia live in tents called *yurts.*
Asia

1. The planet most like earth is venus.
2. We saw the gateway arch in st. louis, missouri.
3. The nile river goes through egypt.
4. Most of the world's highest mountains are in the himalayas.
5. The deepest lake on the planet is lake baikal in russia.
6. The space age began in the 1950s.

Next Step: Write a sentence containing a surprising fact about a geographical place. Write another sentence naming a historical period.

Related Skills Activities

- **Basic Grammar and Writing**
  Using Nouns, p. 375
- ***GrammarSnap***
  Capitalization
- ***SkillsBook***
  Capitalizing Proper Nouns, pp. 41–42
  Capitalizing Historical Periods, p. 46
  Capitalizing Geographic Names and Places, pp. 47–48
- ***Daily Language Workouts***
  Using Maps 1 and 2, pp. 36–39

Answers

1. Earth, Venus
2. Gateway Arch, St. Louis, Missouri
3. Nile River, Egypt
4. Himalayas
5. Lake Baikal, Russia
6. Space Age

Plurals

Most Nouns	Plurals of most nouns are made by adding an *-s*. balloon ➔ balloons shoe ➔ shoes
Nouns Ending in *sh*, *ch*, *x*, *s*, and *z*	The plurals of nouns ending in *sh, ch, x, s,* and *z* are made by adding *-es* to the singular. wish ➔ wishes lunch ➔ lunches box ➔ boxes buzz ➔ buzzes dress ➔ dresses
Nouns Ending in *y*	Nouns that end in *y* with a consonant letter just before the *y* form their plurals by changing the *y* to *i* and adding *-es*. sky ➔ skies story ➔ stories puppy ➔ puppies city ➔ cities Nouns that end in *y* with a vowel before the *y* form their plurals by adding *-s*. monkey ➔ monkeys day ➔ days toy ➔ toys key ➔ keys
Irregular Nouns	Some nouns form a plural by taking on a different spelling. child ➔ children mouse ➔ mice goose ➔ geese

Plurals

■ **Nouns Ending in *sh*, *ch*, *x*, *s*, and *z***

Number your paper from 1 to 15. Write the plural of each noun below.

Example: inch
inches

1. tax
2. pass
3. dash
4. catch
5. six
6. bush
7. watch
8. fox
9. batch
10. kiss
11. lash
12. itch
13. guess
14. waltz
15. bus

Next Step: Write two sentences. Include the plural form of *match* in one and *dish* in the other.

Related Skills Activities

- **Basic Grammar and Writing**
  Singular and Plural Nouns, p. 376
- ***GrammarSnap***
  Plurals of Words Ending in *s*
- ***SkillsBook***
  Plurals 1 and 2, pp. 51–54

Answers

1. taxes
2. passes
3. dashes
4. catches
5. sixes
6. bushes
7. watches
8. foxes
9. batches
10. kisses
11. lashes
12. itches
13. guesses
14. waltzes
15. buses

Numbers

Writing Numbers

Numbers from one to nine are usually written as words; all numbers 10 and above are usually written as numerals.

one four 23 45 365 5,280

Except: Numbers being compared should be kept in the same style.

Students in the choir are between 6 and 10 years old.

Very Large Numbers

You may use a combination of numbers and words for very large numbers.

18 million 1.5 billion

Sentence Beginnings

Use words, not numerals, to begin a sentence.

Eleven students in the class had brown hair.

Numerals Only

Use numerals for any numbers in the following forms:

money $1.50
decimals 98.6
percentages .... 50 percent
pages .... pages 12–21
chapters .... chapter 5
addresses .... 701 Hill St.
dates .... June 6
times .... 3:30 p.m.
statistics .... a score of 5 to 2

Numbers

If the number in a sentence is written correctly, write "OK." If it is not, write it correctly.

Example: There are about twenty peppers in the basket.
20

1. 14 third and fourth graders were absent yesterday.
2. Why are there only fifteen crayons in this box?
3. My grandpa is 59 years old.
4. Kendrick drew ten pictures of his dog.
5. The Hensens drove two hundred and twenty miles to visit family.
6. Ivan can put 9 cherries in his mouth at once!
7. I read forty pages of my book last night.
8. Mexico has 31 states.
9. Seven cars are parked in the Wells' driveway.

Next Step: Draw a picture to illustrate one of the sentences above.

Related Skills Activities

- ***GrammarSnap***
  Commas in Numbers
- ***SkillsBook***
  Writing Numbers, p. 55

Answers

1. Fourteen
2. 15
3. OK
4. 10
5. 220
6. nine
7. 40
8. OK
9. OK

Abbreviations

Common Abbreviations

An **abbreviation** is the shortened form of a word or phrase. Many abbreviations begin with a capital letter and end with a period.

Mrs. Mr. Dr. Sr. Ave. a.m. p.m.

Days of the Week

Sun.	(Sunday)	Thurs.	(Thursday)
Mon.	(Monday)	Fri.	(Friday)
Tues.	(Tuesday)	Sat.	(Saturday)
Wed.	(Wednesday)		

Months of the Year

Jan.	(January)	July	(July)
Feb.	(February)	Aug.	(August)
Mar.	(March)	Sept.	(September)
Apr.	(April)	Oct.	(October)
May	(May)	Nov.	(November)
June	(June)	Dec.	(December)

Acronyms

An acronym is a word formed from the first letter or letters of words in a phrase.

radar (**ra**dio **d**etecting **a**nd **r**anging)
DEAR (Drop Everything And Read)

Initialisms

An initialism is like an acronym, but the initials (letters) are said separately.

CD (compact disc) TV (television)
PTA (Parent-Teacher Association)

Abbreviations 1

■ Common Abbreviations

For each sentence below, write the abbreviation for the underlined word.

Example: Today is <u>Tuesday</u>, July 1.
Tues.

1. I have an appointment with my dentist, <u>Doctor</u> Miller.
2. My last appointment with her was in <u>February</u>.
3. Her office is located on Dry <u>Avenue</u>.
4. My neighbor <u>Mister</u> Link works in the same building.
5. He won't be at work this <u>Friday</u>.
6. He must take a trip to <u>Saint</u> Louis.
7. He wants to visit his father, William P. Link, <u>Senior</u>.

Next Step: Ask a classmate in what month his or her birthday is. Tell each other the abbreviations for your birthday months.

Related Skills Activities

- ***GrammarSnap***
  Capitalization
- ***SkillsBook***
  Using Abbreviations, p. 56

Answers

1. Dr.
2. Feb.
3. Ave.
4. Mr.
5. Fri.
6. St.
7. Sr.

State Abbreviations

Alabama	AL	Kentucky	KY	North Dakota	ND
Alaska	AK	Louisiana	LA	Ohio	OH
Arizona	AZ	Maine	ME	Oklahoma	OK
Arkansas	AR	Maryland	MD	Oregon	OR
California	CA	Massachusetts	MA	Pennsylvania	PA
Colorado	CO	Michigan	MI	Rhode Island	RI
Connecticut	CT	Minnesota	MN	South Carolina	SC
Delaware	DE	Mississippi	MS	South Dakota	SD
District of Columbia	DC	Missouri	MO	Tennessee	TN
Florida	FL	Montana	MT	Texas	TX
Georgia	GA	Nebraska	NE	Utah	UT
Hawaii	HI	Nevada	NV	Vermont	VT
Idaho	ID	New Hampshire	NH	Virginia	VA
Illinois	IL	New Jersey	NJ	Washington	WA
Indiana	IN	New Mexico	NM	West Virginia	WV
Iowa	IA	New York	NY	Wisconsin	WI
Kansas	KS	North Carolina	NC	Wyoming	WY

Address Abbreviations

Avenue	AVE	Heights	HTS	South	S
Boulevard	BLVD	Highway	HWY	Square	SQ
Court	CT	Lane	LN	Station	STA
Drive	DR	North	N	Street	ST
East	E	Road	RD	West	W

Tip: Use these postal abbreviations when addressing envelopes. (See page 212.)

Abbreviations 2

■ **State Abbreviations**

For each state abbreviation below, write out the complete state name. A clue is given for each.

Example: ME (lighthouses)
Maine

1. HI (islands)

2. RI (smallest state)

3. MS (long river)

4. CA (Hollywood)

5. FL (hurricanes)

6. TX (cowboys)

7. NM (not old)

8. AK (biggest state)

9. SD (Mt. Rushmore)

10. NY (skyscrapers)

11. CO (Pike's Peak)

12. KY (horse farms)

13. ID (potatoes)

14. MI (great lake)

Next Step: Write a short paragraph about a state you have visited or would like to visit.

Related Skills Activities

- ***GrammarSnap***
  Capitalization
- ***SkillsBook***
  State Abbreviations, pp. 57–58

Answers

1. Hawaii
2. Rhode Island
3. Mississippi
4. California
5. Florida
6. Texas
7. New Mexico
8. Alaska
9. South Dakota
10. New York
11. Colorado
12. Kentucky
13. Idaho
14. Michigan

Practice Test

For each sentence, look for mistakes in capitalization, abbreviations, or use of numbers. (Write the letter of the line that has a mistake.) If there are no mistakes, write "D."

1. Peter and I asked (A) mr. Lerm for a (B) glass of water. (C) No mistakes (D)
2. 17 kids at school (A) got a letter from (B) Mayor Hillen. (C) No mistakes (D)
3. Aunt Marta would (A) like a visit from us (B) next wednesday. (C) No mistakes (D)
4. Every winter, this (A) area gets two feet (B) or more of snow. (C) No mistakes (D)
5. Our class welcomed (A) a new student from (B) korea in November. (C) No mistakes (D)
6. when Dean went (A) to Hawaii, he surfed (B) some giant waves. (C) No mistakes (D)
7. Sitka is one of the (A) largest alaskan cities, (B) with about 8,800 people. (C) No mistakes (D)
8. At my checkup on Friday, (A) my dentist, Dcr. Wall, (B) told me I am healthy. (C) No mistakes (D)
9. Mom makes sure that I (A) replace my toothbrush (B) every 3 months. (C) No mistakes (D)

Answers

1. B
2. A
3. C
4. D

Answers

5. C
6. A
7. B
8. B
9. C

Related Skills Activities

- ***SkillsBook***
  Mixed Review, pp. 59–60

Improving Spelling

Learning some basic spelling rules can help you spell many words. But remember that there are **exceptions** to the rules. (An exception is a word that doesn't fit the rule.)

Silent *e*

If a word ends with a silent *e*, drop the *e* before adding an ending that begins with a vowel, like *-ed* or *-ing*.

share ➔ shared, sharing

care ➔ cared, caring

Words Ending in *y*

When you write the plurals of words that end in *y*, change the *y* to *i* and add *es*. If the word ends in *ey*, just add *s*. (Also see page 492.)

puppy ➔ puppies　pony ➔ ponies

turkey ➔ turkeys　donkey ➔ donkeys

Consonant Ending

When a one-syllable word with a short vowel needs an ending like *-ed* or *-ing*, the final consonant is usually doubled. *Exception:* Do not double the consonant for words ending in *x*, as in *boxed* or *boxing*.

stop ➔ stopped, stopping　quit ➔ quitter, quitting

swim ➔ swimming, swimmer　star ➔ starred, starring

i* before *e

Use *i* before *e* except after *c* or when these letters "say" *a* as in *neighbor* or *weigh*.

i before *e* words:

friend, piece, relief, believe, audience, chief, fierce

exceptions to *i* before *e* rule:

either, neither, their, height, weird

Spelling Words

The spelling words are listed in alphabetical (ABC) order by their first letter, and then by each following letter. For example, in the "A" column, the words *almost, alone,* and *always* begin with *al*. For these three words, you must look at the third letter to see their alphabetical order.

A
about
afraid
after
again
almost
alone
a lot
always
angry
animal
another
answer
anybody
anyone
April
aren't
around
asked
asleep
August
aunt
author

B
beautiful
because
before
behind
believe
better
bicycle
body
both
bought
break
breakfast
bright
brought
built
bunch

C
cannot
care
catch
caught
cause
change
children
climb
clothes
coming
could
country
cousin

Related Skills Activities

- ***SkillsBook***
  Spelling and Alphabetizing, pp. 61–62

D
dance
daughter
dear
December
decided
didn't
different
dirty
doesn't
done
don't
down
dressed
drive
dropped
during

E
early
earth
either
engine
enough
everyone
everything

F
family
famous
favorite
February
few
field
fight
finally
finished
first
flew
floor
flying
follow
forest
fought
found
Friday
friend
from
front

G
ghost
girl
goes
ground
group
guess
gym

H
half
happen
happiness
have
heard
heart
high
hospital
how
huge
hungry
hurry
hurt

I
idea
I'll
I'm
important
inches
inside
instead
interest
island
isn't
it's

J
January
join
July
June

K
kept
kitchen
knew
knife
knocked
know

L
laugh
learn
leave
library
listen
live
loose
loud
lunch

M
mail
many
March
May
maybe
metal
middle
might
minute
mirror
Monday
monster
morning
mouse
mouth
music
myself

N
near
neighbor
ninety
nobody
noise
north
nothing
November
now

Spelling 1

Write the correct spelling of the missing word in each sentence below. Look at the letters given and the number of blanks for clues.

Example: I enjoy rap, rock, and classical m _ _ _ _.
music.

1. My mother, father, brothers, and sisters are my f _ _ _ _ _.
2. We play basketball in the _ _ m at school.
3. The man who lives next door is my n _ _ _ _ b _ _.
4. Hawaii is an _ s _ _ _ d in the Pacific Ocean.
5. When I hear a joke, I _ _ _ _ h.
6. You might lose a button if it is l _ _ _ _.
7. We borrow books from the _ _ b _ _ _ y.

Next Step: Write a sentence about a song you like. Use a word from page 504 in your sentence.

Related Skills Activities

- ***SkillsBook***
  Spelling and Silent Letters, pp. 63–64
  Spelling Sorts, pp. 65–66

Answers

1. family
2. gym
3. neighbor
4. island
5. laugh
6. loose
7. library

O
o'clock
October
off
often
once
other
our
outside
own

P
paint
paper
parents
past
people
person
phone
picture
piece
pleased
police
poor
president
pretty
probably

Q
question
quick
quiet
quite

R
reached
ready
really
reason
receive
remember
rhyme
right
river
rough
round

S
said
Saturday
scared
school
science
secret
September
sight
since
someone
something
special
stairs
started
straight
strange
strong
Sunday
sure
surprise

T
taught
than
their
then
there
they're
thought
threw
through
Thursday
together
tomorrow
tonight
trouble
truth
Tuesday

U
uncle
understand
until
upon
usual

V
very
visit
voice

W
want
was
watch
wear
weather
Wednesday
went
where
which
while
whole
without
woman
women
won't
world
would
write
wrong

X
X-ray
xylophone

Y
young
your
you're

Z
zero

Spelling 2

For each set of words below, write the correct spelling of the misspelled word.

Example: **a)** person, **b)** quick, **c)** saprize
c) surprise

1. **a)** speshul, **b)** world, **c)** very
2. **a)** through, **b)** rough, **c)** straigth
3. **a)** police, **b)** reddy, **c)** where
4. **a)** shure, **b)** without, **c)** picture
5. **a)** Wendseday, **b)** round, **c)** wrong
6. **a)** strange, **b)** recieve, **c)** usual
7. **a)** thought, **b)** surprise, **c)** ryme
8. **a)** parents, **b)** scool, **c)** remember
9. **a)** zero, **b)** which, **c)** sience
10. **a)** peice, **b)** sure, **c)** women

Next Step: Write five words from page 506 that you might have trouble spelling correctly.

Related Skills Activities

- ***SkillsBook***
  Spelling and Silent Letters, pp. 63–64
  Spelling Sorts, pp. 65–66

Answers

1. special
2. straight
3. ready
4. sure
5. Wednesday
6. receive
7. rhyme
8. school
9. science
10. piece

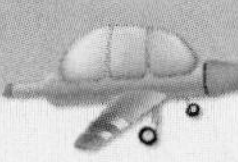

Practice Test

Write the letter of the misspelled word in each group.

1. Ⓐ animal Ⓑ girl Ⓒ write Ⓓ neer
2. Ⓐ beleive Ⓑ Tuesday Ⓒ remember Ⓓ might
3. Ⓐ round Ⓑ comeing Ⓒ while Ⓓ than
4. Ⓐ scool Ⓑ December Ⓒ maybe Ⓓ sure
5. Ⓐ friend Ⓑ question Ⓒ whare Ⓓ please
6. Ⓐ myself Ⓑ dear Ⓒ untill Ⓓ decided
7. Ⓐ because Ⓑ people Ⓒ which Ⓓ leeve
8. Ⓐ coud Ⓑ own Ⓒ knife Ⓓ interest
9. Ⓐ their Ⓑ finally Ⓒ children Ⓓ woud
10. Ⓐ Wendsday Ⓑ catch Ⓒ monster Ⓓ pretty
11. Ⓐ mous Ⓑ wrong Ⓒ high Ⓓ afraid
12. Ⓐ quick Ⓑ first Ⓒ beter Ⓓ another
13. Ⓐ Febuary Ⓑ together Ⓒ both Ⓓ again
14. Ⓐ minite Ⓑ behind Ⓒ guess Ⓓ October
15. Ⓐ group Ⓑ feild Ⓒ women Ⓓ ready
16. Ⓐ idea Ⓑ dressd Ⓒ important Ⓓ November
17. Ⓐ lern Ⓑ early Ⓒ zero Ⓓ parents
18. Ⓐ voice Ⓑ whole Ⓒ world Ⓓ allmost
19. Ⓐ upon Ⓑ recieve Ⓒ lunch Ⓓ half
20. Ⓐ kept Ⓑ past Ⓒ realy Ⓓ science

Answers

1. D
2. A
3. B
4. A
5. C
6. C
7. D
8. A
9. D
10. A

Answers

11. A
12. C
13. A
14. A
15. B
16. B
17. A
18. D
19. B
20. C

Using the Right Word

In your writing, you use words that can be easily confused, such as *blue* and *blew*. This section covers two kinds of problem words that are often confused—*homophones* and *homonyms*.

Homophones are words that sound alike but have different spellings and meanings.

The doghouse was made of wood.
Would Mugsy like it?

Homonyms sound alike *and* are spelled the same, but they have different meanings.

Be careful; don't break that vase!
We should take a break.

ant, aunt	An **ant** is an insect that works hard. My **aunt** is my mom's sister.
ate, eight	We **ate** all the popcorn. (The past tense of *eat* is "ate.") The number **eight** comes between seven and nine.
bare, bear	If you have **bare** feet, you have no shoes or socks on. A **bear** is a big, furry animal.
blew, blue	The wind **blew** hard. (The past tense of *blow* is "blew.") A clear sky is the color **blue**.

Using the Right Word 1

- ant, aunt; ate, eight; bare, bear; blew, blue

For each sentence below, write the word (in parentheses) that is correct.

Example: Does every *(bare, bear)* sleep through the winter?
bear

1. If I slept in a cave all winter, I would turn *(blew, blue)*!
2. Maybe I would be warm enough if *(ate, eight)* big, furry animals slept with me.
3. Serena and her *(ant, aunt)* bought some tomato plants for the garden.
4. One plant was almost *(bare, bear)*.
5. Serena *(ate, eight)* some great tomatoes from that plant a few months later.
6. She noticed an *(ant, aunt)* crawling on one tomato.
7. Serena just *(blew, blue)* it off the tomato.

Next Step: Using two words from the list above, write a sentence about a food you have eaten.

Related Skills Activities

- ***SkillsBook***
  Using the Right Word 1, p. 67

Answers

1. blue
2. eight
3. aunt
4. bare
5. ate
6. ant
7. blew

brake, break	A car's **brake** makes it stop. If you **break** a glass, it shatters into pieces. Taking a **break** means resting for a bit.
buy, by	When you pay for an item, you **buy** it. The word **by** means "near."
cent, scent, sent	One **cent** is the same as one penny. A pine tree's **scent** is the way it smells. We **sent** Aunt Carole a valentine. (The past tense of *send* is "sent.")
close, clothes	**Close** the window so no bugs can get in. People wear **clothes**, such as shirts and pants.
creak, creek	A squeaky kind of sound is called a **creak**. A **creek** is a stream or a tiny river.
dear, deer	Juan is fond of his **dear** grandmother. **Deer** are animals that live in the woods.
dew, do, due	The moisture on the morning grass is **dew**. When you're given a job, always **do** your best. Homework is usually **due** on a certain day.

Using the Right Word 2

- buy, by; cent, scent, sent; close, clothes; dear, deer

Write a word from the list above to complete each sentence.

Example: Some of these flowers have a very strong _____ .
scent

1. I would like to _____ some for my grandma.
2. I need one more _______ to have enough money.
3. My grandma is very _____ to me.
4. The _____ she wears are old, but they always look nice.
5. Once she _____ me a long letter.
6. She described playing in the woods _____ her house when she was young.
7. She remembers leaving corn out for the _____.
8. Grandma often tells me, "Never _____ your mind to new ideas."

Next Step: Write two sentences that show your understanding of the words *by* and *buy*.

Related Skills Activities

- ***SkillsBook***
  Using the Right Word 2, p. 68

Answers

1. buy
2. cent
3. dear
4. clothes
5. sent
6. by
7. deer
8. close

eye, I	A mammal's **eye** allows it to see. **I** love the zoo. (The pronoun *I* refers to the person who is speaking.)
for, four	I made pancakes **for** Mom's birthday breakfast. (*For* tells why something is done.) The number **four** is one more than three.
hare, hair	A **hare** looks like a large rabbit. **Hair** covers a person's head.
heal, heel	Her cut should **heal** within a week. The **heel** is the back part of the foot.
hear, here	We use our ears to **hear** sound. Someone who is **here** is in this place.
heard, herd	We **heard** sirens all night. (The past tense of *hear* is "heard.") A **herd** is a group of animals.
hole, whole	An area that's been hollowed out is a **hole**. Something that is **whole** has nothing missing.
hour, our	One **hour** lasts 60 minutes. **Our** dog barks at strangers. (*Our* shows ownership.)

Using the Right Word 3

■ for, four; hear, here; heard, herd; hour, our

For the sentences below, write the right word from each pair (in parentheses).

Example: My watch tells the date, the *(hour, our)*, the minute, and the second.
hour

1. I got it *(for, four)* my birthday.
2. At night I keep it right *(hear, here)* on my bedside table.
3. Once I *(heard, herd)* its alarm go off at *(for, four)* o'clock in the morning!
4. The alarm also woke up *(hour, our)* three dogs.
5. Of course, they *(hear, here)* every little sound.
6. When they come running, it sounds like a *(heard, herd)* of buffalo!

Next Step: Write a sentence about a time you were frightened. Use one of the words from the list above correctly.

Related Skills Activities

■ ***SkillsBook***
Using the Right Word 3, p. 69

Answers

1. for
2. here
3. heard, four
4. our
5. hear
6. herd

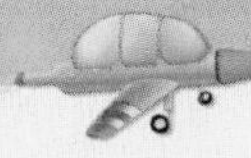

its, it's	The cat licked **its** paw. (*Its* shows ownership.) **It's** hot today! (*It's*—with an apostrophe—is the contraction for "it is.")
knew, new	Dauna **knew** how to read at age four. (The past tense of *know* is "knew.") Something that is **new** is not old.
knight, night	Long ago, a **knight** was a soldier in armor. At **night** it's dark outside.
know, no	To **know** something is to understand it. The opposite of "yes" is "**no.**"
made, maid	Grandma **made** waffles for us. (The past tense of *make* is "made.") A **maid** is someone hired to do housework.
main, mane	The **main** idea is the most important one. The long hair on a horse's neck is its **mane.**
meat, meet	Some people eat the **meat** of animals. We come together to **meet** with others.
one, won	**One** is the number before two. We **won** the game! (The past tense of *win* is "won.")

Using the Right Word 4

■ it's, its; knew, new; know, no; one, won

For each sentence below, write the word (in parentheses) that is correct.

Example: Let's shoot some hoops with my *(knew, new)* ball.
new

1. *(It's, Its)* one of the prizes for a hoops contest I entered.
2. I *(one, won)* third place.
3. I *(knew, new)* I couldn't beat Calvin.
4. I *(know, no)* of only *(one, won)* other player who might have beaten him.
5. While doing a layup, Reggie almost broke the hoop off *(it's, its)* backboard.
6. Calvin wanted *(know, no)* prize other than first.
7. *(It's, Its)* not surprising that he got it!
8. Now he has a *(knew, new)* bike!

Next Step: Write a sentence about entering a contest. Use one of the words from the list above.

Related Skills Activities

■ ***SkillsBook***
Using the Right Word 4, p. 70

Answers

1. It's
2. won
3. knew
4. know, one
5. its
6. no
7. It's
8. new

pair, pare, pear	A **pair** of items is two things. When you trim off the outside of a **pear** or an apple, you **pare** it.
peace, piece	The opposite of war is **peace**. A **piece** of bread is part of a loaf.
plain, plane	Bonita's bedroom is **plain**, not fancy. A **plain** is a large, flat area of land without trees. The shortened word for "airplane" is "**plane**."
read, red	I've **read** that book twice. (The past tense of *read* is "read.") We picked some ripe, **red** tomatoes. (*Red* is a color.)
right, write	**Right** is the opposite of left. Something that is correct is **right**. You put words on paper when you **write**.
road, rode, rowed	A **road** is a path for cars and trucks. Sammy **rode** his tricycle down the driveway. (The past tense of ride is "rode.") The friends **rowed** the boat across the lake. (The past tense of *row* is "rowed.")
scene, seen	A **scene** is a place and its surroundings. The dog had **seen** the rabbit before it took off running. (*Seen* is a way to state "see" in the past tense.)

Using the Right Word 5

■ peace, piece; right, write; road, rode, rowed

For each sentence below, write the word (in parentheses) that is correct.

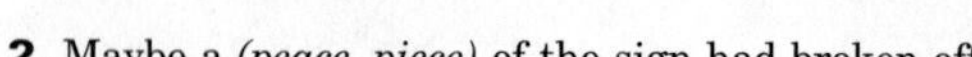

Example: The sign beside the *(road, rode)* wasn't helpful.
road

1. The arrow pointing *(right, write)* only had triangles on it!
2. Maybe a *(peace, piece)* of the sign had broken off.
3. We *(rode, rowed)* on in the car, not knowing where we were.
4. Mom said she'd *(right, write)* someone a letter about it.
5. We wanted to get to the *(peace, piece)* and quiet of the lake.
6. Finally, we put the boat in the water and *(rode, rowed)* away on the gentle waves.

Next Step: Write a sentence about getting lost. Use a word from the list above.

Related Skills Activities

■ ***SkillsBook***
Using the Right Word 5, p. 71

Answers

1. right
2. piece
3. rode
4. write
5. peace
6. rowed

sea, see	A **sea** is a large body of water. People use their eyes to **see**.
sew, so, sow	A needle and thread are needed to **sew**. We were **so** tired. (*So* means "very." *So* can also mean "as a result.") When you plant seeds, you **sow** them.
soar, sore	A high-flying bird is said to **soar**. Muscles that ache are **sore**.
some, sum	Get **some** sleep. (*Some* refers to how much.) A **sum** is the total of numbers added together.
son, sun	A male child is his parents' **son**. The **sun** is the closest star to the earth.
tail, tale	A happy dog wags its **tail**. Colin's story was an exciting **tale** about elves.
their, there, they're	The boys finished **their** homework. (*Their* shows ownership.) If you are here, you cannot be **there**. **They're** outside playing. (*They're* is the contraction for "they are.")
threw, through	Matt **threw** a baseball over the fence. (The past tense of *throw* is "threw.") To go **through** a tunnel, you go in one side and out the other.

Using the Right Word 6

- son, sun; their, there, they're; threw, through

For each section below, decide which word (in parentheses) is correct. Write it on your paper.

Example: In the morning, the *(son, sun)* rises in the east.
sun

1. It peeks *(threw, through)* my bedroom curtains.
2. I have a shade *(their, there, they're)*, but I forget to close it.
3. Dad is Grandma and Grandpa's *(son, sun)*.
4. *(Their, There, They're)* his parents.
5. Once Dad *(threw, through)* a baseball into Grandma's kitchen window.
6. Grandma and Grandpa fixed *(their, there, they're)* window right away.

Next Step: Write a sentence or two about people in your family. Use the word *they're*.

Related Skills Activities

- ***SkillsBook***
  Using the Right Word 6, p. 72

Answers

1. through
2. there
3. son
4. They're
5. threw
6. their

to, two, too	*To* suggests moving toward something. The number **two** is one less than three. *Too* can mean "very" or "also."
waist, waste	Your **waist** is between your chest and hips. You **waste** a thing if you don't use it wisely.
wait, weight	I will stay here and **wait** until you get back. A man's **weight** tells how heavy he is.
way, weigh	Knowing the **way** helps you get somewhere. To find out how heavy you are, **weigh** yourself.
weak, week	The opposite of strong is "**weak.**" A **week** is seven days.
wear, where	Stefan and his brother **wear** jeans every day. **Where** is Scott? (*Where* means "in what place?")
witch, which	A **witch** is a woman who is thought to have magical powers. **Which** magazine do you want? (*Which* identifies one thing out of a group.)
wood, would	**Wood** comes from trees. I **would** vote for you. (*Would* suggests a choice.)
your, you're	**Your** drawing is neat! (*Your* shows ownership.) **You're** an artist. (*You're* is the contraction for "you are."

Using the Right Word 7

■ weak, week; wood, would; your, you're

Write the correct word from the list above to complete each sentence below.

Example: It will be a *week* before school starts again.

1. Did you remember to cover all _________ new books?
2. I think _________ going to do fine in school this year.
3. Raj _________ like summer to last a little longer.
4. He is building a birdhouse out of _________.
5. He might not finish it in just a _________.
6. If he stays up too late working on it, he may feel _________ the next day.
7. You can offer him _______ help if you'd like to.

Next Step: Write two sentences about school. Use the words *your* and *you're* correctly.

Related Skills Activities

■ ***SkillsBook***
Using the Right Word 7, p. 73

Answers

1. your
2. you're
3. would
4. wood
5. week
6. weak
7. your

Practice Test

Read each pair of sentences below. Write the letter of the sentence in which the underlined word is wrong. If both words are correct, write "C."

1. Ⓐ Would you please get ready?
   Ⓑ Its time to go now.
   Ⓒ Correct as is

2. Ⓐ I'd like a peace of that pie.
   Ⓑ It has a wonderful scent.
   Ⓒ Correct as is

3. Ⓐ This road is very bumpy.
   Ⓑ No one rides a bike on it.
   Ⓒ Correct as is

4. Ⓐ Jan herd a noise.
   Ⓑ The cat got a new collar bell.
   Ⓒ Correct as is

5. Ⓐ He wants a pair of blue jeans.
   Ⓑ Will Dad buy them?
   Ⓒ Correct as is

6. Ⓐ Luther sent me a postcard.
   Ⓑ He is spending for months in Florida.
   Ⓒ Correct as is

7. Ⓐ I ate a taco for lunch.
   Ⓑ I had some last weak, too.
   Ⓒ Correct as is

8. Ⓐ An ant is on my sandwich.
   Ⓑ It is not the only one!
   Ⓒ Correct as is

9. Ⓐ Uncle Dave has a bare in his yard.
   Ⓑ Don't worry; it is made of wood.
   Ⓒ Correct as is

10. Ⓐ It has been cloudy for six days.
    Ⓑ When will we see the son again?
    Ⓒ Correct as is

11. Ⓐ Jill rode the bus to the zoo.
    Ⓑ The ride took an our.
    Ⓒ Correct as is

12. Ⓐ Is this you're book?
    Ⓑ Yes—I can tell by its torn cover.
    Ⓒ Correct as is

13. Ⓐ Mr. Lee's son isn't feeling well.
    Ⓑ He is weak and has a fever.
    Ⓒ Correct as is

14. Ⓐ Mark saw eight jays in a tree.
    Ⓑ He could here them, too.
    Ⓒ Correct as is

15. Ⓐ Kenna walked by the river.
    Ⓑ All the trees were bare.
    Ⓒ Correct as is

16. Ⓐ I didn't clothes my dresser drawer.
    Ⓑ I threw a pair of socks toward it.
    Ⓒ Correct as is

Answers

1. B
2. A
3. C
4. A
5. C
6. B
7. B
8. C

Related Skills Activities

- ***SkillsBook***
  Using the Right Word Review, p. 74

Answers

9. A
10. B
11. B
12. A
13. C
14. B
15. C
16. A

Understanding Sentences
Parts of a Sentence

Simple Subject

The subject names someone or something. The subject is often doing something. The **simple subject** is the main word—without any other words—in the complete subject.

My big sister threw the balloon.
(*Sister* is the simple subject.)

My best friend caught the balloon.
(*Friend* is the simple subject.)

Complete Subject

The **complete subject** is the main word along with any other words that describe it.

My big sister threw the balloon.
(*My big sister* is the complete subject.)

The huge balloon is full of water.
(*The huge balloon* is the complete subject.)

Compound Subject

A **compound subject** is made up of two or more simple subjects joined by *and* or *or*.

My big sister and my best friend played catch with the balloon.
(*Sister* and *friend* make up the compound subject.)

Parts of a Sentence 1

■ Complete and Simple Subjects

For each sentence below, write the complete subject.

Example: One famous author of children's books was Theodor Seuss Geisel.
One famous author of children's books

1. Most people know him simply as Dr. Seuss.
2. Odd creatures in fantastic places fill his books.
3. The main character in *Green Eggs and Ham* is Sam-I-Am.
4. A bored brother and sister are entertained by *The Cat in the Hat*.
5. Dr. Seuss's book of wonderful noises is *Mr. Brown Can Moo! Can You?*
6. Dr. Seuss may have taught your parents to read!

Next Step: For each answer you wrote, circle the simple subject. (One is a compound subject, so you will circle two words.)

Related Skills Activities

- **Basic Grammar and Writing**
  Complete Subjects, p. 398
  Simple Subjects and Predicates, p. 400
  Compound Subjects and Predicates, p. 401
- ***GrammarSnap***
  Complete Sentences
  Compound Subjects
- ***SkillsBook***
  Simple and Complete Subjects and Predicates, pp. 77–78
  Subject of a Sentence, pp. 79–80

Answers

1. Most people
2. Odd creatures in fantastic places
3. The main character in *Green Eggs and Ham*
4. A bored brother and sister
5. Dr. Seuss's book of wonderful noises
6. Dr. Seuss

Next Step: Answers

1. people
2. creatures
3. character
4. brother, sister
5. book
6. Dr. Seuss

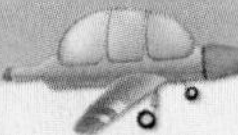

Parts of a Sentence . . .

Simple Predicate (Verb)

The predicate tells what the subject is or does. The **simple predicate** is the main word—the verb—in the complete predicate.

Rocky is the fastest dog on the block.

(*Is* is the simple predicate.)

Rocky runs faster than the other dogs.

(*Runs* is the simple predicate.)

Complete Predicate (Verb)

The **complete predicate** is the verb along with the other words that describe and complete it.

Rocky is the fastest dog on the block.

(*Is the fastest dog on the block* is the complete predicate.)

Rocky runs faster than the other dogs.

(*Runs faster than the other dogs* is the complete predicate.)

Compound Predicate (Verb)

A **compound predicate** is made up of two or more simple predicates (verbs) joined by *and* or *or*.

Rocky runs fast and barks loud.

(*Runs* and *barks* make up the compound predicate.)

Parts of a Sentence 2

■ Complete and Simple Predicates

For each sentence below, write the complete predicate.

Example: Rabbits are mammals with long ears and short tails.
are mammals with long ears and short tails

1. These animals are blind and hairless at birth.
2. Rabbits hop and run fast with their powerful hind legs.
3. They can escape foxes, badgers, and birds of prey.
4. Rabbits are very active at night.
5. Rabbits eat lots of different plants.
6. Many gardeners think of them as pests.

Next Step: For each answer you wrote, circle the simple predicate. (One is a compound predicate, so you will circle two words.)

Related Skills Activities

- **Basic Grammar and Writing**
  Complete Predicates, p. 399
  Simple Subjects and Predicates, p. 400
  Compound Subjects and Predicates, p. 401
- ***GrammarSnap***
  Complete Verbs
- ***SkillsBook***
  Simple and Complete Subjects and Predicates, pp. 77–78
  Predicate of a Sentence, pp. 81–82

Answers

1. are blind and hairless at birth
2. hop and run fast with their powerful hind legs
3. can escape foxes, badgers, and birds of prey
4. are very active at night
5. eat lots of different plants
6. think of them as pests

Next Step: Answers

1. are
2. hop, run
3. can escape
4. are
5. eat
6. think

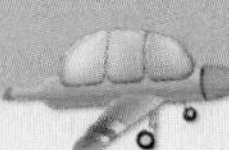

Practice Test

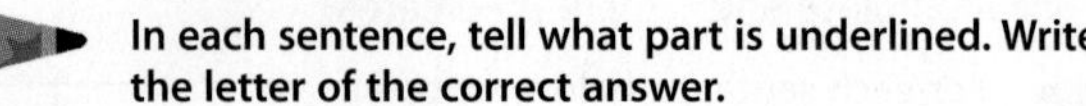

In each sentence, tell what part is underlined. Write the letter of the correct answer.

1. Giraffes are the tallest animals.
   - Ⓐ simple subject
   - Ⓑ complete subject
   - Ⓒ simple predicate
   - Ⓓ complete predicate

2. A baby giraffe is about six feet tall at birth.
   - Ⓐ simple subject
   - Ⓑ complete subject
   - Ⓒ simple predicate
   - Ⓓ complete predicate

3. They can grow to be 18 feet tall!
   - Ⓐ simple subject
   - Ⓑ complete subject
   - Ⓒ simple predicate
   - Ⓓ complete predicate

4. High treetops provide food for giraffes.
   - Ⓐ simple subject
   - Ⓑ complete subject
   - Ⓒ simple predicate
   - Ⓓ complete predicate

5. They use their long tongues and stretchy lips to get leaves.
   - Ⓐ simple subject
   - Ⓑ complete subject
   - Ⓒ simple predicate
   - Ⓓ complete predicate

6. Like a human, a giraffe has seven bones in its neck.
   - Ⓐ simple subject
   - Ⓑ complete subject
   - Ⓒ simple predicate
   - Ⓓ complete predicate

7. Large hooves at the end of long legs help a giraffe balance.
   - Ⓐ simple subject
   - Ⓑ complete subject
   - Ⓒ simple predicate
   - Ⓓ complete predicate

8. These animals can run quite fast.
   - Ⓐ simple subject
   - Ⓑ complete subject
   - Ⓒ simple predicate
   - Ⓓ complete predicate

Answers

1. D
2. C
3. C
4. B

Answers

5. D
6. C
7. B
8. A

Related Skills Activities

- ***SkillsBook***
  Subject and Predicate Review, pp. 83–84

Using the Parts of Speech

All the words in our language fit into eight groups. These word groups are called the **parts of speech**.

Nouns

A **noun** names a person, a place, a thing, or an idea.

classmate Los Angeles bottle joy

Kinds of Nouns

Common Nouns

A **common noun** names any person, place, thing, or idea.

girl	building	team	day
dog	house	window	flower
boy	zoo	sidewalk	lake

Proper Nouns

A **proper noun** names a specific person, place, thing, or idea. Proper nouns are capitalized.

Ann	Willis Tower
Atlanta Braves	Thursday
Central Park	California
Thanksgiving Day	Lake Erie

Nouns 1

■ Common and Proper Nouns

For each sentence below, write one common noun and one proper noun.

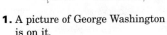

Example: The special quarter for New Jersey came out in 1999.
quarter New Jersey

1. A picture of George Washington is on it.
2. A great big oak tree is on the quarter for Connecticut.
3. Georgia has a peach on its coin.
4. Can you guess which quarter has the Statue of Liberty on it?
5. Maine, the state Mom was born in, has a lighthouse on its quarter.

Next Step: Write a sentence about any state. Include the state's name in your sentence.

Related Skills Activities

- **Basic Grammar and Writing**
  Using Nouns, p. 375+
- ***GrammarSnap***
  Common and Proper Nouns
  Specific Nouns
- ***SkillsBook***
  Nouns, pp. 117–118
  Common and Proper Nouns, pp. 119–120

Answers

1. Common: picture
   Proper: George Washington
2. Common: tree, quarter
   Proper: Connecticut
3. Common: peach, coin
   Proper: Georgia
4. Common: quarter
   Proper: Statue of Liberty
5. Common: state, lighthouse, quarter
   Proper: Maine, Mom

Nouns . . .

Singular Nouns

A **singular noun** names one person, place, thing, or idea.

kid town computer time

Plural Nouns

A **plural noun** names more than one person, place, thing, or idea.

kids towns computers times

Possessive Nouns

A **possessive noun** shows ownership.

My school's colors are blue and white.

Both schools' teams played well.

See page **474** for the rules on forming possessives.

Singular	Plural	Singular possessive	Plural possessive
one person	more than one person	belongs to one person	belongs to more than one person
neighbor	neighbors	neighbor's	neighbors'

Nouns 2

■ Singular and Plural Nouns

Fold your paper in half. Write "singular" on the left and "plural" on the right. Write each noun from the paragraph below in the correct column, like this:

Singular	Plural
Viking	boats

Vikings became famous for their ships. A longship often had the head of a dragon carved into its front end. Colorful sails and 10 oars helped move the wooden ship. Painted shields decorated its sides. What a sight it must have been!

Next Step: Write a sentence or two about any ship you've seen. Underline the singular nouns and circle the plural nouns.

Related Skills Activities

- **Basic Grammar and Writing**
  Singular and Plural Nouns, p. 376
  Possessive Nouns, p. 377
- ***GrammarSnap***
  Nouns
  Plurals of Words Ending in *s*
- ***SkillsBook***
  Singular and Plural Nouns, pp. 121–122
  Possessive Nouns 1 and 2, pp. 123–124

Answers

Singular	Plural
longship	Vikings
head	ships
dragon	sails
end	oars
ship	shields
sight	sides

Pronouns

A **pronoun** is a word that takes the place of a noun.

Karl climbed over the fence.

He could have been hurt.

(The pronoun *he* replaces the noun *Karl*.)

The lunchroom was a busy place.

It was very crowded.

(The pronoun *it* replaces the noun *lunchroom*.)

Kinds of Pronouns

Common Personal Pronouns

Singular Pronouns	Plural Pronouns
I, me, my, mine,	we, us, our, ours,
you, your, yours,	you, your, yours,
he, him, his,	they, them, their,
she, her, hers,	theirs
it, its	

Possessive Pronouns

A **possessive pronoun** shows ownership.

Karl hurt his arm while climbing the fence.
(Karl's arm)

My desk was messy.
(the speaker's desk)

Kendra left her lunch on the table.
(Kendra's lunch)

Pronouns

Possessive Pronouns

For each sentence below, write a possessive pronoun to take the place of the underlined noun or nouns.

Example: Leann kicked Leann's ball into the sky. *(his, her)*
her

1. Then Ralph brought Ralph's ball over. *(his, their)*
2. Leann and Ralph took turns kicking Leann's and Ralph's balls to each other. *(her, their)*
3. Marina and I want to learn how to play Marina's and my new flutes. *(their, our)*
4. Marina got Marina's flute from a cousin. *(his, her)*
5. The flute was missing one of the flute's keys. *(its, their)*
6. Marina's parents had one of the parents' friends repair it. *(their, its)*

Next Step: Write a sentence about a musical instrument. Use the possessive form of *you*.

Related Skills Activities

- **Basic Grammar and Writing**
  Using Pronouns, p. 379
  Possessive Pronouns, p. 380
  How Can I Use Pronouns Correctly?, p. 381
  Plural Pronouns, p. 382
- ***GrammarSnap***
  Pronouns, Subject and Object
  Possessive Pronouns
- ***SkillsBook***
  Personal Pronouns 1 and 2, pp. 125–128
  Pronouns: I and Me, They and Them, pp. 129–130
  Possessive Pronouns, pp. 131–132

Answers

1. his
2. their
3. our
4. her
5. its
6. their

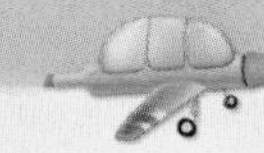

Verbs

A **verb** shows action or links two ideas in a sentence.

The monkey eats a banana. I am happy.

Types of Verbs

Action Verbs

An **action verb** tells what the subject is doing.

Lela eats lots of carrots.

Todd jumped like a kangaroo.

Linking Verbs

A **linking verb** links the subject to a word in the predicate part of a sentence. A linking verb tells something *about* the subject.

My teacher is helpful.
(The verb *is* links *teacher* to *helpful.*)

My friends are happy in our school.
(The verb *are* links *friends* to *happy.*)

Common Linking Verbs: is, are, was, were, am, be, been

Helping Verbs

A **helping verb** comes before the main verb, and it helps state when an action happens.

Pat had called two times.
(*Had* helps the main action verb *called.*)

Pat will be the butler in our play.
(*Will* helps the main linking verb *be.*)

Helping Verbs: has, have, had, will, can, could, should, would, do, did, does, may

Verbs 1

■ **Action, Linking, and Helping Verbs**

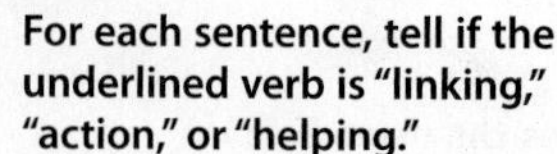

For each sentence, tell if the underlined verb is "linking," "action," or "helping."

Example: My cat's name is Tiger.
linking

1. He does not growl fiercely, though!
2. Tigers are the largest wild cats.
3. A tiger can weigh more than 700 pounds.
4. Tiger cubs stay with their mothers for two years.
5. They live in swamps, forests, and jungles.
6. In 2004, fewer than 5,000 tigers were alive.
7. Without help, they could become extinct.

Next Step: Write a sentence about another wild cat. Use a strong action verb.

Related Skills Activities

- **Basic Grammar and Writing**
  Action Verbs, p. 383
  Linking Verbs, p. 384
  Helping Verbs, p. 385
- ***GrammarSnap***
  Action Verbs
  Helping Verbs
- ***SkillsBook***
  Action and Linking Verbs, pp. 133–134
  Helping Verbs, p. 135

Answers

1. action
2. linking
3. helping
4. action
5. action
6. linking
7. helping

Verbs . . .

Tenses of Verbs

The **tense** of a verb tells when the action takes place. Verb tense is often shown by a word's ending (plays, play*ed*) or with a helping verb (*will* play, *has* played).

Present Tense Verbs

Present tense means the action is happening now or that it happens as a regular event.

Jackie plays on our soccer team.

Our practices help us a lot.

Past Tense Verbs

Past tense means the action happened before the present time, or in the past.

Yesterday Jackie played at Hope Field.

Three girls scored goals.

Future Tense Verbs

Future tense means the action will take place at a later time, or in the future.

Tomorrow Jackie will play goalie.

We will see a soccer video.

Some helping verbs describe the time of the action in more detail.

Jackie has played soccer for three years.

Our coach is planning a tournament.

The soccer field had been a pasture.

Verbs 2

Simple Tenses

For each sentence, identify the tense of the underlined verb. Write "present," "past," or "future."

Example: Inspector Sawyer looks for clues.
present

1. Last year he solved most of his cases.
2. He will retire next year.
3. He will spend his time gardening, fishing, and relaxing.
4. Inspector Sawyer lives in the apartment next door to our family.
5. Usually he walks his dog after dinner.
6. Yesterday he worked late, so I walked his dog.
7. Maybe he will offer me one of his prize tomatoes as a thank-you.

Next Step: Write a sentence about a neighbor. Have a classmate identify the tense of the verb in your sentence.

Related Skills Activities

- **Basic Grammar and Writing**
  How Can I Show Time in My Writing?, pp. 386–387
- ***GrammarSnap***
  Past Tense Verbs
- ***SkillsBook***
  Verbs Tenses 1, 2, and 3, pp. 137–142

Answers

1. past
2. future
3. future
4. present
5. present
6. past
7. future

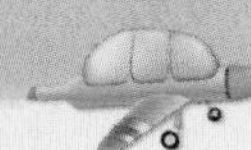

Verbs . . .

Forms of Verbs

Singular Verbs

Use a **singular verb** when the subject is singular. (*Singular* means "one.")

Kayla eats almonds.

(*Eats* is a singular verb.)

Most nouns ending in *s* are plural, but most *verbs* ending in *s* are singular.

Plural Verbs

Use a **plural verb** when the subject is plural. (*Plural* means "more than one.")

The other girls love cashews.

(*Love* is a plural verb.)

Use a verb without an *s* ending for a plural subject.

Regular and Irregular Verbs

Many verbs in our language are **regular**. This means you add *-ed* to form the past tense.

I play.	Yesterday I played.
He kicks.	He has kicked.

Some verbs in our language are **irregular**. You might use a different word to form the past tense, or you might use the same word. (See page 544.)

I see.	I saw.	I have seen.
She writes.	She wrote.	She has written.

Verbs 3

■ Singular and Plural Verbs

Write the correct verb (in parentheses) to complete each sentence.

Example: My family *(have, has)* a new computer.
has

1. I *(type, types)* on an old keyboard.
2. The keys *(stick, sticks)*.
3. My sister *(type, types)* fast on the new keyboard.
4. The new computer *(work, works)* much faster than our old computer did.
5. It *(hold, holds)* more memory, too.
6. My parents *(use, uses)* it more often than they used the old one.
7. Sometimes they *(ask, asks)* for my help!

Next Step: Write a sentence about using computers. Make sure the verb agrees with its subject.

Related Skills Activities

- **Basic Grammar and Writing**
  How Can I Use Verbs Correctly?, p. 388
- ***GrammarSnap***
  Past Tense Verbs
  Subject-Verb Agreement
- ***SkillsBook***
  Regular Verbs, pp. 143–144
  Singular and Plural Verbs, pp. 145–146
  Irregular Verbs, pp. 147–148

Answers

1. type
2. stick
3. types
4. works
5. holds
6. use
7. ask

Common Irregular Verbs

Present Tense	Past Tense	Past Tense with *has, have, had*
am, are, is	was, were	been
begin	began	begun
break	broke	broken
bring	brought	brought
catch	caught	caught
come	came	come
do	did	done
draw	drew	drawn
drive	drove	driven
eat	ate	eaten
fall	fell	fallen
fly	flew	flown
get	got	gotten
give	gave	given
go	went	gone
grow	grew	grown
hide	hid	hidden, hid
know	knew	known
put	put	put
ride	rode	ridden
run	ran	run
see	saw	seen
sing	sang, sung	sung
take	took	taken
throw	threw	thrown
write	wrote	written

Verbs 4

■ Irregular Verbs

For each pair of sentences, write the correct tense of the underlined verb to fill in the blank.

Example: Sometimes we eat pancakes for dinner. Yesterday we *ate* beef burritos for dinner.

1. Please bring your treat to school tomorrow. Last week Tina _______ carrots for a treat.
2. I _____ sick over the weekend. Today I am fine.
3. My dad and I go to the zoo often in summer. Last winter we _______ there twice.
4. The Jameson brothers throw snowballs. Once Jerry _______ one at me, but it missed.
5. Terrell, can you catch this boomerang? Lucy _____ it when she played with it.

Next Step: Write one or two sentences using the past tense of each of these verbs: *sing* and *write*.

Related Skills Activities

- ***GrammarSnap***
  Past Tense Verbs
- ***SkillsBook***
  Irregular Verbs, pp. 147–148

Answers

1. brought
2. was
3. went
4. threw
5. caught

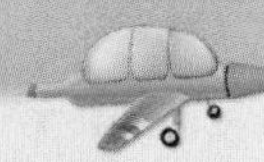

Adjectives

An **adjective** is a word that describes a noun or a pronoun. Adjectives tell *what kind*, *how many*, or *which one*.

Some dogs have funny faces.
(An adjective usually comes before the word it describes.)

The fur on a sheepdog is fluffy.
(An adjective may come after a linking verb like *is* or *are*.)

Kinds of Adjectives

Articles

The articles *a*, *an*, and *the* are adjectives.

A pug is a small dog.
(*A* is used before words beginning with a consonant sound.)

An otterhound is a big dog with a long tail.
(*An* is used before words beginning with a vowel sound.)

Proper Adjectives

Some adjectives are formed from proper nouns. They are always capitalized.

The dingo is an Australian dog.

Compound Adjectives

Some adjectives are made up of more than one word. These adjectives are often hyphenated.

The bulldog is our football team mascot.

A dalmatian has a short-haired coat.

A dachshund has a sausage-shaped body.

Adjectives 1

■ Proper, Common, and Compound Adjectives

Write the adjectives found in each sentence below. Do not include articles.

Example: The poor snowman melts.
poor

1. It is a Texan snowman.
2. A sunbaked area doesn't work well for a snowman.
3. If it were an Alaskan snowman, it wouldn't melt so quickly.
4. In fact, a snowman could have a long life there.
5. The ice-cold air would keep it from melting.
6. Does a snowman take a July vacation at the North Pole?
7. A trip to Florida would be a short vacation for a snowman!

Next Step: Write the two compound adjectives you found in the sentences above.

Related Skills Activities

- **Basic Grammar and Writing**
  Selecting Adjectives, p. 389
- ***GrammarSnap***
  Adjectives
- ***SkillsBook***
  Adjectives 1 and 2, pp. 151–152, 154
  Proper Adjectives, p. 155
  Compound Adjectives, p. 156

Answers

1. Texan
2. sunbaked
3. Alaskan
4. long
5. ice-cold
6. July
7. short

Next Step: Answers

sunbaked, ice-cold

Adjectives . . .

Forms of Adjectives

Positive Adjectives	An adjective describes a noun. A pug has a small face.
Comparative Adjectives	Some adjectives compare two nouns. A bulldog is shorter than a dalmatian. (Many comparative adjectives use the ending *-er.*) Bulldogs are more muscular than poodles. (*More* is used before some comparative adjectives with two or more syllables.)
Superlative Adjectives	Some adjectives compare three or more nouns. That Chihuahua is the smallest dog I have ever seen. (Many superlative adjectives use the ending *-est.*) This golden retriever is the most beautiful dog here. (*Most* is used before some superlative adjectives with two or more syllables.)
Irregular Forms of Adjectives	The following adjectives use different words to make comparisons.

Positive	Comparative	Superlative
good	better	best
bad	worse	worst
many	more	most

Adjectives 2

Comparative and Superlative Adjectives

Choose the comparative or the superlative form of the underlined adjectives to fill in the blanks.

Example: The delivery truck is large, but the garbage truck is larger. *(larger, largest)*

1. A garbage truck is bigger than a pickup truck. Mining trucks are the _______ trucks in the world. *(big, biggest)*
2. Although all trucks are powerful, mining trucks with their two engines are _______ than most trucks. *(more powerful, most powerful)*
3. Mining trucks perform important work, but fire trucks and ambulances perform the _______ work of all. *(more important, most important)*
4. Fire trucks can be fast. However, the _______ vehicle on the road is a car. *(faster, fastest)*
5. A good car uses little fuel. A _______ car will protect the people in it, too. *(better, best)*

Next Step: Write one or two sentences comparing cars and trucks. Use a comparative or superlative adjective in each sentence.

Related Skills Activities

- **Basic Grammar and Writing**
  How Can I Use Adjectives Correctly?, p. 390
- ***GrammarSnap***
  Adjectives
- ***SkillsBook***
  Forms of Adjectives, pp. 157–158

Answers

1. biggest
2. more powerful
3. most important
4. fastest
5. better

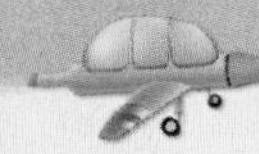

Adverbs

An **adverb** is a word that describes a verb. It tells *how*, *where*, or *when* an action is done.

Desert temperatures drop quickly as the sun goes down.
Desert animals hunt for food nightly.

Kinds of Adverbs

Adverbs of Manner (How)

Adverbs often tell *how* something is done.

The desert sun shines brightly.
The horned viper moves silently.

Adverbs of Place (Where)

Some adverbs tell *where* something happens.

One scientist works nearby.
She stays outside for a long time.

Adverbs of Time (When)

Some adverbs tell *how often* or *when* an action is done.

Sand dunes often change their shape.
A group of scientists explored the desert yesterday.

Adverbs often end with *ly*, but not always. Words like *not, never, very,* and *always* are common adverbs.

Adverbs

Write the adverb that you find in each sentence below. The clue (word) will help you find the adverb.

Example: Alvin said softly, "I have a secret." *(How?)*
softly

1. Then he asked, "Do you want to hear it?" *(When?)*
2. "No," Cedric said, "I'm leaving now." *(When?)*
3. "Are you going far?" Alvin asked. *(Where?)*
4. "No, I'll return soon," Cedric replied as he opened the door. *(When?)*
5. Alvin sadly watched his older brother leave. *(How?)*
6. Cedric called to Alvin, "Tell me your secret later, Al!" *(When?)*
7. "I'll tell you as soon as you get back," he said. *(Where?)*
8. Alvin walked slowly into the kitchen. *(How?)*

Next Step: Write a sentence about a secret. Use an adverb and underline it.

Related Skills Activities

- **Basic Grammar and Writing**
  Selecting Adverbs, p. 391
  How Can I Improve My Writing with Adverbs?, p. 392
- ***GrammarSnap***
  Adverbs
- ***SkillsBook***
  Adverbs 1 and 2, pp. 159–162

Answers

1. Then
2. now
3. far
4. soon
5. sadly
6. later
7. back
8. slowly

Prepositions

A **preposition** is a word that introduces a prepositional phrase.

Todd slept under the covers. (*Under* is a preposition.)
Teddy slept on the chair. (*On* is a preposition.)

Prepositional Phrases

A prepositional phrase begins with a preposition, and it ends with a noun or a pronoun.

Teddy sleeps on his side.

Todd has a stuffed animal, and he always sleeps with it.

Common Prepositions

about	below	near	to
above	beneath	of	toward
across	between	off	under
after	by	on	underneath
against	during	onto	until
along	for	out of	up
among	from	outside	with
around	in	over	within
at	inside	past	without
before	into	since	
behind	like	through	

Prepositions

Write the prepositions you find in each sentence.

Example: The candle flame danced in a warm draft of air.
in, of

1. It was 1889, and Pau read an old book by candlelight.
2. The light formed strange shadows on the ceiling.
3. Pau's cat hid behind the drapes.
4. A spider climbed up a silky thread into its web.
5. The quiet inside his room was scary.
6. Suddenly, there was a knock at the door.
7. "It's time for bed," Pau's dad called to him.
8. As Pau's dad put out the flame, smoke drifted toward the open window.
9. With a sigh, Pau crawled under his covers and went to sleep.

Next Step: Write two sentences about being alone in a quiet room. How many prepositions did you use?

Related Skills Activities

- **Basic Grammar and Writing**
  Using Prepositions, p. 393
- ***GrammarSnap***
  Prepositions and Prepositional Phrases
- ***SkillsBook***
  Prepositions and Prepositional Phrases, pp. 163–164

Answers

1. by
2. on
3. behind
4. up, into
5. inside
6. at
7. for, to
8. toward
9. with, under, to

Conjunctions

A **conjunction** connects words or groups of words.

Coordinating Conjunctions

The most common conjunctions are listed here. They are called **coordinating conjunctions.**

and but or for so yet

We could use skateboards or bikes.
(*Or* connects two words.)

Maya wrote a poem and sang a song.
(*And* connects two phrases.)

We ate early, but we still missed the bus.
(*But* connects two simple sentences.)

Other Conjunctions

Other conjunctions connect ideas in specific ways. Here are some of these conjunctions:

after because when before since

I like to skateboard when it is hot.
After I saw the lightning, I heard the thunder.

Interjections

An **interjection** is a word or phrase used to express strong emotion or surprise.

Interjections

An interjection is followed by an exclamation point or by a comma.

Hey! Slow down! Wow, look at him go!

Conjunctions

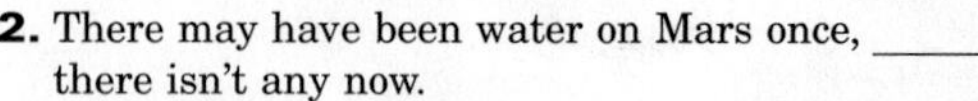

Write a coordinating conjunction *(and, but, or, for, so, yet)* to complete each sentence.

Example: The solar system is made up of eight planets and the sun.

1. Is Mercury ______ Venus the smallest planet?
2. There may have been water on Mars once, ______ there isn't any now.
3. Rock and metal make up some planets, ______ they are called the rocky planets.
4. The gas planets move quickly ______ have many moons.
5. Jupiter has rings, ______ they are lighter rings than Saturn's rings are.
6. Neptune looks blue, ______ the Romans named Neptune after the god of the sea.

Next Step: Write a sentence comparing two of the planets. Use a coordinating conjunction.

Related Skills Activities

- **Basic Grammar and Writing**
  Connecting With Conjunctions, p. 394
  How Can I Use Conjunctions in My Writing?, p. 395
- ***GrammarSnap***
  Coordinating Conjunctions
  Transition Words
- ***SkillsBook***
  Conjunctions, p. 165

Answers

1. or
2. but
3. so
4. and
5. but
6. so

Practice Test

In each sentence, what part of speech is underlined? Write the letter of the correct answer.

1. Do you know who works in your neighborhood?
   Ⓐ pronoun Ⓒ preposition
   Ⓑ interjection Ⓓ verb

2. You will soon notice many workers.
   Ⓐ pronoun Ⓒ adverb
   Ⓑ noun Ⓓ conjunction

3. A letter carrier puts mail in your mailbox.
   Ⓐ pronoun Ⓒ preposition
   Ⓑ interjection Ⓓ verb

4. Waiters or waitresses serve food in restaurants.
   Ⓐ pronoun Ⓒ adverb
   Ⓑ noun Ⓓ verb

5. A police officer helps if you are lost.
   Ⓐ pronoun Ⓒ adverb
   Ⓑ noun Ⓓ verb

6. If you are hurt, a nurse quickly takes care of you.
   Ⓐ pronoun Ⓒ adverb
   Ⓑ adjective Ⓓ verb

7. At the pool, a lifeguard keeps you safe.
   Ⓐ noun Ⓒ preposition
   Ⓑ pronoun Ⓓ conjunction

8. Wow, there are so many things I can do when I grow up!
   Ⓐ pronoun Ⓒ preposition
   Ⓑ interjection Ⓓ conjunction

9. I would really like to be a pilot.
   Ⓐ pronoun Ⓒ adverb
   Ⓑ noun Ⓓ verb

10. Then I could fly a large jet.
    Ⓐ verb Ⓒ preposition
    Ⓑ adjective Ⓓ pronoun

11. Maybe I could visit Hawaii and Alaska.
    Ⓐ conjunction Ⓒ pronoun
    Ⓑ adverb Ⓓ interjection

12. Those would be some long trips!
    Ⓐ adverb Ⓒ pronoun
    Ⓑ noun Ⓓ adjective

Answers

1. A
2. C
3. C
4. B
5. D
6. C

Answers

7. C
8. B
9. B
10. B
11. A
12. D

Related Skills Activities

- ***SkillsBook***
  Verb Review 1, p. 136
  Verb Review 2, p. 149
  Parts of Speech Review 1 and 2, pp. 167–170

Quick Guide: Parts of Speech

Nouns Words that name a person, a place, a thing, or an idea **(Anna, park, scooter, fun)**

Pronouns Words that take the place of nouns **(I, me, you, her, them, ours, theirs)**

Verbs Words that show action or link ideas **(run, jump, is, are)**

Adjectives Words that describe a noun or a pronoun **(old, beautiful, five, the, funny)**

Adverbs Words that describe a verb **(gently, easily, often, nearby)**

Prepositions Words that introduce prepositional phrases **(in, near, under, on top of)**

Conjunctions Words that connect words or groups of words **(and, or, but, when, after)**

Interjections Words (set off by commas or exclamation points) that show emotion or surprise **(Wow, Look out!)**

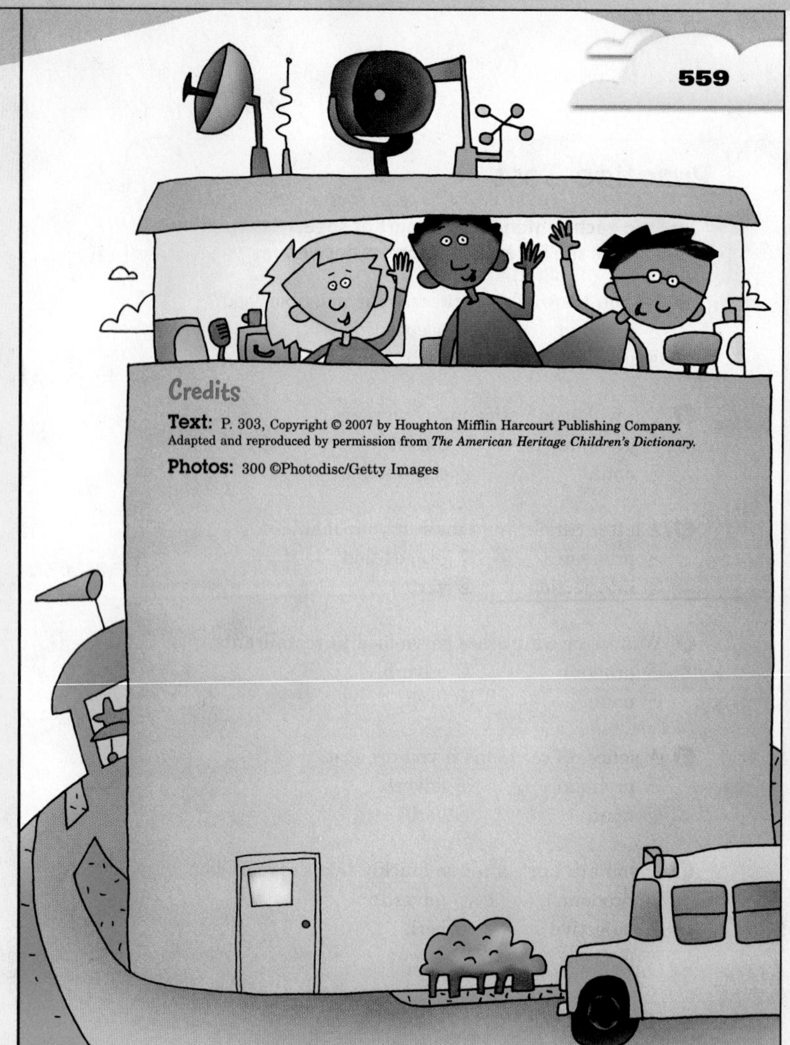

Credits

Text: P. 303, Copyright © 2007 by Houghton Mifflin Harcourt Publishing Company. Adapted and reproduced by permission from *The American Heritage Children's Dictionary.*

Photos: 300 ©Photodisc/Getty Images

Copy Masters

CHECKLISTS

RUBRICS

BENCHMARK PAPERS

RESPONSE SHEETS

GRAPHIC ORGANIZERS

FAMILY CONNECTION LETTERS

UNIT PLANNING AND GETTING STARTED

Copy Masters

Six-Trait Checklist

Ideas

- ☐ focuses on a specific topic
- ☐ contains well-developed and interesting details

Organization

- ☐ has a beginning, middle, and ending
- ☐ has parts that work well and that are in a clear order

Voice

- ☐ has a voice that sounds natural
- ☐ shows that the writer is interested in and excited about the subject

Word Choice

- ☐ contains specific nouns and action verbs
- ☐ uses an appropriate level of language (not too formal or too informal)

Sentence Fluency

- ☐ contains complete sentences
- ☐ flows smoothly from sentence to sentence
- ☐ shows variety in sentence beginnings and lengths

Conventions

- ☐ follows the basic rules of capitalization, punctuation, spelling, and grammar

© Houghton Mifflin Harcourt Publishing Company

Descriptive Writing

Directions Check your writing for capitalization, punctuation, spelling, and grammar.

Conventions Checklist

PUNCTUATION

_____ **1.** Did I use correct end punctuation after each sentence?

_____ **2.** Did I use apostrophes in my contractions *(can't, don't)*?

CAPITALIZATION

_____ **3.** Did I start all my sentences with capital letters?

_____ **4.** Did I capitalize all the names of people?

SPELLING

_____ **5.** Have I carefully checked my spelling?

GRAMMAR

_____ **6.** Have I used the correct verbs *(we are,* not *we is)*?

_____ **7.** Have I used the right words *(there, their, they're; to, two, too)*?

© Houghton Mifflin Harcourt Publishing Company

Narrative Writing

Directions Check your writing for capitalization, punctuation, spelling, and grammar.

Conventions Checklist

PUNCTUATION

_____ 1. Did I use end punctuation after all my sentences?

_____ 2. Did I put quotation marks around words people said?

CAPITALIZATION

_____ 3. Did I start all my sentences with capital letters?

_____ 4. Did I correctly capitalize proper nouns?

SPELLING

_____ 5. Have I carefully checked my spelling?

GRAMMAR

_____ 6. Did I use correct verbs *(he plays,* not *he play)*?

© Houghton Mifflin Harcourt Publishing Company

Expository Writing

Directions Check your writing for capitalization, punctuation, spelling, and grammar.

Conventions Checklist

PUNCTUATION

_____ 1. Did I use end punctuation after all my sentences?

_____ 2. Did I correctly use commas in a series?

CAPITALIZATION

_____ 3. Did I start all my sentences with capital letters?

_____ 4. Did I capitalize all proper names in my essay?

SPELLING

_____ 5. Have I carefully checked my spelling?

GRAMMAR

_____ 6. Have I used the right words *(to, two, too; there, their, they're)*?

© Houghton Mifflin Harcourt Publishing Company

Persuasive Writing

Directions Check your letter for capitalization, punctuation, spelling, and grammar.

Conventions Checklist

PUNCTUATION

_____ 1. Did I use end punctuation after all my sentences?

_____ 2. Did I use commas correctly in dates and addresses?

CAPITALIZATION

_____ 3. Did I begin all my sentences with capital letters?

_____ 4. Did I capitalize names of people, organizations, titles, streets, cities, and states?

SPELLING

_____ 5. Have I carefully checked my spelling?

GRAMMAR

_____ 6. Did I use correct forms of verbs *(go, went, gone)*?

© Houghton Mifflin Harcourt Publishing Company

Book Review

Directions Check your writing for capitalization, punctuation, spelling, and grammar.

Conventions Checklist

PUNCTUATION

_____ 1. Did I use end punctuation after all my sentences?

_____ 2. Did I underline the book's title?

CAPITALIZATION

_____ 3. Did I start all my sentences with capital letters?

_____ 4. Did I capitalize the names of the characters?

SPELLING

_____ 5. Have I carefully checked my spelling?

GRAMMAR

_____ 6. Did I use subjects and verbs that agree *(he races,* not *he race)*?

_____ 7. Did I use the right words *(to, two, too; there, their, they're)*?

© Houghton Mifflin Harcourt Publishing Company

Research Writing

Directions Check your report for punctuation, capitalization, spelling, and grammar.

Conventions Checklist

PUNCTUATION

____ **1.** Did I use correct end punctuation for each sentence?

____ **2.** Did I use commas correctly in my sentences?

CAPITALIZATION

____ **3.** Did I start all my sentences with capital letters?

____ **4.** Did I capitalize all proper nouns and titles?

SPELLING

____ **5.** Have I spelled all my words correctly?

GRAMMAR

____ **6.** Did I use correct verbs *(it flies,* not *it fly)*?

____ **7.** Did I use the right words *(there, their, they're; to, two, too)*?

© Houghton Mifflin Harcourt Publishing Company

6-Point

Rubric for Narrative Writing

Use the following rubric for rating your narrative writing.

Ideas

6 Rich ideas and details make an unforgettable essay!
5 The experience and the details are interesting.
4 The experience is interesting, but it needs more details.
3 The experience isn't clear, and some details don't belong.
2 The narrative should focus on one experience.
1 A new experience or suitable details should be found.

Organization

6 The narrative is arranged superbly!
5 The writing is well organized from beginning to end.
4 Most of the narrative works well.
3 Parts (beginning, middle, or ending) should be stronger.
2 All parts of the essay run together.
1 The narrative needs to be organized.

Voice

6 The voice is original and exciting!
5 The voice sounds exactly like the writer.
4 The voice sounds like the writer most of the time.
3 Sometimes the voice sounds like the writer.
2 The writing does not sound like the writer.
1 The writing has no real voice.

Word Choice

6 The word choice makes a vivid picture!
5 Strong nouns and verbs make clear pictures.
4 Some strong nouns and verbs are used.
3 Many strong words are needed.
2 Some words are overused.
1 Some words make the essay confusing.

Sentence Fluency

6 The sentences are a joy to read!
5 The sentences are clear and varied.
4 Most sentences are clear.
3 Many sentences are choppy.
2 Many sentences are choppy or incomplete.
1 Many sentences are incomplete.

Conventions

6 Conventions are correct.
5 Most conventions are correct.
4 Some errors appear.
3 Errors may confuse the reader.
2 Errors make the writing hard to read.
1 Help is needed to make corrections.

© Houghton Mifflin Harcourt Publishing Company

6-Point

Rubric for Expository Writing

Use this rubric for guiding and rating your expository writing.

Ideas

6 The topic, focus, and details are well developed.
5 The topic is clear and includes many interesting details.
4 The topic is clear. Most of the details tell about the topic.
3 The topic needs to be clearer. More details are needed.
2 The topic is unclear, and the details do not fit.
1 The topic is unclear.

Organization

6 Every part of the essay works perfectly.
5 The beginning, middle, and ending all work well.
4 Most parts of the essay are in order.
3 Some parts of the essay could be better organized.
2 All parts of the essay run together.
1 The organization is confusing.

Voice

6 The voice sounds confident and well informed.
5 The voice sounds well informed.
4 The writer sounds informed in most parts.
3 The writer sounds informed in some parts.
2 The writer sounds unsure.
1 The writer sounds uninterested.

Word Choice

6 Each word is precisely chosen.
5 Specific words explain the topic.
4 Most words in the essay explain the topic.
3 The essay needs more specific words.
2 General or missing words make this essay confusing.
1 Some words are used incorrectly.

Sentence Fluency

6 All sentences are well crafted and varied.
5 Many sentences are well crafted and varied.
4 Most sentences have a variety of lengths and beginnings.
3 Some sentences have varied lengths and beginnings.
2 Many sentences are choppy or incomplete.
1 Many sentences are incomplete and difficult to read.

Conventions

6 The essay uses conventions well.
5 Most conventions are correct.
4 Meaning is clear, but some errors are present.
3 Errors may confuse the reader.
2 Errors make the essay hard to read.
1 Help is needed to make corrections.

© Houghton Mifflin Harcourt Publishing Company

6-Point

Rubric for Persuasive Writing

Use the following rubric for rating your persuasive writing.

Ideas

6 The opinion and reasons are very convincing.
5 The opinion is clear, and all the reasons support it.
4 The opinion is clear, but more reasons would be helpful.
3 The opinion needs to be clearer with more reasons.
2 The opinion is confusing and needs reasons.
1 The writer needs to state an opinion.

Organization

6 Every part of the writing works perfectly.
5 The writing is clearly organized.
4 Most parts are organized and work well.
3 Several parts need to be organized better.
2 All parts of the essay run together.
1 The writing needs to be organized to avoid confusion.

Voice

6 The voice is polite and convincing.
5 The voice is convincing.
4 The voice could be more convincing.
3 The writing exaggerates or has a weak voice.
2 The voice comes and goes.
1 The writing needs voice.

Word Choice

6 Each word is expertly chosen.
5 The words make the opinion and reasons clear.
4 Most words work well.
3 Some words are unclear.
2 Some words make the writing confusing.
1 Help is needed to find better words.

Sentence Fluency

6 The sentences flow beautifully.
5 The sentences read smoothly.
4 A few sentences sound choppy.
3 Many sentences are choppy.
2 Some sentences are choppy or incomplete.
1 Many sentences are incomplete.

Conventions

6 The essay uses conventions well.
5 Most conventions are correct.
4 Some errors are present.
3 Errors may confuse the reader.
2 Errors make the writing hard to read.
1 Help is needed to make corrections.

© Houghton Mifflin Harcourt Publishing Company

5-Point

Rubric for Narrative Writing

Use this rubric for guiding and rating your narrative writing.

Ideas

5 The experience and rich details make an unforgettable essay.
4 The experience is interesting, but it needs more details.
3 The experience isn't clear, and some details don't belong.
2 The narrative should focus on one experience.
1 A new experience or suitable details should be found.

Organization

5 The writing is well organized from beginning to end.
4 Most of the narrative works well.
3 Parts (beginning, middle, or ending) should be stronger.
2 All parts of the essay run together.
1 The narrative needs to be organized.

Voice

5 The voice is original and exciting.
4 The voice sounds exactly like the writer.
3 The voice sounds like the writer most of the time.
2 The writing does not sound like the writer.
1 The writing has no real voice.

Word Choice

5 Strong nouns and verbs make vivid, clear pictures.
4 Some strong nouns and verbs are used.
3 Many strong words are needed.
2 Some words are overused.
1 Some words make the essay confusing.

Sentence Fluency

5 The sentences are clear and varied.
4 Most sentences are clear.
3 Many sentences are choppy.
2 Many sentences are choppy or incomplete.
1 Many sentences are incomplete.

Conventions

5 Conventions are correct.
4 Most conventions are correct.
3 Some errors appear.
2 Errors make the writing confusing and hard to read.
1 Help is needed to make corrections.

© Houghton Mifflin Harcourt Publishing Company

5-Point

Rubric for Expository Writing

Use the following rubric for rating your expository writing.

Ideas

5 The topic, focus, and details are well-developed.
4 The topic is clear and includes many interesting details.
3 The topic is clear. Most of the details tell about the topic.
2 The topic needs to be clearer. More details are needed.
1 The topic is unclear, and the details do not fit.

Organization

5 The beginning, middle, and ending all work well.
4 Most parts of the essay are in order.
3 Some parts of the essay could be better organized.
2 All parts of the essay run together.
1 The organization is confusing.

Voice

5 The voice sounds confident and well-informed.
4 The writer sounds informed in most parts.
3 The writer sounds informed in some parts.
2 The writer sounds unsure.
1 The writer sounds uninterested.

Word Choice

5 Specific words explain the topic.
4 Most words in the essay explain the topic.
3 The essay needs more specific words.
2 General or missing words make this essay confusing.
1 Some words are used incorrectly.

Sentence Fluency

5 All sentences are well crafted and varied.
4 Many sentences are well crafted and varied.
3 Most sentences have a variety of lengths and beginnings.
2 Some sentences have varied lengths and beginnings.
1 Many sentences are incomplete and difficult to read.

Conventions

5 The essay uses conventions well.
4 Most conventions are correct.
3 Meaning is clear, but some errors are present.
2 Errors make the essay confusing and hard to read.
1 Help is needed to make corrections.

© Houghton Mifflin Harcourt Publishing Company

5-Point

Rubric for Persuasive Writing

Use this rubric for guiding and rating your persuasive writing.

Ideas

5 The opinion and reasons are very convincing.
4 The opinion is clear, and all the reasons support it.
3 The opinion is clear, but more reasons would be helpful.
2 The opinion is confusing and needs reasons.
1 The writer needs to state an opinion.

Organization

5 The writing is clearly organized.
4 Most parts are organized and work well.
3 Several parts need to be organized better.
2 All parts of the essay run together.
1 The writing needs to be organized to avoid confusion.

Voice

5 The voice is polite and convincing.
4 The voice is convincing.
3 The voice could be more convincing.
2 The writing exaggerates or has a weak voice.
1 The writing needs voice.

Word Choice

5 Each word is expertly chosen.
4 The words make the opinion and reasons clear.
3 Most words work well.
2 Some words make the writing confusing.
1 Help is needed to find better words.

Sentence Fluency

5 The sentences flow beautifully.
4 The sentences read smoothly.
3 A few sentences sound choppy.
2 Many sentences are choppy.
1 Many sentences are choppy and incomplete.

Conventions

5 The essay uses conventions well.
4 Most conventions are correct.
3 Meaning is clear, but some errors are present.
2 Errors make the writing confusing and hard to read.
1 Help is needed to make corrections.

© Houghton Mifflin Harcourt Publishing Company

4-Point

Rubric for Narrative Writing

Use the following rubric for rating your narrative writing.

Ideas

4 The experience and rich details make an unforgettable essay.
3 The experience is interesting, but it needs more details.
2 The experience isn't clear, and some details don't belong.
1 A new experience or suitable details should be found.

Organization

4 The writing is well organized from beginning to end.
3 Parts (beginning, middle, or ending) should be stronger.
2 All parts of the essay run together.
1 The narrative needs to be organized.

Voice

4 The voice is original and exciting.
3 The voice sounds like the writer most of the time.
2 The writing does not sound like the writer.
1 The writing has no real voice.

Word Choice

4 Strong nouns and verbs make vivid, clear pictures.
3 Some strong nouns and verbs are used.
2 Many strong words are needed.
1 Some words make the essay confusing.

Sentence Fluency

4 The sentences are clear and varied.
3 Most sentences are clear.
2 Many sentences are choppy.
1 Many sentences are incomplete.

Conventions

4 Conventions are correct.
3 Most conventions are correct.
2 Errors make the writing confusing and hard to read.
1 Help is needed to make corrections.

© Houghton Mifflin Harcourt Publishing Company

4-Point

Rubric for Expository Writing

Use this rubric for guiding and rating your expository writing.

Ideas

4 The topic, focus, and details are well-developed.
3 The topic is clear and includes many interesting details.
2 The topic needs to be clearer. More details are needed.
1 The topic is unclear, and the details do not fit.

Organization

4 The beginning, middle, and ending all work well.
3 Most parts of the essay are in order.
2 Some parts of the essay run together.
1 The organization is confusing.

Voice

4 The voice sounds confident and well-informed.
3 The writer sounds informed in most parts.
2 The writer sounds informed in some parts.
1 The writer sounds unsure.

Word Choice

4 Specific words explain the topic.
3 The essay needs more specific words.
2 General or missing words make this essay confusing.
1 Some words are used incorrectly.

Sentence Fluency

4 All sentences are well crafted and varied.
3 Most sentences have a variety of lengths and beginnings.
2 Some sentences have varied lengths and beginnings.
1 Many sentences are incomplete and difficult to read.

Conventions

4 The essay uses conventions well.
3 Meaning is clear, but some errors are present.
2 Errors make the essay confusing and hard to read.
1 Help is needed to make corrections.

© Houghton Mifflin Harcourt Publishing Company

4-Point

Rubric for Persuasive Writing

Use the following rubric for rating your persuasive writing.

Ideas

4 The opinion and reasons are very convincing.
3 The opinion is clear, but more reasons would be helpful.
2 The opinion is confusing and needs reasons.
1 The writer needs to state an opinion.

Organization

4 The writing is clearly organized.
3 Most parts are organized and work well.
2 Several parts need to be organized better.
1 The writing needs to be organized to avoid confusion.

Voice

4 The voice is polite and convincing.
3 The voice could be more convincing.
2 The writing exaggerates or has a weak voice.
1 The writing needs voice.

Word Choice

4 Each word is expertly chosen.
3 Most words work well.
2 Some words make the writing confusing.
1 Help is needed to find better words.

Sentence Fluency

4 The sentences flow beautifully.
3 A few sentences sound choppy.
2 Many sentences are choppy.
1 Many sentences are choppy and incomplete.

Conventions

4 The essay uses conventions well.
3 Meaning is clear, but some errors are present.
2 Errors make the writing confusing and hard to read.
1 Help is needed to make corrections.

© Houghton Mifflin Harcourt Publishing Company

Assessment Sheet

Title *Dancing Drums*

5 Ideas

- Your topic sentence is clear and tells why you will always remember your day at the African festival.
- You might include more sensory details in your middle paragraphs. Describing how the drums sounded or how your bare feet felt as they moved across the wood floor would make your readers feel as if they were dancing next to you.

6 Organization

- Organizing the events in time order helps readers understand how you spent your day.
- Using transitions words, or words that show time, helps connect events in your writing.

5 Voice

- Your writing voice shows that you were doing something that you enjoyed very much.
- You might add a sentence that tells what you were thinking as you moved to the beat of the drums.

6 Word Choice

- Your writing uses strong nouns and verbs that show how delighted you were to learn African dance.
- You bring excitement to your story when you describe feeling the drum beats in your chest.

6 Sentence Fluency

- Your sentences begin in different ways. This makes your essay easy to read.
- Your use of compound verbs in the second and fourth paragraphs makes your writing interesting.

6 Conventions

- Your paper is neat and ready for sharing.
- Your paper is error free!

© Houghton Mifflin Harcourt Publishing Company

Narrative Writing

The Snow Day

One of the best parts of winter is snow! Sometimes it snows a lot. School is cancelled. That's what happened one day. A huge snowstorm closed school. I called my friend Amy. We decided to spend our snow day sledding in the park.

We rode our sleds downhill at the same time. We put our sleds next too each other at the top of the hill. We pushed off. Sometimes Amy reached the bottom first. Sometimes I did.

We decided two go down the hill together. Amy sat in the front and I sat in the back. We pushed off together and started to zoom down the hill. The sled was going so fast that it was hard to steer. Then CRASH! We ran into a bush! Amy went flying and I got my feet caught in the bush! Amy looked like a spider caught in its own spider web. Luckily, no one got hurt.

We decided to use too sleds. It is a safer way to have fun. We stayed at the park until it started to get dark. We pulled our sleds back home. I had a lot of fun that day and, I will never forget it!

© Houghton Mifflin Harcourt Publishing Company

Assessment Sheet

Title *The Snow Day*

5 Ideas

- Your topic sentence is clear and tells how you spent your snow day.
- Your middle paragraphs include details about your day that make the readers feel as if they were riding along with you.

4 Organization

- Organizing the events in time order helps readers understand what happened on your day off from school.
- It would have been easier to follow your story if you had used transitions *(first, then, after the crash).*

5 Voice

- Your writing voice sounds like you are telling the story to a classmate.
- Your writing voice shows you were doing something you enjoy.

5 Word Choice

- Your writing uses strong nouns and verbs that make clear pictures.
- You bring excitement to your story when you paint a picture of Amy sprawled like a spider.

4 Sentence Fluency

- Your sentences begin in different ways. This makes your essay easy to read.
- Some of your sentences in the first two paragraphs are short and choppy. You could combine these to make your writing more interesting.

4 Conventions

- Your paper is neat and ready for sharing.
- Your writing contains errors in the use of "to," "too," and "two." Edit your paragraph to use the correct form of these homophones.
- You do not need to use so many exclamation points. They lose their impact.

© Houghton Mifflin Harcourt Publishing Company

Narrative Writing

Looking for midnight

I got a puppy for my birthday. My puppy is black, it's a boy. It sleep's on a litle rug.

It took me a couple of days. to decide on a name. First I wanted to call him peanut. He is small. Like a peanut. Then I thought about trouble. He is always getting into trouble. Then I made up my mind. I called him midnight. His fur is very dark. Just like the night.

One time midnight ran under the couch. we didnt know. where he was. I was worried. Then I found him. He was scared. Then it was time for schol. I didnt want to go!

© Houghton Mifflin Harcourt Publishing Company

Assessment Sheet

Title *Looking for Midnight*

3 **Ideas**

- The first sentence of your essay tells readers that you are writing about your new puppy.
- You need to focus your essay on only one main idea (what the puppy looks like, how you chose a name, or how he was lost).

4 **Organization**

- You used the transition words "first" and "then" in the second paragraph. These help connect and order your sentences.
- Your essay has a beginning, a middle, and an ending. But they do not focus on only one experience you have had with Midnight.

5 **Voice**

- Your writing voice sounds like you are telling your story to a friend.
- Your writing voice shows that you care about Midnight.

3 **Word Choice**

- Comparing your puppy to a peanut helps readers understand that your young puppy is small.
- You should revise your essay to include more action verbs that make clear pictures for readers.

2 **Sentence Fluency**

- Your essay contains sentence fragments. Remember, a sentence must have a subject and a predicate, or verb. Revise your writing so that every sentence is complete.
- Your essay contains too many short sentences, which makes your writing choppy and difficult to read. Combine pairs of short sentences into one longer sentence.

2 **Conventions**

- Your essay contains many capitalization errors. Check the first word of sentences and the first letter of proper names.
- Your essay includes the contraction for "did not." Contractions need apostrophes.
- You need to proofread your essay for spelling errors ("litle" and "schol").

© Houghton Mifflin Harcourt Publishing Company

Assessment Sheet

Title *Learning by Doing and Going*

6 Ideas

- Your writing begins with a focus sentence that names the topic of your essay and tells why science is your favorite subject.
- Your essay includes exact information that explains why science class is the best part of your school day.

6 Organization

- Your middle paragraphs explain your focus sentence.
- Your ending refers back to your focus sentence and finishes your explanation of why science is your favorite subject.

5 Voice

- Your writer's voice shows that you are interested in learning about the natural world through experiments and field trips.
- Your writer's voice fits your topic and audience.

4 Word Choice

- Your writing includes specific nouns that tell readers exactly what you have investigated through your science experiments.
- You could add sensory details that help readers "see" what you observed during your field trips. You could describe the sounds and scents of the forest you visited on Arbor Day. You could describe how the fallen leaves felt as you picked them up.

6 Sentence Fluency

- Using different sentence beginnings makes your essay easy to read.
- Your writing contains different kinds of sentences that make the essay interesting to read.

6 Conventions

- Your essay is free of spelling and punctuation errors!
- Your essay is neat and ready to publish.

© Houghton Mifflin Harcourt Publishing Company

Expository Writing

How to Bake a Cake

I love to bake cakes because they make a tasty snack. If you are wondering how to bake a cake, and you don't know how, read along. If you follow my directions, you will make the best cake ever!

The first thing you do is go to the store and by your supplies, you need some cake mix eggs milk and oil. Then you go back to your home sweet home. Before you start making your cake, you have to wash your hands and when they are nice and clean, get out a bowl. After that, you poor in the mix and crack the eggs. Then add the milk and oil. Be sure to use a measuring cup to add the write amount!

Next, set your oven to 350° F and as it heats up, stir the batter for about 2 minutes. Then pour the batter into the pan and put it into the oven for 35–45 minutes. The last thing you do is let it cook and wait for a yummy treat.

© Houghton Mifflin Harcourt Publishing Company

Assessment Sheet

Title *How to Bake a Cake*

4 Ideas

- Your writing begins with a focus sentence that names the topic of your essay and tells what you can teach the reader.
- You could be more specific about the items you use when baking a cake. Should the batter be mixed in a large bowl or a small bowl? Should the batter be poured in a metal pan or a glass pan?

6 Organization

- Your middle paragraph answers *how* about your focus sentence.
- You use transition words *(first, then, before, after)* to connect the details given in the middle paragraphs.

4 Voice

- Your writer's voice shows that you are interested in the topic.
- At times, your writer's voice is too casual. You should revise your writing to replace expressions like "home sweet home" and "nice and clean."

4 Word Choice

- Your writing includes specific nouns that tell readers exactly what is needed to make a cake.
- You could add sensory details that "show" readers what happens in each step of the process. You could describe what the batter looks like as the ingredients are blended together. You could describe the scent of the cake.

4 Sentence Fluency

- Using different sentence beginnings makes your essay easy to read.
- The second and third paragraphs of your essay contain some run-on sentences. Correct the run-ons by adding a period and a capital letter.

3 Conventions

- The first sentence of the second paragraph lists the things needed to bake a cake. You should put commas between these items.
- Your essay contains the homophones "by," "poor," and "write." Use a dictionary to make sure you have used the right words.

© Houghton Mifflin Harcourt Publishing Company

Expository Writing

A Kite

I love to fly kites. I like watching them float in the air. Like a bird. I can make my own kite. Do you know how. To make a kite I go get some kite string and stecks. Then I mak a shape. It doesnt have to be a diamond. It can be a circle. Or a square. Or even the shap of an animl. One time I mad a dog kite. it looks like my pet. Do you have a pet. Then you mite want to make a dog kite two. You tape everything together. You tape on some string. Then go to an open place. like a park. Or the beech. Hold the kite in one hand. Hold the string in the other hand, wait for a strong wind. Let go of the kite? Watch it climb into the sky.

© Houghton Mifflin Harcourt Publishing Company

Assessment Sheet

Title *A Kite*

2 Ideas

- Your essay lacks a clear focus. Are you explaining why you like flying kites? Are you describing how to make a kite? You need to decide on the topic.
- Your essay needs more specific details about the topic you select. If you are telling how to make a kite, you need to give information about each step.

2 Organization

- Your essay lacks a clear beginning, middle, and end.
- The first paragraph should have a focus sentence that tells what the essay is about.

4 Voice

- Your writer's voice shows that you enjoy flying kites.
- Your writer's voice shows that you know a lot about making kites.

3 Word Choice

- Comparing a kite to a bird helps readers "see" what it looks like. It also helps them understand why you love flying kites.
- You should use specific nouns that name an exact person, place, thing, or idea.

2 Sentence Fluency

- Your essay contains a number of sentence fragments. Remember that a complete sentence contains a subject and a predicate, or verb. Revise the fragments to make complete sentences.
- Many of your sentences are quite short. This makes the essay choppy and difficult to read.

1 Conventions

- Your essay contains many capitalization errors. Remember to begin every sentence with a capital letter.
- Your essay contains many punctuation errors. Check to see if you ended every question with a question mark, not a period.
- Your essay contains many spelling errors that confuse the reader. You can use a dictionary to find the correct spelling of a word.

© Houghton Mifflin Harcourt Publishing Company

Assessment Sheet

Title *Save Our Recess*

4 Ideas

- Your first paragraph contains an opinion sentence.
- You could make your essay stronger by explaining in your middle paragraph how exercise keeps the body fit and strong. These facts would support your opinion sentence and answer the question *why?*

5 Organization

- Your writing has a clear beginning, middle, and ending.
- Your ending asks the reader to encourage the principal to take your stand on the problem. You might also include a sentence thanking the reader for reading your essay.

6 Voice

- Your writer's voice shows that you know a lot about the problem.
- Your writer's voice sounds confident and determined.

4 Word Choice

- You used the helping verb "should" in your closing. This is a polite way of encouraging your reader to take action on the problem.
- You used the word "kids" five times in your writing! Replace this informal word with a synonym such as "students" or "classmates."

5 Sentence Fluency

- Using different sentence beginnings makes your essay easy to read.
- Your writing includes different kinds of sentences that make your words interesting to a reader.

6 Conventions

- Your writing is error free!
- Your essay is neat and ready to publish.

© Houghton Mifflin Harcourt Publishing Company

Persuasive Writing

New Sidewalks

Dear Mayer Burns,

I am a student who lives on oak lane. I think my neighborhood needs new sidewalks. Right now, the sidewalks are cracked and uneven.

Cracked and uneven sidewalks are very dangerous to anyone moving across them. Walkers can trip and fall. No one enjoys getting hurt! I fell last week. It was painful. My sister has fallen, too. It took many days for her cut to heal. The wheels of a bicycle can get stuck in a rut. The bike stops suddenly. The rider can be thrown off. Even riding a skateboard along an uneven sidewalk can be very dangerous.

Sidewalks are meant to keep people safe. Kids like me are not allowed to ride our bikes in the road. Our parents are always nagging us to stay on the sidewalks. So where are we supposed to ride, huh? We can't use our in-line skates or skateboards either. In the winter, we can't even walk to our friends' houses. The snow piles up on the sides of the road. We are stuck playing in our own yards.

I have been to other streets in our town. Many of them have smooth sidewalks. If other neighborhoods have safe sidewalks, we should, two. You must do something to fix my unsafe street!

Sincerely,

Tia Liang

© Houghton Mifflin Harcourt Publishing Company

Assessment Sheet

Title *New Sidewalks*

4 Ideas

- Your first paragraph tells the reader who you are and contains an opinion sentence.
- Your middle paragraphs support your opinion and answer the question *why?*
- Your essay contains some extra information that does not explain the topic. You should cut these details from your writing. (See paragraph 2.)

6 Organization

- Your writing has a clear beginning, middle, and ending.
- Your middle paragraphs give reasons that are based on facts.
- Your ending asks Mayor Burns to do something about the problem.

4 Voice

- Your writer's voice is convincing and shows you are determined.
- In some parts of your essay, your writer's voice sounds casual. You should revise your writing so that it shows you are serious about the problem.

4 Word Choice

- You use the helping verb "must" in your closing. This verb is not polite to use when writing to an older person. You should replace this verb with "could" or "should."
- You should revise your essay to include a few more specific words.

4 Sentence Fluency

- Your writing includes different kinds of sentences.
- Your middle paragraphs contain some short, choppy sentences. Try combining these sentences by moving a group of words.

4 Conventions

- You have misspelled "Mayor."
- Your forgot to capitalize the first letters of the name of the street you live on.

© Houghton Mifflin Harcourt Publishing Company

Persuasive Writing

A New Pool

Our city is very cold. in the winter and we cannot go swimming. I think franklin park needs a indoor pool. Swimming is good exsersize and we need an indoor pool to stay in good shape. Exsersize is important to everybody. It keep the body fit. And healthy. it is important for kids and for grown ups to. Without exsersize we could all gain about a hundred pounds.

An indoor pool also gives kids something to do and we can meet our frends there and keep busy swimming. If we are busy we will not get into truble. That is good for everybody.

© Houghton Mifflin Harcourt Publishing Company

Assessment Sheet

Title *A New Pool*

2 Ideas

- Your beginning contains a clear opinion sentence.
- Your writing needs more reasons and details to convince readers.

2 Organization

- Your essay lacks middle paragraphs that begin with a topic sentence and contain supporting reasons.
- Your closing does not nicely ask the reader to do something about your idea.

3 Voice

- Your writer's voice shows that you feel strongly.
- In parts of your essay, your writer's voice exaggerates what life without an indoor pool is like.

3 Word Choice

- You should revise your essay to include more strong words that convince the reader.
- You might describe how it feels to be unable to swim during the cold winter months. This might help convince the reader to do something about the issue.

2 Sentence Fluency

- The last paragraph of your writing contains a run-on sentence. This makes your essay hard to read.
- Your writing contains sentence fragments. Check to make sure that every sentence has a subject and a predicate, or verb.

1 Conventions

- Your essay contains many spelling errors. (See "exsersize," "frends," "truble.") Use a dictionary to find the correct spelling of these words.
- Your essay contains capitalization errors. The first word of a sentence and the name of a city begin with a capital letter.

© Houghton Mifflin Harcourt Publishing Company

Assessment Sheet

Use one of the rubrics listed below to rate a piece of writing. Circle the rubric your teacher tells you to use. If you need information about assessing with a rubric, see pages 26–33 in your *Write Source* book.

- Narrative Rubric (pages 122–123)
- Expository Rubric (pages 168–169)
- Persuasive Rubric (pages 212–213)

Title: ______________________________

____ **Ideas**

____ **Organization**

____ **Voice**

____ **Word Choice**

____ **Sentence Fluency**

____ **Conventions**

Evaluator ______________________

© Houghton Mifflin Harcourt Publishing Company

Response Sheet

Writer: ______________________________

Responder: ______________________________

Title: ______________________________

____

What I like:

____

____

____

____

____

____

____

Questions I have:

____

____

____

____

____

____

____

____

© Houghton Mifflin Harcourt Publishing Company

Thinking About Your Writing

Name: ______________________________

Title: ______________________________

____

1. The best part of my essay is . . .

____

____

____

____

____

2. The part that still needs work is . . .

____

____

____

____

____

3. The main thing I learned about my writing is . . .

____

____

____

____

____

© Houghton Mifflin Harcourt Publishing Company

Editing and Proofreading Marks

You can use the marks below to show where and how your writing needs to be changed. Your teachers may also use these marks to point out errors in your writing.

Mark	Meaning	Example	Corrected Example
≡	Capitalize a letter.	*Sable* is a book by Karen hesse.	*Sable* is a book by Karen Hesse.
/	Make a capital letter lowercase.	Tate Marshall loves Dogs.	Tate Marshall loves dogs.
⊙	Add a period.	Mam doesn't want to keep Sable⊙	Mam doesn't want to keep Sable.
ↄ	Take something out.	Doc Winston he will take Sable.	Doc Winston will take Sable.
∧	Insert a word or letter.	Tate was ∧ sad. (very)	Tate was very sad.
∨ ∨ ∨ (' " ")	Insert an apostrophe or a quotation mark.	Sables stealing caused trouble.	Sable's stealing caused trouble.
∧ ∧ ∧ (, ? !)	Insert punctuation.	Tate built a good∧ strong fence.	Tate built a good, strong fence.
⬭ sp.	Correct the spelling error.	Pap was (prowd) sp. of Tate.	Pap was proud of Tate.
¶	Start a new paragraph.	Tate liked to help Pap. ¶ One summer day, Tate had a surprise . . .	Tate liked to help Pap. One summer day, Tate had a surprise . . .

© Houghton Mifflin Harcourt Publishing Company

T-Chart

Topic:

© Houghton Mifflin Harcourt Publishing Company

Sensory Chart

Topic:

See	Hear	Smell	Taste	Touch

© Houghton Mifflin Harcourt Publishing Company

5 W's Chart

Topic: ______________________

Who?	
What?	
When?	
Where?	
Why?	

© Houghton Mifflin Harcourt Publishing Company

Time Line

Topic:

© Houghton Mifflin Harcourt Publishing Company

© Houghton Mifflin Harcourt Publishing Company

Table Diagram

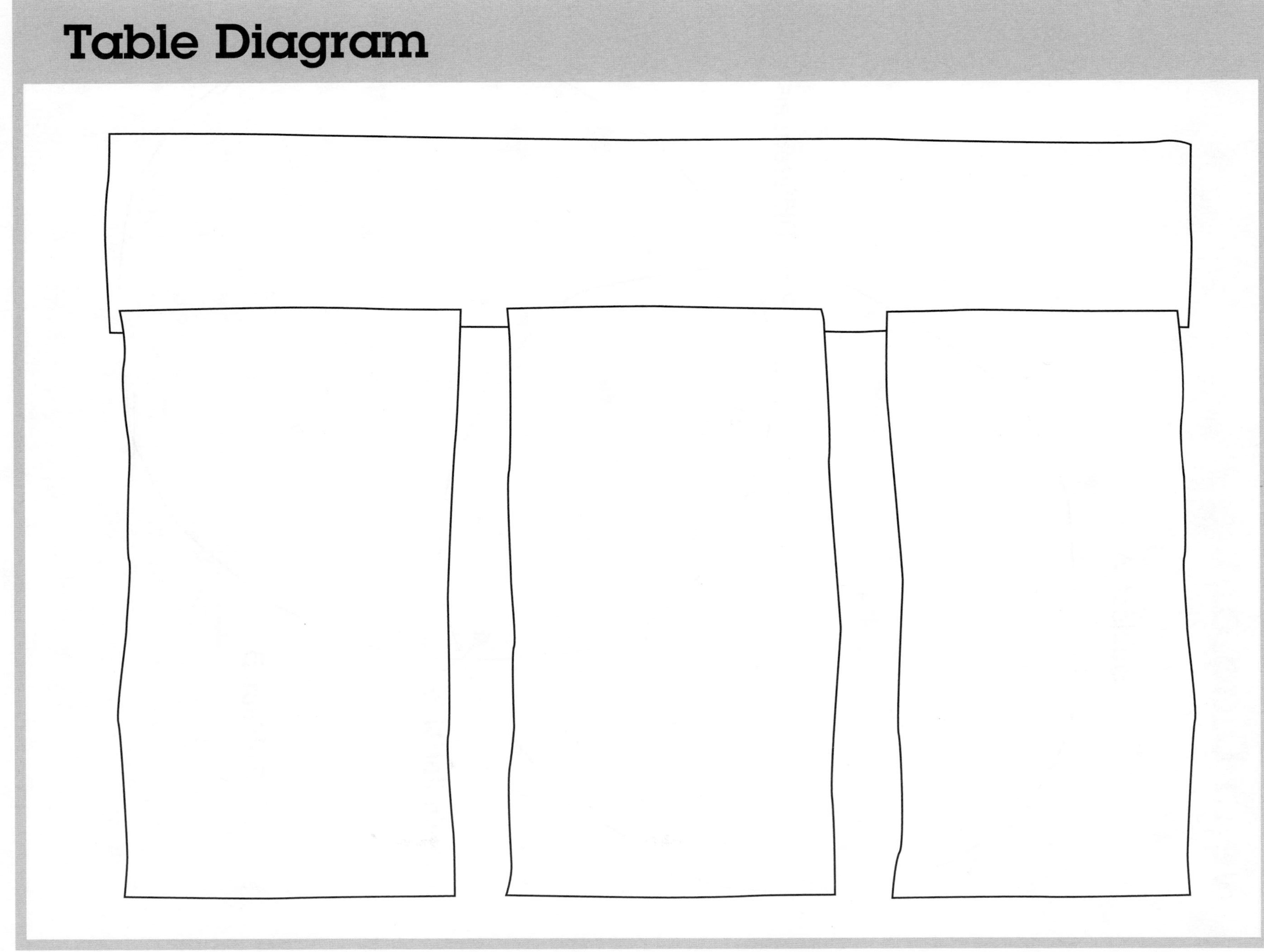

Venn Diagram

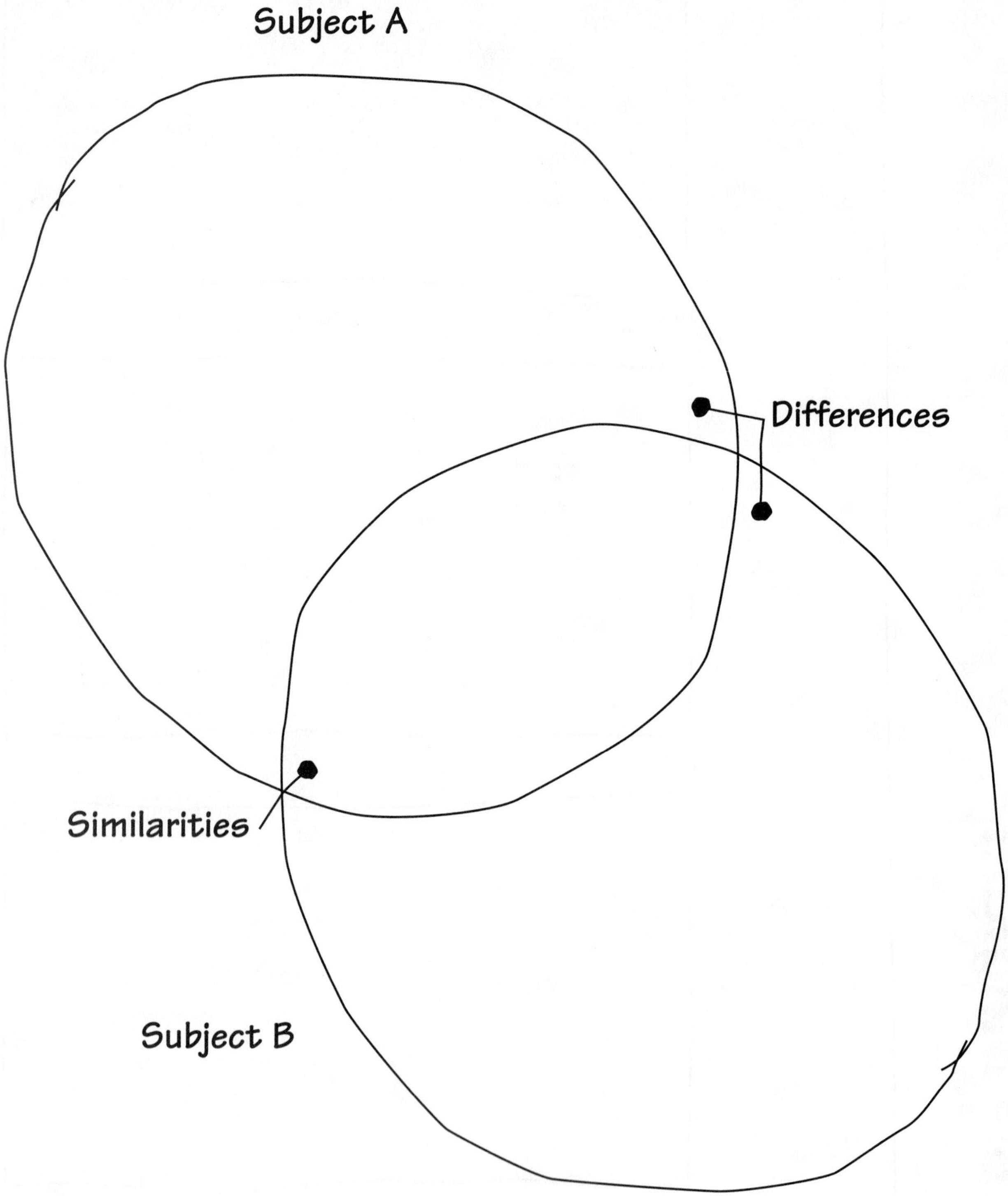

Subject A

Differences

Similarities

Subject B

© Houghton Mifflin Harcourt Publishing Company

Dear Families,

You've probably taught your child the following step-by-step process: *Choose a box of cereal. Get out a bowl and spoon. Pour the cereal into the bowl. Pour milk over the top. Eat the cereal. Put everything away.* Since authors follow steps, too, we're going to learn about the writing process. To **prewrite** is to choose a topic, gather details, and plan. To **write** is to get ideas on paper. To **revise** is to re-read, get feedback, and make needed changes. To **edit** is to check spelling, capital letters, and punctuation. To **publish** is to share the writing with others. We'll also learn about six different qualities, or traits, of good writing—**ideas, organization, voice, word choice, sentence fluency,** and **conventions.** We score the traits like this:

To help your child start thinking about the writing process:

- Read together daily. Talk about how the authors get their ideas and feelings across.
- Provide opportunities to write lists and notes at home.
- While running errands, make up stories about things you see and hear.
- Have family members take turns selecting a "Word of the Day" to use in your dinner conversation.

Thank you!

© Houghton Mifflin Harcourt Publishing Company

Dear Families,

We tell each other about people we meet, places we go, and activities we enjoy. We describe a great pair of shoes in a store window, hoping others can see the shoes in their minds. This type of sharing is fun for speaker and listener alike. As we move into the study of descriptive writing, students will develop these skills by learning to paint "word pictures." We'll use details we can see, hear, smell, taste, and touch. We'll also organize our descriptions in a logical way. The **beginning** gets the reader's attention and tells what will be described. The **middle** gives the details in a certain order, such as top to bottom or left to right. The **ending** shares a final thought or feeling. Finally, we'll reflect on our writing, including what we learned, what we like, and what we want to work on in the future.

To help your child start thinking descriptively:

- Have each family member draw an interesting person, place, or item seen that day, label the details, and tell about it.
- While riding in the car, play a game in which one person describes an object and the others guess what it is.
- As you read together, find examples in which the writer has obvious positive or negative feelings about what is being described. Talk about the specific words used to get the point across.

Thank you!

© Houghton Mifflin Harcourt Publishing Company

Dear Families,

"When I was little . . ." You may have used these words to tell stories about funny, exciting, and memorable events from years gone by. As we move into the study of narrative writing, students will share their own experiences as well as learn about the lives of others. We'll work to make the reader see what we see and feel what we feel. Two traits that are especially important in writing narratives are **organization** and **sentence fluency.** We'll use a time line and write events in order using words such as *first, then, next, as soon as,* and *finally*. We'll also make our writing read more smoothly by blending some short, choppy sentences into longer ones.

To help your child start thinking about narration:

- Help him or her write a letter to a friend or relative telling about a fun experience.
- Write a simple version of a real-life experience, and then cut the sentences apart. Have your child reassemble the events in a logical order.
- Read a biography together. Afterward, ask each other: *What did you like about it? What questions do you have?*
- Help your child start a journal. Provide time to write about one event each night before bedtime.

Thank you!

© Houghton Mifflin Harcourt Publishing Company

Dear Families,

Every day we read for information. We study news articles, follow recipes, and check out Web sites. As the students move into expository writing, they'll learn to explain facts, data, and instructions in their own words. Two important traits in this genre are **ideas** and **word choice.** We'll choose interesting topics. We'll stay focused by adding details that answer *why* and *how.* We'll use description and dialogue to *show* rather than *tell* about our topics. We'll also choose words that show our enthusiasm and use specific nouns to make our writing clearer.

To help your child start thinking about expository text:

- Invite each family member to show and explain a trick or skill that requires at least three steps.
- While traveling in the car, call out a general noun, such as *pet, insect, plant, building, movie, game,* or *book.* Then ask your child to name specific nouns that fit into that category. For example: *pet (dog, cat, gerbil, turtle, parakeet, hamster, mouse, horse, ferret).* Finally, switch roles.
- At dinnertime, ask each family member to name two objects that are important to him or her and to explain why they are important. Then have the rest of the family vote for the object they think would make a more interesting writing topic.

Thank you!

© Houghton Mifflin Harcourt Publishing Company

Dear Families,

As adults, we try to convince children to think or act in certain ways. *Be polite. Stand up straight. Save some of your money for later.* They, in turn, try to persuade us to agree with their ideas. *I'd rather do my homework AFTER supper. Can we go to the zoo this weekend?* As we move into the study of persuasive writing, students will learn to state opinions backed by facts that explain *why.* Two writing traits that help achieve this goal are **voice** and **conventions.** We must express ourselves in strong, but polite language. We must sound convincing by giving accurate information. We must also make sure our meaning is clear by using correct punctuation, spelling, capital letters, and grammar.

To help your child start thinking about persuasion:

- Discuss examples of helpful persuasion, such as a friend suggesting a book to read, and harmful persuasion, such as peer pressure to make fun of a classmate.
- On slips of paper, write real and funny topics for trying to convince someone of something, such as *getting a pet giraffe, where to go on vacation,* and *eating ice cream for breakfast.* Take turns selecting a topic and giving a one-minute persuasive speech.
- Cut out ads from old newspapers or magazines. Together, circle exaggerations the writer uses to try to get you to attend an event or buy a product.

Thank you!

© Houghton Mifflin Harcourt Publishing Company

Dear Families,

Do you remember the book reports you wrote as a child? Are any of those books still treasured favorites? As we move into responding to literature, we'll learn to share our thoughts and feelings about all kinds of reading. One way is to make connections. By thinking about how stories are like our own lives, we learn more about writing and more about ourselves. Another way is to look for the message or theme of a story. What does the main character learn? What can we learn from him or her? We'll practice telling about books without giving away the endings, describing our favorite parts, and comparing fiction and nonfiction books on the same topic. We'll learn to share information using the *3–2-1 Plan* – three important facts, two surprising details, and one thing we wonder about. We'll also study poetry, including why poets choose their topics and styles.

To help your child start thinking about literature response:

- Look through books at home or at the library. Talk about what makes a book seem interesting. The title? The art? The summary on the cover?
- Watch a science or history TV show. Ask one another: *What did you learn? What would you still like to find out?*
- After watching a movie, discuss your favorite characters. Tell what qualities make them act the way they do.
- Invite your child to create a poster, puppet show, or board game about a book he or she enjoys.

Thank you!

© Houghton Mifflin Harcourt Publishing Company

Dear Families,

There once was a student of writing,
Who didn't find verses exciting.
Then one day he wrote
A clever, rhymed note.
His poems are now oh, so inviting!

Do you enjoy limericks? This is just one type of poem we'll learn about as we begin our study of creative writing. Besides poems, we'll write imaginative stories that focus on **characters** (who), **setting** (where and when), and **plot** (what). Then we'll change our stories into plays by separating out the speaking parts, making sure to keep a plot line that includes the **beginning, rising action, high point,** and **ending.** In all of our creative writing, we'll add titles that make our readers want to see where our imaginations have taken us. In short, we'll be having so much fun we'll barely know how hard we're working!

To help your child start thinking creatively:

- Tell an "embellished" story about a childhood event. Have your child guess which details are real and imaginary.
- Read fictional stories together and then make up new endings for them.
- Play a game in which you call out a word, your child says several real or nonsense words that rhyme with it, and you make up a poem using at least two of the words. Then switch roles.

Thank you!

© Houghton Mifflin Harcourt Publishing Company

Dear Families,

Third graders are full of wonder. As a result, they love learning fun facts and dandy details. As we move into our research writing unit, we'll first learn about the helpful resources we have at hand, from books to maps to experts. We'll also study the parts of a nonfiction book, such as the table of contents, glossary, and index. Next, we'll write article summaries that include the main idea and most important details. Finally, we'll craft research reports on topics of interest. We'll learn how to gather information from a variety of sources, take notes, outline, and write with a strong beginning, middle, and end. Then, be prepared for your child's FAVORITE part — telling YOU what he or she has learned!

To help your child start thinking about research:

- Make a list of things you might see in your local library. Next, go on a "treasure hunt" together, marking off items as you find them. Your list might include a fiction book, nonfiction book, magazine, encyclopedia, newspaper, atlas, dictionary, thesaurus, computer, DVD, CD, and librarian.
- Ask a friend or relative if your child may interview him or her. Prepare questions together ahead of time.

Thank you!

© Houghton Mifflin Harcourt Publishing Company

Queridas familias,

Ustedes tal vez les han enseñado a sus hijos el siguiente proceso paso a paso: *Escoge una caja de cereal. Saca un plato hondo y una cuchara. Sirve el cereal en el plato. Sirve la leche en el plato. Cómete el cereal. Guarda todo.* Puesto que los autores también siguen pasos, vamos a aprender sobre el proceso de escritura. **Preescribir** es seleccionar un tema, acumular datos y planear. **Escribir** es poner las ideas en papel. **Revisar** es volver a leer, recibir comentarios y hacer los cambios que sean necesarios. **Editar** es verificar la ortografía, las mayúsculas y la puntuación. **Publicar** es compartir el escrito con los demás. También aprenderemos seis cualidades o rasgos de la buena escritura: **ideas, organización, voz, escogencia de palabras, fluidez de oraciones** y **convenciones.** Calificamos estos rasgos así:

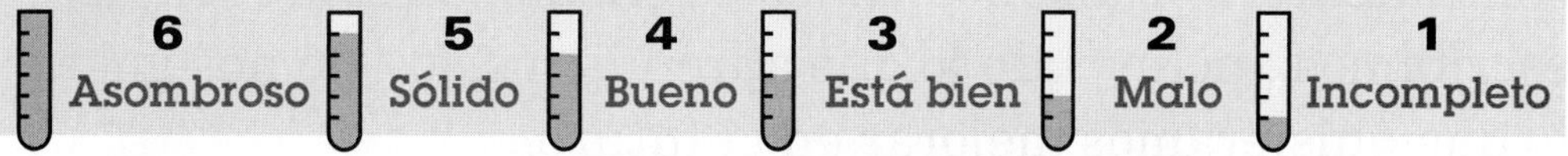

Ayúdele a su hijo a pensar en el proceso de escritura:

- Lean juntos todos los días. Hablen de cómo los autores transmiten sus ideas y sentimientos.
- Suministre oportunidades para escribir notas y listas en casa.
- Cuando hagan diligencias, invéntense historias sobre las cosas que oyen y ven.
- Haga que los miembros de la familia escojan “la palabra del día” para usarla en la conversación durante la cena.

¡Gracias!

© Houghton Mifflin Harcourt Publishing Company

Queridas familias,

Muchas veces hablamos de las personas que conocemos, los lugares que visitamos y las actividades que nos gustan. Describimos un par de zapatos que vimos en una vitrina para que los demás se los imaginen. Esta forma de compartir es divertida para quien habla y quien escucha. A medida que avanzamos en el estudio de la escritura descriptiva, los estudiantes desarrollarán estas destrezas aprendiendo a dibujar "imágenes con palabras". Usaremos detalles que vemos, oímos, olemos, probamos y tocamos. También organizaremos nuestras descripciones de forma lógica. El **principio** atrae la atención del lector y le dice qué se va a describir. El **desarrollo** suministra los detalles en un determinado orden, por ejemplo de arriba abajo o de izquierda a derecha. El **final** expresa un pensamiento o un sentimiento. Por último, vamos a reflexionar sobre lo que escribimos, incluyendo lo que aprendimos, lo que nos gusta y lo que quisiéramos mejorar en el futuro.

Ayúdele a su hijo a pensar descriptivamente:

- Pídale a cada miembro de la familia que dibuje una persona, objeto o lugar interesante que haya visto durante el día. Dígale que marque los detalles y les hable del tema.
- En el auto, jueguen a que una persona describe un objeto mientras que los demás tratan de adivinar de qué objeto se trata.
- Lean juntos. Busquen ejemplos en los que el autor expresa sentimientos positivos o negativos sobre lo que describe. Hablen sobre las palabras que usa para expresar sus ideas.

¡Gracias!

© Houghton Mifflin Harcourt Publishing Company

Queridas familias,

"Cuando yo era pequeño . . ." Usted tal vez ha usado estas palabras para contar historias curiosas, emocionantes o sucesos memorables de años pasados. A medida que avanzamos en el estudio de la escritura narrativa, los estudiantes compartirán sus propias experiencias a la vez que aprenden sobre la vida de los demás. Trabajaremos para que el lector vea lo que nosotros vemos y sienta lo que nosotros sentimos. Dos rasgos muy importantes para escribir narraciones son la **organización** y la **fluidez de oraciones.** Usaremos una línea cronológica para escribir los sucesos en orden, usando palabras como *primero, luego, próximo, tan pronto como* y *finalmente*. También haremos que nuestros escritos se puedan leer más fácilmente, mezclando algunas oraciones cortas con otras más largas.

Ayúdele a su hijo a pensar en la narración:

- Ayúdele a él o ella a escribirle una carta a un amigo o familiar contándole alguna experiencia divertida.
- Escriba una experiencia corta de la vida real. Luego corte las oraciones. Pídale a su hijo que ponga los sucesos en orden lógico.
- Lean juntos una biografía. Luego pregúntense: *¿Qué te gustó? ¿Qué preguntas tienes?*
- Ayúdele a su hijo a comenzar un diario. Antes de irse a la cama, suminístrele cada noche el tiempo necesario para escribir sobre un suceso.

¡Gracias!

© Houghton Mifflin Harcourt Publishing Company

Queridas Familias,

Todos los días leemos para obtener información. Leemos las noticias, practicamos recetas y revisamos los sitios de Internet. A medida que los estudiantes avanzan en el estudio de la escritura explicativa, aprenderán a explicar hechos, datos e instrucciones en sus propias palabras. Dos rasgos importantes de este género son las **ideas** y la **escogencia de palabras**. Seleccionaremos temas interesantes. Mantendremos el enfoque agregando detalles que responden el *por qué* y el *cómo*. Usaremos la descripción y el diálogo para *mostrar* el tema en lugar de *contarlo*. También escogeremos palabras que muestren nuestro entusiasmo y usaremos sustantivos específicos para que nuestra escritura sea más clara.

Ayúdele a su hijo a pensar en textos explicativos.

- Invite a cada miembro de la familia a que muestre y explique un truco o destreza que requiera un mínimo de tres pasos.
- Cuando vayan en el auto, diga un sustantivo común; por ejemplo *mascota, insecto, planta, edificio, película, juego* o *libro.* Luego, pídale a su hijo que nombre sustantivos propios correspondientes a esa categoría, por ejemplo: mascota *(perro, gato, gerbo, tortuga, perico, hámster, ratón, caballo, hurón).* Luego, inviertan los papeles.
- A la hora de cenar, dígale a cada miembro de la familia que nombre dos objetos que le sean importantes y que explique por qué los considera importantes. Luego, pídales a todos que voten por el objeto que les parezca más interesante como tema para escribir.

¡Gracias!

© Houghton Mifflin Harcourt Publishing Company

Queridas familias,

Como adultos, tratamos de convencer a los niños de que piensen o actúen de cierta forma. *Se educado. Párate derecho. Guarda algo de dinero para más adelante.* Al mismo tiempo, ellos tratan de persuadirnos para que estemos de acuerdo con sus ideas. *Preferiría hacer los deberes DESPUÉS de cenar. ¿Podemos ir al zoológico este fin de semana?* A medida que avanzamos en el estudio de la escritura persuasiva, los estudiantes aprenderán a expresar sus opiniones sustentadas en los hechos que explican el *por qué*. Dos rasgos de la escritura que ayudan a lograr esta meta son la **voz** y las **convenciones.** Tenemos que expresarnos en un lenguaje fuerte pero educado. Debemos sonar convincentes suministrando información precisa. También tenemos que asegurarnos de que el significado sea claro usando la puntuación, la ortografía, las mayúsculas y la gramática correctas.

Ayúdele a su hijo a ser persuasivo:

- Discutan ejemplos de persuasión positiva, por ejemplo, un amigo que sugiere un libro para leer; y persuasión negativa, por ejemplo la presión de grupo para burlarse de un compañero de clase.
- En tiras de papel, escriban temas reales y graciosos para tratar de convencer a alguien de hacer cosas como *tener una jirafa de mascota, dónde ir de vacaciones* o *desayunarse con helado.* Seleccionen el tema por turnos, con un discurso persuasivo de un minuto.
- Recorte anuncios de periódicos y revistas viejas. Juntos, encierren en un círculo las exageraciones que usan los autores para convencernos de asistir a un evento o comprar un producto.

¡Gracias!

© Houghton Mifflin Harcourt Publishing Company

Queridas familias,

¿Recuerdan los informes de lectura de libros que escribieron cuando eran niños? ¿Algunos de esos libros siguen siendo sus favoritos? A medida que avanzamos en las reacciones a la literatura, aprenderemos a compartir nuestros pensamientos y sentimientos sobre todo tipo de lectura. Una manera es haciendo conexiones. Cuando pensamos que las historias son como nuestra vida, aprendemos más sobre la escritura y sobre nosotros mismos. Otra forma es buscar el mensaje o el tema de una historia. ¿Qué aprende el personaje principal? ¿Qué podemos aprender de él o ella? Vamos a practicar hablando de libros sin decir cómo terminan, describiremos nuestros apartes favoritos y compararemos libros de ficción y no ficción sobre el mismo tema. Aprenderemos a compartir información usando el *Plan 3–2-1*—tres hechos importantes, dos detalles asombrosos y una cosa que nos pone a pensar. También estudiaremos poesía, incluyendo por qué los poetas escogen sus temas y su estilo.

Ayúdele a su hijo a reaccionar frente a la literatura:

- Miren algunos libros en casa o en la biblioteca. Hablen sobre lo que hace que un libro sea interesante. ¿El título? ¿El arte? ¿El resumen de la portada?
- Miren un programa de ciencia o historia en la televisión. Pregúntense: *¿Qué aprendiste? ¿Qué más te gustaría averiguar?*
- Hablen sobre sus personajes preferidos después de ver una película. Digan qué cualidades los hacen actuar de esa manera.
- Pídale a su hijo que diseñe un cartel, una obra de títeres o un juego de mesa sobre un libro que le guste.

¡Gracias!

© Houghton Mifflin Harcourt Publishing Company

Queridas familias,

Me contaron un cuento muy bueno,
sobre un mico, un perro y un trueno.
Cuando el trueno sonó,
el mico saltó,
y el perro corrió con su dueño.

¿Les gustan los poemas de humor? Estos serán unos de los poemas que aprenderemos durante nuestro estudio de escritura creativa. Además de poemas, escribiremos cuentos imaginarios que se enfocan en los **personajes** (quién), la **escena** (dónde y cuándo), y la **trama** (qué). Luego convertiremos nuestros cuentos en obras para teatro, separando los diálogos y asegurándonos de conservar la trama que incluye **comienzo, aumento de la acción, punto culminante** y **final.** En nuestra escritura creativa, agregaremos títulos que harán pensar a nuestros lectores hasta dónde nos lleva la imaginación. ¡Es decir, nos vamos a divertir tanto que ni siquiera nos daremos cuenta de lo duro que trabajamos!

Ayúdele a su hijo a pensar creativamente:

- Cuéntele una historia adornada de algún suceso de su infancia. Dígale que adivine los detalles reales y los inventados.
- Lean juntos historias de ficción y luego inventen finales nuevos para ellas.
- Jueguen un juego en el que usted dice una palabra y su hijo responde con palabras reales o inventadas que rimen. Invéntese un poema usando al menos dos de esas palabras. Luego cambien los papeles.

¡Gracias!

© Houghton Mifflin Harcourt Publishing Company

Dear Families,

Los niños de tercer grado se asombran con las cosas. Les encanta aprender datos curiosos y detalles graciosos. A medida que avanzamos en nuestra unidad de investigar y escribir, aprenderemos primero acerca de los recursos de ayuda que tenemos a la mano: libros, mapas y expertos. También estudiaremos las partes que componen un libro de no ficción, como la tabla de contenido, el glosario y el índice. Luego escribiremos resúmenes de artículos, incluyendo la idea principal y los detalles más importantes. Finalmente, haremos informes de investigación sobre temas de interés. Aprenderemos a recopilar información de diferentes fuentes, a tomar notas, hacer bosquejos y a escribir un buen principio, desarrollo y final. Entonces prepárese para la parte PREFERIDA de su hijo: ¡contarle a USTED lo que él o ella ha aprendido!

Ayúdele a su hijo a pensar en la investigación:

- Haga una lista de las cosas que pueda ver en la biblioteca municipal. Luego participen juntos en la "búsqueda del tesoro" tachando los objetos de la lista a medida que los encuentran. La lista puede tener un libro de ficción, uno de no ficción, una revista, una enciclopedia, un periódico, un atlas, un diccionario, un tesauro, una computadora, un DVD, un CD y un bibliotecario.
- Pregúntele a un amigo o familiar si su hijo lo puede entrevistar. Preparen juntos las preguntas con anticipación.

¡Gracias!

© Houghton Mifflin Harcourt Publishing Company

Unit Planning

Writing Form

PARAGRAPH

____ days

- **Focus**

- **Skills**

ESSAY

____ days

Prewriting

- **Focus**

- **Skills**

Writing

____ days

- **Focus**

- **Skill**

Revising

____ days

- **Ideas**

- **Organization**

- **Additional Trait**

© Houghton Mifflin Harcourt Publishing Company

Unit Planning (continued)

Editing

____ days

- CAPITALIZATION
- PUNCTUATION
- SPELLING
- GRAMMAR

Workshop

____ days

- IDEAS
- ORGANIZATION
- VOICE
- WORD CHOICE
- SENTENCE FLUENCY
- CONVENTIONS

ACROSS THE CURRICULUM

____ days

- SOCIAL STUDIES
- SCIENCE
- PRACTICAL
- OTHER

© Houghton Mifflin Harcourt Publishing Company

Scavenger Hunt 1: Find the Threes

Directions Find the following "threes" in your book by turning to the pages listed in parentheses.

1. **Three** main parts of a paragraph (pages 44–45)

___

___

___

2. **Three** ways to revise your work (pages 95, 97)

___

___

3. **Three** steps to planning a persuasive letter (pages 188–189)

___

___

___

4. **Three** ways to connect with conjunctions (page 394)

___

___

___

5. **Three** kinds of verbs (page 538)

___

___

6. **Three** things to look for when evaluating a Web site (page 361)

___

___

___

© Houghton Mifflin Harcourt Publishing Company

Scavenger Hunt 2: What Is It?

Directions **Find the answers to the following questions using the index in the back of the book. The underlined words below tell you where to look in the index.**

1. What is conflict?

2. What is rhythm?

3. What is a run-on sentence?

4. What are the traits of writing?

5. What are the editing and proofreading marks?

6. What is an interjection?

© Houghton Mifflin Harcourt Publishing Company

Getting to Know *Write Source*

Directions **Locate the pages in *Write Source* where answers to the following learning tasks can be found. Both the index and the table of contents can help you.**

______________ **1.** Your teacher has asked you to explain the difference between the plot of a story and the theme. You need to look up the definition of each.

______________ **2.** You are writing a paragraph and are not sure of the best way to organize it. You need to know the ways to organize paragraphs.

______________ **3.** You have trouble writing complete sentences. You need to know how to correct sentence fragments.

______________ **4.** Your teacher suggests drawing a life map to choose an experience to write about. You need to know how to draw a life map.

______________ **5.** You are writing a research report and need facts from several sources. You need to know how to use the library to find information.

______________ **6.** Your teacher assigns a fiction book and a nonfiction book to read and instructs you to write about each one in a reading journal. You need to know what to write in a reading journal.

______________ **7.** You want to suggest that third graders become reading buddies to first graders. You need to know how to write a persuasive letter to the principal.

______________ **8.** The words *their* and *they're* confuse you. You need to know which is the right word to use.

______________ **9.** You are writing a short story and your teacher reminds you to follow a plot line. You need to look at a diagram and a description of the parts of a plot line.

______________ **10.** You are writing an expository essay and want to use the six traits of writing to guide you as you write. You need to look at a rubric for expository writing.

© Houghton Mifflin Harcourt Publishing Company

Getting-Started Activity Answers

Scavenger Hunt 1: Find the Threes

1. topic sentence, body sentences, closing sentence
2. cut, add, and move details
3. select a topic, write an opinion sentence, gather reasons
4. connect a series of words, two phrases, and two simple sentences
5. action verbs, linking verbs, helping verbs
6. who publishes it, is it up to date, do all the facts agree

Scavenger Hunt 2: What Is It?

1. a problem or challenge the characters face (pages 271, 280)
2. the pattern of beats in a poem (page 286)
3. two sentences that run together (pages 404)
4. ideas, organization, voice, word choice, sentence fluency, conventions (pages 5, 20–25)
5. symbols and letters that show where and how your writing needs to be changed (pages 461, 594, inside back cover)
6. a word or phrase used to express strong emotion or surprise (pages 554, 558)

Getting to Know *Write Source*

1. 271, 280
2. 422–423
3. 403
4. 441
5. 297–307
6. 352–353
7. 184–213
8. 520
9. 281
10. 160–161

© Houghton Mifflin Harcourt Publishing Company

Index

A

B

D